Coastal Conservation

Coastal ecosystems are centers of high biological productivity, but their conservation is often threatened by numerous and complex environmental factors. Citing examples from the major littoral habitats worldwide, such as sandy beaches, salt marshes, and mangrove swamps, this text characterizes the biodiversity of coastline environments and highlights important aspects of their maintenance and preservation, aided by the analysis of key representative species.

Leaders in the field provide reviews of the foremost threats to coastal networks, including the effects of climate change, invasive species, and major pollution incidents such as oil spills. Further discussion underscores the intricacies of measuring and managing coastline species in the field, taking into account the difficulties in quantifying biodiversity loss due to indirect cascading effects and trophic skew. Synthesizing the current state of species richness with present and projected environmental pressures, the book ultimately establishes a research agenda for implementing and improving conservation practices moving forward.

BROOKE MASLO is Assistant Professor in the Department of Ecology, Evolution, and Natural Resources at Rutgers University in New Jersey. Working in applied conservation biology, her research focuses on evidence-based strategies for the conservation of threatened and endangered species, particularly shorebirds.

JULIE L. LOCKWOOD is Professor and Director of the Graduate Program in Ecology and Evolution at Rutgers University. Her research interests emphasize how species invasions and extinctions combine to shape present-day biodiversity patterns, with a focus on the dynamics of small populations.

Conservation Biology

Executive Editor
Alan Crowden – freelance book editor, UK

Editorial Board
Luigi Boitani – Università di Roma, Italy
Barry Brook – University of Adelaide, Australia
David Brunckhorst – University of New England in Armidale, Australia
Mark Burgman – University of Melbourne, Australia
Abigail Entwistle – Fauna & Flora International (FFI)
Julie Lockwood – Rutgers University, USA
Georgina Mace CBE FRS – Imperial College London, UK
Rob Marrs – University of Liverpool, UK
Helen Regan – University of California, Riverside, USA
David Richardson – Stellenbosch University, South Africa
Helen Schneider – Fauna & Flora International (FFI)
Raman Sukumar – Indian Institute of Science, India
John Wiens – PRBO Conservation Science, California, USA

This series aims to present internationally significant contributions from leading researchers in particularly active areas of conservation biology. It focuses on topics where basic theory is strong and where there are pressing problems for practical conservation. The series includes both authored and edited volumes and adopts a direct and accessible style targeted at interested undergraduates, postgraduates, researchers and university teachers.

Coastal Conservation

Edited by

BROOKE MASLO AND JULIE L. LOCKWOOD
Rutgers University, New Jersey, USA

CAMBRIDGE
UNIVERSITY PRESS

University Printing House, Cambridge CB2 8BS, United Kingdom

Published in the United States of America by Cambridge University Press, New York

Cambridge University Press is part of the University of Cambridge.

It furthers the University's mission by disseminating knowledge in the pursuit of education, learning and research at the highest international levels of excellence.

www.cambridge.org
Information on this title: www.cambridge.org/9781107022799

© Cambridge University Press 2014

First published 2014

Printed in the United Kingdom by TJ International Ltd. Padstow Cornwall

A catalogue record for this publication is available from the British Library

Library of Congress Cataloguing in Publication data
Coastal conservation / edited by Brooke Maslo and Julie L. Lockwood, Rutgers University, New Jersey, USA.
    pages cm
Includes bibliographical references and index.
ISBN 978-1-107-02279-9 (alk. paper)
1. Coastal ecology. 2. Coastal ecosystem health. 3. Shore protection. I. Maslo, Brooke, 1979– editor of compilation. II. Lockwood, Julie L., editor of compilation.
QH541.5.C65C5485 2014
577.5'1–dc23

2014001818

ISBN 978-1-107-02279-9 Hardback
ISBN 978-1-107-60674-6 Paperback

Brooke Maslo dedicates this book to Joanna Burger, Steven N. Handel, and Karl F. Nordstrom.

Julie L. Lockwood dedicates this book to Tabby, Henry, and Tanner Fenn.

Contents

The color plates are to be found between pages 176 and 177.

Contributors

BRENDA E. BALLACHEY US Geological Survey, Alaska Science Center, Anchorage, AK, USA

JAMES L. BODKIN US Geological Survey, Alaska Science Center, Anchorage, AK, USA

ANNETTE C. BRODERICK Centre for Ecology and Conservation, College of Life and Environmental Sciences, University of Exeter, Cornwall Campus, Penryn, UK

AUGUSTO CARDONI Instituto de Investigaciones Marinas y Costeras (IIMyC), Consejo Nacional de Investigaciones Científicas y Técnica, Facultad de Ciencias Exactas y Naturales Universidad Nacional de Mar del Plata, Mar del Plata, Argentina

KENT E. CARPENTER IUCN Species Programme Marine Biodiversity Unit, Global Marine Species Assessment, Biological Sciences, Dominion University, Norfolk, VA, USA

LEANNE C. CULLEN-UNSWORTH Sustainable Places Research Institute, Cardiff University, Cardiff, Wales, UK

FARID DAHDOUH-GUEBAS Laboratoire d'Écologie des Systèmes et Gestion des Ressources, Département de Biologie des Organismes, Faculté des Sciences, Université Libre de Bruxelles – ULB, Campus de la Plaine, Bruxelles, Belgium; Laboratory of Plant Biology and Nature Management, Department of Biology – Faculteit Wetenschappen, Bio-ingenieurswetenschappen, Vrije Universiteit Brussel – VUB, Brussels, Belgium

AMANDA D. DEY 109 Market Lane, Greenwich, NJ 08323, USA

JENIFER E. DUGAN Marine Science Institute, University of California, Santa Barbara, CA, USA

JOANNA C. ELLISON School of Geography and Environmental Studies, University of Tasmania, Launceston, TAS, Australia

BRUNO J. ENS SOVON Dutch Centre for Field Ornithology, SOVON-Texel, Den Burg, Texel, The Netherlands

DAN ESLER US Geological Survey, Alaska Science Center, Anchorage, AK, USA

XIAOJING GAN Ecology Group, Massey University, Palmerston North, New Zealand

MATTHEW H. GODFREY North Carolina Wildlife Resources Commission, Beaufort, NC, USA; Nicholas School of Environment and Earth Sciences, Duke University Marine Lab, Beaufort, NC, USA

BRENDAN J. GODLEY Centre for Ecology and Conservation, College of Life and Environmental Sciences, University of Exeter, Cornwall Campus, Penryn, UK

RUSSELL GREENBERG Migratory Bird Center, Smithsonian Conservation Biology Institute, National Zoological Park, Washington, DC, USA

ROBERT A.R. GULDEMOND Conservation Ecology Research Unit, Department of Zoology and Entomology, University of Pretoria, Hatfield, South Africa

LINDA HARRIS Department of Zoology, Nelson Mandela Metropolitan University, Port Elizabeth, South Africa

LUCY A. HAWKES Centre for Ecology and Conservation, College of Life and Environmental Sciences, University of Exeter, Cornwall Campus, Penryn, UK

DAVID M. HUBBARD Marine Science Institute, University of California, Santa Barbara, CA, USA

JUAN PABLO ISACCH Instituto de Investigaciones Marinas y Costeras (IIMyC), Consejo Nacional de Investigaciones Científicas y Técnica, Facultad de Ciencias Exactas y Naturales Universidad Nacional de Mar del Plata, Mar del Plata, Argentina

ALAN R. JONES Division of Invertebrates, The Australian Museum, Sydney, NSW, Australia

NICO E. KOEDAM Laboratory of Plant Biology and Nature Management, Department of Biology, Faculty of Sciences and Bioengineering Sciences, Vrije Universiteit Brussel – VUB, Brussels, Belgium

KEES KOFFIJBERG SOVON Dutch Centre for Field Ornithology, Nijmegen, The Netherlands

MARIANO LASTRA Department of Ecology and Animal Biology, Faculty of Marine Science, University of Vigo, Vigo, Spain

JULIE L. LOCKWOOD Ecology, Evolution and Natural Resources, Rutgers, The State University of New Jersey, New Brunswick, NJ, USA

RICHARD LOYN Arthur Rylah Institute for Environmental Research, Heidelberg, VIC, Australia

ANTON McLACHLAN University of Sydney, Sydney, NSW, Australia

ILYA M. D. MACLEAN Environment and Sustainability Institute, College of Life and Environmental Sciences, University of Exeter, Cornwall Campus, Penryn, UK

BROOKE MASLO Ecology, Evolution and Natural Resources, Rutgers, The State University of New Jersey, New Brunswick, NJ, USA

CRAIG O. MATKIN North Gulf Oceanic Society, Homer, AK, USA

RONEL NEL Department of Zoology, Nelson Mandela Metropolitan University, Port Elizabeth, South Africa

LAWRENCE J. NILES Conserve Wildlife Foundation of New Jersey, Trenton, NJ, USA

PIETER I. OLIVIER Conservation Ecology Research Unit, Department of Zoology and Entomology, University of Pretoria, Hatfield, South Africa

CHARLES H. PETERSON Institute of Marine Sciences, University of North Carolina, Chapel Hill, Morehead City, NC, USA

BETH A. POLIDORO IUCN Species Survival Commission/Marine Biodiversity Unit, Global Marine Species Assessment, Biological Sciences, Dominion University, Norfolk, VA, USA; School of Mathematics and Natural Sciences, New College of

Interdisciplinary Arts and Sciences, Arizona State University, Phoenix, AZ, USA

STANLEY D. RICE National Marine Fisheries Service, Auke Bay Laboratory, Juneau, AK, USA

ORIN J. ROBINSON Ecology, Evolution and Natural Resources, Rutgers, The State University of New Jersey, New Brunswick, NJ, USA

FELICITA SCAPINI Department of Biology, University of Florence, Firenze, Italy

THOMAS A. SCHLACHER Faculty of Science, Health and Education, The University of the Sunshine Coast, Maroochydore, QLD, Australia

DAVID S. SCHOEMAN Faculty of Science, Health and Education, The University of the Sunshine Coast, Maroochydore, QLD, Australia

RICHARD K.F. UNSWORTH Centre for Sustainable Aquatic Research, College of Science, Swansea University, Swansea, Wales, UK

RUDI J. VAN AARDE Conservation Ecology Research Unit, Department of Zoology and Entomology, University of Pretoria, Hatfield, South Africa

MICHAEL A. WESTON School of Life and Environmental Sciences, Deakin University, Burwood, VIC, Australia

MATTHEW J. WITT Environment and Sustainability Institute, University of Exeter, Cornwall Campus, Penryn, UK

JEAN W.H. YONG Life Sciences, Singapore University of Technology and Design, Singapore

Abbreviations

ARM	Adaptive Resource Management
ASMFC	Atlantic States Marine Fisheries Commission
BEF	biodiversity–ecosystem function
CA	Conditioned Aversion
CPUE	catch per unit effort
CWS	Canadian Wildlife Service
DMS	dimethylsulfide
EFH	essential fish habitat
ENSO	El Nino Southern Oscillation
IOCB	Indian Ocean Coastal Belt
IUCN	International Union for Conservation of Nature
LAZ	littoral active zone
MLLW	mean lower low water
MSX	multinucleated sphere X
NGO	non-governmental organization
ORV	off-road vehicle
PAH	polycyclic aromatic hydrocarbon
PWS	Prince William Sound
SAV	submerged aquatic vegetation
SESA	southeastern South America
TEV	Total Economic Value
TRT	Transitional Range of Temperatures
TSD	temperature-dependent sex determination
USFWS	US Fish and Wildlife Service
WHSRN	Western Hemisphere Shorebird Reserve Network

The conservation of coastal biodiversity

JULIE L. LOCKWOOD AND BROOKE MASLO

OVERVIEW

Defined broadly as the place where the land meets the sea, the coast occupies a profound place of importance in society (UNEP, 2006; Martinez *et al.*, 2007). Because of both sea- and land-derived inputs, coastal ecosystems are centers of high biological productivity, and they provide us with an astounding array of goods and services, including commercial products, dietary protein, fisheries nursery grounds, water filtration, and climate regulation (Burke *et al.*, 2001; Barbier *et al.*, 2011). The coastal landscape has consistently been a preferred location for human settlement, and its attractiveness as such has increased substantially over the past several decades (Small & Nichols, 2003; Coverdale *et al.*, 2013), particularly as a recreational destination and outlet for emotional uplift (Granek *et al.*, 2010). Coastal ecosystems also have immense cultural importance that can transcend socioeconomic groups (UNEP, 2006; Duke *et al.*, 2013). From the chic surf cultures in California and Costa Rica to the subsistence fishing villages in southeast Asia, religious, recreational, and economic cultures are deeply rooted in coastal habitats. Despite this importance, and likely because of it, coastal ecosystems are subject to multiple stressors that have combined to degrade the services they provide across most of their worldwide areal extent (Halpern *et al.*, 2008). Common threats across habitats include overexploitation, pollution, invasive species, and the impacts of climate change.

In this book, we focus on characterizing the biodiversity of coastal ecosystems, and the conservation of these species in the face of multiple, often synergistic, environmental impacts. Coastal biodiversity has largely been overlooked within coastal management frameworks and has proven difficult to adequately account for in systematic conservation planning schemes, leaving its protection in doubt (Stoms *et al.*, 2008; Tallis *et al.*,

Coastal Conservation, eds B. Maslo and J. L. Lockwood. Published by Cambridge University Press.
© Cambridge University Press 2014.

2008; Beger *et al.*, 2010). Yet, biodiversity plays a significant role in both the direct and indirect services provided by coastal ecosystems. In this opening chapter, we provide an overview of coastal biodiversity, highlighting its importance in ecosystem function and the complexities in its measurement and management.

THE COASTAL ECOSYSTEM MOSAIC

It is surprisingly difficult to define what constitutes a 'coast' (Barbier *et al.*, 2008). The most obvious feature of coastlines is the physical merging of ocean and land. From this definition, Burke and colleagues (2001) calculated that there are over 1.5 million linear kilometers of coastline worldwide. However, the influence of the ocean on terrestrial ecosystems extends far inland of the high-tide line, while terrestrial dynamics can impact even the deep trenches of the open ocean (Sheaves, 2009). Where, then, do we draw the line in our definition of the coast? Various authors have drawn this line in different places (e.g. Carter, 1998; Martinez *et al.*, 2007). Following Doody (2000), we define *coastal* to include all nearshore marine, shoreline and maritime terrestrial habitats to the extent of the influence of salt spray. This definition includes habitat such as high-relief rocky coastlines, estuarine/deltaic coastal plains, sandy beaches and dunes, and nearshore tidally influenced marine habitats, such as seagrass beds and mangroves. These habitats share the attributes of being highly dynamic in terms of their erosion–accretion patterns. They are also intimately connected to one another via physical and biological processes (Sheaves, 2009), and it is this level of dynamism and connectivity that is a defining feature of coastal ecosystems.

The habitats that encompass coastal ecosystems have fairly distinct physical and biological boundaries dictated to a large extent by the duration and depth of saltwater inundation and the physical action of waves (Carter, 1998). Within any single habitat there is often also distinct zonation of dominant vegetation, which is a consequence of these same forces (Doody, 2000). Therefore, coastal ecosystems are visually striking by virtue of the juxtaposition of distinct habitat types and, taken together, they form a dynamic collage of land and water habitats (Sheaves, 2009; Barbier, 2012). This feature led Sheaves (2009) to use the term *coastal ecosystem mosaic*, and Barbier (2012) the term *seascape*, to broadly describe coastlines, both acknowledging a high degree of synergy between coastal habitats where the boundaries between them are porous and allow organisms and materials to freely flow from one to another. Although (relatively) easy to define in and of themselves, coastal habitats make up a synergistic and irreducible ecosystem whole.

There is a multitude of ways in which coastal habitats are connected to one another (Sheaves, 2009). There is substantial movement of water, sand, and sediment between habitats (e.g. Schlacher *et al.*, 2008); this movement can be steady and gradual (e.g. tidal or aeolian processes; Davis & Fitzgerald, 2004) or highly episodic (e.g. hurricanes or typhoons; Doody, 2000). Biologically, coastal habitats are connected via plant and animal dispersal and the daily foraging movements and migrations of animals (Sheaves, 2009). This high level of biological connectivity plays a leading role in controlling nutrient transport and recycling between habitats, often with some coastal food webs being subsidized by input from others (e.g. sandy beaches; Schlacher & Connolly, 2009; see also Chapter 3). Many species that utilize coastal ecosystems specialize in one habitat type for part of their life history but move on to others (or off the coast entirely) for the rest (Chapters 9 and 10). Such species require the relatively specialized conditions of coastal habitats for breeding or to escape predation when in a vulnerable state (e.g. larvae or juveniles); however, the remainder of their life requires entirely different ecological conditions. The end result is a highly integrated ecosystem mosaic where one habitat cannot function independently of the others (Heck *et al.*, 2008; Beger *et al.*, 2010).

DEFINING COASTAL BIODIVERSITY

This degree of connectivity of coastal ecosystems has a profound impact on how we define and measure coastal biodiversity. Much like the quandary of defining what a coastal ecosystem is in general, we are faced with making a somewhat arbitrary decision as to what species utilize coastal habitats often enough, or long enough, for us to include them in our biodiversity tally. The easy species to include in our count of coastal biodiversity are those that are restricted to one or more coastal habitats, perhaps even being endemic to one (i.e. being found nowhere else). Many coastal habitats do have endemic species that are also the dominant plant species (e.g. mangroves, salt marsh, seagrass beds); however, there are surprisingly few of them (as long as we exclude coral reefs and islands from the definition of *coastal*, as we do here). As far as we are aware, there is no universally understood explanation for the relative paucity of endemic species in coastal ecosystems. Coastal ecosystems do not occupy a large fraction of either the Earth's terrestrial or oceanic extent, and this may naturally limit the number of endemic species found there. Coastal ecosystems are also highly dynamic through space and time, creating a 'moving target' from an evolutionary point of view. There may simply not be enough time for species to evolve specific adaptations to coastal conditions when these conditions are constantly changing. Or, the occurrence of bountiful resources during pulse events (e.g. fish migrations, spawning events) draws species temporarily only to retreat into more sheltered habitats once resources diminish. No matter the mechanism, the relative paucity of coastal endemics means that coastal ecosystems do not often rank highly in global efforts to document and preserve 'diversity hotspots' (e.g. Myers *et al.*, 2000; Orme *et al.*, 2005). Nevertheless, coastal ecosystems provide some of the best examples of how common and dominant species "[s]hape the world around us" and provide key functions and services (Gaston & Fuller, 2007).

The next obvious species to count are those that require coastal habitats to fulfill a key aspect of their life history but that otherwise range broadly into non-coastal ecosystems. There are many more of these species, they are often found in high abundance in coastal habitats for at least some portion of the year, and they figure prominently in calculations of ecosystem services and conservation decisions (Ronnback, 1999; Martinez *et al.*, 2007; Mcleod *et al.*, 2011; Fourqurean *et al.*, 2012). For example, the seven species of marine turtles use sandy beaches for nesting and their International Union for Conservation of Nature (IUCN) Red List status prompted the protection of critical beach breeding ground (http://www.iucnredlist.org; see also Chapter 10). Similarly, coastal species that are harvested in commercial, recreational, or subsistence fisheries provide a hefty economic benefit to society (Ronnback, 1999; UNEP, 2006). These species are (typically) not endemic to coastal ecosystems as they utilize freshwater or marine ecosystems for some portion of their lives, but without one or more coastal habitats these fisheries will decline, often in a dramatic fashion (e.g. Aburto-Oropeza *et al.*, 2008; Hughes *et al.*, 2009).

Finally, there are those species that can regularly be found in coastal ecosystems, but their entire geographical range extends well outside of coasts either landward or seaward (e.g. Chapters 6, 7, 9). For these species, coastal ecosystems represent one of many suitable potential habitats, and coastal habitats may in fact be somewhat marginal in quality relative to the others they utilize. Some biologists may include these species in their counts of coastal biodiversity and others may not; furthermore, they may make such decisions on a species-by-species basis (e.g. Chapters 6 and 7). The value of conserving these species is an open question. Coastal populations of these species may function as sinks within a larger metapopulation context; therefore, they may be given little conservation value (Kauffman *et al.*, 2004; Fodrie *et al.*, 2009; see also Chapter 6). Or, they may represent unique evolutionary units so that, although they are not considered separate species, their persistence is given high conservation value (e.g. Byun *et al.*, 1997; Wenburg *et al.*, 1998; Zink *et al.*, 2000; see also Chapter 7). For many, perhaps most, widespread species whose ranges can incorporate coastal habitats, we simply do not know which situation pertains.

The chapters in this book delve much deeper into the biodiversity and status of coastal habitats than we do here. Together they highlight two salient and non-mutually exclusive themes. First, many coastal habitats appear simple to the casual human observer due largely to the rarity or even absence of primary producers (e.g. sandy beaches) or to the extreme dominance of only one or two species (e.g. salt marshes, seagrass beds, mangroves, and oyster reefs). This simplicity belies a richly complex array of species, most of which go unseen and unnoticed by human residents of coastal habitats. Second, the integration of land and ocean within coastal habitats creates highly unique species assemblages, even if the species themselves are not uniquely assignable to one or more coastal habitats. In other words, coastal ecosystems may harbor few endemic species, but the species they do harbor create quite distinctive food webs.

COASTAL BIODIVERSITY AND ITS IMPACT ON ECOSYSTEM SERVICES

That coastal habitats provide valuable ecosystem goods and services is now well accepted (Barbier *et al.*, 2011), and the protection of these services increasingly is being used as justification in many coastal zone management plans. What is potentially less understood, and certainly more frequently debated, is the role that coastal biodiversity plays in maintaining these benefits. For direct uses of species, such as fisheries commodities and timber, the importance of species abundance is obvious. However, how species richness affects the delivery of ecosystem services is less clear, but understanding it may be vital to our efforts to conserve coastal ecosystem function (e.g. Zedler *et al.*, 2001; Duffy, 2009).

Coastal ecosystems do not seem to fit in well with traditional biodiversity–ecosystem function (BEF) theory, which predicts a strong linear relationship between species richness and ecological processes (Loreau *et al.*, 2001; Balvanera *et al.*, 2006; Schmid *et al.*, 2009). Many coastal habitats are species-poor, relative to inland habitats. In many cases, species assemblages are comprised of one or a few dominant species (e.g. mangroves, seagrass beds) or have distinct zonation patterns of species occurrence (e.g. salt marsh, dunes), with rare species contributing relatively little to overall biomass. Evidence suggests that, particularly in coastal habitats, the contribution of a species to ecosystem processes is directly related to its biomass (Davies *et al.*, 2011). In this case, the loss of dominant species through coastal degradation can have severe consequences on the provisioning of ecosystem goods and services. Further, compensatory effects of remaining species may be inconsequential (Davies *et al.*, 2011).

Some species losses have simple cause-and-effect relationships. For example, the overexploitation of oysters resulted in a significant depreciation of their value as a fished resource (Chapter 5). However, oyster loss has several additional indirect impacts, which are not as easy to quantify. Declines in water quality, shoreline erosion, and the loss of habitat and resources for other commercially valued fish species top the list. In other cases, impacts of species loss may be decoupled from its impacts. Overharvesting of horseshoe crabs (*Limulus polyphemus*), a marine species, along the Atlantic coast of North America triggered the sharp decline of the red knot (*Calidris canutus rufa*), a terrestrial, long-distance migratory shorebird (Chapter 12). In addition, species additions through deliberate or accidental introductions can alter food webs, change biotic composition, and either directly affect ecosystem function or suppress the ability of a native species to do so (Chapter 8).

Finally, we may not know the specific role a species plays in ecosystem functioning, and there is still much uncertainty about how diversity affects ecosystem processes (Hooper *et al.*, 2005). Answering these questions may change how coastal ecosystem functions are valued as ecosystem services (Barbier *et al.*, 2008; Koch *et al.*, 2009; Barbier, 2012).

CONSERVATION OF COASTAL ECOSYSTEMS

Fully 40% of the world's population in 1995 lived within 100 km of a coast, an increase of over 10% from levels recorded in 1990 (Burke *et al.*, 2001). Human density near coastlines is increasing at a rate nearly three times faster than comparable rates of growth inland (UNEP, 2006). By 2020, three-quarters of the global population is predicted to live within 60 km of the coast (UNCED, 1992). Coastal ecosystems represent some of the most urbanized places on Earth, and as expected, this level of urbanization has taken a heavy toll on the ecological integrity of many coastal habitats (Lotze *et al.*, 2006; UNEP, 2006). However, human settlements are not evenly distributed across habitats or coastlines, leaving some coasts heavily impacted and others virtually untouched (Small & Nichols, 2003; UNEP, 2006; Crain *et al.*, 2009; Halpern *et al.*, 2009). For example, over 60% of mangrove forests occur within, or near, major urban centers, and as a result their conservation status is quite dire (UNEP, 2006; see also Chapter 2). Temperate estuaries, particularly those associated with urban centers and ports, are some of the most degraded ecosystems on Earth, suffering significant impacts from marine pollution, biological invasions, and fisheries collapses (Grosholz, 2002; Kennish, 2002; Kirby, 2004). More generally, those coastal habitats that lie near the outlets of large rivers and urban centers tend to be highly degraded (UNEP, 2006; Halpern et al., 2009). Coastlines that are home to less-dense human settlements and are removed from large river systems are relatively unimpacted (Halpern et al., 2008, 2009).

The list of activities that degrade coastal ecosystems is long with an astonishing variety of direct uses, including fishing, salt production, grazing, fuel wood extraction, and mining (Chapters 2, 3, 5, 7, and 12). These same ecosystems are often also subjected to more indirect and sometimes diffuse stressors, such as terrestrial runoff of nitrogen and phosphorus, invasive species, oil spills, and sea level rise (Chapters 4, 5, 8, and 11). Less understood, but potentially as severe, are the emerging impacts of climate change (Chapters 9 and 10), including rising and warming seas, ocean acidification, increased air temperatures, and more frequent severe storms. The chapters of this book emphasize three conservation themes relative to the effect of these stressors on coastal biodiversity.

First, many stressors co-occur and are synergistic in their impacts on the persistence of one or more species. For example, marine turtles dropped to historically low numbers because of overexploitation over the last century. They are now legally protected from direct sources of mortality across their range, but their recovery is limited both by the loss of beach habitat for nesting due to coastal development and from sea level rise (Chapter 10). Similarly, oyster reefs are degraded by several interacting stressors that then create a positive feedback loop whereby the loss of oysters creates further loss of oysters (Chapter 5). In these instances, conservation managers must mount the nearly herculean effort of untangling the influence of each stressor, ranking their influence relative to one another, and acting to reduce each in turn (Lotze et al., 2006). Nevertheless, it is abundantly clear from reading the chapters in this book that such efforts are desperately needed.

Second, there is mounting evidence that these stressors can affect coastal biodiversity in unexpected and often non-linear ways. There are very clear examples where species have declined in the face of an oil spill (Chapter 11), the arrival of invasive species (Chapter 8), or due to over-exploitation (Chapters 5 and 9). There are other species that are less affected

(Chapter 11), and sometimes even benefit, from these same disturbances (Chapters 8 and 9). Furthermore, some species show short-term responses to stressors, such as oil spills or beach renourishment, while others evince surprisingly long-lived declines in their abundance or distribution due to the same disturbance event (Chapters 3 and 11). Finally, there can be a multitude of 'knock-on' effects of coastal ecosystem stressors on biodiversity whereby the loss or depletion of one species in the food web precipitates massive changes in another (Unsworth *et al.*, 2008; Hughes *et al.*, 2009; see also Chapters 5 and 12). Together, this array of impacts on coastal species renders predictions about how particular stressors will influence biodiversity uncertain.

Finally, the interconnectedness of coastal ecosystems creates a multitude of challenges when considering the conservation of their biodiversity (Sheaves, 2009). Species that utilize coastal ecosystems for all, or part, of their lives integrate processes that occur across biological realms, which are academically, legally, and administratively considered as independent units (Beger *et al.*, 2010). In other words, in coastal ecosystems, biology and management do not often line up neatly with one another. For example, it is unproductive to create conservation plans for seagrasses that ignore their intimate connection with land- and ocean-based processes (Heck *et al.*, 2008; Unsworth *et al.*, 2008; Waycott *et al.*, 2009; see also Chapter 4). Nevertheless, management actions often proceed based on legal and administrative boundaries that treat habitats, and especially land versus oceans, as independent units (Sheaves, 2009; Beger *et al.*, 2010). In many cases, resultant management actions may inadvertently sever critical biological and physical ties between coastal habitats creating counterproductive impacts on coastal biodiversity (e.g. Aburto-Oropeza *et al.*, 2008; Ewel, 2010). More broadly, coastal ecosystems are not easily considered within conservation decision support tools because the spatial information on biological connectivity that is required to do so is scarce and hard to analyze (Stoms *et al.*, 2008; Tallis *et al.*, 2008; Beger *et al.*, 2010).

THE COASTAL CONSERVATION GESTALT

If there is one overriding theme to this book it is that the factors that make coastal biodiversity so interesting are precisely the things that make it so vulnerable to loss. The dynamism and connectivity of coastal ecosystems support a fascinating and diverse set of species. Some species are rare and found only in local coastal habitats, whereas others only use these habitats for a small but critical part of their lives. These species utilize to their full advantage the often physically harsh interface of ocean and land, and they provide inextricable links between these two biological realms. The chapters that follow provide a tour through the major coastal habitats worldwide, allowing readers to glimpse the full array of species they support. This tour is punctuated by the cold realities of species losses and widespread habitat degradation. While the need to act is clear, the challenges associated with managing a dynamic biological mosaic are substantial. We have no doubt that readers will find their own conservation agenda within these pages. We provide a few of our own in the final chapter.

REFERENCES

Aburto-Oropeza O., Ezcurra, E., Danemann, G., *et al.* (2008). Mangroves in the Gulf of California increase fisheries yields. *Proceedings of the National Academy of Sciences of the United States of America*, **105**, 10456–10459.

Balvanera, P., Pfisterer, A. B., Buchmann, N., *et al.* (2006). Quantifying the evidence for biodiversity effects on ecosystem functioning and services. *Ecology Letters*, **9**, 1146–1156.

Barbier, E. B. (2012). Progress and challenges in valuing coastal and marine ecosystem services. *Review of Environmental Economics and Policy*, **6**, 1–19.

Barbier, E. G., Koch, E. W., Silliman, B. R., *et al.* (2008). Coastal ecosystem-based management with non-linear ecological functions and values. *Science*, **319**, 321–323.

Barbier, E. B., Hacker, S. D., Kennedy, C., *et al.* (2011). The value of estuarine and coastal ecosystem services. *Ecological Monographs*, **81**, 169–193.

Beger, M., Grantham, H. S., Pressey, R. L., *et al.* (2010). Conservation planning for connectivity across marine, freshwater and terrestrial realms. *Biological Conservation*, **143**, 565–575.

Burke, L., Kura, Y., Kasem, K., *et al.* (2001). *Coastal Ecosystems.* Washington, DC: World Resources Institute.

Byun, S. A., Koop, B. F. & Reimchen, T. E. (1997). North American black bear mtDNA phylogeography: Implications for morphology and the Haida Gwaii glacial refugium controversy. *Evolution*, **51**, 1647–1653.

Carter, R. W. G. (1998). *Coastal Environments: An Introduction to the Physical, Ecological and Cultural Systems of Coastlines.* New York, NY: Academic Press.

Coverdale, T. C., Herrmann, N. C., Altieri, A. H. & Bertness, M D. (2013). Latent impacts: The role of historical human activity in coastal habitat loss. *Frontiers in Ecology and Environment*, **11**, 69–74.

Crain, C. M., Halpern, B. S., Beck, M. W. & Kappel, C. V. (2009). Understanding and managing human threats to the coastal marine environment. *The Year in Ecology and Conservation: Annals of New York Academy of Science*, **1162**, 39–62.

Davies, T. W., Jenkins, S. R., Kingham, R., *et al.* (2011). Dominance, biomass and extinction resistance determine the consequences of biodiversity loss for multiple coastal ecosystems. *PloS ONE*, **6**, e28362.

Davis, R. A. & Fitzgerald, D. M. (2004). *Beaches and Coasts*. Malden, MA: Blackwell Science.

Doody, J. P. (2000). *Coastal Conservation and Management: An Ecological Perspective*. Boston, MA: Kluwer Academic Publishers.

Duffy, J. E. (2009). Why biodiversity is important to the functioning of real-world ecosystems. *Frontiers in Ecology and Environment*, 7, 437–444.

Duke, N. C., Meynecke, J. O., Dittmann, S., *et al.* (2013). A world without mangroves? *Science*, 317, 41.

Ewel, K. C. (2010). Appreciating tropical coastal wetlands from a landscape perspective. *Frontiers in Ecology and Environment*, 8, 20–26.

Fodrie, J. F., Levin, L. L. & Lucas, A. J. (2009). Use of population fitness to evaluate the nursery function of juvenile habitats. *Marine Ecology Progress Series*, 385, 39–49.

Fourqurean, J. W., Duarte, C. M, Kennedy, H., *et al.* (2012). Seagrass ecosystems as a globally significant carbon stock. *Nature Geoscience*, 5, 505–509.

Gaston, K. J. & Fuller, R. A. (2007). Commoness, population depletion and conservation biology. *Trends in Ecology and Evolution*, 23, 14–19.

Granek, E. F., Polasky, S., Kappel, C. V., *et al.* (2010). Ecosystem services as a common language for coastal ecosystem-based management. *Conservation Biology*, 24, 207–216.

Grosholz, E. (2002). Ecological and evolutionary consequences of coastal invasions. *Trends in Ecology and Evolution*, 17, 22–27.

Halpern, B. S., Walbridge, S., Selkoe, K. A., *et al.* (2008). A global map of human impact on marine ecosystems. *Science*, 319, 948–952.

Halpern, B. S., Ebert, C. M., Kappel, C. V., *et al.* (2009). Global priority areas for incorporating land-sea connections in marine conservation. *Conservation Letters*, 2, 189–196.

Heck, Jr., K. L., Carruthers, T. J. B., Duarte, C. M., *et al.* (2008). Trophic transfers from seagrass meadows subsidize diverse marine and terrestrial consumers. *Ecosystems*, 11, 1198–1210.

Hooper, D. U., Chapin, III, F. S., Ewel, J. J., *et al.* (2005). *Effects of Biodiversity on Ecosystem Processes: Implications for Ecosystem Management*. ESA Public Affairs Office, Position Paper. Ecological Society of America. Jamestown, ND: Northern Prairie Wildlife Research Center.

Hughes, A. R., Williams, S. L., Duarte, C. M., Heck, Jr., K. H. & Waycott, M. (2009). Associations of concern: Declining seagrasses and threatened dependent species. *Frontiers in Ecology and Environment*, 7, 242–246.

Kauffman, M. J., Pollock, J. F. & Walton, B. (2004). Spatial structure, dispersal and management of a recovering raptor population. *American Naturalist*, 164, 582–597.

Kennish, M. J. (2002). Environmental threats and environmental future of estuaries. *Environmental Conservation*, 29, 78–107.

Kirby, M. X. (2004). Fishing down the coast: Historical expansion and collapse of oyster fisheries along continental margins. *Proceedings of the National Academy of Sciences of the United States of America*, 101, 13096–13099.

Koch, E. W., Barbier, E. B., Silliman, B. R., *et al.* (2009). Non-linearity in ecosystem services: Temporal and spatial variability in coastal protection. *Frontiers in Ecology and Environment*, 7, 29–37.

Loreau, M., Naeem, S., Inchausti, P., *et al.* (2001). Biodiversity and ecosystem functioning: Current knowledge and future challenges. *Science*, **294**, 804–808.

Lotze, H. K., Lenihan, H. S., Bourque, B. J., *et al.* (2006). Depletion, degradation, and recovery potential of estuaries and coastal seas. *Science*, **312**, 1806–1809.

Martinez, M. L., Intralawan, A., Vazquez, G., *et al.* (2007). The coasts of our world: Ecological, economic and social importance. *Ecological Economics*, **63**, 254–272.

Mcleod, E., Chmura, G. L., Bouillon, S., *et al.* (2011). A blueprint for blue carbon: Toward an improved understanding of the role of vegetated coastal habitats in sequestering CO_2. *Frontiers in Ecology and Environment*, **9**, 552–560.

Myers, N., Mittermeirer, R. A., Mittermeier, C. G., de Fonseca, G. A. B. & Kent, J. (2000). Biodiversity hotspots for conservation priorities. *Nature*, **403**, 853–858.

Orme, C. D. L., Davies, R. G., Burgess, M., *et al.* (2005). Global hotspots of species richness are not congruent with endemism or threat. *Nature*, **436**, 1016–1019.

Ronnback, P. (1999). The ecological basis for economic value of seafood production supported by mangrove ecosystems. *Ecological Economics*, **29**, 235–252.

Schlacher, T. A. & Connolly, R. M. (2009). Land–ocean coupling of carbon and nitrogen fluxes on sandy beaches. *Ecosystems*, **12**, 311–321.

Schlacher, T. A., Schoeman, D. S., Dugan, J., *et al.* (2008). Sandy beach ecosystems: Key features, sampling issues, management challenges, and climate change impacts. *Marine Ecology*, **29**(S1), 70–90.

Sheaves, M. (2009). Consequences of ecological connectivity: The coastal ecosystem mosaic. *Marine Ecology Progress Series*, **391**, 107–115.

Schmid, B., Balvanera, P., Cardinale, B. J., *et al.* (2009). Consequences of species loss for ecosystem functioning: Meta-analyses of data from biodiversity experiments. In S. Naeem, D. E. Bunker, A. Hector, M. Loreau & C. Perrings (eds.), *Biodiversity, Ecosystem Functioning, & Human Wellbeing*. Oxford: Oxford University Press, pp. 14–29.

Small, C. & Nichols, R. J. (2003). A global analysis of human settlement in coastal zones. *Journal of Coastal Research*, **19**, 584–599.

Stoms, D. M., Davis, F. W., Andelman, S. J., *et al.* (2008). Integrated coastal reserve planning: Making the land–sea connection. *Frontiers in Ecology and Environment*, **3**, 429–436.

Tallis, H., Ferdana, Z. & Gray, E. (2008). Linking terrestrial and marine conservation planning and threats analysis. *Conservation Biology*, **22**, 120–130.

United Nations Conference on Environment and Development (UNCED). (1992). *Protection of the Oceans, All Kinds of Seas, Including Enclosed and Semi-enclosed Seas, and Coastal Areas and the Protection, Rational Use and Development of Their Living Resources*. Agenda 21, Chapter 17. New York, NY: United Nations Divison for Sustainable Development.

Waycott, M., Duarte, C. M., Carruthers, T. J. B., *et al.* (2009). Accelerating loss of seagrasses across the globe threatens coastal ecosystems. *Proceedings of the National Academy of Sciences of the United States of America*, **106**, 12377–12381.

Wenburg, J. K., Bentzen, P. & Foote, C. J. (1998). Microsatellite analysis of genetic population structure in an endangered salmonid: The coastal cutthroat trout (*Oncorhynchus clarki clarki*). *Molecular Ecology*, **7**, 733–749.

United Nations Environment Programme (UNEP). (2006). *Marine and Coastal Ecosystems and Human Well-being: A Synthesis Report Based on the Findings of the Millenium Ecosystem Assessment*. Nairobi: UNEP.

Unsworth, R. K. F., De Leon, P. S., Garrard, S. L., *et al.* (2008). High connectivity of Indo-Pacific seagrass fish assemblages with mangrove and coral reef habitats. *Marine Ecology Progress Series*, **353**, 213–224.

Zedler, J. B., Callaway, J. C. & Sullivan, G. (2001). Declining biodiversity: Why species matter and how their functions might be restored in Californian tidal marshes. *Bioscience*, **51**, 1005–1017.

Zink, R. M., Barrowclough, G. F., Atwood, J. L. & Blackwell-Rago, R. C. (2000). Genetics, taxonomy, and conservation of the threatened California gnatcatcher. *Conservation Biology*, **14**, 1394–1405.

Part I

Biodiversity Status of Coastal Habitats

2

Global patterns of mangrove extinction risk: implications for ecosystem services and biodiversity loss

BETH A. POLIDORO, KENT E. CARPENTER,
FARID DAHDOUH-GUEBAS, JOANNA C. ELLISON,
NICO E. KOEDAM, AND JEAN W.H. YONG

WHAT ARE MANGROVES?

Mangroves are unique plant species found in tropical and subtropical estuarine and nearshore marine regions worldwide. Mangrove species have several physiological adaptations to saline, water-saturated soils, including viviparous or cryptoviviparous seeds that disperse by water, and salt-exclusion or salt-excretion capabilities to cope with high salt concentrations in nearshore saturated soils and sediments. Many species also have specialized aerial roots, or pneumatophores, that enable oxygenation of roots in water-logged soils. Species restricted to tropical intertidal habitat have been defined as "true mangrove" species, while those not exclusive to this habitat are sometimes referred to as "mangrove associates" (Lugo & Snedaker, 1974). Others include as mangroves any tree, shrub, palm, or ground fern exceeding 0.5 m in height and which normally grows in the intertidal zone of tropical coastal or estuarine environments (Duke, 1992). In view of the global variety of mangrove types and their floristics, there are approximately 70 species of mangroves, which are quite taxonomically diverse, as they represent 17 families (Table 2.1). The Mangrove Reference Database and Herbarium provides a larger overview of all known species, subspecies and hybrids (Massó i Alemán et al., 2010).

Compared to other forest types, mangrove forests generally lack an understory and usually exhibit distinct zones of species (Figure 2.1) based on variation in elevation, salinity, and wave action (Duke et al., 1998). Many species are more common in environmental conditions characterized by the low or high intertidal zone, or in the downstream or upstream estuarine

Coastal Conservation, eds B. Maslo and J. L. Lockwood. Published by Cambridge University Press.
© Cambridge University Press 2014.

Table 2.1 *List of mangrove species (excluding hybrids, varieties, and subspecies), estuarine and intertidal position (D, downstream; I, intermediate; U, upstream; L, low; M, middle; H, high), native range (1, Eastern Tropical Pacific; 2, Caribbean; 3, West Africa; 4, East Africa; 5, Asia; 6, Australasia; 7, Oceania), and 2011 IUCN Red List Category (CR, Critically Endangered; EN, Endangered; VU, Vulnerable; NT, Near Threatened; LC, Least Concern; DD, Data Deficient). Presence not indicated for introduced species found outside of their natural biogeographical range (e.g. Rhizophora stylosa in French Polynesia; Bruguiera sexangula, Conocarpus erectus, and Rhizophora mangle in Hawaii; Bruguiera gymnorrhiza and Lumnitzera racemosa in Florida; Avicennia marina in California; Sonneratia apelata in China; and Nypa fruticans in Cameroon and Nigeria). Genus and species nomenclature follow Tomlinson (1986) and Polidoro and colleagues (2010).*

Family	Species	Estuarine position	Intertidal position	Native range	2011 IUCN Red List category
ACANTHACEAE	*Acanthus ebracteatus*	I	M H	5,6	LC
ACANTHACEAE	*Acanthus ilicifolius*	I U	M H	5,6	LC
ACANTHACEAE	*Acanthus volubilis*	U	H	5,6	LC
ACANTHACEAE	*Acanthus xiamenensis*	? ?	? ?	5	DD
ACANTHACEAE	*Avicennia alba*	D	L M	5,6	LC
ACANTHACEAE	*Avicennia bicolor*	D	H	1	VU
ACANTHACEAE	*Avicennia germinans*	D I	M H	1,2,3	LC
ACANTHACEAE	*Avicennia integra*	I	L	6	VU
ACANTHACEAE	*Avicennia marina*	D I	L M H	4,5,6	LC
ACANTHACEAE	*Avicennia officinalis*	I	M	5,6	LC
ACANTHACEAE	*Avicennia rumphiana*	D	H	5,6	VU
ACANTHACEAE	*Avicennia schaueriana*	D	M H	2	LC
ARECACEAE	*Nypa fruticans*	U	L M	5,6	LC
ARECACEAE	*Phoenix paludosa**	U	H	5	NT
BIGNONIACEAE	*Dolichandrone spathacea**	U	M	5,6	LC
BIGNONIACEAE	*Tabebuia palustris**	U	L M	1	VU
COMBRETACEAE	*Conocarpus erectus*	D	H	1,2,3	LC
COMBRETACEAE	*Laguncularia racemosa*	D I	M H	1,2,3	LC
COMBRETACEAE	*Lumnitzera littorea*	I	M	5,6,7	LC
COMBRETACEAE	*Lumnitzera racemosa*	D	M H	4,5,6	LC

Family	Species								
EBENACEAE	Diospyros littorea*		I	U		M	H	5,6	LC
EUPHORBIACEAE	Excoecaria agallocha		I	U		M	H	5,6	LC
EUPHORBIACEAE	Excoecaria indica	D	I		L	M		5,6	DD
FABACEAE	Cynometra iripa*		I	U			H	5,6	LC
FABACEAE	Mora oleifera*		I	U			H	1	VU
LYTHRACEAE	Pemphis acidula	D					H	4,5,6,7	LC
LYTHRACEAE	Sonneratia alba	D			L	M		4,5,6	LC
LYTHRACEAE	Sonneratia apetala				L			5	LC
LYTHRACEAE	Sonneratia caseolaris			U	L			5,6	LC
LYTHRACEAE	Sonneratia griffithii	D		U	L			5	CR
LYTHRACEAE	Sonneratia lanceolata				L			5,6	LC
LYTHRACEAE	Sonneratia ovata	D		U				5,6	NT
MALVACEAE	Brownlowia argentata*			U			H	5,6	DD
MALVACEAE	Brownlowia tersa*			U			H	5	NT
MALVACEAE	Camptostemon philippinense		I		L		H	5	EN
MALVACEAE	Camptostemon schultzii	D	I		L	M		5,6	LC
MALVACEAE	Heritiera fomes			U			H	5	EN
MALVACEAE	Heritiera globosa			U			H	5	EN
MALVACEAE	Heritiera littoralis		I				H	4,5,6	LC
MELIACEAE	Aglaia cucullata			U		M		5	DD
MELIACEAE	Xylocarpus granatum		I	U			H	4,5,6,7	LC
MELIACEAE	Xylocarpus moluccensis					M	H	5,6	LC
MYRSINACEAE	Aegiceras corniculatum		I	U	L			5,6	LC
MYRSINACEAE	Aegiceras floridum				L			5	NT
MYRTACEAE	Osbornia octodonta	D				M	H	5,6	LC
PLUMBAGINACEAE	Aegialitis annulata	D				M	H	5,6	LC
PLUMBAGINACEAE	Aegialitis rotundifolia	D				M	H	5	NT
PTERIDACEAE	Acrostichum aureum*		I				H	2,3,4,5,6	LC
PTERIDACEAE	Acrostichum danaeifolium*		I				H	1,2,3	LC
PTERIDACEAE	Acrostichum speciosum*		I	U			H	5,6	LC

Table 2.1 (cont.)

Family	Species	Estuarine position			Intertidal position			Native range	2011 IUCN Red List category
RHIZOPHORACEAE	*Bruguiera cylindrica*	D	I			M	H	5,6	LC
RHIZOPHORACEAE	*Bruguiera exaristata*		I	U		M	H	5,6	LC
RHIZOPHORACEAE	*Bruguiera gymnorrhiza*	D	I			M	H	4,5,6	LC
RHIZOPHORACEAE	*Bruguiera hainesii*		I				H	5,6	CR
RHIZOPHORACEAE	*Bruguiera parviflora*	D	I			M		5,6	LC
RHIZOPHORACEAE	*Bruguiera sexangula*		I	U		M	H	5,6	LC
RHIZOPHORACEAE	*Ceriops australis*	D	I				H	6	LC
RHIZOPHORACEAE	*Ceriops decandra*		I			M	H	5	NT
RHIZOPHORACEAE	*Ceriops tagal*	D	I			M	H	4,5,6	LC
RHIZOPHORACEAE	*Ceriops zippeliana*		I			M	H	5,6	LC
RHIZOPHORACEAE	*Kandelia candel*	D			L			5	LC
RHIZOPHORACEAE	*Kandelia obovata*	D			L			5	LC
RHIZOPHORACEAE	*Rhizophora apiculata*		I			M		5,6	LC
RHIZOPHORACEAE	*Rhizophora mangle*	D	I			M		2,3	LC
RHIZOPHORACEAE	*Rhizophora mucronata*		I	U	L			4,5,6	LC
RHIZOPHORACEAE	*Rhizophora racemosa*	D	I			M		1,2,3	LC
RHIZOPHORACEAE	*Rhizophora samoensis*	D	I			M		1,6,7	NT
RHIZOPHORACEAE	*Rhizophora stylosa*	D	I		L	M		5,6,7	LC
RUBIACEAE	*Scyphiphora hydrophyllacea*		I				H	5,6	LC
TETRAMERISTACEAE	*Pelliciera rhizophorae*		I	U		M	H	1,2	VU

*May be considered a mangrove associate in some or all regions.

(Adapted from Polidoro *et al.*, 2010.)

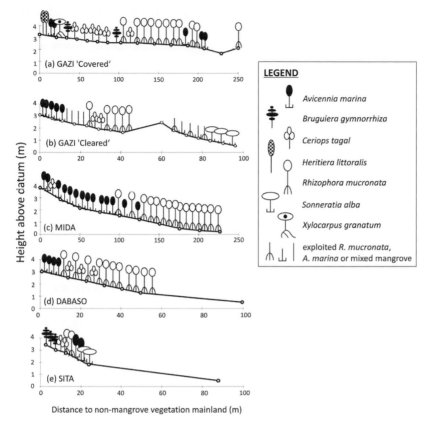

Figure 2.1 Mangrove species distributions observed in five different mangrove areas (a–e) along the coastline of Kenya to illustrate how mangrove species zonation is highly variable due to a number of factors, including variation in environmental conditions and the number and type of species present (adapted from Dahdouh-Guebas *et al.*, 2002).

zones. For example, species found primarily in the upstream estuarine or high intertidal region often have specific freshwater-dominated habitat preference, while other species that have higher inundation tolerance can be found in the downstream estuarine or low intertidal zone and along beaches. However, zonation or correlation with environmental gradients is not always apparent and can be easily disrupted by anthropogenic disturbance (Ellison *et al.*, 2000).

All mangroves disperse their propagules by water, and many mangrove species produce seedlings through vivipary. For many of the mangrove species that reproduce through vivipary or cryptovivipary, an embryo remains on the parent tree for months sometimes before it detaches, germinates, and grows roots (Tomlinson, 1986; Hogarth, 2007). The hypocotyls of some species are more adapted to long-distance dispersal and exhibit a period of postponed dormancy before rooting. A few mangrove species do not reproduce through this process, but rather disperse more conventionally via floating fruits and seeds (Tomlinson, 1986; Hogarth, 2007).

MANGROVE BIODIVERSITY AND ECOSYSTEM SERVICES

Compared to some other coastal habitat-forming species, such as reef-building corals (Carpenter *et al.*, 2008), mangroves are relatively low in global number of species. Unlike many other forests, mangrove forests consist of relatively few species, with 30–40 species in the most diverse sites and only one or a few species present in many places (Duke *et al.*, 1998). The highest numbers of species are found in the Indo-West Pacific, or more specifically in southeast Asia and northern Australia (Ricklefs & Latham, 1993; Duke, 2006; Polidoro *et al.*, 2010). For this reason, many consider the Indo-West Pacific the center of speciation, with mangroves originating here and later disseminating across the Pacific, to the westward coast of the Americas and eastern Africa, and finally to the east and west Atlantic (Hogarth, 2007). An alternate hypothesis, based in part on examination of the fossil record, is that mangroves originated near the Tethys Sea, and diversification occurred in place after the movement of the continents (Ellison *et al.*, 1999). Mangrove species expansion and biogeographical range are considered to be limited by temperature and rainfall patterns, distribution of suitable habitats, and the dispersal properties of individual species, although no universally valid values exist to explain limits (Quisthoudt *et al.*, 2012).

Global mangrove area, estimated to be approximately 138 000 km² in 2000, is less than half of what it was before 1950 and represents only 0.7% of tropical forest area worldwide (FAO, 2007; Giri *et al.*, 2011). Yet, mangrove forests are the economic foundations of many tropical coastal regions (Field *et al.*, 1998), estimated to provide at least US $1.6 billion per year in ecosystem services worldwide 15 years ago (Costanza *et al.*, 1997). More recent studies have estimated that the value of goods and services provided by mangroves can range from US $2000 to $9000 per hectare (Wells *et al.*, 2006). Although the economic value of mangroves can be difficult to quantify, the relatively small number of mangrove species worldwide collectively provide a wealth of services and goods while occupying only 0.12% of the world's total land area (Dodd *et al.*, 2008).

Mangroves protect inland human communities from damage caused by coastal erosion and storms. With their large above-ground aerial root systems and standing crop, mangroves can form a physical barrier against tidal and ocean influences in some regions (Dahdouh-Guebas *et al.*, 2005b; Das & Vincent, 2009). Even in areas where mangrove forests were present but degraded, storm protection was estimated to be much less than in areas where healthy, intact mangrove forests were present (Kairo *et al.*, 2002; Dahdouh-Guebas *et al.*, 2005b). Some studies also have shown that mangroves can use high nitrogen and phosphorus inputs in polluted environments to fuel tree production, acting as a natural filter for pollutants, such as sewage and aquaculture effluent (Robertson & Phillips, 1995; Trott & Alongi, 2000; Kristensen *et al.*, 2011).

Mangroves also serve as both a source and sink for nutrients and sediments for other inshore marine habitats, including seagrass beds and coral reefs (Dorenbosch *et al.*, 2004; Duke *et al.*, 2007; Donato *et al.*, 2011; see also Chapter 4). It is thought that particulate organic matter from mangroves is distributed in sediments in nearby seagrass beds, which through microbial respiration, then provides the carbon dioxide necessary for seagrass photosynthesis (Hemminga *et al.*, 1994). Corals are very vulnerable to sedimentation and excess nutrients, both of which can be trapped by mangrove root systems. Through a net movement of both dissolved and particulate carbon to both seagrasses and corals, mangroves can sequester up to 25.5 million tons of carbon per year (Ong, 1993), and they can provide more than 10% of essential organic carbon to the global oceans (Dittmar *et al.*, 2006). Because mangroves harvest carbon from the atmosphere and transfer it into sediments, they are one of several key coastal ecosystems that play an important role in carbon sequestration and in regulating climate. It is estimated that mangrove sediment carbon stores are approximately five times larger than those found in temperate, boreal, and tropical terrestrial forests (Bouillon, 2011; Donato *et al.*, 2011).

Mangrove forests provide critical habitat for numerous terrestrial, estuarine, and marine species (Robertson & Duke, 1987; Primavera, 1998; Kathiresan & Bingham 2001; Nagelkerken *et al.*, 2008; Ng *et al.*, 2008; Luther & Greenburg, 2009). A variety of terrestrial birds, insects, and reptiles can be found in the upper canopies of mangrove forests, while in the subtidal zone mangrove roots support a large community of marine invertebrates, including barnacles, mollusks, crustaceans, and oysters. Along the coastal zone, sea snakes, otters, dugongs, and several species of cetaceans can be found in mangrove areas. Many species of coastal and pelagic fishes and other taxa rely on mangrove and estuarine areas for primary habitat or for reproductive or juvenile nursing grounds. In this sense, it is estimated that almost 80% of global fish catches are directly or indirectly dependent on mangroves (Sheaves, 2005; Sullivan, 2005; Ellison, 2008).

THREATS TO MANGROVES WORLDWIDE

Mangrove forests are considered to be more susceptible to disturbance than other forests due to their position in wildly dynamic coastal zones that are prone to storms, coastal erosion, and changing river discharges, all of which can suppress successional changes and increase environmental stress (Hogarth, 2007). With almost half (44%) of the world's population living within 150 km of a coastline (Cohen *et al.*, 1997), heavily populated coastal zones have led to the widespread clearing of mangroves for coastal development, aquaculture, agriculture, or resource use. It is estimated that 26% of mangrove forests worldwide are degraded due to overexploitation for fuelwood and timber production (Valiela *et al.*, 2001). Approximately 38% of global mangrove loss has been attributed to the clearing of mangroves solely for aquaculture (Ellison, 2008). Removal of mangroves for fuelwood or aquaculture can contribute directly or indirectly to a number of coastal problems, including a shift in natural tidal flows, alteration of the groundwater table, reduced water quality, release of toxic wastes, introduction of excess nutrients, and changes to natural food chains (Alongi, 2002). Equally worrisome is the expansion of mangrove associates at the expense of true mangrove representatives in certain forests, a concept termed 'cryptic ecologic degradation' and suggested to be responsible for decreased functionality of mangroves (Dahdouh-Guebas *et al.*, 2005a; Koedam & Dahdouh-Guebas, 2008).

As mangroves are the epitome of the terrestrial–marine ecotone, they often effectively connect terrestrial systems with marine ecosystems. For example, the African Eastern Arc mountains (Kenya, Tanzania) and adjacent coastal forests are biodiversity hotspots of global importance. In many places, these terrestrial forests are directly connected hydrologically to mangrove assemblages, which in turn are connected to nearshore seagrass beds and coral reefs. These hydrological and groundwater connections are critical to sustaining the functionality of all of these systems. In many areas, the associated hydrologic connections are fragmented and dissected by deforestation, encroachment, and infrastructure and are rarely viewed and managed as a functional complex comprised of different yet interdependent ecosystems.

Species found primarily in the upstream estuarine or high intertidal regions often have specific freshwater-dominated habitat requirements, are usually patchily distributed, and occupy areas that are generally cleared for the construction of aquaculture ponds or for agriculture. For example, populations of *Heritiera fomes* and *Heritiera globosa* in south and southeast Asia have been severely reduced due to coastal development, the creation of aquaculture ponds, reduction of freshwater from the creation of dams, and expansion of palm and timber plantations (Ong, 2003). In the downstream estuarine and low-intertidal region, many species, such as *Aegiceras floridum*, that have high salinity requirements are experiencing rapid declines due to coastal development and the conversion of tidal wetlands to fish ponds (Primavera *et al.*, 2004).

Climate change is also considered a threat to all mangrove habitats through their sensitivity to sea level rise, particularly where a coastline is subsiding, as is the case in large deltas (Syvitski *et al.*, 2009). Species that occupy a more restricted elevational range or are less abundant than others are the most threatened (Ellison, 2012). With a rise in sea level, the habitat requirements of each species will be disrupted, and species may suffer mortality in their present zones and re-establish at higher elevations, if such migration areas are available (Ellison, 2005; Gilman *et al.*, 2008). Mangrove species at the landward margin are particularly vulnerable to sea level rise if, owing to coastal development or topography, habitat migration or recruitment inland is blocked (Di Nitto *et al.*, 2008). Such species that occur at the landward edge or upstream in tidal estuaries include *Brownlowia tersa, Bruguiera sexangula, Nypa fruticans, Phoenix paludosa, Lumnitzera racemosa, Lumnitzera littorea, Sonneratia caseolaris, Sonneratia lanceolata,* and *Xylocarpus granatum.* Species that are easily dispersed and grow or reproduce rapidly, such as *Rhizophora* species, may adapt better to changing conditions than those that are slower growing and slower to reproduce, such as *Bruguiera, Ceriops,* or *Xylocarpus* species. Maintenance of sediment supply to mangroves and enhancement of mangrove productivity will enhance their adaptive capacity through substrate accretion (Ellison, 2012). Massive sediment deposition can, however, cause mortality (Ellison, 1998).

In the last 100 years, human-facilitated long-distance mangrove plant dispersal has altered some of these species' natural distributions. This process has opened up the possibility for mangroves from different biogeographical regions (Indo-Pacific, tropical Atlantic) to invade the other mangrove forests following their accidental or deliberate introduction (Duke, 1992; Zan *et al.*, 2003; Chimner *et al.*, 2006; Biswas *et al.*, 2007; Fourqurean *et al.*, 2010). In some cases, non-native mangroves growing in foreign mangrove habitats can displace the native mangrove species and alter the natural mangrove ecosystem structure and services. For example, in southern China, as an initial restoration and reforestation effort for degraded mangrove forests, *Sonneratia apetala* (a native of India, Bangladesh, and Sri Lanka) was introduced in 1985 from Bangladesh to the Dong Zhaigang Mangrove Nature Reserve (Hainan Island, China) (Zan *et al.*, 2003). In the northern mangrove areas of China, *S. apetala* is restricted by low winter temperatures, which prevented invasion (Ren *et al.*, 2009). However, uncontrolled colonization into native mangroves did occur in the warmer southern locations of two provinces: Guangdong (Leizhou peninsula, Zhanjiang and Shenzhen) and Hainan island (Dong Zhaigang). At these locations, the rapid growth and invasive nature of *S. apetala* affected the distribution and survival of local native mangrove species. At present, in light of the new data, the relevant authorities and agencies are re-evaluating their mangrove restoration projects and strategies with respect to the use of non-native mangrove species in China.

In the United States, at least four species of Indo-Pacific mangroves (*Bruguiera gymnorrhiza* and *Lumnitzera racemosa* in Florida; *Avicennia marina* in California; *B. sexangula* in Hawaii) have naturalized and spread into the American mangrove forests and tidal wetlands (Duke, 1992; Chimner *et al.*, 2006; Fourqurean *et al.*, 2010). In particular, the more invasive non-native mangrove species, such as *L. racemosa* and *A. marina*, are being targeted for eradication by various land management agencies in California and Florida. It is noteworthy that many other Indo-Pacific mangroves (*B. hainesii*, *Nypa fruticans*, *R. mucronata*, *R. stylosa*, *Heritiera littoralis*, *Ceriops* spp., *Dolichandrone spathacea*, *Kandelia candel*, *A. marina*, *A. officinalis*, *Xylocarpus granatum*) did not persist in Florida, suggesting that Florida may be a marginal environment (one reason being lower temperatures) for these non-native Indo-Pacific mangrove species. However, if non-native mangroves can adapt to the new environment, these mangroves can indeed compete against the native species. Given the importance of native mangroves to the adjacent coastal environment, ecosystem function of local mangrove forests may also change as a consequence of non-native species. Hence, a precautionary approach may be preferred for introducing mangroves, in light of the many examples of natural ecosystem disruption by non-native plant species.

GEOGRAPHIC AREAS AND SPECIES OF CONCERN

Range declines for all mangrove species are occurring in all tropical coastal regions of the world (FAO, 2007). Globally, between 20% and 35% of mangrove area has been lost since approximately 1980 (Valiela *et al.*,

2001; FAO, 2007), and mangrove areas are disappearing at the rate of approximately 1% per year (FAO, 2003, 2007), with estimates as high as 3.6% in the Americas (Valiela *et al.*, 2001), and between 2% and 8% per year in other regions (Miththapala, 2008). Asia has suffered the highest losses (FAO, 2007), primarily due to human impacts (data used in these assessments precede the 2004 Asian tsunami: Valiela *et al.*, 2001). Given their accelerating rate of loss and expected continuation of high exploitation rates (Alongi, 2002), mangrove forests may functionally disappear in as little as 100 years (Duke *et al.*, 2007).

The loss of mangrove forests and individual mangrove species is of great concern, especially as even pristine mangrove areas are species-poor compared with other tropical plant ecosystems and coastal habitats. Globally, 16% of mangroves (11 of 70 species) are considered to be at elevated risk of extinction based on IUCN Red List Criteria (Polidoro *et al.*, 2010; Table 2.1). However, many non-threatened species are also experiencing declines or significant population threats. For many species, there has been significant mangrove area lost within their ranges, even though global population declines for these species are currently estimated to be below the thresholds required for assignment to an IUCN Red List threatened category (Polidoro *et al.*, 2010). Given the alarming rate of decline of mangrove forests in some regions, many species may indeed be threatened at the regional level (IUCN, 2003), or may represent a regionally threatened ecosystem based on a newly developing IUCN Red List for Threatened Ecosystems (Rodriguez *et al.*, 2011).

Mangrove species richness is highest in south and southeast Asia (Figure 2.2), with 56 of the 70 known mangrove species present in this region. Indonesia currently hosts the largest area of mangroves in the world (Spalding *et al.*, 2010; Dahdouh-Guebas, 2011), with more than 30 000 km^2 in 2003 (FAO, 2007), followed by Australia, Mexico, and Brazil. However, Indonesia and the Indo-Malay Philippine Archipelago have the highest rates of mangrove area loss globally, both with an estimated 30% reduction in mangrove area since 1980 primarily due to clearing for the creation of aquaculture ponds and other coastal developments (Primavera, 2000; FAO, 2007). Several species in this region have very restricted ranges and are at elevated risk of extinction. For example, *Camptostemon philippinense* is only present in parts of Indonesia and the Philippines and has an estimated 1200 or fewer individuals remaining due to the extensive removal of mangrove areas for both aquaculture and fuelwood within its very limited range. *Heritiera globosa* has the most restricted distribution in this region as it is only known from western Borneo, where it is patchily distributed and

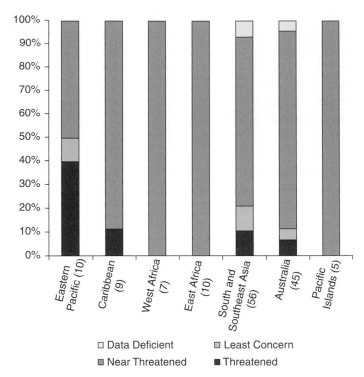

Figure 2.2 Proportion of species in 2011 IUCN Red List Categories per region. Number of true mangrove species present in each region in parentheses.

its riverine habitat has been extensively cleared by logging activities and for the creation of timber and oil palm plantations.

The Sundarbans in southern Bangladesh comprise the largest single block of mangroves in the world. Dominated by a relatively common mangrove species, *Heritiera fomes*, this region is critical habitat for the endangered Royal Bengal Tiger (*Panthera tigris tigris*) and provides crucial protection from cyclonic flooding for millions of human inhabitants. However, with one of the highest densities of human habitation in Asia, the mangroves of the Sundarbans have been extensively cleared and degraded over hundreds of years of human settlement.

The rare *Sonneratia griffithii* is distributed in parts of India and southeast Asia, where a combined 80% loss of all mangrove area has occurred within its patchy range over the past 60 years, with significant losses in Malaysia (Ong, 2003), primarily due to the clearing of mangrove areas for rice farming, aquaculture, and coastal development. This species is already reported to be locally extinct in a number of areas within its range, and > 500 mature individuals are known from India, Myanmar, Thailand, and Malaysia. *Bruguiera hainesii* is an even rarer species and is only known from a few fragmented locations in Indonesia, Malaysia, Thailand, Myanmar, Singapore, Vietnam, the Solomon Islands, and Papua New Guinea (Sheue *et al.*, 2005; Ng *et al.*, 2008). It has very low rates of propagation and germination, and it is estimated that there are < 250 mature individuals remaining. For these species, urgent protection is needed for remaining individuals as well as research to determine minimum viable population size.

After the Indo-Malay Philippine Archipelago, the Caribbean has the second highest rate of mangrove area loss relative to other global regions, with approximately 24% of mangrove area lost over the past quarter-century (FAO, 2007). In the Caribbean, there has been substantial decline of mangrove area due to coastal development; runoff of pollutants, sewage, solid waste, and sediments; clear-cutting for conversion to aquaculture, land fills or agriculture, extraction for fuelwood; pharmaceuticals prospecting; and infrastructure development for tourism. The Central American endemic mangrove, *Pelliciera rhizophorae*, is only known from < 10 patchily distributed populations in Nicaragua, Panama, Colombia, and Costa Rica, and it provides the primary habitat for the mangrove hummingbird (*Amazonina boucardi*). This mangrove species' distribution is thought to be shrinking even further, as its presence is linked with freshwater areas and specific soil types, making it very susceptible to habitat alteration and coastal development.

Mangrove species richness is naturally low at the northern and southern extremities of mangrove global range, such as southern Brazil, the Arabian Peninsula, southern Japan (Ryukyu Islands), southern Australia (Wilson's promontory), and the northern and southern Atlantic coasts of Africa. Species richness is also low in isolated locations, such as the islands in the South Pacific and the Eastern Tropical Pacific. However, the highest proportion of mangrove species at elevated risk of extinction occurs in the Eastern Tropical Pacific (Polidoro *et al.*, 2012). Four of the 10 (40%) mangrove species present along the Pacific coasts of Costa Rica, Panama, and Colombia are listed in one of the three IUCN Red List threatened categories. In this region, *Avicennia bicolor*, *Mora oleifera*, and *Tabebuia palustris* are all rare or uncommon species only known from the Pacific coast of Central America. Extensive clearing of mangroves for settlement, agriculture, and aquaculture ponds are the major causes of mangrove decline in this region (Lugo, 2002). However, owing to sea level rise threats and the vulnerability of low islands, mangrove populations are more at risk from area declines at the extremes of their distribution where mangrove diversity is lowest, such as in the Eastern Tropical Pacific.

CONSEQUENCES OF MANGROVE LOSS ON ECOSYSTEM FUNCTION AND SERVICES

The loss of mangrove forests and individual species not only contributes to the rapid loss of biodiversity and ecosystem function, but it can also negatively impact human livelihoods and the provision of ecosystem services. The loss of mangrove forests and species may indeed be of greatest economic concern in rural, high-poverty areas where subsistence communities rely on mangrove areas for fishing and for direct harvesting of mangroves for fuel, construction, or other economic products (Rönnbäck, 1999; Glaser, 2003; Lopez-Hoffman *et al.*, 2006). In the Gulf of California, for example, where there are only four mangrove species present (*Avicennia germinans, Rhizophora samoensis, Laguncularia racemosa, Conocarpus erectus*), it is estimated that one linear kilometer of *R. samoensis* provides up to 1 hectare of essential marine habitat and provides a median annual value of US $37 000 in the fish and blue crab fisheries (Aburto-Oropez *et al.*, 2008). Geographic areas with high mangrove area loss, or with high numbers of mangrove species at elevated risk of extinction and relatively low mangrove diversity (such as in the Gulf of California in the Eastern Tropical Pacific), are more likely to exhibit loss of ecosystem function and related ecosystem services compared to more species-rich areas.

Among terrestrial vertebrates, more than 850 species are commonly found in mangrove areas, and at least 48 birds, 14 reptiles, 1 amphibian, and 6 mammal species are considered restricted to mangrove ecosystems (Luther & Greenberg, 2009). Of these, approximately 40% that have previously been assessed under IUCN Categories and Criteria are at elevated risk of extinction due to extensive mangrove habitat loss (Luther & Greenberg, 2009). Several types of crabs are keystone organisms in many mangrove forests because they play critical roles in nutrient recycling and bioturbation in mangrove soils (Cannicci *et al.*, 2008). The loss of crabs due to overharvesting, pollution, or habitat loss can in turn decrease growth and succession of mangrove forests (Smith *et al.*, 1991).

In terms of global carbon dioxide emissions associated with land-use change, few studies to date have quantified the potential loss of sediment carbon after mangrove clear-cutting. Some have estimated that up to 50% of carbon stored in the upper 15 cm of sediment may be lost after just 8 years (Granek & Ruttenberg, 2008). In addition to carbon storage, nutrients and carbon from mangrove forests provide essential support to other near-shore marine ecosystems, such as coral reefs and seagrass beds, and enrich coastal food webs and fishery production (Ellison, 2008; Miththapala, 2008). Many mangrove organisms are considered to be equally dependent on carbon of estuarine or pelagic origin, which is carried in by tides (Bouillon et al., 2003, 2005). The loss of mangrove species and forests can therefore change or diminish nearshore marine species community composition. For example, different environmental gradients characterized by a diversity of mangrove species are important for creating a variety of microhabitats, a major factor influencing community composition of fish (Robertson & Blaber, 1992). At a larger scale, the loss of mangrove areas can negatively impact the health and species composition of other connected nearshore ecosystems, such as coral reefs and seagrass areas (Mumby et al., 2004).

The loss of mangrove species and forests, whether found on the land-ward or seaward margin or along more freshwater riverine areas, will have significant impacts on water quality and coastal integrity for human com-munities. For example, water purification services provided by mangrove species in the Muthurajawela Marsh, Sri Lanka are valued at more than US$ 1.8 million per year (Emerton & Kekulandala, 2002). Riverine or freshwater-preferring species, such as Heritiera fomes and Heritiera globosa, buffer coastal rivers and freshwater communities from siltation, erosion, and excess nutrients. In many parts of the world, seaward or fringe man-groves, such as Rhizophora mangle or Rhizophora samoensis that commonly occur along protected coastlines and exposed open waters, are often com-prised of only one or two species. The loss of fringe mangrove species can lead to harmful destruction of coastal areas from storms, erosion, tidal waves, and floods (Ewel et al., 1998; Barbier et al., 2008).

THE WAY FORWARD

There are currently 12 international treaties and instruments that afford some protection, at least on paper, to mangroves in general, some of which have been in force for over 50 years (Table 2.2). However, these interna-tional treaties and instruments can suffer from lack of implementation and enforcement and do not necessarily confer legal protection to mangrove ecosystems. No international treaty or instrument currently addresses con-servation, preservation, or management of particular mangrove species. It is also noteworthy that the lack of any further legislation since 1992 has

Table 2.2 *International conventions and treaties that include protection of mangroves (modified from Ellison & Farnsworth, 1996).*

International convention or treaty	Place	Year
Convention on Nature Protection and Wildlife Preservation in the Western Hemisphere	Washington, DC	1940
Ramsar Convention on Wetlands of International Importance Especially as Waterfowl Habitat	Ramsar	1971
Convention Concerning the Protection of World Cultural and Natural Heritage	Paris	1972
Convention on Prevention of Marine Pollution	London	1972
Convention on International Trade in Endangered Species of Wild Fauna and Flora	Washington, DC	1973
International Convention for the Prevention of Pollution from Ships	London	1973
United Nations Convention on the Law of the Sea	Montego Bay	1982
International Tropical Timber Agreement	Geneva	1983
Convention for Protection and Development of the Marine Environment of the Wider Caribbean Region	Cartagena	1983
Convention on the Control of Transboundary Movements of Hazardous Wastes and their Disposal	Baser	1989
United Nations Convention on Biological Diversity	Rio de Janeiro	1992
United Nations Convention on Climate Change	Rio de Janeiro	1992

roughly coincided with the time period of greatest rate of mangrove area loss in some regions. At a national level, countries such as Indonesia, with its large areas of mangrove forests and high rates of decline, have extensive policies and planning instruments that can be applied to protect mangrove ecosystems but lack unified political, cultural, and economic recognition as a valuable resource to conserve (Sukardjo, 2009). Other countries have weak or vague legislation covering mangrove area usage (Ellison, 2009), or mangroves fall into a legislative gap between marine and land environmental law.

With some exceptions, mangrove areas and species of concern are generally not adequately represented within protected areas. In addition to legislative actions, initiatives are needed on the part of governments, nongovernmental organizations (NGOs), and private individuals to acquire and protect privately owned parcels of coastal land, especially those that contain viable populations of threatened mangrove species (Polidoro *et al.*, 2010). Legislation and management plans to protect or rehabilitate mangrove areas are in place in some countries; however, enforcement is often lacking and specific protection of uncommon or threatened mangrove species is rare.

Outside of formally protected areas, the key to wetland survival is engagement of local communities in sustainable management, with accessible technical support from the scientific community, particularly in baseline assessment of the resource, monitoring, and rehabilitation where required (Ellison, 2009). In the Pacific Islands region, top-down declarations of protected areas have resulted in little protection, while mangroves are effectively managed through community-run conservation areas that are governed by local committees having powers through the village social system.

Mangrove area in some countries, such as Pakistan, Cuba, and Bangladesh, is slightly increasing due to reforestation and restoration efforts (Alongi, 2002). Although regeneration of degraded mangrove areas is thought to be a viable option in some areas (Saenger, 2002; Lewis, 2005; Bosire et al., 2008), successful regeneration is generally only achieved by the planting of monocultures of fast-growing species, such as *Rhizophora* or *Avicennia* species. Many rare and slow-growing species are often not replaced, and many species cannot be easily replanted with success. In sum, mangrove areas may be able to be rehabilitated in some regions, but species and ecosystems cannot be effectively restored.

REFERENCES

Aburto-Oropez, O., Ezcurra, E., Danemann, G., et al. (2008). Mangroves in the Gulf of California increase fishery yields. *Proceedings of the National Academy of Sciences of the United States of America*, **105**, 10456–10459.

Alongi, D. M. (2002). Present state and future of the world's mangrove forests. *Environmental Conservation*, **29**, 331–349.

Barbier, E. B., Koch, E. W., Silliman, B. R., et al. (2008). Coastal ecosystem based management with non-linear ecological functions and values. *Science*, **319**, 321–323.

Biswas, S. R., Choudhury, J. K., Nishat, A. & Rahman, M. M. (2007). Do invasive plants threaten the Sundarbans mangrove forest of Bangladesh? *Forest Ecology and Management*, **245**, 1–9.

Bosire, J. O., Dahdouh-Guebas, F., Walton, M., et al. (2008). Functionality of restored mangroves: A review. *Aquatic Botany*, **89**, 251–259.

Bouillon, S. (2011). Storage beneath mangroves. *Nature Geoscience*, **4**, 282–283.

Bouillon, S., Dahdouh-Guebas, F., Rao, A.V. V. S., Koedam, N. & Dehairs, F. (2003). Sources of organic carbon in mangrove sediments: Variability and possible ecological implications. *Hydrobiologia*, **495**, 33–39.

Bouillon, S., Moens, T. & Dehairs, F. (2005). Carbon sources supporting benthic mineralization in mangrove and adjacent seagrass sediments (Gazi Bay, Kenya). *Biogeosciences*, **1**, 71–78.

Cannicci, S., Burrows, D., Fratini, S., et al. (2008). Faunistic impact on vegetation structure and ecosystem function in mangrove forests: A review. *Aquatic Botany*, **89**, 186–200.

Carpenter, K. E., Abrar, M., Aeby, G., *et al.* (2008). One-third of reef-building corals face elevated extinction risk from climate change and local impacts. *Science*, **321**, 560–563.

Chimner, R. A., Fry, B., Kaneshiro, M. Y. & Cormier, N. (2006). Current extent and historical expansion of introduced mangroves on O'ahu, Hawai'i. *Pacific Science*, **60**, 377–383.

Cohen, J. E., Small, C., Mellinger, A., Gallup, J. & Sachs, J. (1997). Estimates of coastal populations. *Science*, **278**, 1209–1213.

Costanza, R., d'Arge, R., de Groot, R., *et al.* (1997). The value of the world's ecosystem services and natural capital. *Nature*, **387**, 253–260.

Dahdouh-Guebas, F. (2011). World Atlas of Mangroves: Mark Spalding, Mami Kainuma and Lorna Collins (eds), book review. *Human Ecology*, **39**, 107–109.

Dahdouh-Guebas, F., Verneirt, M., Cannicci, S., *et al.* (2002). An exploratory study on grapsid crab zonation in Kenyan mangroves. *Wetlands Ecology and Management*, **10**, 179–187.

Dahdouh-Guebas, F., Hettiarachchi, S., Lo Seen, D., *et al.* (2005a). Transitions in ancient inland freshwater resource management in Sri Lanka affect biota and human populations in and around coastal lagoons. *Current Biology*, **15**, 579–586.

Dahdouh-Guebas, F., Jayatissa, L. P., Di Nitto, D., *et al.* (2005b). How effective were mangroves as a defence against the recent tsunami? *Current Biology*, **15**, 443–447.

Das, S., Vincent, J. R. (2009). Mangroves protected villages and reduced death toll during Indian super cyclone. *Proceedings of the National Academy of Sciences of the United States of America*, **106**, 7357–7360.

Di Nitto, D., Dahdouh-Guebas, F., Kairo, J. G., Decleir, H. & Koedam, N. (2008). Digital terrain modelling to investigate the effects of sea level rise on mangrove propagule establishment. *Marine Ecology Progress Series*, **356**, 175–188.

Dittmar, T., Hertkorn, N., Kattner, G. & Lara, R. J. (2006). Mangroves, a major source of dissolved organic carbon to the oceans. *Global Biogeochemical Cycles*, **20**, GB1012, doi:10.1029/2005GB002570.

Dodd, R. S. & Ong, J. E. (2008). Future of mangrove ecosystems to 2025. In N. V. C. Polunin (ed.), *Aquatic Ecosystems: Trends and Global Prospects*. Cambridge: Cambridge University Press, pp. 172–187.

Donato, D. C., Boone Kauffman, J., Murdiyarso, D., *et al.* (2011). Mangroves among the most carbon-rich forests in the tropics. *Nature Geoscience*, **4**, 293–297.

Dorenbosch, M., van Riel, M. C., Nagelkerken, I. & van der Velde, G. (2004). The relationship of reef fish densities to the proximity of mangrove and seagrass nurseries. *Estuarine, Coastal and Shelf Science*, **60**, 37–48.

Duke, N. C. (1992). Mangrove floristics and biogeography. In A. I. Robertson & D. M. Alongi (eds.), *Tropical Mangrove Ecosystems*. Washington, DC: American Geophysical Union, pp. 63–100.

Duke, N. C. (2006). *Australia's Mangroves: The Authoritative Guide to Australia's Mangrove Plants*. St Lucia: University of Queensland.

Duke, N. C., Pinzon, Z. S. & Prada, M. C. T. (1997). Large-scale damage to mangrove forests following two large oil spills in Panama. *Biotropica*, **29**, 2–14.

Duke, N. C., Ball, M. C. & Ellison, J. C. (1998). Factors influencing biodiversity and distributional gradients in mangroves. *Global Ecology and Biogeography Letters*, **7**, 27–47.

Duke, N. C., Meynecke, J. O., Dittmann, S., *et al.* (2007). A world without mangroves. *Science*, **317**, 41.

Ellison, A. M. (2008). Managing mangroves with benthic biodiversity in mind:
Moving beyond roving banditry. *Journal of Sea Research*, **59**, 2–15.

Ellison, A. M. & Farnsworth, E. J. (1996). Anthropogenic disturbance of Caribbean
mangrove ecosystems: Past impacts, present trends, and future predictions.
Biotropica, **28**, 549–565.

Ellison, A. M., Farnsworth, E. J. & Merkt, R. E. (1999). Origins of mangrove ecosystems and the mangrove biodiversity anomaly. *Global Ecology and
Biogeography*, **8**, 95–115.

Ellison, A. M., Mukherjee, B. B. & Karim, A. (2000). Testing patterns of zonation in
mangroves: Scale-dependence and environmental correlates in the Sundarbans
of Bangladesh. *Journal of Ecology*, **88**, 813–824.

Ellison, J. C. (1998). Impacts of sediment burial on mangroves. *Marine Pollution
Bulletin*, **37**, 420–426.

Ellison, J. C. (2005). Holocene palynology and sea-level change in two estuaries in
southern Irian Jaya. *Palaeogeography, Palaeoclimatology, Palaeoecology*, **220**,
291–309.

Ellison, J. C. (2009). Wetlands of the Pacific Island Region. *Wetlands Ecology and
Management*, **17**, 169–206.

Ellison, J. C. (2012). *Climate Change Vulnerability Assessment and Adaption Planning
for Mangrove Systems*. Washington, DC: WWF US.

Emerton, L. & Kekulandala, L. D. C. B. (2002). *Assessment of the Economic Value of
Muthurajawela Wetland, Occasional Paper 4*. Colombo: IUCN Sri Lanka Country
Office.

Ewel, K. C., Twilley, R. R. & Ong, J. E. (1998). Different kinds of mangrove forests
provide different goods and services. *Global Ecology and Biogeography Letters*, **7**,
83–94.

FAO. (2003). Status and trends in mangrove area extent worldwide. In
M. L. Wilkie & S. Fortuna (eds.), *Forest Resources Assessment Working Paper No.
63*. Rome: Forest Resources Division, FAO. www.fao.org/docrep/007/j1533e/
j1533e00.HTM.

FAO. (2007). *The World's Mangroves 1980–2005, FAO Forestry Paper 153*. Rome:
Forest Resources Division, FAO.

Field, C. B., Osborn, J. G., Hoffman, L. L., *et al.* (1998). Mangrove biodiversity and
ecosystem function. *Global Ecology and Biogeography Letters*, **7**, 3–14.

Fourqurean, J. W., Smith III, T. J., Possley, J., *et al.* (2010). Are mangroves in the
tropical Atlantic ripe for invasion? Exotic mangrove trees in the forests of south
Florida. *Biological Invasions*, **12**, 2509–2522.

Gilman, E., Ellison, J., Duke, N. C. & Field, F. (2008). Threats to mangroves
from climate change and adaptation options: A review. *Aquatic Botany*, **89**,
237–250.

Giri, C., Pchieng, E., Tieszen, L. L., *et al.* (2011). Status and distribution of mangrove
forests of the world using earth observation satellite data. *Global Ecology and
Biogeography*, **20**, 154–159.

Glaser, M. (2003). Interrelations between mangrove ecosystem, local economy and
social sustainability in Caete Estuary, North Brazil. *Wetland Ecology and
Management*, **11**, 265–272.

Granek, E. & Ruttenberg, B. I. (2008). Changes in biotic and abiotic processes following mangrove clearing. *Estuarine, Coastal and Shelf Science*, **80**, 555–562.

Hemminga, M. A., Slim, F. J., Kazungu, J., *et al.* (1994). Carbon outwelling from a mangrove forest with adjacent seagrass beds and coarl reefs (Gazi Bay, Kenya). *Marine Ecology Progress Series*, **106**, 291–301.

Hogarth, P. J. (2007). *The Biology of Mangroves and Seagrasses*. New York, NY: Oxford University Press.

IUCN. (2003). *Guidelines for Application of IUCN Red List Criteria at Regional and National Levels: version 3.0*. http://intranet.iucn.org/webfiles/doc/SSC/ SSCwebsite/Red_List /regional guidelinesEn.pdf.

IUCN. (2011). IUCN Red List of Threatened Species. www.iucnredlist.org.

Kairo, J. G., Dahdouh-Guebas, F., Gwada, P. O., Ochieng, C. & Koedam, N. (2002). Regeneration status of mangrove forests in Mida Creek, Kenya: A compromised or secured future? *Ambio*, **31**, 562–568.

Kathiresan, K., Bingham, B. L. (2001). Biology of mangroves and mangrove ecosystems. *Advances in Marine Biology*, **40**, 81–251.

Koedam, N. & Dahdouh-Guebas, F. (2008). Ecological quality changes precede changes in quantity in mangrove forests. *Science* (E-Letter 02/10/2008).

Kristensen, E., Mangion, P., Tang, M., *et al.* (2011). Microbial carbon oxidation rates and pathways in sediments of two Tanzanian mangrove forests. *Biogeochemistry*, **103**, 143–158.

Lewis III, R. R. (2005). Ecological engineering for successful management and restoration of mangrove forests. *Ecological Engineering*, **24**, 403–418.

Lopez-Hoffman, L., Monroe, L. E., Narvaez, E., Martinez-Ramos, M. & Ackerly, D. D. (2006). Sustainability of mangrove harvesting: How do harvesters perceptions differ from ecological analysis? *Ecology and Society*, **11**, 14.

Lugo, A. E. (2002). Conserving Latin American and Caribbean mangroves: Issues and challenges. *Madera y Bosques*, **8**, 5–25.

Lugo, A. E. & Snedaker, S. C. (1974). The ecology of mangroves. *Annual Reviews of Ecology and Systematics*, **5**, 39–63.

Luther, D. & Greenburg, R. (2009). Mangroves: A global perspective on the evolution and conservation of their terrestrial vertebrates. *Bioscience*, **59**, 602–612.

Massó i Alemán, S., Bourgeois, C., Appeltans, W., *et al.* (2010). The 'Mangrove Reference Database and Herbarium'. *Plant Ecology and Evolution*, **143**, 225–232.

Miththapala, S. (2008). *Mangroves*. Coastal Ecosystems Series, vol. 2. Colombo, Sri Lanka: Ecosystems and Livelihoods Group Asia IUCN.

Mumby, P. J., Edwards, A. J., Arias-Gonzalez, J. E., *et al.* (2004). Mangroves enhance the biomass of coral reef fish communities in the Caribbean. *Nature*, **427**, 533–536.

Nagelkerken, I., Blaber, S., Bouillon, S., *et al.* (2008). The habitat function of mangroves for terrestrial and marina fauna: A review. *Aquatic Botany*, **89**, 155–185.

Ng, P. K. L., Wang, L. K. & Lim, K. K. P. (2008). *Private Lives: An Expose of Singapore Mangroves*. Singapore: Raffles Museum of Biodiversity Research, National University of Singapore.

Ong, J. E. (1993). Mangroves – A carbon source and sink. *Chemosphere*, **27**, 1097–1107.

Ong, J. E. (2003). Plants of the Merbok mangrove, Kedah, Malaysia and the urgent need for their conservation. *Folia Malaysiana*, **4**, 1–18.

Polidoro, B. A., Carpenter, K. E., Collins, L., *et al.* (2010). The loss of species: Mangrove extinction risk and geographic areas of global concern. *PLoS ONE*, **5**, e10095.

Polidoro, B. A., Brooks, T., Carpenter, K. E., *et al.* (2012). Patterns of extinction risk and threat for marine vertebrates and habitat species in the Tropical Eastern Pacific. *Marine Ecology Progress Series*, **448**, 93–104.

Primavera, J. H. (1998). Mangroves as nurseries: Shrimp populations in mangrove and non-mangrove habitats. *Estuarine, Coastal and Shelf Science*, **46**, 457–464.

Primavera, J. H. (2000). Development and conservation of Philippine mangroves: Institutional issues. *Ecological Economics*, **35**, 91–106.

Primavera, J. H., Sadaba, R. B., Lebata, M. J. H. L. & Altamirano, J. P. (2004). *Handbook of Mangroves in the Philippines – Panay*. Philippines: SEAFDEC Aquaculture Department and UNESCO Man and the Biosphere ASPACO Project.

Quisthoudt, K., Schmitz, N., Randin, C. F., et al. (2012). Temperature variation among latitudinal range limits worldwide. *Trees*, **26**, 1919–1931.

Ren, H., Lu, H., Shen, W., *et al.* (2009). *Sonneratia apetala* Buch.Ham in the mangrove ecosystems of China: An invasive species or restoration species? *Ecological Engineering*, **35**, 1243–1248.

Ricklefs, R. E. & Latham, R. E. (1993). Global patterns of diversity in mangrove floras. In R. E. Ricklef & D. Schluter (eds.), *Species Diversity in Ecological Communities*. Chicago, IL: University of Chicago Press.

Robertson, A. I. & Blaber, S. J. M. (1992). Plankton, epibenthos and fish communities. In A. I. Robertson & D. M. Alongi (eds.), *Tropical Mangrove Ecosystems*. Washington, DC: American Geophysical Union. pp. 173–224.

Robertson, A. I. & Duke, N. C. (1987). Mangroves as nursery sites: Comparisons of the abundance and species composition of fish and crustaceans in mangroves and other nearshore habitats in tropical Australia. *Marine Biology*, **96**, 193–205.

Robertson, A. I. & Phillips, M. J. (1995). Mangroves as filters of shrimp pond effluent: Predictions and biogeochemical research needs. *Hydrobiologia*, **295**, 311–321.

Rodriguez, J. P., Rodrigues-Clark, K. M., Baillie, J. E. M., *et al.* (2011). Establishing IUCN Red List criteria for threatened ecosystems. *Conservation Biology*, **25**, 21–29.

Rönnbäck, P. (1999). The ecological basis for economic value of seafood production supported by mangrove ecosystems. *Ecological Economics*, **29**, 235–252.

Saenger, P. (2002). *Mangrove Ecology, Silviculture and Conservation*. Dordrecht: Kluwer Academic Publishers.

Sheaves, M. (2005). Nature and consequences of biological connectivity in mangrove systems. *Marine Ecology Progress Series*, **302**, 293–305.

Sheue, C. R., Yong, J. W. H. & Yang, Y. P. (2005). The Bruguiera (Rhizophoraceae) species in the mangroves of Singapore, especially on the new record and the rediscovery. *Tawania*, **50**, 251–260.

Smith III, T. J., Boto, K. G., Frusher, S. D. & Giddens, R. L. (1991). Keystone species and mangrove forest dynamics: The influence of burrowing by crabs on soil nutrient status and forest productivity. *Estuarine, Coastal and Shelf Science*, **33**, 419–432.

Spalding, M., Kainuma, M. & Collins, L. (2010). *World Atlas of Mangroves*. London: Earthscan.

Sukardjo, S. (2009). Mangroves for national development and conservation in Indonesia: Challenges for the future. *Marine Research in Indonesia*, **34**, 47–61.

Sullivan, C. (2005). *The Importance of Mangroves*. Department of Planning and Natural Resources, Division of Fish and Wildlife, USVI. Fact Sheet #28. http:// ufdc.ufl.edu/UF00093446/00028/3j.

Syvitski, J. P. M., Kettner, K. T., Overeem, I., *et al.* (2009). Sinking deltas due to human activities. *Nature Geoscience*, **2**, 681–687.

Tomlinson, P. B. (1986). *The Botany of Mangroves*. Cambridge: Cambridge University Press.

Trott, L. A. & Alongi, D. M. (2000). The impact of shrimp pond effluent on water quality and phytoplankton biomass in a tropical mangrove estuary. *Marine Pollution Bulletin*, **40**, 947–951.

Valiela, I., Bowen, J. L. & York, J. K. (2001). Mangrove forests: One of the world's threatened major tropical environments. *Bioscience*, **51**, 807–815.

Wells, S., Ravilious, C. & Corcoran, E. (2006). *In the Front Line: Shoreline Protection and Other Ecosystem Services from Mangroves and Coral Reefs*, Cambridge: UNEP World Conservation Monitoring Centre.

Zan, Q. J., Wang, B. S. & Wang, Y. J. (2003). Ecological assessment on the introduced *Sonneratia caseolaris* and *S. apetala* at the mangrove forest of Shenzhen Bay, China. *Acta Botanica Sinica*, **45**, 544–551.

3

Open-coast sandy beaches and coastal dunes

THOMAS A. SCHLACHER, ALAN R. JONES, JENIFER
E. DUGAN, MICHAEL A. WESTON, LINDA HARRIS,
DAVID S. SCHOEMAN, DAVID M. HUBBARD,
FELICITA SCAPINI, RONEL NEL, MARIANO LASTRA,
ANTON McLACHLAN, AND CHARLES H. PETERSON

SYNOPSIS

Beaches and dunes of the open coast form one of the globe's longest ecological interfaces, linking the oceans with the land. These systems are of great importance to society as prime sites for housing and recreation, buffers against storms, and providers of fisheries and mineral resources. By contrast, their unique ecological attributes and biodiversity are much less recognized. In this chapter, we provide a synthesis of the key ecological features and functions of beaches and dunes, outline the main elements of their faunal biodiversity, examine human threats and their biological consequences, and sketch some salient issues in management to achieve conservation of these unique ecosystems. It is apparent that the range of ecosystem goods and services is broad, but nutrient cycling, water filtration, and the provision of habitat and prey for a diverse range of animals are often the key ecological traits. Contrary to common perceptions, beaches and dunes contain a diverse and unique set of species, many of which are found nowhere else. In addition to the complement of highly adapted invertebrates, many wildlife species (e.g. birds, turtles, fishes) are dependent on beaches and dunes for nesting and feeding, and they use these habitats extensively. Human pressures on sandy shorelines and their biodiversity are numerous. Coastal squeeze is, however, the most pervasive, trapping beaches and their biota between the pressures of development from the terrestrial side and the consequences of climate change from the marine side. Beaches are also naturally malleable habitats whose interlinkages, including the exchange of organisms, with the abutting dunes and surf

Coastal Conservation, eds B. Maslo and J. L. Lockwood. Published by Cambridge University Press.
© Cambridge University Press 2014.

zones are essential to their functioning. Unfortunately, human actions intended to arrest the dynamics of beach habitats, such as seawalls and dune stabilizations, run counter to these natural dynamics and generally produce negative environmental outcomes. These present a set of formidable management challenges when the primary goal is to conserve intact ecosystems and biodiversity, calling for more systematic approaches in conservation design and implementation for beach and dune ecosystems.

INTRODUCTION AND BACKGROUND

Values, functions, and ecosystem services of open-coast sandy beaches and coastal dunes

The world's ocean shores are dominated by sandy beaches and coastal dunes, which form the single largest interface between the sea and the land (Bascom, 1980). Humans also concentrate in the coastal zone. By 2020, three-quarters of the global population is predicted to live within 60 km of the shoreline (UNCED, 1992). As populations grow and continue to concentrate in the narrow coastal strip, human use of dunes and beaches will expand its geographic footprint and increase in intensity. Beaches, dunes, and their interconnected surf zones have always been pivotal resources for human society.

Sandy beaches, coastal dunes, and surf zones have outstanding ecological, social, economic, and cultural values, and they provide a diversity of ecosystem services through six broad categories of functions.

1. Provision of habitat and biodiversity

A diversity of plant and animal species, encompassing most phyla, inhabit the three interlinked landscape elements of surf zones, beaches, and coastal dunes. Diversity in these ecosystems arises from a heterogeneity of both living and abiotic elements (McLachlan & Brown, 2006). The diversity of heterotrophs has a broad taxonomic ambit, including microbial diversity in the sands, protozoa in the surf zone, invertebrates from a broad spectrum of body sizes (e.g. micro-, meio-, and macrobenthos), and vertebrates from both the marine (e.g. seabirds, fishes) and terrestrial domain (e.g. shorebirds, mammals, reptiles; Armonies & Reise, 2000; Gheskiere *et al.*, 2002; Foster *et al.*, 2009).

2. Geobiochemical transformations and linkages

Beach ecosystems are important sites of material processing and exchange in the coastal landscape. Nutrient regeneration and water filtration occur in the water body of the surf zones, the sand wedge of beaches, and the soil and aquifers of dunes (Cisneros et al., 2011; Dugan et al., 2011b). Organic matter is supplied to coastal consumers either in the form of in-situ primary production (e.g. phytoplankton in the surf zone) or imports and sequestration of marine matter from the sea (e.g. plant wrack and strandings of animal carcasses) or terrestrial matter from the land (Polis & Hurd, 1996; Schlacher & Connolly, 2009; Kahn & Cahoon, 2012).

3. Cultural connections

Beaches and dunes represent irreplaceable sites of unique spiritual significance for native people (e.g. burial grounds, ceremonial sites, shell middens; Beaton, 1985). Such cultural significance is not confined to historical or ancestral connections with the coastal landscapes of dunes and beaches, but extends into modern times. In many parts of the world, unique surf cultures flourish where beaches have gained near-iconic status; this culturally broad and widespread connection of people with beaches is also extensively exploited in tourism marketing (Gurran & Blakely, 2007).

4. Recreation and socioeconomic associations

Sandy beaches are prime sites for human recreation. More people use beaches for leisure activities than any other type of coastal system (Maguire et al., 2011b), and the value of beach-centered tourism is often higher than other forms (Houston, 2008). Beaches provide recreational opportunities for local people, and they underpin tourism in many areas. The importance of tourism, centered on beaches, is particularly great in small island states or in economies that have morphed from being primarily agriculture- or fisheries-based to relying strongly on coastal tourism (Klein et al., 2004; Barbier et al., 2011).

5. Resource extraction

Since antiquity, humans have exploited the coastal zone, extracting mineral resources and harvesting fish and shellfish. Beaches, dunes, and nearshore waters have always played a central part in such extractive uses (as evidenced by ancient shell and bone middens), and fishing and mining continue to be important activities in many regions around the world (Defeo, 2003; Thornton et al., 2006). Some beaches serve as donor sites for sediments used in beach fill projects elsewhere (Jones et al., 2008).

6. Provision of coastal land

Coastal development was historically concentrated around harbors and estuaries, but in the twentieth century had expanded onto exposed sedimentary coastlines. This trend of ribbon development is driven by beaches being viewed as attractive lifestyle assets (Pilkey *et al.*, 2011), requiring beaches to function as areas for hedonistic activities. To accommodate this culture, coastal dunes must play a dual role, first providing physical building sites and then protecting buildings from erosion and storms (Nordstrom, 2000, 2008; Landry & Hindsley, 2011).

Key traits of beaches and coastal dunes as ecosystems

To the casual observer, sandy beaches appear to be rather simple habitats consisting of a strip of bare sand with few (if any) topographic structures, no attached plants, and few readily apparent animals. Yet beach systems contain structurally heterogeneous habitats that support rich biological communities. For example, the interstitial habitat is especially important for species diversity, with hundreds of species of meiofauna (Brown, 2001). Similarly, avian diversity on open-coast beaches can reach hundreds of species (Foster *et al.*, 2009). Moreover, beaches constitute functionally dynamic ecosystems, belying common notions of plainness (McLachlan, 1983, 2001; Defeo & McLachlan, 2005; McLachlan & Brown, 2006). This diversity of form and function arises from a number of salient physical and ecological features (modified from Schlacher *et al.*, 2008c):

1. **Linkages** between abutting seascape elements are *the* key characteristic of beach systems. Surf zones, beaches, and coastal dunes form a single functional unit, exchanging organisms, sand, organic matter, and nutrients. Beaches are largely open ecosystems, and they connect marine with terrestrial domains through biotic (e.g. animal movement, carrion strandings) and abiotic vectors (e.g. estuarine plumes interacting with beaches, dune aquifers).
2. The **habitat** of the surf–beach–dune unit is a **dynamic** one, formed and altered by variations in sand supply and energy fields from wind, waves, tides, and currents. Habitats are unstable, changing in morphology on several timescales. The shoreline position of these sedimentary coasts is naturally variable.
3. **Energy flows** through the surf–beach–dune ecosystem are underpinned by two distinct sources of organic matter: (1) primary production by phytoplankton and dune plants; and (2) imports of, mostly marine, organic matter (e.g. wrack, carrion). These carbon sources are exploited by a broad range of consumers across several trophic levels, including iconic vertebrates, such as birds and mammals, which are the top predators and scavengers.

Beaches and coastal dunes as critical habitats

Beaches and coastal dunes are important for vertebrates with strong cultural and emotional associations with humans, such as marine turtles, fishes, mammals, and birds. Several species of endangered marine turtles rely on beaches as nesting sites. Conservation of their nesting habitat has become a critical concern because of predictions of heightened erosion under climate change and decreased habitat quality due to shoreline armoring (Fish *et al.*, 2005; Rizkalla & Savage, 2010; see also Chapter 10).

Open-coast beaches and dunes are often overlooked as bird habitat, yet can rival many terrestrial habitats in terms of avian diversity and importance (Dowling & Weston, 1999; Meager *et al.*, 2012). All parts of the sandy littoral zones (i.e. surf zones, non-vegetated beaches, and coastal dunes) host an array of coastal bird species and provide key foraging, shelter and breeding resources (Higgins *et al.*, 1983–2006). Eroding sections of dunes can provide key breeding areas for ground-nesting species, while stable dunes may host burrow-nesting species (e.g. shearwaters), and dune vegetation provides substrates for tree-nesting species (Higgins *et al.*, 1983–2006).

In this chapter we briefly summarize some key aspects of faunal diversity of unvegetated beaches of open coasts, outline the main anthropogenic pressures on sandy shores and coastal dunes, and discuss facets of management for biodiversity conservation of beach and dune ecosystems.

FAUNAL DIVERSITY OF SANDY BEACHES AND COASTAL DUNES

Known diversity of beach animals

At first glance, biodiversity of sandy beaches and dunes appears sparse. Yet beaches and dunes contain a unique faunal biodiversity that encompasses a wide range of animal taxa, many of which live nowhere else. This generally underappreciated faunal diversity comprises three broad elements: (1) resident/endemic/obligate invertebrate species, many of which are direct developers and hence have limited dispersal ability; (2) fish and invertebrate species that use beaches and surf zones for some portion of their life cycle; and (3) wildlife, including birds, reptiles, amphibians, and mammals, with varying degrees of dependence upon beach and dune ecosystems. Resident beach and dune animals often burrow into the shifting sand or have cryptic coloration, making them invisible to a casual visitor. On the wave-swept sand of open-coast beaches where no larger plants grow, most animals are also highly mobile.

The biodiversity of beaches and dunes features many wildlife species, including a number of threatened and endangered birds, mammals, and reptiles, most of which have strong connections to the sea. These wildlife species may be resident on beaches, depend on beaches and dunes for nesting, chick-rearing and pupping (Table 3.1), or use beaches during wintering and migration. Other wildlife are also common, such as raptors, vultures, and mammals, which are opportunistic predators of beach rookeries and nests, or are scavengers of wave-cast carrion. Successful nesting of birds, marine turtles, and some fish requires suitable upper beach and/or dune habitat that is relatively undisturbed by human activity, sparsely vegetated, and not regularly swept by waves during the nesting season (Table 3.1, Figure 3.1; see also Chapter 10).

Invertebrates

Intertidal invertebrate communities of open-coast sandy beaches contain representatives of mobile animals from numerous phyla and classes. The major macroinvertebrate taxa on open-coast beaches are mollusks (clams and snails), arthropods (crustaceans, spiders, and insects), and annelids (polychaetes and oligochaetes) (McLachlan & Brown, 2006). Almost all species are rapid and efficient burrowers, responding to wave-wash, erosion, and turbulence (Ellers, 1995; Brown, 1996). Nemertea (ribbon worms) and a few echinoderms (primarily sand dollars) are also found on the unvegetated part of the beach. The far less well-studied interstitial meiofauna (animals < 1 mm in size and retained on a 30- or 60-micron sieve) can be remarkably diverse in beach sands (Armonies & Reise, 2000; Gheskiere *et al.*, 2002, 2005; Lee & Riveros, 2012).

Reported values of species richness of invertebrates on open-coast beaches vary widely between geographic regions (Soares, 2003; McLachlan & Dorvlo, 2005; Defeo & McLachlan, 2011). Beaches on the west coast of the Americas illustrate this geographic variation well, with large differences in invertebrate species richness between southern California and Chile. Californian beaches have some of the most species-rich intertidal invertebrate assemblages reported for exposed sandy shores, with up to 52 species identified in single surveys and > 100 species (many of which are insects, including a number of flightless beetles) recorded on microtidal beaches in the region (Straughan, 1983; Dugan *et al.*, 2000, 2003). By contrast, a maximum of 14 species are found in single surveys of the intertidal zone of similar beach types in Chile at similar latitudes (Jaramillo & McLachlan, 1993; McLachlan *et al.*, 1993). For other regions (e.g. Spain, Belgium, South Africa, Australia), typical values of species

Table 3.1 *Examples of birds and fish that nest on open-coast sandy beaches and dunes.*

Taxonomic group	Species
Shorebirds	
Plovers	Kentish and *snowy plovers (*Charadrius alexandrinus*, *C. a. nivosus*, *C. a. tenuirostris, C. a. occidentalis*)
	*Piping plover (*Charadrius melodus*)
	Wilson's plover (*Charadrius wilsonia, C. w. crassirostris*)
	White-fronted plover (*Charadrius marginatus*, four subspecies in Africa)
	*Hooded plover (*Thinornis rubricollis*)
	*New Zealand dotterel (*Charadrius obscurus*)
	Red-capped plover (*Charadrius ruficapillus*)
	Killdeer (*Charadrius vociferus*)
Oystercatchers	American oystercatcher (*Haematopus palliatus*)
	Australian pied oystercatcher (*Haematopus ostralegus*)
	*Chatham Island oystercatcher (*Haematopus chathamensis*)
	[1]African black oystercatcher (*Haematopus moquini*)
Lapwings	Masked lapwing (*Vanellus miles*)
Thick Knees/ Stone Curlews	[1]Beach stone-curlew, *Esacus giganteus* or Beach Thick-knee
Seabirds	
Skimmers	Black skimmers (*Rynchops niger niger* and *R. n. intercedens*)
Terns	[1]Damara tern (*Sterna balaenarum*) Africa (Watson *et al.*, 1997)
	*Least tern (**Sternula antillarum antillarum*, **S. a. brownii*)
	*Fairy tern (*Sterna nereis*)
	Crested tern (*Sterna bergii*)
	Caspian tern (*Sterna caspia*)
	Common tern (*Sterna hirundo*)
	Royal tern (*Thalasseus maxima*)
Gulls	Gull-billed tern (*Gelochelidon nilotica*)
	Laughing gull (*Leucophaeus atricilla*)
	Herring gull (*Larus argentatus*)
Penguins	*African or jackass penguin (*Spheniscus demersus*)
	[1]Gentoo penguin (*Pygoscelis papua*)
	King penguin (*Aptenodytes patagonicus*)
Sea turtles (seven species – all are endangered or critically endangered)	*Green sea turtle (*Chelonia mydas*)
	*Flatback sea turtle (*Natator depressa*)
	*Hawksbill sea turtle (*Eretmochelys imbricata*)
	[1]Olive ridley sea turtle (*Lepidochelys olivacea*)
	*Kemp's ridley sea turtle (*Lepidochelys kempii*)
	*Leatherback sea turtle (*Dermochelys coriacea*)
	*Loggerhead sea turtle (*Caretta caretta*)
Fish	California grunion (*Leuresthes tenuis*)

* Currently listed as endangered or threatened.

[1] Vulnerable or near-threatened; IUCN Red List (2006).

Figure 3.1 A colony of jackass penguins (*Spheniscus demersus*) nesting on the upper beach just below the vegetation and above the average reach of tides on a beach in the Western Cape, South Africa (*top*), and a typical shallow nest scrape with snowy plover (*Charadrius novisus*) eggs on a California beach (*bottom*). (Photo credits: (*top*) Les Abernethy, (*bottom*) Callie Bowdish.) (See color plate section.)

richness for marine invertebrates are 25–32 species per beach (McLachlan et al., 1996a; Degraer et al., 1999; Soares, 2003; Rodil & Lastra, 2004; Rodil et al., 2006; Schlacher & Thompson, 2007).

Reported values of species richness for intertidal macroinvertebrates on open-coast beaches are likely to be considerable underestimates. There is a highly diverse assemblage of insects and spiders in the transition zone between the beach and the dunes and in the coastal dunes themselves (Boomsma & Van Loon, 1982; Polis & Hurd, 1995, 1996; Bonte, 2005; Van Dam & Van Dam, 2008; Irmler, 2012; Yamazaki, 2012). However, this component of invertebrate diversity is not customarily included in beach surveys, and there are also impediments in terms of unresolved taxonomies. Similarly, while some data on meiofaunal and microfaunal diversity are available (e.g. Armonies & Reise, 2000), much of it remains to be documented.

At the population level, many resident beach species, particularly those with direct development (i.e. lacking dispersing larvae) appear to be genetically structured, indicating intraspecific diversity (De Matthaeis et al., 1995). By contrast, populations of species that possess planktonic larvae show much less genetic structure (Dawson et al., 2011). Genetic diversity, coupled with phenotypic and behavioral plasticity (Brown, 1996), can be interpreted as an adaptation to the dynamic and instable habitat of sandy shores (Soares et al., 1999).

Fishes

The diversity of fishes inhabiting beaches and surf zones appears to be high but is not well documented in many regions due, in part, to the challenges of sampling the high-energy surf. Although only ~10% of fish species that regularly occur in the surf zone may be considered resident, many species inhabit the low intertidal and surf zones of beaches for significant parts of their life cycle, including breeding, foraging, and as nursery grounds (McLachlan & Brown, 2006).

Surf-zone fishes are conventionally sampled with beach seine nets, with 26 to > 70 species recorded in single surveys and with diversity declining as wave exposure increases (Bennett, 1989; Romer, 1990; Gibson & Robb, 1996; McLachlan & Brown, 2006; Inoue et al., 2008). Surf-zone fish communities are often dominated by a few species and exhibit very high spatial and temporal variability, with many species being opportunistic feeders (Clark et al., 1996). These assemblages also contain a high proportion of juveniles, highlighting the functional importance of surf zones as nursery areas (Watt-Pringle & Strydom, 2003; Pattrick & Strydom, 2008; Haynes et al., 2012; Iseki et al., 2012).

Only the gobiid sand darters (*Kraemeria* spp.) that inhabit the low intertidal zone of coral sand beaches exposed to strong wave action in tropical and subtropical Japan and the Indo-Pacific can be considered true intertidal residents (Tsubaki & Kato, 2009). Beach-nesting fish, such as the California grunion (*Leuresthes tenuis*), depend on the uppermost intertidal zones of open-coast sandy beaches as spawning sites, burying their eggs at the wrack line on spring high tides to incubate there for at least 2 weeks (Martin *et al.*, 2006).

Turtles

All seven species of marine turtles nest exclusively on beaches and fore-dunes (Rumbold *et al.*, 2001; see also Chapter 10; Table 3.1). The nesting behavior of marine turtles has evolved in a setting of natural variability and changing habitat through natural cycles of erosion and shoreline migration. However, lately the conservation of sea turtle nesting habitat has become a critical conservation concern because of predictions of heightened erosion under climate change (Fish *et al.*, 2005). All marine turtle species share broad nesting requirements – deep, relatively loose sand above the high-tide line; the mechanisms by which females choose a beach or a site within a beach for nesting are, surprisingly, not fully resolved (Fuentes *et al.*, 2010). What emerges from work on beaches that have been armored with seawalls is that physical habitat properties can influence turtle nesting frequency and hatching success (Rizkalla & Savage, 2010). It also is likely that turtles may use one or several microhabitat cues in nest site selection, including beach length, width, slope, orientation, vegetation, land use, temperature, dune profiles, and height (Witherington *et al.*, 2011).

Birds

The diverse and abundant invertebrate communities on sandy beaches provide prey for a remarkably species-rich and abundant assemblage of shore-birds in some regions. For example, shorebird density can average > 100 birds per km year-round for some Californian beaches (Hubbard & Dugan, 2003), and 242 species of coastal birds have been recorded on a single Texan sandy beach (Foster *et al.*, 2009).

Beach, dune, and surf-zone habitats support a range of bird guilds, with a wide variety of life-history attributes and ecologies, that exploit coastal resources in many ways (Higgins *et al.*, 1983–2006). Seabirds, including terns, gulls, scoters, grebes, pelicans, loons, and cormorants, feed on fish and invertebrates in the surf and lower intertidal zones. Beaches also function as roosting habitat for many seabird species; this is a critical habitat function that will need to be considered more explicitly in species conservation, especially in the face of direct kills of roosting birds by vehicles and disturbance by human activities. Roosting areas are particularly important for coastal diving birds, such as cormorants and pelicans, which need to dry their feathers regularly.

A variety of bird species nest and rear their often precocial chicks on open-coast beaches and dunes (Tables 3.1 and 3.2). Some seabirds, such as gulls and terns, nest in colonies, mobbing predators to protect their exposed nests and young. Others, particularly plovers and oystercatchers, depend on crypsis to conceal their shallow, solitary nest scrapes (Figure 3.1). Many of these species nest on the dry, upper part of the beach located between the toe of the vegetated foredune and the average reach of high tides, also known as the wrack line. Many terrestrial species also use or prefer coastal dunes (Higgins *et al.*, 1983–2006).

Marine mammals

Pinnipeds, sea otters, and cetaceans feed on invertebrates and fish in the low intertidal and shallow surf zones of sandy beaches (Saayman & Tayler, 1973; Gowans *et al.*, 2007). Many pinnipeds, including endangered species, such as the New Zealand sea lion (*Phocarctos hookeri*), breed and pup on sandy beaches, setting up large colonies that can dominate the habitat seasonally (Berta *et al.*, 2006; Auge *et al.*, 2012). Other species, such as harbor seals (*Phoca vitulina*), haul out on beaches to rest and thermoregulate (Stewart, 1984).

Natural processes affecting animal diversity

The main drivers of intertidal biodiversity on open-coast beaches include four complementary sets of processes: (1) physical features and coastal processes; (2) oceanographic conditions; (3) biological interactions; and (4) population dynamics, all operating across a broad range of temporal and spatial scales. Physical attributes (e.g. slope, wave height, grain size) have been shown to influence intertidal macrobenthic diversity, abundance, and biomass on many beaches worldwide (Soares, 2003; McLachlan & Dorvlo, 2005; Defeo & McLachlan, 2011; Barboza *et al.*, 2012; Gómez & Defeo, 2012; Rodil *et al.*, 2012).

One of the most widely cited predictive models in beach ecology is the relationship between invertebrate metrics (e.g. abundance, biomass, species richness) and beach characteristics (McLachlan, 1990). Generally, wide beaches that slope gently and are built from fine sands contain more species than steeper, shorter, and coarser beaches. Wider beaches tend to be fronted by wide surf zones where most of the wave energy is dissipated across sand bars in multiple rows of breakers. This creates relatively gentle swash flow conditions in the intertidal zone that are favored by many beach species (McArdle & McLachlan, 1992). Conversely, narrow beaches usually have narrow surf zones with no or few breakers. Here, wave energy hits the intertidal zone directly, creating harsh and turbulent water movement in the swash zone, which excludes species (Defeo *et al.*, 2001). Most of the world's exposed beaches are intermediate between these two extremes. Bottom-up drivers (e.g. quantity and quality of organic matter inputs) also affect food webs and biodiversity, especially at higher trophic levels, in many coastal ecosystems, including beaches (e.g. Dugan *et al.*, 2003). These factors can interact with physical drivers to influence coastal food webs and their biodiversity (Box 3.3; Byrnes *et al.*, 2011; Revell *et al.*, 2011).

Intertidal food webs and their biodiversity on beaches depend primarily on organic matter imported from the sea; phytoplankton, marine macro-phytes (e.g. detached large algae and seagrass cast ashore by waves) and carrion provide trophic subsidies that form the base of beach food webs (Box 3.1; Polis & Hurd, 1995, 1996; Colombini & Chelazzi, 2003; McLachlan & Brown, 2006; Rossi *et al.*, 2010; Schlacher & Hartwig, 2013); some energetic contributions can also be made by terrestrial sources in setting close to estuaries that deliver upland material to sea and beach food webs (Bergamino *et al.*, 2012). Primary consumers include suspension-feeding clams, hippid crabs, mysids, and amphipods that filter plankton from the wave wash, and wrack-feeding amphipods, isopods, and insects that feed on drift material deposited at the strandline by waves. Where primary production is relatively low, beaches support scavenging ghost, hermit, and hippid crabs that feed on wave-cast carrion (Schlacher *et al.*, 2007b). The dependence of beach food webs on allochthonous resources results in strong bottom-up effects that propagate upwards to avian and other predators (Figure 3.2, Box 3.1). In temperate regions where planktonic productivity is high, much of the intertidal invertebrate abundance and biomass consists of suspension feeders, such as clams and sand crabs. In regions where large marine algae and seagrass grow close to beaches, smaller invertebrates associated with stranded macrophytes can be abundant and diverse (Dugan *et al.*, 2003; Lastra *et al.*, 2010).

Beach invertebrates and carrion provide prey for shorebirds, seabirds, raptors, fish, and pinnipeds, as well as some terrestrial vertebrates (Carlton & Hodder, 2003). Beaches in developed regions may provide prey resources that are no longer available in coastal wetlands lost to development (Hubbard & Dugan, 2003). Abundant suspension feeders,

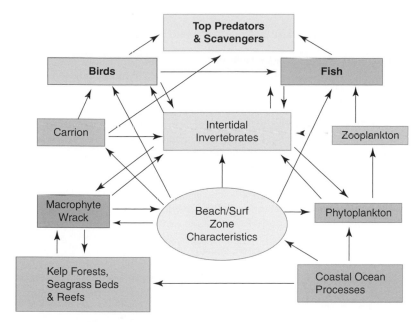

Figure 3.2 Conceptual model of the main functional linkages that characterize food webs of open-coast beaches in temperate regions.

such as clams and sand crabs, that inhabit beaches are important prey resources for shorebirds, herons, seabirds, fish, and pinnipeds, as well as a variety of terrestrial mammals and birds (McLachlan & Brown, 2006; Peterson *et al.*, 2006). Smaller-sized but abundant invertebrates associated with wrack are also important as prey for wildlife, primarily birds and terrestrial mammals (see Box 3.1).

The influence of episodic extreme events, such as hurricanes, cyclones, storms, El Nino Southern Oscillations (ENSOs), earthquakes, and tsunamis on the dynamics of beach and dune ecosystems needs be considered in the conservation and management of these ecosystems and their biodiversity (Box 3.2). Episodic events can cause large impacts and produce lasting changes to beach ecosystems (Arntz *et al.*, 1987; Lucrezi *et al.*, 2010; Harris *et al.*, 2011; Revell *et al.*, 2011; Jaramillo *et al.*, 2012). Ecological changes are mediated or produced via changes to sand supply and characteristics, beach and dune morphology, and mortality of existing populations and communities. Recovery times vary widely; some components may recover rapidly after episodic events (Harris *et al.*, 2011; Jaramillo *et al.*, 2012), while others may take years to decades to recover (Box 3.2; Arntz *et al.*, 1987; Revell *et al.*, 2011).

Box 3.1   Wrack and carrion on beaches – much more to it than mere flotsam

Plant material (e.g. seagrass, large algae) and carrion (animal carcasses) that become stranded on sandy beaches are critical to the functioning of these ecosystems.

(1) Wrack links the nearshore marine zone with the beach and dunes. Marine matter is transferred across the surf zone to become an important source of nutrients in the littoral zone (Colombini & Chelazzi, 2003; Orr *et al.*, 2005b; Colombini *et al.*, 2009; Barreiro *et al.*, 2013).

(2) Wrack provides habitat and food. For example, in California, over 40% of intertidal species depend on wrack as a source of food and habitat. Beaches that are regularly groomed or raked support considerably fewer species of invertebrates at much lower abundance (Llewellyn & Shackley, 1996; Dugan *et al.*, 2003; Rossi *et al.*, 2010; but see Porri *et al.*, 2011).

(3) Wrack forms islands of biodiversity, with larger patches harboring more species (Olabarria *et al.*, 2007; Pelletier *et al.*, 2011; MacMillan & Quijon, 2012).

(4) Wrack underpins food webs culminating in birds. Invertebrates associated with wrack are a key trophic source for coastal birds. Shorebird use of beaches is positively correlated with the availability of wrack and the diversity and abundance of invertebrate prey, as well as beach type and width (Tarr & Tarr, 1987; Dugan *et al.*, 2008; Meager *et al.*, 2012).

(5) Carrion is a high-quality food source that attracts a diversity of vertebrate scavengers, including endangered birds of prey (Rose & Polis, 1998).

Figure Box 3.1 The precocial chicks of many species of beach-nesting shorebirds must feed themselves with beach and dune invertebrates soon after hatching. Prey availability could be a factor in the fledging success of some populations of these species, many of which are threatened or endangered. This young western snowy plover (*Charadrius nivosus*) chick has captured a talitrid amphipod on a California beach – these talitrid amphipods are dependent on wrack as a food source. (Photo credit: Callie Bowdish.) (See color plate section.)

Box 3.2 Beaches and external drivers – an ENSO example

Beaches on open coasts are malleable habitats, continually reshaped by variations in wave regimes, wind strength and direction, and variable sand supply. Changes in ocean dynamics also appear important as determinants of ecological functioning in these ecosystems.

The response of Californian beaches to the 1997–1998 El Nino Southern Oscillation (ENSO) illustrates these links and feedbacks between oceanic conditions and biodiversity in beach ecosystems. These links appear first mediated by changes in the amount of wrack material delivered to the shore. Wrack delivery, in turn, depends on the condition and productivity of nearby reefs and kelp forests, and the availability of upper beach habitat to retain wave-cast wrack, both of which were impacted by the ENSO (Revell *et al.*, 2011).

In these same beaches, wintering shorebirds were sensitive indicators of climatic events and the associated change in beach ecosystem conditions. Species richness and abundance of shorebirds, illustrated here by a numerically dominant wintering species, sanderlings (*Calidris alba*), responded strongly to the 1997–1998 ENSO event in the region. Abundance and diversity of shorebirds remained low through 1999 and had not recovered to pre-ENSO levels after 3 years. This may reflect shorebird mortality during the event and a lack of prey resources on eroded beaches.

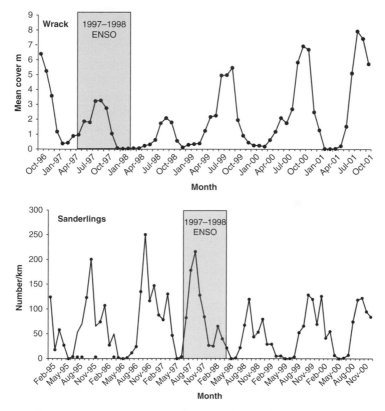

Figure Box 3.2 Fluctuations in the cover of macrophyte wrack (top panel) and sanderling abundance on a California beach in relation to the 1997–1998 ENSO event (shaded area) (Revell *et al.*, 2011).

However, episodic events can also create habitats (Jaramillo *et al.*, 2012). Delivery of sediments from watersheds during heavy rains can supply beaches with sand for years (Barnard *et al.*, 2012). Beach rotations caused by ENSO events can create wider beaches in some areas, while other sections erode intensely (Revell *et al.*, 2011). Washover fans created by hurricanes, or river deltas or spits that form after floods, can create nesting habitat for birds (Cohen *et al.*, 2009).

With few exceptions, habitat requirements (at a micro or macro scale), and the processes that influence them, are poorly understood for coastal birds and wildlife (but see Meager *et al.*, 2012). In particular, many wildlife species, such as shorebirds, turtles, and seabirds, use areas of beaches and dunes that are spatially and temporally dynamic, often with little or no vegetative cover, including in some cases dredge spoils (Erwin *et al.*, 1981). Coastal landscape features that influence wildlife distributions include land-form, complexity of coastlines, intertidal and total area, beach width and slope, relative isolation (as in islands), vegetative cover, proximity to wet-lands, and the degree of urbanization (Nicholls & Baldassarre, 1990; Dugan *et al.*, 2008; LeDee *et al.*, 2008; Meager *et al.*, 2012). Heterogeneity among beach and dune habitats may be as important as specific habitat features.

Coasts can conceivably be fragmented as habitats, even for species capable of flying or swimming; for example, habitat breaks of 50 km (e.g. a large coastal city) may theoretically reduce movement rates of some obligate beach-dwelling birds (Weston *et al.*, 2009). In addition, the narrow strip of beaches and dunes lining the shore can form an important coastal corridor for terrestrial wildlife (Carlton & Hodder, 2003).

Functional links
The diversity and abundance of birds and wildlife in beaches, coastal dunes, and surf zones is not known for most shores. Similarly, landscape ecologists and biogeographers have largely neglected these systems. For example, although overall levels of bird endemism are relatively low in beaches and dunes compared with tropical uplands or islands, coasts support a substantial diversity and abundance of birds, often at critical phases of their life histories, such as during migration and breeding (Higgins *et al.*, 1983–2006). A better understanding of the factors that influence bird and wildlife diversity on beaches and dunes requires better species distribution data than presently exist. Few countries have comprehensive survey data of coastal birds or wildlife; exceptions include areas where surveys have been conducted for threatened species or to guide responses to oil spills (Nicholls & Baldassarre, 1990; Roob *et al.*, 2000; see also Chapter 11).

The functional links between biodiversity and ecological function are known for some components of beaches and dunes but remain unmeasured for many others. Several important ecosystem functions are driven more strongly by physical processes than biodiversity. Such processes include sand storage and transport, wave dissipation and buffering of extreme events, ability to respond dynamically to sea level rise (within limits), water filtration and purification both from terrestrial and marine sources, water storage in dune aquifers, and groundwater discharge through beaches (Schlacher *et al.*, 2008c). Functions that may be more directly affected by biodiversity include the breakdown of organic materials and pollutants, nutrient mineralization and recycling (Box 3.3), community resilience, maintenance of genetic resources, nursery areas for juvenile fishes, nesting sites for turtles, birds, and mammals (Table 3.1), provision of prey resources for birds and terrestrial wildlife, and functional links between terrestrial and marine environments in the coastal zone (McLachlan & Brown, 2006; Schlacher *et al.*, 2008c). In wind-swept sand dunes just landward of the beach, a variety of uniquely adapted plant species take root, acting as ecosystem engineers to modify the unstable sand and shape the dunes, which then affects sand accretion, storage, and erosion as well as biodiversity, community succession and wildlife support (Nordstrom & Mauriello, 2001; Nordstrom *et al.*, 2011).

Beaches are sites of intense biogeochemical processing of organic matter (Box 3.3; Coupland *et al.*, 2007), which contribute to nearshore nutrient and carbon cycling (Pearse *et al.*, 1942; Soares *et al.*, 1997; Rauch & Denis, 2008; Avery *et al.*, 2012; Barreiro *et al.*, 2013). As one of the most important ecosystem functions of beaches, processing of organic matter can be closely tied to biodiversity because it forms critical nutrient and energetic links between marine waters and the beach–dune system (Boxes 3.1 and 3.3; McGwynne *et al.*, 1988; Colombini *et al.*, 2009; Dugan *et al.*, 2011b; Barreiro *et al.*, 2013). Storm-cast wrack can also act as an ecosystem engineer that promotes the establishment and formation of hummock and embryo dunes, and it provides nutrients for colonizing plants (Dugan & Hubbard, 2010; Nordstrom *et al.*, 2011).

Beaches that support surf-zone diatom accumulations can function more like semi-enclosed ecosystems. Here, these resident primary producers in the surf zone support extremely productive intertidal food webs, dominated by suspension feeders (usually clams) that recycle nutrients to the surf zone and support wildlife and fish (Soares *et al.*, 1996, 1997; McLachlan & Brown, 2006). Rich persistent accumulations of surf diatoms that form in the well-developed surf zones of wide sandy beaches of sufficient length have been reported from Australia, New Zealand, South

Box 3.3 Beaches process organic matter and recycle nutrients

Conversions of organic matter through macroscopic food webs, the microbial loop, or bacteria-mediated nutrient mineralization, are ubiquitous in beach systems. On beaches with large accumulations of wrack, rates of carbon respiration can even exceed those measured in tropical rainforests (Coupland *et al.*, 2007).

The deposition, accumulation, and processing of marine macrophyte wrack illustrate these processes well. Intertidal invertebrates quickly consume stranded drift matter, creating particles that are available to the interstitial meiofaunal and microbial communities that affect rapid turnover and remineralization of organic matter (Koop & Field, 1981; Koop & Griffiths, 1982; Griffiths *et al.*, 1983). Invertebrate consumers are capable of consuming between 50% and 70% of the annual input of kelp wrack (> 2 tons/m per year) to beaches (Griffiths *et al.*, 1983; Lastra *et al.*, 2008). Mineralization of wrack on beaches may supply nutrients to nearshore primary producers, such as seagrasses and kelps (Dugan *et al.*, 2011b), creating connectivity and exchange of key resources among abutting ecosystem components.

Figure Box 3.3 A narrow bluff-backed beach that receives high inputs of macrophyte wrack from nearshore giant kelp forests and reefs. These cross-boundary transfers of organic matter (e.g. seagrass, algae, carrion) support high numbers of invertebrate species at high densities. Invertebrates consume a large fraction of the material imported from the sea. Bacteria and meiofauna in the sediment further process this material, and mineralized nutrients are returned to the nearshore zone, further linking abutting components of the surf–beach–dune system. (See color plate section.)

Africa, Brazil, and the northwestern and gulf coasts of the United States (Campbell, 1996).

The role of wildlife in ecosystem functioning is diverse, yet under-appreciated (Sekercioglu, 2006). In coastal environments, wildlife are likely to support a range of ecosystem functions, many related to land-scape connectivity. For example, pollination and seed dispersal of dune plants, alteration of dune geomorphology through burrowing, and regu-lation or support of ecosystem functions through trophic interactions (e.g. onshore transfer of marine nutrients by seabirds, pinnipeds, or turtles) are some of the important ecological functions fulfilled by wildlife species on dunes and beaches.

In summary, much of the faunal diversity of beaches and coastal dunes is undocumented and its roles in ecosystem functioning unexamined. Both adequately cataloging the wealth of species that reside on, and use, sandy beaches and dunes, as well as understanding biological and evolutionary processes that drive this diversity, is required to more effectively address the conservation of these dynamic ecosystems perched on the edge of the sea.

PRESSURES ON BIODIVERSITY AND THEIR EFFECTS

Introduction

Sandy beaches and dunes are squeezed between the continual expansion of coastal settlements on the terrestrial side and the effects of climate change on the marine side (reviewed by Cooper et al., 2009; Jones, 2012). Consequently, sandy beach ecosystems experience numerous anthropogenic pressures, with effects at all levels of biodiversity apparent or probable.

These pressures can be classified in various ways. First, they can be direct (e.g. pollution) or indirect (e.g. damming rivers reduces the sediment supply to beaches). Second, pressures can be hierarchically arranged into a causal chain, starting with ultimate pressures (root causes) and ending with proximate pressures (the immediate factors eliciting a biological response). For example, the growth of human populations and economies constitute ultimate pressures that elicit primary changes in the biogeosphere (e.g. higher atmospheric CO_2 concentrations, coastal development). Increased CO_2 produces second-order effects (e.g. warmer air and water), third-order effects (e.g. sea level rise), and lower-order effects (e.g. beach erosion, habitat loss). Similarly, the lack of public appreciation of beaches as habitat supporting unique assemblages is an ultimate factor leading to many other pressures, such as inadequate beach management and land-use planning. Management often addresses the direct and proximate pressures, while indirect and ultimate pressures are usually ignored, or even welcomed if they result in economic growth. Third, pressures can be classified according to their duration. Those operating for a short time are termed pulse disturbances, whereas those of greater duration are termed press disturbances (Bender *et al.*, 1984); ramp pressures are presses whose effects worsen over time (Lake, 2000). In theory, recovery is possible after pulse disturbances but, in practice, pulse disturbances are often repeated (e.g. beach grooming, nourishment), causing recovery to be incomplete. Finally, pressures and disturbances almost never act in isolation from each other, but rather are usually interactive, additive, or synergistic. Consequently, the magnified effects of co-occurring pressures must be considered, as does the context and scale (e.g. local vs. regional effects), legal requirements, level of economic development, and the availability of scientific/technical expertise.

As well as causing direct mortality, pressures often impact biota by altering or eliminating habitat and resources. Habitat loss, alteration, and fragmentation are particularly important on sandy beaches because the substratum is mobile and subject to various erosive forces. Loss of connectivity is also important as beaches have strong links to dune, nearshore oceanic systems and estuarine systems (Sherman *et al.*, 2002; McLachlan & Brown, 2006; Schlacher & Connolly, 2009).

In addressing pressures and their effects, there has frequently been semantic ambiguity. For example, the term *impact* sometimes refers to a cause and sometimes to an effect, but it is most accurately applied to effects only. The term *pressure* is synonymous with both *threat* and *stressor*, describing human activities that are the causes of change. *Degradation, stress, response,* and *impact* are effects arising from these causes.

A caveat is that the empirical investigation of, and controlled experimentation on, these pressures is often sparse, limiting the confidence and generality of conclusions about impacts. As well, the gradual nature of some pressures (e.g. climate change) may allow assimilation or evolutionary adaptation. For example, the effects of slowly increasing warming or acidification, while potentially serious, cannot be predicted with great confidence. Nonetheless, the combination of available studies and conceptual understanding suggests strongly that sandy shores are vulnerable to numerous pressures (Table 3.2), especially coastal development and climate change (Jones *et al.*, 2007; Cooper *et al.*, 2009; Jones, 2012).

Pressures and biological responses

Arguably the greatest threat to sandy beach ecosystems comes from the interaction of human coastal development and climate change, both of

Table 3.2 *Main pressures on sandy beaches and their impacts.*

Underlying threat	Component pressures and impacts	Key reference(s)
Climate change	**Sea level rise and altered storm and wave regimes**, causing accelerated erosion and shoreline retreat	(Galbraith *et al.*, 2002; Feagin *et al.*, 2005; Webster *et al.*, 2005; Slott *et al.*, 2006; Greaver & Sternberg, 2007; Stockdon *et al.*, 2007; Aiello-Lammens *et al.*, 2011; Harris *et al.*, 2011)
	Increased temperature, affecting phenology, physiology, geographic range, assemblage composition, functional and reproductive traits of beach and dune biota	(Philippart *et al.*, 2003; Stillman, 2003; Schiel *et al.*, 2004; Helmuth *et al.*, 2005; Harley *et al.*, 2006; Hawkes *et al.*, 2007; Ricciardi, 2007; Saba *et al.*, 2007; Byrne, 2011; Doney *et al.*, 2012)
	Altered circulation regimes and upwelling, affecting nearshore primary productivity and larval dispersal	(Hays *et al.*, 2005; Levin, 2006; Barth *et al.*, 2007)
	Altered precipitation, affecting beach aquifers, dune plants, nearshore salinity, and nutrient exports from estuaries	(McLachlan & Turner, 1994; Burnett *et al.*, 2003; Gaston *et al.*, 2006; Greaver & Sternberg, 2007; Schlacher *et al.*, 2008a, 2008d; Schlacher & Connolly, 2009; Fanini *et al.*, 2012a, 2012b)
	Acidification (decreased pH), causing tissue acidosis, reduced calcification	(Feely *et al.*, 2004; Pörtner *et al.*, 2004; Orr *et al.*, 2005a; Raven, 2005; Byrne, 2011)
Recreation	**Off-road Vehicles**, lowering habitat quality and stability, destroying dune vegetation, crushing beach animals, reducing prey for birds and fishes, disturbing and killing wildlife, and altering fauna distribution and behavior	(Godfrey & Godfrey, 1980; Wolcott & Wolcott, 1984; Buick & Paton, 1989; van der Merwe, 1991; Rickard *et al.*, 1994; Williams *et al.*, 2004; Groom *et al.*, 2007; Schlacher *et al.*, 2007b [2008b, 2008e]; Schlacher & Morrison, 2008; Schlacher & Thompson, 2008; Thompson & Schlacher, 2008; Sheppard *et al.*, 2009; Schlacher & Lucrezi, 2010a, 2010b, 2010c; Walker & Schlacher, 2011)
	Trampling and **camping**, impacting cover, abundance, and diversity of dune and beach species	(Hockings & Twyford, 1997; Moffett *et al.*, 1998; Fanini *et al.*, 2005; Schlacher *et al.*, 2011a; Schlacher & Thompson, 2012; Vieira *et al.*, 2012)
	Surf-zone activities (jet skis, boats), adding to noise and chemical pollution, disturbing wildlife	(Davenport & Davenport, 2006)
	Recreational fishing and **bait collecting**, affecting targeted populations of invertebrates and fishes	(Defeo & de Alava, 1995; McLachlan *et al.*, 1996b)
Pollution	**Sewage and stormwater**, changing the chemistry of sand prism, aquifer and nearshore waters and transferring sewage-derived nutrients to beach consumers	(Schlacher & Connolly, 2009)
	Litter is detrimental to invertebrates and wildlife through ingestion and entanglement	(Derraik, 2002; Andrady, 2011; Cole *et al.*, 2011; Hidalgo-Ruz *et al.*, 2012)

Table 3.2 (*cont.*)

Underlying threat	Component pressures and impacts	Key reference(s)
	Heated effluent (thermal pollution) can change intertidal assemblage structure	(Barnett, 1971)
	Oil, metals, and organic contaminants, negatively affecting abundance, diversity, health, and assemblage structure of beach and dune fauna	(Burnett, 1971; Siegel & Wenner, 1984 Haynes *et al.*, 1997; Jones, 2003a; de la Huz *et al.*, 2005; Junoy *et al.*, 2005; Ungherese *et al.*, 2010; Schlacher *et al.*, 2011b)
Construction	**Buildings, infrastructure, roads, etc.** degrade, curtail, or eliminate natural dune habitat and impose noise and light pollution	(Small & Nicholls, 2003; Bird *et al.*, 2004; Longcore & Rich, 2004; Nordstrom, 2008; Nordstrom *et al.*, 2011; Noriega *et al.*, 2012)
Ecologically harmful beach management	**Grooming** (raking, cleaning) eliminates essential habitat and food resources for beach biota, impedes dune formation, lowers beach stability, and disrupts nutrient regeneration	(Llewellyn & Shackley, 1996; Engelhard & Withers, 1999; Dugan *et al.*, 2003; Martin *et al.*, 2006; Garrido *et al.*, 2008; Dugan & Hubbard, 2010; Dugan *et al.*, 2011b; Gilburn, 2012)
	Nourishment causes large-scale mortality of beach invertebrates and may require bulldozing that can crush biota and cause sediment compaction; recovery may be possible if ecologically benign practices are carefully adopted	(Peterson *et al.*, 2000; Peterson & Bishop, 2005; Peterson *et al.*, 2006; Speybroeck *et al.*, 2006; Jones *et al.*, 2008; Schlacher *et al.*, 2012)
	Armoring (seawalls, groins, revetments, breakwaters) disrupts sediment transport, causes beach narrowing, eliminates habitat and lowers fauna occurrence, abundance, and biodiversity, including turtles and birds	(Dugan & Hubbard, 2006; Dugan *et al.*, 2008; Walker *et al.*, 2008; Famini *et al.*, 2009; Rizkalla & Savage, 2010; Dugan *et al.*, 2011a)
Invasive species	**Non-native predators** prey on birds and eggs. **Invasive dune plants** exclude native species and reduce habitat availability and quality. **Non-native algae and seagrass species** change wrack properties	(Inderjit *et al.*, 2006; Maslo & Lockwood, 2009; Burkitt & Wootton, 2011)
Damming of rivers	**Reduction in sediment supply** amplifies erosion	(Sherman *et al.*, 2002; Willis & Griggs, 2003; Finkl & Walker, 2004)
Resource exploitation	**Fisheries** can overharvest target species	(McLachlan *et al.*, 1996b; Kyle *et al.*, 1997; Clark *et al.*, 2002; Defeo, 2003)
	Mining alters, contaminates, or eliminates habitat, imposes mortality, and exacerbates erosion	(Ramirez *et al.*, 2005; Simmons, 2005)

Adapted from Schlacher *et al.*, 2008c.

which are, ultimately, a product of economic and human population growth. Climate change encompasses several proximate, pervasive consequences for beaches, including accelerated erosion (via sea level rise and increased storminess), warming, changed hydrology, and acidification (see Jones, 2012). The extent of ecological response to these pressures may vary from negligible (e.g. evolutionary adaptation or acclimation to falling pH and warming) to extreme (e.g. beach habitat heavily eroded or lost).

Warming of the ocean is already underway and is likely to affect the phenology, physiology, geographical range, composition of beach biota, and some ecological processes (Schiel et al., 2004; Doney et al., 2012). However, these effects may be subtle rather than dramatic; water temperatures will rise less than the air, many beach species can burrow to evade extreme heat, and the change may be sufficiently gradual to allow adaptation or acclimation. The species most vulnerable would be those now living close to their upper thermal limit and unable to shift to cooler latitudes. While larval dispersal may facilitate shifts in some species, those with direct development, such as peracarid crustaceans (an important component of beach macrofauna), would be constrained.

Direct effects of warming include functional and reproductive processes. For example, photosynthesis, decomposition, and nutrient recycling will be accelerated, and egg-laying vertebrates will be affected by warmer temperatures. For beach-nesting birds, warming may reduce the survival of eggs and increase sensitivity to disruption of incubation (Weston & Elgar, 2007). Warming may also have indirect effects on beach biota, including changes to temperature-sensitive plankton (the food of suspension-feeding beach macrofauna) and to the nearshore hydrology, which may affect larval dispersal of beach invertebrates.

Ocean acidification is occurring because of increasing dissolution of atmospheric CO_2. Surface waters are already 0.1 pH units less than pre-industrial levels and are projected to decline between 0.14 and 0.35 units over the twenty-first century (Solomon et al., 2007), changes not seen for about 20 million years (Brewer, 1997). This acidification can potentially affect many biogeochemical conditions and processes and may have influenced the Permian Triassic mass-extinction events (Bambach et al., 2002; Berner, 2002).

Of major significance is the undersaturation of both aragonite and calcite forms of carbonate. This trend may have both physical (e.g. a reduction in the supply of carbonate sediments to beaches) and biological effects (e.g. shelled beach invertebrates, such as mollusks and crustaceans, are calcium-dependent). If mollusk and crustacean shells weaken, these species may become more vulnerable to predation, abrasion, by storms and crushing by vehicles. As well, lower pH can cause tissue acidosis with effects on the development and growth of adults and the larvae of many calcifying beach species (Dupont *et al.*, 2008; Kurihara, 2008; Pörtner, 2008; Byrne, 2011). Alternatively, beach invertebrates may be pre-adapted to lowered pH because the turbulent surf zone may naturally be saturated with CO_2 and the pH of the interstitial water varies naturally over tidal and circadian cycles (Pearse *et al.*, 1942; Pörtner *et al.*, 2004). In consequence, interstitial species, such as nematodes and harpacticoids, can tolerate both varying pH and temperature (Wieser *et al.*, 1974).

Recreation on beaches incorporates several proximate pressures with various impacts. For example, off-road vehicles (ORVs) severely disturb beach and dune habitats, crush invertebrates, destroy dune vegetation, and cause a range of physiological and behavioral changes to the biota of beaches and dunes (Wolcott & Wolcott, 1984; van der Merwe, 1988; Moss & McPhee, 2006; Groom *et al.*, 2007). Camping and trampling in coastal dunes disturbs sensitive foredune areas and can severely affect dune flora and fauna (Schlacher *et al.*, 2011a). These human activities and the mere presence of humans disturb shorebirds, affecting their feeding, reproductive behavior, and survival (Dowling & Weston, 1999; Weston & Elgar, 2005, 2007; Weston *et al.*, 2011). In some instances, temporal decoupling of threat and ecological process can provide some relief for nesting or sensitive beach biota. For example, beach closures during the nesting season are used to protect plovers (Lafferty *et al.*, 2006), and on Mediterranean beaches, sandhopper amphipods recruit in spring while the high tourist season occurs in summer (Fanini *et al.*, 2005).

Pollution of sandy shores involves oil, sewage, metals, plastics, pesticides, fertilizers, light, and sound. Pollution constitutes either a pulse (e.g. oil spill) or a press (e.g. sewage outfall) stressor. Oil spills can affect species through toxic effects on individuals, clogging of animal feeding appendages and reducing oxygen tensions in the sand (de la Huz *et al.*, 2005; Bernabeu *et al.*, 2006). Recovery should be possible from pulse pressures, but this depends on the persistence of the oil in beach sediments and the availability of individuals nearby to recolonize oil-affected areas (Junoy *et al.*, 2005; Schlacher *et al.*, 2011b). It appears that talitrid and exoedicerotid amphipods are sensitive to oil pollution but are able to recover (Jones, 2003a; de la Huz *et al.*, 2005; Barca-Bravo *et al.*, 2008; Ottaviano & Scapini, 2010). However, recovery rates are variable; meiofauna may recover within a year (McLachlan & Harty, 1982), whereas the macrofauna can be affected for many years (Teal & Howarth, 1984). Humans often attempt to ameliorate the effects of oil spills with responses focusing on primarily charismatic vertebrates, generally neglecting other ecosystem components (Weston *et al.*, 2008).

Sewage pollution causes organic enrichment, lowers dissolved oxygen, and raises the redox discontinuity in the sand. These eutrophic effects can cause algal blooms in sheltered bays (Gowen et al., 2000). Metal pollution can reduce both species diversity and abundance of economically valuable species (Castilla, 1983; Haynes et al., 1997). Plastics can be an issue as large particles (ingested by seabirds and turtles), microplastics, and as entanglement agents (Derraik, 2002; Claereboudt, 2004; Andrady, 2011; Cole et al., 2011; Hidalgo-Ruz et al., 2012). Organochlorines, including the pesticide DDT, have been shown to accumulate in beach species, such as hippid crabs (Burnett, 1971). As these are prey for birds, fish, and mammals, there is the potential for trophic transfer, possibly even to humans. Dunes also experience pollution, usually from terrestrial sources. For example, fertilizer from landward agriculture can affect plant communities (Ranwell, 1972). Finally, light and sound from human sources can significantly affect animal behavior (Bird et al., 2004; Longcore & Rich, 2004).

Resource exploitation imposes direct mortality (i.e. fisheries) or severely alters or reduces habitat (e.g. mining). Although the most common fisheries on beaches are small in scale, impacts can be ecologically and economically significant because target species, such as bivalve mollusks, occur in patches that are easily overfished (McLachlan et al., 1996b). Although recovery often occurs, it can be delayed or prevented by other stressors, including erosion. Beaches have long been mined for lime, aggregate, diamonds, and heavy metals. Mining directly damages beach and dune habitat, alters the sediment budget, and exacerbates erosion with negative effects on shorebirds and invertebrates (McLachlan, 1996; Simmons, 2005). Beach communities may also be affected by the dumping of rubble (Fanini et al., 2009).

Non-native species can have large ecological and economic effects in a variety of ecosystems (Mack et al., 2000), but very little is known about such species for open-coast beaches. The coquina clam (Donax variabilis) appears to have been introduced to Egyptian beaches from the Atlantic ocean (El-Ghobashy et al., 2011), and the American hard clam (Mercenaria mercenaria) and Atlantic jackknife clam (Ensis directus) to beaches in northern Spain (Arias & Anadón, 2012). In South Africa, some non-native amphipod species as well as European marram grass (Ammophila arenaria) and coastal she-oak trees (Casuarina equisetifolia) are now present (Mead et al., 2011a, 2011b). Some non-native plants are deliberately planted to stabilize dunes at the expense of native species, or they invade without deliberate human actions (Burkitt & Wootton, 2011). The sublittoral zone fronting the non-vegetated part of beaches can be colonized by invasive algae and seagrasses, altering the composition of the wrack material washed ashore (Piriz et al.,

2003); changed wrack composition and chemistry may be deleterious for local fauna feeding on this beach-cast material (Lastra *et al.*, 2008, 2010). Finally, non-native predators such as dogs, foxes, and cats can prey on birds, chicks, and eggs (Maslo & Lockwood, 2009).

Ironically, some measures designed to manage the shoreline create other problems and become pressures themselves. Examples include armoring, nourishment, grooming, and deliberately introducing species (see above). Armoring (e.g. building of seawalls and similar structures) protects adjacent urban assets from erosion, but has several unwanted ecological effects. Seawalls reduce the size and number of intertidal zones and cause a disproportionate loss of upper beach and dry sand habitat (Dugan & Hubbard, 2006; Dugan *et al.*, 2008). This habitat loss and compression lowers invertebrate numbers, curtails habitats for vertebrates, and limits the deposition of wrack, an essential input to beach food webs (Dugan *et al.*, 2008). Increased erosive forces in front of seawalls can drown a beach over time because natural shoreline retreat is halted by the structure (Pilkey & Wright, 1989). Biota on beaches fronting seawalls may also be more vulnerable to storms and slower to recover from storm impacts (Lucrezi *et al.*, 2010).

Ideally, shorelines should be allowed to respond freely to changes in physical forcing regimes, including landward migration under conditions of higher sea levels. In settled areas, promoting natural landward migration would require moving infrastructure inland to allow the shoreline to recede. While such managed retreat maintains beach habitat, biodiversity, and function, it has enormous economic costs and carries much social uncertainty. In non-urban areas with few societal assets, inland retreat of beaches seems more probable. In the latter case, the ecological effects should be minimal because species are likely to adapt (Scapini *et al.*, 2005; but see Aiello-Lammens *et al.*, 2011). Of course, this option is not available for beaches backed by rocky cliffs; the beach will drown if sea level rises appreciably.

If retreat or quasi-natural shoreline movement is not a viable option, the alternative to arresting shoreline position using a fixed seawall is to restore or maintain eroding beaches through beach nourishment, where sand, often from offshore sources is added to the existing shoreline. This strategy has gained popularity because it maintains both sandy habitat for biota and beach amenities for humans. Of course, the nourishment option is only feasible where sufficient fill sand exists and in countries with adequate financial resources. Nourishment causes a range of negative ecological impacts (Speybroeck *et al.*, 2006). However, if the engineering process consistently and carefully employs best practices (e.g. carefully matched sand, application of very thin layers only, limited bulldozing), it may be regarded as a less ecologically damaging option than structural engineering works (Finkl & Walker, 2004). Although the initial ecological effects are usually severe (Schlacher et al., 2012), recovery of some taxa can occur within months if the properties of the added sediment are closely matched to the original beach sand (Jones et al., 2008). Where fill sediments are poorly matched, ecological impacts may persist for years (Peterson et al., 2000, 2006; see Chapter 10 for the effects of nourishment on marine turtles). Moreover, repeated nourishment episodes (e.g. annual, biannual) can degrade beach biota and inhibit recovery and ecological function (Dolan et al., 2006).

Grooming or raking of urban beaches to remove litter and wrack is widespread but ecologically problematic (Dugan et al., 2003; Dugan & Hubbard, 2010). Although socially desirable, the ecological effects of removing naturally deposited organic material from the beach are significant because this organic material is vital to beach functioning (Llewellyn & Shackley, 1996; Dugan et al., 2003). Wrack plays fundamental roles in nutrient regeneration and carbon processing in beach ecosystems (Coupland et al., 2007). Wrack also promotes beach stability and provides feeding, nesting, and habitat resources for both invertebrates and vertebrates, such as birds, marine turtles, and fish (Colombini & Chelazzi, 2003; Martin et al., 2006). Further, the loss of wrack invertebrates has cascading trophic effects to shorebirds (Dugan et al., 2003). Although grooming is theoretically a pulse disturbance, it is often repeated frequently, delaying or even preventing recovery. If the spatial scale of grooming is large, low-dispersal invertebrate species may need to be translocated and plant seeds added to achieve recovery (Dugan & Hubbard, 2010).

Significance of pressures and their impacts – what matters?
Managers with limited funds need to know which impacts matter (Jones, 2003b). Guidelines have been set for many pollutants, leading to the legal enforcement of water and sediment quality standards. By contrast, understanding the acceptable magnitude of ecological change is poorly developed (Oliver, 1995). In theory, "we need to define – using some form of scientific judgment – what is meant by 'detrimental', 'unacceptable change', 'significant impact', 'reasonable loss', etc." (Fairweather & Cattell, 1990). However, this is highly problematic. Although several criteria for the ecological significance of impacts (e.g. local extinctions, exceeding tolerance limits, loss or reduction of critical breeding habitat, ecosystem stability, primary productivity and assimilative capacity) have been suggested (Duinker & Beanlands, 1986), no consensus definition of an ecologically significant impact has been

reached. Instead, managers generally use value judgments (e.g. number of visitors and money spent at a place, presence of rare/endemic species), or non-biological standards (e.g. surface of beach available for leisure activities, shoreline stability, coastal water quality) to determine actions (Scapini, 2002). In truth, there is unlikely to be a universally acceptable criterion, or threshold, for objectively assessing the degree, duration, or severity of environmental impacts. Judging the limits of acceptable change and valuing biodiversity and naturalness will vary according to a country's or society's historical, cultural, and philosophical roots; it will also depend on its economic development status, financial resources, and the value it places on ecosystems and biodiversity (Scapini, 2010). In this context, ignorance of beach biology and the consequent lack of appreciation of beaches as ecosystems can be a major threat (Fanini *et al.*, 2007).

Despite the complexity of theses ecological, socioeconomic, and cultural issues, it would be useful if pressures and their impacts could be prioritized according to their broad significance or severity. This ranking would depend on the type of pressure, the magnitude and spatial extent of its impacts on biodiversity, and the recovery time from impacts. The following types of pressure are of particular concern for biodiversity conservation (see also Dovers *et al.*, 1996; Salafsky *et al.*, 2002).

1. Pressures with large and/or irreversible effects
For example, coastal development that causes the loss of dune habitat can rarely be reversed (Nordstrom *et al.*, 2011). In some cases, these pressures may be linked to extinctions (Hockey, 1987).

2. Pressures of large spatial scale
Concerning beaches, pressures from climate change are largest because all beaches will be affected (Jones, 2012).

3. Pressures of large temporal scales
Examples of these pressure disturbances are climate change, coastal engineering and urban development because they will affect beaches for centuries (Defeo *et al.*, 2009). Pressure disturbances may elicit a pressure ecological response (i.e. no recovery but an alternative state) unless assimilation or evolutionary adaptation occurs.

4. Ramp pressures
These are a special case of pressure disturbance wherein impacts increase over time (Lake, 2000). Ramp pressures matter greatly, especially if they

incorporate positive feedback loops that cause accelerating ecological effects. The destruction of dune-stabilizing plants is a beach example (Thompson & Schlacher, 2008); climate change may prove to be a ramp pressure.

5. Interactive pressures

Here several processes combine to magnify the effects of each pressure alone. On beaches, the possible shell-weakening effects of acidification may leave calcifying species more vulnerable to storm abrasion, predation, or vehicle crushing (Sheppard et al., 2009). Also, urbanized sections of the coastline are often armored, a situation that amplifies the trampling effects caused by beach visitors (Lucrezi et al., 2009). Further, sections of beaches used for leisure are subject to grooming and impacted by trampling and temporary constructions that may become permanent (Scapini, 2010).

6. Boomerang disturbances

These are pressures that produce unintended effects that rebound negatively on human interests (Webb, 1973). For example, building on dunes accelerates beach erosion, dams trap sediment that would otherwise have supplied beaches, and groyns transfer erosion problems by starving downstream beaches (Nordstrom, 2000).

7. Cumulative effects

Impacts from repeated activities, although individually small, may eventually become unacceptable. This "tyranny of small decisions" is exemplified on beaches by progressive ribbon development, armoring, and urbanization along the coastline (Odum, 1982).

To sum up, pressures leading to irreversible habitat loss or change, biological extirpations, and those operating over large spatial and temporal scales are of most concern. The various effects of climate change are potentially very large, adding to the existing effects of erosion and the cumulative effects of human population growth and coastal urbanization, especially ribbon development. The protection of sandy coastal ecosystems will require increasingly strong management responses to conserve both anthropocentric and ecocentric values.

MANAGEMENT FOR CONSERVATION

What do we manage for?

Management is usually directed toward one or more of the triple bottom-line outcomes – economic, social, and ecological. Ideally, all three can be integrated into social–ecological systems, where managing the environment means seeing humans as integral parts of ecosystems rather than as separate entities. This paradigm shift has come about largely through the realization that biodiversity conservation has dual mandates and outcomes – a moral and ethical imperative, complemented by anthropocentric motives stemming from the positive links between biodiversity and ecosystem goods and services (Millennium Ecosystem Assessment, 2005; Balvanera *et al.*, 2006).

Intact ecosystem goods and services are often vital for poor people in less-developed economies (FAO, 2010). In richer economies, maintaining the high values of human assets at the coast relies, in part, on adequately maintaining these ecosystem goods and services (Barbier *et al.*, 2011; Landry & Hindsley, 2011; Nordstrom *et al.*, 2011). In many situations, environmental management of beaches and the conservation of biodiversity serve economic, social, cultural, and ecological needs. It must also be explicitly recognized that conservation goals and management objectives are inextricably linked to social and economic constraints and demands. These linkages mean that not all conservation actions can be uncritically translated from one area to another. In the context of management and conservation, this paradigm shift is supported by tools, such as systematic conservation planning (Margules & Pressey, 2000), marine spatial planning (Douvere, 2008; Foley *et al.*, 2010), ecosystem-based approaches (McLeod & Leslie, 2009), and active adaptive management (Folke *et al.*, 2002).

Challenges

Globally, there are few conservation areas specifically designated to protect entire beach and dune ecosystems and their biodiversity (Defeo *et al.*, 2009). Those that do exist are either incidental or are in place to protect a sensitive or important feature of a sandy shore, such as shorebird and turtle nesting sites, penguin roosting sites in New Zealand, and clam preserves (or at least closed fishery areas) in New Zealand and California. Whole-beach and dune ecosystems are, however, seldom protected, or protected areas are not well managed (e.g. the use of ORVs in conservation zones; Thompson & Schlacher, 2008).

Why are beach ecosystems so poorly represented in existing reserves? This situation has arisen because of four factors: (1) limited awareness of the ecological values of beaches, including their biodiversity (Dugan *et al.*, 2010); (2) societal demands on beach and dune systems to support primarily utilitarian uses (Schlacher *et al.*, 2007a); (3) perceptions that beaches are resilient to human impacts – a misconception that certainly does not apply for the sensitive dunes backing beaches (e.g. Santoro *et al.*, 2012); and

(4) piecemeal planning and conservation actions that focus on single problems but neglect issues at the scale of landscapes and entire ecosystems (James, 2000a, 2000b). For example, most management of ocean beaches is done to protect ocean-front housing and other assets without much or any regard to conserving or sustaining natural resources or ecological processes (Peterson & Estes, 2001).

Unfortunately, for beach–dune systems, economic and social considerations still dominate management approaches characterized by a hazards and playgrounds focus (James, 2000a), whereas conservation is largely neglected (Schlacher *et al.*, 2006). Here we broadly address management for biodiversity conservation outcomes and briefly examine two aspects under this perspective: (1) the properties of sandy beaches and coastal dunes that may be particularly relevant for conservation and management; and (2) the use of systematic conservation planning and related spatial techniques for beaches and dunes. We suggest a vision statement for the conservation of open-coast beaches and dunes (Box 3.4), and we synthesize the key messages into a set of core strategies to guide conservation and management actions (Box 3.5). We also provide a list of management measures (Table 3.3) that will in most cases produce positive environmental outcomes for beaches and dunes at the local scale.

Properties of beaches and dunes particularly relevant for conservation
Sandy beaches have a number of attributes with important implications for biodiversity conservation and management in these systems.

1. Linked habitats
The appropriate functional unit for management is a tripartite system that comprises three closely interlinked elements – surf zones, non-vegetated beaches, and coastal dunes. The continual exchange of sand, nutrients, organisms, and organic matter couple these elements into a single functional unit, namely the littoral active zone (LAZ; McLachlan & Brown, 2006).

2. Dynamic habitats
Sandy coasts are malleable, undergoing considerable changes in shape, size, and shoreline position, driven by variations in sea level, wave energy (including storms), and sediment supply and transport (Bird, 2000).

3. Narrow, finite, and fragmented habitats
Sandy shores and coastal dunes are compressed into a narrow strip along the ocean margins, and there is no option for replacement (e.g.

Box 3.4   Suggested vision, objectives, and strategies for sandy beach conservation and management

Vision

A comprehensive, adequate, and representative network of beaches and coastal dunes successfully protected from unsustainable human uses and impacts.

Objectives

1. To ensure sufficient representation of biodiversity (genetic through to habitat) and ecological function (at all scales).
2. To create and maintain a network of beaches that is of sufficient size and configuration to maintain viable populations as well as biological connectivity among sandy beach habitats and biota.
3. To achieve efficient and effective protection of natural assets (e.g. species, habitats, processes).
4. To provide, if possible, for environmentally benign and sustainable human uses, including sustainable fisheries.
5. To create setback lines that allow beaches and dunes to migrate in response to changing external drivers, including predicted sea level rise.

Strategies

1. State explicit conservation goals for beaches and dunes.
2. Manage surf zones, beaches, and dunes as a single geomorphic unit – the littoral active zone (LAZ).
3. Comprehensively identify and map ecological values in the LAZ.
4. Implement ecosystem-based conservation planning and spatial zoning.
5. Seek and foster political support for beach conservation.
6. Align management objectives with conservation goals.
7. Include sea level rise projections in long-term planning.

---

compensatory habitat) for beaches and dunes lost to human development or other forces. Beaches and dunes also have variable length, being fragmented by other coastal features (e.g. estuaries, rocky headlands) and, increasingly, by urban settlements (Nordstrom, 2000).

4. Dual threats from the land and the sea

Beaches are increasingly becoming trapped between the impacts of climate change from the sea and development from the land (coastal squeeze; *sensu* Schlacher *et al.*, 2006). Human stressors are amplified in the narrow coastal band formed by beaches and dunes.

Table 3.3 *Examples of on-ground management actions that can produce positive environmental outcomes on beaches and dunes and that are congruent with the vision for sandy beach conservation (Box 5.4) and the related strategies (Box 5.5). These actions are important tools in local coastal management but should always be used to support more comprehensive strategies at larger scales.*

Principle	Intervention aim	Action
Manage for interlinked habitats	Rehabilitate sand dunes	Planting appropriate dune vegetation should only be done to replace plant cover that has been lost due to human interference, not to stabilize dune systems beyond their natural dynamics; non-vegetated areas should be maintained as such where these exist naturally.
	Build and replace dunes	Constructing dunes is appropriate in highly developed coastal areas where dunes have been eliminated or severely truncated. Dunes are usually created by beach scarping (bulldozing), sand fences, and vegetation plantings.
Avoid hard-engineering as a management intervention	Use scientifically determined setback lines	Avoiding development that is inappropriately sited on primary dunes (and the subsequent need to defend it with seawalls in the longer term) by implementing scientifically determined setback lines, which also serve to keep the littoral active zone (LAZ) intact and functional.
	Nourish beaches with sediment	Nourishment projects should only be undertaken using techniques that reduce environmental impacts to the resident fauna (e.g. match sediments, apply only very thin layers).
Protect sensitive features on sandy shores	Reduce trampling impacts	Manage visitors, directing access to beach via boardwalks to avoid trampling of dune vegetation; any fences must be constructed and sited in such a way that movement of organisms and exchange of sand and organic matter is not altered significantly.
	Decrease impacts from vehicles	Closing beaches and dunes to all non-essential motorized traffic; ban all recreational vehicles from beaches and dunes.
	Provide/enhance habitat for endangered species	Restoring degraded habitats, including foraging areas; shield artificial lights (for nesting turtles).

Table 3.3 (cont.)

Principle	Intervention aim	Action
Include biodiversity and ecosystem services/processes explicitly in conservation and management	Reduce disturbance to wildlife	Codes of conduct, education, and legal restrictions on visitor activities, including beach closures (e.g. banning flash photography, dogs, access to sensitive areas, etc.).
	Protect rare and endangered species	Protecting species of low population size, restricted range, or other vulnerable features usually requires habitat conservation or restoration with large benefits for other elements of the ecosystem; particularly successful knock-on effects when species with large home-ranges, such as birds of prey, are protected.
	Lower mortality of eggs, chicks, hatchlings	Fencing nests to prevent access by predators (feral or invasive species) and humans. Use of Conditioned Aversion to teach introduced predators to avoid shorebird eggs (Box 3.6).
	Reduce incidence of invasive species	Species eradication programs (e.g. weeding, seeding of native species, fire-ant controls, predator removal, etc.).
	Mitigate detrimental effects of beach grooming	Because removing wrack from beaches also removes habitat and organisms and disrupts nutrient cycling, limiting beach cleaning has large and multiple environmental benefits.

Sources: Dowling & Weston, 1999; Nordstrom & Weston, 1999; Lafferty, 2001; Greene, 2002; Dugan *et al.*, 2003; Williams *et al.*, 2004; Bertolotti & Salmon, 2005; Nordstrom, 2005; Peterson & Bishop, 2005; Ferreira *et al.*, 2006; Peterson *et al.*, 2006; Sergio *et al.*, 2006; Speybroeck *et al.*, 2006; Waayers *et al.*, 2006; Nordstrom, 2008; Maguire *et al.*, 2009; Maslo & Lockwood, 2009; Williams *et al.*, 2009; Dugan & Hubbard, 2010; Lettink *et al.*, 2010; Doherty & Heath, 2011; Maslo *et al.*, 2011; McIntyre & Heath, 2011; Nordstrom *et al.*, 2011; Maslo *et al.*, 2012; Santoro *et al.*, 2012; Vranjic *et al.*, 2012; Weston *et al.*, 2012.

5. Low resilience of dunes

Sandy beaches and dunes are physically abutting systems, but differ some-what in their degree of resilience to human use and modifications. Beaches can physically withstand some forms of low-impact human uses, whereas dunes are highly sensitive and have very low tolerances to all forms of human use (Groom *et al.*, 2007). The biota of both beaches and dunes are sensitive to most forms of human use. Major modifications (e.g. development, disruptions to sand transport) have large impacts on beaches and dunes alike (Defeo *et al.*, 2009).

6. Endangered species

Dunes and beaches support endangered plant and animal species, including the critical life-history stages of marine turtles and shorebirds, and species that require large home-ranges or other natural habitat features, such as birds of prey (Varland *et al.*, 2008).

7. Metapopulations and isolated populations

Some invertebrate beach species have pelagic larvae that disperse widely, creating metapopulations across a series of fragmented beaches (Defeo & McLachlan, 2005). The dispersal of adults by storms may support the metapopulation dynamics of species without pelagic larvae, which might otherwise exist in discrete, isolated populations (Harris *et al.*, 2011). Fragmentation of populations and ensuing metapopulation dynamics may also occur in coastal vertebrates such as birds.

8. High-value ecosystem services

Beaches and dunes are highly valued by humans (e.g. storm protection, recreation areas, real estate, fisheries, etc.) and are important ecological elements of the nearshore and coastal zone (e.g. foraging areas for birds, nutrient regeneration and water filtration, etc.). Arguably, beaches are the globe's most valuable commodity at the land–ocean interface, potentially heightening conflicts between socioeconomic and environmental demands (Landry & Hindsley, 2011).

9. Mineral deposits

Coastal dunes contain valuable mineral deposits, placing additional pressure on these finite systems (Lubke & Avis, 1998).

10. *Increasingly urbanized and settled*

Human populations are becoming increasingly concentrated in coastal cities and smaller settlements. More beaches and dunes will front larger urban and peri-urban conurbations in the future (Noriega *et al.*, 2012).

Ecosystem-based spatial conservation planning for sandy beaches

An important practical question is how to make decisions about the number, size, location, and spatial configuration of dune and beach areas to address conservation goals. Systematic conservation planning (Margules & Pressey, 2000) can be used to identify ecologically important areas that are irreplaceable, based on spatial patterns of biodiversity, habitats, and ecosystem services (processes). Projections of sea level rise should be used to understand which of these areas are likely to maintain their integrity on a 50- or 100-year timescale. Ideally, generous setback lines would be set to ensure the persistence of beaches, underpinned by adopting a precautionary principle. The dunes in these areas would benefit from formally recognized protection in the form of reserves.

In a second step, a cumulative threat assessment (Halpern *et al.*, 2008; Teck *et al.*, 2010) should be applied to identify particularly threatened beaches that are affected by multiple stressors. Planning tools can then be used to disaggregate cumulative stressors, either spatially through zoning of activities, or temporally by seasonal closures, for example. The intent of this planning would be first to build resilience into the irreplaceable and sustainable areas, and second, to reduce pressure on highly stressed beaches that serve as supporting areas (primarily in ecosystem functions) for the irreplaceable beaches.

Legislation and policy

The role of legislation and policy in ecosystem-based spatial conservation planning is to ensure that political or management responsibilities cater to ecological processes. Management at local, provincial/state and/or national/federal levels must take bioregional scales and processes into account. Countries generally do not have beach-specific legislation; beaches are presumed to be sufficiently represented under the banner of integrated coastal zone management or other forms of coastal legislation (James, 2000b).

There exists a need for beaches to be represented specifically in policy and in environmental legislation; a spatial planning approach is probably required to achieve this objective. There is also the widespread problem of multi-jurisdictional issues, where different levels of government either co-govern the same part of the coastline or responsibilities are split between

Box 3.5 Core strategies in sandy beach and dune conservation and management

1. Conserve ecological values

Coastal conservation and management must explicitly recognize the multiple and diverse ecological values of beaches and dunes (beyond their utilitarian values) and set targets to conserve them effectively.

2. Manage for interlinked habitats

Sandy coasts, including their surf zones, beaches, and dunes, must be managed as interlinked and dynamic functional units (e.g. littoral cells). It is important to minimize disruptions to the supply and transport of sand and all other processes that limit the exchange of material (including organisms) between the dunes, beaches, and surf.

3. Protect sensitive and irreplaceable features

Sensitive and irreplaceable features of beaches and dunes require higher protection investment. These include but are not limited to: (1) all sites of archaeological, spiritual, or cultural significance; (2) all dune areas and their flora and fauna; (3) nesting sites for sea turtles and birds; (4) feeding and roosting areas for birds, including raptors; (5) the water table; (6) fishery areas; and (7) areas with high wilderness/naturalness quality.

4. Limit seawalls and similar engineering structures

Because engineering works, particularly seawalls, generally have negative environmental consequences, their construction should be kept to a minimum from a conservation perspective.

5. Reduce impacts from beach nourishment

Beach nourishment (i.e. adding sand to eroded beaches) causes impacts on the local fauna. Nourishment works should use engineering techniques that can limit these impacts (e.g. application of thin layers, matching sediments, leaving unnourished refuge islands).

6. Leave wrack on the beach

Whenever and wherever possible, organic material deposited on the upper beach near the dunes (wrack, beachcast) should be left in place as it forms a vital source of food and habitat for beach animals. Raking beaches severely disrupts food chains and destroys critical habitats.

7. Ban vehicles from beaches and dunes

Non-essential motorized traffic (e.g. recreational off-road vehicles) is highly detrimental to beaches and dunes, severely impacting habitats and a wide range of species.

habitat types and activities (e.g. state manages dunes, local government manages the non-vegetated beach and vehicle traffic, federal government legislates on threatened species, department of transport regulates watercraft). Legislation should simplify jurisdictions along coastlines to foster consistent and efficient management for good conservation outcomes.

Lines in the sand: some core strategies

It is important to understand that conserving beach and dune habitats relies heavily on keeping sand budgets and transport processes intact.

Box 3.6 Training foxes on beaches not to eat eggs

In many of the world's beaches, invasive or superabundant terrestrial animal pests create conservation problems. Prominent among these are predators, often mammalian, which prey intensively on species that are often not well adapted to cope with the nature or extent of depredation. This is especially true during vulnerable life-history stages, such as breeding. For example, comparatively small birds are unable to defend against many predators meaning their nutritious eggs are preyed upon by predators such as snakes, foxes, stoats, cats, racoons, ghost crabs, or rats.

Many options exist for the management of pest predators on beaches, but few are entirely successful. Predator numbers can be reduced by culling, baiting, or immunocontraception, or by using ecological approaches, such as reinstating apex predators. Specific prey species benefit from predator exclusion or the provision of shelter to facilitate escape from predators (Maguire *et al.*, 2011a). Another approach for territorial, intelligent, generalist predators is to train them not to eat prey of conservation significance. This is done by creating an association between a prey type and a negative stimulus, such as illness. This can cause the predator to avoid subsequent consumption of the specific prey and is known as Conditioned Aversion (CA). For territorial predators, the predator may become the protector(!), as it excludes untrained conspecifics and does not consume the prey of conservation significance.

Maguire and colleagues (2009) examined the rate of red fox (*Vulpes vulpes*) predation of artificial eggs that mimicked eggs of the threatened beach-nesting hooded plover (*Thinornis rubricollis*). Foxes are a major cause of reproductive failure among hooded plovers. Following an initial take by foxes, eggs treated with an aversive agent experienced lower rates of depredation compared with untreated eggs, suggesting that foxes were avoiding eggs after being trained. Questions remain regarding how long the training will last, the predator-specificity of the training, and whether CA is a viable management tool on other beaches and in dunes. A key advantage of CA is that it can be used in areas where roaming domestic dogs are common – places where fox baiting or trapping is often considered incompatible with public support of conservation efforts.

Box 3.6 (cont.)

Figure Box 3.6 Red fox preying upon eggs in the foredunes of an Australian beach. (Photo credit: Thomas Schlacher.) (See color plate section.)

Recognizing the importance of physical processes in sandy shore ecosystems is fundamental to the management and conservation of these dynamic shorelines (Komar, 1998). One of the most effective approaches to managing the LAZ for ecological value and function is the use of setback lines (Ferreira *et al.*, 2006). The action of major storms and episodic events can, in fact, help create the microhabitat heterogeneity needed to maintain biodiversity in these ecosystems. For example, storm-produced washover fans on barrier islands are preferred nesting areas for endangered piping plovers (*Charadrius melodus*) on the east coast of the US (Cohen *et al.*, 2009). These washover fans are ephemeral features that re-vegetate over time and therefore lose value as nesting area. However, more than the beach or dunes needs to be considered, as numerous other processes from upcoast or upstream have the potential to compromise these systems. Delivery of sand to the littoral zone by streams and rivers is an important large-scale process crucial to beach health (Willis & Griggs, 2003; Masters, 2006). Reductions in sand supply from upcoast or upstream can drastically reduce beach widths and drive habitat conversion (e.g. beach to cobble or bedrock). Sandshed management will be increasingly important for maintaining beach health in some regions (Revell *et al.*, 2007). There are a number of core strategies (Box 3.5) that emerge from examining the theory and practice of beach and dune conservation and from the discussion of pressures that matter most (see previous section). There is also a range of practical intervention options available that should be effective in achieving positive conservation outcomes at the small scale (Table 3.3). We recommend that these be implemented as part of a larger program that is more thoroughly designed, using techniques of systematic conservation planning, sea level rise forecasting, or similar approaches. Above all, effective conservation of the unique biodiversity of ocean beaches and coastal dunes is ultimately contingent upon society placing a greater value on maintaining the ecological properties of these systems and committing the will and resources to conserve them into the future.

REFERENCES

Aiello-Lammens, M. E., Chu-Agor, M. L., Convertino, M., *et al.* (2011). The impact of sea-level rise on Snowy Plovers in Florida: Integrating geomorphological, habitat, and metapopulation models. *Global Change Biology*, **17**, 3644–3654.

Andrady, A. L. (2011). Microplastics in the marine environment. *Marine Pollution Bulletin*, **62**, 1596–1605.

Arias, A. & Anadón, N. (2012). First record of *Mercenaria mercenaria* (Bivalvia: Veneridae) and *Ensis directus* (Bivalvia: Pharidae) on Bay of Biscay, Iberian Peninsula. *Journal of Shellfish Research*, **31**, 57–60.

Armonies, W. & Reise, K. (2000). Faunal diversity across a sandy shore. *Marine Ecology Progress Series*, **196**, 49–57.

Arntz, W. E., Brey, T., Tarazona, J. & Robles, A. (1987). Changes in the structure of a shallow sandy beach community in Peru during an El Nino event. *South African Journal of Marine Science*, **5**, 645–658.

Auge, A. A., Chilvers, B. L., Mathieu, R. & Moore, A. B. (2012). On-land habitat preferences of female New Zealand sea lions at Sandy Bay, Auckland Islands. *Marine Mammal Science*, **28**, 620–637.

Avery, G. B., Kieber, R. J., Taylor, K. J. & Dixon, J. L. (2012). Dissolved organic carbon release from surface sand of a high energy beach along the Southeastern Coast of North Carolina, USA. *Marine Chemistry*, **132–133**, 23–27.

Balvanera, P., Pfisterer, A. B., Buchmann, N., *et al.* (2006). Quantifying the evidence for biodiversity effects on ecosystem functioning and services. *Ecology Letters*, **9**, 1146–1156.

Bambach, R. K., Knoll, A. H. & Sepkoski, J. J. (2002). Anatomical and ecological constraints on Phanerozoic animal diversity in the marine realm. *Proceedings of the National Academy of Sciences of the United States of America*, **99**, 6854–6859.

Barbier, E. B., Hacker, S. D., Kennedy, C., *et al.* (2011). The value of estuarine and coastal ecosystem services. *Ecological Monographs*, **81**, 169–193.

Barboza, F. R., Gómez, J., Lercari, D. & Defeo, O. (2012). Disentangling diversity patterns in sandy beaches along environmental gradients. *PLoS ONE*, **7(7)**, e40468.

Barca-Bravo, S., Servia, M. J., Cobo, F. & Gonzalez, M. A. (2008). The effect of human use of sandy beaches on developmental stability of *Talitrus saltator* (Montagu, 1808) (Crustacea, Amphipoda). A study on fluctuating asymmetry. *Marine Ecology – Evolutionary Perspective*, **29**, 91–98.

Barnard, P. L., Hubbard, D. M. & Dugan, J. E. (2012). Beach response dynamics of a littoral cell using a 17-year single-point time series of sand thickness. *Geomorphology*, **139**, 588–598.

Barnett, P. R. O. (1971). Some changes in intertidal sand communities due to thermal pollution. *Proceedings of the Royal Society of London. Series B, Biological Sciences*, **177**, 353–364.

Barreiro, F., Gómez, M., López, J., Lastra, M. & de la Huz, R. (2013). Coupling between macroalgal inputs and nutrients outcrop in exposed sandy beaches. *Hydrobiologia*, **700**, 73–84.

Barth, J. A., Menge, B. A., Lubchenco, J., et al. (2007). Delayed upwelling alters nearshore coastal ocean ecosystems in the northern California current. *Proceedings of the National Academy of Sciences of the United States of America*, **104**, 3719–3724.

Bascom, W. (1980). *Waves and Beaches: The Dynamics of the Ocean Surface.* Garden City, NY: Anchor Press.

Beaton, J. M. (1985). Evidence for a coastal occupation time-lag at Princess Charlotte Bay (North Queensland) and implications for coastal colonization and population growth theories for Aboriginal Australia. *Archaeology in Oceania*, **20**, 1–20.

Bender, E. A., Case, T. J. & Gilpin, M. E. (1984). Perturbation experiments in community ecology: Theory and practice. *Ecology*, **65**, 1–13.

Bennett, B. A. (1989). The fish community of a moderately exposed beach on the southwestern Cape coast of South Africa and an assessment of this habitat as a nursery for juvenile fish. *Estuarine, Coastal and Shelf Science*, **28**, 293–305.

Bergamino, L., Lercari, D. & Defeo, O. (2012). Terrestrial trophic subsidy in sandy beaches: Evidence from stable isotope analysis in organic matter sources and isopod *Excirolana armata*. *Aquatic Biology*, **14**, 129–134.

Bernabeu, A. M., de la Fuente, M. N., Rey, D., et al. (2006). Beach morphodynamics forcements in oiled shorelines: Coupled physical and chemical processes during and after fuel burial. *Marine Pollution Bulletin*, **52**, 1156–1168.

Berner, R. A. (2002). Examination of hypotheses for the Permo-Triassic boundary extinction by carbon cycle modeling. *Proceedings of the National Academy of Sciences of the United States of America*, **99**, 4172–4177.

Berta, A., Sumich, J. L. & Kovacs, K. M. (2006). *Marine Mammals: Evolutionary Biology.* San Diego, CA: Academic Press.

Bertolotti, L. & Salmon, M. (2005). Do embedded roadway lights protect sea turtles? *Environmental Management*, **36**, 702–710.

Bird, B. L., Branch, L. C. & Miller, D. L. (2004). Effects of coastal lighting on foraging behavior of beach mice. *Conservation Biology*, **18**, 1435–1439.

Bird, E. C. F. (2000). *Coastal Geomorphology: An Introduction.* Chichester: John Wiley.

Bonte, D. (2005). Anthropogenic induced changes in nesting densities of the dune-specialised digger wasp *Bembix rostrata* (Hymenoptera: Sphecidae). *European Journal of Entomology*, **102**, 809–812.

Boomsma, J. J. & Van Loon, A. J. (1982). Structure and diversity of ant communities in successive coastal dune valleys. *Journal of Animal Ecology*, **51**, 957–974.

Brewer, P. G. (1997). Ocean chemistry of the fossil fuel CO_2 signal: The haline signal of 'business as usual'. *Geophysical Research Letters*, **24**, 1367–1369.

Brown, A. C. (1996). Behavioural plasticity as a key factor in the survival and evolution of the macrofauna on exposed sandy beaches. *Revista Chilena de Historia Natural*, **69**, 469–474.

Brown, A. C. (2001). Ecology of sandy beaches. In J. H. Steele, S. A. Thorpe & K. K. Turekian (eds.), *Encyclopedia of Ocean Sciences*. San Diego, CA: Academic Press, pp. 2496–2504.

Buick, A. M. & Paton, D. C. (1989). Impact of off-road vehicles on the nesting success of hooded plovers *Charadrius rubricollis* in the Coorong region of South Australia. *Emu*, **89**, 159–172.

Burkitt, J. & Wootton, L. (2011). Effects of disturbance and age of invasion on the impact of the invasive sand sedge, *Carex kobomugi*, on native dune plant populations in New Jersey's coastal dunes. *Journal of Coastal Research*, **27**, 182–193.

Burnett, R. (1971). DDT residues: Distribution of concentrations in *Emerita analoga* (Stimpson) along coastal California. *Science*, **174**, 606–608.

Burnett, W. C., Bokuniewicz, H., Huettel, M., Moore, W. S. & Taniguchi, M. (2003). Groundwater and pore water inputs to the coastal zone. *Biogeochemistry*, **66**, 3–33.

Byrne, M. (2011). Impact of ocean warming and ocean acidification on marine invertebrate life history stages. *Oceanography and Marine Biology: An Annual Review*, **49**, 1–42.

Byrnes, J. E., Reed, D. C., Cardinale, B. J., *et al.* (2011). Climate-driven increases in storm frequency simplify kelp forest food webs. *Global Change Biology*, **17**, 2513–2524.

Campbell, E. E. (1996). The global distribution of surf diatom accumulations. *Revista Chilena de Historia Natural*, **69**, 495–501.

Carlton, J. T. & Hodder, J. (2003). Maritime mammals: Terrestrial mammals as consumers in marine intertidal communities. *Marine Ecology Progress Series*, **256**, 271–286.

Castilla, J. C. (1983). Environmental impact in sandy beaches of copper mine tailings at Chañaral, Chile. *Marine Pollution Bulletin*, **14**, 459–464.

Cisneros, K. O., Smit, A. J., Laudien, J. & Schoeman, D. S. (2011). Complex, dynamic combination of physical, chemical and nutritional variables controls spatio-temporal variation of sandy beach community structure. *PloS ONE*, **6**, e23724.

Claereboudt, M. R. (2004). Shore litter along sandy beaches of the Gulf of Oman. *Marine Pollution Bulletin*, **49**, 770–777.

Clark, B., Hauck, M., Harris, J., Salo, K. & Russell, E. (2002). Identification of subsistence fishers, fishing areas, resource use and activities along the South African coast. *South African Journal of Marine Science*, **24**, 425–437.

Clark, B. M., Bennett, B. A. & Lamberth, S. J. (1996). Factors affecting spatial variability in seine net catches of fish in the surf zone of False Bay, South Africa. *Marine Ecology Progress Series*, **131**, 17–34.

Cohen, J. B., Houghton, L. M. & Fraser, J. D. (2009). Nesting density and reproductive success of piping plovers in response to storm- and human-created habitat changes. *Wildlife Monographs*, **173**, 1–24.

Cole, M., Lindeque, P., Halsband, C. & Galloway, T. S. (2011). Microplastics as contaminants in the marine environment: A review. *Marine Pollution Bulletin*, **62**, 2588–2597.

Colombini, I. & Chelazzi, L. (2003). Influence of marine allochthonous input on sandy beach communities. *Oceanography and Marine Biology. An Annual Review*, **41**, 115–159.

Colombini, I., Mateo, M. A., Serrano, O., *et al.* (2009). On the role of *Posidonia oceanica* beach wrack for macroinvertebrates of a Tyrrhenian sandy shore. *Acta Oecologica – International Journal of Ecology*, **35**, 32–44.

Cooper, J. A. G., Anfuso, G. & Del Rio, L. (2009). Bad beach management: European perspective. *Geological Society of America, Special Papers*, **460**, 167–179.

Coupland, G. T., Duarte, C. M. & Walker, D. I. (2007). High metabolic rates in beach cast communities. *Ecosystems*, **10**, 1341–1350.

Davenport, J. & Davenport, J. L. (2006). The impact of tourism and personal leisure transport on coastal environments: A review. *Estuarine, Coastal and Shelf Science*, **67**, 280–292.

Dawson, M. N., Barber, P. H., Gonzalez-Guzman, L. I., *et al.* (2011). Phylogeography of *Emerita analoga* (Crustacea, Decapoda, Hippidae), an eastern Pacific Ocean sand crab with long-lived pelagic larvae. *Journal of Biogeography*, **38**, 1600–1612.

De la Huz, R., Lastra, M., Junoy, J., Castellanos, C. & Viéitez, J. M. (2005). Biological impacts of oil pollution and cleaning in the intertidal zone of exposed sandy beaches: Preliminary study of the "Prestige" oil spill. *Estuarine, Coastal and Shelf Science*, **65**, 19–29.

De Matthaeis, E., Cobolli, M., Mattoccia, M. & Scapini, F. (1995) Geographic variation in *Talitrus saltator* (Crustacea, Amphipoda) – Biochemical evidence. *Bollettino di Zoologia*, **62**, 77–84.

Defeo, O. (2003). Marine invertebrate fisheries in sandy beaches: An overview. *Journal of Coastal Research*, SI**35**, 56–65.

Defeo, O. & de Alava, A. (1995). Effects of human activities on long-term trends in sandy beach populations: The wedge clam *Donax hanleyanus* in Uruguay. *Marine Ecology Progress Series*, **123**, 73–82.

Defeo, O. & McLachlan, A. (2005). Patterns, processes and regulatory mechanisms in sandy beach macrofauna: A multi-scale analysis. *Marine Ecology Progress Series*, **295**, 1–20.

Defeo, O. & McLachlan, A. (2011). Coupling between macrofauna community structure and beach type: A deconstructive meta-analysis. *Marine Ecology Progress Series*, **433**, 29–41.

Defeo, O., Gomez, J. & Lercari, D. (2001). Testing the swash exclusion hypothesis in sandy beach populations: The mole crab *Emerita brasiliensis* in Uruguay. *Marine Ecology Progress Series*, **212**, 159–170.

Defeo, O., McLachlan, A., Schoeman, D. S., *et al.* (2009). Threats to sandy beach ecosystems: A review. *Estuarine, Coastal and Shelf Science*, **81**, 1–12.

Degraer, S., Mouton, I., De Neve, L. & Vincx, M. (1999). Community structure and intertidal zonation of the macrobenthos on a macrotidal, ultra-dissipative sandy beach: Summer–winter comparsion. *Estuaries and Coasts*, **22**, 742–752.

Derraik, J. G. B. (2002). The pollution of the marine environment by plastic debris: A review. *Marine Pollution Bulletin*, **44**, 842–852.

Doherty, P. J. & Heath, J. A. (2011). Factors affecting piping plover hatching success on Long Island, New York. *Journal of Wildlife Management*, **75**, 109–115.

Dolan, R., Donoghue, C. & Stewart, D. (2006). Long-term impacts of tidal inlet bypassing on the swash zone filter feeder *Emerita talpoida* at Oregon Inlet and Pea Island, North Carolina. *Shore & Beach*, **74**, 23–27.

Doney, S. C., Ruckelshaus, M., Duffy, J. E., *et al.* (2012). Climate change impacts on marine ecosystems. *Annual Review of Marine Science*, 4, 11–37.

Douvere, F. (2008). The importance of marine spatial planning in advancing ecosystem-based sea use management. *Marine Policy*, 32, 762–771.

Dovers, S. R., Norton, T. W. & Handmer, J. W. (1996). Uncertainty, ecology, sustainability and policy. *Biodiversity and Conservation*, 5, 1143–1167.

Dowling, B. & Weston, M. A. (1999). Managing a breeding population of the hooded plover *Thinornis rubricollis* in a high-use recreational environment. *Bird Conservation International*, 9, 255–270.

Dugan, J. E. & Hubbard, D. M. (2006). Ecological responses to coastal armouring on exposed sandy beaches. *Shore & Beach*, 74, 10–16.

Dugan, J. E. & Hubbard, D. M. (2010). Loss of coastal strand habitat in southern California: The role of beach grooming. *Estuaries and Coasts*, 33, 67–77.

Dugan, J. E., Hubbard, D. M., Engle, J. M., *et al.* (2000). Macrofauna communities of exposed sandy beaches on the southern California mainland and Channel Islands. In D. R. Brown, K. L. Mitchell & H. W. Chang (eds.), *Fifth California Islands Symposium, OCS Study, MMS 99–0038*, pp. 339–346.

Dugan, J. E., Hubbard, D. M., McCrary, M. D. & Pierson, M. O. (2003). The response of macrofauna communities and shorebirds to macrophyte wrack subsidies on exposed sandy beaches of southern California. *Estuarine, Coastal and Shelf Science*, 58, 25–40.

Dugan, J. E., Hubbard, D. M., Rodil, I. F., Revell, D. L. & Schroeter, S. (2008). Ecological effects of coastal armoring on sandy beaches. *Marine Ecology*, 29, 160–170.

Dugan, J. E., Defeo, O., Jaramillo, E., *et al.* (2010). Give beach ecosystems their day in the sun. *Science*, 329, 1146.

Dugan, J. E., Airoldi, L., Chapman, M. G., Walker, S. J. & Schlacher, T. A. (2011a). Estuarine and coastal structures: Environmental effects, a focus on shore and nearshore structures. In E. Wolanski & D. S. McLusky (eds.), *Treatise on Estuarine and Coastal Science*, vol. 8. Waltham, MA: Academic Press, pp. 17–41.

Dugan, J. E., Hubbard, D. M., Page, H. M. & Schimel, J. P. (2011b). Marine macrophyte wrack inputs and dissolved nutrients in beach sands. *Estuaries and Coasts*, 34, 839–850.

Duinker, P. N. & Beanlands, G. E. (1986). The significance of environmental impacts: An exploration of the concept. *Environmental Management*, 10, 1–10.

Dupont, S., Havenhand, J., Thorndyke, W., Peck, L. & Thorndyke, M. (2008). Near-future level of CO2-driven ocean acidification radically affects larval survival and development in the brittlestar *Ophiothrix fragilis*. *Marine Ecology Progress Series*, 373, 285–294.

El-Ghobashy, A. E., Mahmad, S. Z., Kandeel, S. K. & El-Ghitany, A. H. (2011). Factors associated with the distribution of the invasive bivalve clams *Donax variabilis* (Say,1822) at the area of the Mediterranean Coast preferred by marine fish larvae, New Damietta, Egypt. *Journal of American Science*, 7, 1051–1062.

Ellers, O. (1995). Behavioral control of swash-riding in the clam *Donax variabilis*. *Biological Bulletin*, 189, 120–127.

Engelhard, T. & Withers, K. (1999). Biological effects of mechanical beach raking in the upper intertidal zone on Padre Island National Seashore, Texas. *Gulf Research Reports*, 10, 73–74.

Erwin, R. M., Galli, J. & Burger, J. (1981). Colony site dynamics and habitat use in Atlantic coast seabirds. *Auk*, **98**, 550–561.

Fairweather, P. G. & Cattell, F. C. R. (1990). Priorities for pollution ecology research: Impact assessment. *Bulletin of the Ecological Society of Australia*, **20**, 37–38.

Fanini, L., Cantarino, C. M. & Scapini, F. (2005). Relationships between the dynamics of two *Talitrus saltator* populations and the impacts of activities linked to tourism. *Oceanologia*, **47**, 93–112.

Fanini, L., El Gtari, M., Ghlala, A., El Gtari-Chaabkane, T. & Scapini, F. (2007). From researchers to primary school: Dissemination of scientific research results on the beach. An experience of environmental education at Nefza, Tunisia. *Oceanologia*, **49**, 145–157.

Fanini, L., Marchetti, G. M., Scapini, F. & Defeo, O. (2009). Effects of beach nourishment and groynes building on population and community descriptors of mobile arthropodofauna. *Ecological Indicators*, **9**, 167–178.

Fanini, L., Gecchele, L. V., Gambineri, S., *et al.* (2012a). Behavioural similarities in different species of sandhoppers inhabiting transient environments. *Journal of Experimental Marine Biology and Ecology*, **420–421**, 8–15.

Fanini, L., Marchetti, G. M., Baczewska, A., Sztybor, K. & Scapini, F. (2012b). Behavioural adaptation to different salinities in the sandhopper *Talitrus saltator* (Crustacea: Amphipoda): Mediterranean vs Baltic populations. *Marine and Freshwater Research*, **63**, 275–281.

FAO. (2010). *The State of the World Fisheries and Aquaculture 2010*. Rome: FAO.

Feagin, R. A., Sherman, D. J. & Grant, W. E. (2005). Coastal erosion, global sea-level rise, and the loss of sand dune plant habitats. *Frontiers in Ecology and the Environment*, **3**, 359–364.

Feely, R. A., Sabine, C. L., Lee, K., *et al.* (2004). Impact of anthropogenic CO_2 on the $CaCO_3$ system in the oceans. *Science*, **305**, 362–366.

Ferreira, O., Garcia, T., Matias, A., Taborda, R. & Dias, J. A. (2006). An integrated method for the determination of set-back lines for coastal erosion hazards on sandy shores. *Continental Shelf Research*, **26**, 1030–1044.

Finkl, C. W. & Walker, H. J. (2004). Beach nourishment. In M. Schwartz (ed.), *The Encyclopedia of Coastal Science*. Dordrecht: Kluwer Academic, pp. 37–54.

Fish, M. R., Cote, I. M., Gill, J. A., *et al.* (2005). Predicting the impact of sea-level rise on Caribbean sea turtle nesting habitat. *Conservation Biology*, **19**, 482–491.

Foley, M. M., Halpern, B. S., Micheli, F., *et al.* (2010). Guiding ecological principles for marine spatial planning. *Marine Policy*, **34**, 955–966.

Folke, C., Carpenter, S. R., Elmqvist, T., *et al.* (2002). Resilience and sustainable development: Building adaptive capacity in a world of transformations. *Ambio*, **31**, 437–440.

Foster, C. R., Amos, A. F. & Fuiman, L. A. (2009). Trends in abundance of coastal birds and human activity on a Texas barrier island over three decades. *Estuaries and Coasts*, **32**, 1079–1089.

Fuentes, M., Dawson, J., Smithers, S., Hamann, M. & Limpus, C. (2010). Sedimentological characteristics of key sea turtle rookeries: Potential implications under projected climate change. *Marine and Freshwater Research*, **61**, 464–473.

Galbraith, H., Jones, R., Park, R., *et al.* (2002). Global climate change and sea level rise: Potential losses of intertidal habitat for shorebirds. *Waterbirds*, **25**, 173–183.

Garrido, J., Olabarria, C. & Lastra, M. (2008). Colonization of wrack by beetles (Insecta, Coleoptera) on a sandy beach of the Atlantic coast. *Vie et Milieu*, **58**, 223–232.

Gaston, T. F., Schlacher, T. A. & Connolly, R. M. (2006). Flood discharges of a small river into open coastal waters: Plume traits and material fate. *Estuarine, Coastal and Shelf Science*, **69**, 4–9.

Gheskiere, T., Hoste, E., Kotwicki, L., *et al.* (2002). The sandy beach meiofauna and free-living nematodes from De Panne. *Bulletin de l'Institut Royal des Sciences Naturelles de Belgique*, **72**, 43–49.

Gheskiere, T., Vincx, M., Urban-Malinga, B., *et al.* (2005). Nematodes from wave-dominated sandy beaches: Diversity, zonation patterns and testing of the iso-communities concept. *Estuarine, Coastal and Shelf Science*, **62**, 365–375.

Gibson, R. N. & Robb, L. (1996). Piscine predation on juvenile fishes on a Scottish sandy beach. *Journal of Fish Biology*, **49**, 120–138.

Gilburn, A. S. (2012). Mechanical grooming and beach award status are associated with low strandline biodiversity in Scotland. *Estuarine, Coastal and Shelf Science*, **107**, 81–88.

Godfrey, P. J. & Godfrey, M. (1980). Ecological effects of off-road vehicles on Cape cod. *Oceanus*, **23**, 56–67.

Gómez, J. & Defeo, O. (2012). Predictive distribution modeling of the sandy-beach supralittoral amphipod *Atlantorchestoidea brasiliensis* along a macroscale estuarine gradient. *Estuarine, Coastal and Shelf Science*, **98**, 84–93.

Gowans, S., Würsig, B. & Karczmarski, L. (2007). The social structure and strategies of delphinids: Predictions based on an ecological framework. *Advances in Marine Biology*, **53**, 195–294.

Gowen, R. J., Mills, D. K., Trimmer, M. & Nedwell, D. B. (2000). Production and its fate in two coastal regions of the Irish Sea: The influence of anthropogenic nutrients. *Marine Ecology Progress Series*, **208**, 51–64.

Greaver, T. L. & Sternberg, L. S. L. (2007). Fluctuating deposition of ocean water drives plant function on coastal sand dunes. *Global Change Biology*, **13**, 216–223.

Greene, K. (2002). Beach nourishment: A review of the biological and physical impacts. *Atlantic States Marine Fisheries Commission: Habitat Management Series*, **7**, 1–43.

Griffiths, C. L., Stenton-Dozey, J. M. E. & Koop, K. (1983). Kelp wrack and the flow of energy through a sandy beach ecosystem. *Developments in Hydrobiology*, **19**, 547–556.

Groom, J. D., McKinney, L. B., Ball, L. C. & Winchell, C. S. (2007). Quantifying off-highway vehicle impacts on density and survival of a threatened dune-endemic plant. *Biological Conservation*, **135**, 119–134.

Gurran, N. & Blakely, E. (2007). Suffer a sea change? Contrasting perspectives towards urban policy and migration in coastal Australia. *Australian Geographer*, **38**, 113–131.

Halpern, B. S., Walbridge, S., Selkoe, K. A., *et al.* (2008). A global map of human impact on marine ecosystems. *Science*, **319**, 948–952.

Harley, C. D. G., Hughes, A. R., Hultgren, K. M., *et al.* (2006). The impacts of climate change in coastal marine systems. *Ecology Letters*, **9**, 228–241.

Harris, L., Nel, R., Smale, M. & Schoeman, D. (2011). Swashed away? Storm impacts on sandy beach macrofaunal communities. *Estuarine, Coastal and Shelf Science*, **94**, 210–221.

Hawkes, L. A., Broderick, A. C., Godfrey, M. H. & Godley, B. J. (2007). Investigating the potential impacts of climate change on a marine turtle population. *Global Change Biology*, **13**, 923–932.

Haynes, D., Leeder, J. & Rayment, P. (1997). A comparison of the bivalve species *Donax deltoides* and *Mytilus edulis* as monitors of metal exposure from effluent discharges along the Ninety Mile Beach, Victoria, Australia. *Marine Pollution Bulletin*, **34**, 326–331.

Haynes, P. S., Brophy, D. & McGrath, D. (2012). Variability in the early life stages of juvenile plaice (*Pleuronectes platessa*) on west of Ireland nursery grounds: 2000–2007. *Journal of the Marine Biological Association of the United Kingdom*, **92**, 395–406.

Hays, G. C., Richardson, A. J. & Robinson, C. (2005). Climate change and marine plankton. *Trends in Ecology and Evolution*, **20**, 337–344.

Helmuth, B., Kingsolver, J. G. & Carrington, E. (2005). Biophysics, physiological ecology, and climate change: Does mechanism matter? *Annual Review of Physiology*, **67**, 177–201.

Hidalgo-Ruz, V., Gutow, L., Thompson, R. C. & Thiel, M. (2012). Microplastics in the marine environment: A review of the methods used for identification and quantification. *Environmental Science and Technology*, **46**, 3060–3075.

Higgins, P. J., Peter, J. M., Steele, W. K. & Marchant, S. J. J. F. (1983–2006). *The Handbook of Australian, New Zealand and Antarctic Birds*. Melbourne: Oxford University Press.

Hockey, P. A. R. (1987). The influence of coastal utilisation by man on the presumed extinction of the Canarian black oystercatcher *Haematopus meadewaldoi* Bannerman. *Biological Conservation*, **39**, 49–62.

Hockings, M. & Twyford, K. (1997). Assessment and management of beach camping within Fraser Island World Heritage Area, South East Queensland. *Australian Journal of Environmental Management*, **4**, 25–39.

Houston, J. R. (2008). The economic value of beaches – A 2008 update. *Shore & Beach*, **76**, 22–26.

Hubbard, D. M. & Dugan, J. E. (2003). Shorebird use of an exposed sandy beach in southern California. *Estuarine Coastal and Shelf Science*, **58**, 41–54.

Inderjit, C. D., Ranelletti, M. & Kaushek, S. (2006). Invasive marine algae: An ecological perspective. *Botanical Reviews*, **72**, 153–178.

Inoue, T., Suda, Y. & Sano, M. (2008). Surf zone fishes in an exposed sandy beach at Sanrimatsubara, Japan: Does fish assemblage structure differ among microhabitats? *Estuarine, Coastal and Shelf Science*, **77**, 1–11.

Irmler, U. (2012). Effects of habitat and human activities on species richness and assemblages of staphylinidae (Coleoptera) in the Baltic sea coast. *Psyche*, **2012**, Article ID 879715, doi:10.1155/2012/879715.

Iseki, T., Miyauchi, Y. & Fujii, T. (2012). Residence pattern of the ayu *Plecoglossus altivelis altivelis* larvae and juveniles occurring in the surf zone of a sandy beach, Niigata Prefecture, northern Sea of Japan. *Fisheries Science*, **78**, 55–65.

James, R. J. (2000a). From beaches to beach environments: Linking the ecology, human-use and management of beaches in Australia. *Ocean and Coastal Management*, **43**, 495–514.

James, R. J. (2000b). The first step for the environmental management of Australian beaches: Establishing an effective policy framework. *Coastal Management*, **28**, 149–160.

Jaramillo, E. & McLachlan, A. (1993). Community and population responses of the macroinfauna to physical factors over a range of exposed sandy beaches in South-Central Chile. *Estuarine, Coastal and Shelf Science*, **37**, 615–624.

Jaramillo, E., Dugan, J. E., Hubbard, D. M., *et al.* (2012). Ecological implications of extreme events: Footprints of the 2010 earthquake along the Chilean coast. *PloS ONE*, **7**, e35348.

Jones, A. (2003a). Ecological recovery of amphipods on sandy beaches following oil pollution: An interim assessment. *Journal of Coastal Research*, SI35, 66–73.

Jones, A. R., (2003b). Impacts on ecosystem health – What matters? In: G. Albrecht (ed.), *Proceedings of the Airs Waters Places Transdisciplinary Conference on Ecosystem Health in Australia*. Newcastle, Australia: University of Newcastle, pp. 208–223.

Jones, A. R. (2012). Climate change and sandy beach ecosystems. In E. A. Beever & J. L. Belant (eds.), *Ecological Consequences of Climate Change*. Boca Raton, FL: CRC Press, pp. 133–162.

Jones, A. R., Gladstone, W. & Hacking, N. J. (2007). Australian sandy-beach eco-systems and climate change: Ecology and management. *Australian Zoologist*, **34**, 190–202.

Jones, A. R., Murray, A., Lasiak, T. A. & Marsh, R. E. (2008). The effects of beach nourishment on the sandy-beach amphipod *Exoediceros fossor*: Impact and recovery in Botany Bay, New South Wales, Australia. *Marine Ecology – Evolutionary Perspective*, **29**(S1), 28–36.

Junoy, J., Castellanos, C., Vieitez, J. M., de la Huz, M. R. & Lastra, M. (2005). The macroinfauna of the Galician sandy beaches (NW Spain) affected by the Prestige oil-spill. *Marine Pollution Bulletin*, **50**, 526–536.

Kahn, A. E. & Cahoon, L. B. (2012). Phytoplankton productivity and photophysiology in the surf zone of sandy beaches in North Carolina, USA. *Estuaries and Coasts*, **35**, 1393–1400.

Klein, Y. L., Osleeb, J. P. & Viola, M. R. (2004). Tourism-generated earnings in the coastal zone: A regional analysis. *Journal of Coastal Research*, **20**, 1080–1088.

Komar, P. D. (1998). *Beach Processes and Sedimentation*. Englewood Cliffs, NJ: Prentice-Hall.

Koop, K. & Field, J. G. (1981). Energy transformation by the supralittoral isopod *Ligia dilatata* Brandt. *Journal of Experimental Marine Biology and Ecology*, **53**, 221–233.

Koop, K. & Griffiths, C. L. (1982). The relative significance of bacteria, meio- and macrofauna on an exposed sandy beach. *Marine Biology*, **66**, 295–300.

Kurihara, H. (2008). Effects of CO_2-driven ocean acidification on the early devel-opmental stages of invertebrates. *Marine Ecology Progress Series*, **373**, 275–284.

Kyle, R., Robertson, W. D. & Birnie, S. L. (1997). Subsistence shellfish harvesting in the Maputaland Marine Reserve in northern KwaZulu-Natal, South Africa: Sandy beach organisms. *Biological Conservation*, **82**, 173–182.

Lafferty, K. D. (2001). Disturbance to wintering western snowy plovers. *Biological Conservation*, **101**, 315–325.

Lafferty, K. D., Goodman, D. & Sandoval, C. P. (2006). Restoration of breeding by snowy plovers following protection from disturbance. *Biodiversity and Conservation*, **15**, 2217–2230.

Lake, P. S. (2000). Disturbance, patchiness, and diversity in streams. *Journal of the North American Benthological Society*, **19**, 573–592.

Landry, C. E. & Hindsley, P. (2011). Valuing beach quality with hedonic property models. *Land Economics*, **87**, 92–108.

Lastra, M., Page, H. M., Dugan, J. E., Hubbard, D. M. & Rodil, I. F. (2008). Processing of allochthonous macrophyte subsidies by sandy beach consumers: Estimates of feeding rates and impacts on food resources. *Marine Biology*, **154**, 163–174.

Lastra, M., Schlacher, T. A. & Olabarria, C. (2010). Niche segregation in sandy beach animals: An analysis with surface-active peracarid crustaceans on the Atlantic coast of Spain. *Marine Biology*, **157**, 613–625.

LeDee, O. E., Cuthbert, F. J. & Bolstad, P. V. (2008). A remote sensing analysis of coastal habitat composition for a threatened shorebird, the piping plover (*Charadrius melodus*). *Journal of Coastal Research*, **24**, 719–726.

Lee, M. R. & Riveros, M. (2012). Latitudinal trends in the species richness of free-living marine nematode assemblages from exposed sandy beaches along the coast of Chile (18–42°S). *Marine Ecology*, **33**, 317–325.

Lettink, M., Norbury, G., Cree, A., *et al.* (2010). Removal of introduced predators, but not artificial refuge supplementation, increases skink survival in coastal duneland. *Biological Conservation*, **143**, 72–77.

Levin, L. A. (2006). Recent progress in understanding larval dispersal: New directions and digressions. *Integrative and Comparative Biology*, **46**, 282–297.

Llewellyn, P. J. & Shackley, S. E. (1996). The effects of mechanical beach cleaning on invertebrate populations. *British Wildlife*, **7**, 147–155.

Longcore, T. & Rich, C. (2004). Ecological light pollution. *Frontiers in Ecology and the Environment*, **2**, 191–198.

Lubke, R. A. & Avis, A. M. (1998). A review of the concepts and application of rehabilitation following heavy mineral dune mining. *Marine Pollution Bulletin*, **37**, 546–557.

Lucrezi, S., Schlacher, T. A. & Walker, S. J. (2009). Monitoring human impacts on sandy shore ecosystems: A test of ghost crabs (*Ocypode* spp.) as biological indicators on an urban beach. *Environmental Monitoring and Assessment*, **152**, 413–424.

Lucrezi, S., Schlacher, T. A. & Robinson, W. (2010). Can storms and shore armouring exert additive effects on sandy-beach habitats and biota? *Marine and Freshwater Research*, **61**, 951–962.

Mack, R. N., Simberloff, D., Lonsdale, W. M., *et al.* (2000). Biotic invasions: Causes, epidemiology, global consequences, and control. *Ecological Applications*, **10**, 689–710.

MacMillan, M. R. & Quijon, P. A. (2012). Wrack patches and their influence on upper-shore macrofaunal abundance in an Atlantic Canada sandy beach system. *Journal of Sea Research*, **72**, 28–37.

Maguire, G. S., Stojanovic, D. & Weston, M. A. (2009). Conditioned taste aversion reduces fox depredation on model eggs on beaches. *Wildlife Research*, **36**, 702–708.

Maguire, G. S., Duivenvoorden, A. K., Weston, M. A. & Adams, R. (2011a). Provision of artificial shelter on beaches is associated with improved shorebird fledging success. *Bird Conservation International*, **21**, 172–185.

Maguire, G. S., Miller, K. K., Weston, M. A. & Young, K. (2011b). Being beside the seaside: Beach use and preferences among coastal residents of south-eastern Australia. *Ocean and Coastal Management*, **54**, 781–788.

Margules, C. R. & Pressey, R. L. (2000). Systematic conservation planning. *Nature*, **405**, 243–253.

Martin, K. T., Speer-Blank, R., Pommerening, J., Flannery, K. & Carpenter, K. (2006). Does beach grooming harm grunion eggs? *Shore & Beach*, **74**, 17–22.

Maslo, B. & Lockwood, J. L. (2009). Evidence-based decisions on the use of predator exclosures in shorebird conservation. *Biological Conservation*, **142**, 3213–3218.

Maslo, B., Handel, S. N. & Pover, T. (2011). Restoring beaches for Atlantic coast piping plovers (*Charadrius melodus*): A classification and regression tree analysis of nest-site selection. *Restoration Ecology*, **19**, 194–203.

Maslo, B., Burger, J. & Handel, S. N. (2012). Modeling foraging behavior of piping plovers to evaluate habitat restoration success. *Journal of Wildlife Management*, **76**, 181–188.

Masters, P. M. (2006). Holocene sand beaches of southern California: ENSO forcing and coastal processes on millennial scales. *Palaeogeography, Palaeoclimatology, Palaeoecology*, **232**, 73–95.

McArdle, S. B. & McLachlan, A. (1992). Sand beach ecology: Swash features relevant to the macrofauna. *Journal of Coastal Research*, **8**, 398–407.

McGwynne, L. E., McLachlan, A. & Furstenburg, J. P. (1988). Wrack break-down on sandy beaches. Its impact on interstitial meiofauna. *Marine Environmental Research*, **25**, 213–232.

McIntyre, A. F. & Heath, J. A. (2011). Evaluating the effects of foraging habitat restoration on shorebird reproduction: The importance of performance criteria and comparative design. *Journal of Coastal Conservation*, **15**, 151–157.

McLachlan, A. (1983). Sandy beach ecology – A review. In A. McLachlan & E. Erasmus (eds.), *Sandy Beaches as Ecosystems*. Boston, MA: Junk Publishers, pp. 5–44.

McLachlan, A. (1990). Dissipative beaches and macrofauna communities on exposed intertidal sands. *Journal of Coastal Research*, **6**, 57–71.

McLachlan, A. (1996). Physical factors in benthic ecology: Effects of changing sand particle size on beach fauna. *Marine Ecology Progress Series*, **131**, 205–217.

McLachlan, A. (2001). Coastal beach ecosystems. In S. A. Levin (ed.), *Encyclopedia of Biodiversity*. San Diego, CA: Academic Press, pp. 741–751.

McLachlan, A. & Brown, A. C. (2006). *The Ecology of Sandy Shores*. Burlington, MA: Academic Press.

McLachlan, A. & Dorvlo, A. (2005). Global patterns in sandy beach macrobenthic communities. *Journal of Coastal Research*, **21**, 674–687.

McLachlan, A. & Harty, B. (1982). Effects of crude oil on the supralittoral meiofauna of a sandy beach. *Marine Environmental Research*, **7**, 71–79.

McLachlan, A. & Turner, I. (1994). The interstitial enivronment of sandy beaches. *Marine Ecology – Pubblicazioni della Stazione Zoologica di Napoli I*, **15**, 177–211.

McLachlan, A., Jaramillo, E., Donn, Jr., T. E. & Wessels, F. (1993). Sandy beach macrofauna communities and their control by the physical environment: A geographical comparison. *Journal of Coastal Research*, **15**, 27–38.

McLachlan, A., Deruyck, A. & Hacking, N. (1996a). Community structure on sandy beaches – Patterns of richness and zonation in relation to tide range and latitude. *Revista Chilena de Historia Natural*, **69**, 451–467.

McLachlan, A., Dugan, J. E., Defeo, O., *et al.* (1996b). Beach clam fisheries. *Oceanography and Marine Biology – An Annual Review*, **34**, 163–232.

McLeod, K. & Leslie, H. (eds.) (2009). *Ecosystem-based Management for the Oceans*. Washington, DC: Island Press.

Mead, A., Carlton, J. T., Griffiths, C. L. & Rius, M. (2011a). Introduced and crypto-genic marine and estuarine species of South Africa. *Journal of Natural History*, **45**, 2463–2524.

Mead, A., Carlton, J. T., Griffiths, C. L. & Rius, M. (2011b). Revealing the scale of marine bioinvasions in developing regions: A South African re-assessment. *Biological Invasions*, **13**, 1991–2008.

Meager, J. J., Schlacher, T. A. & Nielsen, T. (2012). Humans alter habitat selection of birds on ocean-exposed sandy beaches. *Diversity and Distributions*, **18**, 294–306.

Millennium Ecosystem Assessment. (2005). *Ecosystems and Human Well-being: Synthesis*. Washington, DC: Island Press.

Moffett, M. D., McLachlan, A., Winter, P. E. D. & De Ruyck, A. M. C. (1998). Impact of trampling on sandy beach macrofauna. *Journal of Coastal Conservation*, **4**, 87–90.

Moss, D. & McPhee, D. P. (2006). The impacts of recreational four-wheel driving on the abundance of the ghost crab (*Ocypode cordimanus*) on a subtropical sandy beach in SE Queensland. *Coastal Management*, **34**, 133–140.

Nicholls, J. L. & Baldassarre, G. A. (1990). Habitat associations of piping plovers wintering in the United Strates. *Wilson Bulletin*, **102**, 581–590.

Nordstrom, K. F. (2000). *Beaches and Dunes on Developed Coasts*. Cambridge: Cambridge University Press.

Nordstrom, K. F. (2005). Beach nourishment and coastal habitats: Research needs to improve compatibility. *Restoration Ecology*, **13**, 215–222.

Nordstrom, K. F. (2008). *Beach and Dune Restoration*. Cambridge: Cambridge University Press.

Nordstrom, K. F. & Mauriello, M. N. (2001). Restoring and maintaining naturally-functioning landforms and biota on intensively developed barrier islands under a no-retreat alternative. *Shore & Beach*, **69**, 19–28.

Nordstrom, K. F., Lampe, R. & Vandemark, L. M. (2000). Reestablishing naturally functioning dunes on developed coasts. *Environmental Management*, **25**, 37–51.

Nordstrom, K. F., Jackson, N. L., Kraus, N. C., *et al.* (2011). Enhancing geomorphic and biologic functions and values on backshores and dunes of developed shores: A review of opportunities and constraints. *Environmental Conservation*, **38**, 288–302.

Noriega, R., Schlacher, T. A. & Smeuninx, B. (2012). Reductions in ghost crab populations reflect urbanization of beaches and dunes. *Journal of Coastal Research*, **28**, 123–131.

Odum, W. E. (1982). Environmental degradation and the tyranny of small decisions. *Bioscience*, **32**, 728–729.

Olabarria, C., Lastra, M. & Garrido, J. (2007). Succession of macrofauna on macro-algal wrack of an exposed sandy beach: Effects of patch size and site. *Marine Environmental Research*, **63**, 19–40.

Oliver, J. K. (1995). Is the 'limits of acceptable change' concept useful for environ-mental managers? A case study from the Great Barrier Reef Marine Park. In G. C. Grigg, P. T. Hale & D. Lunney (eds.), *Conservation Through Sustainable Use of Wildlife*. Brisbane: Centre for Conservation Biology, University of Queensland, pp. 131–139.

Orr, J. C., Fabry, V. J., Aumont, O., *et al.* (2005a). Anthropogenic ocean acidification over the twenty-first century and its impact on calcifying organisms. *Nature*, **437**, 681–686.

Orr, M., Zimmer, M., Jelinski, D. E. & Mews, M. (2005b). Wrack deposition on different beach types: Spatial and temporal variation in the pattern of subsidy. *Ecology*, **86**, 1496–1507.

Ottaviano, O. & Scapini, F. (2010). Can fluctuating asymmetry in *Talitrus saltator* (Montagu, 1808) (Crustacea, Amphipoda) populations be used as a bioindicator of stress on sandy beach ecosystems? *Oceanologia*, **52**, 259–280.

Pattrick, P. & Strydom, N. A. (2008). Composition, abundance, distribution and seasonality of larval fishes in the shallow nearshore of the proposed Greater Addo Marine Reserve, Algoa Bay, South Africa. *Estuarine, Coastal and Shelf Science*, **79**, 251–262.

Pearse, A. S., Humm, H. J. & Wharton, G. W. (1942). Ecology of sand beaches at Beaufort, NC. *Ecological Monographs*, **12**, 135–190.

Pelletier, A. J. D., Jelinski, D. E., Treplin, M. & Zimmer, M. (2011). Colonisation of beach-cast macrophyte wrack patches by talitrid amphipods: A primer. *Estuaries and Coasts*, **34**, 863–871.

Peterson, C. H. & Bishop, M. J. (2005). Assessing the environmental impacts of beach nourishment. *Bioscience*, **55**, 887–896.

Peterson, C. H. & Estes, J. A. (2001). Conservation and management of marine communities. In M. D. Bertness, S. D. Gaines & M. E. Hay (eds.), *Marine Community Ecology*. Sunderland, MA: Sinauer, pp. 469–507.

Peterson, C. H., Hickerson, D. H. M. & Johnson, G. G. (2000). Short-term consequences of nourishment and bulldozing on the dominant large invertebrates of a sandy beach. *Journal of Coastal Research*, **16**, 368–378.

Peterson, C. H., Bishop, M. J., Johnson, G. A., D'Anna, L. M. & Manning, L. M. (2006). Exploiting beach filling as an unaffordable experiment: Benthic intertidal impacts propagating upwards to shorebirds. *Journal of Experimental Marine Biology and Ecology*, **338**, 205–221.

Philippart, C. J. M., van Aken, H. M., Beukema, J. J., *et al.* (2003). Climate-related changes in recruitment of the bivalve *Macoma balthica*. *Limnology and Oceanography*, **48**, 2171–2185.

Pilkey, O. H. & Wright, H. L. (1989). Seawalls versus beaches. *Journal of Coastal Research*, Special Issue, **4**, 41–67.

Pilkey, O. H., Neal, W. J., Cooper, J. A. G. & Kelley, J. T. (2011). *The World's Beaches: A Global Guide to the Science of the Shoreline*. Berkeley, CA: University of California Press.

Piriz, M. L., Eyras, M. C. & Rostagno, C. M. (2003). Changes in biomass and botanical composition of beach-cast seaweeds in a disturbed coastal area from Argentine Patagonia. *Journal of Applied Phycology*, **15**, 67–74.

Polis, G. A. & Hurd, S. D. (1995). Extraordinarily high spider densities on islands – Flow of energy from the marine to terrestrial food webs and the absence of predation. *Proceedings of the National Academy of Sciences of the United States of America*, **92**, 4382–4386.

Polis, G. A. & Hurd, S. D. (1996). Linking marine and terrestrial food webs: Allochthonous input from the ocean supports high secondary productivity on small islands and coastal land communities. *American Naturalist*, **147**, 396–423.

Porri, F., Hill, J. M. & McQuaid, C. D. (2011). Associations in ephemeral systems: The lack of trophic relationships between sandhoppers and beach wrack. *Marine Ecology Progress Series*, **426**, 253–262.

Pörtner, H. O. (2008). Ecosystem effects of ocean acidification in times of ocean warming: A physiologist's view. *Marine Ecology Progress Series*, **373**, 203–217.

Pörtner, H. O., Langenbuch, M. & Reipschlager, A. (2004). Biological impact of elevated ocean CO2 concentrations: Lessons from animal physiology and earth history. *Journal of Oceanography*, **60**, 705–718.

Ramirez, M., Massolo, S., Frache, R. & Correa, J. A. (2005). Metal speciation and environmental impact on sandy beaches due to El Salvador copper mine, Chile. *Marine Pollution Bulletin*, **50**, 62–72.

Ranwell, D. S. (1972). *Ecology of Salt Marshes and Sand Dunes*. London: Chapman & Hall.

Rauch, M. & Denis, L. (2008). Spatio-temporal variability in benthic mineralization processes in the eastern English Channel. *Biogeochemistry*, **89**, 163–180.

Raven, J. (2005). *Ocean Acidification Due to Increasing Atmospheric Carbon Dioxide*. London: The Royal Society.

Revell, D. L., Marra, J. J. & Griggs, G. B. (2007). Sandshed management. *Journal of Coastal Research*, **SI50**, 93–98.

Revell, D. L., Dugan, J. E. & Hubbard, D. M. (2011). Physical and ecological responses of sandy beaches to the 1997–98 El Nino. *Journal of Coastal Research*, **27**, 718–730.

Ricciardi, A. (2007). Are modern biological invasions an unprecedented form of global change? *Conservation Biology*, **21**, 329–336.

Rickard, C. A., McLachlan, A. & Kerley, G. I. H. (1994). The effects of vehicular and pedestrian traffic on dune vegetation in South Africa. *Ocean and Coastal Management*, **23**, 225–247.

Rizkalla, C. E. & Savage, A. (2010). Impact of seawalls on loggerhead sea turtle (*Caretta caretta*) nesting and hatching success. *Journal of Coastal Research*, **27**, 166–173.

Rodil, I. F. & Lastra, M. (2004). Environmental factors affecting benthic macrofauna along a gradient of intermediate sandy beaches in northern Spain. *Estuarine, Coastal and Shelf Science*, **61**, 37–44.

Rodil, I., Lastra, M. & Sánchez-Mata, A. (2006). Community structure and intertidal zonation of the macroinfauna in intermediate sandy beaches in temperate latitudes: North coast of Spain. *Estuarine, Coastal and Shelf Science*, **67**, 267–279.

Rodil, I. F., Compton, T. J. & Lastra, M. (2012). Exploring macroinvertebrate species distributions at regional and local scales across a sandy beach geographic continuum. *PLoS ONE*, **7**(6), e39609.

Romer, G. S. (1990). Surf zone fish community and species response to a wave energy gradient. *Journal of Fish Biology*, **36**, 279–287.

Roob, R., Edmunds, M. & Ball, D. (2000). Victorian oil spill response atlas: Biological resources, macroalgal communities in central Victoria. *Australian Marine Ecology*, **109**, 42 pp.

Rose, M. D. & Polis, G. A. (1998). The distribution and abundance of coyotes: The effects of allochthonous food subsidies from the sea. *Ecology*, **79**, 998–1007.

Rossi, F., Olabarria, C., Incera, M. & Garrido, J. (2010). The trophic significance of the invasive seaweed *Sargassum muticum* in sandy beaches. *Journal of Sea Research*, **63**, 52–61.

Rumbold, D. G., Davis, P. W. & Perretta, C. (2001). Estimating the effect of beach nourishment on *Caretta caretta* (loggerhead sea turtle) nesting. *Restoration Ecology*, **9**, 304–310.

Saayman, G. S. & Tayler, C. K. (1973). Social organisation of inshore dolphins (*Tursiops aduncus* and *sousa*) in the Indian Ocean. *Journal of Mammalogy*, **54**, 993–996.

Saba, V. S., Santidrian-Tomillo, P., Reina, R. D., *et al.* (2007). The effect of the El Nino Southern Oscillation on the reproductive frequency of eastern Pacific leatherback turtles. *Journal of Applied Ecology*, **44**, 395–404.

Salafsky, N., Margoluis, R., Redford, K. H. & Robinson, J. G. (2002). Improving the practice of conservation: A conceptual framework and research agenda for conservation science. *Conservation Biology*, **16**, 1469–1479.

Santoro, R., Jucker, T., Prisco, I., *et al.* (2012). Effects of trampling limitation on coastal dune plant communities. *Environmental Management*, **49**, 534–542.

Scapini, F. (ed.) (2002). *Baseline Research for the Integrated Sustainable Management of Mediterranean Sensitive Coastal Ecosystems: A Manual for Coastal Managers, Scientists and All Those Studying Coastal Processes and Management in the Mediterranean*. Firenze: Istituto Agronomico per l'Oltremare, Società Editrice Fiorentina.

Scapini, F. (2010). Mediterranean coastal areas at risk between conservation and development. In F. Scapini & G. Ciampi (eds.), *Coastal Water Bodies: Nature and Culture Conflicts in the Mediterranean*. Dordrecht: Springer Science, pp. 1–20.

Scapini, F., Chelazzi, L., Colombini, I., Fallaci, M. & Fanini, L. (2005). Orientation of sandhoppers at different points along a dynamic shoreline in southern Tuscany. *Marine Biology*, **147**, 919–926.

Schiel, D. R., Steinbeck, J. R. & Foster, M. S. (2004). Ten years of induced ocean warming causes comprehensive changes in marine benthic communities. *Ecology*, **85**, 1833–1839.

Schlacher, T. A. & Connolly, R. M. (2009). Land–ocean coupling of carbon and nitrogen fluxes on sandy beaches. *Ecosystems*, **12**, 311–321.

Schlacher, T. A. & Hartwig, J. (2013). Bottom-up control in the benthos of ocean-exposed sandy beaches. *Austral Ecology*, **38**, 177–189.

Schlacher, T. A. & Lucrezi, S. (2010a). Experimental evidence that vehicle traffic changes burrow architecture and reduces population density of ghost crabs on sandy beaches. *Vie et Milieu – Life and Environment*, **60**, 313–320.

Schlacher, T. A. & Lucrezi, S. (2010b). Compression of home ranges in ghost crabs on sandy beaches impacted by vehicle traffic. *Marine Biology*, **157**, 2467–2474.

Schlacher, T. A. & Lucrezi, S. (2010c). Impacts of off-road vehicles (ORVs) on burrow architecture of ghost crabs (Genus *Ocypode*) on sandy beaches. *Environmental Management*, **45**, 1352–1362.

Schlacher, T. A. & Morrison, J. M. (2008). Beach disturbance caused by off-road vehicles (ORVs) on sandy shores: Relationship with traffic volumes and a new method to quantify impacts using image-based data acquisition and analysis. *Marine Pollution Bulletin*, **56**, 1646–1649.

Schlacher, T. A. & Thompson, L. M. C. (2007). Exposure of fauna to off-road vehicle (ORV) traffic on sandy beaches. *Coastal Management*, **35**, 567–583.

Schlacher, T. A. & Thompson, L. M. C. (2008). Physical impacts caused by off-road vehicles (ORVs) to sandy beaches: Spatial quantification of car tracks on an Australian barrier island. *Journal of Coastal Research*, **224**, 234–242.

Schlacher, T. A. & Thompson, L. (2012). Beach recreation impacts benthic invertebrates on ocean-exposed sandy shores. *Biological Conservation*, **147**, 123–132.

Schlacher, T. A., Schoeman, D. S., Lastra, M., *et al.* (2006). Neglected ecosystems bear the brunt of change. *Ethology, Ecology & Evolution*, **18**, 349–351.

Schlacher, T. A., Dugan, J., Schoeman, D. S., *et al.* (2007a). Sandy beaches at the brink. *Diversity and Distributions*, **13**, 556–560.

Schlacher, T. A., Thompson, L. M. C. & Price, S. (2007b). Vehicles versus conservation of invertebrates on sandy beaches: Quantifying direct mortalities inflicted by off-road vehicles (ORVs) on ghost crabs. *Marine Ecology – Evolutionary Perspective*, **28**, 354–367.

Schlacher, T. A., Connolly, R. M., Skillington, A. J. & Gaston, T. F. (2008a). Can export of organic matter from estuaries support zooplankton in nearshore, marine plumes? *Aquatic Ecology*, **43**, 383–393.

Schlacher, T. A., Richardson, D. & McLean, I. (2008b). Impacts of off-road vehicles (ORVs) on macrobenthic assemblages on sandy beaches. *Environmental Management*, **41**, 878–892.

Schlacher, T. A., Schoeman, D. S., Dugan, J. E., *et al.* (2008c). Sandy beach ecosystems: Key features, sampling issues, management challenges and climate change impacts. *Marine Ecology – Evolutionary Perspective*, **29**(S1), 70–90.

Schlacher, T. A., Skillington, A. J., Connolly, R. M., Robinson, W. & Gaston, T. F. (2008d). Coupling between marine plankton and freshwater flow in the plumes off a small estuary *International Review of Hydrobiology*, **6**, 641–658.

Schlacher, T. A., Thompson, L. M. C. & Walker, S. J. (2008e). Mortalities caused by off-road vehicles (ORVs) to a key member of sandy beach assemblages, the surf clam *Donax deltoides*. *Hydrobiologia*, **610**, 345–350.

Schlacher, T. A., de Jager, R. & Nielsen, T. (2011a). Vegetation and ghost crabs in coastal dunes as indicators of putative stressors from tourism. *Ecological Indicators*, **11**, 284–294.

Schlacher, T. A., Holzheimer, A., Stevens, T. & Rissik, D. (2011b). Impacts of the 'Pacific Adventurer' oil spill on the macrobenthos of subtropical sandy beaches. *Estuaries and Coasts*, **34**, 937–949.

Schlacher, T. A., Noriega, R., Jones, A. & Dye, T. (2012). The effects of beach nourishment on benthic invertebrates in eastern Australia: Impacts and variable recovery. *Science of the Total Environment*, **435**, 411–417.

Schoeman, D. S. & Richardson, A. J. (2002). Investigating biotic and abiotic factors affecting the recruitment of an intertidal clam on an exposed sandy beach using a generalized additive model. *Journal of Experimental Marine Biology and Ecology*, **276**, 67–81.

Sekercioglu, C. H. (2006). Increasing awareness of avian ecological function. *Trends in Ecology and Evolution*, **21**, 464–471.

Sergio, F., Newton, I., Marchesi, L. & Pedrini, P. (2006). Ecologically justified charisma: Preservation of top predators delivers biodiversity conservation. *Journal of Applied Ecology*, **43**, 1049–1055.

Sheppard, N., Pitt, K. A. & Schlacher, T. A. (2009). Sub-lethal effects of off-road vehicles (ORVs) on surf clams on sandy beaches. *Journal of Experimental Marine Biology and Ecology*, **380**, 113–118.

Sherman, D. J., Barron, K. M. & Ellis, J. T. (2002). Retention of beach sands by dams and debris basins in southern California. *Journal of Coastal Research*, SI**36**, 662–674.

Siegel, P. & Wenner, A. (1984). Abnormal reproduction of the sand crab *Emerita analoga* in the vicinity of a nuclear generating station in southern California. *Marine Biology*, **80**, 341–345.

Simmons, R. E. (2005). Declining coastal avifauna at a diamond-mining site in Namibia: Comparisons and causes. *Ostrich*, **76**, 97–103.

Slott, J. M., Murray, A. B., Ashton, A. D. & Crowley, T. J. (2006). Coastline responses to changing storm patterns. *Geophysical Research Letters*, **33**, L18404.

Small, C. & Nicholls, R. J. (2003). A global analysis of human settlement in coastal zones. *Journal of Coastal Research*, **19**, 584–599.

Soares, A. G. (2003). Sandy beach morphodynamics and macrobenthic communities in temperate, subtropical and tropical regions: A macroecological approach. PhD thesis, University of Port Elizabeth, Port Elizabeth, South Africa.

Soares, A. G., McLachlan, A. & Schlacher, T. A. (1996). Disturbance effects of stranded kelp on populations of the sandy beach bivalve *Donax serra* (Röding). *Journal of Experimental Marine Biology and Ecology*, **205**, 165–186.

Soares, A. G., Schlacher, T. A. & McLachlan, A. (1997). Carbon and nitrogen exchange between sandy beach clams (*Donax serra*) and kelp beds in the Benguela Coastal Upwelling Region. *Marine Biology*, **127**, 657–664.

Soares, A. G., Scapini, F., Brown, A. C. & McLachlan, A. (1999). Phenotypic plasticity, genetic similarity and evolutionary inertia in changing environments. *Journal of Molluscan Studies*, **65**, 136–139.

Solomon, S., Qin, D., Manning, M., *et al.* (2007). Technical summary. In S. Solomon, D. Qin, M. Manning, *et al.* (eds.), *Climate Change 2007: The Physical Science Basis. Contribution of Working Group I to the Fourth Assessment Report of the Intergovernmental Panel on Climate Change*. Cambridge: Cambridge University Press, pp. 19–91.

Speybroeck, J., Bonte, D., Courtens, W., *et al.* (2006). Beach nourishment: An ecologically sound coastal defence alternative? A review. *Aquatic Conservation – Marine and Freshwater Ecosystems*, **16**, 419–435.

Stewart, B. S. (1984). Diurnal hauling patterns of harbor seals at San Miguel Island, California. *Journal of Wildlife Management*, **48**, 1459–1461.

Stillman, J. H. (2003). Acclimation capacity underlies susceptibility to climate change. *Science*, **301**, 65–65.

Stockdon, H. F., Sallenger, A. H., Holman, R. A. & Howd, P. A. (2007). A simple model for the spatially-variable coastal response to hurricanes. *Marine Geology*, **238**, 1–20.

Straughan, D. (1983). Ecological characteristics of sandy beaches in the Southern California Bight. In A. McLachlan & T. Erasmus (eds.), *Sandy Beaches as Ecosystems: Proceedings of the 1st International Symposium on Sandy Beaches, Port Elizabeth, South Africa, 17–21 January 1983. Developments in Hydrobiology*. The Hague: W. Junk, pp. 441–447.

Tarr, J. G. & Tarr, P. W. (1987). Seasonal abundance and the distribution of coastal birds on the northern Skeleton Coast, South West Africa/Namibia. *Madoqua*, **15**, 63–72.

Teal, J. M. & Howarth, R. W. (1984). Oil spill studies: A review of ecological effects. *Environmental Management*, **8**, 27–43.

Teck, S. J., Halpern, B. S., Kappel, C. V., *et al.* (2010). Using expert judgment to estimate marine ecosystem vulnerability in the California Current. *Ecological Applications*, **20**, 1402–1416.

Thompson, L. M. C. & Schlacher, T. A. (2008). Physical damage to coastal foredunes and ecological impacts caused by vehicle tracks associated with beach camping on sandy shores: A case study from Fraser Island, Australia. *Journal of Coastal Conservation*, **12**, 67–82.

Thornton, E. B., Sallenger, A., Sesto, J. C., *et al.* (2006). Sand mining impacts on long-term dune erosion in southern Monterey Bay. *Marine Geology*, **229**, 45–58.

Tsubaki, R. & Kato, M. (2009). Intertidal slope of coral sand beach as a unique habitat for fish: Meiobenthic diet of the transparent sand dart, Kraemeria cunicularia (Gobiidae). *Marine Biology*, **156**, 1739–1749.

Ungherese, G., Mengoni, A., Somigli, S., *et al.* (2010). Relationship between heavy metals pollution and genetic diversity in Mediterranean populations of the sandhopper *Talitrus saltator* (Montagu) (Crustacea, Amphipoda). *Environmental Pollution*, **158**, 1638–1643.

United Nations Conference on Environment and Development (UNCED). (1992). *Protection of the Oceans, All Kinds of Seas, Including Enclosed and Semi-enclosed Seas, and Coastal Areas and the Protection, Rational Use and Development of Their Living Resources.* Agenda 21, Chapter 17. New York, NY: United Nations Divison for Sustainable Development.

Van Dam, A. R. & Van Dam, M. H. (2008). Impact of off-road vehicle use on dune endemic Coleoptera. *Annals of the Entomological Society of America*, **101**, 411–417.

Van der Merwe, D. (1988). *The Effects of Off-road Vehicles (ORV's) on Coastal Ecosystems – A Review*. Institute for Coastal Research Report No. 17. Port Elizabeth, South Africa: University of Port Elizabeth.

Van der Merwe, D. (1991). Effects of off-road vehicles on the macrofauna of a sandy beach. *South African Journal of Science*, **87**, 210–213.

Varland, D. E., Powell, L. A., Kenney, M. K. & Fleming, T. L. (2008). Peregrine falcon survival and resighting frequencies on the Washington coast, 1995–2003. *Journal of Raptor Research*, **42**, 161–171.

Vieira, J. V., Borzone, C. A., Lorenzi, L. & de Carvalho, F. G. (2012). Human impact on the benthic macrofauna of two beach environments with different morpho-dynamic characteristics in southern Brazil. *Brazilian Journal of Oceanography*, **60**, 135–148.

Vranjic, J. A., Morin, L., Reid, A. M. & Groves, R. H. (2012). Integrating revegetation with management methods to rehabilitate coastal vegetation invaded by Bitou bush (*Chrysanthemoides monilifera* ssp *rotundata*) in Australia. *Austral Ecology*, **37**, 78–89.

Waayers, D., Newsome, D. & Lee, D. (2006). Observations of non-compliance behaviour by tourists to a voluntary code of conduct: A pilot study of turtle tourism in the Exmouth region, Western Australia. *Journal of Ecotourism*, **5**, 211–222.

Walker, S. J. & Schlacher, T. A. (2011). Impact of a pulse human disturbance experiment on macrofaunal assemblages on an Australian sandy beach. *Journal of Coastal Research*, **27**, 184–192.

Walker, S. J., Schlacher, T. A. & Thompson, L. M. C. (2008). Habitat modification in a dynamic environment: The influence of a small artificial groyne on macro-faunal assemblages of a sandy beach. *Estuarine Coastal and Shelf Science*, **79**, 24–34.

Watt-Pringle, P. & Strydom, N. A. (2003). Habitat use by larval fishes in a temperate South African surf zone. *Estuarine, Coastal and Shelf Science*, **58**, 765–774.

Webb, L. J. (1973). *Environmental Boomerang*. Milton: Jacaranda Press.

Webster, P. J., Holland, G. J., Curry, J. A. & Chang, H. R. (2005). Changes in tropical cyclone number, duration, and intensity in a warming environment. *Science*, **309**, 1844–1846.

Weston, M. A. & Elgar, M. A. (2005). Disturbance to brood-rearing hooded plover *Thinornis rubricollis*: Responses and consequences. *Bird Conservation International*, **15**, 193–209.

Weston, M. A. & Elgar, M. A. (2007). Responses of incubating hooded plovers (*Thinornis rubricollis*) to disturbance. *Journal of Coastal Research*, **23**, 569–576.

Weston, M. A., Dann, P., Jessop, R. *et al.* (2008). Can oiled shorebirds and their nests and eggs be successfully rehabilitated? A case study involving the threatened hooded plover *Thinornis rubricollis* in south-eastern Australia. *Waterbirds*, **31**, 127–132.

Weston, M. A., Ehmke, G. C. & Maguire, G. S. (2009). Manage one beach or two? Movements and space-use of the threatened hooded plover (*Thinornis rubricollis*) in south-eastern Australia. *Wildlife Research*, **36**, 289–298.

Weston, M. A., Ehmke, G. C. & Maguire, G. S. (2011). Nest return times in response to static versus mobile human disturbance. *Journal of Wildlife Management*, **75**, 252–255.

Weston, M. A., Dodge, F., Bunce, A., Nimmo, D. G. & Miller, K. K. (2012). Do temporary beach closures assist in the conservation of breeding shorebirds on recreational beaches? *Pacific Conservation Biology*, **18**, 47–55.

Wieser, W., Ott, J., Schiemer, F. & Gnaiger, E. (1974). An ecophysiological study of some meiofauna species inhabiting a sandy beach at Bermuda. *Marine Biology*, **26**, 235–248.

Williams, J. A., Ward, V. L. & Underhill, L. G. (2004). Waders respond quickly and positively to the banning of off-road vehicles from beaches in South Africa. *Wader Study Group Bulletin*, **104**, 79–81.

Williams, K. J. H., Weston, M. A., Henry, S. & Maguire, G. S. (2009). Birds and beaches, dogs and leashes: Dog owners' sense of obligation to leash dogs on beaches in Victoria, Australia. *Human Dimensions of Wildlife*, **14**, 89–101.

Willis, C. M. & Griggs, G. B. (2003). Reductions in fluvial sediment discharge by coastal dams in California and implications for beach sustainability. *Journal of Geology*, **111**, 167–182.

Witherington, B., Hirama, S. & Mosier, A. (2011). Sea turtle responses to barriers on their nesting beach. *Journal of Experimental Marine Biology and Ecology*, **401**, 1–6.

Wolcott, T. G. & Wolcott, D. L. (1984). Impact of off-road vehicles on macroinvertebrates of a mid-Atlantic beach. *Biological Conservation*, **29**, 217–240.

Yamazaki, K. (2012). Seasonal changes in seaweed deposition, seaweed fly abundance, and parasitism at the pupal stage along sandy beaches in central Japan. *Entomological Science*, **15**, 28–34.

4

Biodiversity, ecosystem services, and the conservation of seagrass meadows

RICHARD K.F. UNSWORTH AND LEANNE
C. CULLEN-UNSWORTH

INTRODUCTION

Seagrass meadows are soft sediment intertidal to subtidal benthic habitats that are comprised of a group of plants adapted to life in the sea (den Hartog, 1970; Hemminga & Duarte, 2000). Seagrasses comprise one of the world's most widespread habitats in shallow coastal waters; they are found on all of the world's continents except Antarctica. Seagrass habitat can be patchy, but is more commonly comprised of continuous vegetation, which can be thousands of square kilometers in size. It is these large swaths that are referred to as seagrass *beds* or *meadows* (terms that are interchangeable). Seagrass meadows occur in sheltered intertidal and shallow subtidal areas on sand or mud substratum (and occasionally in among boulders). Current documented distributions include 125 000 km² of seagrass meadows; however, recent estimates suggest that these meadows could cover up to 600 000 km² of the coastal ocean (Duarte *et al.*, 2010).

Seagrasses are marine angiosperms belonging to the order Helobiae and comprising two families – Potamogetonaceae and Hydrocharitaceae (den Hartog, 1970). Seagrass plants are rhizomatous (they have stems extending horizontally below the sediment surface) and modular, composed of repeating units (ramets) that exhibit clonal growth (Hemminga & Duarte, 2000). In contrast to other submerged marine plants (e.g. seaweeds or algae), seagrasses flower, develop fruit, and produce seeds (Ackerman, 2006). They have true roots and internal gaseous and nutrient transport systems (Kuo & den Hartog, 2006). The functional definition for seagrass plants encompasses only 72 species. Three seagrass species are considered endangered and 10 are at elevated risk of extinction; however, the gross majority of species are considered common (Short *et al.*, 2011). It is the common abundance of these species, rather than their rarity, that makes

Coastal Conservation, eds B. Maslo and J. L. Lockwood. Published by Cambridge University Press.
© Cambridge University Press 2014.

them important. Seagrasses provide habitat, meaning they have a major functional role in supporting various stages in the life cycles of other organisms. For this reason, and with their extensive root–rhizome system and well-developed canopy, seagrasses, like reef-building organisms, are termed foundation species (Hughes et al., 2009).

Several environmental parameters determine the distribution of seagrass meadows. These parameters include biophysical conditions that regulate the physiological activity and morphology of seagrasses, such as temperature, salinity, depth, substrate type, day length, light availability, water currents, wave action, epiphytes, and diseases. Biologically driven parameters include the availability of seeds and vegetative fragments. Anthropogenic influences often drive conditions that commonly inhibit available plant resources, such as excess nutrients and high sediment loading. Various combinations of these parameters will permit, encourage, or eliminate seagrass from a given location (Coles et al., 2011).

Biodiversity and ecosystem services

Seagrasses provide myriad ecosystem goods and services that are critical for human well-being (Costanza et al., 1997; Duffy et al., 2005; Duffy, 2006; Duarte et al., 2008). Among these ecosystem services is the production of large quantities of organic material that supports complex food webs and consequently food production. The physical structure of seagrass meadows provides shelter and nursery grounds for many other species, including commercially important faunal species. In this way, seagrass both directly and indirectly supports important subsistence and commercial fisheries, both within the seagrass and other connected habitats. Other important ecosystem services include the filtering of nutrients and sediments, and accumulation and recycling of organic and inorganic materials; oxygenation of the water column and sediments; and providing coastal protection from storms through the sediment stabilization. These ecosystem services are of high value to humanity, and some efforts have been made to quantify this value in monetary terms. Costanza and colleagues (1997) estimated a value of more than US $19 000 per hectare per year for combined seagrass/algae beds based on their nutrient cycling service alone. Green and Short (2003) quote sources estimating commercial fisheries value in Florida to be approximately US $47.8 million per year, and Unsworth and others (2010) estimated a minimum value for seagrass fisheries in Indonesia to be US $140 million (Table 4.1). In addition to some of the tangible socio-economic and ecological values of seagrass meadows, these systems are linked to many traditional ways of life and have multiple intangible values,

Table 4.1 *Economic values for seagrass meadows extracted from the literature. Values for carbon sink and carbon standing stock are based on extrapolation of the ecological study to European Union climate exchange variable carbon price of US $20/ton.*

Service	Study	Location	Value (US $/ha/year)
Fisheries exploitation	Watson *et al.*, 1993	Queensland, Australia	3500
Fisheries production	Author unknown	Indian River Lagoon, USA	1862
Fisheries production	McArthur & Boland, 2006	South Australia	133
Fisheries standing stock	Unsworth *et al.*, 2010	Wakatobi, Indonesia	47–109
Nutrient cycling	Costanza *et al.*, 1997	Globally	19,004
Restoration	Thorhaug, 1990	USA	1236
Restoration	Engeman *et al.*, 2008	Florida, USA	140,752
Use values	UNEP, 2004	SE Asia	215,000
Use values	Kuriandewa *et al.*, 2003	South China Sea	80,226
Carbon storage	Lavery *et al.*, 2013	Australia	386
Total Economic Value	Dirhamsyah, 2007	East Bintan, Indonesia	2287

representing an important cultural resource for coastal communities worldwide (Table 4.2).

The provision of shelter, feeding, and nursery grounds are critical ecosystem services delivered by seagrass systems globally, as evidenced by the presence of diverse and abundant fauna with high economic value in seagrass meadows. These ecosystem services, valuable in their own right, also have consequential positive feedback roles that provide additional ecosystem service support. In temperate eelgrass (*Zostera marina*) meadows, secondary production (from seagrass epiphytes) is a critical determinant of fish yield, and this productivity is highly influenced by invertebrate grazing. The maintenance of this productivity is therefore important to support seagrass fisheries. Experimental evidence has shown that algal grazer species diversity (e.g. isopods) enhances this secondary production, increasing the ecosystem service provision of seagrass meadows (Duffy *et al.*, 2003). Similar experiments have demonstrated that grazer diversity is also important for providing resistance within the seagrass system, and

Table 4.2 *Components of seagrass meadows that contribute to Total Economic Value (TEV).*

Use values				Non-use values	
Consumptive	Non-consumptive	Indirect	Other	Existence and bequest	Intrinsic
Fisheries	Tourism	Coastal protection	Option value (e.g. maintenance of system for future use)	Knowledge of system existence and continued existence for enjoyment by future generations	Biodiversity
Aquarium trade (e.g. seahorses)	Research	Biological support (e.g. fish nursery)			Species richness
	Education				Existence with no human use
Curio trade (e.g. shells)	Recreation	Global life support (e.g. oxygen production)			
Bioprospecting (e.g. sponges)	Culture				
Construction materials	Religion				
Food & animal feed					

Adapted from Cullen, 2007.

through the stability of this secondary production, to environmental stressors, such as increased temperature and freshwater inputs (Blake & Duffy, 2010). This result illustrates a link between biodiversity and the provision of ecosystem services for humans and demonstrates that biodiversity may also enhance the capacity of seagrass meadows to continue to provide ecosystem services in the face of future significant environmental change.

Current status and trends

Despite the high ecological and socioeconomic value of seagrass meadows, these habitats are being lost globally at unprecedented rates (Short & Wyllie-Echeverria, 1996; Duarte, 2002; Orth et al., 2006; Waycott et al., 2009). Since 1980, it is estimated that around 110 km² per year of seagrass have been lost, and since 1990 the rate of loss is estimated at 7% of the total global seagrass area per year (Waycott et al., 2009). Although some large-scale and local losses of seagrass habitat can be attributed to natural events and cycles, human population expansion is now the most serious cause of decline. Increasing anthropogenic inputs to the coastal oceans and destructive activities in coastal regions are primarily responsible for the worldwide deterioration and loss of seagrasses (Short & Wyllie-Echeverria, 1996). The consequences of this loss are often difficult to identify and/or measure, mostly due to limited information available to determine cause and effect. Where information does exist, data indicate the decimation of many fisheries and significant mortality of many species of conservation importance. For example, the cyclone that hit the coastline of Queensland, Australia in February 2011 decimated an extensive area of seagrass and resulted in 1200 green turtles (*Chelonia mydas*) and 180 dugongs (*Dugong dugon*) (both species dependent on seagrass for food) being washed ashore dead or in a state of very poor health (Bell & Ariel, 2011). Further evidence exists in the analysis of long-term fisheries data from Norway, which demonstrate that the loss and temporal variability (e.g. natural short-term declines) of seagrass meadows significantly and negatively affects cod (*Gadus* spp.) and pollack (*Pollachius* spp.) fish stocks due to reduced habitat, shelter, and associated resources (Fromentin et al., 1998).

To stimulate appropriate action for protection, several high-profile reviews have sought to highlight the key values of seagrass meadows (e.g. Orth et al., 2006; Duarte et al., 2008; Short et al., 2011). However, the majority of the resultant discussion has focused on the floral value of seagrass meadows and the threats to their existence, with only limited consideration of the consequences of seagrass loss to marine fauna. Therefore, in this chapter, we focus on seagrass conservation through a biodiversity and ecosystem service lens. We discuss the mechanisms though which seagrass meadows support faunal biodiversity, including fisheries, and discuss the factors driving faunal biodiversity loss in seagrass meadows and the anthropocentric (or ecosystem service) implications of this loss. We conclude the chapter by discussing future research needs to support evidence-based conservation management planning and action.

ECOSYSTEM SERVICES AND PEOPLE

Over a billion people live within 50 km of a seagrass meadow, far more than live near coral reefs or mangrove forests, yet only a small fraction of these billion people even know seagrass exists (Dennison, 2009). These seagrass meadows provide numerous ecosystem services that are critical for human well-being (Table 4.2), defined as "the benefits that humans derive, directly or indirectly, from ecological functions" (Costanza *et al.*, 1997). Seagrass meadows act as major global carbon sinks, contribute to global nitrogen cycling, and provide productive habitat supporting world fisheries (Costanza *et al.*, 1997; E. L. Jackson *et al.*, 2001; Duarte *et al.*, 2010; Unsworth & Cullen, 2010). The services that seagrass ecosystems provide have been highlighted for their significant economic value, particularly in terms of the role they play in nutrient cycling (Costanza *et al.*, 1997). Other well-evidenced ecosystem services include provision of physical shelter and nursery habitat for commercially important faunal species, sediment stabilization and coastal protection, production of organic material that supports a complex food web and fisheries productivity, biodiversity protection, water filtration (sediment trapping), and the cycling of important global atmospheric gases, particularly CO_2, as well as the production of oxygen (Christiansen *et al.*, 1981; Duarte & Cebrian, 1996; Hemminga & Duarte, 2000; Beck *et al.*, 2001). Although the mechanism is poorly understood, seagrasses are also thought to have an important role in the cycling of dimethylsulfide (DMS) (Lopez & Duarte, 2004), which, due to its action in cloud formation, may have a significant impact on the Earth's climate. In many locations, seagrass meadows are also economically important for the habitat they create for cultivating seaweed. Additionally, we suggest that the provision of rich commercial and subsistence fishing grounds may represent an as-yet unappreciated role of seagrass in food security in an era of rapid global environmental change (Anderson, 1989; Watson *et al.*, 1993; de la Torre-Castro & Rönnbäck, 2004; Unsworth & Cullen, 2010).

Although seagrass meadows cover only 0.1–0.2% of the global oceans (Hemminga & Duarte, 2000), they contribute a figure an order of magnitude greater than this to total marine primary production (Duarte & Cebrian, 1996). Further, the role of seagrass in the carbon cycle is increasingly acknowledged as a mechanism for long-term carbon capture and storage, which is recognized as a viable strategy for combating increasing levels of atmospheric CO_2 (Irving et al., 2011). Additional intangible services that seagrass meadows provide include those of a social, cultural, and spiritual nature. The lives of many within coastal communities are closely intertwined with seagrass meadows, and numerous indigenous peoples have close cultural and spiritual links to seagrass habitats, which include their use in cultural and religious ceremonies (Felger et al., 1980).

Action is urgently required to improve understanding, raise awareness, and protect the many valuable and some as-yet underappreciated ecosystem services provided by seagrass meadows. Further evidence is required to support appropriate action. However, the complexity inherent in ecosystems means that we will rarely understand their workings mechanistically; therefore, maintenance of biodiversity may serve as a useful proxy for a system state that provides multiple ecosystem services. The chances of maintaining these ecosystem services over time will be improved through the maintenance of high biodiversity (Duffy, 2009; Palumbi et al., 2009). From an alternative perspective, management to conserve biodiversity will provide ecosystem service benefits, which serves as one rationale for increased conservation efforts (Duffy, 2009).

Food security

Worldwide, marine fisheries provide a vital source of protein for millions of people, and in some countries in excess of 60% of the animal protein consumed by people is from the sea (UNEP-WCMC, 2006). The Food and Agriculture Organization of the United Nations (FAO) calculates that fish account for 16% of the global population's intake of animal protein and 6% of all protein consumed. Globally, fish provide more than 1.5 billion people with almost 20% of their average per-capita intake of animal protein, and 3 billion people with at least 15% of this protein (FAO, 2010). The implications for maintaining the security of this food source are far-reaching; however, it is well acknowledged that the majority of the world's fisheries are at risk (Pauly et al., 1998, 2002). To meet the needs of the predicted human population of 2050, an additional 75 million tons of protein from fish and aquatic invertebrates will be required, representing a 50% increase in current supply (Rice & Garcia, 2011).

The role of seagrass in supporting food security is yet to be documented, although correlations between seagrass and fisheries productivity are emerging (Warren *et al.*, 2010). Important fisheries in their own right, seagrass meadows also play a significant role in coral reef and other fisheries productivity. Unsworth and colleagues (2010) highlight the high local subsistence and direct financial value of seagrass meadows in the Indo-Pacific region, where reliance of fishers on seagrass meadows, rather than coral reefs, as a fishing ground, contradicts the emphasis of management, monitoring, and conservation efforts placed primarily on coral reef habitats. Seagrass meadows have also been shown by Unsworth and Cullen (2010) to have a hidden role in Indo-Pacific fisheries productivity, which was previously attributed to other habitats. Seagrass meadows support commercially important species as well as species with high economic value for subsistence. Few faunal species utilize seagrass meadows throughout their entire life, but their use of this habitat can have a significant cascade effect, supporting thriving adult populations with high fisheries value (Gillanders, 2006). This link has been clearly demonstrated for King George whiting (*Sillaginodes punctata*) in South Australia, for example, which uses seagrass meadows as a nursery habitat (Connolly, 1994).

In the northeast Atlantic, the role of seagrass meadows in fisheries is less clear (E. L. Jackson *et al.*, 2001), and there is inadequate knowledge of seagrass distribution, status, and long-term trends. Information is required that clearly explains any links between seagrass meadows and regionally important fisheries. Recognition of the importance of native coastal habitats is reflected in the many European policies and directives aimed at reducing and reversing seagrass loss, but the positive benefits of these actions have been minimal (Airoldi & Beck, 2007). Typically, fisheries management in places such as Europe through the EU common fisheries policy does not recognize the role that different habitats, such as seagrass, play in supporting fish stocks, and protection is exclusively seen from the perspective of biodiversity protection rather than ecosystem service provision. Further information is required to evince the current and historical and hence future potential role of seagrass meadows in European fisheries so that seagrass conservation is seen as beneficial to society.

DRIVERS OF BIODIVERSITY

Understanding the relationship between a habitat and its associated fauna provides valuable insights for improved conservation efforts, particularly for preserving the ecological functions of increasingly degraded and fragmented habitats (Bentley *et al.*, 2000, Hauser *et al.*, 2006). These habitat–fauna links are critical even at small spatial scales, where habitat variability and localized habitat destruction are significant factors in controlling faunal abundance and diversity (Bell & Westoby, 1986; Hauser *et al.*, 2006). In degraded ecosystems, a major concern for resource managers is the survivorship of diverse faunal assemblages as floral habitat becomes fragmented and/or lost. Habitat fragmentation is arguably one of the greatest contributors to the loss of biological diversity (Wilcox & Murphy, 1985). With increased degradation, fragmentation, and loss of seagrass, understanding and elucidating the links between seagrass flora and fauna will support recognition of the value of these meadows and demonstrate the urgency for conservation action. Not only is it important for conservation managers to understand how habitat variability and fragmentation impact biodiversity, but also what resources within that habitat provide the necessary support for biodiversity.

Seagrass meadows exhibit high primary and secondary productivity and as such support highly diverse and abundant fish and invertebrate communities (Gillanders, 2006; Unsworth *et al.*, 2008). However, other autotrophs present within the seagrass habitat contribute significantly to total primary productivity and consequently to resource provision for higher trophic organisms (Nakaoka, 2005). Seagrass epiphytes, for example, can contribute 20–60% of seagrass meadow primary productivity (Hemminga & Duarte, 2000). Other important primary producers in seagrass meadows include benthic macroalgae and phytoplankton (Nakaoka, 2005). While seagrass provides a large surface area for colonization and habitat for shelter, the primary productivity of this flora is commonly not the major direct source of carbon and nitrogen for higher trophic levels of the food web. Most seagrass meadow invertebrate herbivores utilize epiphytic algae, as do many herbivorous fish (e.g. siganids in the tropical seas). The mechanism by which seagrass productivity enters the food web and supports a biodiverse fauna is largely through the detrital food chain, as more seagrass biomass enters into the decomposition process than is consumed by plant herbivores (Duarte & Cebrian, 1996, Heck *et al.*, 2008).

The presence of seagrass habitat and its abundance of primary producers stimulate a faunal abundance, diversity, and biomass that is higher than adjacent non-vegetated habitats. To date, studies have typically described and quantified fish communities or invertebrate infauna. Or such studies have made comparisons between areas covered by, or lacking, seagrass demonstrating that seagrass presence increases faunal species richness, abundance, and diversity. For example, eelgrass (*Zostera muelleri*) meadows in New Zealand have been shown to have a median of 23 taxa compared to sandy areas with a median of just four taxa (Battley *et al.*, 2011). However, although this example demonstrates a general trend, there are exceptions to the rule. A study from South Australia, while recording biodiversity differences between subtidal seagrass meadows and sand flats, demonstrated no significant difference between seagrass meadows and sand flats in the intertidal area (Jenkins et al., 1997). This result may be a consequence of the temporary nature of the intertidal habitat being available only during high tide and therefore limiting habitat value, but the example illustrates how, although we understand some of the major floral diversity structuring processes in seagrass meadows, we still have much to learn about the key drivers of seagrass faunal biodiversity.

GLOBAL PATTERNS OF SEAGRASS BIODIVERSITY

Together with other marine flora and fauna, seagrasses have their center of genetic richness in the Indo-West Pacific (Fortes, 1991; Allen & Werner, 2002; Bell & Smith, 2004). Twenty-four of the world's 72 seagrass floral species across 9 of the world's 13 seagrass genera occur in the Indo-West Pacific, adapted to a wide range of environmental conditions. In stark contrast to this diversity, the North Atlantic supports two species of seagrass from a single genus. Global patterns of seagrass floral biodiversity are generally mirrored by their associated faunal communities. In the Indo-Pacific, individual seagrass meadows have been shown to support over 80 species of fish (Unsworth et al., 2007c), while those in the North Atlantic typically support only 20–30 species (Jackson et al., 2006; Joseph et al., 2006). A review of studies conducted across Indonesia suggests that Indonesian seagrass collectively supports over 300 species of fish (Tomascik et al., 1997; see Figures 4.1–4.4). Intensive monitoring of seagrass fisheries in the Wakatobi National Park in Indonesia has found > 250 species of fish inhabiting seagrass around a single island (Operation Wallacea, unpublished data).

While there are clear regional differences in floral and faunal diversity, the influence of latitude is less clear. A review by Virnstein and others (1983) demonstrates that the diversity and density of various seagrass epifaunal groups show inconsistent latitudinal patterns. Diversity of decapod and amphipod crustaceans increased significantly with decreasing latitude, but diversity of isopods and fishes is not influenced significantly by latitude. An explanation for these trends remains elusive; however, the findings are of renewed interest as researchers consider the impacts of climate change on species distributions.

Altered environmental conditions resulting from climate change are likely to be most pronounced over latitudinal gradients, with some marine

Figure 4.1 Left eye flounder (*Bothus* sp.) in a seagrass meadow (*Thalassia hemprichii*) in Indonesia. (See color plate section.)

ecosystem studies already reporting significant change. For example, meta-analyses of fish assemblages in European tidal estuaries provide evidence of a northward migration of species with changing sea surface temperatures (Nicolas *et al.*, 2011). Other examples come from seagrass meadows in the Gulf of Mexico, where fish assemblages are increasingly influenced by

Figure 4.2 Banded sea-krate (*Laticauda colubrina*) in a seagrass meadow (*Thalassia hemprichii*) in Indonesia. (See color plate section.)

Figure 4.3 Cockles in a dwarf eelgrass (*Zostera noltii*) seagrass meadow in South Wales, UK. (See color plate section.)

Figure 4.4 Stony coral (*Acropora* sp.) in a mixed *Cymodocea serrulata* seagrass meadow in Green Island, Australia. (See color plate section.)

species of tropical and subtropical origin as sea-surface temperatures rise (Fodrie *et al.*, 2010). Knowledge of these shifts and migrations is founded on the availability of historical and long-term ecological data describing seagrass fish assemblages in specific locations. In many localities, however, such detailed seagrass faunal biodiversity information is largely unavailable, and temporal trends are not described.

HABITAT DEGRADATION, PATCHINESS, AND FRAGMENTATION

Seagrass degradation and loss can be manifest in different ways, impacting differently the role of seagrass as habitat for associated fauna. Deterioration can be observed as a gradual decline in the density of the seagrass (e.g. reduced shoot density, biomass, or percentage cover) and/or as the loss of sections of a meadow, causing increased patchiness or leading to the meadow becoming discontinuous and fragmented into smaller sections. A decline in seagrass density affects its capacity to provide structurally complex habitat, while seagrass meadow fragmentation will impact the wider landscape ecology of the ecosystem creating less continuous habitats with reduced connectivity between them.

Habitat complexity

Coupled with decreased structural complexity is an altered habitat usage regime by faunal species (Bentley *et al.*, 2000; Attum *et al.*, 2006). Decreased habitat complexity may alter the potential for new fauna to settle in seagrass meadows by reducing the availability of space and niche diversity (Orth *et al.*, 1984; Unsworth *et al.*, 2007b, providing less shelter from predation and physical stress and/or reducing food availability by limiting sediment trapping (Hicks, 1985; Verweij *et al.*, 2006).

Greater complexity generally increases the density of faunal assemblages in seagrass meadows, but faunal populations will reach a maximum as complexity creates habitat that becomes too difficult to forage within and the resultant energy expenditure outweighs the benefits of such foraging. Juvenile and small fish density are therefore expected to reach a population maximum at a higher level of complexity than mature and larger fish that may have difficulty moving within densely vegetated habitat. However, a range of studies spanning several geographic regions, seagrass species, and faunal groups, have described varying relationships between structural complexity and faunal assemblages (Unsworth *et al.*, 2007b). Other variables, such as resource availability, may also contribute to the abundance and diversity of faunal species. Therefore, the relationship between habitat complexity and faunal diversity is not simple.

Understanding the influence of increased habitat patchiness and/or fragmentation is important for the management (and potential mitigation) of anthropogenic activities that result in direct mechanical damage to seagrass meadows. Destructive activities include bait digging, anchoring or mooring, propeller scarring, cockle raking (pulling a rake though surface sediments to collect cockles) and vehicle (tractor and 4×4) usage, as well as coastal developments or land-use changes that may result in large-scale removal of seagrass meadows. These activities can have considerable direct impact on seagrass habitat provision by fragmenting a continuous meadow into a series of isolated smaller areas or creating increased patchiness. For example, in Porth Dinllaen on the coast of North Wales, UK, moorings alone have resulted in a 10% decrease of seagrass cover due to the scouring action of mooring chains as they slacken and rest on the seabed after high water (Egerton, 2011). The issues at Portth Dinllaen are in addition to clearly visible wheel marks from vehicle use and widespread damage from anchors. The ecosystem service consequences of this type of loss remain poorly understood, and further work is required to document the impacts and guide management action.

Landscape ecology and fragmentation

In a management context, the impacts of habitat fragmentation can be considered using the concept of a minimal viable habitat plot (Hirst & Attrill, 2008). Application of the principles of this concept requires a landscape ecology approach. Landscape ecology is concerned with the consequences of spatial patterns on ecological processes and provides a means to estimate the ecological value of the spatial arrangements of habitats and habitat patches (Salita et al., 2003). Although spatial habitat patterns have been a major focus of terrestrial ecology for decades, the approach has only recently begun to obtain traction in the marine environment, and more recently within the field of seagrass ecology (Salita et al., 2003; Jackson et al., 2006). From a conservation and management perspective, this is a particularly important approach, as a relatively small seagrass patch may be of high conservation value if adjacent to a large meadow; however, its conservation value may be limited if the patch is isolated from other seagrass.

Although seagrass landscape ecology studies are limited in number, those that do exist have demonstrated that fragmentation of seagrass into less continuous habitat does not have the resultant simple linear relationship with faunal species and abundance that might be expected. The relationship between fauna and habitat has been shown to be a positive parabolic one for some seagrass-dependent fish species, with highest fish abundances in both continuous (95% cover) and fragmented (16% cover) seagrass landscapes (Bostrom et al., 2011). Research suggests that conditions are suboptimal for fish at 55–65% cover (Salita et al., 2003; Bostrom et al., 2011). Explanations used to rationalize this parabolic relationship between fish and habitat include the availability of food and/or predation risk. Seagrass landscape studies, although scientifically robust, are currently spatially and geographically limited and require verification over broader and deeper hierarchical landscape scales.

Studies in the UK on *Zostera marina* (Hirst & Attrill, 2008) have shown no impact of habitat size on infaunal abundance and diversity. This result suggests that even very small patches can have high faunal diversity and abundance. As Bostrom and colleagues (2011) point out, such studies are limited in number, and further research is urgently required investigating the relationships between larger motile fauna, seagrass floral species, and patch dynamics.

The edge effect

Researchers have considered how ecological roles are altered, as seagrass becomes more fragmented and more patches form. Changes in seagrass area and orientation (e.g. increased patchiness or fragmentation) can result in patches having increased meadow edge to area ratios. Like terrestrial forests, seagrass meadows when fragmented can exhibit ecologically different roles at these edges, known as the edge effect. Edge effects are the diverse physical and biotic alterations associated with the artificial boundaries of fragments and are considered dominant drivers of change in fragmented landscapes (Gates & Gysel, 1978; Saunders *et al.*, 1991; Ries *et al.*, 2004). Edge effects can have serious positive or negative impacts on species diversity and composition, community dynamics and ecosystem functioning (Saunders *et al.*, 1991).

Habitat fragmentation and the edge effect also impact faunal behavior. Optimal foraging theory predicts that species prefer to forage at locations providing the greatest benefit at lowest energetic cost (Kotler *et al.*, 2010; Smith *et al.*, 2011). Where habitat edges provide increased food availability in the absence of additional costs, such as predation or increased energy use, it can be expected that forager abundance is greatest (Smith *et al.*, 2011).

Predator avoidance

In seagrass meadows, an additional manifestation of the edge effect is that predation risk is also increased along edges (Irlandi *et al.*, 1995; Bologna & Heck, 1999; Peterson & Heck, 2001). However, predation risk with respect to landscape structure and patch dynamics shows parabolic distribution with increased risk in larger patches and connected ecosystems due to higher predator densities (Hovel & Lipcius, 2001; Laurel *et al.*, 2003). Predation is therefore proposed as an explanation for the avoidance by fauna of very patchy as well as continuous vegetation (Salita *et al.*, 2003). An example of this behavior is evident in juvenile cod (*Gadus morhua*), which forage in seagrass meadows for zooplankton and invertebrates over unvegetated habitat but reduce their risk of predation by using the structure provided by patchy seagrass vegetation rather than continuous meadow (Laurel *et al.*, 2003; Thistle *et al.*, 2010).

Implications for management

The scenarios presented above demonstrate the complexity involved in trying to predict the effects of habitat fragmentation on faunal composition and abundance. Conclusions are largely species- or area-specific, which illustrates the need for further ecological community-level investigations into the role of variable seagrass landscapes in supporting biodiversity and hence ecosystem service provision.

Habitat fragmentation results in the need for decisions to be made about the relative merits of protecting, and possibly reconnecting, small fragments of seagrass. Increasingly (and perhaps worryingly) regulatory authorities and conservation managers of terrestrial as well as marine ecosystems pose the question "what is the smallest viable patch size for supporting biodiversity?" This question brings us back to the idea of a minimum viable habitat plot, but from an alternative perspective to that of justifying the protection of even small areas of seagrass as discussed earlier in the chapter. Research aiming to answer this question may be contentious, and the interpretation of results is highly context-specific and therefore not necessarily transferable.

SEAGRASS BIODIVERSITY IN A CONNECTED SEASCAPE

Seagrass meadows are not isolated systems. Like all marine habitats, they are connected by water, which facilitates the movement of living and dead organic material (Hiddink, 2003; Sheaves, 2005; Mumby, 2006; Heck *et al.*, 2008; Unsworth *et al.*, 2009). Habitat connectivity exists at a variety of levels of biological organization and manifests itself through passive or active dispersal of organisms between habitat types. Tropical seagrass meadows, for example, are connected to coral reefs through the passive movement of floral seagrass and macroalgal flotsam (Stapel *et al.*, 1996; Wernberg *et al.*, 2006), as well as through the active movement of migratory fish. The pinfish (*Lagodon rhomboides*), found along the southeast Atlantic and Gulf coasts of the US, actively connects seagrass with adjacent habitats through its migration between subtidal seagrass, intertidal salt marsh, and mudflats for foraging (Hettler, 1989; Irlandi & Crawford, 1997). Migration benefits pinfish, as it facilitates individuals' access to food resources while allowing them to access shelter as the tide drops and exposes salt marsh at low tide. In this way, habitat connectivity can enhance the reproductive productivity or survivorship of migratory species.

Research from the Comoros and Tanzania has shown that the presence of seagrass habitat can also positively influence densities of adult fish on adjacent coral reefs (Dorenbosch *et al.*, 2005). This observation is attributed to the provision of additional nursery and feeding grounds by the seagrass, which indirectly enhances the adult reef fish population. Similar findings from the Caribbean demonstrate how mangrove connectivity enhances the biomass of coral reef fish populations in the same way (Mumby *et al.*, 2003).

Habitats can also be interconnected genetically though the passive dispersal of larvae, which can be transported over large distances (Levin, 2006; Stephens *et al.*, 2006). This genetic connectivity is beneficial as it can enhance the resilience and survivorship potential of floral and faunal populations through access to a more diverse genetic structure. Recent studies on seagrass reproduction have highlighted the key role that dispersal of gametes between connected habitats plays in the maintenance and persistence of seagrass populations (Kendrick *et al.*, 2012).

Habitat connectivity is important within the life cycles of many faunal groups, including crustaceans, mollusks, and fish, where different habitats are utilized as feeding or nursery grounds during different life-cycle stages (Kneib & Wagner, 1994; Laegdsgaard & Johnson, 2001; Hiddink, 2003; Unsworth *et al.*, 2007a). Habitat usage often depends on the specific nutritional needs of individuals at different developmental stages (de la Moriniere *et al.*, 2003); however, the regularity of migrations and the mechanisms underpinning the process remain poorly understood in coastal ecosystems (Parrish, 1989; Fortes, 1991; Sheaves, 2005).

Seagrass meadows are not only connected to adjacent marine habitats through the provision of nursery and feeding grounds, but their productivity also provides a trophic subsidy for a range of diverse and remote marine and terrestrial communities (Heck *et al.*, 2008). This subsidy is evidenced by the accumulation of seagrass detritus in the deep sea and on land (visible as seagrass wrack along the shoreline) where entire consumer communities depend upon it (Wolff, 1976). The high turnover of seagrasses (i.e. growth, degradation, consumption, and regrowth of leaves) means that they can provide critical consumer subsidy for multiple terrestrial animals, including some rodents, brant geese (*Branta bernicla*), and widgeon (*Anas* spp.)

(Heck *et al.*, 2008). Seagrass loss therefore has the capacity to impact species and communities at multiple ecological scales.

The disconnected seascape

Worldwide, a pattern of declining health and abundance of coastal habitats closely associated to seagrass meadows continues (Gardner *et al.*, 2003; Cote *et al.*, 2005; Airoldi & Beck, 2007; Waycott *et al.*, 2009). This loss persists despite strategies to safeguard these biodiverse ecosystems from a range of stressors, such as eutrophication, pollution, and overharvesting. Loss of coral reefs and mangroves in the tropics are well documented (see Chapter 2); however, in temperate regions, other highly biodiverse and productive bio-genic coastal habitats, such as oyster reefs, mussel beds, worm reefs, and salt marshes, all commonly closely associated to seagrass meadows, have also undergone large-scale loss and degradation (Airoldi & Beck, 2007; J. B. C. Jackson *et al.*, 2001; see also Chapters 5 and 7). The loss of an adjacent or associated habitat and reduced connectivity can result in cascade effects on ecosystem biodiversity and productivity. For example, loss of nursery habitat has been found in the Caribbean to result in reduced fish biomass on adjacent reefs (Mumby *et al.*, 2003). In North Carolina, motile organisms seeking refuge on alternative nearby habitat after displacement (due to habitat degradation) have been shown to cause the depletion of epibenthic crustacean (prey) populations (Lenihan *et al.*, 2001). Although there is extensive literature on how habitat degradation directly impacts within-habitat fauna, surprisingly little attention has been given to how the effects propagate through space and time beyond the immediate area and habitat affected (Newell, 1970). A better understanding of the connections and dynamic flows between habitats and ecosystems is required to support the development of appropriate coastal management and conservation strategies (Harborne *et al.*, 2006).

SEAGRASS REGIME CHANGES AND ALTERNATIVE STABLE STATES

Seagrass meadows have the capacity to regulate their own environment through mechanisms of positive feedback (Herman *et al.*, 2001; Rietkerk *et al.*, 2004). They achieve this in many ways, one of which is by enhancing sediment and organic matter trapping (Moriarty & Boon, 1989; de Boer, 2007), which potentially increases light availability. Other positive feed-backs that enhance the ability of seagrass to manipulate environmental conditions to receive the resources necessary for production in a submerged low-light environment include competition with algae for nutrients, over-shading phytoplankton, providing habitat for algal grazing zooplankton, and in some cases the production of alleopathic compounds that reduce algal growth. These feedback mechanisms are critical given that seagrasses typically have high light requirements, about 20% of incident light at the sediment surface, and are particularly sensitive to altered environmental conditions (Duarte, 1991; Dennison et al., 1993; Zimmerman et al., 1995).

Through environmental manipulation, seagrasses may stimulate their own growth and survival capacity and can therefore be classified as ecosystem engineers (Koch, 2001; Cardoso et al., 2004). This activity has further positive impacts on associated biodiversity. Conversely, seagrass degradation and loss results in a reduced capacity to engineer and can lead to negative feedbacks (i.e. reduced environmental suitability and hence diminished environmental regulation and recovery potential).

Over the last century, seagrasses have become increasingly affected by human activities, with severe declines often characterized by sudden loss of entire meadows (Orth et al., 2006; Waycott et al., 2009). Loss is usually linked to decreased light intensity, eutrophication and/or increased sedimentation, or direct mechanical disturbance. In many areas seagrass meadows fail to recover once the initial stress has subsided. Instead, the system settles into an alternative stable state of high turbidity, increased suspended sediments, and/or anoxic sediments that preclude seagrass establishment (van der Heide et al., 2007; Carr et al., 2010). This alternative stable state can be catastrophic for faunal biodiversity. If an inhospitable alternative stable state is reached it may not be possible for seagrass to recolonize and, through their action as ecosystem engineers, return the system to a more desirable state. However, under favorable baseline conditions (e.g. high light with low suspended sediments), seagrass loss due to a specific stressor may not result in a shift to an alternative stable state, and recovery may be possible after the loss-inducing stressor is removed. Different baseline conditions also influence the importance of seagrass feedback mechanisms. For example, a meta-analysis of 83 seagrass meadows across Europe demonstrates that in exposed locations, the seagrass–sediment–light feedback mechanism is of greater importance than in sheltered estuaries where other parameters, such as eutrophication, are equally as important as sediment loading in controlling light availability (van der Heide et al., 2012).

Understanding the positive feedback and alternative stable states of seagrass systems is critical for improved management of seagrass meadows and the biodiversity that they support. Seagrass habitat management also has implications for adjacent and connected habitats within the seascape that are benefited by the ecosystem services derived from seagrass meadows. Typically, a high-light environment of reduced suspended sediment benefits all photosynthetic organisms. This trend is evident in tropical marine systems where corals grow in shallow waters where, without the presence of seagrass, sediment disturbance may arguably be too great. In temperate European eelgrass meadows, the photosynthetic dinoflagellate-containing anemone, *Anemonia viridis*, may also arguably benefit from high light induced by seagrass-positive (light) feedbacks.

Seagrass meadows can also have positive feedback mechanisms that act within the sediment and which are complementary to feedbacks occurring within the water column. In conditions of reduced sedimentary organic matter and/or where sediments are largely anoxic (such as on a mudflat), seagrass meadows oxygenate the sediment and deliver a source of organic matter (Agawin & Duarte, 2002; Frederiksen & Glud, 2006), which typically stimulates enhanced biodiversity and species richness. Recent experimental studies combined with meta-analysis have revealed that this positive feedback mechanism of oxygenation and sulfide reduction is not caused by seagrass alone, but that it is assisted by the symbiosis present within gills of Lucinid bivalves with sulfide-oxidizing bacteria (van der Heide *et al.*, 2012). This faunal–bacterial–seagrass interaction is mutually beneficial and increases seagrass productivity.

THREATS TO SEAGRASS

Global threats to seagrasses are increasing, which puts the ecosystem services they provide at risk. In some areas of southeast Asia, the extent of estimated seagrass loss during the last 50 years is greater than 50% (Kirkman & Kirkman, 2002). In Europe, land reclamation, coastal development, overfishing, and pollution over the past centuries have nearly eliminated seagrass meadows, with most countries estimating losses of between 50% and 80%. Well-documented threats to seagrasses include nutrient loading, sediment runoff, physical disturbance, disease, commercial fishing practices, aquaculture, overgrazing, algal blooms, and global climate change (Orth *et al.*, 2006; Williams, 2007; Richards *et al.*, 2010; Rasheed & Unsworth, 2011). Another less well-understood threat comes from invasive species.

The impacts of invasive species on ecosystem functioning and the provision of ecosystem services is a fundamental issue in conservation ecology, but, in general, the consequences of invasive species on ecosystem processes and ecological interactions remain poorly understood (Tomas *et al.*, 2011a).

A lack of experimental data on ecological effects within seagrass systems, particularly for community structure and function, means that further research is required to improve understanding to help mitigate for the impacts of invasive species (Williams, 2007; Williams & Smith, 2007).

Seagrass meadows are home to multiple non-native species (see Chapter 8), but their cumulative effect has been virtually unstudied. Approximately 56 non-native species, mainly invertebrates and seaweeds, have been introduced to seagrass meadows (Williams, 2007), with hull-fouling and aquaculture being the most significant sources (Williams & Smith, 2007). Invasive seaweeds impact seagrass systems by changing the competitive relationships within the habitat. This impact is demonstrated by a high abundance of invasive seaweeds, their monopolization of space, and the concomitant reduction in abundance and biomass of native macrophytes. Altered faunal biodiversity has also been identified as an impact of invasive seaweeds although the mechanisms of this effect are not clear (Schaffelke & Hewitt, 2007). The most common invasive species in seagrass systems include seaweeds from the Caulerpa and Sargassum families and the Asian mussel (*Musculista senhousia*) (Williams, 2007). The macroalga *Caulerpa taxifolia*, in particular, has led to seagrass decline probably because *Caulerpa* thrives better than native seagrasses in a *Caulerpa*-modified environment (Holmer *et al.*, 2009). Evidence from eelgrass beds in Atlantic Canada and elsewhere has also documented seagrass decline due to sediment disruption and direct feeding action of the invasive green crab (*Carcinus maenas*).

Predator–prey interactions can be strongly influenced by non-native species, with invasive seaweeds in particular a growing global concern. Although there is some evidence of the positive effects of invasive algae through basal habitat and niche diversification within seagrass meadows (Thomsen, 2010; Deudero *et al.*, 2011), most studies describe negative impacts on seagrass meadows (Williams & Smith, 2007). Tomas and others (2011b) highlight the negative impacts of sea grapes (*Caulerpa racemosa*) on urchin performance in the field, which explains how this widespread invasive alga is not eradicated by the grazing pressure of native herbivores. Given the ecological and economic importance of sea urchins, negative impacts of invasive seaweeds on their performance within seagrass meadows can have a widespread cascade effect on ecosystem function and ecosystem service provision (Tomas *et al.*, 2011a). More often, herbivores prefer native to non-native seaweeds, and so for this reason they are unlikely to control the spread of invasives. Compounding the problem, anthropogenic influences, such as increased nutrients, can enhance invasive seaweed growth. Undisturbed marine communities can be at least initially resistant to most non-native seaweeds aside from the siphonous green species; however, habitat disturbance and eutrophication can facilitate and increase invasion (Williams & Smith, 2007).

The disruption caused by invasive species contributes to seagrass decline, changes in biodiversity, and reduced resilience of seagrass meadows. The presence of invasives may also compromise seagrass restoration efforts (Williams, 2007; Malyshev & Quijon, 2011). Maintaining seagrass density and meadow size can offer resistance to non-native species (Williams, 2007), and early detection, rapid response, and control measures will minimize invasive spread (Schaffelke & Hewitt, 2007).

SEAGRASS AND SHIFTING BASELINES

Available literature on seagrass meadows is largely based upon the conclusions of research across gradients of seagrass status, from locations perceived to be degraded to those of an apparent pristine or healthy status. However, seagrass meadows in the twenty-first century are largely not considered to be in pristine condition. As human populations have expanded over the last 2000 years, marine resource exploitation has typically left the world's seagrass meadows devoid of key components of their food web (Jackson, 2001). Tropical seagrass meadows have been depleted of megaherbivores, such as dugongs, manatees (*Trichechus* spp.), and green turtles (Jackson, 2001), and more generally, tropical marine ecosystems in many locations are now devoid or depleted of major predatory species (Andrews & Whitaker, 1994; Stevens et al., 2000; Jackson, 2001; Platt et al., 2007). With continued high extraction rates of marine fauna (large predatory fish, smaller herbivorous fish, and invertebrates), many populations are under threat (Fortes, 1990; Ainsworth et al., 2008; Unsworth & Cullen, 2010), with abundances often declining by an order of magnitude within a decade (Ainsworth et al., 2008; Exton, 2009). The specific impacts of these changes on the seagrass system are not clear, but there is increasing evidence that seagrass communities are defined by top-down predator control (Eklof et al., 2009). This trend of declining predator abundance may therefore result in further cascade effects, such as loss of predators leading to increased urchin abundance with associated episodes of seagrass overgrazing, the result being a loss of cover or changes in seagrass assemblage structure (Rose, 1999). Overexploitation is therefore considered a major driver of seagrass loss (Heck & Valentine, 2007; Moksnes et al., 2008; Eklof et al., 2009). Further experimental evidence from turtle exclusion studies demonstrates a reduction in the resilience potential of seagrass meadows to eutrophication driven by reduced herbivory

(Christianen *et al.*, 2011). It has also been hypothesized that in the past, high turtle density likely resulted in Caribbean seagrass (*Thalassia testudinum*) shoots growing to double the length of current mean recorded size, probably stimulated by very high rates of herbivory (Jackson, 2001).

Recognition that an intact seagrass food web enhances the resilience and ecosystem service value of a seagrass meadow has significant implications for future management and conservation of these systems. However, developing conservation strategies that work toward achieving a historic baseline is problematic due to the phenomenon of shifting baseline syndrome (e.g. Papworth *et al.*, 2009). In a seagrass context, this manifests itself as the present generation of stakeholders, including scientists, resource managers, fishers, and tourists, having a different idea of normality, or what is pristine, than those in the past. Current stakeholders do not recognize what a pristine seagrass meadow might look like and how it may function.

Consequently, current conservation efforts do not aspire to a fully functioning pristine ecosystem, but rather to a *relatively* well-functioning one. The shifting baseline concept also applies to the historical distribution of seagrass meadows and their restoration, particularly in locations where loss has been extreme, such as in Europe. This presents a problem when human perceptions of change represent all the information available to be used as a basis for conservation or management action. It is useful in this instance to take an interdisciplinary approach to evidencing the value of seagrass meadows that includes aspects of historical ecology.

PRIORITIZING SEAGRASS CONSERVATION

Seagrass meadows are connected habitats that play a critical and increasingly recognized role within global marine ecosystems. As such, concern for seagrass meadows is essential for the development of a comprehensive approach to integrated marine and coastal management. However, these important ecosystem service providers remain marginalized within conservation agendas, principally because marine conservation priorities do not recognize the full socioeconomic and ecological value of goods and services that seagrasses provide (Duarte *et al.*, 2008; Unsworth & Cullen, 2010). As mentioned earlier, the links between seagrass and food security are yet to be shown across scales, although correlations between seagrass presence and fisheries productivity are emerging (Warren *et al.*, 2010), which may support calls for renewed management initiatives that prioritize seagrass protection. Currently, ~72 countries have seagrass habitats under some kind of protection (Green & Short, 2003); however, this protection is largely a consequence of co-location within Marine Protected Areas designated for other habitats.

Globally, seagrass status is uncertain and greater efforts are required to document their status and protect these valuable systems. While conservation actions rightly look toward protecting biodiversity and focus on rare or endangered species or systems, it is often the common uncharismatic species like seagrasses that have a far greater ecosystem-scale role (Gaston & Fuller, 2008). The conservation of foundation species, such as canopy-forming plants, reef-building organisms, and seagrasses, is important because the services these species provide can be degraded long before the foundation species disappear (Hughes et al., 2009). Historical records reveal that it is mostly common species rather than rare ones that have undergone substantial and serious rapid declines, typically without first becoming threatened with imminent extinction. Loss of common species is confounded by the limited ability of humans to perceive small incremental declines until it is too late (Gaston & Fuller, 2008). This trend leads further to long-term conservation objectives and perceptions of loss becoming affected by shifting baselines (Papworth et al., 2009). While the majority of floral seagrass species are not currently at risk and are common, the habitats they create are being lost at a rate of 7% annually (Waycott et al., 2009), along with the ecosystem services they provide. This loss has further serious consequences for ecologically rare species residing in seagrass or for those that are vulnerable to extinction (Hughes et al., 2009).

Seagrass meadows are not necessarily aesthetically pleasing or immediately charismatic habitats. They can be found in muddy, turbid water conditions, which do not impress in magazines as colorful, biodiverse wonders of the world. However, these uncharismatic ecosystems do support IUCN Red List threatened species and are undoubtedly an important socioeconomic and ecological resource that requires protection (Unsworth & Cullen, 2010).

The recent recognition of seagrasses within climate mitigation strategies as carbon capture and storage systems adds to their global value, along with, we would argue, recognition that seagrasses may represent a source of food security in a rapidly changing global environment. We therefore need to adopt new, and crucial, evidence-based marine conservation strategies that place seagrass meadows securely and high up on the conservation agenda. Following the rationale that increased biodiversity supports multiple ecosystem services, managing to maximize biodiversity may represent a pathway to ensuring long-term maintenance of an acceptable balance between the conflicting demands for multiple ecosystem services from seagrass meadows (Duffy, 2009). However, conservation and management actions will be strengthened by further developing our understanding of the complex sociocultural values of these ecosystems as well as deepening our ecological understanding. Considering the potential influence of shifting baseline syndrome, it will also be beneficial to investigate historical seagrass and coupled seagrass–fishery trends. The global seagrass resource may be vastly underestimated in relation to the limited conservation management currently afforded seagrass habitats (Duarte et al., 2008; Unsworth et al., 2010).

AN AGENDA FOR FUTURE RESEARCH

Biodiversity and habitat conservation measures often give only secondary consideration to seagrass habitats. There appears to be a significant misalignment between current conservation efforts for biodiversity, ecosystem services, and seagrass meadows, and further research is required to provide clear evidence of how they are linked and to demonstrate how these linkages are modified across seascape and regional scales and by anthropogenic activities. These linkages also need to be placed in the context of conservation that can promote the future resilience of seagrass meadows. Seagrass meadows are an underappreciated resource requiring interdisciplinary attention within the international research agenda to provide evidence in support of a new marine management regime.

We need to explore patterns of biodiversity at regional and global scales and further investigate the key drivers of seagrass faunal biodiversity. We also require further evidence of the relationships between larger motile fauna, seagrass floral species, and patch dynamics as well as the mechanisms underpinning migration between habitats in coastal ecosystems. Our current knowledge of the socioeconomic impacts of invasive species remains limited, and more research evidencing the ecological and socioeconomic impacts will support the development of appropriate management action to help minimize and mitigate impacts of invasive species. Major research gaps specific to invasives include community-level ecological studies and economic assessments.

Applied interdisciplinary research on ecosystem function and socioeconomic value is called for with case studies to show the food security value of seagrass meadows. In our changing global environment, research should interact with understanding critical issues, such as water quality, ocean acidification, and climate change, and the impacts of these on seagrass productivity as well as seagrass-associated and -dependent fauna (Unsworth et al., 2012a). Of benefit will be the development of an agenda to support understanding of the factors that will lead to increased seagrass resilience and hence increased biodiversity resilience in the face of environmental change. Researchers are only just beginning to develop an understanding of the influence of biodiversity on ecosystem service provision in the marine environment (e.g. Duffy, 2006), and there is still much to understand about how habitats, such as seagrass meadows, respond to changes in functional as well as species diversity, and how these factors interact with processes, such as climate change and ocean acidification (Unsworth *et al.*, 2012a, 2012b).

Historical information and trends can be used to inform research and subsequent resource management, which is particularly important in terms of developing an agenda for habitat restoration that creates functionally important systems contributing valuable ecosystem services. Improved economic estimates and financial valuations are also required. An understanding of resource economics can support understanding of exploitation to improve the chances of achieving effective management.

With marine conservation efforts generally focused elsewhere, the consequences of seagrass decline are receiving inadequate attention. The scope of conservation efforts needs to be expanded and placed in the context of sustainable long-term exploitation of the whole marine environment. An understanding of the importance of seagrass meadows through improved and widespread research and education is required to gain support for the conservation of these dynamic, potentially highly resilient, and valuable systems.

REFERENCES

Ackerman, J. D. (2006). Seagrass reproduction of seagrasses: Pollination in the marine context. In A. W. D. Larkum, R. J. Orth & C. M. Duarte (eds.), *Seagrasses: Biology, Ecology and Their Conservation*. London: Springer, pp. 89–109.

Agawin Sr., N. & Duarte, C. M. (2002). Evidence of direct particle trapping by a tropical seagrass meadow. *Estuaries*, **25**(6), 1205–1209.

Ainsworth, C. H., Pitcher, J. & Rotinsulu, C. (2008). Evidence of fishery depletions and shifting cognitive baselines in Eastern Indonesia. *Biological Conservation*, **141**, 848–859.

Airoldi, L. & Beck, M. W. (2007). Loss, status and trends for coastal marine habitats of Europe. *Oceanography and Marine Biology*, **45**, 345–405.

Allen, G. R. & Werner, T. B. (2002). Coral reef fish assessment in the 'coral triangle' of southeastern Asia. *Environmental Biology of Fishes*, **65**, 209–214.

Anderson, E. E. (1989). Economic benefits of habitat restoration: Seagrass and the Virginia hard-shell blue crab fishery. *North American Journal of Fisheries Management*, **9**, 140–149.

Andrews, H. V. & Whitaker, R. (1994). Status of the saltwater crocodile (*Crocodylus porosus*) in North Andaman island. *Hamadryad*, **19**, 79–92.

Attum, O., Eason, P., Cobbs, G. & el Din, S. M. B. (2006). Response of a desert lizard community to habitat degradation: Do ideas about habitat specialists/generalists hold? *Biological Conservation*, **133**, 52–62.

Battley, P. F., Melville, D. S., Schuckard, R. & Ballance, P. F. (2011). *Zostera muelleri* as a structuring agent of benthic communities in a large intertidal sandflat in New Zealand. *Journal of Sea Research*, **65**, 19–27.

Beck, M. W., Heck, K. L., Able, K. W., *et al.* (2001). The identification, conservation, and management of estuarine and marine nurseries for fish and invertebrates. *Bioscience*, **51**, 633–641.

Bell, I. & Ariel, E. (2011). Dietary shift in green turtles. *Seagrass-Watch News*, Issue **44**, p. 32.

Bell, J. D. & Westoby, M. (1986). Abundance of macrofauna in dense seagrass is due to habitat preference, not predation. *Oecologia (Berlin)*, **68**, 205–209.

Bell, J. J. & Smith, D. (2004). Ecology of sponge assemblages (Porifera) in the Wakatobi region, south-east Sulawesi, Indonesia: Richness and abundance. *Journal of the Marine Biological Association of the United Kingdom*, **84**, 581–591.

Bentley, J. M., Catterall, C. P. & Smith, G. C. (2000.) Effects of fragmentation of araucarian vine forest on small mammal communities. *Conservation Biology*, **14**, 1075–1087.

Blake, R. E. & Duffy, J. E. (2010). Grazer diversity affects resistance to multiple stressors in an experimental seagrass ecosystem. *Oikos*, **119**, 1625–1635.

Bologna, P. A. X. & Heck, K. L. (1999). Macrofaunal associations with seagrass epiphytes: Relative importance of trophic and structural characteristics. *Journal of Experimental Marine Biology and Ecology*, **242**, 21–39.

Bostrom, C., Pittman, S. J., Simenstad, C. & Kneib, R. T. (2011). Seascape ecology of coastal biogenic habitats: Advances, gaps, and challenges. *Marine Ecology Progress Series*, **427**, 191–217.

Cardoso, P. G., Pardal, M. A., Lillebo, A. I., *et al.* (2004). Dynamic changes in seagrass assemblages under eutrophication and implications for recovery. *Journal of Experimental Marine Biology and Ecology*, **302**, 233–248.

Carr, J., D'odorico, P., Mcglathery, K. & Wiberg, P. (2010). Stability and bistability of seagrass ecosystems in shallow coastal lagoons: Role of feedbacks with sediment resuspension and light attenuation. *Journal of Geophysical Research-Biogeosciences*, **115**, G03011, doi:10.1029/2009JG001103.

Christianen, M. J. A., Govers, L. L., Bouma, T. J., *et al.* (2011). Marine megaherbivore grazing may increase seagrass tolerance to high nutrient loads. *Journal of Ecology*, **100**, 546–560.

Christiansen, C., Christoffersen, H., Dalsgaard, J. & Nornberg, P. (1981). Coastal and near-shore changes correlated with die-back in eel-grass (*Zostera marina*, L). *Sedimentary Geology*, **28**, 163–173.

Coles, R. G., Grech, A., Rasheed, M. A., *et al.* (2011). Seagrass ecology and threats in the tropical Indo-Pacific bioregion. In R. S. Pirog (ed.), *Seagrass: Ecology, Uses and Threats*. Hauppauge: Nova Science Publishers, pp. 225–240.

Connolly, R. (1994). The role of seagrass as preferred habitat for juvenile *Sillaginodes punctata* (cuv. & val.) (sillaginidae, pisces): Habitat selection or feeding? *Journal of Experimental Marine Biology and Ecology*, **180**, 39–47.

Costanza, R., D'arge, R., de Groot, R., *et al.* (1997). The value of the world's ecosystem services and natural capital. *Nature*, **387**, 253–260.

Cote, I. M., Gill, J. A., Gardner, T. A. & Watkinson, A. R. S. (2005). Measuring coral reef decline through meta-analyses. *Philosophical Transactions of the Royal Society of London, Series B, Biological Sciences*, **360**, 385–395.

Cullen, L. C. (2007). Marine resource dependence, resource use patterns and identification of economic performance criteria within a small island community: Kaledupa, Indonesia. PhD Thesis, University of Essex, Colchester, UK.

De Boer, W. F. (2007). Seagrass–sediment interactions, positive feedbacks and critical thresholds for occurrence: A review. *Hydrobiologia*, **591**, 5–24.

De la Moriniere, E. C., Pollux, B. J. A., Nagelkerken, I., *et al.* (2003). Ontogenetic dietary changes of coral reef fishes in the mangrove–seagrass–reef continuum: Sable isotopes and gut-content analysis. *Marine Ecology Progress Series*, **246**, 279–289.

De la Torre-Castro, M. & Rönnbäck, P. (2004). Links between humans and seagrasses – An example from tropical East Africa. *Ocean and Coastal Management*, **47**, 361–387.

Den Hartog, C. (1970). *The Seagrasses of the World*. Amsterdam: North Holland Publishing.

Dennison, W. C. (2009). Seagrasses: Biology, ecology and conservation. *Botanica Marina*, **52**, 367.

Dennison, W. C., Orth, R. J., Moore, K. A., *et al.* (1993). Assessing water quality with submersed aquatic vegetation: Habitat requirements as barometers of Chesapeake Bay health. *Bioscience*, **43**, 86–94.

Deudero, S., Box, A., Alos, J., Arroyo, N. L. & Marba, N. (2011). Functional changes due to invasive species: Food web shifts at shallow *Posidonia oceanica* seagrass beds colonized by the alien macroalga *Caulerpa racemosa*. *Estuarine, Coastal and Shelf Science*, **93**, 106–116.

Dirhamsyah. (2007). Economic valuation of the seagrass beds of East Bintan, Riau Archipelago. *Oseanologi dan Limnologi di Indonesia*, **33**, 257–270.

Dorenbosch, M., Grol, M. G. G., Christianen, M. J. A., Nagelkerken, I. & van der Velde, G. (2005). Indo-Pacific seagrass beds and mangroves contribute to fish density coral and diversity on adjacent reefs. *Marine Ecology Progress Series*, **302**, 63–76.

Duarte, C. M. (1991). Allometric scaling of seagrass form and productivity. *Marine Ecology Progres Series*, **77**, 289–300.

Duarte, C. M. (2002). The future of seagrass meadows. *Environmental Conservation*, **29**, 192–206.

Duarte, C. M. & Cebrian, J. (1996). The fate of marine autotrophic production. *Limnology and Oceanography*, **41**, 1758–1766.

Duarte, C. M., Dennison, W. C., Orth, R. J. W. & Carruthers, T. J. B. (2008). The charisma of coastal ecosystems: Addressing the imbalance. *Estuaries and Coasts*, **31**, 233–238.

Duarte, C. M., Marba, N., Gacia, E., *et al.* (2010). Seagrass community metabolism: Assessing the carbon sink capacity of seagrass meadows. *Global Biogeochemical Cycles*, **24**, GB4032, doi:10.1029/2010GB003793.

Duffy, J. E. (2006). Biodiversity and the functioning of seagrass ecosystems. *Marine Ecology Progress Series*, **311**, 233–250.

Duffy, J. E. (2009). Why biodiversity is important to the functioning of real-world ecosystems: Managing ecosystems to promote biodiversity can have important practical benefits. *Frontiers in Ecology and the Environment*, **7**, 437–444.

Duffy, J. E., Richardson, J. P. & Canuel, E. A. (2003). Grazer diversity effects on ecosystem functioning in seagrass beds. *Ecology Letters*, **6**, 881.

Duffy, J. E., Richardson, J. P. & France, K. E. (2005). Ecosystem consequences of diversity depend on food chain length in estuarine vegetation. *Ecology Letters*, **8**, 301–309.

Egerton, J. (2011). *Management of the Seagrass Bed at Porth Dinllaen. Initial Investigation Into the Use of Alternative Mooring Systems*. Report for Gwynedd Council.

Eklof, J. S., Frocklin, S., Lindvall, A., et al. (2009). How effective are MPAs? Predation control and 'spill-in effects' in seagrass–coral reef lagoons under contrasting fishery management. *Marine Ecology Progress Series*, **384**, 83–96.

Engeman, R. M., Duquesnel, J. A., Cowan, E. M., et al. (2008). Assessing boat damage to seagrass bed habitat in a Florida park from a bioeconomics perspective. *Journal of Coastal Research*, **24**, 527–532.

Exton, D. A. (2009). Nearshore fisheries of the Wakatobi. In J. Clifton & R. K. F. Unsworth (eds.), *Marine Conservation and Research in the Coral Triangle: The Wakatobi Marine National Park*. New York, NY: Nova Scientific, pp. 193–207.

FAO (Food and Agriculture Organization of the United Nations). (2010). *The State of World Fisheries and Aquaculture*. www.fao.org/docrep/013/i1820e/i1820e00.htm.

Felger, R. S., Moser, M. B. & Moser, E. W. (1980). Seagrasses in Seri Indian culture. In R. C. Phillips & C. P. Mcroy (eds.), *Handbook of Seagrass Biology, an Ecosystem Perspective*. New York, NY: Garland STPM Press, pp. 260–276.

Fodrie, F. J., Heck, Jr., K. L., Powers, S. P., Graham, W. M. & Robinson, K. L. (2010). Climate-related, decadal-scale assemblage changes of seagrass-associated fishes in the northern Gulf of Mexico. *Global Change Biology*, **16**, 48–59.

Fortes, M. D. (1990). *Seagrasses: A Resource Unknown in the ASEAN Region*. Manila, Philippines: International Center for Living Aquatic Resources Management.

Fortes, M. D. (1991). Seagrass–mangrove ecosystems management: A key to marine coastal conservation in the ASEAN region. *Marine Pollution Bulletin*, **23**, 113–116.

Frederiksen, M. S. & Glud, R. N. (2006). Oxygen dynamics in the rhizosphere of *Xostera marina*: A 2-dimensional planar optode study. *Limnology and Oceanography*, **51**, 1072–1083.

Fromentin, J. M., Stenseth, N. C., Gjosaeter, J., Johannessen, T. & Planque, B. (1998). Long-term fluctuations in cod and pollack along the Norwegian Skagerrak coast. *Marine Ecology Progress Series*, **162**, 265–278.

Gardner, T. A., Cote, I. M., Gill, J. A., Grant, A. & Watkinson, A. R. (2003). Long-term region-wide declines in Caribbean corals. *Science*, **301**, 958–960.

Gaston, K. J. & Fuller, R. A. (2008). Commonness, population depletion and conservation biology. *Trends in Ecology and Evolution*, **23**, 14–19.

Gates, J. E. & Gysel, L. W. (1978). Avian nest dispersion and fledging success in field–forest ecotones. *Ecology*, **59**, 871–883.

Gillanders, B. M. (2006). Seagrasses, fish, and fisheries. In A. W. D. Larkum, R. J. Orth & C. M. Duarte (eds.), *Seagrasses: Biology, Ecology and Their Conservation*. London: Springer, pp. 503–536.

Green, E. P. & Short, F. (2003). *World Atlas of Seagrasses*. Prepared by the UNEP World Conservation Monitoring Centre. Berkeley, CA: University of California Press.

Harborne, A., Mumby, P., Micheli, F., *et al.* (2006). The functional value of Caribbean coral reef, seagrass and mangrove habitats to ecosystem processes. *Advances in Marine Biology*, **50**, 57–189.

Hauser, A., Attrill, M. J. & Cotton, P. A. (2006). Effects of habitat complexity on the diversity and abundance of macrofauna colonising artificial kelp holdfasts. *Marine Ecology Progress Series*, **325**, 93–100.

Heck, K. L. & Valentine, J. F. (2007). The primacy of top-down effects in shallow benthic ecosystems. *Estuaries and Coasts*, **30**, 371–381.

Heck, K. L., Carruthers, T. J. B., Duarte, C. M., *et al.* (2008). Trophic transfers from seagrass meadows subsidize diverse marine and terrestrial consumers. *Ecosystems*, **11**, 1198–1210.

Hemminga, M. A. & Duarte, C. M. (2000). *Seagrass Ecology*. Cambridge: Cambridge University Press.

Herman, P. M. J., Middleburg, J. J. & Heip, C. H. R. (2001). Benthic community structure and sediment processes on an intertidal flat: Results from the ECOFLAT project. *Continental Shelf Research*, **21**, 2055–2071.

Hettler, W. F. (1989). Food habits of juveniles of spotted seatrout and gray snapper in Western Florida Bay. *Bulletin of Marine Science*, **44**, 155–162.

Hicks, G. R. F. (1985). Biomass and production estimates for an estuarine meio-benthic copepod, with an instantaneous assessment of exploitation by flatfish predators. *New Zealand Journal of Ecology*, **8**, 125–127.

Hiddink, J. G. (2003). Modelling the adaptive value of intertidal migration and nursery use in the bivalve *Macoma balthica*. *Marine Ecology Progress Series*, **252**, 173–185.

Hirst, J. A. & Attrill, M. J. (2008). Small is beautiful: An inverted view of habitat fragmentation in seagrass beds. *Estuarine, Coastal and Shelf Science*, **78**, 811–818.

Holmer, M., Marba, N., Lamote, M. & Duarte, C. M. (2009). Deterioration of sediment quality in seagrass meadows (*Posidonia oceanica*) invaded by macroalgae (*Caulerpa* sp.). *Estuaries and Coasts*, **32**, 456–466.

Hovel, K. A. & Lipcius, R. N. (2001). Habitat fragmentation in a seagrass landscape: Patch size and complexity control blue crab survival. *Ecology*, **82**, 1814–1829.

Hughes, A. R., Williams, S. L., Duarte, C. M., Heck, K. L. & Waycott, M. (2009). Associations of concern: Declining seagrasses and threatened dependent species. *Frontiers in Ecology and the Environment*, **7**, 242–246.

Irlandi, E. A. & Crawford, M. K. (1997). Habitat linkages: The effect of intertidal saltmarshes and adjacent subtidal habitats on abundance, movement, and growth of an estuarine fish. *Oecologia*, **110**, 222–230.

Irlandi, E. A., Ambrose, W. G. & Orlando, B. A. (1995). Landscape ecology and the marine environment: How spatial configuration of seagrass habitat influences growth and survival of the bay scallop. *Oikos*, **72**, 307–313.

Irving, A. D., Connell, S. D. & Russell, B. D. (2011). Restoring coastal plants to improve global carbon storage: Reaping what we sow. *PLoS ONE*, **6**, e18311.

Jackson, E. L., Rowden, A. A., Attrill, M. J., Bossey, S. J. & Jones, M. B. (2001). The imporance of seagrass beds as a habitat for fishery species. *Oceanography and Marine Biology*, **39**, 269–303.

Jackson, E. L., Attrill, M. J. & Jones, M. B. (2006). Habitat characteristics and spatial arrangement affecting the diversity of fish and decapod assemblages of seagrass (*Zostera marina*) beds around the coast of Jersey (English Channel). *Estuarine, Coastal and Shelf Science*, **68**, 421–432.

Jackson, J. B. C. (2001). What was natural in the coastal oceans? *Proceedings of the National Academy of Sciences of the United States of America*, **98**, 5411–5418.

Jackson, J. B. C., Kirby, M. X., Berger, W. H., *et al.* (2001). Historical overfishing and the recent collapse of coastal ecosystems. *Science*, **293**, 629–637.

Jenkins, G. P., May, H. M. A., Wheatley, M. J. & Holloway, M. G. (1997). Comparison of fish assemblages associated with seagrass and adjacent unvegetated habitats of Port Phillip Bay and Corner Inlet, Victoria, Australia, with emphasis on commercial species. *Estuarine, Coastal and Shelf Science*, **44**, 569–588.

Joseph, V., Locke, A. & Godin, J. G. J. (2006). Spatial distribution of fishes and decapods in eelgrass (*Zostera marina* L.) and sandy habitats of a New Brunswick estuary, eastern Canada. *Aquatic Ecology*, **40**, 111–123.

Kendrick, G. A., Waycott, M., Carruthers, T. J. B., *et al.* (2012). The central role of dispersal in the maintenance and persistence of seagrass populations. *Bioscience*, **62**, 56–65.

Kirkman, H. & Kirkman, J. A. (2002). The management of seagrasses in Southeast Asia. *Bulletin of Marine Science*, **71**, 1379–1390.

Kneib, R. T. & Wagner, S. L. (1994). Nekton use of vegetated marsh habitats at different stages of tidal inundation. *Marine Ecology Progress Series*, **106**, 227–238.

Koch, E. M. (2001). Beyond light: Physical, geological, and geochemical parameters as possible submersed aquatic vegetation habitat requirements. *Estuaries*, **24**, 1–17.

Kotler, B. P., Brown, J., Mukherjee, S., Berger-tal, O. & Bouskila, A. (2010). Moonlight avoidance in gerbils reveals a sophisticated interplay among time allocation, vigilance and state-dependent foraging. *Proceedings of the Royal Society of London, Series B, Biological Sciences*, **277**, 1469–1474.

Kuo, J. & den Hartog, C. (2006). Seagrass morphology, anatomy, and ultrastructure. In A. W. D. Larkum, R. J. Orth & C. M. Duarte (eds.), *Seagrasses: Biology, Ecology and Their Conservation*. London: Springer, pp. 51–87.

Kuriandewa, T. E., Kiswara, W., Hutomo, M. & Soemodihardjo, S. (2003). The seagrasses of Indonesia. In E. P. Green & F. T. Short (eds.), *World Atlas of Seagrasses*. Prepared by the UNEP World Conservation Monitoring Centre, Berkeley, CA: University of California Press, pp. 171–184.

Laegdsgaard, P. & Johnson, C. R. (2001). Why do fish utilise mangrove habitats? *Journal of Experimental Marine Biology and Ecology*, **257**, 229–253.

Laurel, B. J., Gregory, R. S. & Brown, J. A. (2003). Settlement and distribution of age-0 juvenile cod, *Gadus morhua* and *G-ogac*, following a large-scale habitat manipulation. *Marine Ecology Progress Series*, **262**, 241–252.

Lavery, P. S., Mateo, M. A., Serrano, O. & Rozaimi, M. (2013). Variability in the carbon storage of seagrass habitats and its implications for global estimates of blue carbon ecosystem service. *PLoS ONE*, **8**(9); e73748. doi: 10.1371/journal.pone.0073748.

Lenihan, H. S., Peterson, C. H., Byers, J. E., *et al.* (2001). Cascading of habitat degradation: Oyster reefs invaded by refugee fishes escaping stress. *Ecological Applications*, **11**, 764–782.

Levin, L. A. (2006). Recent progress in understanding larval dispersal: New directions and digressions. *Integrative and Comparative Biology*, **46**, 282–297.

Lopez, N. I. & Duarte, C. M. (2004). Dimethyl sulfoxide (DMSO) reduction potential in Mediterranean seagrass (*Posidonia oceanica*) sediments. *Journal of Sea Research*, **51**, 11–20.

Malyshev, A. & Quijon, P. A. (2011). Disruption of essential habitat by a coastal invader: New evidence of the effects of green crabs on eelgrass beds. *ICES Journal of Marine Science*, **68**, 1852–1856.

McArthur, L. C. & Boland, J. W. (2006). The economic contribution of seagrass to secondary production in South Australia. *Ecological Modelling*, **196**, 163–172.

Moksnes, P. O., Gullstrom, M., Tryman, K. & Baden, S. (2008). Trophic cascades in a temperate seagrass community. *Oikos*, **117**, 763–777.

Moriarty, D. J. W. & Boon, P. I. (1989). Interactions of seagrasses with sediment and water. In A. W. D. Larkum, A. J. Mccomb & S. A. Shepherd (eds.), *Biology of Seagrasses: A Treatise on the Biology of Seagrasses with Special Reference to the Australian Region*. New York, NY: Elsevier.

Mumby, P. (2006). Connectivity of reef fish between mangroves and coral reefs: Algorithms for the design of marine reserves at seascape scales. *Biological Conservation*, **128**, 215–222.

Mumby, P. J., Edwards, A. J., Arias-Gonzalez, J. E., *et al.* (2003). Mangroves enhance the biomass of coral reef communities in the Caribbean. *Nature*, **427**, 533–536.

Nakaoka, M. (2005). Plant–animal interactions in seagrass beds: Ongoing and future challenges for understanding population and community dynamics. *Population Ecology*, **47**, 167–177.

Newell, R. G. (1970). *The Biology of Intertidal Animals*. London: Elek.

Nicolas, D., Chaalali, A., Drouineau, H., *et al.* (2011). Impact of global warming on European tidal estuaries: Some evidence of northward migration of estuarine fish species. *Regional Environmental Change*, **11**, 639–649.

Orth, R. J., Heck, K. L. & van Montfrans, J. (1984). Faunal communities in seagrass beds: A review of the influence of plant structure and prey characteristics on predator-prey relationships. *Estuaries*, **7**, 339–350.

Orth, R. J., Carruthers, T. J. B., Dennison, W. C., *et al.* (2006). A global crisis for seagrass ecosystems. *Bioscience*, **56**, 987–996.

Palumbi, S. R., Sandifer, P. A., Allan, J. D., *et al.* (2009). Managing for ocean biodiversity: Creating a national biodiversity conservation agenda to sustain marine ecosystem services. *Frontiers in Ecology and the Environment*, **7**, 204–211.

Papworth, S. K., Rist, J., Coad, L. & Milner-Gulland, E. J. (2009). Evidence for shifting baseline syndrome in conservation. *Conservation Letters*, **2**, 93–100.

Parrish, J. D. (1989). Fish communities of interacting shallow-water habitats in tropical oceanic regions. *Marine Ecology Progress Series*, **58**, 143–160.

Pauly, D., Christensen, V., Dalsgaard, J., Froese, R. & Torres, F. (1998). Fishing down marine food webs. *Science*, **279**, 860–863.

Pauly, D., Christensen, V., Guenette, S., *et al.* (2002). Towards sustainability in world fisheries. *Nature*, **418**, 689–695.

Peterson, B. J. & Heck, K. L. J. (2001). Positive interactions between suspension-feeding bivalves and seagrass – A facultative mutualism. *Marine Ecology Progress Series*, **213**, 143–155.

Platt, S. G., Tasirin, J. S., Hunowu, I., Siwu, S. & Rainwater, T. R. (2007). Recent distribution records of estuarine crocodiles (*Crocodylus porosus*) in northern Sulawesi, Indonesia. *Herpetological Bulletin*, **100**, 13–17.

Rasheed, M. & Unsworth, R. K. F. (2011). Long-term climate-associated dynamics of a tropical seagrass meadow: Implications for the future. *Marine Ecology Progress Series*, **422**, 93–103.

Rice, J. C. & Garcia, S. M. (2011). Fisheries, food security, climate change and biodiversity: Characteristics of the sector and perspectives on emerging issues. *ICES Journal of Marine Science*, **68**, 1343–1353.

Richards, C. L., Wares, J. P. & Mackie, J. A. (2010). Evaluating adaptive processes for conservation and management of estuarine and coastal resources. *Estuaries and Coasts*, **33**, 805–810.

Ries, L., Fletcher, R. J., Battin, J. & Sisk, T. D. (2004). Ecological responses to habitat edges: Mechanisms, models, and variability explained. *Annual Review of Ecology, Evolution and Systematics*, **35**, 491–522.

Rietkerk, M., Dekker, S. C., de Ruiter, P. C. & van de Koppel, J. (2004). Self-organized patchiness and catastrophic shifts in ecosystems. *Science*, **305**, 1926–1929.

Rose, C. D. (1999). Overgrazing of a large seagrass bed by the sea urchin *Lytechinus variegatus* in Outer Florida Bay. *Marine Ecology Progress Series*, **190**, 211–222.

Salita, J. T., Ekau, W. & Saint-Paul, U. (2003). Field evidence on the influence of seagrass landscapes on fish abundance in Bolinao, northern Philippines. *Marine Ecology Progress Series*, **247**, 183–195.

Saunders, D. A., Hobbs, R. J. & Margules, C. R. (1991). Biological consequences of ecosystem fragmentation – A review. *Conservation Biology*, **5**, 18–32.

Schaffelke, B. & Hewitt, C. L. (2007). Impacts of introduced seaweeds. *Botanica Marina*, **50**, 397–417.

Sheaves, M. (2005). Nature and consequences of biological connectivity in mangrove systems. *Marine Ecology Progress Series*, **302**, 293–305.

Short, F. T. & Wyllie-Echeverria, S. (1996). Natural and human-induced disturbance of seagrasses. *Environmental Conservation*, **23**, 17–27.

Short, F. T., Polidoro, B., Livingstone, S. R., et al. (2011). Extinction risk assessment of the world's seagrass species. *Biological Conservation*, **144**, 1961–1971.

Smith, T. M., Hindell, J. S., Jenkins, G. P., Connolly, R. M. & Keough, M. J. (2011). Fine-scale spatial and temporal variations in diets of the pipefish *Stigmatopora nigra* within seagrass patches. *Journal of Fish Biology*, **78**, 1824–1832.

Stapel, J., Nijboer, R. & Philipsen, B. (1996). Initial estimates of the export of leaf litter from a seagrass bed in the Spermonde Archipelago, South Sulawesi, Indonesia. In J. Kuo, R. C. Phillips, D. I. Walker & H. Kirkman (eds.), *Seagrass Biology: Proceedings of an International Workshop, Rottnest Island, Western Australia, 25–29 January 1996*. Faculty of Sciences, Crawley: The University of Western Australia.

Stephens, S. A., Broekhuizen, N., Macdiarmid, A. B., et al. (2006). Modelling transport of larval New Zealand abalone (*Haliotis iris*) along an open coast. *Marine and Freshwater Research*, **57**, 519–532.

Stevens, J. D., Bonfil, R., Dulvy, N. K. & Walker, P. (2000). The effects of fishing on sharks, rays and chimaeras (chondrichthyans), and the implications for marine ecosystems. *ICES Journal of Marine Science*, **57**, 476–494.

Thistle, M. E., Schneider, D. C., Gregory, R. S. & Wells, N. J. (2010). Fractal measures of habitat structure: Maximum densities of juvenile cod occur at intermediate eelgrass complexity. *Marine Ecology Progress Series*, **405**, 39–56.

Thomsen, M. S. (2010). Experimental evidence for positive effects of invasive seaweed on native invertebrates via habitat-formation in a seagrass bed. *Aquatic Invasions*, **5**, 341–346.

Thorhaug, A. (1990). Restoration of mangroves and seagrasses — Economic benefits for fisheries and mariculture. In J. J. Berger (ed.), *Environmental Restoration: Science and Strategies for Restoring the Earth*. Washington, DC: Island Press, pp. 265–279.

Tomas, F., Box, A. & Terrados, J. (2011a). Effects of invasive seaweeds on feeding preference and performance of a keystone Mediterranean herbivore. *Biological Invasions*, **13**, 1559–1570.

Tomas, F., Cebrian, E. & Ballesteros, E. (2011b). Differential herbivory of invasive algae by native fish in the Mediterranean Sea. *Estuarine, Coastal and Shelf Science*, **92**, 27–34.

Tomascik, T., Mah, J. A., Nontji, A. & Moosa, K. M. (1997). *The Ecology of the Indonesian Seas (Part II)*. Oxford: Oxford University Press, Periplus Editions (HK).

UNEP. (2004). *Seagrass in the South China Sea*. UNEP/GEF/SCS Technical Publication No. 3.

UNEP-WCMC. (2006). *In the Front Line: Shoreline Protection and Other Ecosystem Services from Mangroves and Coral Reefs*. Cambridge: UNEP-WCMC.

Unsworth, R. K. F. & Cullen, L. C. (2010). Recognising the necessity for Indo-Pacific seagrass conservation. *Conservation Letters*, **3**, 63–73.

Unsworth, R. K. F., Bell, J. J. & Smith, D. J. (2007a). Tidal fish connectivity of reef and seagrass habitats in the Indo-Pacific. *Journal of the Marine Biological Association of the United Kingdom*, **87**, 1287–1296.

Unsworth, R. K. F., de Grave, S., Jompa, J., Smith, D. J. & Bell, J. J. (2007b). Faunal relationships with seagrass habitat structure: A case study using shrimp from the Indo-Pacific. *Marine and Freshwater Research*, **58**, 1008–1018.

Unsworth, R. K. F., Wylie, E., Smith, D. J. & Bell, J. J. (2007c). Diel trophic structuring of seagrass bed fish assemblages in the Wakatobi Marine National Park, Indonesia. *Estuarine, Coastal and Shelf Science*, **72**, 81–88.

Unsworth, R. K. F., Salinas de Leon, P., Garrard, S., *et al.* (2008). High connectivity of Indo-Pacific seagrass fish assemblages with mangrove and coral reef habitats. *Marine Ecology Progress Series*, **353**, 213–224.

Unsworth, R. K. F., Garrard, S. L., de Leon, P. S., *et al.* (2009). Structuring of Indo-Pacific fish assemblages along the mangrove–seagrass continuum. *Aquatic Biology*, **5**, 85–95.

Unsworth, R. K. F., Cullen, L. C., Pretty, J. N., Smith, D. J. & Bell, J. J. (2010). Economic and subsistence values of the standing stocks of seagrass fisheries: Potential benefits of no-fishing marine protected area management. *Ocean and Coastal Management*, **53**, 218–224.

Unsworth, R. K. F., Collier, C. J., Henderson, G. M. & Mckenzie, L. J. (2012a). Tropical seagrass meadows modify seawater carbon chemistry: Implications for coral reefs impacted by ocean acidification. *Environmental Research Letters*, **7**, 024026.

Unsworth, R. K. F., Rasheed, M. A., Chartbrand, K. M. & Roelofs, A. J. (2012b). Solar radiation and tidal exposure as environmental drivers of *Enhalus acoroides* dominated seagrass meadows. *PLoS ONE*, **7**(3), e34133.

Van der Heide, T., van Nes, E. H., Geerling, G. W., *et al.* (2007). Positive feedbacks in seagrass ecosystems: Implications for success in conservation and restoration. *Ecosystems*, **10**, 1311–1322.

Van der Heide, T., Govers, L. L., de Fouw, J., et al. (2012). A three-stage symbiosis forms the foundation of seagrass ecosystems. *Science*, **336**, 1432–1434.

Verweij, M. C., Nagelkerken, I., de Graaff, D., *et al.* (2006). Structure, food and shade attract juvenile coral reef fish to mangrove and seagrass habitats: A field experiment. *Marine Ecology Progress Series*, **306**, 257–268.

Virnstein, R. W., Nelson, W. G. & Howard, R. K. (1983). Latitudinal gradients in seagrass epifauna, especially amphipods. *Estuaries*, **6**, 254.

Warren, M. A., Gregory, R. S., Laurel, B. J. & Snelgrove, P. V. R. (2010). Increasing density of juvenile Atlantic (*Gadus morhua*) and Greenland cod (*G. ogac*) in association with spatial expansion and recovery of eelgrass (*Zostera marina*) in a coastal nursery habitat. *Journal of Experimental Marine Biology and Ecology*, **394**, 154–160.

Watson, R. A., Coles, R. G. & Lee Long, W. J. (1993). Simulation estimates of annual yield and landed value for commercial penaeid prawns from a tropical seagrass habitat, northern Queensland, Australia. *Marine and Freshwater Research*, **44**, 211–220.

Waycott, M., Duarte, C. M., Carruthers, T. J. B., *et al.* (2009). Accelerating loss of seagrasses across the globe threatens coastal ecosystems. *Proceedings of the National Academy of Sciences of the United States of America*, **106**, 12377–12381.

Wernberg, T., Vanderklift, M. A., How, J. & Lavery, P. S. (2006). Export of detached macroalgae from reefs to adjacent seagrass beds. *Oecologia*, **147**, 692–701.

Wilcox, B. A. & Murphy, D. D. (1985). Conservation strategy: The effects of fragmentation on extinction. *American Naturalist*, **125**, 879–887.

Williams, S. L. (2007). Introduced species in seagrass ecosystems: Status and concerns. *Journal of Experimental Marine Biology and Ecology*, **350**, 89–110.

Williams, S. L. & Smith, J. E. (2007). A global review of the distribution, taxonomy, and impacts of introduced seaweeds. *Annual Review of Ecology, Evolution and Systematics*, **38**, 327–359.

Wolff, T. (1976). Utilization of seagrass in the deep sea. *Aquatic Botany*, **2**, 161–174.

Zimmerman, R. C., Reguzzoni, J. L. & Alberte, R. S. (1995). Eelgrass (*Zostera marina*) transplants in San Francisco Bay: Role of light availability on metabolism, growth and survival. *Aquatic Botany*, **51**, 67–86.

5

Cascading effects of global oyster reef loss on the health of estuaries

BROOKE MASLO

ESTUARINE HEALTH AND BIODIVERSITY

Estuaries are transition ecotones where freshwater from the land drains into the sea. Classically defined as semi-enclosed coastal bodies of water with a connection to the open sea and within which seawater is measurably diluted with freshwater derived from land drainage (Pritchard, 1967), estuaries are characterized by a continuous exchange of tidal flows that create a marked salinity gradient from the limnetic zone (where the river enters the estuary) to the mouth of the estuary (Venice System, 1959). Estuarine habitat types include shallow open water, mudflats, fresh- and saltwater marshes, oyster reefs, seagrass beds, mangrove forests, and river deltas (Davis & Fitzgerald, 2004). Complex patterns of sedimentation, water circulation, geomorphology, and energetics make estuaries some of the most productive ecosystems in the world (Kennish, 2002).

Due to their tremendous habitat diversity, estuaries support a broad array of both resident and transient organisms, with taxonomic groups ranging from benthic meiofauna and macrophytes to wading birds and large cetaceans. This biodiversity, in turn, promotes proper estuarine functioning and the provisioning of ecosystem goods and services (Barbier *et al.*, 2011). Healthy estuaries support the persistence of commercial fisheries, provide nursery habitats for many commercially and ecologically important species, and maintain water quality through filtration and detoxification mechanisms (Granek *et al.*, 2010). Therefore, they are of high economic and ecological importance. However, the continued viability and health of estuarine systems rely heavily on multiple complex interactions between various trophic levels and abiotic factors, held in a delicate balance that maintains the integrity of the system.

Coastal Conservation, eds B. Maslo and J. L. Lockwood. Published by Cambridge University Press.
© Cambridge University Press 2014.

Humans place tremendous stress on estuarine systems, through direct exploitation of resources and indirect degradation effects. Contemporary estuarine systems suffer from fisheries overexploitation, habitat modification, point and non-point source pollution, nutrient enrichment, and freshwater diversions (Kennish, 2002). While intact estuarine systems are resilient to moderate disturbances, the magnitude and intensity of anthropogenic perturbations over the last 300 years has resulted in significant shifts in biotic communities (Lotze et al., 2006). Over 50% of mangroves and salt marshes, 30% of coral reefs, and 29% of seagrasses have been lost or degraded by human impacts (Waycott et al., 2009; Deegan et al., 2012; see also Chapters 2, 4, and 7). In addition, over 90% of formerly economically, structurally, or functionally important estuarine species have been severely depleted (Lotze et al., 2006). This loss of biodiversity and ecosystem function has resulted in increased susceptibility to biological invasions, further declines in water quality, and reduced resilience to anthropogenic and natural disturbance (Lotze et al., 2006; Barbier et al., 2011). Exploitation, eutrophication, sedimentation, and other stressors continue to heavily impact estuarine systems, presenting significant challenges to management and restoration efforts. While species recovery has occurred in some situations, the current overwhelming cumulative effects of multiple drivers are preventing recovery of most species (Worm et al., 2006). Comprehensive restructured management efforts may be necessary to redirect many species to a promising trajectory of recovery.

The historic decline of oyster reefs provides a consummate illustration of the cascading effects of biodiversity loss in estuarine systems. Approximately 85% of the world's oyster reefs have been lost, with many estuaries experiencing complete functional extinction (Beck et al., 2011). In this chapter, I discuss the historic causes and continued drivers of global oyster reef loss, the influence of oysters on estuarine processes, and the additive effects of multiple stressors in preventing oyster recovery.

ECOLOGY AND REPRODUCTIVE BIOLOGY OF OYSTERS

Oysters are bivalve mollusks in the family Ostreidae, and include species in the *Crassostrea*, *Ostrea*, *Saccostrea*, and *Ostreola* genera. As eurytopic ectotherms, oysters inhabit dynamic estuarine systems across both temperate and subtropical regions and can thrive in a wide range of salinities and temperatures. Oysters are true filter-feeders, consuming phytoplankton, detritus, and microalgae (Newell & Langdon, 1996). During feeding, water is drawn across the gills by specialized cilia. Particulates within the water stream are encased in mucus inside the oyster and transported toward the labial palps, where they are sorted before reaching the mouth. Particulates not accepted as food are cast as pseudofeces just outside the shell. Digested food particles are then ejected from the shell cavity as feces (EOBRT, 2007).

Oysters are protandrous hermaphrodites, maturing as males and then transitioning into females at an older age (Guo et al., 1998). Size and body condition appear to influence the sex of individual oysters; females are generally larger but may transition back to males annually in response to environmental, nutritional, and physical stresses (Thompson et al., 1996). Gametogenesis occurs with a rise in water temperature, and spawning is triggered by a combination of environmental stimuli, including water temperature, salinity, food availability, and physiochemical factors (Galtsoff, 1964; Hayes & Menzel, 1981). In most temperate regions, spawning is seasonal; however, spawning can occur continuously throughout the year where appropriate conditions are sustained (Hofmann et al., 1992). Fertilization occurs both internally and externally, depending on the species. Males and females in the genus Crassostrea, for example, release gametes into the water column, while females in the genus Ostrea draw sperm into the shell cavity for fertilization and partial larval development (NRC, 2004).

Following fertilization, the embryo transitions through several free-swimming, planktotrophic larval (veliger) stages over a period of several weeks, undergoing a series of morphological changes. Larval dispersal through the water column occurs via both passive and active transport and is influenced by a series of environmental factors, including water circulation, salinity, and chemical cues (Tamburri et al., 1992; Dekshenieks et al., 1996; Newell et al., 2005b). During the final stage (pediveliger), larvae possess a well-developed foot that enables them to travel along the bottom of the water column in search of a suitable attachment substrate.

Settlement occurs when the pediveliger cements itself to the substrate and undergoes permanent metamorphosis, becoming oyster spat. Oyster settlement is largely influenced by several reef patch characteristics. Suitable substrate is defined as a sediment-free, three-dimensional structure with significant vertical relief (Brumbaugh & Coen, 2009). Oyster larvae have been shown to settle on several hard substrates, including concrete, marl, limestone, and other bivalve shell (Soniat et al., 1991; Soniat & Burton, 2005; ASMFC, 2007; Nestlerode et al., 2007); however, evidence demonstrates that oyster shell itself is the ideal substrate for larval settlement (e.g. Bartol & Mann, 1999; Coen & Luckenbach, 2000). Natural oyster reefs consist of live, dead, and disarticulated oyster shell cemented together to form a complex, vertical structure. The interstitial spaces between the shells provide oyster spat with protection from predation, dessication, and ice scour. In addition, both live oysters and oyster shell may release chemicals that attract larvae and trigger metamorphosis (Zimmer-Faust & Tamburri, 1994). Reefs with significant vertical relief also receive greater spat recruitment due to reduced hypoxia and sedimentation higher in the water column (Powers et al., 2009).

Water circulation patterns around a reef also affect larval settlement success. As larvae are carried along with the current, they must actively descend upon a reef before being swept past it (Fuchs et al., 2013). Larger reef patches provide more settlement area, while rough substrates promote greater bottom drag and turbulence relative to soft sediments (Whitman & Reidenbach, 2012). These forces may interact to promote larval settlement (Fuchs & Reidenbach, unpublished data, 2013).

Although oysters have a broad range of environmental tolerances, sustained conditions at either extreme can affect optimal growth and vitality (EOBRT, 2007). For example, growth rate increases in warmer water temperatures, with oysters capable of growth year-round in many tropical locations. Eastern oysters (Crassostrea virginica) reach harvest size (76–90 mm) in the Gulf of Mexico within 24 months of settling (Berrigan et al., 1991), but harvest size in the colder Long Island Sound, New York, typically is reached in 4–5 years (Shumway, 1996). Warmer water temperatures also contribute to earlier gonadal development and spawning, and increased larval development and settling success. However, extremely high water temperatures can result in lowered ciliary action and filtration rate, inhibiting feeding and growth. These effects can be exacerbated by low salinities, which also limit pseudofeces production and raise mortality rates. Low salinities can be beneficial to some oysters by suppressing disease and lowering predation rates (Carnegie & Burreson, 2011). Optimal salinities vary substantially between species; eastern oysters prefer 14–28 ppt (EOBRT, 2007), while Pacific oysters (Crassostrea gigas) and mangrove oysters (C. rhizophorae) thrive in 32–36 ppt and 44 ppt, respectively (Korringa, 1952).

Other important factors influencing oyster growth are turbidity and sedimentation. Because oyster reefs are predominantly located in soft-bottomed habitats subject to dynamic environmental conditions, they are adapted to tolerate moderate sediment levels. However, oysters can easily be overwhelmed by significant sediment loading. Excessive sedimentation can bury up to 90% of the surface area of low-lying reefs within 16 months (Lenihan, 1999). Siltation also causes extended periods of hypoxia/anoxia across much of a low-lying reef or at the base of taller reefs, interfering with proper pumping and filtration rates and often resulting in mortality (Lenihan & Peterson, 1998; EOBRT, 2007). In addition, turbid waters reduce light levels within the water column, which may disrupt larval settlement behavior. Oyster larvae exhibit phototaxis, with light prompting individuals to seek and settle on the undersurfaces or within the interstitial spaces of intact reefs to avoid predation. In lowered light levels, larvae are less active and will instead settle on the exposed upper surfaces of the substrate. Finally, high levels of siltation lower the pH of estuarine water, spurring negative effects on both embryonic development and larval growth (Calabrese & Davis, 1966).

These evolved adaptations and life-history traits have allowed oysters to persist in a dynamic system for centuries. By engineering their own eco-system in an otherwise barren benthic landscape, oysters are able to acquire adequate nutrients, avoid predation, and reproduce successfully. By tempering environmental conditions to maintain the habitat in which they live, oysters have a pronounced positive impact on the estuarine ecosystem.

IMPACTS OF OYSTER REEFS ON ESTUARINE BIODIVERSITY

Oyster reefs are one of the most critical habitats for the maintenance of biodiversity in estuarine systems (Table 5.1); indeed, the loss of oyster reefs is strongly associated with declines in biodiversity across coastal habitats (Lotze et al., 2006; Airoldi et al., 2008). The epitome of an ecosystem engineer, oysters create biogenic habitat on an otherwise barren, soft-bottomed estuarine floor, and in doing so have tremendous influence on estuarine communities and food webs. The conglomeration of both live and dead oyster shell cemented together creates a complex, three-dimensional structure suitable as habitat for myriad resident and transient species (Coen et al., 1999; Kennedy & Sanford, 1999). Interstitial spaces within the reef structure serve as refugia from predators and environmental stressors (Lenihan & Peterson, 1998; Dumbauld et al., 2000). Unexploited, disease-free reefs can extend several hectares across the estuarine floor and reach up to 4 m in height (Lenihan & Peterson, 1998), creating bountiful aggregations of prey species (Breitburg, 1999). In addition, oysters serve as nursery habitat for several commercially important estuarine species (Beck et al., 2001; Lenihan et al., 2001; Heck et al., 2003). The abundance and diversity of the faunal community supported by oyster reefs rivals that of other structured estuarine habitats, particularly submerged aquatic vegetation (SAV; Glancy et al., 2003; Grabowski et al., 2005; Hosack et al., 2006; Shervette & Gelwick, 2008).

Table 5.1 *Ecosystem goods and services provided by oysters and oyster reefs.*

Broad category	Specific service provided	Key references
Habitat	Essential fish habitat (EFH)	Coen et al., 1999; Harding & Mann, 2001a, 2010; Lenihan et al., 2001; Tallman & Forrester, 2007; Marenghi & Ozbay, 2010
	Ecologically important species	Breitburg et al., 1995; Breitburg, 1999; Eggleston, 1999; Dumbauld et al., 2000; Meyer & Townsend, 2000; Harding & Mann, 2001b; Cranfield et al., 2004; Grabowski et al., 2005; Luckenbach et al., 2005; Tolley & Volety, 2005; Rodney & Paynter, 2006; Quan et al., 2009, 2012; Summerhayes et al., 2009; Marenghi & Ozbay, 2010; Markert et al., 2010
	Amelioration of adjacent estuarine habitats	Everett et al., 1995; Meyer et al., 1997; Henderson & O'Neill, 2003; Newell & Koch, 2004; Wall et al., 2008
Fishery commodity	Oyster production	Lenihan et al., 1995; Lenihan & Peterson, 1998; Bartol & Mann, 1999; Coen et al., 1999; Kennedy & Sanford, 1999; Lenihan, 1999; Coen & Luckenbach, 2000; Mann & Powell, 2007; Schulte et al., 2009
	Augmented fish production	Coen et al., 1999, Breitburg et al., 2000; Peterson et al., 2003
Water quality	Filtration (removal of phytoplankton and sediment, turbidity reduction)	Newell et al., 2002; Cressman et al., 2003; Newell, 2004; Grizzle et al., 2006, 2008; Shervette & Gelwick, 2008; Zu Ermgassen et al., 2013
	Benthic–pelagic coupling/nutrient cycling	Dame et al., 1984, 1985, 1989
	Eutrophication control/denitrification	Nelson et al., 2004; Newell, 1988, 2004; Newell et al., 2002, 2005; Cerco & Noel, 2007; Piehler & Smyth, 2011
Coastal defense	Wave attenuation/erosion reduction	Meyer et al., 1997; Piazza et al., 2005
Species interactions	Trophic dynamics	Jackson et al., 2001; Baird et al., 2004; Grabowski & Powers, 2004
Carbon sequestration	Greenhouse gas reduction	Peterson & Lipcius, 2003
Landscape diversification	Synergies among habitats	Micheli & Peterson, 1999; Peterson et al., 2003; Grabowski et al., 2005
Recreational value	Sport fishing	Lipton, 2004

Oyster reefs are essential for the persistence of oysters themselves in estuarine environments, forming the foundation for all other faunal interactions. As discussed above, oyster shell reefs are the ideal substrate for larval recruitment because they induce settlement through chemical cues and serve as refugia from predators (Tamburri *et al.*, 1992; Bartol & Mann, 1999). Reefs also mitigate the effects of environmental stress on oysters by elevating them above sediment accumulations and the hypoxic/anoxic zone (Lenihan & Peterson, 1998). The success of a restored eastern oyster metapopulation in the Great Wicomico River (Chesapeake Bay) was largely attributed to the high vertical relief of the reef structure (Schulte *et al.*, 2009). Increases in oyster densities on each reef, in turn, amplified juvenile recruitment, with both phenomena contributing to long-term sustainability. Reefs also accelerate water flows, thereby boosting the delivery of suspended food particles to oysters and improving their growth and survival (Lenihan *et al.*, 1995; Lenihan, 1999). As a fishery commodity, oyster production (as measured in biomass harvested) is a valuable resource (e.g. Kennedy & Sanford, 1999; Lenihan & Peterson, 2004). Unexploited reefs in eastern oyster sanctuaries in North Carolina and Virginia are valued at approximately $51 217 per hectare in 2011 US dollars (Grabowski *et al.*, 2012). However, over a century of overharvesting and the resultant destruction of reef habitats has reduced the harvest value of degraded reefs to US $2640 per hectare, based on 1991 oyster yield data (Rothschild *et al.*, 1994; Grabowski & Peterson, 2007).

Richness and diversity of the macrofaunal community increase in the presence of oyster reefs as well (Coen *et al.*, 1999; Cranfield *et al.*, 2004; Shervette & Gelwick, 2008). A study in the Hawkesbury River, Australia, documented a total of 39 epifaunal taxa from 8 major taxonomic groups on Sydney rock oyster (*Saccostrea glomerata*) reefs, including several polychaetes, nine bivalve species, six crustacean orders, three gastropod species, three chiton species, and one species each of arachnid, ascidian, and fish (Summerhayes *et al.*, 2009). Quan and colleagues (2009) experienced similar results in the Yangtze River Estuary, China, documenting a diverse epibenthic macrofaunal community of 28 species (11 mollusks, 4 annelids, and 2 fishes) on a constructed jinjiang oyster (*Crassostrea rivularis*) reef. In addition, this reef supported 50 nekton species, including 31 fishes, 9 shrimps, and 10 crabs. Well-represented faunal groups included anchovies, puffers, gobies, and mullets. As a non-native species, oysters can have positive impacts on native communities in some cases as well. Invasive Pacific oyster reefs in the Wadden Sea of Lower Saxony, Germany, demonstrate higher species richness, abundance, biomass, and diversity than native blue mussel (*Mytilus edulis*) beds (Markert *et al.*, 2010). Other documented fauna supported by oyster reefs include sponges, bryozoans, hydroids, tunicates, corals, anemones, amphipods, isopods, and decapods (Coen *et al.*, 1999; Meyer & Townsend, 2000; Cranfield *et al.*, 2004).

Oyster reefs are particularly important to commercial fisheries because they support at least one life stage of many economically valuable species (Coen *et al.*, 1999; Peterson *et al.*, 2003; Grabowski *et al.*, 2005). Coen and colleagues (1999) identified 79 resident, facultative, and transient species of finfish utilizing reefs in Maryland, Virginia, North Carolina, South Carolina, and Texas, many of which are of commercial or recreational importance. Notable species included black sea bass (*Centropristis striata*), American eel (*Anguilla rostrata*), and summer flounder (*Paralichthys dentatus*). Striped bass (*Morone saxatilis*) individuals are larger and more abundant on oyster reefs than soft bottoms in the Chesapeake Bay (Harding & Mann, 2003), and total catch per unit effort (CPUE) of blue crabs (*Callinectes sapidus*) in the Chesapeake Bay is significantly greater for natural oyster bars than either sand bars or restored oyster habitat (Harding & Mann, 2010).

Oyster aquaculture systems can also serve as suitable habitat for commercial fishes. Nine of the 57 taxa caught in eastern oyster floating aquaculture cages were part of a recreational or commercial fishery in Delaware, including mummichog (*Fundulus heteroclitus*), spotted seat trout (*Cynoscion nebulosus*), and bay anchovy (*Anchoa mitchilli*) (Marenghi & Ozbay, 2010). Tallman and Forrester (2007) noted that both scup (*Stenotomus chrysops*) and tautogs (*Tautoga onitis*) were more abundant on oyster grow-out cages than on adjacent rocky reefs or an artificial reef.

Habitat provisioning results in direct augmentation of commercial and recreational fish populations, increasing the value of oyster reefs to these industries and far surpassing the economic value of harvested oysters alone (Grabowski *et al.*, 2012). Peterson and colleagues (2003) estimated that oyster reefs contribute an additional 2.6 kg of fish and large mobile crustaceans per 10 m^2 of restored oyster reef in the southeastern US. The authors reported that restored oyster reefs had the highest impact on bay anchovies, two species of goby, and stone crabs (*Menippe mercenaria*). Economic value of this additional fish production is estimated at US \$3.70 per 10 m^2 of reef (Grabowski & Peterson, 2007), and the resultant commercial fish value per hectare of oyster reef is US \$4123 per year in 2011 dollars (Grabowski *et al.*, 2012). Given the current poor conditions of oyster reefs globally, these estimates may be conservative.

Richness and abundance of faunal communities are directly related to oyster reef condition, with oyster population structure and reef structural complexity serving as critical factors (Breitburg *et al.*, 2000; Luckenbach *et al.*, 2005; Coen *et al.*, 2007). Restored reefs in the Yangtze River Estuary, China, showed increases in community metrics (species richness, abundance, and biomass) concurrent with the rising number and density of market-sized Suminoe oysters (*Crassostrea ariakensis*) over a five-year period (Quan *et al.*, 2012). Similarly, Rodney and Paynter (2006) found significantly more fauna and epifauna, including xanthid crabs, amphipods, and demersal fish, on three- to five-year-old restored eastern oyster reefs when compared to adjacent degraded reefs. These studies suggest that the current status of oyster reefs worldwide has significant negative impacts on estuarine biodiversity.

IMPACTS OF OYSTER REEFS ON ESTUARINE HEALTH

Oyster reef habitat provides many additional ecosystem services that are crucial to the health of estuarine systems (Table 5.1), including improved water quality, stabilization of coastal habitats, and landscape diversification (Grabowski & Peterson, 2007). Although the effects of oysters on water quality are not completely understood, scientific evidence increasingly suggests that impacts can be significant at both local and larger scales (Coen *et al.*, 2007).

Water quality enhancements are achieved through seston filtration, denitrification, and benthic–pelagic coupling. Oysters are capable of removing large quantities of particulate matter from the water column, reducing both phytoplankton and suspended sediments (French McCay *et al.*, 2003; Zu Ermgassen *et al.*, 2013). Field experiments have demonstrated the ability of eastern oysters to remove up to 37% of the seston from the water column as it passes over the reef and reduce chlorophyll *a* concentrations by 25% and 13% downstream of intertidal reefs in North Carolina and South Carolina, respectively (Cressman *et al.*, 2003; Grizzle *et al.*, 2006, 2008). In addition, denitrification services provided by oysters can reduce eutrophication, harmful algal blooms, and hypoxia levels in estuarine systems. Cerco and Noel (2007) estimate that a 10% increase in existing eastern oyster biomass in the Chesapeake Bay would reduce nitrogen loading by 30 000 kg per day. Denitrification predominantly occurs through benthic–pelagic coupling, where particles and nutrients are transferred from the water column to the benthos (Bayne & Hawkins, 1992). Oysters accomplish this through the deposition of pseudofeces, removing nitrogen at high rates and with high efficiency (Piehler & Smyth, 2011). These benthic–pelagic interactions also reduce phytoplankton biomass and turbidity

(Newell *et al.*, 2005a). The resultant improved water clarity increases light penetration, benefitting the growth of submerged aquatic vegetation (Newell & Koch, 2004).

As three-dimensional intertidal structures, oyster reefs influence the flow velocity and circulation patterns of estuarine waters. By slowing flow, oyster reefs promote organic matter deposition downstream of the reef, which enhances larval settlement of fishes and invertebrates (Breitburg *et al.*, 1995; Lenihan, 1999). Reefs also can serve as breakwaters that attenuate waves, reduce erosion, and protect adjacent shorelines and other estuarine habitats. Oyster cultch (fossilized shell) added to the lower intertidal edge of smooth cordgrass (*Spartina alterniflora*) salt marshes in North Carolina significantly improved sediment stabilization within the marsh habitat and greatly reduced the erosive wave forces of a 10-h storm event (Meyer *et al.*, 1997). Even small fringing reefs may be a valuable tool to protect shorelines in low-energy environments (Piazza *et al.*, 2005). However, wave height plays a major role in the ability of reefs to dissipate wave energy, particularly for submerged aquatic vegetation (Smith *et al.*, 2009). Therefore, reefs must be in close proximity to adjacent habitats for maximum protection.

The role oyster reefs play within the broader estuarine ecosystem is still being investigated; however, studies suggest that the landscape setting around the reef can influence ecosystem processes in adjacent habitats (Grabowski *et al.*, 2005). For example, larval dispersal and settlement is affected by water circulation; therefore, oyster density on individual reefs and its resultant water quality effects will vary by location (Coen *et al.*, 2007; Plutchak *et al.*, 2010). In addition, reefs adjacent to extensive salt marsh may reduce the reef's value as biogenic habitat (Geraldi *et al.*, 2009), while reefs isolated from submerged aquatic vegetation and marsh hold greater benefits for juvenile fishes (Grabowski *et al.*, 2005). Oyster reefs may also act as corridors or stepping-stones for fish species traveling between habitat patches (Irlandi & Crawford, 1997; Micheli & Peterson, 1999). Additional research can further quantify the effects of oysters on landscape diversification in estuarine systems.

CURRENT STATUS AND THREATS OF OYSTER REEFS

Oyster reef habitats throughout the world are in dire condition, with approximately 85% of oyster reefs being lost worldwide (Figure 5.1). Seventy percent and 63% of the 144 bays and 40 ecoregions, respectively, examined by Beck and colleagues (2009, 2011) have < 10% of their historic reefs remaining. Abundance in 37% of these bays and 28% of these ecoregions is at < 1%,

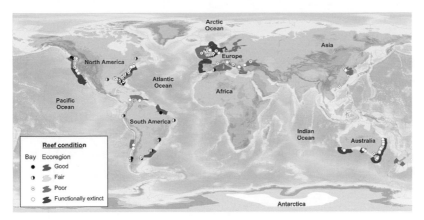

Figure 5.1 Global condition of oyster reefs, based on Beck and colleagues' (2009) examination of 144 bays and 44 ecoregions. Current conditions are ranked based on the percentage of reefs remaining compared to historical abundance: good (< 50% lost), fair (50–89% lost), poor (90–99% lost), and functionally extinct (> 99% lost). Reprinted from Beck *et al.* (2011) with permission from *Bioscience*. (See color plate section.)

indicating functional extinction of both an ecological and economic resource. Where oysters do occur, densities and size of individuals are significantly reduced. Perhaps the most cited illustration of the magnitude of oyster loss occurs in the Chesapeake Bay, where the adult eastern oyster population in the upper reaches has declined by 99.7% (Wilberg *et al.*, 2011). From an estimated virgin abundance of 311 billion individuals, current estimates report only 851 million individuals, with continued increases in mortality (Wilberg *et al.*, 2011). Habitat area has also declined by an estimated 57–63% between 1980 and 2000 (Smith *et al.*, 2005; Wilberg *et al.*, 2011). The situation is comparable throughout much of the world. For example, the population of Chilean oysters (*Ostrea chilensis*) in the Fouvaux Strait, New Zealand, was estimated in 1999 at < 4% of that prior to commercial fishery operations in 1867 and has only increased to ~20% after management of the *Bonamia exitiosa* epizootic (Cranfield *et al.*, 1999; Beck *et al.*, 2009). In Strangford Lough, Northern Ireland, a 1997 survey documented European flat oyster (*Ostrea edulis*) individuals in only two of six survey regions and estimated oyster density in these two locations to be 0.0022 and 0.0005 individuals/m², respectively (Kennedy & Roberts, 1999). A detailed listing of the current conditions of oyster reefs on a global scale can be found in Beck and colleagues (2009).

The destruction of oyster reefs worldwide is a conglomeration of synergistic impacts of both historical and current stressors that form a negative

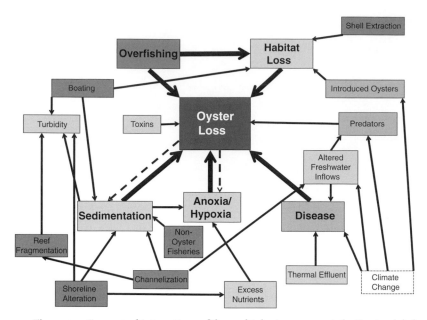

Figure 5.2 Conceptual interactions of the multiple stressors contributing to global oyster decline. Primary threats (overfishing, habitat loss, sedimentation, anoxia/hypoxia, and disease) are in bold type, and the severity of additional threats are indicated by font size. Weighted arrows represent the most influential interactions between multiple stressors, while dotted arrows represent a feedback loop between environmental degradation and oyster loss. Biological threats appear in mid-gray, environmental threats in light gray, and anthropogenic threats in dark gray. (See color plate section.)

feedback loop to further exacerbate the decline of global oyster reefs (Figure 5.2). The path of degradation for each species is similar, beginning with the intense pressure of commercial fisheries (Kirby, 2004; Beck *et al.*, 2011). Oysters have a long history of exploitation, but populations were not affected by the early harvesting practices of indigenous people (Rothschild *et al.*, 1994). Implementation of large-scale commercial fishing operations allowed oyster landings to increase significantly, resulting in the appreciable loss of large-bodied adult oysters (Wilberg *et al.*, 2011). Because the sex ratio of large oysters is female-biased, harvesting of market-sized oysters directly affects the fecundity of a given oyster population. Overfishing continued in most cases, despite the implementation of protective laws and fishing restrictions, until the collapse of the commercial fishery (Rothschild *et al.*, 1994; Kirby, 2004). Despite the depauperate conditions of oyster reefs worldwide, oysters continue to be harvested on a grand scale today, predominantly along the east and Gulf coasts of North America (Beck *et al.*, 2011).

Most detrimental to the persistence of oysters were the aggressive fishing practices implemented in the 1800s, particularly dredges and trawlers, which remove or destroy oyster substrate during harvest operations (Rothschild et al., 1994; Lenihan & Peterson, 2004; Mackenzie, 2007). In the mid-1900s, the use of hydraulic-powered patent tongs introduced an even greater destructive force to the already imperiled reefs (Rothschild et al., 1994). Loss of vertical relief and structural complexity of the reefs left oysters vulnerable to the negative effects of siltation and hypoxia, resulting in further oyster mortality and reduced juvenile recruitment (Lenihan & Peterson, 1998; Mackenzie, 2007). In addition, overharvesting of individual reefs, combined with the destruction of reef segments for navigation channels, fragmented the entire reef system, severely limiting spawning success (Eggleston, 1999). Loss of interconnected reef networks contributed to the decline of water quality through resuspension of particulates, further inhibiting oyster survival (Mann, 2000; EOBRT, 2007). Despite the poor condition of global oyster reefs, contemporary fisheries management continues to promote destructive practices, and there are incidences of fisheries collapse as late as the 1990s and 2000s (Valero & Caballero, 2003; Virvilis & Angelidis, 2006).

While fishing and habitat loss explain the bulk of oyster decline, the effects of eutrophication, disease, sedimentation, and non-native species interact and continue to challenge oyster recovery (Jackson et al., 2001). Disease introductions exacerbated already elevated mortality levels across several regions. While the path of introduction for many parasites remains unknown, the occurrence of some parasites and pathogens have been linked to human-mediated modes of dispersal. Of the 18 oyster disease agents identified by Ruesink and colleagues (2005), three were spread to naïve conspecific populations through brood stock transplants, and two were introduced via non-native brood stock. In one case, European flat oysters introduced to the US were infected with the protozoan, *Bonamia ostreae*. Individuals transplanted back to their native region of Europe carried the disease with them and infected populations there. These diseases had (and still have) catastrophic effects on already depleted oyster populations. The introduction of *Haplosporidium nelsoni*, the causative agent of multinucleated sphere X (MSX), to the Chesapeake Bay from Asia around 1957 resulted in > 90% mortality of eastern oysters in high salinity areas (Burreson et al., 2000; Carnegie & Burreson, 2011). *Marteilia sydneyi*, the native protozoan that causes QX disease in Australian Sydney rock oyster aquaculture, results in > 90% mortality of non-resistant individuals (Nell, 2007). While development of resistance in some oyster species has been documented (Carnegie & Burreson, 2011), disease continues to impact the recovery of oysters worldwide.

Oysters are also negatively impacted by myriad additional non-native species. Because native and introduced oysters tend to differ in their tolerance of environmental conditions, competition may not be an influential factor (Ruesink et al., 2005). However, where native and non-native species do overlap, non-native species often outcompete natives (Richardson et al., 1993; Baker, 1995; Grabowski & Powers, 2004). The thinner shells of non-native Suminoe oysters allows them to grow faster than native eastern oysters in North Carolina (Grabowski & Powers, 2004); however, having thinner shells does make them more susceptible to predation by blue crabs (Bishop & Peterson, 2005). Perhaps more threatening to oyster populations is the effect of non-native oyster pests, including mudworms and drilling snails (Mackenzie, 2007; Buhle & Ruesink, 2009). The disappearance of Sydney rock oysters and Australian flat oysters (Ostrea angasi) from eastern Australia is likely the result of an invasive mudworm (Polydora sp.) introduced with oyster stock from New Zealand (Ogburn et al., 2007). Another major oyster pest, the Atlantic oyster drill (Urosalpinx cinerea), has been introduced to several regions worldwide and impacts many oyster species. Native to the eastern Atlantic seaboard, the Atlantic oyster drill thrives in naïve habitats where it is free from specialized predators (Faasse & Ligthart, 2007).

Marine pollution has tremendous impacts on the health and vitality of oysters in estuarine systems, and the decline of oysters has coincided with increases in sediments and nutrients entering waterways through stormwater runoff and sewage dumping (Paerl et al., 1998; Kennish, 2002). Increased siltation collects at the base of reefs, increasing hypoxia and anoxia levels and preventing larval settlement (Lenihan & Peterson, 1998; Mackenzie, 2007; Brumbaugh & Coen, 2009). Excessive sedimentation also increases the susceptibility of individuals to parasites (Lenihan, 1999; Ogburn et al., 2007). Nutrient loading in the water, concurrent with the loss of oysters through overfishing and habitat loss, shifts primary productivity from the benthos to plankton leading to eutrophication. While moderate eutrophication may enhance the primary productivity of oysters (Kirby & Miller, 2005), it usually occurs at levels high enough to generate algal production that can smother or suffocate oysters of all life stages.

Several anthropogenic factors add to the continued loss of oysters and reef habitat as well. Shell mining of extinct and extant reefs for lime and other byproducts depletes reef structure and contributes to oyster mortality (Hargis & Haven, 1999; NRC, 2004). Harvesting practices for non-oyster fisheries (e.g. clam dredging, shrimp trawling) can increase siltation on adjacent oyster reefs (Dugas et al., 1997). Wakes generated by intensive recreational boating erodes existing reefs, increases sediment loads, and transports larvae to exposed shell margins where they are vulnerable to dessication (Grizzle et al., 2002; Wall et al., 2005). Changes in hydrology through freshwater diversions, stormwater inputs, and channelization can also significantly impact oyster health by affecting predation rates and disease-related mortality and increasing suspended solids in the water column (Dugas et al., 1997; Mackenzie, 2007; but see Klinck et al., 2002). Toxins entering estuaries through oil spills, industrial effluents, and other point sources have serious detrimental effects at all life stages (Dauer et al., 2000; Wintermeyer & Cooper, 2003). Shoreline armoring practices (bulkheads, revetments, etc.) increase erosion and turbidity and promote sediment and nutrient loading through stormwater runoff (EOBRT, 2007). Finally, superheated effluent from power plant cooling stations can reduce larval stock density and impact spat recruitment (EOBRT, 2007).

The impacts of climate change are less well-studied. Although shell accretion rates of healthy oyster bars can outpace predicted sea level rise (Grabowski et al., 2012), restored oyster bars have a short life expectancy due to sediment burial, negative species interactions, and other poorly understood factors (Mann & Powell, 2007). In addition, acidification of estuarine waters through CO_2 enrichment can affect calcification rates in oyster larvae, ultimately reducing growth rates (Miller et al., 2009). Warmer water temperatures may increase spawning and growth rates at the northern extent of a species' range, improving estuarine water quality through increased filtration rates. However, conditions may be reversed at the southern extent, where water temperatures may contribute to higher mortality. Furthermore, shifting environmental conditions (i.e. water circulation, salinity) can influence the distribution of predators, competitors, and parasites (Powell et al., 2012). Therefore, if current trends continue, oyster reefs will remain highly vulnerable to climate-induced changes.

RESTORATION OF OYSTER REEFS

Attempts to restore oysters commenced as early as the mid-1800s, when resource managers in Australia and the US began the importation of non-native oyster stock to replenish diminished reefs (Kirby, 2004; NRC, 2004). Since that time, several additional restoration initiatives have been implemented (Table 5.2), primarily with the goal of maintaining oysters as a fisheries resource. In the Chesapeake Bay, the predominant restoration methods

Table 5.2 *Past and present oyster restoration strategies.*

Activity		Description
Stock enhancement		
	Brood stock sanctuaries	Protected natural or constructed reefs where oyster harvest is restricted in an effort to enhance natural recruitment
	Wild seed transplanting	Young oysters or spat are collected from existing reefs and relocated to reefs that have the potential to support oysters but where natural recruitment is low
	Hatchery seed transplanting	Oyster hatcheries promote the growth of spat on shells, which are then transplanted on reefs that have the potential to support oysters but where natural recruitment is low
	Selectively bred aquaculture stock	Oyster spat that has been selectively bred for disease resistance is transplanted onto reefs in regions where disease prevalence is high
Habitat enhancement		
	Substrate addition	Hard substrate (usually oyster or clam shell) is added to degraded reefs or on soft-bottom in areas where reefs formerly existed or where there is potential for reef establishment. Other materials for substrate addition include lime, marl, concrete, coal ash, and granite
	Bar cleaning	A power dredge is used to remove all live oysters from a bar, and the empty shells are returned as substrate after the sediment is removed
	Bagged/bagless dredging	A power dredge is dragged across an oyster bar, stirring up oysters and sediment. With bagged dredging, oysters are brought aboard the dredge, culled, and returned to the bar. In bagless dredging, sediments are carried away in the current and oyster shell settles back onto the reef
	Shell bags	Mesh bags are filled with shell (usually oyster or whelk) and positioned and secured side-by-side in the intertidal zone, jump-starting natural recruitment of oysters and vertical accretion of reef structure. Usually done by volunteers
	Oyster mats	Adult oysters are secured in a vertical position onto aquaculture-grade mesh mats and placed over degraded reefs to enhance recruitment
Oyster gardening		Volunteers steward floating oyster aquaculture cages attached to bulkheads or docks on both private and public property

Table 5.2 (*cont.*)

Activity	Description
Shell recycling	Consumers are encouraged to bring dead oyster shells to recycling stations to secure materials for substrate addition projects. Shells are quarantined before use to minimize risk of disease transmission
Spat catching	Volunteers suspend a small cage with clean oyster shells from a rope attached to private docks and bulkheads and record the number of spat that attach to the substrate. The information is used to identify areas of pronounced natural recruitment to determine appropriate sites for restoration projects

between 1990 and 2007 were seed transplanting and substrate addition (Kennedy *et al.*, 2011). The former strategy involves harvesting and relocating juveniles to degraded reefs, while substrate addition generally involves the placement of oyster shell (or other hard substrate) on degraded reef bases (NRC, 2004; Kennedy *et al.*, 2011). Seed stock can come from wild populations or aquaculture hatcheries (Mann & Powell, 2007; Carlsson *et al.*, 2008). Other fishery-based strategies include bar cleaning and bagged/bagless dredging.

One of the biggest challenges to successful restoration is that the majority of past restoration projects have been implemented with the goal of maintaining oysters as a fished commodity (Beck *et al.*, 2009, 2011). Repleted oyster reefs are left open for harvesting rather than being restricted until the population and habitat recover (Coen & Luckenbach, 2000; Kennedy *et al.*, 2011). Therefore, most restored reefs operate as a "put-and-take" fishery and continue to degrade (Hargis & Haven, 1999).

Unfortunately, oysters and oyster reef habitats still are not afforded the same protections as other imperiled species or critical ecosystems, despite the data published over the last decade on their population status and ecological function (Beck *et al.*, 2011). Very few oyster sanctuaries exist globally, and oysters are only rarely considered in marine protected area (MPA) planning (Beck *et al.*, 2009). Oysters are not even provided the same protections given to other commercial fisheries. Whereas fishery restrictions are generally implemented once stocks drop below 10%, oysters continue to be harvested in areas with < 1% of their historical abundance remaining (Beck *et al.*, 2009). These continued trends undermine restoration efforts from the start.

Only within the last two decades have oyster reefs been recognized for their value as habitat and ecosystem service providers (Grabowski & Peterson, 2007; Grabowski *et al.*, 2012). Since that time, enhancement of ecological function has become a goal for oyster restoration (Seaman, 2007; Beck *et al.*, 2011), and subsequent initiatives have enjoyed some success. Examples include a metapopulation of 9 reef complexes comprising 35 ha in the Great Wicomico River (Virginia) that was successfully restored in 2004, and > 56% of constructed reefs of varying ages surveyed in central and northern North Carolina that successfully increased oyster density, vertical relief, and spat recruitment compared with baseline conditions (Powers *et al.*, 2009; Schulte *et al.*, 2009). In both cases, restored reefs were protected from harvest, emphasizing the importance of promoting sustainability in oyster fishery management.

However, even in the absence of oyster harvesting, successful restoration is hindered by the suite of threats that impact oyster survival. Many of the remaining restored reefs surveyed in northern North Carolina (referenced above) failed because of burial by sediment and poor water quality (Powers *et al.*, 2009). More importantly, given the short lifespan of dead oyster shell (exacerbated by heavy sediment loads), substrate addition can be prohibitively expensive as a long-term strategy (Mann & Powell, 2007). In addition, oyster disease mortality reduces vertical accretion rates of reefs, imposing a further limitation to substrate addition efforts (Powell & Klinck, 2007). Finally, there is a common misconception among resource managers that non-native oysters can replace natives (Beck *et al.*, 2011). While the life history of oysters may suggest that non-natives can produce several desirable outcomes, their introduction could have severe deleterious effects on native ecosystems (Ruesink *et al.*, 2005). Because documentation of successful native oyster restoration projects exists (Powers *et al.*, 2009; Schulte *et al.*, 2009), introduction of non-native oysters is not recommended as a viable strategy by conservation practitioners (Beck *et al.*, 2009).

Oyster restoration for ecosystem services is carried out using a variety of practices, including those mentioned previously. Community-based restoration efforts have also become very popular in recent times. In some regions of the US, local consumers are encouraged to bring their oyster shells to recycling stations rather than disposing of them. The shells are quarantined for 1–3 months to reduce disease transmission potential before being used for substrate addition projects (Bushek *et al.*, 2004; Brumbaugh & Coen, 2009). The use of shell bags is also employed for small-scale, community-based restoration initiatives. Volunteers fill mesh bags with shell (oyster or whelk) and lay them side-by-side within the intertidal zone, forming the structural foundation of an eventual oyster reef (Taylor & Bushek, 2008). Other popular community-based tools include oyster gardening and spat catching, where citizen scientists steward floating aquaculture cages secured to bulkheads or docks (Rossi-Snook et al., 2010). While these small-scale approaches are seldom monitored for success (Coen & Luckenbach, 2000; Brumbaugh & Coen, 2009), public education and outreach has been shown to be a powerful tool in promoting conservation priorities.

Innovative techniques and complex modeling are now being implemented as a means to reverse the trajectory of oyster populations worldwide. Habitat suitability and optimization models to identify prime restoration methods and develop effective strategies exist for several regions (e.g. Volety et al., 2005; Barnes et al., 2007; North et al., 2010; Starke et al., 2011; Pollack et al., 2012). New methodologies continue to develop, including oyster seed mats, reef blocks, and other contained cultch designs (Wall, 2004; Stokes et al., 2012). Finally, research to further understand and improve oyster dispersal, settlement, and disease resistance is ongoing (e.g. Narvaez et al., 2012; Wang et al., 2012; Fuchs et al., 2013).

REVERSING THE TIDE: OYSTER RECOVERY AND THE FUTURE OF ESTUARIES

Successful estuarine recovery will be achieved when the system contains sufficient biotic and abiotic resources to continue its development without further assistance or subsidy (SER, 2004). Given their massive water filtration capabilities, oysters will play a significant role in achieving this goal, but their populations must recover for this to occur. While independent projects can promote the restoration of oysters at a local scale, a global strategy is needed to achieve successful conservation. Beck and colleagues (2009) laid out detailed recommendations to recover global oyster reefs, including reef protection and restoration, prevention of non-native species introductions and sustainable fisheries management. The fourth pillar of this multipronged strategy is water quality improvement, presenting an obvious Catch-22. If oysters are to recover, estuarine health must improve; but if estuarine health is to improve, oysters must recover.

While overharvesting and destructive fishing practices have relatively straightforward solutions (albeit difficult to implement), improving water quality presents a complex challenge. Pollutants enter estuarine environments along multiple pathways, the origins of which are not always known. Dispersal of these contaminants throughout the water column and bottom sediments is not uniform and is subject to perturbations from storms and other dynamic events. Anthropogenic inputs to estuaries are difficult to regulate, particularly in developing countries where management of human overpopulation and poverty overshadow resultant environmental threats (Kennish, 2002). Therefore, comprehensive watershed management remains a lofty goal.

The challenge moving forward is to promote oyster recovery in the presence of marine pollutants, which will require an understanding of which contaminants in a given estuary are driving water quality decline and at what threshold levels oyster recovery is feasible. The creation of broadly applicable, quantitative ecological models can assist in the development of site-specific water quality restoration targets and triggers for intervention. Vigilant monitoring of important parameters will allow resource managers to adaptively manage oyster reefs, consequently redirecting estuaries on a self-sustaining trajectory toward recovery.

REFERENCES

Airoldi, L., Balata, D. & Beck, M. W. (2008). The gray zone: Relationships between habitat loss and marine diversity and their applications in conservation. *Journal of Experimental Marine Biology and Ecology*, **366**, 8–15.

ASMFC. (2007). *The Importance of Habitat Created by Shellfish and Shell Beds Along the Atlantic Coast of the US.* Prepared by L. D. Coen and R. Grizzle, with contributions by J. Lowery and K. T. Paynter. Washington, DC: ASMFC.

Baird, D., Christian, R. R., Peterson, C. H. & Johnson, G. A. (2004). Consequences of hypoxia on estuarine ecosystem function: Energy diversion from consumers to microbes. *Ecological Applications*, **14**, 805–822.

Baker, P. (1995). Review of ecology and fishery of the Olympia oyster, *Ostrea lurida* with annotated bibliography. *Journal of Shellfish Research*, **14**, 501–518.

Barbier, E. B., Hacker, S. D., Kennedy, C., *et al.* (2011). The value of estuarine and coastal ecosystem services. *Ecological Monographs*, **81**, 169–193.

Barnes, T. K., Volety, A. K., Chartier, K., Mazzotti, F. J. & Pearlstine, L. (2007). A habitat suitability index model for the eastern oyster (*Crassostrea virginica*), a tool for restoration of the Caloosahatchee Estuary, Florida. *Journal of Shellfish Research*, **26**, 949–959.

Bartol, I. & Mann, R. (1999). Small-scale patterns of recruitment on a constructed intertidal reef: The role of spatial refugia. In M. W. Luckenbach, R. Mann & J.A. Wesson (eds.), *Oyster Reef Habitat Restoration: A Synopsis and Synthesis of Approaches.* Gloucester Point, VA: Virginia Institute of Marine Science Press, pp. 159–170.

Bayne, B. L. & Hawkins, A. J. S. (1992). Ecological and physiological aspects of herbivory in benthic suspension-feeding molluscs. In D. M. John, S. J. Hawkins & J. H. Price (eds.), *Plant–Animal Interactions in the Marine Benthos.* Systematics Association Special Vol. 46. Oxford: Clarendon Press, pp. 265–288.

Beck, M. W., Heck, Jr., K. L., Able, K. W., *et al.* (2001). The identification, conservation, and management of estuarine and marine nurseries for fish and invertebrates. *Bioscience*, **51**, 633–641.

Beck, M. W., Brumbaugh, R. D., Airoldi, L., *et al.* (2009). *Shellfish Reefs at Risk: A Global Analysis of Problems and Solutions*. Arlington, VA: The Nature Conservancy.

Beck, M. W., Brumbaugh, R. D., Airoldi, L., *et al.* (2011). Oyster reefs at risk and recommendations for conservation, restoration, and management. *Bioscience*, **61**, 107–116.

Berrigan, M., Candies, T., Cirino, J., *et al.* (1991). *The Oyster Fishery of the Gulf of Mexico, United States: A Regional Management Plan*. No. 24. Ocean Springs, MS: Gulf States Marine Fisheries Commission.

Bishop, M. J. & Peterson, C. H. (2005). Constraints to *Crassostrea ariakensis* aquaculture: Season and method of culture strongly influence success of grow-out. *Journal of Shellfish Research*, **24**, 497–502.

Breitburg, D. L. (1999). Are three-dimensional structures, and healthy oyster population the keys to an ecologically interesting, and important fish community? In M. W. Luckenbach, R. Mann & J.A. Wesson (eds.), *Oyster Reef Habitat Restoration: A Synopsis and Synthesis of Approaches*. Gloucester Point, VA: Virginia Institute of Marine Science Press, pp. 239–250.

Breitburg, D. L., Palmer, M. A. & Loher, T. (1995). Larval distributions and the spatial patterns of settlement of an oyster reef fish – Responses to flow and structure. *Marine Ecology Progress Series*, **125**, 45–60.

Breitburg, D. L., Coen, L. D., Luckenbach, M. W., *et al.* (2000). Oyster reef restoration: Convergence of harvest and conservation strategies. *Journal of Shellfish Research*, **19**, 371–377.

Brumbaugh, R. D. & Coen, L. D. (2009). Contemporary approaches for small-scale oyster reef restoration to address substrate versus recruitment limitation: A review and comments relevant for the Olympia oyster, *Ostrea lurida* Carpenter 1864. *Journal of Shellfish Research*, **28**, 147–161.

Buhle, E. R. & Ruesink, J. L. (2009). Impacts of invasive oyster drills on Olympia oyster (*Ostrea lurida* Carpenter 1864) recovery in Willapa Bay, Washington, United States. *Journal of Shellfish Research*, **28**, 87–96.

Burreson, E. M., Stokes, N. A. & Friedman, C. S. (2000). Increased virulence of an introduced pathogen: *Haplosporidium nelson* (MSX) in the eastern oyster *Crassostrea virginica*. *Journal of Aquatic Animal Health*, **12**, 1–8.

Bushek, D., Richardson, D., Bobo, M. Y. & Coen, L. D. (2004). Quarantine of oyster shell cultch reduces the abundance of *Perkinsus marinus*. *Journal of Shellfish Research*, **23**, 369–373.

Calabrese, A. & Davis, H. C. (1966). The pH tolerance of embryos of *Mercenaria mercenaria* and *Crassostrea virginica*. *Biological Bulletin*, **131**, 427–436.

Carlsson, J., Carnegie, R. B., Cordes, J. F., *et al.* (2008). Evaluating recruitment contribution of a selectively bred aquaculture line of the oyster, *Crassostrea virginica* to be used in restoration efforts. *Journal of Shellfish Research*, **27**, 1117–1124.

Carnegie, R. B. & Burreson, E. M. (2011). Declining impact of an introduced pathogen: *Haplosporidium nelsoni* in the oyster *Crassostrea virginica* in Chesapeake Bay. *Marine Ecology Progress Series*, **432**, 1–15.

Cerco, C. F. & Noel, M. R. (2007). Can oyster restoration reverse cultural eutrophication in Chesapeake Bay? *Estuaries and Coasts*, **30**, 331–343.

Coen, L. D. & Luckenbach, M. W. (2000). Developing success criteria for evaluating oyster reef restoration: Ecological function or resource exploitation? *Ecological Engineering*, **15**, 323–343.

Coen, L. D., Luckenbach, M. W. & Breitburg, D. L. (1999). The role of oyster reefs as essential fish habitat: A review of current knowledge and some new perspectives. *American Fisheries Society Symposium*, **22**, 438–454.

Coen, L. D., Brumbaugh, R. D., Bushek, D., *et al.* (2007). Ecosystem services related to oyster restoration. *Marine Ecology Progress Series*, **341**, 303–307.

Cranfield, H. J., Michael, K. P. & Doonan, I. J. (1999). Changes in the distribution of epifaunal reefs and oysters during 130 years of dredging for oysters in Foveaux Strait, southern New Zealand. *Aquatic Conservation: Marine and Freshwater Ecosystems*, **9**, 461–483.

Cranfield, H. J., Rowden, A. A., Smith, D. P., Gordon, K. P. & Michael, K. P. (2004). Macrofaunal assemblages of benthic habitat of different complexity and the proposition of a model of biogenic reef habitat regeneration in Foveaux Strait, New Zealand. *Journal of Sea Research*, **52**, 109–125.

Cressman, K. A., Posey, M. H., Mallin, M. A., Leonard, L. A. & Alphin, T. D. (2003). Effects of oyster reefs on water quality in a tidal creek estuary. *Journal of Shellfish Research*, **22**, 753–762.

Dame, R. F., Zingmark, R. G. & Haskin, E. (1984). Oyster reefs as processors of estuarine material. *Journal of Experimental Marine Biology and Ecology*, **83**, 239–247.

Dame, R. F., Wolaver, T. G. & Libes, S. M. (1985). The summer uptake and release of nitrogen by an intertidal oyster reef. *Netherlands Journal of Sea Research*, **19**, 265–268.

Dame, R. F., Spurrier, J. D. & Wolaver, T.G. (1989). Carbon, nitrogen and phosphorus processing by an oyster reef. *Marine Ecology Progress Series*, **54**, 249–256.

Dauer, D. M., Ranasinghe, J. A. & Weisberg, S. B. (2000). Relationship between benthic community condition, water quality, sediment quality, nutrient loads, and land use patterns in Chesapeake Bay. *Estuaries*, **23**, 80–96.

Davis, R. A. & Fitzgerald, D. M. (2004). *Beaches and Coasts*. Malden, MA: Blackwell Science.

Deegan, L. A., Johnson, D. S., Warren, R. S., *et al.* (2012). Coastal eutrophication as a driver of salt marsh loss. *Nature*, **490**, 388–392.

Dekshenieks, M. M., Hoffman, E. E., Klink, J. M. & Powell, E. N. (1996). Modeling the vertical distribution of oyster larvae in response to environmental conditions. *Marine Ecology Progress Series*, **136**, 97–110.

Dugas, R. J., Joyce, E. A. & Berrigan, M. A. (1997). History and status of the oyster, *Crassostrea virginica*, and other molluscan fisheries of the Gulf of Mexico. In C. L. MacKenzie, Jr., V. G. Burrell, Jr., A. Rosenfield & W. L. Hobart (eds.), *The History, Present Condition, and Future of the Molluscan Fisheries of North and Central America and Europe*. NOAA Technical Report. NMFS 127, pp. 187–210.

Dumbauld, B. R., Visser, E. P., Armstrong, D. A., *et al.* (2000). Use of oyster shell to create habitat for juvenile Dungeness crab in Washington coastal estuaries: Status and prospects. *Journal of Shellfish Research*, **19**, 379–386.

Eggleston, D. B. (1999). Application of landscape principles to oyster reef habitat restoration. In M. W. Luckenbach, R. Mann & J. A. Wesson (eds.), *Oyster Reef Habitat Restoration: A Synopsis and Synthesis of Approaches.* Gloucester Point, VA: Virginia Institute of Marine Science Press, pp. 213–227.

EOBRT, Eastern Oyster Biological Review Team. (2007). *Status Review of the Eastern Oyster* (Crassostrea virginica). Report to the National Marine Fisheries Service, Northeast Regional Office. 16 February 2007. NOAA Technical Memo. NMFS F/SPO-88.

Everett, R. A., Ruiz, G. M. & Carlton, J. T. (1995). Effect of oyster mariculture on submerged aquatic vegetation: An experimental test in a Pacific Northwest estuary. *Marine Ecology Progress Series,* **125,** 205–217.

Faasse, M. & Ligthart, M. (2007). The America oyster drill, *Urosalpinx cinerea* (Say, 1822), introduced to The Netherlands – Increased risks after ban on TBT. *Aquatic Invasions,* **2,** 402–406.

French McCay, D. P., Peterson, C. H., DeAlteris, J. T. & Catena, J. (2003). Restoration that targets function as opposed to structure: Replacing lost bivalve production and filtration. *Marine Ecology Progress Series,* **264,** 197–212.

Fuchs, H. L., Hunter, E. J., Schmitt, E. L. & Guazzo, R. A. (2013). Active downward propulsion by oyster larvae in turbulence. *Journal of Experimental Marine Biology,* **216,** 1458–1469.

Galtsoff, P. S. (1964). The American oyster *Crassostrea virginica* Gmelin. *Fishery Bulletin,* **64,** 1–480.

Geraldi, N. R., Powers, S. P., Heck, K. L. & Cebrian, J. (2009). Can habitat restoration be redundant? Response of mobile fishes and crustaceans to oyster reef restoration in marsh tidal creeks. *Marine Ecology Progress Series,* **389,** 171–180.

Glancy, T. P., Frazer, T. K., Cichra, C. E. & Lindberg, W. J. (2003). Comparative patterns of occupancy by decapod crustaceans in seagrass, oyster, and marsh-edge habitats in a northeast Gulf of Mexico estuary. *Estuaries,* **26,** 1291–1301.

Grabowski, J. H. & Peterson, C. H. (2007). Restoring oyster reefs to recover ecosystem services. In K. Cuddington, J. E. Byers, W. G. Wilson & A. Hastings (eds.), *Ecosystem Engineers: Plants to Protists.* London: Elsvier, pp. 281–298.

Grabowski, J. H. & Powers, S. P. (2004). Habitat complexity mitigates trophic transfer on oyster reefs. *Marine Ecology Progress Series,* **277,** 291–295.

Grabowski, J.H., Hughes, A. R., Kimbro, D. L. & Dolan, M. L. (2005). How habitat setting influences restored oyster reef communities. *Ecology,* **86,** 1926–1935.

Grabowski, J. H., Brumbaugh, R. D., Conrad, R. F., *et al.* (2012). Economic valuation of ecosystem services provided by oyster reefs. *Bioscience,* **62,** 900–909.

Granek, E. F., Polasky, S., Kappel, C. V., *et al.* (2010). Ecosystem services as a common language for coastal ecosystem-based management. *Conservation Biology,* **24,** 207–216.

Grizzle, R. E., Adams, J. R. & Walters, L. J. (2002). Historical changes in intertidal oyster (*Crassostrea virginica*) reefs in a Florida lagoon potentially related to boating activities. *Journal of Shellfish Research,* **21,** 749–756.

Grizzle, R. E., Greene, J. K., Luckenbach, M. W. & Coen, L. D. (2006). A new in situ method for measuring seston uptake by suspension-feeding bivalve molluscs. *Journal of Shellfish Research,* **25,** 643–649.

Grizzle, R. E., Greene, J. K. & Coen, L. D. (2008). Seston removal by natural and constructed intertidal eastern oyster (*Crassostrea virginica*) reefs: A comparison with previous laboratory studies, and the value of in situ methods. *Estuaries and Coasts*, **31**, 1208–1220.

Guo, X., Hedgecock, D., Hershberger, W. K., Cooper, K. & Allen, Jr., S. K. (1998). Genetic determinants of protandric sex in the Pacific oyster, *Crassostrea gigas* Thunberg. *Evolution*, **52**, 394–402.

Harding, J. M. & Mann, R. (2001a). Diet and habitat use by bluefish, *Pomotomus saltatrix*, in a Chesapeake Bay estuary. *Environmental Biology of Fishes*, **60**, 401–409.

Harding, J. M. & Mann, R. (2001b). Oyster reefs as fish habitat: Opportunistic use of restored reefs by transient fishes. *Journal of Shellfish Research*, **20**, 951–959.

Harding, J. M. & Mann, R. (2003). Influence of habitat on diet and distribution of striped bass (*Morone saxatilis*) in a temperate estuary. *Bulletin of Marine Science*, **72**, 841–851.

Harding, J. M. & Mann, R. (2010). Observations of distribution, size, and sex ratio of mature blue crabs, *Callinectes sapidus*, from a Chesapeake Bay tributary in relation to oyster habitat and environmental factors. *Bulletin of Marine Science*, **86**, 75–91.

Hargis, W. J. & Haven, D. S. (1999). Chesapeake oyster reefs, their importance, destruction, and guidelines for restoring them. In M. W. Luckenbach, R. Mann & J. A. Wesson (eds.), *Oyster Reef Habitat Restoration: A Synopsis and Synthesis of Approaches*. Gloucester Point, VA: Virginia Institute of Marine Science Press, pp. 329–358.

Hayes, P. F. & Menzel, R. W. (1981). The reproductive cycle of early setting *Crassostrea virginica* (Gmelin) in the northern Gulf of Mexico, and its implications for population recruitment. *Biological Bulletin*, **160**, 80–88.

Heck, Jr., K. L., Hays, G. & Orth, R. J. (2003). Critical evaluation of the nursery role hypothesis for seagrass meadows. *Marine Ecology Progress Series*, **253**, 123–136.

Henderson, J. & O'Neill, L. J. (2003). *Economic Values Associated with Construction of Oyster Reefs by the Corps of Engineers*, EMRRP Technical Notes Collection (ERDC TN-EMRRP-ER-01). Vicksburg, MS: US Army Engineer Research and Development Center.

Hofmann, E. E., Powell, E. N., Klinck, J. M. & Wilson, E. A. (1992). Modeling oyster populations. 3. Critical feeding periods, growth, and reproduction. *Journal of Shellfish Research*, **11**, 399–416.

Hosack, G. R., Dumbauld, B. R., Ruesink, J. L. & Armstrong, D. A. (2006). Habitat associations of estuarine species: Comparisons of intertidal mudflat, seagrass (*Zostera marina*), and oyster (*Crassostrea gigas*) habitats. *Estuaries and Coasts*, **29**, 1150–1160.

Irlandi, E. A. & Crawford, M. K. (1997). Habitat linkages: The effect of intertidal saltmarshes and adjacent subtidal habitats on abundance, movement, and growth of an estuarine fish. *Oecologia*, **110**, 222–230.

Jackson, J. B. C., Kirby, M. X., Berger, W. H., *et al.* (2001). Historical overfishing and the recent collapse of coastal ecosystems. *Science*, **293**, 629–638.

Kennedy, R. J. & Roberts, D. (1999). A survey of the current status of the flat oyster *Ostrea edulis* in Stragford Lough, Northern Ireland, with a view to the restoration of its oyster beds. *Biology and Environment: Proceedings of the Royal Irish Academy*, **99B**, 79–88.

Kennedy, V. S. & Sanford, L. P. (1999). Characteristics of relatively unexploited beds of the eastern oyster, *Crassostrea virginica*, and early restoration programs. In M. W. Luckenbach, R. Mann & J. A. Wesson (eds.), *Oyster Reef Habitat Restoration: A Synopsis and Synthesis of Approaches.* Gloucester Point, VA: Virginia Institute of Marine Science Press, pp. 25–46.

Kennedy, V. S., Breitburg, D. L., Christman, M. C., *et al.* (2011). Lessons learned from efforts to restore oyster populations in Maryland and Virginia, 1990–2007. *Journal of Shellfish Research*, **30**, 719–731.

Kennish, M. J. (2002). Environmental threats and environmental future of estuaries. *Environmental Conservation*, **29**, 78–107.

Kirby, M. X. (2004). Fishing down the coast: Historical expansion and collapse of oyster fisheries along continental margins. *Proceedings of the National Academy of Sciences of the United States of America*, **101**, 13096–13099.

Kirby, M. X. & Miller, H. M. (2005). Response of a benthic suspension feeder (*Crassostrea virginica* Gmelin) to three centuries of anthropogenic eutrophication in Chesapeake Bay. *Estuarine, Coastal and Shelf Science*, **62**, 679–689.

Klinck, J. M., Hofmann, E. E., Powell, E. N. & Dekshenieks, M. M. (2002). Impact of channelization on oyster production: A hydrodynamic-oyster population model for Galveston Bay, Texas. *Environmental Modeling and Assessment*, **7**, 273–289.

Korringa, P. (1952). Recent advances in oyster biology. *Quarterly Review of Biology*, **27**, 266–308.

Lenihan, H. S. (1999). Physical–biological coupling on oyster reefs: How habitat structure influences individual performance. *Ecological Monographs*, **69**, 251–275.

Lenihan, H. S. & Peterson, C. H. (1998). How habitat degradation through fishery disturbance enhances impacts of hypoxia on oyster reefs. *Ecological Applications*, **8**, 128–140.

Lenihan, H. S. & Peterson, C. H. (2004). Conserving oyster reef habitat by switching from dredging and tonging to diver-harvesting. *Fishery Bulletin*, **102**, 298–305.

Lenihan, H. S., Peterson, C. H. & Allen, J. M. (1995). Does flow also have a direct effect on growth of active suspension feeders? An experimental test with oysters. *Limnology and Oceangraphy*, **41**, 1359–1366.

Lenihan, H. S., Peterson, C. H., Byers, J. E., *et al.* (2001). Cascading of habitat degradation: Oyster reefs invaded by refugee fishes escaping stress. *Ecological Applications*, **11**, 764–782.

Lipton, D. (2004). The value of improved water quality to Chesapeake Bay boaters. *Marine Resource Economics*, **19**, 265–270.

Lotze, H. K., Lenihan, H. S., Bourque, B. J., *et al.* (2006). Depletion, degradation, and recovery potential of estuaries and coastal seas. *Science*, **312**, 1806–1809.

Luckenbach, M. W., Coen, L. D., Ross, Jr., P. G. & Stephen, J. A. (2005). Oyster reef habitat restoration: Relationships between oyster abundance and community development based on two studies in Virginia and South Carolina. *Journal of Coastal Research*, **40**, 64–78.

Mackenzie, C. L. (2007). Causes underlying the historical decline in eastern oyster (*Crassostrea virginica* Gmelin, 1791) landings. *Journal of Shellfish Research*, **26**, 927–938.

Mann, R. (2000). Restoring the oyster reef communities in the Chesapeake Bay: A commentary. *Journal of Shellfish Research*, **19**, 335–339.

Mann, R. & Powell, E. N. (2007). Why oyster restoration goals in the Chesapeake Bay are not and probably cannot be achieved. *Journal of Shellfish Research*, **26**, 905–917.

Marenghi, F. P. & Ozbay, G. (2010). Floating oyster, *Crassostrea virginica* Gmelin 1791, aquaculture as habitat for fishes and macroinvertebrates in Delaware inland bays: The comparative value of oyster clusters and loose shell. *Journal of Shellfish Research*, **29**, 889–904.

Markert, A., Wehrmann, A. & Kroncke, I. (2010). Recently established *Crassostrea*-reefs versus native *Mytilus*-beds: Differences in ecosystem engineering affects the macrofaunal communities (Wadden Sea of Lower Saxony, southern German Bight). *Biological Invasions*, **12**, 15–32.

Meyer, D. L. & Townsend, E. C. (2000). Faunal utilization of created intertidal eastern oyster (*Crassostrea virginica*) reefs in the southeastern United States. *Estuaries*, **23**, 34–45.

Meyer, D. L., Townsend, E. C & Thayer, G. W. (1997). Stabilization and erosion control of oyster cultch for intertidal marsh. *Restoration Ecology*, **5**, 93–99.

Micheli, F. & Peterson, C. H. (1999). Estuarine vegetated habitats as corridors for predator movements. *Conservation Biology*, **13**, 869–881.

Miller, A. W., Reynolds, A. C., Sobrino, A. & Riedel, G. F. (2009). Shellfish face uncertain future in high CO_2 world: Influence of acidification on oyster larvae calcification and growth in estuaries. *PLoS ONE*, **4**, e5661.

Narváez, D. A., Klinck, J. M., Powell, E. N. *et al.* (2012). Circulation and behavior controls on dispersal of eastern oyster (*Crassostrea virginica*) larvae in Delaware Bay. *Journal of Marine Research*, **70**, 411–440.

Nell, J. (2007). *Diseases of Sydney Rock Oysters*. Profitable and Sustainable Primary Industries, Primefact 589. NSW Department of Primary Industries. www.extension.org/sites/default/files/Diseases%20of%20Sydney%20Rock%20Oysters.pdf.

Nelson, K. A., Leonard, L. A., Posey, M. H., Aplin, T. D. & Mallin, M. A. (2004). Using transplanted oyster (*Crassosstrea virginica*) beds to improve water quality in small tidal creeks: A pilot study. *Journal of Experimental Marine Biology and Ecology*, **298**, 347–368.

Nestlerode, J. A., Luckenbach, M. W. & O'Brien, F. X. (2007). Settlement and survival of the oyster *Crassostrea virginica* on created oyster reef habitats in Chesapeake Bay. *Restoration Ecology*, **15**, 273–283.

Newell, R. I. E. (1988). Ecological changes in Chesapeake Bay: Are they the result of overharvesting the American oyster, Crassostrea virginica? In M. P. Lynch & E. C. Krome (eds.), *Understanding the Estuary: Advances in Chesapeake Bay Research*. Solomons, MD: Chesapeake Research Consortium, pp. 536–546.

Newell, R. I. E. (2004). Ecosystem influences of natural and cultivated populations of suspension-feeding bivalve mollusks: A review. *Journal of Shellfish Research*, **23**, 51–61.

Newell, R. I. E. & Koch, E. W. (2004). Modeling seagrass density and distribution in response to changes in turbidity stemming from bivalve filtration and seagrass sediment stabilization. *Estuaries*, **27**, 793–806.

Newell, R. I. E. & Langdon, C. J. (1996). Mechanisms and physiology of larval and adult feeding. In V. S. Kennedy, R. I. E. Newell & A. F. Eble (eds.), *The Eastern*

Oyster Crassostrea virginica. College Park, MD: Maryland Sea Grant College, University of Maryland, pp. 185–229.

Newell, R. I. F., Cornwell, J. C. & Owens, M. S. (2002). Influence of simulated bivalve biodeposition and microphytobenthos on sediment nitrogen dynamics: A laboratory study. *Limnology and Oceanography*, **47**, 1367–1379.

Newell, R. I. E., Fisher, T. R., Holyoke, R. R. & Cornwall, J. C. (2005a). Influence of eastern oysters on nitrogen and phosphorus regeneration in Chesapeake Bay, USA. In R. F. Dame & S. Olenin (eds.), *The Comparative Roles of Suspension Feeders in Ecosystems*. Dordrecht: Springer, pp. 93–120.

Newell, R. I. E., Kennedy, V. S., Manuel, J. L. & Merritt, D. (2005b). *Behavioral Responses of* Crassostrea ariakensis *and* Crassostrea virginica *Larvae to Environmental Change Under Spatially Realistic Conditions*. Final report to Maryland Department of Natural Resources, Annapolis, MD.

North, E. W., King, D. M., Xu, J., *et al.* (2010). Linking optimization and ecological models in a decision support tool for oyster restoration and management. *Ecological Applications*, **20**, 810–866.

NRC, National Research Council. (2004). *Nonnative Oysters in the Chesapeake Bay*. Washington, DC: National Academies Press.

Ogburn, D. M., White, I. & McPhee, D. P. (2007). The disappearance of oyster reefs from eastern Australian estuaries – Impact of colonial settlement or mudworm invasion? *Coastal Management*, **35**, 271–287.

Paerl, H. W., Pinckney, J. L., Fear, J. M. & Peierls, B. L. (1998). Ecosystem responses to internal and watershed organic matter loading: Consequences for hypoxia in the eutrophying Neuse River Estuary, North Carolina, USA. *Marine Ecology Progress Series*, **166**, 17–25.

Peterson, C. H. & Lipcius, R. N. (2003). Conceptual progress towards predicting quantitative ecosystem benefits of ecological restorations. *Marine Ecology Progress Series*, **264**, 297–307.

Peterson, C. H., Grabowski, J. H. & Powers, S. P. (2003). Estimated enhancement of fish production resulting from restoring oyster reef habitat: Quantitative valuation. *Marine Ecology Progress Series*, **264**, 249–264.

Piazza, B. P., Banks, P. D. & La Peyre, M. K. (2005). The potential for created oyster shell reefs as a sustainable shoreline protection strategy in Louisiana. *Restoration Ecology*, **13**, 499–506.

Piehler, M. E. & Smyth, A. R. (2011). Habitat-specific distinctions in estuarine denitrification affect both ecosystem function and services. *Ecosphere*, **2**, art. 12, doi:10.1890/ES10-00082.1.

Plutchak, R., Major, K., Cebrian, J., *et al.* (2010). Impacts of oyster reef restoration on primary productivity and nutrient dynamics in tidal creeks of the north central Gulf of Mexico. *Estuaries and Coasts*, **33**, 1355–1364.

Pollack, J. B., Cleveland, A., Palmer, T. A., Reisinger, A. S. & Montagna, P. A. (2012). A restoration suitability index model for the eastern oyster (*Crassostrea virginica*) in the Mission-Aransas Estuary, TX, USA. *PLoS ONE*, **7**, e40839.

Powell, E. N. & Klinck, J. M. (2007). Is oyster shell a sustainable resource? *Journal of Shellfish Research*, **26**, 181–194.

Powell, E. N., Klinck, J. M., Guo, X., *et al.* (2012). Can oysters *Crassostrea virginica* develop resistance to Dermo Disease in the field: The impediment posed by climate change. *Journal of Marine Research*, **70**, 309–355.

Powers, S. P., Peterson, C. H., Grabowski, J. H. & Lenihan, H. S. (2009). Success of constructed oyster reefs in no-harvest sanctuaries: Implications for restoration. *Marine Ecology Progress Series*, **389**, 159–170.

Pritchard, D. W. (1967). What is an estuary: Physical standpoint. In G. H. Lauff (ed.), *Estuaries*. Washington, DC: American Association for the Advancement of Science, Publication 83, pp. 3–5.

Quan, W., Zhu, J., Ni, Y., Shi, L. & Chen, Y. (2009). Faunal utilization of constructed intertidal oyster (*Crassostrea rivularis*) reef in the Yangtze River Estuary, China. *Ecological Engineering*, **35**, 1466–1475.

Quan, W., Humphries, A., Shen, X. & Chen, Y. (2012). Oyster and associated benthic macrofaunal development on a created intertidal oyster (*Crassostrea ariakensis*) reef in the Yangtze River Estuary, China. *Journal of Shellfish Research*, **31**, 599–610.

Richardson, C. A., Seed, R., Alroumaihim, E. M. H. & McDonald, L. (1993). Distribution, shell growth and predation of the New Zealand oyster, *Tiostrea* (=*Ostrea*) *lutaria* Hutton, in the Menai Strait, North Wales. *Journal of Shellfish Research*, **12**, 207–214.

Rodney, W. S. & Paynter, K. T. (2006). Comparisons of macrofaunal asemblages on restored and non-restored oyster reefs in mesohaline regions of Chesapeake Bay in Maryland. *Journal of Experimental Marine Biology and Ecology*, **335**, 39–51.

Rossi-Snook, K., Ozbay, G. & Marenghi, F. (2010). Oyster (*Crassostrea virginica*) gardening program for restoration in Delaware's inland bays, USA. *Aquaculture International*, **18**, 61–67.

Rothschild, B. J., Ault, J. S., Goulletquer, P. & Heral, M. (1994). Decline of the Chesapeake Bay oyster population: A century of habitat destruction and overfishing. *Marine Ecology Progress Series*, **111**, 29–39.

Ruesink, J. L., Lenihan, H. S., Trimble, A. C., *et al.* (2005). Introduction of non-native oysters: Ecosystem effects and restoration implications. *Annual Review of Ecology, Evolution and Systematics*, **36**, 643–689.

Schulte, D. M., Burke, R. P. & Lipcius, R. N. (2009). Unprecedented restoration of a native oyster metapopulation. *Science*, **325**, 1124–1128.

Seaman, W. (2007). Artificial habitats and the restoration of degraded marine ecosystems and fisheries. *Hydrobiologia*, **580**, 143–155.

Shervette, V. R. & Gelwick, F. (2008). Seasonal and spatial variations in fish and macroinvertebrate communities of oyster and adjacent habitats in a Mississippi estuary. *Estuaries and Coasts*, **31**, 584–596.

Shumway, S. E. (1996). Natural environmental factors. In V. S. Kennedy, R. I. E. Newell & A. F. Eble (eds.), *The Eastern Oyster* Crassostrea virginica. College Park, MD: Maryland Sea Grant College, University of Maryland, pp. 467–513.

Smith, G. F., Bruce D. G., Roach, E. B., *et al.* (2005). Assessment of recent habitat conditions of eastern oyster *Crassostrea virginica* bars in mesohaline Chesapeake Bay. *North American Journal of Fisheries Management*, **25**, 1569–1590.

Smith, K. A., North, E. W., Shi, F., *et al.* (2009). Modeling the effects of oyster reefs and breakwaters on seagrass growth. *Estuaries and Coasts*, **32**, 748–757.

Society for Ecological Restoration International, SER. (2004). *SER International Primer on Ecological Restoration*. SERI Science and Policy Working Group. Washington, DC: SER.

Soniat, T. M. & Burton, G. M. (2005). A comparison of the effectiveness of sandstone and limestone as cultch for oysters, *Crassostrea virginica*. *Journal of Shellfish Research*, **24**, 483–485.

Soniat, T. M., Broadhurst, R. C. & Haywood, III, E. L. (1991). Alternatives to clamshell as cultch oysters, and the use of gypsum for the production of cultchless oysters. *Journal of Shellfish Research*, **10**, 405–410.

Starke, A., Levinton, J. S. & Doall, M. (2011). Restoration of *Crassostrea virginica* (Gmelin) to the Hudson River, USA: A spatiotemporal modeling approach. *Journal of Shellfish Research*, **30**, 671–684.

Stokes, S., Wunderink, S., Lowe, M. & Gereffi, G. (2012). *Restoring Gulf Oyster Reefs: Opportunities for Innovation*. Durham, NC: Duke Center on Globalization, Governance, and Competitiveness, Duke University. www.cggc.duke.edu/pdfs/CGGC_Oyster-Reef-Restoration.pdf.

Summerhayes, S. A., Bishop, M. J., Leigh, A. & Kelaher, B. P. (2009). Effects of oyster death and shell disarticulation on associated communities. *Journal of Experimental Marine Biology and Ecology*, **379**, 60–67.

Tallman, J. C. & Forrester, G. E. (2007). Oyster grow-out cages function as artificial reefs for temperate fishes. *Transactions of the American Fisheries Society*, **136**, 790–799.

Tamburri, M. N., Zimmer-Faust, R. K. & Tamplin, M. L. (1992). Natural sources and properties of chemical inducers mediating settlement of oyster larvae: A re-examination. *Biological BulletinI*, **183**, 327–338.

Taylor, J. & Bushek, D. (2008). Intertidal oyster reefs can persist and function in a temperate North American Atlantic estuary. *Marine Ecology Progress Series*, **361**, 301–306.

Thompson, R. J., Newell, R. I. E., Kennedy, V. S. & Mann, R. (1996). Reproductive processes and early development. In V. S. Kennedy, R. I. E. Newell & A. F. Eble (eds.), *The Eastern Oyster* Crassostrea virginica. College Park, MD: Maryland Sea Grant College, University of Maryland, pp. 335–370.

Tolley, S. G. & Volety, A. K. (2005). The role of oysters in habitat use of oyster reefs by resident fishes and decapod crustaceans. *Journal of Shellfish Research*, **24**, 1007–1012.

Valero, A. L. & Caballero, Y. Q. (2003). *A Practitioner's Guide for the Culture of Marine Bivalves in the Colombian Caribbean Sea: Pearly Oysters, Oysters, and Scallops*. Serie de Documentos Generales, no. 10. Invemar Cargraphics.

Venice System. (1959). Symposium on the classification of brackish waters, Venice, April 8–14, 1958. *Archivio di Oceanografia e Limnologia*, **11**(Suppl.), 1–248.

Virvilis, C. & Angelidis, P. (2006). Presence of the parasite *Marteilia* sp. in the flat oyster (*Ostrea edulis* L.) in Greece. *Aquaculture*, **259**, 1–5.

Volety, A. K., Barnes, T., Pearlstine, L. & Mazzoti, F. (2005). Habitat suitability index model for the American oyster, *Crassostrea virginica:* Implications for restoration and enhancement of oysters in SW Florida estuaries. *8th International Conference on Shellfish Restoration*. Brest, France.

Wall, C. C., Peterson, B. J. & Gobler, C. J. (2008). Facilitation of seagrass *Zostera marina* productivity by suspension-feeding bivalves. *Marine Ecology Progress Series*, **357**, 165–174.

Wall, L. M. (2004). Recruitment and restoration of the oyster *Crassostrea virginica* in areas with intense boating activity in Mosquito Lagoon, Florida. Master's thesis, University of South Central Florida, Orlando, FL.

Wall, L. M., Walters, L. J., Grizzle, R. E. & Sacks, P. E. (2005). Recreational boating activity on the recruitment and survival of the oyster *Crassostrea virginica* on intertidal reefs in Mosquito Lagoon, Florida. *Journal of Shellfish Research*, **24**, 965–973.

Wang, Z., Haidvogel, D., Bushek, D., *et al.* (2012). Circulation and water properties and their relationship to the oyster disease, MSX, in Delaware Bay. *Journal of Marine Research*, **70**, 279–308.

Waycott, M., Duarte, C. M., Carruthers, T. J. B, *et al.* (2009). Accelerating loss of seagrasses across the globe threatens coastal ecosystems. *Proceedings of the National Academy of Sciences of the United States of America*, **106**, 12377–12381.

Whitman, E. R. & Reidenbach, M. A. (2012). Benthic flow environments affect recruitment of *Crassostrea virginica* larvae to an intertidal oyster reef. *Marine Ecology Progress Series*, **463**, 177–191.

Wilberg, M. J., Livings, M. E., Barkman, J. S., Morris, B. T. & Robinson, J.M. (2011). Overfishing, disease, habitat loss, and potential extirpation of oysters in upper Chesapeake Bay. *Marine Ecology Progress Series*, **436**, 131–144.

Wintermyer, M. L. & Cooper, J. M. (2003). Dioxin/furan and polychlorinated biphenyl concentrations in eastern oyster (*Crassostrea virginica*, Gmelin) tissues and the effects on egg fertilization and development. *Journal of Shellfish Research*, **22**, 737–746.

Worm, B., Barbier, E. B., Beaumont, N., *et al.* (2006). Impacts of biodiversity loss on ocean ecosystem services. *Science*, **314**, 787–790.

Zimmer-Faust, R. K. & Tamburri, M. (1994). Chemical identity and ecological implications of a waterborne, larval settlement cue. *Limnology and Oceanography*, **39**, 1075–1087.

Zu Ermgasson, P. S. E., Spalding, M. D., Grizzle, R. E. & Brumbaugh, R. D. (2013). Quantifying the loss of a marine ecosystem service: Filtration by the eastern oyster in US estuaries. *Estuaries and Coasts*, **36**, 36–43.

6

Biodiversity status of coastal dune forests in South Africa

RUDI J. VAN AARDE, ROBERT A. R. GULDEMOND, AND
PIETER I. OLIVIER

INTRODUCTION

People tend to settle close to the sea and hence place disproportionate pressure on coastlines and associated habitats, such as dune forests. Dune forests, by definition, are limited to a narrow belt along a coastline. Edge effects, area limitations, isolation, and the ebb and flow of climatic conditions accentuate the sensitivity of dune forests to human-made disturbances, which may put extraordinary pressures on the species living within them. This also holds for South Africa, where some 20 million people (40% of the population) live within 100 km of the coast (Department of Environmental Affairs, http://www.environ ment.gov.za/). Associated economic development and reliance on natural resources transform and fragment coastal landscapes and bring about habitat loss that may challenge the persistence of species (Arthurton *et al.*, 2006).

Coastal forests in South Africa are relatively young (Lawes, 1990), harbor few endemic species (van Wyk & Smith, 2001), are naturally fragmented and embedded in matrices of contrasting landscapes (Berliner, 2009). By designation, coastal forests are sensitive to disturbance, but relatively high ecological resilience provides for their potential to recover following the withdrawal of these stressors (van Aarde *et al.*, 1996; Wassenaar *et al.*, 2005; Grainger *et al.*, 2011). Protecting or restoring dune forests to meet conservation targets or to regain ecosystem services makes sense but calls for an evaluation of the prevailing status, as well as identifying the threats and opportunities related to aspects of their biological diversity. We address these issues here.

DEFINING SOUTH AFRICA'S DUNE FORESTS

The 3650-km long South African coastline runs from Namibia in the west to Mozambique in the east (Figure 6.1). This coastline is exposed to different

Coastal Conservation, eds B. Maslo and J. L. Lockwood. Published by Cambridge University Press.

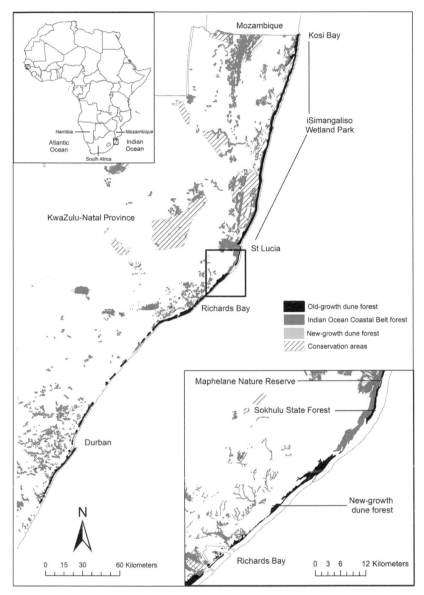

Figure 6.1 New- and old-growth dune forests are situated at the northern end of the South African east coast. The iSimangaliso Wetland Park, stretching from Kosi Bay in the north to the Maphelane Nature Reserve in the south, is the largest area that formally protects dune forests. We have been conducting structured ecological surveys for some 20 years in the new-growth forests north of Richards Bay and old-growth forests in the Sokhulu State Forests. (See color plate section.)

climatic and ecological conditions due to the cold Agulhas and warmer Benguela oceanic systems. The western coastline has an arid climate and contains no forests. Along the southern and eastern seaboards of South Africa one may find forests due to a more temperate and subtropical climate that sometimes extends to the hinterland across the mountain ranges and coastal plains (Mucina & Rutherford, 2006). Only 7% of terrestrial South Africa is climatically suitable for forests, yet as a biome forests account for < 0.6% of the country (Low & Rebelo, 1996; Mucina & Rutherford, 2006).

Forests in South Africa are fragmented, and most of the patches are very small (< 100 ha; Berliner, 2009), most likely due to climate conditions and fire over millennia (Geldenhuys, 1992; Eeley et al., 1999). Forests in South Africa also have a wide distribution and are surrounded either by the Fynbos, Savanna, Grassland, Albany Thicket or the Indian Ocean Coastal Belt biomes (Mucina & Rutherford, 2006). Subsequently, different types of forests are recognized within the forest biome, and often a certain patch may be given a different name by authors that use different criteria to classify them (i.e. Lubke et al., 1997; Midgley et al., 1997; von Maltitz et al., 2003).

Broadly, South Africa harbors two main forest types, Afromontane and the Indian Ocean Coastal Belt (IOCB) Forests, with an intermediate Coastal Scarp Forest located between the two groups (Lawes et al., 2004). Dune forests fall entirely within the IOCB and account for 2.5% of the total forested areas in South Africa (Berliner, 2009). The IOCB covers a narrow strip (< 10 to ~35 km wide) along the 800 km long eastern seaboard of the Indian Ocean. It extends south from southern Mozambique through KwaZulu-Natal and into the Eastern Cape Province (Mucina & Rutherford, 2006; see Figure 2.1). This biome forms the southernmost example of the East African Tropical Coastal Forest, which extends northwards along the Mozambican, Tanzanian, Kenyan, and southern Somalian coastlines, where forests generally have a larger inland extent than those seen in South Africa (Burgess & Clarke, 2000). Other forest types in the IOCB biome include coastal lowland, mangrove, riparian, sand, scarp, and swamp forests (Mucina & Rutherford, 2006). These ecotypes differ from dune forests and from each other in species composition, recruitment and regeneration patterns, as well as in their evolutionary history; and at ~20 000 years of age are at least twice as old as dune forests (Lawes, 1990). Only dune forests are exclusively situated within the coastal zone, whereas the other forests may also be found further inland.

The climate of the Holocene interglacial period provides for the typical tropical affinity of the IOCB biome (Lawes et al., 2007). The southbound shift of the Intertropical Convergence Zone and the weakening of the high-pressure system due to heating of the land surface cause humid air to flow toward the southern parts of Africa during the austral summers (Tyson, 1986; Lawes, 1990). These weather systems and the proximity of the warm Agulhas Current close to the eastern coastline enable tropical conditions to persist along this coastline at relatively high latitudes (Mucina & Rutherford, 2006).

The weather of the IOCB gradually changes from north to south along the coast. In summer, the northern parts tend to be relatively hot and humid but less so toward the southern regions. Winters are mild in the north and relatively cold in the south. Frost is seldom recorded, and rainfall is fairly consistent across the biome at around 1200 mm per year (Mucina & Rutherford, 2006). Rain falls throughout the year in the northern parts of the biome, but mostly during the summer months in the southern regions.

Dune forests are situated on porous and leached sand deposits left by a regressing Indian Ocean during the end of the last glacial period 8000– 10 000 years ago (Tinley, 1985). Strong winds during arid periods blew these dunes into a characteristic parabolic shape and rolling topography (von Maltitz *et al.*, 2003). The dunes run parallel to the shoreline and vary in height from a few meters closer to the high-water mark to ~80 m further inland with the highest vegetated dune exceeding 180 m (Tinley, 1985).

It follows that dune forests by their fragmented nature, location, and relatively young age may be disturbance-prone, especially in the presence of climate change-associated disruptions that are becoming typical of coastlines throughout the world (i.e. Klein & Nicholls, 1999). The extraordinary variety of species associated with these forests, their associations with other biomes, and restrictions imposed by ecological realities are best understood by considering biodiversity at the three popular levels of academic endeavor – species, habitats, and processes.

SPECIES

Vegetation

A South African dune forest consists of well-developed tree, shrub, and herb layers. In general, a dune forest is rich in plant species and has a canopy of 12–15 m in height (Ferreira & van Aarde, 2000; Mucina & Rutherford, 2006). The understory is usually between 0.2 and 2 m high with a litter layer that provides niche space for a variety of biological activity, although soils here tend to be relatively poor in minerals and somewhat acidic (van Aarde *et al.*, 1998; Ferreira & van Aarde, 2000, Kumssa *et al.*, 2004).

Non-deciduous trees, such as coastal red milkwood (*Mimusops caffra*), white milkwood (*Sideroxylon inerme*), white pear (*Apodytes dimidiata*), natal apricot (*Dovyalis longispina*), and quar (*Psydrax obovata*) are some of the more common species in the tree canopy layer (Mucina & Rutherford, 2006). The sweet thorn (*Acacia karroo*), a widespread deciduous pioneer tree species, dominates in disturbed as well as new-growth forests < 50 years old (van Aarde *et al.*, 1996). Coastal silver oak (*Brachylaena discolour*), bush tick berry (*Chrysanthemoides monilifera*), and forest num-num (*Carissa bispinosa*) are also frequently found in the understory, while the herbaceous layer is sometimes dominated by buckweed (*Isoglossa woodii*), Chinese violet (*Asystasia gangetica*), and wart ferns (*Microsorum scolopendria*) (Grainger, 2011). Herbaceous and woody vines, such as dwaba-berry (*Monanthotaxis caffra*), Cape grape (*Rhoicissus tomentosa*), and coastal currant (*Searsia nebulosa*), add to the structure of dune forests (Mucina & Rutherford, 2006).

We have identified 85 species of tree (woody plants > 1.7 m high) and 56 species of herbaceous plants over 18 years of research in two patches of old-growth dune forests (Sokhulu State Forest and Maphelane Nature Reserve; Figure 6.1). Four tree species were very common and accounted for > 75% of the cumulative mean abundance, 6 were common (50–74%) and 13 were rare (25–49%), whereas no less than 62 tree species were very rare and accounted for < 25% (Table 6.1).

We considered the most typical species in old-growth dune forests as those that contributed more than 50% to the mean cumulative abundance (very common and common species defined above). Dominant species in the tree community include understory trees, such as the large-leaf dragon tree (*Dracaena aletriformis*) and black bird-berry (*Psychotria capensis*), as well as subcanopy and canopy species, such as the acorn jackal-berry (*Diospyros natalensis*), African coca-tree (*Erythroxylum emarginatum*), Zulu cherry-orange

Table 6.1 *The number of species of trees, herbs, millipedes, and birds in each cumulative abundance quartile recorded over 18 years in two patches of old-growth dune forests in the Sokhulu State Forest and Maphelane Nature Reserve. Information extracted from Grainger (2011).*

	Very common	Common	Rare	Very rare
Cumulative abundance	> 75%	> 50–74%	> 25–49%	< 25%
Trees	4	6	13	62
Herbs	1	4	6	45
Millipedes	1	1	2	12
Birds	3	6	8	70

(*Teclea gerrardii*), natal ironplum (*Drypetes natalensis*), sea guarri (*Euclea race-mosa* subsp. *sinuate*), dune soap-berry (*Deinbollia oblongifolia*), poison olive (*Peddiea africana*), and giant pock ironwood (*Chionanthus peglerae*).

For the herbaceous community, dominant species include the patchily distributed buckweed, which is characteristic of dune forest throughout our study region and further north (Ferreira & van Aarde, 2000; Griffiths *et al.*, 2010). Other species include large forest asparagus (*Asparagus falcatus*), river nettle (*Laportea peduncularis*), and forest burr (*Pupalia lappacea*). The climber Bloubokkietou (*Pyrenacantha scandens*) is also a common species in old-growth dune forests. Importantly, however, none of the tree and herb species that we recorded in the old-growth dune forests are considered endemic, and they may also be found in other forest types or adjacent savanna and grassland (Grainger, 2011).

In some places, the vegetation on coastal dunes closely follows progression and erosion of sand from beaches (Lubke *et al.*, 1997). Pioneer communities on lower dune ridges close to the high-water mark often are dominated by inkberry (*Scaevolia plumieri*) (Peter *et al.*, 2003), while grasses, such as coastal rat-tail grass (*Sporobolus virginicus*) and blady grass (*Imperata cylindrical*) and the forb, *Helichrysum asperum*, colonize areas behind these dune ridges. Sands behind the foredunes are dominated by woody scrubs, such as big num-num (*Carissa macrocarpa*). Bush clumps establish further away from the shoreline and are eventually followed by dune forests where tall trees dominate; deterministic observations posit this as an alternative successional pathway of regenerating dune forests to the one described below (Avis, 1992; Lubke *et al.*, 1992a).

On most sand dunes natural and made-made disturbances are followed by ecological succession characterized by a directional progression when senescent pioneer trees (mainly sweet thorn) are replaced by secondary species typical of old-growth dune forests (Grainger & van Aarde, 2012a). Consequently, the present cordon of dune forest comprises patches of varying sizes that represent different seral stages ranging in age from a few years to ~80 years old. Physiognomically older patches represent old-growth dune forests, and our recent assessment suggests that there may be 191 of these patches along the eastern coastline (Olivier *et al.*, 2013).

Vertebrates
Mammals
Some 15% of the 295 mammals listed for southern Africa may occur in dune forests, but these species mainly occur in adjacent forests, savanna,

and grasslands (Skinner & Smithers, 1990). We have recorded 28 mammal species over a period of 18 years in both new- and old-growth dune forests. Large herbivores are mostly absent, whereas bushbuck (*Tragelaphus scriptus*), bushpig (*Potamochoerus porcus*), and red duiker (*Cephalophus natalensis*) are the most prevalent mesoherbivores (Boyes *et al.*, 2011). Rodents and shrews are widely distributed in dune forests, and their numbers vary greatly across space and time (Ferreira & van Aarde, 2000). Early successional stages of new-growth forests are dominated by widespread generalists, such as the multimammate mouse (*Mastomys natalensis*) and the pouched mouse (*Saccostomus campestris*), while later stages provide for forest specialists, such as the red veld rat (*Aethomys chrysophilus*) and Angoni vlei rat (*Otomys angoniensis*), albeit always occurring in low numbers (Ferreira & van Aarde, 2000).

Species living in dune forests that are considered important to conservation in South Africa include a subspecies of Samango monkey (*Cercopethicus mitis erythrarchus*), endemic to South Africa and living mainly in protected areas (Boyes *et al.*, 2011). The forest shrew (*Myosorex sclateri*) and four-toed elephant shrew (*Petrodromus tetradactylus*) are listed as endangered due to habitat loss, while the tree hyrax (*Dendrohyrax arboreus*), blue duiker (*Philantomba monticola*), and suni (*Neotragus moschatus zuluensis*) are listed as vulnerable species due to habitat loss or the bush meat trade (Friedman & Daly, 2004).

Birds

Dune forests support many birds, and we have recorded at least 135 species. The number of species noted annually since 1993 ranges from 39 to 90 species per survey. Birds of the region appear sensitive to landscape-level disturbance, and assemblages in exotic plantations and patches of grasslands (some transient and an apparent seral stage of dune forest succession) differ from those of new- and old-growth dune forests (see Niemand, 2001). Forest succession has cascading effects on relative abundances, species richness, and number of guilds, all of which increase with regeneration age (Kritzinger, 1996). However, the lack of suitable nesting places and a well-developed undergrowth may still inhibit specialist forest species from colonizing new-growth dune forests (Kritzinger & van Aarde, 1998).

Based on the cumulative abundances calculated from structured transect surveys in old-growth dune forests (Table 6.1), only the yellow-bellied greenbul (*Chlorocichla falviventris*), green-backed camaroptera (*Camaroptera brachyura*), and the collared sunbird (*Hedydipna collaris*) are considered very common. Six species are common and include yellow-breasted apalis

(*Apalis flavida*), dark-backed weaver (*Ploceus bicolour*), terrestrial brownbul (*Phyllastrephus terrestris*), black-backed puffback (*Dryoscopus cubla*), eastern olive sunbird (*Cyanomitra olivacea*), and the yellow-rumped tinkerbird (*Pogoniulus bilineatus*). Eight bird species are considered rare, and an additional 70 species are considered very rare. None of the birds we recorded are restricted to dune forests, and they may also occur in other forest types or adjacent savanna, woodlands, and grasslands.

Only some of the very rare bird species are of special conservation concern. Dune forests provide winter habitat for the endangered spotted ground thrush (*Zoothera guttata*), an altitudinal migrant that has experienced extensive range reduction. Three other birds, the eastern bronze-naped pigeon (*Columba delegorguei*), mangrove kingfisher (*Halcyon senegaloides*), and southern-banded snake eagle (*Circaetus fasciolatus*), living in dune forests are also considered vulnerable (Barnes, 2000).

Reptiles

Based on the South African Reptile Conservation Assessment (http://sarca. adu.org.za), approximately 10% of the 480 species of reptiles listed for southern Africa may occur in dune forests. We have recorded 19 of these during fieldwork on other taxa. The Setaro's dwarf chameleon (*Bradypodion setaroi*) was previously thought to be a South African endemic and was listed as endangered due to a relatively limited distribution and the threat of habitat loss. However, the IUCN now lists it as Least Concern, as much of its distribution is under formal protection (IUCN, 2012). The Gaboon adder (*Bitis gabonica*) has recently been afforded special protective status in South Africa in response to excessive collection for the illegal pet trade. Moreover, and although not directly linked with dune forests per se, sand dunes above the high-tide level provide nesting places for leatherback (*Dermochelys coriacea*) and loggerhead turtles (*Caretta caretta*) (Branch, 1998).

Amphibians

The "Maputaland amphibian assemblage", which includes the low-lying coastal areas of KwaZulu-Natal, has more species of frogs than any other biogeographic area surveyed during the South African Frog Atlas Project in 2004. On average, 30 species were recorded per half-degree grid cell (Minter *et al.*, 2004). Forests along the east coast provide ideal habitat for amphibians and may explain why this region has been identified as a diversity hotspot and region of high endemism for amphibians (Measey, 2011). We have recorded 23 frog species in dune forests during surveys on other taxa, including the endangered Pickersgill's reed frog (*Hyperolius pickersgilli*), which is considered an endemic species to the region.

Invertebrates

Dune forests are rich in invertebrates, and systematic or ecological studies in new- and old-growth dune forests include those done on ants (Majer & de Kock, 1992), coleopteran beetles (van Aarde *et al.*, 1996), dung beetles (Davis *et al.*, 2003), millipedes (Redi *et al.*, 2005), soil invertebrates (Kumssa *et al.*, 2004), and spiders (Dippenaar-Schoeman & Wassenaar, 2002, 2006). Transient and successional vegetation changes that develop either in response to rehabilitation, or spontaneously following disturbances, provide for colonization by a variety of invertebrate taxa (van Aarde *et al.*, 1996; Davis *et al.*, 2003; Redi *et al.*, 2005; Wassenaar *et al.*, 2005). Similar to the other taxa, dune forests have no endemic invertebrate species. For instance, we have recorded 21 millipede species to date in new- and old-growth forests, but these also occur in adjoining forests and woodland habitats. Using structured survey data, a similar pattern to other taxa in species assemblage is prevalent for millipedes (Table 6.1), with 1 very common and 1 common species, 2 rare species, and 12 very rare species. Only one of the two millipede species listed as endangered for our study region, the Zululand black millipede (*Doratogonus zuluensis*), has been recorded during our survey work.

SPATIAL GRADIENTS IN SPECIES COMPOSITION AND RICHNESS

Species richness tends to decline from the lower tropical toward the higher temperate latitudes (Gaston, 2000). Geldenhuys (1992) demonstrated a trend of decreasing floristic diversity from north to south for both inland and coastal forests in South Africa. Similarly, Lawes and colleagues (2007) described a southward decrease in species richness for birds, frogs, and butterflies in coastal forests. However, this pattern is complicated by the close relationship between the coastline and the hinterland where an exchange of coastal species and the adjacent habitats may account for the high species richness observed in dune forests (Lawes, 1990; Lawes *et al.*, 2007).

Notably, some species reach their northernmost distribution along dune forests in South Africa, such as the tree hyrax, brown scrub robin (*Cercotrichas signata*), red-fronted tinkerbird (*Pogoniulus pusillus*), and natal tree frog (*Leptopelis natalensis*). Dune forest also has a close affinity with the tropics further north in Africa (Burgess & Clarke, 2000), and several species are at the southern end of their distributional range. Examples here include thick-tailed bushbaby (*Otolemur crassicaudatus*), Livingstone's turaco (*Tauraco livingstonii*), Gaboon adder, Setaro's dwarf chameleon, violet worm lizard (*Zygaspis violacea*), and the sand peawood (*Craibia zimmermannii*).

The role played by dune forests when these species disperse or during the processes that shape community structures has not been adequately assessed. Taking into account the recognized degree of local variation in habitat types and species distribution across the region, it would be unwise to interpret local patterns and processes without considering dune forests' role within a regional context. Local scale is important, especially considering the responses of species to natural and human-induced disturbances.

In some places along the coast, the continuous supply of sand through wave action allows for new coastal habitats to develop (Tinley, 1985). These habitats are colonized by pioneer species at the start of a successional process toward maturely developed thicket or forest communities (Weisser *et al.*, 1982). Species richness, cover, stature, and biomass increase as succession progresses, but early seral stages do not support forest specialists, which only reside in later stages (Grainger & van Aarde, 2012a). Senescence of the dominant pioneer sweet thorn trees leaves gaps in the canopy, which are colonized by secondary pioneer species, such as white stinkwood (*Celtis africana*) and coastal red milkwood, that are also typical of canopy gaps in old-growth dune forest (Grainger & van Aarde, 2013). Canopy gaps in new-growth dune forests, therefore, do not reset succession but rather are a critical factor in the regeneration of dune forests.

HABITAT AND LANDSCAPE REALITIES

Geographic and ecological realities render dune forests both distinctive and sensitive to regional dynamics and local disturbance. Dune forests are narrow and consequently exposed to edge effects, the intensity of which depends on how dune forests differ from the adjoining wetlands, grasslands, savanna, other forest types, stands of exotic plantations or sugar cane fields and stretches dominated by informal urban developments. Species from different adjoining habitats may structure dune forest assemblages, some of which originate from the hinterland or from along the coast, most notably the more tropical coastal forests to the north and the temperate forests to the south.

Given this landscape perspective, dune forests comprise a collection of species assembled from three or more habitat types that existed prior to relatively recent climate conditions (6000–8000 years ago) that were

Table 6.2 *Number of tree, mammal, bird, reptile, and amphibian species in dune forests that may also be found in adjoining habitats from the hinterland (savanna, grasslands, and wetlands), other forest types (Afromontane, mangrove, riparian, sand, scarp, and swamp forests), or are at the extreme of their northern or southernmost coastal distributional ranges in South Africa.*

Taxon[†]	Adjoining habitat	Other forest types	Northernmost distributional range	Southernmost distributional range
Trees	122	24	16	21
Mammals	26	1	2	4
Birds	105	19	8	3
Reptiles	19	0	0	3
Amphibians	18	1	0	4

[†]The numbers of tree and bird species are from records collected during our structured surveys over 18 years in new- and old-growth dune forests north of Richards Bay, South Africa. Reptile and amphibian numbers are incidental species records during the same period. Mammal records include 28 species that we have seen in dune forests and 5 more listed in Skinner and Smithers (1990).

conducive to dune forest development. A dune forest may be a meeting ground of species that are typical of other habitats, which can either withstand, or are favored by, the subtropical weather conditions. This idea seems to find support in many species that live in dune forests and also occur either in adjoining savanna, grasslands, wetlands in the hinterland, or other forest types in the region, or are at the extremes of their coastal distributional ranges (Table 6.2).

Dune forests also mark the edge of the distributional range of several hinterland species, and these may occur in numbers well below those recorded in their core distributional ranges (see Caughley & Sinclair, 1994). In addition, the peninsular effect dictates a decrease in species number from the base to the extreme of the peninsula (Simpson, 1964). From this pattern, we can expect dune forest assemblages to comprise forest specialists at the extreme of their tropical northern or temperate southern distributional ranges, and generalists typical of savanna and grasslands (Table 6.2). It then follows that assemblages in dune forests are made up of a few common generalists and many apparent rare species, a prediction supported by the summary information in Table 6.1. Collectively, these species contribute to the richness of dune forests and may play an important but yet undetermined role in the persistence of assemblages in the greater landscape mosaic.

The proximity of dune forests to a variety of other habitats and the expected large species pool in its vicinity accommodates species that can fill niches where dune forests were disturbed. This pattern may explain the relatively fast rate of ecological succession that marks post-disturbance regeneration of dune forest (see Wassenaar *et al.*, 2005; Grainger & van Aarde, 2012a). Post-disturbance areas of new-growth dune forests represent a collection of transient habitat and include life forms typical for savanna, shrublands, and grasslands. The rate at which some of these species colonize is a function of landscape features, such as area, distance, and edge, whereas others are driven by local habitat conditions generated during the aging of new-growth forests (Grainger *et al.*, 2011). This element adds to the adaptive capacity of dune forests to change and may ease regeneration after natural or human-induced disturbances. In part, it also may explain the persistence and resilience of dune forests despite their exposure to a long history of disturbance.

The structure, composition, and connectivity of the heterogeneous landscape clearly have strong effects on ecological processes, diversity, and composition of species in dune forests (Grainger *et al.*, 2011). However, dispersal and recruitment limitation may interfere with natural successional processes (Boyes *et al.*, 2011). The success of plant dispersal in dune forests, for example, is limited by distance (isolation effects) and dispersal vector availability (Grainger, 2011; Grainger *et al.*, 2011).

THREATS

Dune forests have been subjected to intense exploitation by people for ~1600 years dating back to the Iron Age (Feely, 1980); since the arrival of Europeans to the region, 70% of dune forests along KwaZulu-Natal coastline have been lost (Olivier *et al.*, 2013). Current figures suggest that 56% of dune forests are transformed, with commercial plantations serving as the biggest contributor, representing 17% of the total area (Berliner, 2005).

Forests here experience some of the highest population pressures in the country with an estimated density of 60 people per hectare living within a 5-km radius of forest patches (Berliner, 2009). Three important exotic invasive plants for the region, triffid weed (*Chromolaena odorata*), lantana (*Lantana camara*), and common guava (*Psidium guajava*), proliferate in areas where people live. The increased population pressure linked to peri-urban and urban development may also degrade dune forests directly due to timber and fuelwood extraction, overexploitation of plants and animals for food and traditional medicines, and land clearance for agriculture, housing, commercial plantations, and mining (Lawes *et al.*, 2004). The loss of ecosystem services, such as protection from rough seas and storms, erosion control, water catchment and purification, and carbon sequestration may in turn threaten people that depend on dune forests for their livelihoods (Barbier *et al.*, 2011).

The modification of wetlands, grasslands, and savanna woodlands adjacent to dune forests may also have direct effects on dune forest persistence and development. For instance, if savanna woodlands rather than sugar cane fields surround forest fragments, woodland birds that also occur in dune forests may benefit from the woodland structure when dispersing, whereas a homogeneous and treeless landscape may inhibit such movements. Dune forest fragments may therefore become more isolated due to changes in the surrounding landscape. Furthermore, habitat modification may result from high levels of herbivory by cattle and other herbivores, arresting succession through differential mortality of seedlings (Boyes *et al.*, 2011). Exposure to disturbed surrounding habitats also increases the probability of invasive plants colonizing dune forests, which may also change natural successional processes (Lubke, 2004; Grainger & van Aarde, 2012a).

CONSERVATION

Dune forests in South Africa fall within a biodiversity hotspot and are situated at the southern end of the Maputaland Centre of Endemism (van Wyk & Smith, 2001; Küper *et al.*, 2004). These forests may be valued for their role in conservation, especially for Maputaland-endemic species that tend to have a limited distribution and are consequently sensitive to habitat loss and fragmentation (see Guldemond & van Aarde, 2010). Coastal dunes are also excessively exposed to anthropogenic disturbances, such as tourism-related development and mineral extraction (Lubke *et al.*, 1992b). Furthermore, their geographic location in relatively high rainfall regions makes them suitable for commercial forestry, placing even more pressure through the establishment of non-native plantations.

The relatively high diversity, but lack of endemism within dune forests themselves could be due to their relatively young age and recent expansion (Lawes *et al.*, 2007), which provided little evolutionary time for the development of unique species or subspecies (McLachlan, 1991). However, the near lack of known endemic species (except for possibly some millipede species) should not detract from the conservation importance of dune forests.

The protection of dune forests in isolation of other habitat types may lead to misplaced conservation initiatives, especially when considering that these forests and adjoining habitats collectively may provide for the spatial structuring of species populations. Such populations may operate either as a classical metapopulation, partially connected, or a mainland-island system (Olivier *et al.*, 2009). Within this paradigm, dune forests function either as a source or a sink, but mostly as the latter. The persistence of dune forests therefore depends on their continuing connectivity to source populations to allow for dispersal through which assemblages are maintained or may regenerate following disturbance (Olivier *et al.*, 2013). This postulate finds support in our modeling of spatial occupancy, illustrating that the presence of more than half of the tree and bird species in new-growth forests can be explained by landscape parameters such as edge, isolation, and area, while patch age explains the presence of the remaining species in these taxa (Grainger *et al.*, 2011).

Furthermore, Trimble and van Aarde (2011) recorded a precipitous decline in richness and population numbers of nearly 60% of bird species in new- and old-growth dune forests over the last two decades, possibly due to regional forces because species with wide ranges declined more rapidly than those with narrow ranges. Dune forests do not function in isolation, but rather are part of a regional landscape that collectively responds to disturbances and provides for the persistence of both local and regional species pools (see Fairbanks *et al.*, 2001). We subscribe to incentives that seek to encapsulate a range of landscapes to conserve not only species, but also a variety of habitats and linkages between landscapes, to ensure the persistence of ecological processes. Fortunately, some conservation incentives are in place and others are in various stages of development.

Just over 36% of dune forests along the coastline from Kosi Bay in KwaZulu-Natal to the Kei River Mouth in the Eastern Cape are being conserved (Berliner, 2005). At 23%, the biggest contributor comes from national and provincial parks, wilderness areas, and special protected forests. The iSimangaliso Wetland Park is the largest protected area in the region, a 3320-km^2 World Heritage Site that protects 280 km of dune forests along the coastline stretching from Kosi Bay to the Maphelane Nature Reserve, just south of St Lucia (Figure 6.1). State forests, where people are allowed to harvest, have almost 13% of the protected forests under their jurisdiction, while private lands contribute < 1% of dune forest protection.

THE FUTURE OF DUNE FORESTS

The dune forests in South Africa's northern sectors of the east coast appear to be well protected. However, this is not the case further south from Richards Bay toward Durban and beyond (Figure 6.1). Dune forests there are fragmented, and actions to establish linkages between existing dune forest patches are a high priority. This connectivity strategy also holds for patches of other forest types adjacent to or further inland that may share species. Maintaining natural processes to restore dune forests, such as dispersal and colonization, is possible (van Aarde *et al.*, 1996; Grainger *et al.*, 2011). For instance, Olivier and colleagues (2013) calculated that forests along the east coast of South Africa harbor an extinction debt of 14 bird species. Prevention of future extinctions may therefore depend on protecting and restoring ecological functions that operate at landscape scales.

Dune forest restoration is also a valid and legal land-use option, which at the same time is ecologically attractive and sustainable, and it also provides for opportunities to test ecological theories about the mechanisms behind the reassembling of forest communities. In addition, understanding how species use the surrounding landscape matrix and forest patches may also provide valuable insight to managing the landscape to complement forest persistence.

The scientific information needed to ensure conservation efficiency is lacking, however. For instance, some 229 studies have been published on South African forests between 1990 and 2010, 93 of which focused on the forests in the IOCB biome (CERU, unpublished data). Not a single publication focuses on amphibians or reptiles in dune forests. Furthermore, 14 of the 16 studies on forest restoration in South Africa focus on a single site (see van Aarde *et al.*, 1996; Wassenaar *et al.*, 2005; Grainger *et al.*, 2011). Establishing links between dune forest fragments and the other forests along the east coast is dependent upon on a firm knowledge base of how these ecosystems interact, if they are dependent upon each other, and how they may respond to disturbance.

The long-term challenge for the preservation of dune forests in South Africa is to make people understand and appreciate the value of intact forests. For instance, tradition dictates that local people should use and benefit from forests, such as having access to medicinal plants (Grainger & van Aarde, 2012b). On the other hand, dune forests may not appear to hold a great deal of worth beyond the intrinsic value of nature. However, dune forests have immediate and future benefits for the people living just inland from them. The most obvious is as a barrier to the destructive forces of the Indian Ocean. In 2007, a storm destroyed some commercial and private property, as well as rural livelihoods along the South African east coast. The worst-affected areas were those with no indigenous dune forests to dissipate the force of the waves. With climate change predicted to increase storm events, the value of a barrier to protect human life and livelihood becomes increasingly apparent (i.e. Roberts, 2008).

The benefit of restoring degraded forests, and conserving intact ones, spreads wider than for dune forests alone or for South African forests in general, or even beyond our boundaries (i.e. Rey-Benayas *et al.*, 2009; Bullock *et al.*, 2011). The metaphorical tide of habitat loss is as violent and virulent as any actual coastal storm. Studying, describing, and mimicking natural processes during the restoration and protection of dune forests ultimately determine the persistence of these habitats for future generations.

REFERENCES

Arthurton, R., Korateng, K., Forbes, T., *et al.* (2006). Coastal and marine environments. In J. C. Mohamed-Katerere & M. Sabet (eds.), *Africa Environment Outlook 2*. Malta: Progress Print, pp. 155–195.

Avis, A. M. (1992). Coastal dune ecology and management in the eastern Cape. PhD thesis, Rhodes University, Grahamstown.

Barbier, E. B., Hacker, S. D., Kennedy, C., *et al.* (2011). The value of estuarine and coastal ecosystem services. *Ecological Monographs*, **81**, 169–193.

Barnes, K. N. (2000). *The Eskom Red Data Book of Birds of South Africa, Lesotho and Swaziland*. Randburg: BirdLife South Africa.

Berliner, D. D. (2005). *Systematic Conservation Planning for the Forest Biome of South Africa*. Pretoria: Department of Water Affairs and Forestry.

Berliner, D. D. (2009). Systematic conservation planning for South Africa's forest biome: An assessment of the conservation status of South Africa's forests and recommendations for their conservation. PhD thesis, University of Cape Town, Cape Town.

Branch, B. (1998). *Field Guide to the Snakes and Other Reptiles of Southern Africa*. Cape Town: Struik Publishers.

Boyes, L. J., Gunton, R. M., Griffiths, M. E. & Lawes, M. J. (2011). Causes of arrested succession in coastal dune forest. *Plant Ecology*, **212**, 21–32.

Bullock, J. M., Aronson, J., Newton, A. C., Pywell, R. F. & Rey-Benayas, J. M. (2011). Restoration of ecosystem services and biodiversity: Conflicts and opportunities. *Trends in Ecology and Evolution*, **26**, 541–549.

Burgess, N. D. & Clarke, G. P. (2000). *Coastal Forests of Eastern Africa*. Gland: IUCN Forest Conservation Programme.

Caughley, G. & Sinclair, A. R. E. (1994). *Wildlife Ecology and Management*. Cambridge, MA: Blackwell Sciences.

Davis, A. L. V., van Aarde, R. J., Scholtz, C. H. & Delport, J. H. (2003). Convergence between dung beetle assemblages of a post-mining vegetational chrononsequence and unminded dune forest. *Restoration Ecology*, **11**, 29–42.

Dippenaar-Schoeman, A. S. & Wassenaar, T. D. (2002). A checklist of the ground-dwelling spiders of coastal dune forest at Richards Bay, South Africa (Arachnida, Araneae). *Bulletin of the British Arachnological Society*, **12**, 275–279.

Figure 3.1 A colony of jackass penguins (*Spheniscus demersus*) nesting on the upper beach just below the vegetation and above the average reach of tides on a beach in the Western Cape, South Africa. (Photo credit: Les Abernethy.)

Figure 3.1 (cont.) A typical shallow nest scrape with snowy plover (*Charadrius novisus*) eggs on a California beach. (Photo credit: Callie Bowdish.)

Figure Box 3.1 The precocial chicks of many species of beach-nesting shorebirds must feed themselves with beach and dune invertebrates soon after hatching. Prey availability could be a factor in the fledging success of some populations of these species, many of which are threatened or endangered. This young western snowy plover (*Charadrius nivosus*) chick has captured a talitrid amphipod on a California beach – these talitrid amphipods are dependent on wrack as a food source. (Photo credit: Callie Bowdish.)

Figure Box 3.3 A narrow bluff-backed beach that receives high inputs of macrophyte wrack from nearshore giant kelp forests and reefs. These cross-boundary transfers of organic matter (e.g. seagrass, algae, carrion) support high numbers of invertebrate species at high densities. Invertebrates consume a large fraction of the material imported from the sea. Bacteria and meiofauna in the sediment further process this material, and mineralized nutrients are returned to the nearshore zone, further linking abutting components of the surf–beach–dune system.

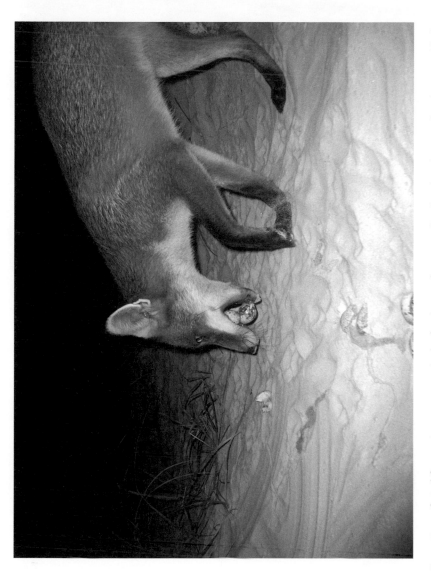

Figure Box 3.6 Red fox preying upon eggs in the foredunes of an Australian beach. (Photo credit: Thomas Schlacher.)

Figure 4.1 Left eye flounder (*Bothus* sp.) in a seagrass meadow (*Thalassia hemprichii*) in Indonesia.

Figure 4.2 Banded sea-krate (*Laticauda colubrina*) in a seagrass meadow (*Thalassia hemprichii*) in Indonesia.

Figure 4.3 Cockles in a dwarf eelgrass (*Zostera noltii*) seagrass meadow in South Wales, UK.

Figure 4.4 Stony coral (*Acropora* sp.) in a mixed *Cymodocea serrulata* seagrass meadow in Green Island, Australia.

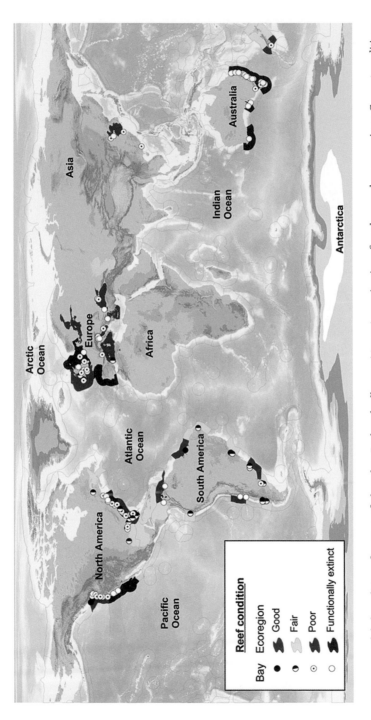

Figure 5.1 Global condition of oyster reefs, based on Beck and colleagues' (2009) examination of 144 bays and 44 ecoregions. Current conditions are ranked based on the percentage of reefs remaining compared to historical abundance: good (< 50% lost), fair (50–89% lost), poor (90–99% lost), and functionally extinct (> 99% lost). Reprinted from Beck *et al.* (2011) with permission from *Bioscience*.

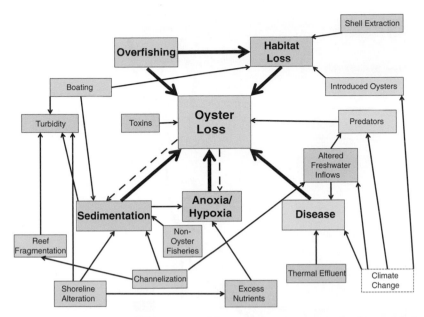

Figure 5.2 Conceptual interactions of the multiple stressors contributing to global oyster decline. Primary threats (overfishing, habitat loss, sedimentation, anoxia/hypoxia, and disease) are in bold type, and the severity of additional threats are indicated by font size. Weighted arrows represent the most influential interactions between multiple stressors, while dotted arrows represent a feedback loop between environmental degradation and oyster loss. Biological threats appear in blue, environmental threats in green, and anthropogenic threats in tan.

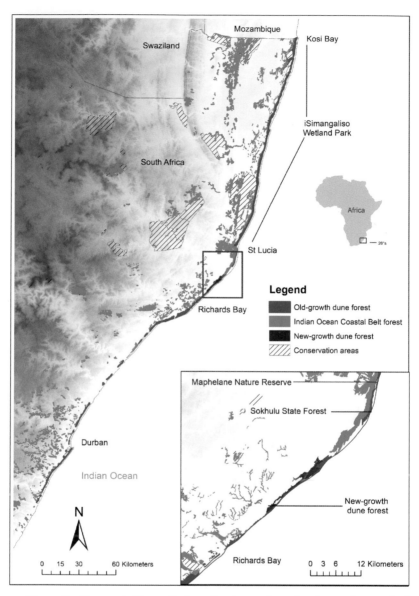

Figure 6.1 New- and old-growth dune forests are situated at the northern end of the South African east coast. The iSimangaliso Wetland Park, stretching from Kosi Bay in the north to the Maphelane Nature Reserve in the south, is the largest area that formally protects dune forests. We have been conducting structured ecological surveys for some 20 years in the new-growth forests north of Richards Bay and old-growth forests in the Sokhulu State Forests.

Figure 7.2 Subtle variation in marsh vegetation leads to different avifaunas in South American salt marshes: denseflower cordgrass (*Spartina densiflora*) and smooth cordgrass (*S. alterniflora*) marsh undisturbed and disturbed by cattle grazing and sewage discharge, respectively. The most common bird species associated with each marsh are shown: (**a**) spot-winged crake; (**b**) bay-capped wren-spinetail (*Spartonoica maluroides*); (**c**) southern lapwing (*Vanellus chilensis*); (**d**) Correndera pipit; (**e**) yellow-winged blackbird (*Agelasticus thilius*); (**f**) Chimango caracara (*Milvago chimango*).

Figure 7.4 Two endemic salt marsh birds from western North America: Alameda song sparrow (*Melospiza melodia pusillula*) from south San Francisco Bay and Belding's savannah sparrow (*Passerculus sandwichensis beldingi*) from southern California.

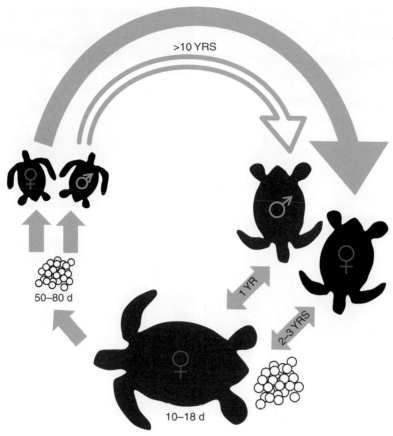

Figure 10.1 Schematic showing the generalized life cycle of marine turtles. Adult female turtles visit the nesting beach every 2–3 years, laying up to eight clutches of eggs at 10- to 18-day intervals. Adult male turtles are thought to visit the nesting beach annually. Nests (with 80–140 eggs) incubate for between 50 and 80 days, with incubation temperature determining hatchling sex. Hatchling and juvenile sea turtles develop in cryptic and poorly understood nursery areas before recruiting back to the adult foraging areas some decades later.

Figure 10.2 **(a)** Nesting beach may be lost through coastal squeeze, where beach is eroded but coastal development prevents its retreat (here valuable coastal property in North Carolina, USA is defended by sand bags); **(b)** hatchling deformities, such as this two-headed green turtle (*Chelonia mydas*) from a nest in Cyprus, may result from altered nest incubation temperatures; **(c)** nests can be washed out by storms and unusually high tides. This nest has been exposed in the bank of an escarpment; **(d)** eggs that may fail to develop due to unusually high incubation temperatures or non-viable incubation conditions may be moved to hatcheries. (Photo credits: (a) Matthew Godfrey, (c) David Wright, (b, d) Lucy Hawkes.)

Dippenaar-Schoeman, A. S. & Wassenaar, T. D. (2006). A checklist of spiders from the herbaceous layer of a coastal dune forest ecosystem at Richards Bay, KwaZulu-Natal, South Africa (Arachnida, Araneae). *African Invertebrates*, **47**, 63–70.

Eeley, H. A. C., Lawes, M. J. & Piper, S. E. (1999). The influence of climate change on the distribution of indigenous forest in KwaZulu-Natal, South Africa. *Journal of Biogeography*, **26**, 595–617.

Fairbanks, D. H. K., Reyers, B. & van Jaarsveld, A. S. (2001). Species and environment representation: Selecting reserves for the retention of avian diversity in KwaZulu-Natal, South Africa. *Biological Conservation*, **98**, 365–379.

Feely, J. M. (1980). Did Iron Age man have a role in the history of Zululand's wilderness landscapes? *South African Journal of Science*, **76**, 150–152.

Ferreira, S. M. & van Aarde, R. J. (2000). Maintaining diversity through intermediate disturbances: Evidence from rodents colonizing rehabilitating dunes. *African Journal of Ecology*, **38**, 286–294.

Friedmann, Y. & Daly, B. (2004). *Red Data Book of the Mammals of South Africa: A Conservation Assessment*. Conservation Breeding Specialist Group (SSG/IUCN). Parkview: Endangered Wildlife Trust.

Gaston, K. J. (2000). Global patterns in biodiversity. *Nature*, **405**, 220–227.

Geldenhuys, C. J. (1992). Richness, composition and relationships of the floras of selected forests in southern Africa. *Bothalia*, **22**, 205–233.

Grainger, M. J. (2011). An evaluation of coastal dune forest rehabilitation through ecological succession. PhD thesis, University of Pretoria, Pretoria.

Grainger, M. J. & van Aarde, R. J. (2012a). Is succession-based management of coastal dune forest restoration valid? *Ecological Restoration*, **30**, 200–208.

Grainger, M. J. & van Aarde, R. J. (2012b). The resilience of the medicinal plant community of rehabilitating coastal dune forests, KwaZulu-Natal, South Africa. *African Journal of Ecology*, **50**, 120–123.

Grainger, M. J. & van Aarde, R. J. (2013). The role of canopy gaps in the regeneration of coastal dune forest. *African Journal of Ecology*, **51**, 11–20.

Grainger, M. J., van Aarde, R. J. & Wassenaar, T. D. (2011). Landscape composition influences the restoration of subtropical coastal dune forest. *Restoration Ecology*, **19**, 111–120.

Griffiths, M. E., Tsvuura, Z., Franklin, D. C. & Lawes, M. J. (2010). Pollination ecology of *Isoglossa woodii*, a long lived, synchronously monocarpic herb from coastal forests in South Africa. *Plant Biology*, **12**, 495–502.

Guldemond, R. A. R. & van Aarde, R. J. (2010). Forest patch size and isolation as drivers of bird species richness in Maputaland, Mozambique. *Journal of Biogeography*, **37**, 1884–1893.

IUCN. (2012). The IUCN Red List of Threatened Species. Version 2012.2. www.iucnredlist.org. Downloaded 17 October 2012.

Klein, R. J. T. & Nicholls, R. J. (1999). Assessment of coastal vulnerability to climate change. *Ambio*, **28**, 182–197.

Kritzinger, J. J. (1996). Avian community structure on rehabilitating coastal dune forests in northern KwaZulu-Natal, South Africa. MSc thesis, University of Pretoria, Pretoria.

Kritzinger, J. J. & van Aarde, R. J. (1998). The bird communities of rehabilitating coastal dunes at Richards Bay, KwaZulu-Natal. *South African Journal of Science*, **94**, 71–78.

Kumssa, D. B., van Aarde, R. J. & Wassenaar, T. D. (2004). The regeneration of soil micro-arthropod assemblages in a rehabilitating coastal dune forest at Richards Bay, South Africa. *African Journal of Ecology*, **42**, 346–354.

Küper, W., Sommer, J. H., Lovett, J. C., *et al.* (2004). Africa's hotspots redefined. *Annals of the Missouri Botanical Garden*, **91**, 525–535.

Lawes, M. J. (1990). The distribution of the Samango monkey (*Cercopithecus mitis erythrarchus* Peters, 1852 and *Cercopithecus mitis labiatus* I. Geoffroy, 1843) and forest history in southern Africa. *Journal of Biogeography*, **17**, 669–680.

Lawes, M. J., Midgley, J. J & Chapman, C. A. (2004). South Africa's forests: The ecology and sustainable use of indigenous timber resources. In M. J. Lawes, H. A. C. Eeley, C. M. Shackleton & B. G. S. Geach (eds.), *Indigenous Forests and Woodlands in South Africa: Policy, People and Practice*. Scottsville: University of KwaZulu-Natal Press, pp. 31–63.

Lawes, M. J., Eeley, H. A. C., Findlay, N. J. & Forbes, D. (2007). Resilient forest faunal communities in South Africa: A legacy of palaeoclimatic change and extinction filtering? *Journal of Biogeography*, **34**, 1246–1264.

Low, A. B. & Rebelo, A. G. (1996). *Vegetation of South Africa, Lesotho and Swaziland*. Pretoria: Department of Environmental Affairs and Tourism.

Lubke, R. A. (2004). Vegetation dynamics and succession on sand dunes of the eastern coasts of Africa. In M. L. Martinez & N. P. Psuty (eds.), *Coastal Dunes Ecology and Conservation*. Berlin: Springer-Verlag, pp. 67–73.

Lubke, R. A., Avis, A. M. & Phillipson, P. B. (1992a). Vegetation and floristics. In *Environmental Impact Assessment. Eastern Shores of Lake St Lucia (Kingsa/Trojan Lease Area)*, vol. 1, part 1. Grahamstown: Coastal and Environmental Services, pp. 189–247.

Lubke, R. A., Moll, J. B. & Avis, A. M. (1992b). Rehabilitation ecology. In *Environmental Impact Assessment. Eastern Shores of Lake St Lucia (Kingsa/Trojan Lease Area)*, vol. 1, part 1. Grahamstown: Coastal and Environmental Services, pp. 251–303.

Lubke, R. A., Avis, A. M., Steinke, T. D. & Boucher, C. (1997). Coastal vegetation. In R. M. Cowling, D. M. Richardson & S. M. Pierce (eds.), *Vegetation of Southern Africa*. Cambridge: Cambridge University Press, pp. 300–321.

MacLachlan, A. (1991). Ecology of coastal dunes. *Journal of Arid Environments*, **21**, 229–243.

Majer, J. D. & de Kock, A. E. (1992). Ant recolonization of sand mines near Richards Bay, South Africa: An evaluation of progress with rehabilitation. *South African Journal of Science*, **88**, 31–36.

Measey, G. J. (2011). *Ensuring a Future for South Africa's Frogs: A Strategy for Conservation Research*. Pretoria: South African National Biodiversity Institute.

Midgley, J. J., Cowling, R. M., Seydack, A. H. W. & van Wyk, G. F. (1997). Forest. In R. M. Cowling, D. M. Richardson & S. M. Pierce (eds.), *Vegetation of Southern Africa*. Cambridge: Cambridge University Press, pp. 278–299.

Minter, L. R., Burger, M., Harrison, J. A., *et al.* (2004). *Atlas and Red Data Book of the Frogs of South Africa, Lesotho and Swaziland*. Washington, DC: Smithsonian Institution.

Mucina, L. & Rutherford, M. C. (2006). *The Vegetation of South Africa, Lesotho and Swaziland*. Pretoria: South African National Biodiversity Institute.

Niemand, L. J. (2001). The contribution of the bird community of the regenerating coastal dunes at Richards Bay to regional diversity. MSc thesis, University of Pretoria, Pretoria.

Olivier, P. I., van Aarde, R. J. & Ferreira, S. M. (2009). Support for a metapopulation structure among mammals. *Mammal Review*, **39**, 178–192.

Peter, C. I., Ripley, B. S. & Robertson, M. P. (2003). Environmental limits to the distribution of *Scaevola plumieri* along the South African coast. *Journal of Vegetation Science*, **14**, 89–98.

Redi, B. H., van Aarde, R. J. & Wassenaar, T. D. (2005). Coastal dune forest development and the regeneration of millipede communities. *Restoration Ecology*, **13**, 284–291.

Rey-Benayas, J. M., Newton, A. C., Diaz, A. & Bullock, J. M. (2009). Enhancement of biodiversity and ecosystem services by ecological restoration: A meta-analysis. *Science*, **325**, 1121–1124.

Roberts, D. (2008). Thinking globally, acting locally – Institutionalizing climate change at the local government level in Durban, South Africa. *Environment & Urbanisation*, **20**, 521–537.

Simpson, G. G. (1964). Species density of North American recent mammals. *Systematic Zoology*, **13**, 57–73.

Skinner, J. D. & Smithers, R. N. H (1990). *The Mammals of the Southern African Sub-region*. Cape Town: Struik Publishers.

Tinley, K. L. (1985). *The Coastal Dunes of South Africa: A Synthesis*. Pretoria: Council for Scientific and Industrial Research.

Trimble, M. J. & van Aarde, R. J. (2011). Decline of birds in a human modified coastal dune forest landscape in South Africa. *PLoS ONE*, **6**(1), e16176.

Tyson, P. D. (1986). *Climatic Change and Variability in Southern Africa*. Cape Town: Oxford University Press.

Van Aarde, R. J., Ferreira, S. M., Kritzinger, J. J., *et al.* (1996). An evaluation of habitat rehabilitation on coastal dune forests in northern KwaZulu-Natal, South Africa. *Restoration Ecology*, **4**, 334–345.

Van Aarde, R. J., Smit, A.-M. & Claassens, A. S. (1998). Soil characteristics of rehabilitating and unmined coastal dune forests. *Restoration Ecology*, **6**, 102–110.

Van Wyk, A. E. & Smith, G. F. (2001). *Regions of Floristic Endemism in Southern Africa*. Pretoria: Umdaus Press.

Von Maltitz, G., Mucina, L., Geldenhuys, C., *et al.* (2003). *Classification System for South African Indigenous Forests*. Pretoria: Department of Water Affairs and Forestry.

Wassenaar, T. D., van Aarde, R. J., Pimm, S. L. & Ferreira, S. M. (2005). Community convergence in disturbed subtropical dune forest. *Ecology*, **86**, 655–666.

Weisser, P. J., Garland, I. F. & Drews, B. K. (1982). Dune advancement 1937–1977 at the Mlalazi Nature Reserve, Natal, South Africa and preliminary vegetation-succession chronology. *Bothalia*, **14**, 127–130.

7

The distribution and conservation of birds of coastal salt marshes

RUSSELL GREENBERG, AUGUSTO CARDONI, BRUNO
J. ENS, XIAOJING GAN, JUAN PABLO ISACCH,
KEES KOFFIJBERG, AND RICHARD LOYN

INTRODUCTION

Salt and brackish coastal marshes (coastal salt marsh) are distributed thinly along the mid- to high-latitude coastlines of all the major continents except Antarctica. Where coastlines are protected and supplied with a source of sediment, grasses and shrubs colonize and stabilize the substrate, paving the way for further marsh accretion. Salt marshes form along lagoons protected by barrier islands, at the mouths of river deltas and along the edges of protected estuaries. Salt marshes are widely distributed, but account for a small amount of land cover. Although precise quantification of the current extent of salt marsh is lacking, an estimate of 60 000 km^2 seems reasonable (Greenberg *et al.*, 2006b). Salt marsh vegetation is replaced by mangrove forest between 32°N and 40°S or coexists with it at higher tidal levels (see Chapter 2). Whatever the exact amount of extant salt marsh, it is clear that it is a fraction of what existed even a century ago. The direct and indirect effects of human activity are particularly acute for salt marshes, as most of the human population lives on or near the coasts or within the watershed that feeds the estuaries where marsh grows (Rickey & Anderson, 2004).

Salt marshes show a great deal of similarity throughout the world in their simple vegetative structure punctuated by tidal sloughs and their low floristic diversity. In general, they are dominated by one to a few species of salt-tolerant grasses and shrubs (mostly of the Chenopodiaceae), often showing distinct zonation associated with the frequency of tidal inundation and salinity (Figure 7.1). However, marshes along the different continental

Coastal Conservation, eds B. Maslo and J. L. Lockwood. Published by Cambridge University Press.
© Cambridge University Press 2014.

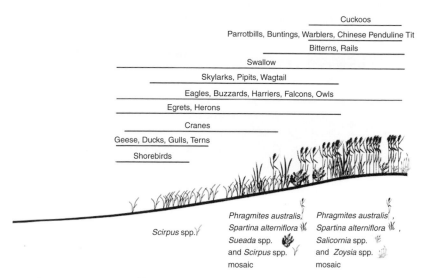

Figure 7.1 Zonation of birds in a Chinese salt marsh. Lower marshes are locally dominated by *Suaedia*, *Zoysia*, and *Salicornia*, and upper marshes have a diversity of reeds (*Phragmites*, *Scirpus*) and shrubs (e.g. yin chen hao, *Artemisia capillaris*).

shorelines are unique, showing differences in the dominant plant taxa, source of the colonizing fauna, specifics of the tidal regime, frequency of storm disturbance, and the tremendous variation in human activity and use. While similar to the eye, even within a region subtle differences in marsh structure give rise to distinct biotic assemblages (Figure 7.2).

Salt marshes have long been recognized for the host of ecosystem services they provide; however, their role in the conservation of biological diversity is less understood, even for well-studied taxa, such as birds. The main reason for this lack of attention is that salt marshes provide habitat for only a few breeding and resident avian species, and only temporary roosting and foraging sites for a much larger list of avian species. Furthermore, research and salt marsh conservation efforts are often regionally focused and lack a global perspective. In this chapter, we provide a needed overview of the world's salt marshes by providing regional information from marshes found along the shoreline of five continents. We examine the overall avifauna (by far the best-documented salt marsh fauna), particularly noting specialized taxa and their conservation status and providing the context of the regional and globally shared threats they face. The regions examined are China, Australia, western Europe (with a focus on the Wadden Sea), southeastern South America (Argentina, Uruguay, and Brazil), and North America. The goals of such an

Figure 7.2 Subtle variation in marsh vegetation leads to different avifaunas in South American salt marshes: denseflower cordgrass (*Spartina densiflora*) and smooth cordgrass (*S. alterniflora*) marsh undisturbed and disturbed by cattle grazing and sewage discharge, respectively. The most common bird species associated with each marsh are shown: (**a**) spot-winged crake; (**b**) bay-capped wren-spinetail (*Spartonoica maluroides*); (**c**) southern lapwing (*Vanellus chilensis*); (**d**) Correndera pipit; (**e**) yellow-winged blackbird (*Agelasticus thilius*); (**f**) Chimango caracara (*Milvago chimango*). (See color plate section.)

exercise are to highlight both the general phenomena and the unique aspects of different marsh systems throughout the world.

GLOBAL VARIATION IN COASTAL SALT MARSH

Although we believe it is critical to take a global view of coastal salt marsh conservation to identify common threats and possible conservation solutions, it is equally important to evaluate the unique features of each system so that conservation measures are appropriate to that system.

Extent of marshes

Despite a 50% decline in marsh area due to rice and salt production and aquaculture since 1950, the China coast still supports ~22 000 km² of coastal salt marsh, mostly along the Yellow Sea (Zhao, 1996). Similarly, despite losses of over 70% of the original North American coastal wetlands, salt marshes are extensive along the eastern and southern coasts of North America where they cover ~15 000 km². Salt marshes of the west coast of the United States are limited in extent (~440 km²), of which ~70% are associated with the San Francisco Bay. The estimate for coastal salt marsh area in Australia is 6020 km² (N. Montgomery, Ozestuaries, personal communication, 2012), with the greatest extent found along the tropical coast in a zone adjacent to mangrove vegetation (Adam, 2009). Only 660 km² (11%) of salt marsh is found in New South Wales, Victoria, Tasmania, and South Australia combined (N. Montgomery, personal communication, 2012). Salt marshes in Europe are found around estuaries in the British Isles and along the coasts of the Wadden and Baltic Seas. The area of European salt marshes is ~450 km² for the British Isles and 950 km² for the rest of western Europe (Dijkema, 1990). Additional pockets of salt marsh are found along the Mediterranean Sea and Persian Gulf (Chapman, 1977). Temperate salt marshes in southeastern South America (SESA) are distributed from southern Brazil, through Uruguay to Argentina. Salt marshes from south of Brazil to northern Patagonia in Argentina cover an extent of 2133 km² (Argentina, 2045 km²; Uruguay, 25 km²; Brazil, 62 km²; Isacch et al., 2006). The largest salt marshes are found predominantly in the northern part of SESA, most notably the Patos Lagoon in Brazil, Bahia Samborombon at the mouth of the Rio de la Plata in Argentina, and big bay systems, such as Bahía Blanca and Bahia Anegada in Argentina (Isacch et al., 2006).

The floristic composition of salt marshes

Just considering low marsh (the region at or below the mean high-tide line), global coastal marshes divide into those that are dominated by grasses (primarily *Spartina* spp.), which include the Atlantic and Gulf coasts of North America and the Atlantic coast of South America, and those that are dominated by small halophytic shrubs, primarily in the Chenopodeacea (predominantly *Sarcocornia* and *Suaedia* spp.), including China (Xu & Zhao, 2005; Figure 7.1), Australia (Boon, 2011), the west coast of North America, southern and western Europe, and small areas (such as Patatagonia) in South America (Isacch et al., 2006). This provides a major habitat dichotomy, as *Spartina* species provide more cover than the Chenopods and also support more taxa associated with interior grasslands (e.g. *Ammodramus* sparrows in North America).

Tidal flux, freshwater flow, and zonation

Tidal marsh vegetation tends to be dominated by few species. The factors that determine the floristics and vegetative structure are many, but two main gradients are particularly important: tidal flux and freshwater input. Besides affecting the salinity and vegetation, the tidal intensity determines both the physical environment that birds have to face on a once- or twice-daily basis, and also the input of nutrients, or productivity, of the system. Tidal flux varies on a large geographic scale, with low tidal ranges along the Gulf coast of the United States, northern portion of SESA, southern Europe, Australia, and southern China, and large tidal ranges at higher latitudes along the Atlantic coast. Variation due to the position of a marsh in an estuarine system can be greater than what is driven by latitude and position in an oceanic basin. Natural freshwater input, which has been altered greatly for most marsh systems, varies by region, season, and position in a particular estuarine system. The input of stream or river water can be augmented directly by precipitation from storms. Important for the study of bird diversity (and biodiversity as a whole), the interplay between tidal and freshwater inputs results in a gradient in vegetation and physical environment as one moves from the estuarine or oceanic edge to the interior of a marsh. This often takes the form of distinct zonation, with large differences between high marsh (above the mean high-tide line) and low marsh. The implications of regional gradients and local zonation have yet to be explored fully for coastal marsh bird distribution and conservation (Isacch *et al.*, 2013).

A typical zonation pattern can be illustrated with Chinese marshes (Figure 7.1); the open flats of the low marsh are sparsely covered with *Suaedia, Zoysia,* and *Salicornia,* and upper marshes have a diversity of reeds (*Phragmites, Scirpus*) and shrubs (e.g. yin chen hao, *Artemisia capillaris*). Marshes of the warm temperate Australian coastlines also support two distinct salt marsh types – short salt marsh, dominated by beaded glasswort (*Sarcocornia quinqueflora*), and tall salt marsh, dominated by more substantial woody shrubs, including shrubby glasswort (*Sclerostegia arbuscula*) in the tidal zone and herbaceous plants, such as grey glasswort (*Halosarcia halocnemoides*) or black-seeded samphire (*H. pergranulata*) in ephemeral saltpan wetlands.

Western European marshes show a unique pattern of zonation where low areas comprise active sedimentation devoid of most vegetation except common glasswort (*Salicornia europaea*) and Townsend's cordgrass (*Spartina townsendii*). From the average, we cross through three zones. The lower zone consists of *Pucinellia* species, sea wormwood (*Artemisia maritima*), and herbaceous seepweed (*Suaeda maritima*), among others. Higher up is a meadow-like vegetative zone of *Cochlearia* species, goose tongue (*Plantago maritima*), triangle orache (*Atriplex prostrata*), *Spergularia* species and seaside arrowgrass (*Triglochin maritima*), which backs up to an upper edge, usually a dike. On the British Isles, mid-marsh zones are dominated by *Spartina*, which has spread considerably with the advent of Townsend's cordgrass and the hybrid English cordgrass (*S. anglica*). In more sandy areas, mid-marsh zones are dominated by *Salicornia*, with upper zones covered with *Puccinellia*, *Juncus*, *Scheonoplectus*, *Carex*, and *Festuca* species with patches of *Phragmites* reeds along the upper edges.

Variation in SESA marshes comes at a more regional level. The northern portion of SESA is dominated by brackish marsh, with true salt marsh primarily occurring in the south and being dominated by chickenclaws (*Sarcocornia perennis*) and smooth cordgrass (*Spartina alterniflora*) (Isacch et al., 2006). Brackish marshes are dominated mainly by denseflower cordgrass (*Spartina densiflora*) and also by *Juncus* and *Scirpus* species in the upper parts (Isacch et al., 2006), and all are primary habitat for land birds using coastal marshes (Isacch et al., 2013).

Upper marsh zones in eastern North America are often a mix of several *Spartina* species, such as saltmeadow cordgrass (*S. patens*) and big cordgrass (*S. cynosuroidesi*) in the south and Townsend's cordgrass in the north, saltgrass (*Distichlis spicata*), and marsh elder (*Iva frutescens*) and *Baccharis* shrubs. Black needle-rush (*Juncus roemerianus*) dominates brackish marshes, and upper estuaries also support *Typha*, *Scirpus*, and other *Juncus* species along with several forbs. In San Francisco Bay (which holds most of the marsh of the North American Pacific coast), a band of *Salicornia* with a narrow outer zone of California cordgrass (*Spartina foliosa*) dominates the lower tidal zones, with a diversity of shrubs found in the upper zones (i.e. *Grindelia*, *Atriplex*, and *Baccharis*). Brackish marshes, such as those of the Suisun Bay and lower Sacramento Delta, are dominated by rushes (i.e. *Scheonopectus* and *Juncus* species).

Inland salt marshes

In many regions, salt marshes are restricted to the coast and offer a stark contrast to interior freshwater marshes. In some arid regions, however, salt marshes fringe inland bodies of waters and often share a floristic similarity to coastal salt marsh. This probably has a biogeographic influence, as selection for adaptive divergence in coastal marshes is reduced in the presence of similar interior habitats.

Stands of chenopod shrubs, similar to those that characterize many Australian coastal salt marshes, grow in large parts of arid regions of inland Australia, reaching their greatest density near salt lakes where they would clearly be classified as salt marsh. However, salt marshes have strong floristic similarities with chenopod shrublands in even drier environments, such as stony gibber plains (which may be extremely dry deserts for many years). These chenopod shrublands have been considered a type of salt marsh (Adam, 2009). Some inland lakes represent previous marine incursions in recent geological time and hence may deserve consideration as relictual coasts. A more pragmatic reason for considering them here is that they offer quite similar habitat for birds and support a similar suite of bird guilds despite differences at the species level. Salt marshes are a common feature of the Great Basin of North America and the Pampas region of Argentina. While North American coastal marsh specialists are not found in interior salt marshes, the two species most closely associated with coastal salt marshes in SESA are found also around interior alkali grasslands and marshes (Cardoni *et al.*, 2013).

COASTAL MARSH AS A HABITAT FOR BIRDS

See the Appendix for basic characteristics of salt marsh avifaunas of China, Australia, southeast South America, Europe, and North America.

Breeding birds

Coastal marshes on different continents and coastlines show considerable similarity in their use by birds. Coastal marshes are generally species-poor in the number of nesting birds, generally between 10 and 20 species, consisting primarily of small passerines, raptors, shorebirds, and rails (Greenberg *et al.*, 2006b; Figure 7.3). The total number of birds recorded in salt marshes can be quite high, however. For example, at least 148 bird species make some use of salt marsh or chenopod shrublands in Australia. In a study of the most common salt marsh type in SESA (denseflower cordgrass marsh), a continent known for its very bird diversity, Cardoni (2011) found only 9 breeding species with ~80% of nests corresponding with only 2 species: bay-capped wren-spinetail (*Spartonoica maluroides*) and Chimango caracara (*Milvago chimango*). In fairness, the nine species may be a slight underestimate, as a few other species characteristic of the Pampas occasionally nest in SESA salt marshes (Isacch *et al.*, 2013), particularly those associated with disturbances, such as grazing or eutrophication.

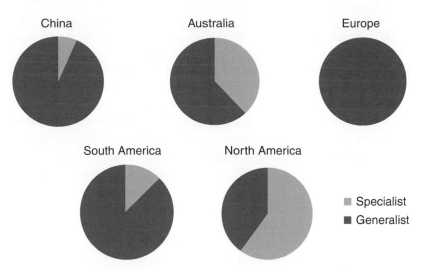

Figure 7.3 Proportion of specialist species within the breeding avifauna of salt marshes in different continents. Specialist classification is inclusive of species that are listed as possible specialists (> 75% of the total population in salt marshes) and also includes species for which at least one subspecies is a salt marsh specialist.

Generally, few aquatic species nest within the salt marsh vegetation. These include shorebirds (e.g. common redshank, *Tringa totanus*), dabbling ducks (e.g. wigeons, mallards, pintails), and secretive marsh birds (i.e. rails, crakes, and bitterns). In Australia, a somewhat larger range of aquatic species have been found nesting in salt marshes, including Australian pelicans (*Pelecanus conspicillatus*) (Quinn & Lacey, 1999; Menkhorst, 2010), brolgas (*Grus rubicunda*) (Loyn, personal observation), and silver gulls (*Chroicocephalus novaehollandiae*).

Zonation plays a critical role in local species diversity. Upper zones with less tidal influence, lower salinity and more floristic and structural diversity, tend to support more species but fewer specialists (Isacch *et al.*, 2013). For example, the tidal reed beds (*Phragmites*) of Eurasian marshes support a particularly high diversity of species that are found both in tidal and non-tidal (non-coastal) reed beds. Chinese coastal reed beds support breeding populations of several species of reed warbler (*Acrocephalus* spp.), reed bunting (*Emberiza schoeniclus*), reed parrotbill (*Paradoxornis heudei*), and vinous-throated parrotbill (*Sinosuthora webbiana*).

Similarly, along the Atlantic coast of North America, the upper marsh level is often a heterogeneous mixture of shrubs and a diversity of salt-tolerant grasses. In these areas, typical marsh birds are present, such as marsh wrens (*Cistithorus palustris*), common yellowthroats (*Geothlypis trichas*), and (particularly in brackish areas) red-winged blackbirds (*Agelaius phoeniceus*), along with species associated with scrubland, such as yellow warbler (*Dendroica petechia*), willow flycatcher (*Empidonax trailii*), and even painted buntings (*Passerina ciris*). In Australia, tall salt marsh attracts all the salt marsh specialists at comparable levels of abundance but not the open-ground insectivores. White-fronted chats (*Epthianura albifrons*) and striated field wrens (*Calamanthus fuliginosus*) are among the most common species in tall salt marsh, along with a range of other insectivores typical of forest and woodland (e.g. Horsfield's bronze-cuckoo (*Chrysococcyx basalis*), brown thornbill (*Acanthiza pusilla*), white-browed scrubwren (*Sericornis frontalis*) and superb fairy-wren (*Malurus cyaneus*)), and one species associated with swamps (little grassbird, *Megalurus gramineus*). Blue-winged (*Neophema chrysostoma*), elegant (*N. elegans*), and orange-bellied (*N. chrysogaster*) parrots visit tall salt marsh when the relevant plants produce seed in winter and spring (Loyn *et al.*, 1986).

Fewer species occupy the lower, more open vegetated tidal flats of salt marsh systems, although these more physiologically harsh zones tend to support more specialized plants and animals. For example, North American salt marshes, primarily the low marsh zones, are dominated by one or two species of Emberizid sparrow (per site), but among the 20 or so total taxa, we find mostly salt marsh specialists (Figure 7.4).

Many coastlines support few or no salt marsh specialized birds, even in the low true salt marsh zones. European marshes are dominated by birds typical of the open country, such as the Eurasian skylark (*Alauda arvensis*), reed bunting, and meadow pipit (*Anthus pratensis*). In other parts of Eurasia, the most common species is the widespread zitting cisticola (*Cisticola juncidis*), a species found in a variety of low vegetated flats outside the tidal zone. In Australia, short salt marsh provides nesting habitat for few species other than the Australasian pipit (*Anthus australis*) and white-fronted chat. Although the zonal patterns of vegetation and birds are generally well described, how the use of the different zones are integrated over the life cycle of mobile organisms, such as birds, is poorly documented. Among the possibilities that need further exploration are the following: (1) birds can rely on the upper zone for nest and roost cover while feeding on the productive, but less protected flats; (2) birds can also use the upper zones for refuge from the highest tides; (3) populations can show patterns of dominance-mediated habitat use that is based on distribution with respect to tidal zones; (4) the more thickly vegetated upper zone can serve as a

Figure 7.4 Two endemic salt marsh birds from western North America: Alameda song sparrow (*Melospiza melodia pusillula*) from south San Francisco Bay and Belding's savannah sparrow (*Passerculus sandwichensis beldingi*) from southern California. (See color plate section.)

refuge for newly fledged young; and (5) for species that breed in multiple zones, tradeoffs might exist between protection from predators that invade from the marsh edge in lower zones versus the greater chance of tidal flooding in the center of the marsh (Greenberg *et al.*, 2006a; Cervencl *et al.*, 2011).

Non-breeding birds

Birds from other habitats and regions often migrate through coastal salt marshes during the non-breeding season. Although tidal marshes have a sparse and species-poor seed bank (Leck, 1989), at some times of year certain plants produce seed crops (e.g. *Spartina, Schoenoplectus,* and *Sarcocornia*) that are used by visiting granivorous birds (primarily passerines and dabbling ducks, but also several parrots in Australia) during the winter months (dry season). In China, species breeding in *Phragmites* beds, in particular, are joined by a host of other land birds who feed primarily on seeds and arthropods (Gan *et al.,* 2010). Granivorous species, such as the great pampa finch (*Embernagra platensis*) and grassland yellow finch (*Sicalis luteola*), opportunistically use denseflower cordgrass marshes in SESA, associated with increasing seed production caused by bioturbation for burrowing crabs (*Neohelice granulata*) (Cardoni *et al.,* 2007). In southeastern Australia, however, flocks of granivorous birds visit low salt marsh in winter when the beaded glasswort produces seed (Loyn *et al.,* 1986). The most common species are the non-native European goldfinch (*Carduelis carduelis*) and native blue-winged parrot, the latter being classified as a seasonal salt marsh specialist. Two other salt marsh specialists also feed in these low salt marshes – the critically endangered orange-bellied parrot, a winter migrant from Tasmania, and the elegant parrot. In northern Europe, salt marsh is one of the preferred habitats of twite (*Carduelis flavirostris*), a small seed-eating Cardueline finch with an otherwise limited habitat distribution in winter. Granivory of salt marsh plants by migratory birds may contribute to the connectivity of marsh systems, at least within a hemisphere. Dispersal by birds may account for the curiously wide distribution of many of the common species. For example, smooth cordgrass is distributed in low marsh from North to South America and through the Caribbean. Vivian-Smith and Stiles (1994) documented that waterfowl can potentially disperse the seeds, which become attached to their plumage and feet. This phenomenon could also occur with longer-distance migrants, such as shorebirds (Popp *et al.,* 2011). Alternatively, smooth cordgrass in the east coast of South America could be one of the first examples of human-mediated dispersal of *Spartina*.

Salt marsh, particularly if it is of short vegetation stature, is often heavily used for roosting by shorebirds and waterfowl (Summers, 1977; Ferns, 1992). Shorebirds and waders, in particular, may require the marsh edge for roosting during high tides. In Australia, low marsh often attracts flocks of Australian shelduck (*Tadorna tadornoides*), Australian pelican, royal spoonbill (*Platalea regia*), Pacific golden plover (*Pluvialis fulva*), sharp-tailed sandpiper (*Calidris acuminata*), and eastern curlew (*Numenius madagascar-iensis*) (Loyn, 1978; Loyn *et al.*, 2001). Out in the open, shorebirds and waterfowl are highly vulnerable to predation by accipiters and falcons (Page & Whitacre, 1975; Cresswell & Whitfield, 1994), and marshes may afford some protection. However, waterbirds roosting near salt marshes in SESA can be susceptible to predation by wild cats that are hidden in the vegetation (Canepuccia *et al.*, 2008). Salt marshes, with their thick vegeta-tion, supports primarily harriers (*Circus spp.*) and short-eared owls (*Asio flammeus*) as its primary raptor species. For this reason, salt marshes may be a critical buffer habitat for shorebirds and aquatic birds. Marshes may be critical to the conservation of a broader diversity of estuarine birds than the marsh specialists.

Along all coastlines, a number of wading birds, terns, and shorebirds forage along tidal pools within the salt marsh (Chavez-Ramirez & Slack, 1995). When salt marshes flood with tidal water, rain, or local runoff, they provide pools that may attract a range of waterbirds, depending on many factors, including salinity. Species using this microhabitat include water-fowl, herons and egrets, terns and shorebirds (Loyn, 1978; Chavez-Ramirez & Slack, 1995). Sometimes pools are deliberately constructed in salt marshes to attract waterbirds or control mosquitoes (Spencer *et al.*, 2009). Geese and dabbling ducks also graze within marshes (Charman & Macey, 1978; Rowcliffe *et al.*, 1995), potentially acting as ecosystem engi-neers. Along the Hudson Bay (and locally along the Atlantic coast), large flocks of snow geese (*Chen caerulescens*) graze salt marshes and can denude areas causing long-term damage, an increasing phenomenon as goose populations have expanded in recent decades (Jefferies *et al.*, 2006).

Global distribution of salt marsh specialization

Coastal marshes support a relatively small number of breeding bird species, but the proportion of breeding taxa that are restricted to salt marshes, at least in a substantial portion of their range, can be large. However, the degree of endemism varies greatly between coastlines. One of the great mysteries of tidal marsh biogeography is that, while North American marshes support as many as 33 specialist subspecies (depending on your taxonomy), representing 12 species, and one fully specialist species, such local specialization is rarely observed in other continents. Sparrows of the family Emberizidae are the dominant land birds of salt marshes along all the North American coastlines. Six species of sparrow with 20 different subspecies (based on classification of the American Ornithologists Union) breed in salt marshes. A coastline can have from one to five species, but given a tendency to specialize on vegetation zones, any one site usually has one species (two in the mid-Atlantic region). Salt marsh sparrow taxa are either completely specialized on tidal marshes or tidal marsh is their preferred habitat. Only the salt marsh sparrow (*Ammodramus caudacutus*) is completely restricted to salt marsh, although the seaside sparrow (*A. maritimus*) is nearly so.

Other than sparrows, seven species have at least one subspecies that is completely or largely restricted to salt marshes, at least for a portion of their range, including a warbler, crake, rail, New World blackbird, and a wren (see Appendix). Clapper rail (*Rallus longirostris*) is strongly associated with salt marshes on the Pacific, Atlantic, and Gulf coasts. Although the black rail (*Laterallus jamaicensis*) is found scattered in interior sites in California and the Midwest, the greatest concentrations are in salt marshes. The American black duck (*Anas rubripes*) is restricted to salt and brackish marshes in the southern part of its range. The eastern willet (*Catoptrophorus semipalmatus semipalmatus*) is restricted to nesting in salt marshes, although it forages on nearby beaches and mudflats and migrates and winters in a variety of other littoral habitats. The marsh wren has a series of subspecies in the southeast US that are largely restricted to tidal marsh. Many North American specialist taxa have some type of conservation listing, primarily at the state level (see Appendix). Subspecies on the federal endangered or threatened species list include three subspecies of clapper rail. The Belding's savannah sparrow (*Passerculus sandwichensis beldingi*) is considered endangered in California, as is the large-billed savannah sparrow (*P. s. rostratus*) in Mexico.

Some information on population size and trend is available for North American taxa (see Appendix). These data come from a variety of different sources with variable data quality and analytical certainty, but it is clear that the localized distribution of habitat imposes strict population limits. Most taxa range from the hundreds (as in the case of the light-footed clapper rail (*Rallus longirostrus levipes*) of southern California) to tens of thousands, which is low compared to most North American species (PIF, 2007).

The lack of specialized salt marsh taxa is not obviously related to the extent of coastal marshland in a region. China, with its (historically) extensive marshland, supports only one possible specialist, the Saunders's gull (*Larus saundersi*) (Cao *et al.*, 2008; Jiang *et al.*, 2010). The main nesting habitats for this species are seepweed-dominated (*Suaeda* spp.) salt marshes (Chu *et al.*, 1999; Jiang *et al.*, 2002). However, due to the loss of salt marshes this species breeds in artificial interior wetlands that have been established just inland from the coast. The Saunders's gull was listed as

"Vulnerable" by the IUCN because of its low population estimate, which is expected to decline at an increasing rate due to habitat loss and disturbance in the breeding and non-breeding areas (Cao *et al.*, 2008; IUCN, 2011).

No specialist species or subspecies of bird is known from European salt marshes, although for both Europe and China, many breeding bird species to a large extent depend on salt marshes as important breeding habitat within the region. One possible factor for Eurasian marshes is the long history of human impact; however, the poor fossil record for passerines makes it impossible to determine whether bird taxa were present but now extirpated. A few species are known to occur primarily during the non-breeding season in European salt marshes, including the twite in the British Isles and the rock pipit (*Anthus petrosus*) along the Wadden Sea (Dierschke, 2002).

Fourteen Australian bird species and three subspecies can be considered salt marsh specialists. Most of them make some use of other habitats, including wetland fringes and low shrublands with similar structure to salt marsh, but they do not occur in those habitats as commonly as in salt marsh, at least at some times of the year. Four of the species are parrots that nest in habitat other than salt marsh but make extensive use of salt marsh in the non-breeding season. Six of the species (including the four parrots) occur in temperate salt marsh, and four others – slender-billed thornbill (*Acanthiza iredalei*), rufous fieldwren (*Calamanthus campestris*), white-winged fairy-wren (*Malurus leucopterus*), and yellow chat (*Epthianura corcea*) – occur in salt marsh in arid parts of Australia and the tropical north (see Appendix). The western population of slender-billed thornbills is listed as nationally vulnerable, and two populations of yellow chat are listed as endangered. The remaining species are found mainly in arid parts of Australia. Orange chats predominantly occur in salt marshes around ephemeral lakes. White-winged fairy-wrens also occupy those habitats, but also occur in dry chenopod shrublands, and the pied honeyeater (*Certhionyx variegatus*), thick-billed grasswren (*Amytornis textilis*), and gibberbird (*Ashbyia lovensis*) favor dry chenopod shrublands. Gibberbirds inhabit sparse, stony chenopod shrublands (gibber plains) with the least claim to be considered as a salt marsh specialist. Four bird genera are represented mainly or exclusively by salt marsh specialists (*Neophema* 4/7, *Calamanthus* 2/2, *Ephthianura* 3/4, and *Ashbyia* 1/1), and the latter two of these genera form a distinctive subfamily of birds, recently shown as closely related to the honeyeaters, Meliphagidae (Christidis & Boles, 2008). In all these genera, most of the non-specialist species make significant use of salt marsh and similar habitats so that the association with salt marsh remains strong across the entire genus. Hence the evolution of salt marsh specialists happened long ago in evolutionary time. The Australian interior has gone through a range of mesic–xeric cycles and has often been more humid than at present, with changing coastlines as sea levels rose and fell. Therefore, it is likely that coastal salt marsh has played a strong role in the evolution of salt marsh specialists. Salt has also accumulated in some inland landscapes from aerial deposition over long periods of geological time.

Whereas in Australia, being restricted to salt marsh and similar chenopod-dominated habitats is characteristic of species across an entire genus, most of the specialized taxa in North America are well-marked subspecies with very shallow genetic structure (Greenberg *et al.*, 2006b). Perhaps the presence of interior salt marshes, which may have been larger during the earlier periods of the Pleistocene, and a reduced effect of glaciation compared to northern continents allowed for the persistence of salt marsh species and deeper divergence times in Australia. In North America, a majority of the extant taxa probably colonized current salt marshes since the retreat of the glaciers.

While we have emphasized breeding endemics, at least one threatened species in Australia, the orange-bellied parrot, is known to depend upon salt marshes in winter. These birds breed in woodland patches in southwest Tasmania, feeding in adjacent buttongrass moorland, and winter in salt marsh in coastal Victoria and Tasmania. Listed as Critically Endangered in Australia, the global population has declined from > 120 in the 1970s to ~30 in 2012.

The two bird species that show the strongest association with SESA salt marshes are the bay-capped wren-spinetail and the spot-winged crake (*Porzana spiloptera*) (Isacch & Cardoni, 2011; Cardoni *et al.*, 2013). Both are of conservation concern at the global scale (Birdlife International, http://www.birdlife.org). Both species also use interior wetlands (many of which are saline) and grasslands, but they are locally abundant in salt marshes and may be deemed salt marsh specialists when more quantitative data are available. Specifically, it should be noted that bay-capped wren-spinetail use almost exclusively denseflower cordgrass marshes along SESA. Furthermore, bay-capped wren-spinetail, a member of the predominantly South American family Furnariidae, shows phenotypic differences in bill shape and plumage coloration between populations inhabiting brackish (inland) versus salt marshes (coastal) (Cardoni *et al.*, 2013). With the possible exception of the spinetail and crake, no specialist species or subspecies of breeding bird has been described from South American salt marshes. While over 1000 km north of the main coastal marsh zone of

SESA, the paraná (or marsh antwren, *Stymphalornis acutirostris*), a species in the Thamnophilidae family first described in 1995, is apparently endangered and largely restricted to fresh–brackish tidal marshes of estuaries of Paraná, Brazil (Reinert *et al.*, 2007; IUCN, 2011). The paucity of salt marsh endemics in South America is particularly surprising in light of the high diversity of the South American avifauna.

THREATS TO SALT MARSHES

Because of their limited distribution, association with heavily developed coastlines and location at the outflow of large watersheds devoted to agriculture and human settlement, the integrity of salt marsh systems is threatened globally. Even in regions with relatively low population density, salt marshes are disproportionately affected by development. Even in a country with low overall human population density, such as Australia, coastal marshes have been subjected to many anthropogenic pressures, threats, and modifications mainly arising from agriculture and urban and industrial development (Laegdsgaard *et al.*, 2009; Boon, 2011). These pressures are similar to those operating elsewhere in the world because in parts of Australia, human populations are heavily concentrated near the coast with a strong beach culture (Silliman *et al.*, 2009).

Actual land uses that contribute to salt marsh loss have varied through time and between coastlines and estuaries. Salt production involving the formation of evaporating ponds has been a long-standing cause of marsh conversion in areas of high insolation, such as southern Europe, California, Australia, and China. Salt production is on the decline in Europe, Australia, and North America, and many of the old salt evaporation ponds are being restored as salt marsh (e.g. San Francisco Bay). Salt marshes in urban areas have been preferred sites to place airports, landfills, low-income housing developments, and a host of land-expensive projects that need to be isolated from the city itself. Salt marshes in areas with tourist development are often converted to resorts and small harbors (Glenn *et al.*, 1996).

Simple habitat loss has been the greatest threat to the biological diversity of coastal marshes. Probably > 40% of original North American coastal wetland area has been filled and developed (Horwitz, 1978). Wetland loss has been extremely high along the estuaries of the west coast of the US, with >79% estimated loss from the San Francisco Bay.

Conversion of coastal marsh to other land uses or urbanization has stabilized along some coastlines (or even reversed through restoration), such as the North American shoreline. Loss of coastal marsh in SESA is minimal with a few notable exceptions, such as the 10% of marsh loss by landfill in Patos Lagoon, Brazil (Costa *et al.*, 2009). However, without proactive conservation, marsh habitat can be lost, even in seemingly stable areas. Furthermore, marsh loss continues to be significant along certain coastlines. In northern Europe, salt marsh areas have also been reclaimed for industrial and port development and urbanization (Dijkema *et al.*, 1984). In many of these areas, salt marshes are bordered by dikes and seawalls on the landward side to prevent flooding of the hinterland. These salt marshes will be lost if sedimentation cannot keep up with sea level rise (Dijkema *et al.*, 1984).

In China, more than 100 000 km^2 of tidal area have been reclaimed over the last 60 years, largely for aquacultural ponds and agricultural fields, and this activity has created irreversible changes to coastal ecosystems and resulted in additional negative impacts, such as acceleration of tidal marsh degeneration, erosion and contamination, siltation of shipping channels, reduction of carbon pools, habitat fragmentation for threatened species, and loss of stepping stones for some migratory birds (Chen *et al.*, 2000; Ma *et al.*, 2004; Cao & Wong, 2007). Most middle to high intertidal zones, which are the main salt marsh areas, have degenerated due to the incessant reclamations. For example, in Shuangtaizi estuary, ~1200 km^2 of *Phragmites* habitat, which held the majority of salt marsh in the 1980s, has been completely enclosed within a dike and fragmented by development, leaving only 28 km^2 of *Suaeda* marsh in the intertidal area in 2004 (Ji & Zhou, 2010). The southern Yangtze estuaries and north Hangzhou Bay used to have extensive salt marshes and mudflats (400 km^2) in the 1980s, providing quality stopover sites for many thousands of migratory shorebirds in the spring. However, the intertidal zone in this region was reduced to < 200 km^2 in 2003 (Ge, 2007), and the remaining intertidal zone completely disappeared in 2004 when a dike was built close to shore (Li *et al.*, 2008). Consequently, in the southern Yangtze estuaries (survey area 80 km^2), the number of shorebirds recorded during their northward migration dropped from ~1300 individuals of 33 species per day in 1998 to only 1115 individuals of 23 species during the entire season in 2010 (Hu & Lu, 2000; Heng *et al.*, 2011).

Cattle grazing and pre-grazing burning of the vegetation represent the main anthropogenic disturbances affecting SESA salt marshes (Isacch *et al.*, 2004; Cardoni, 2011; Isacch & Cardoni, 2011; Cardoni *et al.*, 2012). Northern SESA salt marshes develop along the coastal area of the Río de la Plata grasslands, a region supporting a vast livestock industry and a rapidly increasing arable agriculture (Soriano *et al.*, 1991). Croplands replaced grasslands in most of the region, leaving natural or semi-natural grasslands conserved only in areas that naturally limit agricultural develop-ment (Viglizzo *et al.*, 2001), such as coastal marshes. Consequently, cattle are being moved to salt marshes (Bilenca & Miñarro, 2004).

Frequently recorded salt marsh species, such as the bay-capped wren-spinetail and sedge wren (*Cistothorus platensis*), only use salt marshes with extensive cover of tall grass without or with only low levels of cattle grazing and burning (Figure 7.2), while Hudson's canastero (*Asthenes hudsoni*) uses tall marshes with high levels of cattle grazing (Cardoni, 2011; Isacch & Cardoni, 2011). Otherwise, heavily grazed marshes become functionally short grass prairies and support the avifauna appropriate to this habitat, such as the correndera pipit (*Anthus correndera*), bar-winged cinclodes (*Cinclodes fuscus*), and southern lapwing (*Vanellus chilensis*) (Isacch *et al.*, 2004; Cardoni, 2011; Isacch & Cardoni, 2011).

European salt marshes have been grazed and harvested for hay since their most recent post-glacial development began over 5000 years ago. More importantly, European marshes have been actively reclaimed as agricultural and grazing land for the past 400 years through the construc-tion of seawalls that prevent tidal flow (Hazeldon & Boorman, 2001). The original extent of tidal marsh may have been on the order of 1000 km^2 for Great Britain and 3000 km^2 along the northern European mainland. Dijkema (1990) estimated that 70% of the remaining European salt marsh is exploited. Grazing remains the most common human use of European salt marshes. When grazing is too intense, a short sward develops that is not attractive to breeding birds but is favored by geese outside their breeding season. Brackish salt marshes in the Baltic, on the other hand, are threatened when grazing is stopped or reduced; reed beds, tall grasses, and woodlands increase at the cost of the halophytic vegetation characteristic of salt marshes in Europe. Extensive salt marsh areas have also been reclaimed in recent centuries to be converted into agricultural polders and flood-free pastures. Along the mainland coast of the Wadden Sea, for many centuries new development of salt marshes was encouraged by stimulating sedimen-tation through a system of groins and ditches, followed by land reclamation. Currently, the area is protected as part of the Natura 2000 network and a World Heritage Site. Marshes in China are often heavily grazed, harvested for paper production, and mined for crabs and worms for food and fish bait (Boulord *et al.*, 2011). In contrast, although North American salt marshes were grazed and harvested for hay production in past centuries, it is not currently a common practice. In recent decades, marsh burning is mostly restricted to the creation of forage for fur-producing and hunted wildlife, and its effect on bird diversity remains controversial (Mitchell *et al.*, 2006).

Marshes along urbanized estuaries are subject to direct loss due to development and indirect degradation resulting from nitrification and the accumulation of pollutants. Many estuaries border industrial sites, which provide a point source for contaminants. Sewage discharge associated with increased urban development has a particularly high impact on vegetation below the average high-tide line growing without the influx of freshwater (Cardoni *et al.*, 2011). Discharge provides fertilization, which boosts smooth cordgrass growth and attracts species, such as bay-capped wren-spinetail and yellow-winged blackbird (*Agelasticus thilius*), from nearby interior and coastal habitats by providing cover and food (Cardoni *et al.*, 2011; Figure 7.2). Smooth cordgrass marsh, however, is frequently flooded and can possibly serve as an ecological trap because birds breeding in this transformed habitat are vulnerable to nest failure (Cardoni *et al.*, 2011). On the other hand, the increase of smooth cordgrass biomass production generated by increased nutrient loading increases detrital production, which also increases dead vegetation deposition (wrack). Wrack creates areas devoid of vegetation, which promote the use of the salt marsh by species from open habitats (e.g. correndera pipit, bar-winged cinclodes, shorebirds). This small-scale habitat disturbance can be important in maintaining species diversity (Grime, 1977).

Pollutants, such as excess nutrients, heavy metals, and pesticides, are a threat to all North American marsh systems. Much of the inputs are due to runoff from agricultural and industrialized areas upstream. Increases in nitrogen and other nutrients from agricultural runoff have favored the invasive common reed (*Phragmites australis*) in high marsh and, in low to mid-marsh, the spread of smooth cordgrass at the expense of a diversity of other grasses and forbs (Bertness *et al.*, 2002; Rickey & Anderson, 2004). Heavy metals often accumulate in marshes as well, but much of the load is sequestered in the halophytic plant tissue and sediment (Duarte *et al.*, 2010). Mercury arrives in salt marshes both from runoff and from atmospheric dispersion and precipitation and undergoes methylization, whereby it becomes biologically active, threatening salt marsh fauna (Williams *et al.*, 1994). Mercury damage is thought to be particularly acute in salt marshes, and high levels of mercury have been documented in species that consume invertebrates, such as the salt marsh sparrow (Shriver *et al.*, 2006). Most studies that document locally high mercury concentrations in the tissues of salt marsh-breeding sparrows have focused on the northeastern US, which is both highly industrialized and the recipient of atmospheric mercury from the interior (Shriver *et al.*, 2006). The consequences of moderate to high levels of mercury in the tissues of birds have not been assessed.

Pesticides are applied directly to marshes to control mosquito populations, although the amount used has declined over time and much of it is
specific to larval metamorphosis in mosquitoes (Dale, 1993; Rey *et al.*,
2012). Still, because of the widespread use of chemical agents, it is important to initiate some studies on the possible impact of various treatments on
marsh ecology and marsh bird populations. Other management
approaches, such as ditching, open water management, and biological
controls have been adopted (Daiber, 1986). The impact of structural management (such as pond creation) on birds is mixed, with some indication
that waterfowl may use these features, whereas marsh specialists may
decline in the areas (Mitchell *et al.*, 2006).

Salt marshes are notably species-poor, with vegetation zones often
dominated by a single species of plant. Therefore, non-native plant species
can come to dominate a zone previously occupied by a native species and
dramatically change the entire terrestrial community. Non-native common
reed is an issue in eastern North America, and the spread of non-native
Spartina (primarily smooth cordgrass) has affected western North America,
China, and parts of Australia. The effect of such invasions is poorly documented, but recent research in North America has shown that *Phragmites*
invasion favors certain generalist species, such as marsh wrens, over tidal
marsh specialists, such as seaside and salt marsh sparrows (Benoit &
Askins, 1999). At low density, patches of *Phragmites* may increase diversity
by providing song perches for some species, but ultimately reed beds form
monocultures with limited sites for nesting and low food resources. Control
of monocultural *Phragmites* involves both burning and herbicide applications, and examples of long-term recovery of native *Spartina* marsh are few.

For the purposes of increasing sedimentation and reducing erosion,
non-native *Spartina* species were intentionally introduced to the coastal
regions of China in 1979, but they quickly replaced native plants and
converted the intertidal zone into *Spartina*-dominated salt marshes
(Qin & Zhong, 1992; An *et al.*, 2007). Over the past three decades,
Spartina expanded its geographical range widely along the east coast and
estuarine wetlands in China (Wang *et al.*, 2006; An *et al.*, 2007). The
intertidal zone is already very narrow due to reclamation activities, so the
occupation of *Spartina* served only to intensify the loss of native salt
marshes. Along most of the coastline of Jiangsu province, *Spartina* is the
only salt marsh plant species now found outside the dikes. Not only did
Spartina change the vegetation composition, but it also altered the habitat
structure and food resources for birds at Chongming Dongtan, leading to
the degradation and further loss of suitable habitat for many birds (Gan

et al., 2009, 2010; Ma *et al.*, 2011). Smooth cordgrass was purposefully introduced to reclaim tidally inundated land in China. Unlike eastern North America, where cordgrass is native, *Spartina* marshes in China support few birds and no specialist taxa. Only the grass warblers are found there in greater numbers than in the native *Phragmites* and *Scirpus* marshes (Gan *et al.*, 2009, 2010). Non-native *Spartina* is also invading the Pacific coast of North America. In the San Francisco Bay, *Spartina* (Daehler & Strong, 1996) has been shown to create a reproductive trap for breeding populations of the endemic subspecies of song sparrow (*Melospiza melodia pusillula*). Sparrow nests in cordgrass growing below the mean high-tide line (which was formerly unvegetated) are likely to be tidally flooded (Nordby *et al.*, 1991). English cordgrass is a high-profile invasive plant in some salt marshes in Australia and New Zealand, but its impact has been local, and it is now subject to primarily chemical control efforts (Kriwoken & Hedge, 2000).

Marshes along urbanized estuaries are degraded simply due to the reduction in tidal and freshwater inflow, as well as sedimentation. Along the Hudson River estuary, marshes have become increasingly saline as water is impounded and diverted upstream, and the vegetation has shifted from tidal freshwater and brackish to salt marshes over the past century (Marshall, 2004). These brackish marshes have been increasingly dominated by common reed. Similarly, freshwater flow into the San Francisco Bay estuaries has declined by 40% over the past century (Nichols *et al.*, 1986), causing saltwater intrusion into the upper brackish estuaries and delta. Agricultural development in the watershed that feeds estuaries can enhance sedimentation, whereas diking and seawall protection (such is common in northern Europe) can disrupt sedimentation. Sediment loads flowing from the Yellow River in China have declined dramatically between 1950 and 2005 due to a series of large dam projects, increases in soil conservation practices, and changes in rainfall and water use (Wang *et al.*, 2007). How important the inputs of sediment, nutrients, and contaminants are depends on the catchment size for the estuary that feeds the marsh as well as the industrial development in the immediate area. Particularly negatively impacted salt marshes are found in the large coastal estuaries of China, San Francisco, the mid-Atlantic US, and the estuary of the Rio de la Plata.

The small, isolated marshes of southern California have suffered from urban development, fragmentation, and changes in hydrology, thereby favoring monocultural patches of American glasswort (*Salicornia virginica*) (Zedler *et al.*, 2001). Hydrological changes include a large reduction in natural freshwater flow during the rainy season and a muting of tidal action.

Colorado River delta marshes in the Gulf of California were greatly reduced when a series of dams were constructed upstream to feed irrigation projects, once again reducing freshwater inflow (Glenn, 1996). With many of these dams filling up, a resurgence of some flow has allowed for the possibility of recovery of the remaining degraded marsh systems.

The Deepwater Horizon oil rig explosion of 2010 highlighted the vulnerability of coastal marshes. Some of these marshes are located near areas of offshore drilling, but many more are situated near shipping lanes and are highly vulnerable to catastrophic and chronic low-level petroleum spills (Wiese & Ryan, 2003). While short-term impacts on arthropod assemblages (the food base for most salt marsh birds) have been detected (McCall & Pennings, 2012), the long-term effect on bird populations has yet to be determined (but see Chapter 11). Effects of oil are known to be particularly persistent in coastal marshes, sometimes lasting decades (Kingston, 2002).

Located on the coast and sensitive to temperature regimes, salt marshes are particularly vulnerable to climate change (Hughes, 2004; Woodrey *et al.*, 2012). Sea level rise and increased storm surges are probably the foremost resultant impacts. Even in areas experiencing high sedimentation rates, rising seas at a moderate to high level (which are often exacerbated by the geomorphology of estuaries) may outpace marsh accretion. Species vulnerability analyses have demonstrated considerable reduction and fragmentation in habitat (Shriver & Gibbs, 2004). Species with reproductive output already constrained by regular tidal flooding, such as salt marsh sparrows in northeastern US, will have to cope with an increase in storm surges, which may make century-events annual occurrences in some estuaries (Bayard & Elphick, 2011; Tebaldi *et al.*, 2012). Van de pol and colleagues (2010) showed through simulations based on real reproductive data on six salt marsh-nesting species that the unpredictable storm surges will likely cause local declines. They argue that restored low marsh may actually act as an ecological trap as birds are unable to predict future catastrophic flooding.

Ultimately, sea level rise may force a migration of marsh habitat inland. However, many estuaries have geomorphologies that will retard the retreat of marshland (Strauss *et al.*, 2012). More importantly, estuaries surrounded by human development will provide little opportunity for the inland shift (Straus *et al.*, 2012). Perhaps in less-developed areas of Australia, South America, and Mexico, we will be able to see a natural shift of salt marsh habitat, but in North America, Europe, and China, this seems unlikely without a specific management plan for land bordering marshes.

Climate change has other impacts as well. Salt marsh is an unbuffered habitat, exposed to insolation, which can cause thermal stress. Tidal flooding can limit the ability of birds to escape into cover to avoid the direct effects of solar radiation. Their main physiological mechanism for cooling is evapotranspiration, and water use is increased by the windy conditions common to many coastal marshes. Because saltwater use is physiologically stressful for most birds, water balance is particularly critical for species restricted to salt marshes with high summer temperatures. Increasing summer temperatures would exacerbate heat and water issues, but this has received relatively little attention (Greenberg *et al.*, 2012). Summer temperatures may have the greatest impact on reproduction, vis-à-vis reduced clutch size or egg and nestling survival, which may determine southern edges of distributions (Etterson *et al.*, 2011). Increasing winter temperatures are likely to have indirect effects in areas bordering on the subtropics; mangroves, which are physiologically limited by cold temperatures, will encroach upon salt marshes as conditions become more favorable (Stuart *et al.*, 2007; see Chapter 2). In the temperate zone, patterns of freshwater inflow can be expected to change. Presumably semi-arid and arid regions that are expected to face increased drought will see further reduction in freshwater flow, but some areas (such as SESA) may see an increase in freshwater. Rainfall in the northern area of SESA has increased in the last 100 years (Canepuccia *et al.*, 2008), probably as a by-product of climate change. Related to climate change, the increase in atmospheric CO_2 has produced short-term increases in primary productivity of salt marsh grasses, particularly when accompanied by an increase in soil nitrogen (Langley & Megonigal, 2010). In the longer term, climate change may favor a shift in plant composition from C3 plants, such as common reed, to C4 plants. One experimental study demonstrated that wintering populations of a seed-eating songbird is highly limited by food supply (Danner, 2012), which is mediated by weather. Increases in winter temperature and food supply (due to increased plant growth and seed production) could boost the winter carrying capacity of coastal marshes for granivorous birds (which globally includes a diverse group of sparrows, waterfowl, parrots, etc.). However, it is not yet clear that increased primary productivity results in increased seed production. Relating these trophic connections to changes in CO2 and climate is a ripe area for further investigation.

PROSPECTS FOR THE FUTURE

Coastal marshes are highly localized ecosystems that are impacted by heavy land use, urbanization, changes in hydrology, toxins and pollutants, habitat modification, and invasive species. Although many of the impacts are shared among all coastal marshes, the relative importance of different management issues varies considerably across continents. Most of the coastal areas we have discussed, as well as many others, support efforts to protect and restore the coastal wetlands that focus on the appropriate local issues. Grazing and burning may be the most important issue in South America, but contamination may be more important along more industrialized coastlines in North America and Europe. Salt marshes continue to be lost to development, but along many of the more urbanized coastlines, actual loss of marsh has slowed, and some restoration is in progress. However, restored salt marshes are often small ghosts of the systems they replaced and suffer from many kinds of degradation. Furthermore, the boxing in of small protected or restored marshes by upland development both impinges on the avifauna of existing wetlands and reduces the flexibility to accommodate the migration of marshlands in response to sea level rise.

Because salt marshes are already so heavily impacted, simply protecting them from development is not an alternative that will lead to healthier ecosystems. While modified hydrology is one of the greatest threats to salt marshes, restoration of more natural hydrology is also a dominant tool for transforming salt marshes back into habitats that will support the full range of bird diversity, especially ones that will support salt marsh specialists. Although some success has been reported for restoring vegetation (Zedler *et al.*, 2001; Roman & Burdick, 2012), the long-term impact of restoring natural water flows on marsh birds, particularly specialist species, is controversial and needs more long-term research. Marshes restored with marsh vegetation and greater freshwater and tidal flow will continue to suffer from many other environmental impacts, such as fragmentation, contamination, and non-native species invasions. It would seem that a higher-profile, internationally cooperative effort to develop the theoretical framework and technologies for salt marsh restoration is needed to address the magnitude of the problem.

AN INTERNATIONAL CONFEDERACY OF SALT MARSH CONSERVATION BIOLOGISTS

Although each coastline and estuary is unique, many of the issues facing biological conservation of coastal salt marsh would greatly benefit by taking a more global approach. We would envision that organizing salt marsh conservation biology under some sort of global confederacy would offer the umbrella for some more global approaches, such as the following.

1. Develop a uniform global inventory of the distribution of tidal marshes, categorized by salinity and vegetation type, and made available on a website to tidal marsh researchers throughout the world, similar to the Mangrove Atlas (Spalding *et al.*, 1997). Such an inventory is being developed by the Marine Assessment and Decision Support Programme at UNEP-WCMC, but how it will be disseminated for researchers and policy-makers is unclear.

2. Increase research on the (Pleistocene, Holocene, and very recent) history of tidal marshes, focusing on their extent, distribution, and floral composition through time. Every effort should be made to apply the research broadly and with an explicitly geographic comparative component. Results of such a comprehensive historical survey could be presented along with the current tidal marsh distribution in a web atlas that is periodically revised and updated.

3. Standardize inventory and monitoring data for tidal marsh fauna and flora, and conduct more comparative work focused on tidal marsh taxa (vertebrate, invertebrate, and floristic) living along different coastlines. Such data may exist already in the published or gray literature, but need to be compiled into usable and accessible formats. In cases where published data are lacking, faunal inventories should be initiated.

4. Conduct more globally integrated work on the role of physiological, trophic, life historical, and social factors in shaping adaptations to tidal marsh environments. Along with this, we need to develop models for the factors that drive and inhibit divergence of tidal marsh populations from their inland source and sister populations. These activities will emphasize the adaptive uniqueness of tidal marsh forms.

5. Foster more internationally cooperative work on the principles of salt marsh restoration, focusing particularly on ecologically sound methods for invasive plant species control and restitution of more natural tidal flow, hydrology, and sedimentation so that lessons can be learned between these various systems that are so similar, yet different.

6. Raise awareness of the critical issues facing salt marsh conservation on a global scale. Continue to elevate the international importance of critical coastal wetlands through RAMSAR and other forms of outreach to the public and policy communities.

ACKNOWLEDGMENTS

We would like to thank the following people for providing information used in this chapter: Danny Rogers, David Melville, Simba Chen, Zhijun Ma,

Qiang Ma, and Lin Zhang. Nadav Nur (Point Reyes Bird Observatory) provided population estimates for San Francisco Bay birds. DAC and JPI works were supported by CONICET, UNMdP, ANPCyT, and CREO.

REFERENCES

Adam, P. (2009). Australian saltmarshes in global context. In N. Saintilan (ed.), *Australian Saltmarsh Ecology*. Collingwood: CSIRO Publishing, pp. 1–21.

An, S. Q. (2003). *Ecological Engineering of Wetlands*. Beijing: Chemical Industry Press.

An, S. Q., Gu, B. H., Zhou, C. F., *et al.* (2007). Spartina invasion in China: Implications for invasive species management and future research. *Weed Research*, **47**, 183–191.

Bayard, T. S. & Elphick, C. S. (2011). Planning for sea-level rise: Quantifying patterns of saltmarsh sparrow (*Ammodramus caudacutus*) nest flooding under current sea-level conditions. *Auk*, **128**, 393–403.

Beadell, J., Greenberg, R., Droege, S. & Royle, J. A. (2003). Distribution, abundance, and habitat affinities of the coastal plain swamp sparrow. *Wilson Bulletin*, **115**, 38–44.

Benoit, L. K. & Askins, R. A. (1999). Impact of the spread of Phragmites on the distribution of birds in Connecticut tidal marshes. *Wetlands*, **19**, 194–208.

Bertness, M. D., Ewanchuk, P. J. & Silliman, B. R. (2002). Anthropogenic modification of New England salt marsh landscapes. *Proceedings of the National Academy of Sciences of the United States of America*, **99**, 1395–1398.

Bilenca, D. & Miñarro, F. (2004). *Identificación de Areas Valiosas de Pastizales en Las Pampas y Campos Argentinos, Uruguay y Sur de Brasil (AVPs)*. Buenos Aires: Fundación Vida Silvestre.

BirdLife International. (2004). *Birds in Europe 2*. Cambridge: BirdLife International.

Boon, P. I. (2011). Saltmarshes. In: *Understanding the Western Port Environment: A Summary of Current Knowledge and Priorities for Future Research*. Docklands, Victoria: Melbourne Water, pp. 116–133.

Boulord, A., Wang, T.-H., Wang, X.-M. & Song, G.-X. (2011). Impact of reed harvesting and smooth cordgrass *Spartina alterniflora* invasion on nesting reed parrotbill *Paradoxornis heudei*. *Bird Conservation International*, **21**, 25–35.

Canepuccia, A. D., Farias, A., Escalante, A. H., *et al.* (2008). Differential responses of marsh predators to rainfall-induced habitat loss and subsequent variations in prey availability. *Canadian Journal of Zoology*, **86**, 407–418.

Cao, L., Barter, M. A. & Wang, X. (2008). Saunders's gull: A new population estimate. *Bird Conservation International*, **18**, 301–306.

Cao, M. C., Liu, G. H., Shan, K., *et al.* (2010). A multi-scale assessment of habitat suitability of red-crowned crane at the Yellow River Delta Nature Reserve, Shandong, China. *Biodiversity Science*, **18**, 283–291.

Cao, W. Z. & Wong, M. H. (2007). Current status of coastal zone issues and management in China: A review. *Environment International*, **33**, 985–992.

Cardoni, D. A. (2011). Adaptaciones evolutivas y respuestas a la actividad antrópica de aves de marismas del atlántico sudoccidental: un análisis a diferentes escalas temporales. PhD thesis, Universidad Nacional de Mar del Plata, Argentina.

Cardoni, D. A., Isacch, J. P. & Iribarne, O. O. (2007). Indirect effects of the burrowing crab (*Chasmagnathus granulatus*) in the habitat use of salt marsh birds. *Estuaries and Coasts*, **30**, 382–389.

Cardoni, D. A., Isacch, J. P., Fanjul, M. E., Escapa, M. & Iribarne, O. O. (2011). Relationship between anthropogenic sewage discharge, marsh structure and bird assemblages in a SW Atlantic salt marsh. *Marine Environmental Research*, **71**, 122–130.

Cardoni, D. A., Isacch, J. P. & Iribarne, O. O. (2012). Effects of cattle grazing and fire on the abundance, habitat selection, and nesting success of the bay-capped wren-spinetail (*Spartonoica maluroides*) in coastal saltmarshes of the Pampas region. *Condor*, **114**, 803–811.

Cardoni, D. A., Greenberg, R., Maldonado, J. E. & Isacch, J. P. (2013). Morphological adaptation to coastal marshes in spite of limited genetic structure in the Neotropical passerine *Spartonoica maluroides* (Aves: Furnariidae). *Biological Journal of Linnaean Society*, **109**, 78–91.

Cervencl, A., Esser, W., Maier, M., *et al.* (2011). Can differences in incubation patterns of common redshanks *Tringa totanus* be explained by variations in predation risk? *Journal of Ornithology*, **152**, 1033–1043.

Chapman, V. J. (ed.). (1977). Wet coastal ecosystems. In *Ecosystems of the World*, vol. 1. Amsterdam: Elsevier Scientific.

Charman, K. & Macey, A. (1978). The winter grazing of saltmarsh vegetation by dark-bellied Brent geese. *Wildfowl*, **29**, 153–162.

Chavez-Ramirez, F. & Slack, R. D. (1995). Differential use of coastal marsh habitats by nonbreeding wading birds. *Colonial Waterbirds*, **18**, 166–171.

Chen, M. R., Han, X. F. & Liu, S. Q. (2000). The effects of reclamation and sustainable development on coastal zone in Shanghai. *China Soft Science*, **12**, 115–120.

Christidis, L. & Boles, W. E. (2008). *Systematics and Taxonomy of Australian Birds*. Collingwood: CSIRO Publishing.

Chu, Z. Y., Yang, S. Z., Qiao, Z. Z. & Ye, E. Q. (1999). Conservation of the Saunder's gull breeding colony at the Luanhe Estuary. *Chinese Biodiversity*, **7**, 20–23.

Costa, C. S. B., Iribarne, O. O. & Farina, J. M. (2009). Human impacts and threats to the conservation of South American salt marshes. In B. R. Silliman, E. D. Grosholz & M. D. Bertness (eds.), *Human Impacts on Salt Marshes: A Global Perspective*. Los Angeles, CA: University of California Press, pp. 337–359.

Cresswell, W. & Whitfield, D. P. (1994). The effects of raptor predation on wintering wader populations at the Tyningharne estuary, southeast Scotland. *Ibis*, **136**, 223–232.

Daehler, C. C. & Strong, D. R. (1996). Status, prediction and prevention of introduced cordgrass *Spartina* spp. invasions in Pacific estuaries, USA. *Biological Conservation*, **78**, 51–58.

Daiber, F. C. (1986). *Conservation of Tidal Marsh*. New York, NY: Van Nostrand Reinhold Co.

Dale, P. (1993). Australian wetlands and mosquito control – Contain the pest and sustain the environment. *Wetlands Australia*, **12**, 1–12.

Danner, R. M. (2012). The effects of limited winter food availability on the population dynamics, energy reserves, and feather molt of the swamp sparrow. PhD thesis, Virginia Polytechnic and State University, Blacksburg, VA.

Dierschke, J. (2002). Vorkommen und Habitatwahl des Strandpiepers *Anthus petrosus* im deutschen Wattenmeer. [Occurrence and habitat use of rock pipit *Anthus petrosus* in the German Wadden Sea.] *Vogelwelt*, **123**, 125–134.

Dijkema, K. S. (1987). Geography of salt marshes in Europe. *Zeitschrift fur Geomorphologie*, **31**, 489–499.

Dijkema, K. S. (1990). Salt and brackish marshes around the Baltic Sea and adjacent parts of the North Sea: Their vegetation and management. *Biological Conservation*, **51**, 191–209.

Dijkema, K. S., Beeftink, W. G., Doody, J. P., *et al.* (1984). Salt marshes in Europe. *Nature and Environment Series*, **30**, 1–178.

Duan, Y. B., Tian, X. H., Zhu, S. Y., *et al.* (2011). Make use of nest-site of oriental white stork in the Yellow River Estuary Nature Reserve. *Acta Ecologica Sinica*, **31**, 666–672.

Duarte, B., Caetano, M. & Almeida, P. R. (2010). Accumulation and biological cycling of heavy metal in four salt marsh species, from Tagus estuary (Portugal). *Environmental Pollution*, **75**, 1661–1668.

Etterson, M. A., Olsen, B. J., Greenberg, R. & Shriver, W. G. (2011). Sources, sinks, and model accuracy. In J. Liu, V. Hull, A. Morzillo & J. Wiens (eds.), *Sources, Sinks, and Sustainability Across Landscapes*. New York, NY: Cambridge University Press, pp. 273–290.

Ferns, P. N. (1992). *Bird Life of Coasts and Estuaries*. Cambridge: Cambridge University Press.

Gan, X. J., Zhang, K. J., Tang, S. M., Li, B. & Ma, Z. J. (2006). Three new records of birds in Shanghai: *Locustella pleskei* (Pleske's warbler), *Megalurus pryeri* (Japanese swamp warbler) and *Acrocephalus concinens* (blunt-winged paddyfield warbler). *Journal of Fudan University (Natural Science)*, **45**, 417–420.

Gan, X. J., Cai, Y. T., Choi, C. Y., *et al.* (2009). Potential impacts of invasive *Spartina alterniflora* on spring bird communities at Chongming Dongtan, a Chinese wetland of international importance. *Estuarine Coastal and Shelf Science*, **83**, 211–218.

Gan, X. J., Choi, C. Y., Wang, Y., *et al.* (2010). Alteration of habitat structure and food resources by invasive smooth cordgrass affects habitat use by wintering salt-marsh birds at Chongming Dongtan, East China. *Auk*, **12**, 317–327.

Garnett, S. T. (1987). Aerial surveys of waders (Aves: Charadriiformes) along the coast of north-eastern Australia. *Australian Wildlife Research*, **14**, 521–528.

Ge, Z. M. (2007). *The Research on the Characters of Migratory Waterbird Communities and the Habitats Restoration Strategy at the Yangtze River Mouth*. Shanghai: East China Normal University.

Glenn, E. P., Lee, C., Felger, R. & Zengel, S. (1996). Effects of water management on the wetlands of the Colorado River Delta, Mexico. *Conservation Biology*, **10**, 1175–1186.

Greenberg, R., Elphick, C., Nordby. J. C., *et al.* (2006a). Flooding and predation: Trade-offs in the nesting ecology of tidal-marsh sparrows. *Studies in Avian Biology*, **32**, 96–109.

Greenberg, R., Maldonado, J., Droege, S. & McDonald, M. V. (2006b). Tidal marshes: A global perspective on the evolution and conservation of their terrestrial vertebrates. *Bioscience*, **56**, 675–685.

Greenberg, R., Danner, R. M., Olsen, B. J. & Luther, D. (2012). High temperatures explain bill size in salt marsh sparrows. *Ecography*, **35**, 146–152.

Grime, J. P. (1977). Evidence for the existence of three primary strategies in plants and its relevance to ecological and evolutionary theory. *American Naturalist*, 111, 1169–1195.

Hazelden, J. & Boorman, L. A. (2001). Soils and 'managed retreat' in South East England. *Soil Use and Management*, 17, 150–154.

Heng, N. N., Niu, J. Y., Zhang, B. & Wang, T. H. (2011). Habitat selection of shore-birds in the intertidal mudflat of Nanhui coasts. *Journal of Fudan University (Natural Science)*, 50, 276–310.

Higgins, P. J. (ed.). (1999). *Handbook of Australian, New Zealand and Antarctic Birds*, vol. 4: Parrots to Dollarbird. Melbourne: Oxford University Press.

Higgins, P. J. & Davies, S. J. J. F. (eds.). (1996). *Handbook of Australian, New Zealand and Antarctic Birds*, vol. 3: Snipe to Pigeons. Melbourne: Oxford University Press.

Higgins, P. J. & Peter, J. M. (eds.). (2002). *Handbook of Australian, New Zealand and Antarctic Birds*, vol. 6: Pardalotes to Shrike-thrushes. Melbourne: Oxford University Press.

Higgins, P. J., Peter, J. M. & Steele, W. K. (eds.). (2001). *Handbook of Australian, New Zealand and Antarctic Birds*, vol. 5: Tyrant-flycatchers to Chats. Melbourne: Oxford University Press.

Higgins, P. J., Peter, J. M. & Cowling, S. J. (eds.). (2006). *Handbook of Australian, New Zealand and Antarctic Birds.*, vol. 7: Boatbill to Starlings. Melbourne: Oxford University Press.

Horwitz, E. L. (1978). *Our Nations Wetlands*. Washington, DC: Council on Environmental Quality.

Hu, W. & Lu, J. J. (2000). The research on shorebirds' community structure of spring in San Jia Gang. *Journal of East China Normal University (Natural Science)*, 4, 106–109.

Huang, Z. Y., Sun, Z. H., Yu, K., *et al.* (1993). *Bird Resources and Habitats in Shanghai*. Shanghai: Fudan University Press.

Hughes, R. G. (2004). Climate change and loss of saltmarshes: Consequences for birds. *Ibis*, 146, 21–28.

Isacch, J. P. & Cardoni, D. A. (2011). Different grazing strategies are necessary to conserve endangered grassland birds in short and tall salty grasslands of the flooding Pampas. *Condor*, 113, 724–734.

Isacch, J. P., Holz, S., Ricci, L. & Martínez, M. M. (2004). Post-fire vegetation change and bird use of a salt marsh in coastal Argentina. *Wetlands*, 24, 235–243.

Isacch, J. P., Costal, C. S. B., Rodríguez-Gallego, L., *et al.* (2006). Distribution of salt marsh plant communities associated with environmental factors along a latitudinal gradient on the SW Atlantic coast. *Journal of Biogeography*, 33, 888–900.

Isacch, J. P., Cardoni, D. A. & Iribarne, O. (2013). Diversity and habitat distribution of birds in coastal marshes and comparisons with surrounded upland habitats in southeastern South America. *Estuaries and Coasts*, doi: 10.1007/12237-013-9655-7.

IUCN. (2011). IUCN Red List of Threatened Species, Version 2011.2. www.iucn-redlist.org. Accessed 15 September 2012.

Jefferies, R. L., Jano, A. P. & Abraham, K. F. (2006). A biotic agent promotes large-scale catastrophic change in the coastal marshes of Hudson Bay. *Journal of Ecology*, 94, 234–242.

Ji, Y. H. & Zhou, G. S. (2010). Transformation of vegetation structure in China's Liaohe Delta during 1988–2006. *Chinese Journal of Plant Ecology*, 34, 359–367.

Jiang, H. X., Chu, G. Z. & Hou, Y. Q. (2002). Breeding habitat selection of Saunders' gull *Larus saundersi* in Yancheng of Jiangsu Province. *Acta Ecologica Sinica*, 22, 999–1004.

Jiang, H. X., Hou, Y. Q., Chu, G. Z., *et al.* (2010). Breeding population dynamics and habitat transition of Saunders's gull *Larus saundersi* in Yancheng National Nature Reserve, China. *Bird Conservation International*, 20, 13–24.

Jing, K. (2005). Stopover ecology of shorebirds in Chongming Dongtan, Shanghai. PhD thesis, Fudan University, Shanghai.

JMMB. (2010). *Trends of migratory and wintering waterbirds in the Wadden Sea 1987/ 88–2008/09*. Wilhelmshaven, Germany. www.waddensea-secretariat.org.

JMBB. (2011). *Trends in breeding birds in the Wadden Sea 1991–2006*. Wilhelmshaven, Germany. www.waddensea-secretariat.org.

Kingston, P. F. (2002). Long-term environmental impacts of oil spills. *Spill Science and Technology Bulletin*, 7, 53–61.

Koffijberg, K., Blew, J., Eskildsen, K., *et al.* (2003). *High Tide Roosts in the Wadden Sea*, Wadden Sea Ecosystem No. 16. Wilhelmshaven, Germany: Common Wadden Sea Secretariat, Joint Monitoring Group of Migratory Birds in the Wadden Sea.

Koffijberg, K., Dijksen, L., Hälterlein, B., *et al.* (2006). *Breeding Birds in the Wadden Sea in 2001. Results from the Total Survey in 2001 and Trends in Numbers Between 1991–2001*. Wadden Sea Ecosystem No. 22. Wilhelmshaven, Germany: Common Wadden Sea Secretariat, Trilateral Monitoring and Assessment Group, Joint Monitoring Group of Breeding Birds in the Wadden Sea.

Kriwoken, L. K. & Hedge, P. (2000). Exotic species and estuaries: Managing *Spartina anglica* in Tasmania, Australia. *Ocean and Coastal Management*, 43, 573–584.

Laegdsgaard, P., Kelleway, J., Williams, R. J. & Harty, C. (2009). Protection and management of coastal saltmarsh. In N. Saintilan (ed.), *Australian Saltmarsh Ecology*. Collingwood: CSIRO Publishing, pp. 179–210.

Langley, J. A. & Megonigal, J. P. (2010). Ecosystem response to elevated CO_2 levels limited by nitrogen-induced plant species shift. *Nature*, 466, 96–99.

Laursen, K., Blew, J., Eskildsen, K., *et al.* (2010). *Migratory Waterbirds in the Wadden Sea 1987–2008*. Wadden Sea Ecosystem No. 30. Wilhelmshaven, Germany: Common Wadden Sea Secretariat, Joint Monitoring Group of Migratory Birds in the Wadden Sea.

Leck, M. A. (1989). Wetland seed banks. In M. A. Leck, V. T. Parker & R. L. Simpson (eds.), *Ecology of Soil Seed Banks*. San Diego, CA: Academic Press, pp. 283–306.

Li, G. D., Zhou, Y. X., Tian, B., Liu, Z. G. & Zheng, Z. S. (2008). Shanghai estuarine and coastal wetlands change analysis based on remote sensing and GIS. *Journal of Jilin University (Earth Science Edition)*, 38, 219–323.

Loyn, R. H. (1978). A survey of birds in Westernport Bay, Victoria, 1973–74. *Emu*, 78, 11–19.

Loyn, R. H., Lane, B. A., Chandler, C. & Carr, G. W. (1986). Ecology of orange-bellied parrots *Neophema chrysogaster* at their main remnant wintering site. *Emu*, 86, 195–206.

Loyn, R. H., Dann, P. & McCulloch, E. (2001). Important wader sites in the East Asian–Australasian flyway: 1. Western Port, Victoria, Australia. *The Stilt*, 38, 39–53.

Ma, Z. J., Li, B., Zhao, B., *et al.* (2004). Are artificial wetlands good alternatives to natural wetlands for waterbirds? A case study on Chongming Island, China. *Biodiversity and Conservation*, **13**, 333–350.

Ma, Z. J., Gan, X. J., Choi, C. Y., *et al.* (2007). Wintering bird communities in newly-formed wetland in the Yangtze River estuary. *Ecological Research*, **22**, 115–124.

Ma, Z., Gan, X., Cai, Y., Chen, J. & Li, B. (2011). Effects of exotic *Spartina alterniflora* on the habitat patch associations of breeding saltmarsh birds at Chongming Dongtan in the Yangtze River estuary, China. *Biological Invasions*, **13**, 1673–1686.

Marchant, S. & Higgins, P. J. (eds.). (1990). *Handbook of Australian, New Zealand and Antarctic Birds*, vol. 1: Ratites to Ducks. Melbourne: Oxford University Press.

Marchant, S. & Higgins, P. J. (eds.). (1993). *Handbook of Australian, New Zealand and Antarctic Birds*, vol. 2: Raptors to Lapwings. Melbourne: Oxford University Press.

Marshall, S. (2004). The meadowlands before the commission: Three centuries of human use and alteration of the Newark and Hackensack meadows. *Urban Habitats*, **2**, 4–27.

McCall, B. D. & Pennings, S. C. (2012). Disturbance and recovery of salt marsh arthropod communities following BP Deepwater Horizon oil spill. *PLoS ONE*, **7**, e32735.

Menkhorst, P. (2010). *A Survey of Colonially Breeding Birds on Mud Islands, Port Phillip, Victoria, with an Annotated List of All Terrestrial Vertebrates*, Arthur Rylah Institute Technical Report 206. Heidelberg, Victoria: Department of Sustainability and Environment.

Mitchell, L. R., Gabrey, S., Marra, P. P. & Erwin, R. M. (2006). Impacts of marsh management on coastal-marsh bird habitats. *Studies in Avian Biology*, **32**, 155–175.

Nichols, F. H., Cloern, J. E., Luoma, S. N. & Peterson, D. H. (1986). The modification of an estuary. *Science*, **231**, 567–573.

Nordby, J. C., Cohen, A. Beissinger, S. R. (1991). Effects of a habitat-altering invader on nesting sparrows: An ecological trap? *Biological Invasions*, **11**, 565–575.

Page, G. & Whitacre, D. F. (1975). Raptor predation on wintering shorebirds. *Condor*, **77**, 73–83.

PIF, Partners in Flight. (2007). Land Bird Population Estimate Data Base. rmbo.org/pif_db/laped/about.aspx.

Popp, M., Mirré, V. & Brochmann, C. A. (2011). A single mid-Pleistocene long-distance dispersal by a bird can explain the extreme bipolar disjunction in crowberries (*Empetrum*). *Proceedings of the National Academy of Sciences of the United States of America*, **108**, 6520–6525.

Qin, P. & Zhong, C. X. (1992). *Applied Studies on* Spartina. Beijing: Ocean Press.

Quinn, D. & Lacey, G. (1999). *Birds of French Island*. Richmond: Spectrum Publications.

Reinert, B. L., Bornschein, M. R. & Firkowski, C. (2007). Distribuição, tamanho populacional, hábitat e conservação do bicudinho-do-brejo *Stymphalornis acutirostris* Bornschein, Reinert e Teixeira, 1995 (Thamnophilidae). *Revista Brasileira de Ornitologia*, **15**, 493–519.

Rey, J. R., Walton, W. W., Wolfe, R. J., *et al.* (2012). North American wetlands and mosquito control. *International Journal of Environmental Research and Public Health*, **9**, 4537–4605.

Rickey, M. A. & Anderson, R. C. (2004). Effects of nitrogen addition on the invasive grass *Phragmites australis* and a native competitor *Spartina pectinata*. *Journal of Applied Ecology*, **41**, 888–896.

Roman, C. T. & Burdick, D. M. (eds.). (2012). *Tidal Marsh Restoration: A Synthesis of Science and Management*. Washington, DC: Island Press.

Rowcliffe, J. M., Watkinson, A. R., Sutherland, W. J. & Vickery, J. A. (1995). Cyclic winter grazing patterns in Brent geese and the regrowth of salt-marsh grass. *Functional Ecology*, **9**, 931–941.

Shan, K., Zhang, C. H. & Zhang, H. Y. (2007). Migration behavior of crane to south in Yellow River Delta Nature Reserve. *Chinese Journal of Wildlife*, **28**, 36–38.

Shriver, W. G. & Gibbs, J. P. (2004). Projected effects of sea-level rise on the population viability of seaside sparrows (*Ammodramus maritimus*). In H. R. Akcakaya, M. A. Burgman, O. Kindvall, *et al.* (eds.), *Species Conservation and Management: Case Studies*. New York, NY: Oxford University Press, pp. 397–409.

Shriver, W. G., Evers, D. C., Hodgman, T. P. & MacCulloch, B. J. (2006). Hg in sharp-tailed sparrows breeding in coastal wetlands. *Environmental Bioindicators*, **1**, 129–135.

Silliman, B. R., Grosholz, E. D. & Bertness, M. D. (eds.). (2009). *Human Impacts on Salt Marshes: A Global Perspective*. Berkeley, CA: University of California Press.

Soriano, A., León, R. J. C., Sala, O. E., *et al.* (1991). Río de la Plata grasslands. In R. T. Coupland (ed.), *Ecosystems of the World 8A, Natural Grasslands, Introduction and Western Hemisphere*. New York, NY: Elsevier, pp. 367–407.

Spalding, M. F., Blasco, F. & Field, C. D. (1997). *World Mangrove Atlas*. International Society for Mangrove Ecosystems. www.unep-wcmc.org/world-mangrove-atlas_451.html.

Spencer, J., Monamy, V. & Breitfuss, M. (2009). Saltmarsh as habitat for birds and other vertebrates. In N. Saintilan (ed.), *Australian Saltmarsh Ecology*. Collingwood: CSIRO Publishing, pp. 149–165.

Starks, J., Brown, P., Loyn, R. & Menkhorst, P. (1992). Twelve years of winter counts of the orange-bellied parrot *Neophema chrysogaster*. *Australian Bird Watcher*, **14**, 305–312.

Strauss, B. H., Ziemlinski, R., Weiss, J. L. & Overpeck, J. T. (2012). Tidally adjusted estimates of topographic vulnerability to sea level rise and flooding for the contiguous United States. *Environmental Research Letters*, **7**, 014033. doi:10.1088/1748-9326/7/1/014033.

Stuart, S. A., Choat, B., Martin, K. C., Holbrook, N. M. & Ball, M. C. (2007). The role of freezing in setting the latitudinal limits of mangrove forests. *New Phytologist*, **173**, 576–583.

Summers, S. W. (1977). Distribution, abundance, and energy relationships of waders (Aves: Charadrii) and Langebaan Lagoon. *Transaction of the Royal Society of South Africa*, **42**, 483–495.

Tebaldi, C., Strauss, B. H. & Zervus, C. E. (2012). Modeling sea level rise impacts on storm surges along the US coasts. *Environmental Research Letters*, **7**, 014032. doi:10.1088/1748-9326/7/1/014032.

US Fish and Wildlife Service. (2002). *Birds of Conservation Concern 2002*. Arlington, VA: Division of Migratory Bird Management. migratorybirds.fws.gov/reports/bcc2002.pdf.

Van de Pol, M., Ens, B. J., Heg, D., *et al.* (2010). Do changes in the frequency, magnitude and timing of extreme climatic events threaten the population viability of coastal birds? *Journal of Applied Ecology*, **47**, 720–730.

Viglizzo, E. F., Lertora, F., Pordomingo, A. J., *et al.* (2001). Ecological lessons and applications from one century of low external-input farming in the Pampas of Argentina. *Agriculture, Ecosystem and Environment*, **83**, 6–81.

Vivian-Smith, G. & Stiles, E. W. (1994). Dispersal of salt marsh seeds on the feet and feathers of waterfowl. *Wetlands*, **14**, 316–319.

Wang, H., Yang, Z., Saito, Y. I., *et al.* (2007). Stepwise decreases of the Huanghe (Yellow River) sediment load (1950–2005): Impacts of climate change and human activities. *Global and Planetary Change*, **57**, 331–354.

Wang, Q., An, S. Q., Ma, Z. J., *et al.* (2006). Invasive *Spartina alterniflora*: Biology, ecology and management. *Acta Phytotaxonomica Sinica*, **44**, 559–588.

Wiese, F. K. & Ryan, P. C. (2003). The extent of chronic marine oil pollution in southeastern Newfoundland waters assessed through beached bird surveys 1984–1999. *Marine Pollution Bulletin*, **46**, 1090–1101.

Williams, T. P., Bubb, J. M. & Lester, J. N. (1994). Metal accumulation within salt marsh environments: A review. *Marine Pollution Bulletin*, **28**, 277–290.

Woodrey, M. S., Rush, S. A., Cherry, J. A., *et al.* (2012). Understanding the potential impact of global climate change on marsh birds in the Gulf of Mexico region. *Wetlands*, **32**, 35–49.

Xu, H. F. & Zhao, Y. L. (2005). *Comprehensive Surveys in Chongming Dongtan Nature Reserve for Migratory Birds, Shanghai.* Beijing: Chinese Forestry Publishing House.

Zedler, J. B., Callaway, J. C. & Sullivan, G. (2001). Declining biodiversity: Why species matter and how their functions might be restored in Californian tidal marshes. *Bioscience*, **51**, 1005–1017.

Zembal, R. & Hoffmann, S. M. (2010). *Belding's Savannah Sparrow Survey: 2010, Conservation and Recovery Report 2010–03.* Sacramento, CA: California Department of Fish and Game.

Zembal, R., Hoffmann, S. M. & Koneeny, J. (2010). *Status and Distribution of the Light-footed Clapper Rail in California. A report to the California Department of Fish and Game.* Sacramento, CA: California Department of Fish and Game.

Zhang, X. L., Xu, Z. J., Zhang, Z. H., Gu, D. Q. & Ye, S. Y. (2010). Review on degradation of coastal wetland of Northern China Sea. *Geological Review*, **56**, 561–567.

Zhao, D. C. (1996). *Vegetation of Coastal China.* Beijing: Ocean Press.

APPENDIX

Breeding bird species of Chinese coastal marshes, with information on breeding and conservation status, habitat use, and distribution.

	Migratory status[a]	Breeding region[b] *	Nesting in coastal marsh	Habitat type	Conservation status[c]
Saunders's gull *Larus saundersi*	M	North/Mid	YES	Nests in low and sparse *Suaeda* spp.-dominated marshes, feeds on low intertidal zone or artificial fish ponds	VU
Oriental stork *Ciconia boyciana*	M	North/Mid	NO	Feeds in *Phragmites*-dominated habitats in Yellow River Delta	EN, I
Yellow bittern *Ixobrychus sinensis*	R–M	North/Mid/South	YES	*Phragmites* and *Spartina* habitats	LC
Schrenck's bittern *Ixobrychus eurhythmus*	M	North/Mid/South	?	*Phragmites* and *Spartina* habitats	LC
Cinnamon bittern *Ixobrychus cinnamomeus*	R–M	North/Mid/South	YES	*Phragmites* and *Spartina* habitats	LC
Black bittern *Dupetor flavicollis*	M	North/Mid/South	?	*Phragmites* and *Spartina* habitats	LC
Chinese pond heron *Ardeola bacchus*	R–M	North/Mid/South	NO	Feeds along the creek and bare ground in coastal marshes	LC
Eastern cattle egret *Bubulcus coromandus*	R–M	North/Mid/South	NO	Feeds along the creek and bare ground in coastal marshes	LC
Grey heron *Ardea cinerea*	R–M	North/Mid	NO	Feeds along the creek, bare ground, and *Scirpus* habitat in coastal marshes	LC
Purple heron *Ardea purpurea*	R–M	North/Mid	?	Feeds along the creek, bare ground, and *Scirpus* habitat in coastal marshes	LC
Great egret *Ardea alba*	R–M	North/Mid/South	NO	Feeds along the creek, bare ground, and *Scirpus* habitat in coastal marshes	LC
Intermediate egret *Egretta intermedia*	R–M	Mid/South	NO	Feeds along the creek, bare ground, and *Scirpus* habitat in coastal marshes	LC
Little egret *Egretta sacra*	R–M	North/Mid/South	NO	Feeds along the creek, bare ground, and *Scirpus* habitat in coastal marshes	LC
Chinese egret *Egretta eulophotes*	M	North/Mid/South	NO	In Hong Kong only fed in shallow tidal water	VU, II
Black-eared kite *Milvus lineatus*	R–M	North/Mid/South	NO		LC, II

Breeding bird species of Chinese coastal marshes, with information on breeding and conservation status, habitat use, and distribution. (cont.)

	Migratory status[a]	Breeding region[b] *	Nesting in coastal marsh	Habitat type	Conservation status[c]
Common kestrel *Falco tinnunculus*	R–M	North/Mid/South	NO	*Phragmites, Spartina,* and *Scirpus* habitats	LC, II
Slaty-breasted rail *Gallirallus striatus*	R	Mid/South	YES	Nests in *Phragmites* and *Spartina* habitats in Chongming Dongtan	LC
Water rail *Rallus aquaticus*	R	Mid/South	YES	Nests in *Phragmites* and *Spartina* habitats in Chongming Dongtan	LC
White-breasted waterhen *Amaurornis phoenicurus*	R–M	Mid/South	YES	*Phragmites* and *Spartina* habitats in Chongming Dongtan	LC
Ruddy-breasted crake *Porzana fusca*	R–M	North/Mid/South	YES	*Phragmites* and *Spartina* habitats in Chongming Dongtan	LC
Red-crowned crane *Grus japonensis*	M	North	NO	Reed bed and *Suaeda* habitat in Shuangtaizi estuary	EN, I
Grey-headed lapwing *Vanellus cinereus*	M	North/Mid/South	YES	*Scirpus* habitat in Chongming Dongtan	LC
Lesser coucal *Centropus bengalensis*	R–M	Mid/South	?		LC, II
Indian cuckoo *Cuculus micropterus*	M	North/Mid/South	NO		LC
Common cuckoo *Cuculus canorus*	M	North/Mid	NO	Parasitizes the nest of Oriental reed warbler in *Phragmites* and *Spartina* habitats in Chongming Dongtan	LC
Grass owl *Tyto longimembris*	R–M	Mid/South	YES	Nests in *Spartina* habitats in Chongming Dongtan	LC, II
White-throated kingfisher *Halcyon smyrnensis*	R	South	NO		LC
Black-capped kingfisher *Halcyon pileata*	R–M	North/Mid/South	NO	*Phragmites* and *Spartina* habitats in Chongming Dongtan	LC
Common kingfisher *Alcedo atthis*	R	North/Mid/South	NO	*Phragmites* and *Spartina* habitats in Chongming Dongtan	LC

Species	Status	Region	Breeding	Habitat	IUCN
Common hoopoe *Upupa epops*	R–M	North/Mid	NO	Feeds in *Phragmites* and *Spartina* habitats in Chongming Dongtan	LC
Long-tailed shrike *Lanius schach*	R	Mid/South	NO	Feeds in *Phragmites* and *Spartina* habitats in Chongming Dongtan	LC
Oriental skylark *Alauda gulgula*	R–M	Mid/South	NO	*Scirpus* habitat in Chongming Dongtan	LC
Barn swallow *Hirundo rustica*	R–M	North/Mid/South	NO	Feeds above intertidal zone in Chongming Dongtan	LC
Red-rumped swallow *Cecropis daurica*	M	North/Mid/South	NO	Feeds above intertidal zone in Chongming Dongtan	LC
Oriental reed warbler *Acrocephalus orientalis*	M	North/Mid/South	YES	Nests in *Phragmites* and *Spartina* habitats in Chongming Dongtan	–
Black-browed reed warbler *Acrocephalus bistrigiceps*	M	North/Mid/South	YES	*Phragmites* and *Spartina* habitats in Chongming Dongtan	LC
Blunt-winged warbler *Acrocephalus concinens*	M	North/Mid	YES	*Phragmites* and *Spartina* habitats in Chongming Dongtan	LC
Marsh grassbird *Locustella pryeri*	R–M	North/Mid	YES	Nests in *Spartina*-dominated habitats in Chongming Dongtan	NT
Zitting cisticola *Cisticola juncidis*	R–M	North/Mid/South	YES	Nests in *Phragmites*-dominated habitats in Chongming Dongtan	LC
Plain prinia *Prinia inornata*	R	Mid/South	?	*Scirpus*- and *Phragmites*-dominated habitats in Chongming Dongtan	LC
Reed parrotbill *Paradoxornis heudei*	R	North/Mid	YES	Nests in *Phragmites* in Chongming Dongtan	NT
Vinous-throated parrotbill *Sinosuthora webbiana*	R	North/Mid/South	YES	*Phragmites* and *Spartina* habitats in Chongming Dongtan	LC
Eurasian tree sparrow *Passer montanus*	R	North/Mid/South	NO	*Phragmites* and *Spartina* habitats in Chongming Dongtan	LC
White wagtail *Motacilla alba*	M	North/Mid	NO	*Scirpus*, *Phragmites*, and *Spartina* habitats in Chongming Dongtan	LC

Breeding bird species of Chinese coastal marshes, with information on breeding and conservation status, habitat use, and distribution. (cont.)

	Migratory status[a]	Breeding region[b] *	Nesting in coastal marsh	Habitat type	Conservation status[c]
Striated heron *Butorides striata*	R–M	North/Mid/South	NO		LC
Watercock *Gallicrex cinerea*	M	North/Mid/South	?		LC
Common moorhen *Gallinula chloropus*	R–M	North/Mid/South	?	Breeds in the reed beds in the artificial fishing pond in Chongming, Dongtan	LC
Common coot *Fulica atra*	M	North/Mid	?	Breeds in the reed beds in the artificial fishing pond in Chongming, Dongtan	LC
Little tern *Sternula albifrons*	M	North/Mid/South	?	Breed in the reed beds in the artificial fishing pond in Chongming, Dongtan	LC
Whiskered tern *Chlidonias hybrida*	M	North/Mid/South	?	Breed in the reed beds in the artificial fishing pond in Chongming, Dongtan	LC
White-winged tern *Chlidonias leucopterus*	M	North/Mid/South	?	Breed in the reed beds in the artificial fishing pond in Chongming, Dongtan	LC

Sources: Chu *et al.*, 1999; Jiang *et al.*, 2002a, 2002b; Gan *et al.*, 2006; Cao *et al.*, 2008; Jiang *et al.*, 2010; Duan *et al.*, 2011; Ma *et al.*, 2011; Zhang, personal communication, 2011; Melville, personal communication, 2012.
[a] Migratory status (M, migrant; R, resident; R–M, partial migrant).
[b] Breeding region (North, north coast of China, including Liaoning, Hebei, Tianjing; Mid, middle coast of China, including Shandong, Jiangsu, Shanghai, Zhejiang; South, south coast of China, including Fujian, Guangdong, Guangxi, Hainan).
[c] Conservation status (EN, Endangered; VU, Vulnerable; NT, Near-Threatened; LC, Least Concern (IUCN, 2011); I, wildlife under first class protection in China; II, wildlife under second class protection in China).
* As defined by IUCN, 2011; X. J. Gan, personal observation.

Migratory and wintering bird species in Chinese coastal marshes, with information on conservation status and habitat use.

	Migratory status[a]	Migratory/ wintering species[b]	Wintering region[c] *	Habitat type in coastal marsh (Evidence)	Conservation status[d]
Japanese quail *Coturnix japonica*	M	M/W	Mid/South	Reed beds	NT
Swan goose *Anser cygnoides*	M	M/W	Mid/South	*Scirpus* habitat, mainly feeds on corms of *Scirpus* in Chongming Dongtan	VU
Bean goose *Anser fabalis*	M	M/W	Mid/South	*Scirpus* habitat, mainly feeds on corms of *Scirpus* in Chongming Dongtan	LC
Greylag goose *Anser anser*	M	M/W	Mid/South	*Scirpus* habitat, mainly feeds on corms of *Scirpus* in Chongming Dongtan	LC
Greater white-fronted goose *Anser albifrons*	M	M/W	Mid/South	*Scirpus* habitat, mainly feeds on corms of *Scirpus* in Chongming Dongtan	LC, II
Lesser white-fronted goose *Anser erythropus*	M	M/W	Mid	*Scirpus* habitat, mainly feeds on corms of *Scirpus* in Chongming Dongtan	VU
Snow goose *Chen caerulescens*	M	W	Mid		LC
Brent goose *Branta bernicla*	M	W	Mid	Lagoon in Shandong	LC
Mute swan *Cygnus olor*	M	M/W	North/Mid		LC, II
Tundra swan *Cygnus columbianus*	M	M/W	Mid/South	*Scirpus* habitat, mainly feeds on corms of *Scirpus* in Chongming Dongtan	LC, II
Whooper swan *Cygnus cygnus*	M	W	Mid	Mainly feeds on *Zostera* in lagoon in Rongcheng Shandong	LC, II
Gadwall *Anas strepera*	M	M/W	Mid/South	*Scirpus* habitat, mainly feeds on seeds, corms, and rhizomes of *Scirpus* in Chongming Dongtan	LC
Falcated duck *Anas falcata*	M	M/W	Mid/South	*Scirpus* habitat, mainly feeds on seeds, corms, and rhizomes of *Scirpus* in Chongming Dongtan	NT

Migratory and wintering bird species in Chinese coastal marshes, with information on conservation status and habitat use. (cont.)

	Migratory status[a]	Migratory/ wintering species[b]	Wintering region[c]*	Habitat type in coastal marsh (Evidence)	Conservation status[d]
Eurasian wigeon *Anas penelope*	M	M/W	Mid/South	*Scirpus* habitat, mainly feeds on seeds, corms, and rhizomes of *Scirpus* in Chongming Dongtan	LC
Mallard *Anas platyrhynchos*	M	M/W	Mid/South	*Scirpus* habitat, mainly feeds on seeds, corms, and rhizomes of *Scirpus* in Chongming Dongtan	LC
Spot-billed duck *Anas zonorhyncha*	M	M/W	Mid/South	*Scirpus* habitat, mainly feeds on seeds, corms, and rhizomes of *Scirpus* in Chongming Dongtan	LC
Northern shoveler *Anas clypeata*	M	M/W	Mid/South	*Scirpus* habitat, mainly feeds on seeds, corms, and rhizomes of *Scirpus* in Chongming Dongtan	LC
Northern pintail *Anas acuta*	M	M/W	Mid/South	*Scirpus* habitat, mainly feeds on seeds, corms, and rhizomes of *Scirpus* in Chongming Dongtan	LC
Garganey *Anas querquedula*	M	M/W	Mid/South	*Scirpus* habitat, mainly feeds on seeds, corms, and rhizomes of *Scirpus* in Chongming Dongtan	LC
Baikal teal *Anas formosa*	M	M/W	Mid/South	*Scirpus* habitat in Chongming Dongtan	VU
Eurasian teal *Anas crecca*	M	M/W	Mid/South	*Scirpus* habitat, mainly feeds on seeds, corms, and rhizomes of *Scirpus* in Chongming Dongtan	LC
Black stork *Ciconia nigra*	M	M/W	Mid/South	*Scirpus* habitat in Chongming Dongtan	LC, I
Oriental stork *Ciconia boyciana*	M	M/W	Mid/South	*Scirpus* habitat in Chongming Dongtan	EN, I
Great bittern *Botaurus stellaris*	M	M/W	Mid/South	*Phragmites* and *Spartina* habitats	LC
Striated heron *Butorides striata*	R–M	M/W	South		LC
Chinese pond heron *Ardeola bacchus*	R–M	M/W	Mid/South		LC

Common name / Scientific name				Notes	Status
Eastern cattle egret *Bubulcus coromandus*	R–M	M/W	South	Feeds along the creek and bare ground in coastal marshes	LC
Grey heron *Ardea cinerea*	R–M	M/W	Mid/South	Feeds along the creek, bare ground, and *Scirpus* habitat in coastal marshes	LC
Purple heron *Ardea purpurea*	R–M	M/W	Mid/South	Feeds along the creek, bare ground, and *Scirpus* habitat in coastal marshes	LC
Great egret *Ardea alba*	R–M	M/W	Mid/South	Feeds along the creek, bare ground, and *Scirpus* habitat in coastal marshes	LC
Intermediate egret *Egretta intermedia*	R–M	M/W	Mid/South	Feeds along the creek, bare ground, and *Scirpus* habitat in coastal marshes	LC
Little egret *Egretta sacra*	R–M	M/W	Mid/South	Feeds along the creek, bare ground, and *Scirpus* habitat in coastal marshes	LC
Chinese egret *Egretta eulophotes*	M	M	–		VU, II
Black-winged kite *Elanus caeruleus*	M	M	Mid/South		LC, II
White-tailed sea eagle *Haliaeetus albicilla*	M	M/W	North/Mid	*Scirpus* habitat in Chongming Dongtan	LC, II
Eastern marsh harrier *Circus spilonotus*	M	M/W	Mid/South	*Phragmites* and *Spartina* habitats in Chongming Dongtan	LC, II
Hen harrier *Circus cyaneus*	M	M/W	Mid/South	*Phragmites* and *Spartina* habitats in Chongming Dongtan	LC, II
Pied harrier *Circus melancleucos*	M	M/W	Mid/South	*Phragmites* and *Spartina* habitats in Chongming Dongtan	LC, II
Eastern buzzard *Buteo japonicus*	M	M/W	Mid/South		LC, II
Upland buzzard *Buteo hemilasius*	M	M/W	North/Mid		LC, II
Golden eagle *Aquila chrysaetos*	M	M/W	North/Mid		LC, II
Eastern imperial eagle *Aquila heliaca*	M	M	–		VU, I

Migratory and wintering bird species in Chinese coastal marshes, with information on conservation status and habitat use. (cont.)

	Migratory status[a]	Migratory/ wintering species[b]	Wintering region[c] *	Habitat type in coastal marsh (Evidence)	Conservation status[d]
Greater spotted eagle *Aquila clanga*	M	M/W	Mid/South		VU, II
Common kestrel *Falco tinnunculus*	R–M	M/W	North/Mid/South	*Phragmites, Spartina,* and *Scirpus* habitats in Chongming Dongtan	LC, II
Eurasian hobby *Falco subbuteo*	M	M/W	South		LC, II
Amur falcon *Falco amurensis*	M	M	–		LC, II
Swinhoe's rail *Coturnicops exquisitus*	M	W	Mid/South	*Phragmites* habitats in Chongming Dongtan	VU, II
Slaty-breasted rail *Gallirallus striatus*	R	W	Mid/South	*Phragmites* and *Spartina* habitats in Chongming Dongtan	LC
Water rail *Rallus aquaticus*	R	W	Mid/South	*Phragmites* and *Spartina* habitats in Chongming Dongtan	LC
White-breasted waterhen *Amaurornis phoenicurus*	R	W	Mid/South	*Phragmites* and *Spartina* habitats in Chongming Dongtan	LC
Baillon's crake *Porzana pusilla*	M	M/W	Mid/South	In fishing pond covered by *Phragmites* near coast in Rudong, Jiangsu	LC
Ruddy-breasted crake *Porzana fusca*	R–M	W	Mid/South	Record in Chongming Dongtan	LC
Watercock *Gallicrex cinerea*	M	M	North/Mid/South	*Scirpus* habitat in Chongming Dongtan	LC
Common moorhen *Gallinula chloropus*	R–M	W	North/Mid/South	*Phragmites* and *Spartina* habitats in Chongming Dongtan	LC

Species				Habitat	Status
Common coot *Fulica atra*	M	M/W	North/Mid		LC
Siberian crane *Grus leucogeranus*	M	M/W	North/Mid	*Scirpus* habitat, mainly feeds on corms of *Scirpus* in Chongming Dongtan, reed bed in Yellow River Delta Shandong	CR, I
Sandhill crane *Grus canadensis*	M	V		*Scirpus* habitat, mainly feeds on corms of *Scirpus* in Chongming Dongtan, reed bed in Yellow River Delta Shandong	LC, II
White-naped crane *Grus vipio*	M	M/W	North/Mid	*Scirpus* habitat, mainly feeds on corms of *Scirpus* in Chongming Dongtan, reed bed in Yellow River Delta Shandong	VU, II
Common crane *Grus grus*	M	M/W	North/Mid	*Scirpus* habitat, mainly feeds on corms of *Scirpus* in Chongming Dongtan, reed bed in Yellow River Delta Shandong	LC, II
Hooded crane *Grus monacha*	M	M/W	North/Mid	*Scirpus* habitat, mainly feeds on corms of *Scirpus* in Chongming Dongtan, reed bed in Yellow River Delta Shandong	VU, I
Red-crowned crane *Grus japonensis*	M	M/W	North/Mid	Reed bed and *Suaeda* habitats in Yellow River Delta Shandong and Yancheng Jiangsu	EN, I
Pacific golden plover *Pluvialis fulva*	M	M/W	Mid/South	*Scirpus* habitat in Chongming Dongtan	LC
Grey plover *Pluvialis squatarola*	M	M/W	Mid/South	*Scirpus* habitat in Chongming Dongtan	LC
Common ringed plover *Charadrius hiaticula*	M	M	–	*Scirpus* habitat in Chongming Dongtan	LC
Little ringed plover *Charadrius dubius*	M	M/W	South	*Scirpus* habitat in Chongming Dongtan	LC
Kentish plover *Charadrius alexandrinus*	M	M/W	Mid/South	*Scirpus* habitat in Chongming Dongtan	LC

Migratory and wintering bird species in Chinese coastal marshes, with information on conservation status and habitat use. (cont.)

	Migratory status[a]	Migratory/ wintering species[b]	Wintering region[c] *	Habitat type in coastal marsh (Evidence)	Conservation status[d]
Lesser sand plover *Charadrius mongolus*	M	M/W	Mid/South	*Scirpus* habitat in Chongming Dongtan	LC
Greater sand plover *Charadrius leschenaultii*	M	M/W	South	*Scirpus* habitat in Chongming Dongtan	LC
Oriental plover *Charadrius veredus*	M	M	–	*Scirpus* habitat in Chongming Dongtan	LC
Eurasian woodcock *Scolopax rusticola*	M	M/W	Mid/South	*Scirpus* habitat in Chongming Dongtan	LC
Jack snipe *Lymnocryptes minimus*	M	M	–	?	LC
Pintail snipe *Gallinago stenura*	M	M/W	South		LC
Swinhoe's snipe *Gallinago megala*	M	M/W	South	*Scirpus* habitat in Chongming Dongtan	LC
Common snipe *Gallinago gallinago*	M	M/W	Mid/South	*Scirpus*, *Phragmites*, and *Spartina* habitats in Chongming Dongtan	LC
Long-billed dowitcher *Limnodromus scolopaceus*	M	V	–	*Scirpus* habitat in Chongming Dongtan	LC
Asian dowitcher *Limnodromus semipalmatus*	M	M	–	*Scirpus* habitat in Chongming Dongtan	NT
Black-tailed godwit *Limosa limosa*	M	M	–	*Scirpus* habitat in Chongming Dongtan	NT

Species				Habitat	Status
Bar-tailed godwit *Limosa lapponica*	M	M	–	*Scirpus* habitat in Chongming Dongtan	LC
Whimbrel *Numenius phaeopus*	M	M/W	South	*Scirpus* habitat in Chongming Dongtan	LC
Eurasian curlew *Numenius arquata*	M	M	–	*Scirpus* habitat in Chongming Dongtan	NT
Eastern curlew *Numenius madagascariensis*	M	M/W	North/Mid/South	*Scirpus* habitat in Chongming Dongtan	VU
Spotted redshank *Tringa erythropus*	M	M/W	Mid/South	*Scirpus*, bare ground in *Phragmites* and *Spartina* habitats in Chongming Dongtan	LC
Common redshank *Tringa totanus*	M	M/W	Mid/South	*Scirpus* habitat in Chongming Dongtan	LC
Marsh sandpiper *Tringa stagnatilis*	M	M/W	South	*Scirpus* habitat in Chongming Dongtan	
Common greenshank *Tringa nebularia*	M	M/W	Mid/South	*Scirpus*, bare ground in *Phragmites* and *Spartina* habitats in Chongming Dongtan	LC
Nordmann's greenshank *Tringa guttifer*	M	M	–	*Scirpus* habitat in Chongming Dongtan	EN
Wood sandpiper *Tringa glareola*	M	M/W	Mid/South	*Scirpus* habitat in Chongming Dongtan	LC
Grey-tailed tattler *Tringa brevipes*	M	M	–	*Scirpus* habitat in Chongming Dongtan	LC
Terek sandpiper *Xenus cinereus*	M	M	–	*Scirpus* habitat in Chongming Dongtan	LC
Great knot *Calidris tenuirostris*	M	M	–	*Scirpus* habitat in Chongming Dongtan	VU
Ruddy turnstone *Arenaria interpres*	M	M	–	*Scirpus* habitat in Chongming Dongtan	LC
Red knot *Calidris canutus*	M	M	–	*Scirpus* habitat in Chongming Dongtan	LC

Migratory and wintering bird species in Chinese coastal marshes, with information on conservation status and habitat use. *(cont.)*

	Migratory status[a]	Migratory/ wintering species[b]	Wintering region[c] *	Habitat type in coastal marsh (Evidence)	Conservation status[d]
Sanderling *Calidris alba*	M	M/W	Mid/South	*Scirpus* habitat in Chongming Dongtan	LC
Red-necked stint *Calidris ruficollis*	M	M/W	South	*Scirpus* habitat in Chongming Dongtan	LC
Little stint *Calidris minuta*	M	M	–	*Scirpus* habitat in Chongming Dongtan	LC
Long-toed stint *Calidris subminuta*	M	M	–	*Scirpus* habitat in Chongming Dongtan	LC
Temminck's stint *Calidris temminckii*	M	M/W	South	*Scirpus* habitat in Chongming Dongtan	LC
Sharp-tailed sandpiper *Calidris acuminata*	M	M	–	*Scirpus* habitat in Chongming Dongtan	LC
Curlew sandpiper *Calidris ferruginea*	M	M	–	*Scirpus* habitat in Chongming Dongtan	LC
Dunlin *Calidris alpina*	M	M/W	North/Mid/ South	*Scirpus* habitat in Chongming Dongtan	LC
Spoon-billed sandpiper *Eurynorhynchus pygmeus*	M	M	–	*Scirpus* habitat in Chongming Dongtan	CR
Broad-billed sandpiper *Limicola falcinellus*	M	M	–	*Scirpus* habitat in Chongming Dongtan	
Ruff *Philomachus pugnax*	M	M	–	*Scirpus* habitat in Chongming Dongtan	

Species	Status	Distribution	Habitat	Conservation
Oriental pratincole *Glareola maldivarum*	M	–	*Scirpus* habitat in Chongming Dongtan	LC
Black-headed gull *Chroicocephalus ridibundus*	M/W	North/Mid/South	*Scirpus* habitat in Chongming Dongtan	LC
Saunders's gull *Larus saundersi*	M/W	Mid/South	*Spartina* habitats in Rudong, Jiangsu	VU
Relict gull *Ichthyaetus relictus*	M/W	North/Mid	*Spartina* habitats in Rudong, Jiangsu	VU, I
Heuglin's gull *Larus heuglini*	M	–	*Scirpus* habitat in Chongming Dongtan	LC
Vega gull *Larus vegae*	M/W	North/Mid	*Scirpus* habitat in Chongming Dongtan	LC
Yellow-legged gull *Larus cachinnans*	M/W	Mid/South	*Scirpus* habitat in Chongming Dongtan	LC
Oriental scops owl *Otus sunia*	R–M	–	*Scirpus, Phragmites,* and *Spartina* habitats in Chongming Dongtan	LC, II
White-throated needletail *Hirundapus caudacutus*	M	–		LC
Silver-backed needletail *Hirundapus cochinchinensis*	M	–	*Scirpus* habitat in Chongming Dongtan	LC, II
Fork-tailed swift *Apus pacificus*	R–M	–		LC
House swift *Apus nipalensis*	M	–		LC

Migratory and wintering bird species in Chinese coastal marshes, with information on conservation status and habitat use. (cont.)

	Migratory status[a]	Migratory/ wintering species[b]	Wintering region[c] *	Habitat type in coastal marsh (Evidence)	Conservation status[d]
White-throated kingfisher *Halcyon smyrnensis*	R	W	South		LC
Black-capped kingfisher *Halcyon pileata*	R–M	W	South		LC
Common kingfisher *Alcedo atthis*	R	W	North/Mid/South	*Phragmites* and *Spartina* habitats in Chongming Dongtan	LC
Pied kingfisher *Ceryle rudis*	R	W	Mid/South		LC
Common hoopoe *Upupa epops*	M	M/W	Mid/South	Feeds in *Phragmites* and *Spartina* habitats in Chongming Dongtan	LC
Eurasian wryneck *Jynx torquilla*	M	M/W	Mid/South	Roosts in *Phragmites* habitats in Chongming Dongtan	LC
Long-tailed shrike *Lanius schach*	R	W	Mid/South	Feeds in *Phragmites* and *Spartina* habitats in Chongming Dongtan	LC
Chinese penduline tit *Remiz consobrinus*	M	M/W	Mid/South	Feeds on seeds and arthropods in *Phragmites* habitats in Chongming Dongtan	LC
Sand martin *Riparia riparia*	M	M/W	North/Mid/South	Feeds above intertidal zone in Chongming Dongtan	LC
Asian stubtail *Urosphena squameiceps*	M	M/W	South	*Phragmites* and *Spartina* habitats in Chongming Dongtan	LC
Dusky warbler *Phylloscopus fuscatus*	M	M/W	South	*Phragmites* and *Spartina* habitats in Chongming Dongtan	LC
Radde's warbler *Phylloscopus schwarzi*	M	M	–	*Phragmites* and *Spartina* habitats in Chongming Dongtan	LC

Common name / Scientific name				Habitat	Status
Yellow-browed warbler *Phylloscopus inornatus*	M	M/W	South	*Phragmites* and *Spartina* habitats in Chongming Dongtan	LC
Arctic warbler *Phylloscopus borealis*	M	M/W	South	*Phragmites* and *Spartina* habitats in Chongming Dongtan	LC
Pale-legged warbler *Phylloscopus tenellipes*	M	M	–	*Phragmites* and *Spartina* habitats in Chongming Dongtan	LC
Eastern crowned warbler *Phylloscopus coronatus*	M	M	–	*Phragmites* and *Spartina* habitats in Chongming Dongtan	LC
Streaked reed warbler *Acrocephalus sorghophilus*	M	M	–	*Phragmites* and *Spartina* habitats in Chongming Dongtan	VU
Lanceolated warbler *Locustella lanceolata*	M	M	–	*Phragmites* and *Spartina* habitats in Chongming Dongtan	LC
Pallas's grasshopper warbler *Locustella certhiola*	M	M	–	*Phragmites* and *Spartina* habitats in Chongming Dongtan	LC
Middendorff's grasshopper warbler *Locustella ochotensis*	M	M	–	*Phragmites* and *Spartina* habitats in Chongming Dongtan	LC
Styan's grasshopper warbler *Locustella pleskei*	M	M	–	*Phragmites* and *Spartina* habitats in Chongming Dongtan	VU
Marsh grassbird *Locustella pryeri*	R–M	W	Mid/South	*Phragmites* and *Spartina* habitats in Chongming Dongtan	NT
Zitting cisticola *Cisticola juncidis*	R–M	W	Mid/South	*Phragmites* and *Spartina* habitats in Chongming Dongtan	LC

Migratory and wintering bird species in Chinese coastal marshes, with information on conservation status and habitat use. (cont.)

	Migratory status[a]	Migratory/wintering species[b]	Wintering region[c] *	Habitat type in coastal marsh (Evidence)	Conservation status[d]
Goldcrest *Regulus regulus*	M	M/W	Mid/South	*Phragmites* and *Spartina* habitats in Jiuduansha, Shanghai	
Reed parrotbill *Paradoxornis heudei*	R	W	North/Mid	Nests in *Phragmites* in Chongming Dongtan	NT
Vinous-throated parrotbill *Sinosuthora webbiana*	R	W	North/Mid/South	*Phragmites* and *Spartina* habitats in Chongming Dongtan	LC
Scaly thrush *Zoothera dauma*	M	M/W	Mid/South	*Phragmites* and *Spartina* habitats in Chongming Dongtan	LC
Grey-backed thrush *Turdus hortulorum*	M	M/W	Mid/South	*Phragmites* and *Spartina* habitats in Jiuduansha, Shanghai	LC
Eyebrowed thrush *Turdus obscurus*	M	M/W	Mid/South	*Phragmites* and *Spartina* habitats in Chongming Dongtan	LC
Pale thrush *Turdus pallidus*	M	M/W	Mid/South	*Phragmites* and *Spartina* habitats in Chongming Dongtan	LC
Dusky thrush *Turdus eunomus*	M	M/W	Mid/South	*Phragmites* and *Spartina* habitats in Chongming Dongtan	–
Bluethroat *Luscinia svecica*	M	M/W	Mid/South	*Phragmites* and *Spartina* habitats in Chongming Dongtan	LC
Siberian rubythroat *Luscinia calliope*	M	M/W	Mid/South	*Phragmites* and *Spartina* habitats in Chongming Dongtan	LC
Siberian blue robin *Luscinia cyane*	M	M/W	Mid/South	*Phragmites* and *Spartina* habitats in Chongming Dongtan	LC
Rufous-tailed robin *Luscinia sibilans*	M	M/W	South	*Phragmites* and *Spartina* habitats in Chongming Dongtan	LC

Species				Habitat	Status
Orange-flanked bluetail *Tarsiger cyanurus*	M	M/W	Mid/South	*Phragmites* and *Spartina* habitats in Chongming Dongtan	LC
Daurian redstart *Phoenicurus auroreus*	M	M/W	Mid/South	*Phragmites* and *Spartina* habitats in Chongming Dongtan	LC
Yellow-rumped flycatcher *Ficedula zanthopygia*	M	M	–	*Phragmites* and *Spartina* habitats in Chongming Dongtan	LC
Narcissus flycatcher *Ficedula narcissina*	M	M	–	*Phragmites* and *Spartina* habitats in Chongming Dongtan	LC
Mugimaki flycatcher *Ficedula mugimaki*	M	M	–	*Phragmites* and *Spartina* habitats in Chongming Dongtan	LC
Eurasian tree sparrow *Passer montanus*	R	W	North/Mid/South	*Phragmites* and *Spartina* habitats in Chongming Dongtan	LC
Eastern yellow wagtail *Motacilla tschutschensis*	M	M/W	South	*Phragmites* and *Spartina* habitats in Chongming Dongtan	–
White wagtail *Motacilla alba*	M	M/W	South	*Scirpus* habitat in Chongming Dongtan	LC
Richard's pipit *Anthus richardi*	M	M/W	South	*Phragmites* and *Spartina* habitats in Chongming Dongtan	LC
Oliver-backed pipit *Anthus hodgsoni*	M	M/W	South	*Scirpus*, *Phragmites*, and *Spartina* habitats in Chongming Dongtan	LC
Pechora pipit *Anthus gustavi*	M	M	–	*Phragmites* and *Spartina* habitats in Chongming Dongtan	LC
Chestnut-eared bunting *Emberiza fucata*	M	M/W	Mid/South	*Phragmites* and *Spartina* habitats in Chongming Dongtan	LC
Little bunting *Emberiza pusilla*	M	M/W	Mid/South	*Phragmites* and *Spartina* habitats in Chongming Dongtan	LC

Migratory and wintering bird species in Chinese coastal marshes, with information on conservation status and habitat use. (cont.)

	Migratory status[a]	Migratory/ wintering species[b]	Wintering region[c] *	Habitat type in coastal marsh (Evidence)	Conservation status[d]
Yellow-throated bunting *Emberiza elegans*	M	M/W	Mid/South	*Phragmites* and *Spartina* habitats in Chongming Dongtan	LC
Yellow-breasted bunting *Emberiza aureola*	M	M/W	South	*Phragmites* and *Spartina* habitats in Chongming Dongtan	VU
Black-faced bunting *Emberiza spodocephala*	M	M/W	Mid/South	*Phragmites* and *Spartina* habitats in Chongming Dongtan	LC
Pallas's bunting *Emberiza pallasi*	M	M/W	North/Mid/ South	*Phragmites* and *Spartina* habitats in Chongming Dongtan	LC
Ochre-rumped bunting *Emberiza yessoensis*	M	M/W	Mid/South	*Phragmites* and *Spartina* habitats in Chongming Dongtan	NT
Reed bunting *Emberiza schoeniclus*	M	M/W	Mid/South	*Phragmites* and *Spartina* habitats in Chongming Dongtan	LC

Sources: Huang et al., 1993; Jing, 2005; Gan et al., 2006, 2009, 2010; Ma et al., 2007; Shan et al., 2007; Cao et al., 2010; Zhang et al., 2010; Ma, personal communication, 2011; Zhang, personal communication, 2011.
[a] Migratory status (M, migrant; R, resident; R–M, partial migrant; V, vagrant).
[b] Migratory/wintering species (migratory or wintering species in coast of China: M, migratory species; W, wintering species).
[c] Wintering region (North, north coast of China, including Liaoning, Hebei, Tianjing; Mid, middle of coastal China, including Shandong, Jiangsu, Shanghai, Zhejiang; South, south coast of China, including Fujian, Guangdong, Guangxi, Hainan).
[d] Conservation status (CR, Critically Endangered; EN, Endangered; VU, Vulnerable; NT, Near-Threatened; LC, Least Concern (IUCN, 2011); I, wildlife under first class protection in China; II, wildlife under second class protection in China).
* As defined by IUCN, 2011; X. J. Gan, personal observation.

Australian salt marsh specialists and selected other bird species that often use salt marshes with information on guild, distribution, and breeding status.

Guild	Species		Code
Waterbirds*			
	Australian shelduck	*Tadorna tadornoides*	L
	Little curlew	*Numenius minutus*	IN, L, NB
	Eastern curlew	*Numenius madagascariensis*	CL, NB
Land birds other than insectivores			
*Carnivores**	Swamp harrier	*Circus approximans*	
Nectarivores	Pied honeyeater	*Certhionyx variegatus*	IN
Frugivores	Silvereye	*Zosterops lateralis*	C, T, NB
Seed-eaters	**Blue-winged parrot**	*Neophema chrysostoma*	NB
	Elegant parrot	*Neophema elegans*	NB
	Orange-bellied parrot	*Neophema chrysogaster*	C, NB
	Rock parrot	*Neophema petrophila*	C, NB
	Scarlet-chested parrot	*Neophema splendida*	IN, NB
	Ground parrot	*Pezoporus wallicus*	C, NB
	Night parrot	*Pezoporus occidentalis*	IN, ???
	House sparrow	*Passer domesticus*	NB, I
	European goldfinch	*Carduelis carduelis*	NB, I
Insectivorous land birds that feed from			
Open air	Welcome swallow	*Hirundo neoxena*	NB
Canopy or tall shrubs	Horsfield's bronze-cuckoo	*Chalcites basalis*	
	Brown thornbill	*Acanthiza pusilla*	C, T
	Inland thornbill	*Acanthiza apicalis*	IN, T
Low shrubs	**White-winged fairy-wren**	*Malurus leucopterus*	IN, L
	Thick-billed grasswren	*Amytornis textilis*	IN
	Striated fieldwren	*Calamanthus fuliginosus*	C, T
	Rufous fieldwren	*Calamanthus campestris*	IN, T
	Slender-billed thornbill	*Acanthiza iredalei*	L, #
	Chestnut-breasted whiteface	*Aphelocephala pectoralis*	IN, L
	Orange chat	*Epthianura aurifrons*	IN, L
	Yellow chat	*Epthianura crocea*	IN, L
	White-fronted chat	*Epthianura albifrons*	L
	Crimson chat	*Epthianura tricolor*	IN, L
	Chestnut-rumped thornbill	*Acanthiza uropygialis*	IN
	Little grassbird	*Megalurus gramineus*	T
Damp ground below shrubs	White-browed scrubwren	*Sericornis frontalis*	C, T

Australian salt marsh specialists and selected other bird species that often use salt marshes with information on guild, distribution, and breeding status. (*cont.*)

Guild	Species		Code
Open ground	**Gibberbird**	*Ashbyia lovensis*	IN, L
	Australasian pipit	*Anthus novaeseelandiae*	L
	Superb fairy-wren	*Malurus cyaneus*	C
	Yellow-rumped thornbill	*Acanthiza chrysorrhoa*	L, NB
	Australian magpie	*Cracticus tibicen*	L, NB
	Flame robin	*Petroica phoenicea*	L, NB
	Willie wagtail	*Rhipidura leucophrys*	L, NB
	Eurasian skylark	*Alauda arvensis*	C, L, I
	Horsfield's bushlark	*Mirafra javanica*	L

Sources: Observations by author RL; Marchant & Higgins, 1990, 1993, 1999; Higgins & Davies, 1996; Higgins *et al.*, 2001, 2006. Higgins & Peter, 2002. Species classed as specialists are shown in bold (estimated >75% associated with salt marsh or chenopod shrublands).

C, only in coastal salt marsh; IN, only in inland or northern Australia; L, only in low salt marsh; T, only in tall salt marsh; NB, usually as a non-breeding visitor, seasonally or breeding in other habitats nearby; I, introduced to Australia.

#, subspecies *A.i.iredaleyi* in inland chenopod shrublands; *A.i.rosinae* in coastal salt marsh; *A.i.hedleyi* in inland heath and low chenopod shrublands.

???, extremely rare and little known species, which has been recorded from inland chenopod shrublands.

*Guild includes many additional species (see text).

Characteristic birds of southeastern South America (SESA) coastal marshes with information on abundance, breeding, migratory and conservation status.

Species		Relative abundance[a]	Breeding	Migratory status[b]	Conservation status[c]
Typical salt marsh species					
Long-winged harrier	*Circus buffoni*	+	Yes	R	
Cinereous harrier	*Circus cinereus*	+	Yes	R	
Milvago chimango	**Chimango caracara**	+++	Yes	R	
South American painted snipe	*Nycticryphes semicollarus*	+	?	R	
Dot-winged crake	*Porzana spiloptera*	++	Yes	R	VU
Short-eared owl	*Asio flammeus*	+	Yes	R	
Bay-capped wren-spinetail	**Spartonoica maluroides**	+++	Yes	R–M	NT
Sedge wren	*Cistothorus platensis*	++	Yes	R–M	EP
Great pampa finch	*Embernagra platensis*	++	Yes	R	
Grassland yellow finch	*Sicalis luteola*	++	Yes	R	
Yellow-winged blackbird	*Agelasticus thilius*	+	Yes	R	
Species only associated with disturbed salt marshes					
Southern lapwing	**Vanellus chilensis**	++	No	R	
Correndera pipit	*Arthus correndera*	+++	No	R	
Hudson's canastero	*Asthenes hudsoni*	++	Yes	R	
Bar-winged cinclodes	*Cinclodes fuscus*	++	No	R	
Austral negrito	*Lessonia rufa*	+	No	M	
Species not associated with salt marsh habitats, but occasionally use it					
Rufous-collared sparrow	*Zonotrichia capensis*		No		
Spotted nothura	**Nothura maculosa**		No		
Red-winged tinamou	*Rhynchotus rufescens*		No		
Yellow-billed pintail	*Anas georgica*		Yes		
Maguari store	*Ciconia maguari*		No		
Cocoi heron	*Ardea cocoi*				
Great egret	*Ardea alba*		No		

Characteristic birds of southeastern South America (SESA) coastal marshes with information on abundance, breeding, migratory and conservation status. (cont.)

Species		Relative abundance[a]	Breeding	Migratory status[b]	Conservation status[c]
Snowy egret	*Egretta thula*		No		
Cattle egret	*Bubulcus ibis*		No		
Striated heron	*Butorides striata*		No		
Whistling heron	*Syrigma sibilatrix*		No		
Black-crowned night heron	*Nycticorax nycticorax*		No		
Stripe-backed bittern	*Ixobrychus involucris*		No		
Pinnated bittern	*Botaurus pinnatus*		No		
White-faced ibis	*Plegadis chihi*		No		
Southern caracara	*Caracara plancus*		No		
Plumbeous rail	*Pardirallus sanguinolentus*		?		
Rufous-sided crake	*Laterallus melanophaius*		No		
Common moorhen	*Gallinula chloropus*		No		
Red-gartered coot	*Fulica armillata*		No		
White-winged coot	*Fulica leucoptera*		No		
Black-necked stilt	*Himantopus mexicanus*		No		
Lesser yellowlegs	*Tringa flavipes*		No	M	
Common snipe	*Gallinago gallinago*		No		
Barn owl	*Tyto alba*		No		
Smooth-billed ani	*Crotophaga ani*		No		
Nacunda nighthawk	*Chordeiles nacunda*		No		
Wren-like rushbird	*Phleocryptes melanops*		Yes		
Curve-billed reedhaunter	*Limnornis curvirostris*		No		
Freckle-breasted thornbird	*Phacellodomus striaticollis*		No		
Sulphur-throated spinetail	*Cranioleuca sulphurifera*		No		
Pale-breasted spinetail	*Synallaxis albescens*		No		
Fork-tailed flycatcher	*Tyrannus savana*		No		
Spectacled tyrant	*Hymenops perspicillatus*		Yes		

Common name	Scientific name			
Many-coloured rush-tyrant	*Tachuris rubrigastra*			No
Crested doradito	*Pseudocolopteryx sclateri*			?
Warbling doradito	*Pseudocolopteryx flaviventris*			Yes
Great kiskadee	*Pitangus sulphuratus*			No
Black-and-white monjita	*Xolmis dominicanus*	VU		?
Yellow-browed tyrant	*Satrapa icterophrys*			No
Long-tailed reed finch	*Doracospiza albifrons*			Yes
Barn swallow	*Hirundo rustica*		M	No
Sand martin	*Riparia riparia*		M	No
Cliff swallow	*Petrochelidon pyrrhonota*		M	No
Brown-chested martin	*Progne tapera*		M	No
Blue-and-white swallow	*Pygochelidon cyanoleuca*		M	No
Tawny-headed swallow	*Alopochelidon fucata*		M	No
White-rumped swallow	*Tachycineta leucorrhoa*		M	No
White-rumped swallow	*Tachycineta leucorrhoa*		M	No
House wren	*Troglodytes aedon*			No
Chestnut-capped blackbird	*Chrysomus ruficapillus*			No
Brown-and-yellow marshbird	*Pseudoleistes virescens*			No
White-browed blackbird	*Sturnella superciliaris*			No
Shiny cowbird	*Molothrus bonariensis*			No
	Rare species			?
Speckled rail	*Coturnicops notatus*	IC		

[a]Relative abundance (+++, very common; ++, common; +, scarce).
[b]Migratory status (M, migrant; R, resident; R–M, partial migrant).
[c]Conservation status: EP, Endangered; VU, Vulnerable; NT, Near-Threatened; IC, insufficiently known (IUCN, 2011).

Birds of the Waddell Sea salt marshes with information on use (breeding, feed, roosting).

Species		Marsh use[a]
Eurasian spoonbill	*Platalea leucorodia*	Breeding
Barnacle goose	*Branta leucopsis*	Feeding
Dark-bellied brent goose	*Branta bernicla bernicla*	Feeding, roosting*
Red-breasted merganser	*Mergus serrator*	Breeding
Eurasian wigeon	*Anas penelope*	Feeding, roosting*
Northern pintail	*Anas acuta*	Feeding
Eurasian teal	*Anas crecca*	Feeding
Eurasian oystercatcher	*Haematopus ostralegus*	Breeding, roosting
Pied avocet	*Recurvirostra avosetta*	Breeding, roosting
Common ringed plover	*Charadrius hiaticula*	Roosting
Kentish plover	*Charadrius alexandrinus*	Roosting
Grey plover	*Pluvialis squatarola*	Roosting
Dunlin	*Calidris alpina*	Roosting
Curlew sandpiper	*Calidris ferruginae*	Roosting
Common redshank	*Tringa totanus*	Breeding, roosting
Spotted redshank	*Tringa erythropus*	Roosting
Bar-tailed godwit	*Limosa lapponica*	Roosting
Eurasian curlew	*Numenius arquata*	Roosting*
Black-headed gull	*Chroicophalus ridibundus*	Breeding, roosting
Common gull	*Larus canus*	Roosting
European herring gull	*Larus argentatus*	Roosting
Common tern	*Sterna hirundo*	Breeding
Gull-billed tern	*Gelochelidon nilotica*	Breeding, feeding
Horned lark	*Eremophila alpestris*	Feeding
Skylark	*Alauda arvensis*	Breeding
Rock pipit	*Anthus petrosus*	Feeding
Meadow pipit	*Anthus pratensis*	Breeding
Reed bunting	*Emberiza schoeniclus*	Breeding
Twite	*Carduelis flavirostris*	Feeding

Sources: Koffijberg *et al.*, 2003, 2006; Laursen *et al.*, 2010.

[a] For roosting only species were selected of which > 50% of all high-tide roosts are situated at salt marshes. Among these, those marked with * preferably stay in salt marsh vegetation during high tide, others preferably disperse over salt marshes and fringes of mudflats in front of the marshes.

Characteristic birds of coastal marshes of North America with information on coastline of occurrence and breeding status.

Species		Coast[a]	Breeding
American bittern	*Botaurus lentiginosus*	AGP	
Great blue heron	*Ardea herodias*	AGP	
Great egret	*Aredea alba*	AGP	
Reddish egret	*Egretta rufescens*	AG	
Snowy egret	*Egretta thula*	AG	
Little blue heron	*Egretta caerulea*	AG	
Tricolored heron	*Egretta tricolor*	AG	
Black-crowned night heron	*Nycticorax nicticorax*	AGP	
Yellow-crowned night heron	*Nyctanassa violacea*	AG	
White ibis	*Eudocimus albus*	AG	
White-faced ibis	*Plegadis chihi*	GP	
Glossy ibis	*Plegadis falcinellis*	AG	
Roseate spoonbill	*Ajaia ajaia*	AG	
Canada goose	*Branta canadensis*	AGP	
Brant	*Branta bernicula*	AP	
Snow goose	*Chen caerulescens*	AG	
Mallard	*Anas platyrhynchos*	AGP	+
Mottled duck	*Anas fulvigula*	AG	+
American black duck	*Anas rubripes*	A	+
Gadwall	*Anas strepera*	AGP	+
Northern pintail	*Anas acuta*	AGP	
American wigeon	*Anas americana*	AGP	
Northern shoveler	*Anas clypeata*	AGP	
Blue-winged teal	*Anas discolor*	AGP	+
Cinnamon teal	*Anas canoptera*	P	
Green-winged teal	*Anas crecca*	AGP	
Ruddy duck	*Oxyura jamaicensis*	AGP	
Northern harrier	*Circus cyaneus*	AGP	+
American coot	*Fulica americana*	AGP	
Clapper rail	*Rallus longirostris*	AGP	+
Sora	*Porzana carolina*	AGP	
Yellow rail	*Coturnicops noveboracensis*	G	
Black rail	*Laterallus jamaicensis*	AGP	+
American oystercatcher	*Haematopus palliatus*	AGP	
American avocet	*Recurvirostra americana*	AGP	
Black-necked stilt	*Himantopus mexicanus*	AGP	
Greater yellowlegs	*Tringa melanoleuca*	AGP	
Lesser yellowlegs	*Tringa flavipes*	AGP	
Willet	*Catoptrophorus semipalmatus*	AGP	
Long-billed curlew	*Numenius mericanus*	AGP	
Marbled godwit	*Limosa fedoa*	AGP	
Dunlin	*Calidris alpina*	AGP	
Least sandpiper	*Calidris minutilla*	AGP	
Short-billed dowitcher	*Limnodromus griseus*	AGP	

Characteristic birds of coastal marshes of North America with information on coastline of occurrence and breeding status. (cont.)

Species		Coast[a]	Breeding
Forster's tern	*Sterna foresteri*	AGP	
Gull-billed tern	*Sterna nilotica*	AG	
Short-eared owl	*Aso flammeus*	AP	
Willow flycatcher	*Empidonax trailii*	A	
Fish crow	*Corvus ossifragus*	AGP	
Sedge wren	*Cistothorus platensis*	AG	
Marsh wren	*Cistothorus palustris*	AGP	+
Yellow warbler	*Dendroica petechia*	A	+
Common yellowthroat	*Geothlypis trichas*	AGP	+
Seaside sparrow	*Ammodramus maritimus*	AG	+
Nelson's sparrow	*Ammodramus nelsoni*	A	+
Saltmarsh sparrow	*Ammodramus caudicutus*	A	+
Savannah sparrow	*Passerculus sandwichensis*	AP	+
Song sparrow	*Melospiza melodia*	AP	+
Swamp sparrow	*Melospiza georgiana*	AG	+
Red-winged blackbird	*Aegalius phoeniceus*	AGP	+
Common grackle	*Quiscalus quiscula*	AG	
Boat-tailed grackle	*Quiscalus major*	AG	+

[a] A, Atlantic coast; G, Gulf coast; P, Pacific coast.

Overview of species depending on salt marshes in the Wadden Sea, along with their conservation status and trend. For explanation see text.

Species		EU Bird Directive	SPEC category[a]	European threat status[b]	Trend, breeding[c]	Trend, non-breeding
Barnacle goose	Branta leucopsis	x		Vulnerable	Not breeding	++
Dark-bellied brent goose	Branta bernicla		SPEC 3	Vulnerable	Not breeding	o
Eurasian wigeon	Anas penelope			Secure	No data	o
Northern pintail	Anas acuta		SPEC 3	Declining	No data	+
Eurasian teal	Anas crecca			Secure	Not breeding	−
Red-breasted merganser	Mergus serrator			Secure	+	No data
Eurasian oystercatcher	Haematopus ostralegus			Secure	o	−
Pied avocet	Recurvirostra avosetta	x		Secure	−	−
Common ringed plover	Charadrius hiaticula			Secure	−	+
Kentish plover	Charadrius alexandrinus	x		Declining	−	−
Grey plover	Pluvialis squatarola			Secure	Not breeding	o
Dunlin	Calidris alpina	x	SPEC 3	Depleted (breeding)	Not breeding	−
Curlew sandpiper	Calidris ferruginea			Not evaluated	Not breeding	?
Common redshank	Tringa totanus		SPEC 2	Declining	−	o
Spotted redshank	Tringa erythropus		SPEC 3	Declining	Not breeding	−
Bar-tailed godwit	Limosa lapponica	x		Secure	Not breeding	+
Eurasian curlew	Numenius arquata		SPEC 2	Declining	−	o
Black-headed gull	Chroicophalus ridibundus			Secure	−	−
Common gull	Larus canus		SPEC 2	Depleted	+	o

Overview of species depending on salt marshes in the Wadden Sea, along with their conservation status and trend. For explanation see text. (cont.)

Species		EU Bird Directive	SPEC category[a]	European threat status[b]	Trend, breeding[c]	Trend, non-breeding
European herring gull	*Larus argentatus*			Secure	–	–
Gull-billed tern	*Gelochelidon nilotica*	x	SPEC 3	Vulnerable	?	No data
Horned lark	*Eremophila alpestris*			Secure	Not breeding	No data
Rock pipit	*Anthus petrosus*			Secure	Not breeding	No data
Twite	*Carduelis flavirostris*			Secure	Not breeding	No data

[a]SPEC 1, species of global concern; SPEC 2, species concentrated in Europe and with an Unfavorable Conservation Status; SPEC 3, species not concentrated in Europe but with an Unfavorable Conservation Status in Europe (Birdlife International, 2004).
[b]*Source*: Birdlife International, 2004.
[c]*Source*: JMMB, 2010, 2011.

North American species with at least one subspecies specialized on coastal marshes, with information on population size and conservation status.

Taxon		Surveys	Population size	Recent trends
Black rail (*Laterallus jamaicensis*)	*jamaicensis coturniculus*	Playback surveys in California and along east coast	30 000 (California subspecies)	Bird of Conservation Concern – USFWS, 2002 *L. j. coturniculus* Threatened (California), Wildlife of Special Concern (Arizona), Endangered (Mexico)
Clapper rail (*Rallus longirostris*)	*obsoletus* group (*levipes, obsoletus, yumanensis, beldingi*) *crepitans* group	BBS (48 routes)	390 (Light footed) 1200 (California) Eastern (no estimate)	*R. l. levipes, obsoletus,* and *yumanensis* are Federal and California Endangered. *R. l. levipes* Endangered (Mexico) *R. l. yumanensis* Threatened (Mexico)
Eastern willett (*Tringa semipalmata*)	*semipalmatus*	BBS	50 routes (no estimate)	
Marsh wren (*Cistothorus palustris*)	*palustris waynei griseus marianae*	BBS (17 routes)	2000 (two Atlantic coastal subspecies combined)	*C. p. griseus* and *C. p. marianae* Subspecies of Conservation Concern (Florida)
Common yellowthroat (*Geothlypis trichas*)	*sinuosa*		No estimate	Bird of Conservation Concern (USFWS, 2002) Species of Special Concern (California)
Seaside sparrow (*Ammodramus maritimus*)	Atlantic Coast group Gulf Coast group	BBS (27 routes)	110 000	*A. m. mirabilis* Endangered *A. m. nigrescens*) Extinct Species of National Conservation Concern (USFWS, 2002)
Nelson's sharp-tailed sparrow (*Ammodramus nelson*)		BBS (15 routes)	50 000 Acadian	

North American species with at least one subspecies specialized on coastal marshes, with information on population size and conservation status. (cont.)

Taxon		Surveys	Population size	Recent trends
Saltmarsh sharp-tailed sparrow (*Ammodramus caudacutus*)	*caudacutus diversus*	Several state- and refuge-based point count surveys	50 000–250 000 (based on extrapolations from mark recapture studies)	Species of National Conservation Concern (USFWS, 2002)
Savannah sparrow (*Passerculus sandwichensis*)	*rostratus* (group) *beldingi* (group)	Five-year surveys – California Fish & Game	2900 (Southern California population of *beldingi*)	*P. s. beldingi* Endangered (California), Threatened (Mexico) *P. s. rostratus* Species of Special Concern (California), Special Protection (Mexico).
Song sparrow (*Melospiza melodia*)	*pusillula, samuelis maxillaris*	Periodic surveys (point counts – DISTANCE estimate)	15 000 pairs (*pusillula*) 77 000 pairs (*samuelis*) 44 000 pairs (*maxillaries*)	All three subspecies Bird of Conservation Concern (USFWS, 2002) Species of Special Concern (California)
Coastal plain swamp sparrow (*Melospiza georgiana*)	*nigrescens*	BBS (15 routes) Annual point counts along Delaware Shore	3000 pairs (BBS) 10–15 000 pairs	Subspecies of Conservation Concern (Maryland and Delaware)
Boat-tailed grackle (*Quiscalus major*)		BBS (66 routes outside Florida)	1.5 million outside Florida	

Sources: Beadell *et al.*, 2003; PIF, 2007; Zembal & Hoffmann, 2010; Zembal *et al.*, 2010; Greenberg *et al.*, unpublished data, 2012; PRBO, personal communication, 2012; Shriver *et al.*, unpublished data, 2012.

Part II

Emerging Threats

8

The impacts of invasive species on coastal marine ecosystems

JULIE L. LOCKWOOD AND ORIN J. ROBINSON

INTRODUCTION

Invasive species are an increasing presence in coastal marine ecosystems, and their ecological and economic impacts have been sometimes severe (Rilov & Crooks, 2009). Such impacts have stirred academic interest as well as directed policy and management actions designed to ameliorate or forestall further negative consequences (Ruiz *et al.*, 2000). We review two key pieces of invasion ecology that dictate how we study the impact of coastal marine invaders, and we set available empirical evidence generated from research on marine invaders in this context. We show that significant gaps remain in our knowledge of the impacts of coastal marine invaders. These gaps include bias in the taxonomic groups and coastal habitats studied, incomplete documentation of ecological impacts, and scientific uncertainty in when negative impacts are likely to occur and how long they may persist. These gaps combine to inhibit comprehensive regulatory actions that are aimed at reducing the inflow of non-native species into coastal waters and executing effective eradication or control measures for those species that impose negative impacts.

THE INVASION PROCESS

One of the consistent themes across chapters in this volume is that invasive species can cause major changes to coastal ecosystems (e.g. Chapters 4 and 5). As is true across a variety of other ecosystems, coastal marine invaders can impose significant stress on co-occurring native species exacerbating what is already a precarious existence for many species (Rilov & Crooks, 2009; see also Chapter 7). Despite their occasionally large impacts, coastal marine invaders are only a small subset of all the non-native species established in

Coastal Conservation, eds B. Maslo and J. L. Lockwood. Published by Cambridge University Press.
© Cambridge University Press 2014.

coastal ecosystems, and a yet smaller subset of all the non-native species that were transported into these ecosystems and released there (Ruiz *et al.*, 2000; Miller & Ruiz, 2009). In other words, of all the coastal marine species which have been entrained in a transport process (e.g. via ballast water, aquaria trade), only a fraction of them will go on to garner attention as having become widespread and imposing negative impacts on native species and ecosystems, or having become "invasive." There is much general debate about what that invasive fraction may be, but it can be as low as 10% and as high as 50% depending on the taxa considered and the habitat into which non-natives are released (Ricciardi *et al.*, 2013). Even the highest estimated fraction of 50% indicates that there are as many non-native species in an ecosystem that do not have recorded impacts as there are those that do.

The above realization focuses our attention on determining which non-natives constitute the invasive fraction, and what factors play a role in determining membership in this group. Blackburn and colleagues (2011) conceptualize the invasion process as a series of four stages, where each stage involves a series of barriers that a species must pass through to reach the next stage. Briefly, individuals of a species must initially be entrained in a transportation vector and moved to, and released at, a location to which they are clearly non-native. These released individuals have to survive in this new location, and reproduce at such a rate, that they establish a self-sustaining population. Finally, the established non-native population must experience substantial population growth and range expansion to be considered invasive (Blackburn *et al.*, 2011). It is at this latter stage that invasive species tend to affect changes on co-occurring native species and local ecosystem processes (Lockwood *et al.*, 2013).

WHAT IS IMPACT, EXACTLY?

For conservation biologists and applied ecologists, the interest in invasive species stems mostly from their negative impact on co-occurring native species and the ecosystems in which they are embedded (Simberloff *et al.*, 2005). Impacts can be generated at any biological level ranging from changes in the genetic diversity of native individuals to alterations of an entire ecosystem (Lockwood *et al.*, 2013). Many of these impacts have economic consequences and can be, and have been, measured using monetary metrics (Pimentel *et al.*, 2005). A comprehensive definition of impact comes from Ricciardi and colleagues (2013), who state that an impact is "a measurable change to the properties of an ecosystem by a non-native species". These authors note that this definition allows for the possibility that every established non-native species can have impacts simply by co-occurring with native species, that these impacts can be small or large and positive or negative in sign, and that they can vary substantially through time and space (Ricciardi *et al.*, 2013). This definition differs from those used in policy or management in that the latter usage usually implies that only large and negative effects are considered "impacts" (Ricciardi *et al.*, 2013).

The lack of a consistent definition for impact has led to very few attempts to create a theory of impact or derive meaningful hypotheses that can help us predict when and where impacts are likely to occur (cf. Ricciardi *et al.*, 2013). This failure makes it difficult to make meaningful comparisons of impacts across species, locations, or through time (Thiele *et al.*, 2010). In an effort to remedy this issue, Parker and colleagues (1999) created a general formula for measuring invasive species' impacts; $I = R \times A \times E$. In this equation, impact (I) is a product of the species' abundance (A), its geographical extent (R, or range size), and its per-individual ecological effects (E). Widespread and abundant non-native species that also have a high per-individual effect will show the largest impacts, and vice versa for low-impact invaders.

There have been several significant updates to the concepts developed by Parker and colleagues (1999). These include recognition that per-individual effects of invasive species may scale with abundance, creating non-linearities in impact across a range of conditions, and that per-individual effects can vary substantially across the geographical extent of the invader, and these spatial differences matter in how we calculate overall impact (Thiele *et al.*, 2010). More generally, there is a profound lack of empirical data on the relationship between abundance and impact, as measured ecologically or economically (Yokomizo *et al.*, 2009). The assumed linear relationship in the Parker and colleagues (1999) equation is but one of at least four potential ways in which impact scales according to abundance (Figure 8.1; Yokomizo *et al.*, 2009). Finally, per-individual effects can be divided into those that are unique to the species involved, or are more generally applicable and therefore easily measured and compared (Thomsen *et al.*, 2011). Therefore, how per-individual effects are measured becomes a critical component to the extent to which invasive species impacts can be compared.

A final complicating facet of invasive species' impact is that it can vary substantially through time (Strayer *et al.*, 2006). The most obvious way in which impacts can vary is via changes in abundance of the invader through time. Species that are in the early phase of exponential growth, for example, will inherently show comparatively smaller ecological impacts than they will once they reach higher abundances. However, not all invasive species follow standard population growth models. For example, any species that

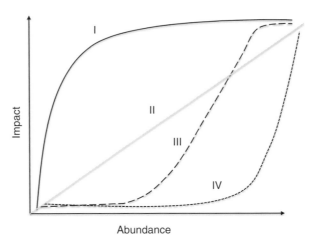

Figure 8.1 Theoretical abundance–impact curves relating the population size of an invasive species with its impact on co-occurring native species or the local ecosystem in which it has established. These four possibilities (I to IV) were first described by Yokomizo and colleagues (2009) in relation to economic impacts, and we continue their use here generalizing impacts to include ecological factors. The impact formula of Parker and colleagues (1999) assumes a Type II abundance–impact curve, which we represent in gray and consider the default assumption. Non-linear abundance–impact curves can be generated through a variety of mechanisms, and there is considerable value in documenting these. However, an understanding of which curve obtains in any one situation can greatly benefit efforts in ameliorating the impacts of this species (see text).

shows a substantial lag in their population growth, where they stay at low numbers for very long periods of time, will tend to impart few ecological impacts during this lag only to become highly abundant after the lag has ended (Crooks & Soule, 1999). Some invasive species will reach very high abundances and then decline in numbers sometimes down to near extinction (Simberloff & Gibbons, 2004). These population collapses suggest that invasive species that currently are very abundant and having large impacts on native species may not always be harmful (Lockwood et al., 2013). These more complex population dynamics create real dilemmas for those charged with managing invasive species (see below; Crooks, 2005).

THE IMPACT OF COASTAL MARINE INVADERS

Coastal marine ecosystems harbor large numbers of non-native species and have done so since at least the dawn of maritime commerce (Carlton, 1999; Ruiz et al., 1999). The most common pathway by which non-native species arrive in coastal ecosystems is within a ship's ballast water or as a hull-fouling organism (Ruiz *et al.*, 2000; Minchin *et al.*, 2009). Any bay or estuary that is home to a major port city (either now or in the past) will have had relatively large numbers of non-native species established there (Ruiz *et al.*, 2000). Many more non-native species find their way into coastal marine ecosystems as accidental introductions via commercial ventures (e.g. mariculture) or through the release of individual organisms into coastal waters by aquaria hobbyists or retailers that no longer wish to keep their pets (Fofonoff *et al.*, 2009; Minchin *et al.*, 2009). Non-native species are less common in other coastal habitats, such as rocky shorelines and shallow estuaries, in part because these habitats are not typically associated with large cities and are not commercial ports of call (Preisler *et al.*, 2009). However, these coastal areas can be secondarily invaded via the range expansion of established invaders out of nearby major port areas or by the inadvertent transfer of non-native species along a coastline via the ballast or hull of smaller boats (e.g. recreational boats) or other local-scale vectors (Preisler *et al.*, 2009; Ruiz *et al.*, 2011).

No matter the mechanism of transport and release, the number of non-native species in coastal ecosystems is very large and set to increase into the future (Ruiz *et al.*, 1999). Bax and colleagues (2003) report that one new estuarine or marine non-native species has established every 32 weeks in San Francisco Bay, and every 85 weeks in well-studied (large) ports in the US, Australia, and New Zealand. In every published account of the temporal rate at which non-native species are appearing in coastal marine ecosystems, the rate of establishment is increasing, sometimes exponentially (e.g. Cohen & Carlton, 1998; Ruiz *et al.*, 2000). Furthermore, as climate continues to warm and commercial shipping traffic shifts pole-wards in response, the likelihood of non-native species appearing in very high- and low-latitude coastal ecosystems will increase (Hewitt *et al.*, 2009; de Rivera *et al.*, 2011).

In the context of the invasion process model of Blackburn and colleagues (2011), we can state with certainty that coastal marine ecosystems have had a long-duration inflow of non-native species and that this "invasion tap" is being opened yet wider as the climate warms and global trade expands in magnitude and geographical scope (Carlton, 1999). From a conservation perspective, we should be asking what the massive inflow of non-native species does to the native species that occupy coastal ecosystems (Bax *et al.*, 2003). Below, we review the existing literature published on the impacts of coastal marine invaders and quantify trends in the taxonomic, geographical, biological, and temporal aspects of research on coastal marine invaders.

We searched for relevant peer-reviewed articles by entering all combinations of the keyword "invas*", with each of the following: "marine", "coast*", "marsh", "estuar*", "dune", "bay", "beach", and "nearshore OR near shore" into Web of Science® and Google Scholar®. We retained only those articles that included an assessment of the impacts of an invasive coastal marine species. We also culled only those examples that involved habitats that were regularly submerged under seawater or were heavily influenced by the ocean dynamics (e.g. high salt marsh). After these criteria were applied, there were a total of 101 publications that provided details on the impacts of 99 invasive populations. From this set, we recorded: (1) the biological level in which impacts were studied (i.e. genes to ecosystem); (2) whether an ecological impact was explicitly recorded, and if so, if the effect was positive or negative; (3) the duration of study in years; (4) the habitat type considered; and (5) the broad taxonomic group under investigation.

Like other more restrictive reviews of marine invader impacts (e.g. Ruiz et al., 1999; Byers, 2009), and perhaps surprising as a core reason for interest in invasive species is their impact, we found a large number of published research never explicitly measured an effect of the invader on native species or ecosystems (Figure 8.2). These articles included studies of geographical distribution (e.g. Araújo et al., 2011), population genetics (e.g. Ben-Shlomo et al., 2010), diet (e.g. Baines & Fisher, 2007), life-history

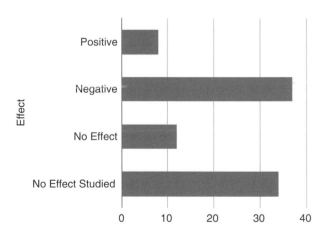

Figure 8.2 The impact (positive, negative, no effect, or no effect studied) reported for all invasive species targeted in the publications we review here. Most published research on coastal marine invaders did not explicitly document an effect, and when they did, the number of negative effects was twice that of positive or no effects.

traits (e.g. Bishop & Peterson, 2006), and many other characteristics of invasive species in coastal systems. Of those that did record an impact, twice as many recorded negative impacts than positive or no impacts. There were equal numbers of studies that recorded positive or no impacts (Figure 8.2). We define positive impacts to be a positive change in a measured property and vice versa for a negative impact. Whether any measured change is good or bad relative to a conservation goal is not always clear, and we do not presume to make that assessment here. Certainly, the value of this change must vary according to who is placing value on the property itself (Thieltges et al., 2006; Rilov, 2009; Lockwood et al., 2013).

Positive impacts have been described in reference to salt marsh in Chapter 7 and seagrass beds in Chapter 4. Within our review, two illustrative instances involve *Spartina* providing important resources for native species. In a study of the Yangtze River estuary, Wang and colleagues (2008) showed that native crab abundance and biomass were higher in *Spartina* marshes than in marshes comprised of native grasses. They also conducted feeding preference experiments that showed that native crabs consumed twice as much smooth cordgrass (*Spartina alterniflora*) than the native marsh grasses. Similarly, Hindell and Warry (2010) used stable isotope analysis to show that *Spartina* was an important contributor to the biomass of a fish that is (depending on the life stage) two or three trophic levels above plants.

The number of no-effect results stemmed from field and laboratory studies that showed that a non-native species known to be invasive elsewhere did not directly interact with or impact the native flora and fauna of the area under direct investigation. For example, Barnard and colleagues (2006) found that the veliger stage of the well-known invasive zebra mussel (*Dreissena polymorpha*) occupied a trophic position in the St. Lawrence estuarine transition zone that was novel and had no direct interaction with the other major constituents of that food web. The zebra mussel veligers did not compete with native zooplankton for resources, nor were they an important carbon source for higher trophic levels. Another well-known invader in coastal systems that was found to have no effect on a local community of native species was the ctenophore, *Mnemiopsis leidyi*. Known to be a predator of fish eggs (Monteleone & Duguay, 1988), *M. leidyi* was found to actively select against Baltic cod (*Gadus morhua callarias*) eggs in the presence of other food items and was determined to be no direct threat to the Baltic cod population (Jaspers et al., 2011).

A potential interpretation of Figure 8.2 is that negative impacts far outpace positive or no impacts. However, it was impossible to gauge from our review whether the number of recorded negative impacts were truly a

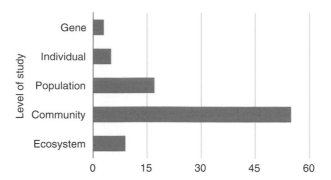

Figure 8.3 The biological level (genetic, individual, population, community, or ecosystem) at which impacts of each coastal marine invader was studied. Most published research pertains to population- and community-level impacts.

common feature of coastal marine invaders, or if research agendas and funding sources target species with suspected or known negative impacts, driving up the number of published negative results. There is certainly evidence derived from a wider swath of invasion studies that species with larger impacts are more likely to have received research attention (Pysek *et al.*, 2008). We suggest that the results in Figure 8.3 are driven to some extent by the motivation to conduct research; however, it is unclear to what degree. Teasing apart the influence of research effort from realized impact across a range of coastal marine invaders would repay greatly in our understanding of how common negative impacts are in this ecosystem.

A closer look at the publications that recorded either positive or negative impact showed that most studies failed to provide statistical effect sizes for the impacts they documented. The publication of effect sizes is critical to our ability to conduct quantitative meta-analyses (Fernandez-Duque & Valeggia, 1994), which is a sorely needed avenue of research across all invasion studies, including marine invasions (Ruiz *et al.*, 1999; Byers, 2009). In the context of the impact of invasive species, the publication of effect sizes takes on added importance as these values allow for the construction of empirical abundance–impact curves as in Figure 8.1. They also allow for the direct comparison of impacts of the same species across locations or through time, thereby uncovering more nuanced mechanisms for when and how impacts can occur (Ruiz *et al.*, 1999; Byers, 2009). Related to the lack of published effect sizes, we found authors also rarely couched their results within the context of broader impact currencies like those derived from Parker and colleagues (1999). This gap adds an additional barrier to our ability to compare impacts across species, populations, or ecosystems.

Our review indicates that the vast majority of research on the impacts of coastal marine invaders focused on community-level interactions, documenting, for example, competitive and predatory interactions with native species (e.g. Byers, 2009; Figure 8.3). Population- and ecosystem-level impacts were modestly well studied. This research typically considered the impacts of invaders on the population dynamics of co-occurring native species (e.g. Ruesink *et al.*, 2005), or the alteration of physical features of ecosystems by invasive species (e.g. Crooks, 2009). We show that there are very few examples of research on the individual and genetic impacts of marine invaders, a trend also apparent across chapters in this volume. The pattern evident in Figure 8.3 reflects the broader allocation of research effort across biological levels in invasion ecology in general (Parker *et al.*, 1999; Lockwood *et al.*, 2013). Nevertheless, there is no reason to expect that *realized* ecological impacts are distributed across biological levels in this manner, which highlights the need to expand the existing purview of research.

The overwhelming majority of the research we reviewed reported on results derived from less than 3 years of data acquisition, with many results stemming from studies lasting less than a year (Figure 8.4). Fewer than 5 studies lasted over 10 years in duration, albeit these exceptions were very long duration studies that reported on data that spanned > 20 years. The short duration of study that we report here matches patterns derived from across a larger set of invasion studies (Strayer *et al.*, 2006). Perhaps unsurprisingly, the predominance of studies that last < 4 years matches the length of time required to obtain a PhD, and the typical duration of a research grant (see also Pimm, 1991). However, the lack of long-term studies on the impact

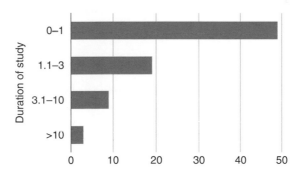

Figure 8.4 The number of years that data were collected within the publications we review here. The vast majority of published research on coastal marine invaders reports on results from < 4 years of data acquisition.

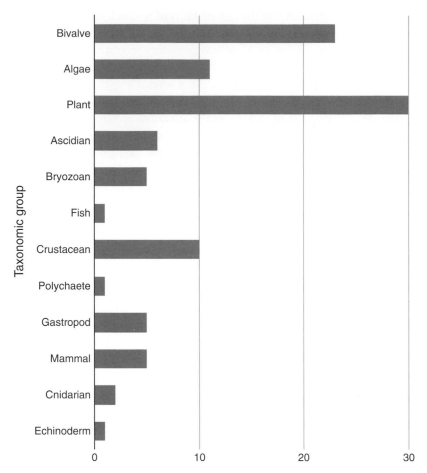

Figure 8.5 The taxonomic identity of invasive species within the publications we review here. The breadth of taxa reflects the unique nature of coastal ecosystems; however, the focus on a few taxa (e.g. plants) is common across all invasion studies (see text).

of marine invaders is a glaring gap in our understanding of how such effects may wax and wane through time (Byers, 2009). For example, the short duration of research largely prevents mechanistic understanding of both lag phases and collapses and what these complex population dynamics mean for impacts on native species and ecosystems.

We found that plants, bivalves, algae, and crustaceans were the most common taxonomic groups studied (Figure 8.5). This taxonomic focus broadly reflects trends found by Pysek and colleagues (2008), who reviewed a wider range of habitat types. Our results disagree with those of Pysek *et al.*

(2008) due largely to the unique taxonomic composition of coastal marine invaders. For example, we record a variety of invertebrates that are principally found in marine environments (e.g. bryozoans, ascidians, and cnidarians). It is not clear whether the taxonomic trends we found reflect true differences in the identity of species that will impose impacts, or if the species in these groups (or single species within these groups) have garnered more research and funding attention because of previously known impacts. Either interpretation suggests that plants, algae, and bivalves tend to be more harmful than other groups within coastal marine ecosystems. However, we consider this a tenuous conclusion that deserves more attention using data that can clearly tease apart the influence of regularity of study from commonness of impact.

We found that the coastal habitats most often studied were estuaries, intertidal systems, and salt marshes (Figure 8.6). Almost certainly this reflects the fact that these ecosystems surround, or are home to, large port cities, and therefore large numbers of non-native species have established there (e.g. Preisler *et al.*, 2009). This trend across habitats may also reflect the taxonomic trends reported in Figure 8.5. There are more plants and bivalves, for example, within estuaries and salt marshes than in mudflats or dunes. We again run into the question of whether impacts are more common in estuaries and salt marshes, or whether there are a few species that are known to cause large impacts in these habitats and thus there is comparatively more money and time spent investigating them. Nevertheless, Figure 8.6 suggests that a few select habitats are receiving the lion's share of attention regarding invasive species impacts, perhaps to the detriment of our understanding of how invasive species impact other habitats.

A CONSERVATION AND RESEARCH AGENDA

There is plenty of evidence that the most efficient way to prevent invasive species impacts is to prevent the invasion from happening in the first place (e.g. Keller *et al.*, 2007). Coastal marine ecosystems are some of the most highly invaded places in the world (Ruiz *et al.*, 1999; Crooks & Rilov, 2009), in large part because of the enormous colonization and propagule pressure associated with commercial shipping (Minchin *et al.*, 2009). The need to curtail the number of non-native species that are transported and released into coastal marine ecosystems has been recognized for several decades now (Ruiz *et al.*, 1999). Almost all the attention devoted to realizing this goal has focused on regulation of ballast water or preventing hull fouling (Bax *et al.*, 2003; Hewitt *et al.*, 2009). This focus is certainly warranted, as

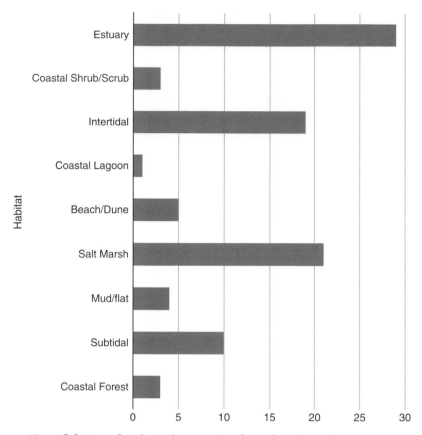

Figure 8.6 Most often the studies we review focused on salt marshes, estuaries, or intertidal zones. This focus is warranted given the number of non-native species established in these habitats; however, the impacts of invasive species within other habitats may be under-documented as a result.

commercial and recreational ships have been, and continue to be, enormous sources for the delivery of non-native species.

Other commercial ventures, such as mariculture and the marine ornamental pet trade, have increased in their importance as vectors of non-native species over the past decade (Bax *et al.*, 2003). In particular, the number of marine species that are imported within the pet trade is vast and growing (Tissot *et al.*, 2010). Zajicek and colleagues (2009) report that 1500 fish species, 200 coral species, and 500 invertebrate species representing tens of millions of individuals are sold worldwide each year in the marine ornamental pet trade. Certainly many of these species will be housed in locations far from coastal marine waters (Weigle *et al.*, 2005); however, enough will be released into coastal waters by frustrated aquaria owners and retailers that this vector stands to deliver a wide variety of newly established non-native species over the coming decades (Zajicek *et al.*, 2009).

If the invasion of coastal marine ecosystems is to be addressed in a comprehensive fashion, these non-shipping vectors must receive policy and management attention aimed at reducing the risk that these vectors will introduce new invaders (Bax *et al.*, 2003; Weigle *et al.*, 2005). Because these species are purposefully imported (rather than moved as byproducts of commerce; e.g. ballast water), there exist both top-down and voluntary mechanisms for regulating the extent to which these vectors introduce non-native species (Campbell, 2009). Many of these approaches deserve more scrutiny as to their effectiveness, and there appears to be little cross-over in risk assessment approaches developed for terrestrial and marine ecosystems (e.g. Weigle *et al.*, 2005).

Even the best risk assessment protocols will not forestall the establishment of invasive species (Lockwood *et al.*, 2013), and the evolving nature of commerce ensures that policies directed at reducing the introduction of invasive species will always be 'behind the eight-ball' (Minchin *et al.*, 2009). What is the most effective way to respond to the recent establishment of a non-native species that is deemed likely to become invasive? The answer is clear: act quickly to eradicate the incipient population before it becomes so abundant and widespread that it is economically and politically infeasible to remove (Crooks & Soule, 1999; Simberloff, 2003; Bodey *et al.*, 2010). The need to act quickly and decisively puts a high premium on developing eradication protocols that make clear the lines of authority needed to enact eradication, determining the range of socially acceptable methods that can be used to kill non-native individuals, and the source of readily available funding to undertake these actions (Bax *et al.*, 2001; Thresher & Kuris, 2004; Wotton & Hewitt, 2004).

Comprehensive risk assessment and rapid response eradication campaigns depend greatly on our ability to determine which non-native species are likely to cause unacceptable impacts on what native ecosystems (Hewitt *et al.*, 2009). To do this well, we must have a much better understanding of how and when invasive species impact native ecosystems (Ruiz *et al.*, 1999; Crooks & Rilov, 2009; Ricciardi *et al.*, 2013). However, even when coastal marine invaders are widespread and are known to cause impacts, an understanding of how these effects are manifest is critical to the strategies employed to ameliorate them (Ruiz *et al.*, 1999; Ketternring & Adams, 2011). For example, the abundance–impact curves of Figure 8.1 suggest very different goals for management. If the impact of an invasive species follows curves I or II, many individuals of the invader must be removed before measurable and acceptable reductions in impact will occur. In contrast, if impact followed curve IV, even moderate success in controlling the invader will pay off (Yokomizo *et al.*, 2009). There should be equally relevant insights to control efforts gained from comparing invasive species effects across their geographical range and through time (Ruiz *et al.*, 1999; Byers, 2009). To achieve these goals, our review suggests existing research must fill several knowledge gaps.

Perhaps the more worrisome gap is the failure of existing research to explicitly document the effects of invaders on native species or ecosystem properties, and when this is done, failing to report the associated statistical effect size(s) (see also Ruiz *et al.*, 1999; Byers, 2009). These information gaps create substantial obstacles to efforts to compare or generalize invasive species impacts across populations, species, and locations. They also hinder effective management by failing to specify (or acknowledge) that documented impacts may be exclusive to the time and place of study (e.g. Thieltges *et al.*, 2006; Hacker *et al.*, 2012). Filling this gap would be greatly facilitated by developing a generally accepted definition of 'impact' (*sensu* Ricciardi *et al.*, 2013), and realistic ways of measuring and reporting these impacts. Despite the simplicity of the Parker and colleagues (1999) impact equation, it is far easier to collect comprehensive information on either abundance or range size than it is for per-individual effects (Thiele *et al.*, 2010). Those working in coastal marine ecosystems could lead the way in this effort by agreeing to systematically collect and report basic information on any (or all) elements of this equation (e.g. Zaiko *et al.*, 2011). This effort would pay off for managers and scientists, even if it were restricted to one or a few taxa (Ruiz *et al.*, 1999).

The lack of long-term research on the impacts of coastal marine invaders serves as an additional impediment to providing empirical evidence for (or against) any of the theoretical abundance–impact curves (Figure 8.1). Long-term studies also allow us to document the prevalence of population growth lags and collapses, and when these are likely to occur. When lags are present, managers may make the mistake of assuming these rare species will *always* remain rare and thus devote their limited resources to other currently troublesome invaders. However, once these species emerge from their lag, they quickly increase in abundance and potentially cause some level of impact (Crooks & Soule, 1999). In such cases, a manager has missed a relatively long-lived opportunity to eradicate a species that was destined to become a harmful invader (Crooks, 2005). Population collapses suggest the exact opposite management problem in that such species will quickly reach very high abundances likely producing notable impacts, but these impacts will naturally wane through time without any management input (Strayer *et al.*, 2006). In this instance, managers may have expended scarce resources addressing a problem that will, to some extent, take care of itself. The current state of invasion research provides us with precious little help in identifying lagging or collapsing invaders (Lockwood *et al.*, 2013). Simply documenting the prevalence of lagged or collapsed populations of coastal marine invaders would prove highly relevant.

Our understanding of the impacts of coastal marine invaders is largely limited to their community-level effects, and we may be missing substantial issues related to the genetic and behavioral integrity of native species or the functioning of invaded ecosystems (e.g. Kimbro *et al.*, 2009). Such impacts are understudied across the board (Parker *et al.*, 1999; Lockwood *et al.*, 2013), but their importance within coastal marine ecosystems seems relatively large (Grosholz, 2002; Ruesnik *et al.*, 2005). For example, estuaries provide enormous benefits via their production of ecosystem services (Barbier *et al.*, 2011). Any alteration of these services due to invasive species will therefore have wide-ranging implications for human economies and welfare (Crooks, 2009). Related is the reliance of human society on coastal marine fisheries (Casal, 2006). Certainly, fisheries can be impacted by the competition or predation of native fishes imposed by invasive species (Byers, 2009; Rilov, 2009). However, they can be equally impacted by a change in the genetic integrity of native fish populations, or a change in these natives' behavior or individual well-being (e.g. Walton *et al.*, 2002; Conrad *et al.*, 2011). Whether impacts at these biological levels are more prevalent than those at the community level is an open question, but an expanded effort at documenting impacts across biological levels should have wide-ranging payoffs (Grosholz, 2002).

Finally, there is a clear need to expand the taxonomic breadth and range of coastal habitats studied in regards to the impacts of invasive species (Preisler *et al.*, 2009). Some of the trends we report above are justified given the likely (but often unproven) differences in the numbers of non-native species within certain taxonomic groups or habitats. More attention should be paid to groups and places that are more likely to harbor invasive species, but the absolute number of invasive species within a habitat type may not translate directly into the degree of impact imposed on that habitat (Zaiko *et al.*, 2011). For example, the large number of invasive species within estuaries may, taken together, impose lower overall negative impacts than the one invasive species that radically transforms sandy beaches (Chapter 3) or seagrass beds (Chapter 4). As of now we are incapable of making such comparisons because sandy beaches and seagrasses have not been well studied in regards to invasive species. Furthermore, without a consistent metric to measure invasive species impacts, making these judgments will continue to be difficult.

CONCLUSION

Coastal ecosystems are some of the most highly invaded locations in the world, a distinction that is likely to become even more dramatic as the pace and extent of global commerce continues to expand (Bax et al., 2001). Given the unique biodiversity of these ecosystems, and their profound importance in supporting human societies (Chapter 1), one might expect considerable investment in documenting which of the thousands of non-native species that occupy these habitats will become invasive and what can be done about those that do (Bax et al., 2003). On a limited scale, there has been considerable political, economic, and scientific capital expended on reducing the inflow of non-natives species into coastal ecosystems through ballast water and hull fouling (Bax et al. 2003; Hewitt et al., 2009). This is not a bad investment given the role these vectors play in transporting and releasing non-native species. However, as our review indicates, and others have highlighted (e.g. Bax et al., 2003), there are still major gaps in how scientists and managers approach the problem of coastal marine invaders. These gaps clearly reflect broader issues within invasion ecology, and their resolution is not something that can be solved overnight. However, the payoff for conserving coastal biodiversity can be substantial and path-breaking.

REFERENCES

Araújo, R., Violante, J., Pereira, R., et al. (2011). Distribution and population dynamics of the introduced seaweed Grateloupia turuturu (Halymeniaceae, Rhodophyta) along the Portuguese coast. Phycologia, 50, 392–402.

Baines, S. B., Fisher, N. S. & Cole, J. J. (2007). Dissolved organic matter and persistence of the invasive zebra mussel (Dreissena polymorpha) under low food conditions. Limnology and Oceanography, 52, 70–78.

Barbier, E. B., Hacker, S. D., Kennedy, C., et al. (2011). The value of estuarine and coastal ecosystem services. Ecological Monographs, 81, 169–193.

Barnard, C., Martineau, C., Frenette, J., Dodson, J. J. & Vincent, W. F. (2006). Trophic position of zebra mussel veligers and their use of dissolved organic carbon. Limnology and Oceanography, 51, 1473–1484.

Bax, N., Carlton, J. T., Mathews-Amos, A., et al. (2001). The control of biological invasions in the world's oceans. Conservation Biology, 15, 1234–1246.

Bax, N., Williamson, A., Aguero, M., Gonzalez, E. & Geeves, W. (2003). Marine invasive alien species: A threat to global biodiversity. Marine Policy, 27, 313–323.

Ben-Shlomo, R., Reem, E., Douek, J. & Rinkevich, B. (2010). Population genetics of the invasive ascidian *Botryllus schlosseri* from South American coasts. *Marine Ecology Progress Series*, **412**, 85–92.

Bishop, M. J. & Peterson, C. H. (2006). When r-selection may not predict introduced-species proliferation: Predation of a nonnative oyster. *Ecological Applications*, **16**, 718–730.

Blackburn, T. M., Pysek, P., Bacher, S., *et al.* (2011). A proposed united framework for biological invasions. *Trends in Ecology and Evolution*, **26**, 333–339.

Bodey, T. W., Bearhop, S., Roy, S. S., Newton, J. & McDonald, R. A. (2010). Behavioral responses of invasive American mink *Neovison vison* to an eradication campaign, revealed by stable isotope analysis. *Journal of Applied Ecology*, **47**, 114–120.

Byers, J. E. (2009). Competition in marine invasions. In G. Rilov & J. A. Crooks (eds.), *Biological Invasions in Marine Ecosystems*. Ecological Studies 204. Berlin: Springer, pp. 245–258.

Campbell, M. (2009). An overview of risk assessment in a marine biosecurity context. In G. Rilov & J. A. Crooks (eds.), *Biological Invasions in Marine Ecosystems*. Ecological Studies 204. Berlin: Springer, pp. 353–374.

Carlton, J. T. (1999). The scale and ecological consequences of biological invasions in the world's oceans. In O. T. Sandlund, P. J. Schei & A. Viken (eds.), *Invasive Species and Biodiversity Management*. Dordrecht: Kluwer Academic Publishers, pp. 195–212.

Casal, C. M. V. (2006). Global documentation of fish introductions: The growing crisis and recommendations for action. *Biological Invasions*, **8**, 3–11.

Cohen, A. N. & Carlton, J. T. (1998). Accelerating invasion rate in a highly invaded estuary. *Science*, **279**, 555–558.

Conrad, J. L., Weinersmith, K. L., Brodin, T., Saltz, J. B. & Sih, A. (2011). Behavioural syndromes in fishes: A review with implications for ecology and fisheries management. *Journal of Fish Biology*, **78**, 395–435.

Crooks, J. A. (2005). Lag times and exotic species: The ecology and management of biological invasions in slow-motion. *Ecoscience*, **12**, 316–329.

Crooks, J. A. (2009). The role of exotic marine ecosystem engineers. In G. Rilov & J. A. Crooks (eds.), *Biological Invasions in Marine Ecosystems*. Ecological Studies 204. Berlin: Springer, pp. 287–304.

Crooks, J. A. & Rilov, G. (2009). Future directions for marine invasion research. In G. Rilov & J. A. Crooks (eds.), *Biological Invasions in Marine Ecosystems*. Ecological Studies 204. Berlin: Springer, pp. 621–626.

Crooks, J. A. & Soule, M. E. (1999). Lag times in population explosions of invasive species: Causes and implications. In O. T. Sandlund, P. J. Schei & A. Viken (eds.), *Invasive Species and Biodiversity Management*. Dordrecht: Kluwer Academic Publishers, pp. 103–126.

De Rivera, C. E., Steves, B. P., Fofonoff, P. W., Hines, A. H. & Ruiz, G. M. (2011). Potential for high-latitude marine invasions along western North America. *Diversity and Distributions*, **17**, 1198–1209.

Fernandez-Duque, E. & Veleggia, C. (1994). Meta-analysis: A valuable tool in conservation research. *Conservation Biology*, **8**, 555–561.

Fofonoff, P. W., Ruiz, G. M., Hines, A. H., Steves, B. D. & Carlton, J. T. (2009). Four centuries of biological invasions in tidal waters of the Chesapeake Bay Region. In

G. Rilov & J. A. Crooks (eds.), *Biological Invasions in Marine Ecosystems*. Ecological Studies 204. Berlin: Springer, pp. 479–506.

Grosholz, E. (2002). Ecological and evolutionary consequences of coastal invasions. *Trends in Ecology and Evolution*, **17**, 22–27.

Hacker, S. D., Zarnetske, P., Seabloom, E., *et al.* (2012). Subtle differences in two non-native congeneric beach grasses significantly affect their colonization, spread and impact. *Oikos*, **121**, 138–148.

Hewitt, C. L., Everett, R. A., Parker, N. & Campbell, M. L. (2009). Marine bioinvasion management: Structural framework. In G. Rilov & J. A. Crooks (eds.), *Biological Invasions in Marine Ecosystems*. Ecological Studies 204. Berlin: Springer, pp. 327–334.

Hindell, J. S. & Warry, F. Y. (2010). Nutritional support of estuary perch (*Macquaria colonorum*) in a temperate Australian inlet: Evaluating the relative importance of invasive *Spartina*. *Estuarine, Coastal and Shelf Science*, **90**, 159–167.

Jaspers, C., Titelman, J., Hansson, L. J., Haraldsson, M. & Ditlefsen, C. R. (2011). The invasive ctenophore *Mnemiopsis leidyi* poses no threat to Baltic cod eggs and larvae. *Limnology and Oceanography*, **56**, 431–439.

Keller, R. P, Lodge, D. M. & Finnoff, D. C. (2007). Risk assessment for invasive species produces net bioeconomic benefits. *Proceedings of the National Academy of Sciences of the United States of America*, **104**, 203–207.

Ketternring, K. M. & Adams, C. R. (2011). Lessons learned from invasive plant control experiments: A systematic review and meta-analysis. *Journal of Applied Ecology*, **48**, 970–979.

Kimbro, D. L., Grosholz, E. D., Baukus, A. J., *et al.* (2009). Invasive species cause large-scale loss of native California oyster habitat by disrupting trophic cascades. *Oecologia*, **160**, 563–575.

Lockwood, J. L., Hoopes, M. F. & Marchetti, M. P. (2013) *Invasion Ecology*, 2nd edn. London: Wiley-Blackwell Publishers.

Miller, A. W. & Ruiz, G. M. (2009). Differentiating successful and failed invaders: Species pools and the importance of defining vector, source and recipient regions. In G. Rilov & J. A. Crooks (eds.), *Biological Invasions in Marine Ecosystems*. Ecological Studies 204. Berlin: Springer, pp. 153–172.

Minchin, D., Gollasch, S., Cohen, A. N., Hewitt, C. L. & Olenin, S. J. (2009). Characterizing vectors of marine invasion. In G. Rilov & J. A. Crooks (eds.), *Biological Invasions in Marine Ecosystems*. Ecological Studies 204. Berlin: Springer, pp. 109–116.

Monteleone, D. M. & Duguay, L. E. (1988). Laboratory studies of predation by the ctenophore *Mnemiopsis leidyi* on the early stages in the life history of the bay anchovy, *Anchoa mitchilli*. *Journal of Plankton Research*, **10**, 359–372.

Parker, I. M., Simberloff, D., Lonsdale, W. M., *et al.* (1999). Impact: Toward a framework for understanding the ecological effects of invaders. *Biological Invasions*, **1**, 3–19.

Pimentel, D., Zuniga, R. & Morrison, D. (2005). Update on the environmental and economic costs associated with alien-invasive species in the United States. *Ecological Economics*, **52**, 273–288.

Pimm, S. L. (1991). *The Balance of Nature?* Chicago, IL: University of Chicago Press.

Preisler, R. K., Wasson, K., Wolff, W. J. & Tyrrell, M. C. (2009). Invasion of estuaries vs the adjacent open coast: A global perspective. In G. Rilov & J. A. Crooks (eds.),

Biological Invasions in Marine Ecosystems. Ecological Studies 204. Berlin: Springer, pp. 587–604.

Pysek, P., Richardson, D. M., Pergl, J., *et al.* (2008). Geographical and taxonomic biases in invasion ecology. *Trends in Ecology and Evolution,* **23,** 237–244.

Ricciardi, A., Hoopes, M. F., Marchetti, M. P. & Lockwood, J. L. (2013). Progress toward understanding the ecological impacts of non-native species. *Ecological Monographs,* **83,** 263–282.

Rilov, G. (2009). The integration of invasive species into marine ecosystems. In G. Rilov & J. A. Crooks (eds.), *Biological Invasions in Marine Ecosystems.* Ecological Studies 204. Berlin: Springer, pp. 241–244.

Rilov, G. & Crooks, J. A. (2009). Marine bioinvasions: Conservation hazards and vehicles for ecological understanding. In G. Rilov & J. A. Crooks (eds.), *Biological Invasions in Marine Ecosystems.* Ecological Studies 204. Berlin: Springer, pp. 3–12.

Ruesink, J. L., Lenihan, H. S., Trimble, A. C., *et al.* (2005). Introduction of non-native oysters: Ecosystem effects and restoration implications. *Annual Review of Ecology, Evolution and Systematics,* **36,** 643–689.

Ruiz, G. M., Fofonoff, P., Hines, A. H. & Grosholz, E. D. (1999). Non-indigenous species as stressors in estuarine and marine communities: Assessing the impacts and interactions. *Limnology and Oceanography,* **44,** 950–972.

Ruiz, G. M., Fofonoff, P. W., Carlton, J. T., Wonham, M. J. & Hines, A. H. (2000). Invasions of coastal marine communities in North America: Apparent patterns, processes, and biases. *Annual Reviews in Ecology, Evolution and Systematics,* **31,** 481–531.

Ruiz, G. M., Fofonoff, P. W., Steves, B., Foss, S. F. & Shiba, S. N. (2011). Marine invasion history and vector analysis of California: A hotspot for western North America. *Diversity and Distributions,* **17,** 362–373.

Simberloff, D. (2003). Eradication: Preventing invasions at the outset. *Weed Science,* **51,** 247–253.

Simberloff, D. & Gibbons, L. (2004). Now you see them, now you don't: Population crashes of established introduced species. *Biological Invasions,* **6,** 161–172.

Simberloff, D., Parker, I. M. & Windle, P. N. (2005). Introduced species policy, management, and future research. *Frontiers in Ecology and the Environment,* **3,** 12–20.

Strayer, D. L., Eviner, V. T., Jeschke, J. M. and Pace, M. L. (2006). Understanding the long-term effects of species invasions. *Trends in Ecology and Evolution,* **21,** 645–651.

Thiele, J., Kollmann, J., Markussen, B. & Otte, A. (2010). Impact assessment revisited: Improving the theoretical basis for management of invasive alien species. *Biological Invasions,* **12,** 2025–2035.

Thieltges, D. W., Strasser, M. & Reise, K. (2006). How bad are invaders in coastal waters? The case of the American slipper limpet *Crepidula fornicata* in western Europe. *Biological Invasions,* **8,** 1673–1680.

Thresher, R. E. & Kuris, A. M. (2004). Options for managing invasive marine species. *Biological Invasions,* **6,** 295–300.

Tissot, B. N., Best, B. A., Borneman, E. H., *et al.* (2010). How U.S. ocean policy and market power can reform the coral reef wildlife trade. *Marine Policy,* **34,** 1385–1388.

Thomsen, M. S., Wernberg, T., Oldern, J. D., Griffin, J. N. & Silliman, B. R. (2011). A framework to study the context-dependent impact of marine invasions. *Journal of Experimental and Marine Biology and Ecology*, **400**, 322–327.

Walton, W. C., MacKinnon, C., Rogriquez, L. F., Proctor, C. & Ruiz, G. M. (2002). Effect of an invasive crab upon a marine fishery: Green crab, *Carcinus maena*, predation upon a venerid clam, *Katelysia scalarina*, in Tasmania (Australia). *Journal of Experimental Marine Biology and Ecology*, **272**, 171–189.

Wang, J., Zhang, Z. X., Nie, M., *et al.* (2008). Exotic *Spartina alterniflora* provides compatible habitats for native estuarine crab *Sesarma dehaani* in the Yangtze River estuary. *Ecological Engineering*, **34**, 57–64.

Weigle, S. M., Smith, L. D., Carlton, J. T. & Pederson, J. (2005). Assessing the risk of introducing exotic species via the live marine species trade. *Conservation Biology*, **19**, 213–223.

Wotton, D. M. & Hewitt, C. L. (2004). Marine biosecurity post-border management: Developing incursion response systems for New Zealand. *New Zealand Journal of Marine and Freshwater Resources*, **38**, 553–559.

Yokomizo, H., Possingham, H. P., Thomas, M. B. & Buckley, Y. M. (2009). Managing the impact of invasive species: The value of knowing the density-impact curve. *Ecological Applications*, **19**, 376–386.

Zaiko, A., Lehtiniemi, M., Narscius, A. & Olenin, S. (2011). Assessment of bioinvasion impacts on a regional scale: A comparative approach. *Biological Invasions*, **13**, 1739–1765.

Zajicek, P., Hardin, S. & Watson, C. (2009). A Florida marine ornamental pathway risk analysis. *Reviews in Fisheries Science*, **17**, 156–169.

9

Climate change and conservation of waders

ILYA M. D. MACLEAN

INTRODUCTION

The world's climate is changing rapidly. In the last 50 years, global temperatures on land have risen by approximately 1°C, and over the next 100 years a further rise in temperatures of at least 2°C is expected (IPCC, 2007). This rise may not seem like much, but the rate of temperature change is unprecedented in recent history, and many animals and plants are struggling to keep pace (Chen *et al.*, 2011). Wading birds (Charadrii) are particularly susceptible to climate change (Maclean & Wilson, 2011). Many species travel over large sections of the globe during the course of their annual cycle and use habitats in many different biomes and climate zones (Piersma & Lindstrom, 2004). The majority of waders breed in the high Arctic, a region warmer now than at any time in the last 125 000 years and undergoing further warming at a rate almost twice that of the global average. Other species breed in freshwater marshes, which are threatened by increased drought. During the winter periods, the majority of waders move to coastal habitats where they experience climate-related threats associated with the marine environment. Global sea level rose ~17 cm during the last century, but the rate in the last decade is nearly double that of the last century (Church & White, 2006). Significant habitat loss and change has occurred as a result, and even greater changes are expected in the future (Chu-Agor *et al.*, 2010). The magnitude of future changes in sea level are very difficult to predict because of uncertainties associated with understanding the extent of polar ice sheet loss. However, the last time polar regions were significantly warmer than at present for an extended period, reductions in polar ice volume led to 4–6 m of sea level rise (IPCC, 2007). Marine invertebrate prey of waders are also susceptible to changes

Coastal Conservation, eds B. Maslo and J. L. Lockwood. Published by Cambridge University Press.
© Cambridge University Press 2014.

in ocean chemistry. Ocean acidity has increased by ~30% as a result of higher levels of dissolved carbon dioxide, with concomitant deleterious impacts on calcifying organisms (Orr *et al.*, 2005). Moreover, temperature increases and changes in ocean circulation patterns have been linked with reductions in dissolved oxygen in coastal and marine systems, with extremely damaging consequences for the fauna associated with these habitats (Grantham *et al.*, 2004). Many of these species are part of the food web on which waders rely.

In this chapter, I present an overview of the impacts of climate change on waders. I start by reviewing the growing body of evidence that shows that waders are affected by climate change. I then explore how some of these effects are likely to have deleterious consequences. In so doing, I aim to give a balanced overview of climate-driven impacts on this group of birds. Not all effects are harmful. Some species have expanded their range as a consequence of warming temperatures (Maclean *et al.*, 2008a), and others are expected to benefit through higher survival (van de Pol *et al.*, 2010). Moreover, significant knowledge gaps and scientific challenges remain, giving rise to considerable uncertainties. Some of the major challenges and possible ways in which future ecologists might overcome these difficulties are also presented. Finally, I explore some of the opportunities that exist for helping waders cope with climate change and discuss how these could be integrated with conservation policies and legislation.

RESPONSES TO CLIMATE CHANGE

Phenological change

Phenology – the timing of seasonal activities of animals and plants – is perhaps the simplest process in which to track changes in the ecology of species in response to climate change (Walther *et al.*, 2002). Quantitative assessment of phenological changes across numerous species overwhelmingly suggests that the timing of seasonal events has indeed changed. However, most evidence comes from biological events associated with the timing of the onset of spring, and responses at other times of year are less clear-cut (Parmesan & Yohe, 2003; Parmesan, 2006). In the Northern Hemisphere, first leaf and bloom dates and last spring freeze dates have advanced by between 1 and 1.5 days per decade since the 1950s (Schwartz *et al.*, 2006). Waders, too, have advanced their phenology in spring. In the Netherlands, there is a tradition of collecting lapwing (*Vanellus vanellus*) eggs for consumption, and because of financial and ceremonial rewards, search intensity in the early season is extremely high. Between 1930 and

2003, a period in which spring temperatures increased, the first date that eggs were collected advanced by approximately two weeks (Both *et al.*, 2005). This advance can predominantly be explained by increasing spring temperatures and wetter winters, with little variance remaining to be explained by other factors, such as habitat change. Similar advances in the timing of the breeding season of lapwings were demonstrated by Musters and colleagues (2010), although no such advancement was noted in black-tailed godwits (*Limosa limosa*). Whereas lapwings are short-distance migrants in the Netherlands, black-tailed godwits originate from much further south. It has been hypothesized that the magnitude of phenological advancement is dependent on the migratory strategy adopted by species, which might help to explain these differences. The evolutionary causes and consequences of phenological advancement and the relevance of environmental cues triggering breeding cycle events are discussed later in this chapter.

Although much of the work on phenological advancement in waders has come from the Netherlands, where good long-term data sets exist, there is growing evidence from elsewhere. In North America, the timing of arrival of western sandpipers (*Calidris mauri*) corresponds with the timing of snowmelt, although late snowmelts do delay breeding, suggesting that phenological shifts do not necessarily fully compensate for environmental changes (Niehaus & Ydenberg, 2006). In central Europe, four studied wader species advanced the timing of their spring migration by an average of 11 days (range: 1–40 days) between 1964 and 2005 (Adamik & Pietruszkova, 2008). In Iceland, similar advances have been noted, although overall the associations between arrival dates and annual temperatures were weak (Boyd & Petersen, 2006). Evidence for changes in the timing of biological events in autumn are typically less coherent, with delays, advances, and non-significant trends in migration timing noted, for example (Adamik & Pietruszkova, 2008). However, this variation is to be expected given that earlier arrival facilitates earlier completion of the breeding cycle, whereas milder temperatures delay the need to depart to overwintering grounds.

One of the great ecological concerns with phenological response to climate change is that the phenology of different trophic levels responds at different rates, causing mismatch between the timing of peak food requirements and food availability (Both & Visser, 2001; Walther *et al.*, 2002). Although much of the evidence for this is from non-wader species, particularly great tits (*Parus major*) (Perrins, 1991; Buse *et al.*, 1999; Both *et al.*, 2005), there is also evidence of mistiming in waders (Pearce-Higgins *et al.*, 2005; Visser & Both, 2005). For example, since the mid-1960s, the modeled mean first-clutch hatch date of golden plover (*Pluvarius apricaria*) in the UK has advanced more quickly than the peak of tipulid emergence, the prey they feed their chicks (Pearce-Higgins *et al.*, 2005). This observation would suggest that the ways in which the biological rhythms of this species and its prey respond to temperature cues and environmental constraints do not necessarily match. As long-distance migrants, waders are especially vulnerable to problems associated with responding appropriately to climate change. At their wintering grounds, migrants cannot accurately predict the phenology of their breeding grounds and, as a solution, they have evolved climate-independent clock mechanisms to start their spring migration (Both, 2007). These endogenous mechanisms have become maladaptive because of climate change, and at present many bird species are thought to be arriving too late at their breeding sites (e.g. Both & Visser, 2001; Rubolini *et al.*, 2011).

Distribution shifts

It is generally agreed that climatic regimes influence species' distributions, often because species are physiologically constrained to live within certain climatic limits (Sunday *et al.*, 2012). With general warming trends, one would expect these "climate envelopes" to shift toward cooler latitudes (Walther *et al.*, 2002), and indeed, numerous studies have demonstrated this shift (Parmesan & Yohe, 2003; Root *et al.*, 2003; Chen *et al.*, 2011). There is strong evidence, particularly from Europe, that waders are among the species that have redistributed in response to milder winters. For example, in the UK the distributions of eight out of nine common wader species that overwinter on estuaries changed markedly between the mid-1970s and early 1990s (Austin & Rehfisch, 2005). During mild winters, the proportion of these waders' populations decreased in the mild southwest but increased in the cool northeast. Across northern Europe, the story is subtly different. Although the "centers of gravity" of populations of seven species of wader occurring in internationally important numbers underwent substantial shifts of up to 119 km between 1976 and 2000, generally in a northeasterly direction, this pattern appears to be predominantly driven by range expansion rather than wholesale range shifts. Large increases in numbers occurring in the Baltic and North Sea coast of Germany have occurred, but along the milder Atlantic coast of France, populations have remained relatively stable (Maclean *et al.*, 2005, 2006, 2008a).

A recent global meta-analysis suggested that many terrestrial species do not fill their potential thermal ranges as predicted by their thermal tolerance limits (Sunday *et al.*, 2012). High temperatures do not appear to be a main determinant of range extents at the warmer margins, whereas other factors such as water availability or biological interactions seem to be more important at their colder margins. In the UK, there is a clear non-temperature-related disadvantage associated with waders overwintering in the milder southwest, but a temperature-related disadvantage associated with overwintering on the colder east coast. On average, estuaries on the west coasts of Britain have sandier sediments than those on the east coast and support a lower biomass of the invertebrate prey of waders. On the east coast, estuaries are more productive, but the birds have a higher risk of thermally induced mortality (Austin & Rehfisch, 2005). Consequently, the observed shift in wader distribution toward the northeast may represent a shift in the balance between these two opposing forces. During milder winters, the birds benefit from better foraging opportunities on the east coast but are not as severely at risk of thermally induced mortality. Along the mild Atlantic coast of France, however, there are several productive estuaries that continue to host high wader numbers and consequently no direct reason to migrate in milder winters.

Interestingly, a more recent study in France adds a further dimension to this picture. Across 23 wader species associated with estuaries along the Atlantic coast, there was a dramatic shift between 1973 and 2009 in the composition of wader assemblages toward a community dominated by species associated with milder climates (Godet et al., 2011). At first glance this shift appears to contradict previous findings in Maclean and colleagues (2008a,b), which suggest that cold-climate species have not declined in this region. However, the study by Godet and colleagues included a wider range of wader species, with the addition of several populations of species that overwinter predominantly in southern Europe and Africa. There was no evidence of consistent declines in populations of species associated with colder climates. The change in assemblage appears to be driven by increases in species associated with warm climates rather than declines in those associated with cold climates, which is essentially the same as that found by Maclean and others (2008a,b).

Changes in vital rates

Although climate change can cause modifications in geographical distribution and the timing of biological events, another important effect is the influence on demographic parameters. It is well known that adverse weather affects bird survival and can do so either directly or indirectly. Direct effects result because the rate of heat loss from a bird's body increases as temperatures decrease and wetting of the feathers by rain reduces their effectiveness to act as insulation (Robinson et al., 2007). Although the latter is not a major problem for most adult waders, which tend to have waterproof feathers, it can be a problem for juveniles. In cold, wet conditions, birds have to invest more energy in maintaining their body temperature, and individuals failing to meet these increased costs may die. This effect is particularly severe for resident passerine species (Robinson *et al.*, 2007), but it also applies to migratory waders, such as common redshank and red knot (Wiersma & Piersma, 1994; Insley *et al.*, 1997). Under warmer conditions, such effects are likely to become less severe, with beneficial consequences for the survival of individual birds. However, the majority of bird species are limited in the amount of energy they are able to store as fat reserves, principally because excess weight increases the energetic cost of flight, as well as leading to increased predation risk as escape flight ability is impaired (Gosler *et al.*, 1995). Body weight (and hence condition) is therefore maintained in an extremely dynamic fashion, with a number of factors influencing a bird's fattening decisions. Short, unexpected periods of adverse weather can disrupt the delicate balance of tradeoffs, causing large-scale mortality of waders over very short periods of time (Clark, 2004, 2009). Climate change also has the potential to affect wader mortality deleteriously, either directly by increasing the variability of weather conditions at a given location or by acting as a trigger for waders to undergo range or phenological shifts that expose them to more variable weather conditions.

Indirect effects of climate and weather on survival are also important and occur primarily through influencing the abundance and availability of food supply. Just as climate and weather affects birds, the quality, availability, and accessibility of prey is also affected, with survival consequences for waders due to altered intake rates. Such factors may be more important in the non-breeding period when many populations, particularly those that winter in the Northern Hemisphere, may be food-limited (Robinson *et al.*, 2005). Extended periods of frost or snow cover may prevent ground-feeding birds from foraging, leading to increased rates of mortality and hence a reduction in population size (Robinson *et al.*, 2007). While the risk of such events is lower in coastal areas where saline influences reduce the risk of water freezing, low temperatures and high rainfall have been shown to adversely affect the foraging success of many migratory waders (Pienkowski, 1983; Insley *et al.*, 1997). A warming climate is likely to increase the survival rates of many waterbird species at higher latitudes, although it is probably more likely to benefit residents than migrants as the majority of migrant species spend the non-breeding season in warmer areas. Consequently, there may be increased competition between residents and migrants during the breeding season.

Many waders are migratory and require favorable conditions at stopover sites to successfully complete their journey. Although direct evidence is lacking for waders, other waterbird species (i.e. wildfowl) have benefited from climate change due to increased food availability on staging grounds (Kery *et al.*, 2006). Climatic conditions on the pole-ward spring journey are likely to be particularly important. This expectation is based on two factors. First, there is a greater evolutionary imperative to arrive early on the breeding grounds rather than leave early from these same grounds in the autumn. The first arrivals secure the best breeding territories and hence increased reproductive success (Kokko, 1999). Second, mortality during spring migration has less chance to be compensated for by other mortality factors than on autumn migration. Mortality during the winter is often significant and is likely to be density-dependent, so that many individuals that die during the autumn migration may have died in the winter anyway. However, this is less likely to be the case in long-lived species, such as Eurasian oystercatchers (*Haematopus ostralegus*) (Robinson *et al.*, 2009).

As with survival, climatic conditions can influence reproductive productivity both directly and indirectly. Direct effects result because young chicks may be particularly susceptible to hypothermia due to their small size and undeveloped plumage. In warmer regions, they may also be susceptible to heat stress. Indirect effects result because climatic conditions can also influence the amount of food that parents are able to collect for their offspring. Several studies have documented relationships between wader fledging success and temperature (Schekkerman *et al.*, 1996; Hotker & Sebebade, 2000; Meltofte *et al.*, 2008), with higher temperatures generally leading to higher reproductive productivity. Productivity on breeding grounds can have carry-over effects on wintering grounds. In parts of the UK, for example, the proportion of overwintering juvenile dunlin (*Calidris alpina*) is strongly correlated with summer temperatures in the Arctic. The highest proportion of juveniles occurred at intermediate temperatures, suggesting that as temperatures continue to increase in the UK, productivity of dunlins may decline (Beale *et al.*, 2006). Indirect effects occur primarily because cold and/or wet weather can limit the overall abundance of activity levels of invertebrate prey. Although evidence of this phenomenon for waders is lacking, it has been well documented in other bird species, and the mechanisms seem entirely relevant to waders (Foster, 1974; Davics & Green, 1976; Avery & Krebs, 1984). Indirect effects can also occur as a result of more complex ecological interactions. For example, temperature affects the size of lemming (*Lemmus* and *Dicrostonyx* spp.) populations in the tundra (Oksanen & Oksanen, 1992). In years when lemmings are scarce, avian and mammalian predators turn their attention to bird nests, reducing the breeding success of the ground-nesting wader species (Underhill *et al.*, 1993). Predicted warmer climates are likely to have severe negative impacts on wader populations that breed in the Arctic via increased nest predation rates.

Climate can also affect productivity by changing the time interval suitable for breeding. For example, populations of many waders breeding in the high Arctic spend the winter in coastal areas of Europe and Africa. Climate warming has created a longer window of suitable conditions for waders breeding in the high Arctic. Although the implications of earlier arrival and onset of breeding of northern waders are currently unexplored, these behavioral changes may provide these species with greater opportunities for multi-brooding or clutch replacement after a failed breeding attempt (Rehfisch & Crick, 2003). Furthermore, earlier breeding may present juveniles and post-breeding adults with a longer period in which to grow and improve their body condition before migrating south at the end of the Arctic summer. In contrast, however, it is also possible that warmer temperatures in the Arctic may lead to increases in precipitation there, such that snow cover is retained for longer (Maclean *et al.*, 2008b). Under such circumstances, waders that attempt to arrive earlier on their breeding grounds may be faced with prolonged snow cover that could affect their productivity. Furthermore, increased snow cover and delayed melt could delay their breeding, which may be detrimental given the short window of opportunity that they have for breeding at high latitudes before temperatures start to fall again (Maclean *et al.*, 2008b). Therefore, the overall extent to which the window of opportunity for breeding in the Arctic is altering through time is not so clear and depends largely on the relative degree of change in temperature and precipitation.

LOSS OF HABITAT AND CHANGES IN HABITAT QUALITY

Climate change will also affect the extent and quality of habitats. Rising sea levels are particularly likely to affect coastal habitats, both through changing their extent and altering their quality due to more frequent tidal inundation and changes in estuarine morphology. The extent to which sea level rise has, and will, continue to lead to habitat loss in coastal habitats depends largely on whether man-made features preventing landward migration are in place. For example, in Suffolk County, New York, USA, the breeding habitat of the federally threatened piping plover (*Charadrius melodius*) is predicted to increase as a result of sea level rise if landward migration of habitats is uninhibited. However, if plover habitat is unable to migrate, then potential habitat loss will be in the region of 5–12% (Seavey et al., 2011).

The extent to which prevention of landward migration affects coastal areas is likely to be habitat-specific. Evidence from salt marshes in southeast England, an important feeding and nesting habitat for many waders, indicates that coastal squeeze does not necessarily lead to loss of marsh area because marshes accrete vertically and maintain their elevation with respect to sea level where the supply of sediment is sufficient. In contrast, organogenic marshes and those in areas where sediment is more limiting may be more susceptible to sea level rise (Hughes, 2004). Similar mixed results have been reported from the United States (Erwin et al., 2006).

Intertidal mudflats, however, may be more threatened. Modeled changes in the extent of intertidal foraging habitat for waders at five locations in the US suggest loss of current intertidal habitat in the range of 20–70% by 2100, even under conservative global warming scenarios (Galbraith et al., 2002). In China, similar dramatic losses of habitat are predicted. Modeled predictions of the effects of sea level rise on coastal wetlands loss in the Yangtze Estuary suggest losses of ~40% (Tian et al., 2010). This area is an important staging ground for many waders using the East Asian–Australasian flyway, such as the critically endangered spoon-billed sandpiper (Eurynorhynchus pygmeus).

Sea level rise can also have an effect on habitat quality. Rising seas cause changes in estuarine morphology, which in turn affects sediments (Crooks, 2004). Wader densities are largely dependent on the availability of their invertebrate prey, itself affected by the nature of sediment. Some models suggest that, as a consequence of sea level rise, changes in coastal geomorphology will result in sandier sediments (Austin & Rehfisch, 2003). Sandy sediments tend to host a lower biomass of the invertebrate prey of waders, so in addition to habitat loss, sea level rise may also result in a reduction in habitat quality. The quality of several types of low-lying coastal habitats, but notably coastal grazing marsh, saline lagoons, and salt marsh are likely to be adversely affected by inundation. Saltwater flooding poses a significant threat to these habitats as many of their associated flora and fauna tolerate a finite range in salinity or flooding conditions (Mitchell et al., 2007). In many instances, these events will have deleterious consequences for waders, which typically occur at high density in coastal freshwater and brackish lagoons (Warnock et al., 2002; Thaxter et al., 2010).

Other climate-related factors are also likely to have an effect on habitat quality. Globally, precipitation is generally predicted to increase in the tropics and polar regions but decrease at mid-latitudes (IPCC, 2007). Combined with warmer temperatures, this is likely to reduce water availability in habitats important to waders (Robinson *et al.*, 2009). Many waders rely on areas of shallow, small-scale flooding, particularly during the breeding season (Eglington *et al.*, 2008). Shallow water bodies are particularly vulnerable to drying out and may do so much more often in a future altered climate.

The overall effects of habitat loss or change on wader populations cannot necessarily be inferred directly, mainly because it cannot be assumed that all areas of habitat host equal densities of waders, nor that all areas are at their biological carrying capacity for waders. Two broad approaches have been used to model the population-level impacts of habitat loss. Both are based on understanding how demographic parameters are affected by environmental change, but the two approaches differ somewhat in the way they do this.

The first approach, here termed phenomenological modeling, uses empirically derived functions to model the demography of populations. Intrinsic population growth and the degree of density-dependence are estimated and some element of environmental stochasticity assumed (Sutherland, 2006). Often these approaches also include a spatial component. Populations are not considered in isolation, but immigration and emigration between populations is also quantified within a metapopulation framework. This method was used to model the impacts of sea level rise-induced habitat change on populations of snowy plover (*Charadrius nivosus*) in California (Aiello-Lammens *et al.*, 2011). The results projected that the population size of this species will decline faster than the habitat area loss or the reduction in carrying capacity supported by the remaining habitat. This result demonstrates the necessity of incorporating population dynamics in assessing the impacts of sea level rise on coastal species.

The other approach relies on understanding the behavioral decisions individuals make in choosing breeding habitat and uses this to derive associated demography to make predictions from first principles. The starting point is usually to assume that individuals will settle where they gain the highest fitness (i.e. they follow an ideal free distribution; Fretwell & Lucas, 1969). The next step is to understand the negative feedbacks of population size (i.e. resource depletion) upon distribution and performance. These mechanisms are used to determine key questions about the consequences of habitat loss or modification; for example, will individuals move elsewhere, or are all alternative breeding or feeding sites full? The critical question then is how much the population is likely to change as a result of habitat loss or modification. To answer this, it is necessary to derive population parameters and then incorporate these into models that link habitat loss and population size. The advantage of the behavior-based modeling approach is that it does not suffer from extrapolation problems to the same degree as other methods. Information is derived from first principles, and while some factors, such as future food supply, cannot be extrapolated without some risk of error, the extent to which birds attempt and have the means to maximize energy intake is less likely to change to a significant degree. Consequently, this approach has gained considerable popularity in recent years and has been widely used to predict the effects of habitat loss on waders (e.g. Gill *et al.*, 2001; Stillman *et al.*, 2005; West & Caldow, 2006).

SCIENTIFIC CHALLENGES ASSOCIATED WITH MODELING FUTURE RESPONSES TO CLIMATE CHANGE

Changes in phenology

To understand the true implications of phenological mismatches on the persistence of wader populations, it is necessary to understand the mechanisms that drive the biology of their seasonal activities. These mechanisms could be twofold. First, there can be a micro-evolutionary (genetic) response to the selection pressures for the earlier onset of biological events, such as breeding. Second, the waders can show a phenotypically plastic response (i.e. they modify their behavior) to trends in weather or climate on their wintering ground and/or along their migratory routes. If spring arrives earlier on the wintering grounds, spring migration will also start earlier, facilitating earlier onset of breeding. Given the evidence that a mistiming between wader breeding and peak production of their prey is occurring, we suggest that evolutionary changes are not happening sufficiently quickly. Inappropriate cues only matter within a bird's lifetime rather than through evolutionary time. Nevertheless, there is evidence that at least some changes in biological timing are evolutionarily rather than phenotypically driven. For example, Jonzen and colleagues (2006) show that long-distance migrants have advanced their spring arrival in Scandinavia by more than short-distance migrants and that the beginning of their migratory journey is also earlier. Because the cues used by these migrants to trigger departure from their wintering grounds are uncorrelated with climate change on the breeding grounds, the authors propose that such advancement is a demonstration that evolutionary changes have occurred. Otherwise, how else would the birds "know" to depart earlier? However, others have argued that this phenomenon is more likely to be a result of faster migration in response to improved environmental conditions (Both, 2007), and at present the debate remains unresolved.

Distribution shifts

Several studies have also attempted to model future changes in species distributions (Huntley et al., 2007). Perhaps the most widely used method of modeling the impact of climate change on species distributions is the application of bioclimatic envelope models (Beaumont et al., 2007), which are based on the assumption that species ranges are determined by climate. For example, Eurasian oystercatchers breeding in the UK are predicted to expand into more inland areas in eastern England (Berry et al., 2001). Using a broadly similar approach, Rehfisch and colleagues (2004) use relationships between the current distributions and abundances of waders overwintering on non-estuarine sites in the UK and predict northward and eastward wintering range shifts toward their breeding grounds.

Although widely used, bioclimatic envelope modeling has (at least) three limitations (Heikkinen et al., 2006). First, the approach tends to ignore factors that affect distributions independent of climate suitability, such as the spatial configuration of habitats. Challenging new methods that integrate metapopulation and climate envelope models or account for spatial–demographic process will need to be developed to address such issues. Second, non-climatic factors, such as habitat, are often not included in climate envelope models (Berry et al., 2001). Although habitat quality theoretically can be incorporated into the modeling framework, quantifying how habitats might change under future climate scenarios is much harder. Third, and allied to this problem, is the core assumption that it is climate that limits the distribution of species. It has been suggested that for many species the association between species and climate are no better than would be expected by chance (Beale et al., 2008). Evidence suggests that terrestrial organisms often do not fill their entire thermal niche. The warmer margins of species ranges appear to be set by other factors, potentially biotic interactions (Sunday et al., 2012). To overcome this problem, better understanding of species interactions under future climate scenarios is required. Despite these limitations, however, independent validations across numerous taxa indicate that climate envelope models are reasonably able to provide predictive future ranges, albeit not necessarily with a precision that makes it suitably useful from a conservation planning perspective (Araujo et al., 2005).

Population modeling

The size of all populations is essentially controlled, at a fundamental level, through the balance of two demographic rates, the rate at which new individuals are born into the population (fecundity or productivity) and the rate at which old individuals leave the population (Newton, 1988). A number of detailed population studies of waders have shown that reasons for changes in population size can be explained by understanding variation in these demographic rates (Gosscustard *et al.*, 1995; Atkinson *et al.*, 2003). Some studies have also used demographic models to predict the effects of environmental change on wader population size and persistence at specific locations (Durell *et al.*, 2006; van de Pol *et al.*, 2010). In practice, however, modeling the effects of climate change on populations, particularly over larger areas, is extremely difficult (Sutherland, 2006). Population models depend on three fundamental tenants of population dynamics: (1) populations increase in the absence of intraspecific competition (intrinsic population growth); (2) at higher population levels this growth rate is reduced as a result of intraspecific competition (density-dependence); and (3) stochasticity (i.e. random events) can produce deviations from a deterministic equilibrium (i.e. a pre-determinable stable state). However, field measurement of intrinsic population growth usually entails either looking at population changes over time or measuring demographic components and combining these. In so doing, empirically derived intrinsic population growth rates are confounded with density-dependent growth. Similarly, measuring density-dependence is problematic. Doing so usually entails using a time series to plot the change in population size between each time interval against the total population size. Unless there is no census error, or census error can be measured exactly (which is rarely the case), then density-dependence will be overestimated using this method (Freckleton *et al.*, 2006). Stochasticity is difficult to measure simply because it relies on long runs of population data collected in a consistent way. Another problem is that population models can potentially suffer from the same failings of extrapolation, as current relationships between demographic rates and environmental conditions may not hold true in the future. When using population models to predict the consequences of climate change, one of the most common approaches is to correlate demographic parameters with components of climate change. If current relationships do not hold true into the future, as they may well not given the wide array of non-linear relationships observed in nature, then any projections are unlikely to hold true.

Possible future directions

The challenge of predicting how waders and other species will respond to climate change remains a difficult hurdle to overcome, as the methods used to date have their merits and drawbacks. Statistical methods, such as climate envelope models, are conceptually easy to understand, and to some extent have provided useful and meaningful predictions (Pearson & Dawson, 2003). However, they are constrained by the fact that observed spatial and temporal relationships between species and their environment may not hold true in the future. Process-based models circumvent this problem to some degree, but can often be difficult to parameterize (Sutherland, 2006). The rapid increase in computer-processing power may help to circumvent some of these issues, insofar as they could, in theory, permit non-linear process-based models to be parameterized by iteration using spatial and/or temporal observations (see Nash & Walker-Smith, 1987 for a review). While many of the methods are old, they require considerable computational power when applied to complex models. Perhaps for that reason the approach remains relatively underutilized and tested in ecological contexts. The rapid increase in the use of Bayesian approaches in ecological settings is in part because of the ability of these approaches to handle and conveniently combine sources of uncertainty (McCarthy, 2007), but while it allows known unknowns to be quantified, it cannot handle unknown unknowns. Adaptive management is widely advocated as response to all forms of uncertainty. In reality, however, it is almost never carried out because the changes in management usually have to be severe in order to bring about detectable changes in a reasonable time, and the political risks of such management are usually considered too high (Sutherland, 2006). The scientific challenges associated with modeling future responses to climate change remain significant. It is promising, however, that both the overall magnitude and the relative degree of threat predicted to be facing different species in different parts of the world is broadly supported by observed responses (Maclean & Wilson, 2011). Despite the uncertainties, predicted ecological responses to climate change are broadly correct.

HELPING WADERS COPE WITH CLIMATE CHANGE

Site management

One of the most effective potential means of helping waders cope with climate change is active site management. Many wetlands hosting high densities of waders, including those in coastal areas, form part of human-modified landscapes. The suitability of wetland systems for waders is linked closely to the watershed or catchment of which they are a part. Consequently, they are influenced greatly by terrestrial processes, including many human uses or modifications of land and water. There is considerable scope to alter these hydrological regimes in a manner that favors waders (Baron *et al.*, 2002). Similarly, the risk to coastal areas from sea level rise may be ameliorated by managed realignment. In most parts of the globe, coastal areas are heavily used by humans, and in many places coastal defenses are in place to prevent flooding and erosion. Soft-engineering approaches to coastal management seem like a logical and sound approach that could help to minimize habitat loss. Nevertheless, being a comparatively new approach, the long-term effectiveness of such schemes is poorly understood (French, 2006). Until further evidence-based studies are carried out, it would seem wise to monitor effectiveness and proceed with caution. Moreover, although integrated shoreline and catchment management offer opportunities for managing habitats in a way that ensures their suitability for waders, inevitably the needs of biodiversity will compete with land uses. Consequently, although scientific knowledge goes some way to informing wader habitat management, for the science to be implemented, it will need to be integrated with the political agenda that dictates land use.

Protected area networks

If species approaching their climatic limits cannot adapt to the new climate and cannot be maintained in their present locations by management, they will only survive if they move into remaining suitable areas. Facilitating dispersal is a valuable way of helping species cope with climate change. Although waders theoretically are capable of dispersing very long distances, the food on which they rely often has relatively poor dispersal abilities. Consequently, particularly for those species with food-specialist requirements, waders may be adversely affected by high climate change velocity (Davey et al., 2012).

One of the most effective means of assisting species dispersal is to ensure that there is an adequate network of protected areas. Although the extent to which waders will be able to disperse through landscapes is partially dependent on the availability of suitable habitat in the wider countryside, a network of protected areas, each relatively close to the others, is likely to facilitate wader dispersal and help ensure that species displaced by unsuitable climate have a refuge (Mitchell et al., 2007). In so doing, four factors will help to ensure their effectiveness (Maclean et al., 2008b). First, protected areas should be situated toward the colder range limits of the species for which they are designed to facilitate protection. Second, they should be targeted at areas where they can contribute most to developing an ecological network, for example, by being situated between two existing wetlands. Third, they should be located in areas predicted to become drier, but likely to remain within relevant flyways. Lastly, they should be located in areas which are toward the start or finish of long and arduous migration journeys, such as to the north and south of the Sahara, or at critical staging sites along the East Asian–Australasian flyway.

Perhaps the biggest barriers to such common-sense approaches are the policy frameworks surrounding wetland protection. Although legislation, such as the Ramsar Convention and European Commission Habitats and Birds directives, is specifically designed to ensure a strategic, international approach to wetland conservation, the systems for designating protected sites tend to concentrate on waterbird numbers at the time of designation rather than on likely numbers in a future altered climate. Therefore, recent climate colonizers to a country are often not protected directly (Maclean & Austin, 2009). This gap in coverage is inevitable given the need to rely on actual rather than predicted data, but it highlights the need for regular reviews of protected area features.

Management of the wider countryside

Although protected area networks provide one means of facilitating climate-induced range shifts, wader dispersal could also be facilitated by appropriate management of the wider countryside. Although waders concentrate in coastal areas, which act as natural dispersal corridors to some extent, significant numbers also occur at freshwater sites. Small, shallow water bodies, or seasonally flooded areas within otherwise unsuitable habitats, are likely to act as stepping stones, aiding the pole-ward redistribution of waders and the prey items on which they rely as the climate warms. The concept of connectivity across landscapes is well accepted by policy-makers (Mitchell et al., 2007; FWS, 2011), but as with other facets of conservation, conflicting land-use pressures make it much more difficult to accomplish in practice. In developed countries, one of the best means of achieving appropriate management of the wider countryside would be to integrate such management into other relevant policies, such as agri-environment schemes in Europe and the Wetlands Conservation Act in North America (Mitchell et al., 2007; FWS, 2011). In developing countries, people living in the vicinity of wetlands often exercise more power than governments over the use of wetland resources (Maclean et al., 2012). Integrating local people's needs into wetland conservation policy is likely to be the most effective means of ensuring the conservation of wetland complexes at a landscape scale (Mafabi, 2000). As the world's climate continues to change, it will become increasingly important for nature conservation to transcend national boundaries so that the status of waders and other species can be assessed in their entirety. In so doing, tools for monitoring and conserving waders that have arisen as a result of site-based concerns will need to be reapplied. Developing countries, being least-equipped to implement these tools, may well be faced with the brunt of this challenge.

REFERENCES

Adamik, P. & Pietruszkova, J. (2008). Advances in spring but variable autumnal trends in timing of inland wader migration. *Acta Ornithologica*, **43**, 119–128.

Aiello-Lammens, M. E., Chu-Agor, M. L., Convertino, M., *et al.* (2011). The impact of sea-level rise on snowy plovers in Florida: Integrating geomorphological, habitat, and metapopulation models. *Global Change Biology*, **17**, 3644–3654.

Araujo, M. B., Pearson, R. G., Thuiller, W. & Erhard, M. (2005). Validation of species-climate impact models under climate change. *Global Change Biology*, **11**, 1504–1513.

Atkinson, P. W., Clark, N. A., Bell, M. C., *et al.* (2003). Changes in commercially fished shellfish stocks and shorebird populations in the Wash, England. *Biological Conservation*, **114**, 127–141.

Austin, G. E. & Rehfisch, M. M. (2003). The likely impact of sea level rise on waders (Charadrii) wintering on estuaries. *Journal for Nature Conservation (Jena)*, **11**, 43–58.

Austin, G. E. & Rehfisch, M. M. (2005). Shifting nonbreeding distributions of migratory fauna in relation to climatic change. *Global Change Biology*, **11**, 31–38.

Avery, M. I. & Krebs, J. R. (1984). Temperature and foraging successs of great tits *Parus major* hunting for spiders. *Ibis*, **126**, 33–38.

Baron, J. S., Poff, N. L., Angermeier, P. L., *et al.* (2002). Meeting ecological and societal needs for freshwater. *Ecological Applications*, **12**, 1247–1260.

Beale, C. M., Dodd, S. & Pearce-Higgins, J. W. (2006). Wader recruitment indices suggest nesting success is temperature-dependent in Dunlin *Calidris alpina*. *Ibis*, **148**, 405–410.

Beale, C. M., Lennon, J. J. & Gimona, A. (2008). Opening the climate envelope reveals no macroscale associations with climate in European birds. *Proceedings of the National Academy of Sciences of the United States of America*, **105**, 14908–14912.

Beaumont, L. J., Pitman, A. J., Poulsen, M. & Hughes, L. (2007). Where will species go? Incorporating new advances in climate modelling into projections of species distributions. *Global Change Biology*, **13**, 1368–1385.

Berry, P. M., Vanhinsberg, D., Viles, H. A., *et al.* (2001). Impacts on terrestrial environments. In P. A. Harrison, P. M. Berry & T. P. Dawson (eds.), *Climate Change and Nature Conservation in Britain and Ireland: Modelling Natural Resource Responses to Climate Change (The MONARCH Project)*. Oxford: UKCIP Technical Report.

Both, C. (2007). Comment on "Rapid advance of spring arrival dates in long-distance migratory birds". *Science*, **315**, 598.

Both, C. & Visser, M. E. (2001). Adjustment to climate change is constrained by arrival date in a long-distance migrant bird. *Nature*, **411**, 296–298.

Both, C., Piersma, T. & Roodbergen, S. P. (2005). Climatic change explains much of the 20th century advance in laying date of northern lapwing *Vanellus vanellus* in The Netherlands. *Ardea*, **93**, 79–88.

Boyd, H. & Petersen, A. (2006). Spring arrivals of migrant waders in Iceland in the 20th century. *Ringing & Migration*, **23**, 107–115.

Buse, A., Dury, S. J., Woodburn, R. J. W., Perrins, C. M. & Good, J. E. G. (1999). Effects of elevated temperature on multi-species interactions: The case of pedunculate oak, winter moth and tits. *Functional Ecology*, **13**, 74–82.

Chen, I. C., Hill, J. K., Ohlemuller, R., Roy, D. B. & Thomas, C. D. (2011). Rapid range shifts of species associated with high levels of climate warming. *Science*, **333**, 1024–1026.

Chu-Agor, M. L., Munoz-Carpena, R., Kiker, G., Emanuelsson, A. & Linkov, I. (2010). Exploring vulnerability of coastal habitats to sea level rise through global sensitivity and uncertainty analyses. *Environmental Modelling & Software*, **26**, 593–604.

Church, J. A. & White, N. J. (2006). A 20th century acceleration in global sea-level rise. *Geophysical Research Letters*, **33**, 4.

Clark, J. A. (2004). Ringing recoveries confirm high mortality in severe winters. *Ringing & Migration*, **22**, 43–50.

Clark, J. A. (2009). Selective mortality of waders during severe weather. *Bird Study*, **56**, 96–102.

Crooks, S. (2004). The effect of sea-level rise on coastal geomorphology. *Ibis*, **146**, 18–20.

Davey, C. M., Chamberlain, D. E., Newson, S. E., Noble, D. G. & Johnston, A. (2012). Rise of the generalists: Evidence for climate driven homogenization in avian communities. *Global Ecology and Biogeography*, **21**, 568–578.

Davies, N. B. & Green, R. E. (1976). Development and ecological significance of feeding techniques in reed warbler (*Acrocephalus scirpaceus*). *Animal Behaviour*, **24**, 213–229.

Durell, S., Stillman, R. A., Caldow, R. W. G., *et al.* (2006). Modelling the effect of environmental change on shorebirds: A case study on Poole Harbour, UK. *Biological Conservation*, **131**, 459–473.

Eglington, S. M., Gill, J. A., Bolton, M., *et al.* (2008). Restoration of wet features for breeding waders on lowland grassland. *Journal of Applied Ecology*, **45**, 305–314.

Erwin, R. M., Cahoon, D. R., Prosser, D. J., Sanders, G. M. & Hensel, P. (2006). Surface elevation dynamics in vegetated *Spartina* marshes versus unvegetated tidal ponds along the mid-Atlantic coast, USA, with implications to waterbirds. *Estuaries and Coasts*, **29**, 96–106.

Foster, M. S. (1974). Rain, feeding behavior, and clutch size in tropical birds. *Auk*, **91**, 722–726.

Freckleton, R. P., Watkinson, A. R., Green, R. E. & Sutherland, W. J. (2006). Census error and the detection of density dependence. *Journal of Animal Ecology*, **75**, 837–851.

French, P. W. (2006). Managed realignment – The developing story of a comparatively new approach to soft engineering. *Estuarine, Coastal and Shelf Science*, **67**, 409–423.

Fretwell, S. D. & Lucas, H. L. J. (1969). On territorial behavior and other factors influencing habitat distribution in birds, Part 1, theoretical development. *Acta Biotheoretica*, **19**, 16–36.

FWS, Fish and Wildlife Service (2011). *Rising to the Challenge: Strategic Plan for Responding to Accelerating Climate Change*. Washington, DC: US Fish and Wildlife Service.

Galbraith, H., Jones, R., Park, R., *et al.* (2002). Global climate change and sea level rise: Potential losses of intertidal habitat for shorebirds. *Waterbirds*, **25**, 173–183.

Gill, J. A., Sutherland, W. J. & Norris, K. (2001). Depletion models can predict shorebird distribution at different spatial scales. *Proceedings of the Royal Society of London, Series B, Biological Sciences*, **268**, 369–376.

Godet, L., Jaffre, M. & Devictor, V. (2011). Waders in winter: Long-term changes of migratory bird assemblages facing climate change. *Biology Letters*, **7**, 714–717.

Gosler, A. G., Greenwood, J. J. D. & Perrins, C. (1995). Predation risk and the cost of being fat. *Nature*, **377**, 621–623.

Gosscustard, J. D., Caldow, R. W. G., Clarke, R. T., Durell, S. & Sutherland, W. J. (1995). Deriving population parameters from individual variations in foraging behaviour. 1. Empirical game-theory distribution model of oystercatcher *Haematopus ostralegus* feeding on mussels *Myilus edulis*. *Journal of Animal Ecology*, **64**, 265–276.

Grantham, B. A., Chan, F., Nielsen, K. J., *et al.* (2004). Upwelling-driven nearshore hypoxia signals ecosystem and oceanographic changes in the northeast Pacific. *Nature*, **429**, 749–754.

Heikkinen, R. K., Luoto, M., Araujo, M. B., *et al.* (2006). Methods and uncertainties in bioclimatic envelope modelling under climate change. *Progress in Physical Geography*, **30**, 751–777.

Hotker, H. & Sebebade, A. (2000). Effects of predation and weather on the breeding success of avocets *Recurvirostra avosetta*. *Bird Study*, **47**, 91–101.

Hughes, R. G. (2004). Climate change and loss of saltmarshes: Consequences for birds. *Ibis*, **146**, 21–28.

Huntley, B., Green, R. E., Collingham, Y. C. & Willis, S. G. (2007). *A Climatic Atlas of European Breeding Birds*. Barcelona: Lynx Edicions.

Insley, H., Peach, W., Swann, B. & Etheridge, B. (1997). Survival rates of redshank *Tringa totanus* wintering on the Moray Firth. *Bird Study*, **44**, 277–289.

IPCC. (2007). *Climate Change 2007: Synthesis Report. Contribution of Working Groups I, II and III to the Fourth Assessement Report of the Intergovernmental Panel on Climate Change*, Geneva, Switzerland: IPCC.

Jonzén, N., Lindén, A., Ergon, T., *et al.* (2006). Rapid advance of spring arrival dates in long-distance migratory birds. *Science*, **312**, 1959–1961.

Kery, M., Madsen, J. & Lebreton, J. D. (2006). Survival of Svalbard pink-footed geese *Anser brachyrhynchus* in relation to winter climate, density and land-use. *Journal of Animal Ecology*, **75**, 1172–1181.

Kokko, H. (1999). Competition for early arrival in migratory birds. *Journal of Animal Ecology*, **68**, 940–950.

Maclean, I. M. D. & Austin, G. E. (2009). Waterbirds, climate change and wildlife conservation in Britain. *British Wildlife*, **20**, 250–256.

Maclean, I. M. D. & Wilson, R. J. (2011). Recent ecological responses to climate change support predictions of high extinction risk. *Proceedings of the National Academy of Sciences of the United States of America*, **108**, 12337–12342.

Maclean, I., Austin, G. & Rehfisch, M. (2005). Climate-mediated changes in the distribution and abundance of over-wintering waders in Europe. *Alauda*, **73**, 277.

Maclean, I. M. D., Austin, G. E. & Rehfisch, M. M. (2006). Are responses to climate change temperature dependent? Population changes in over-wintering migratory shorebirds. *Journal of Ornithology*, **147**, 26.

Maclean, I. M. D., Austin, G. E., Rehfisch, M. M., *et al.* (2008a). Climate change causes rapid changes in the distribution and site abundance of birds in winter. *Global Change Biology*, **14**, 2489–2500.

Maclean, I. M. D., Rehfisch, M. M., Delany, S. & Robinson, R. A. (2008b). *The Effects of Climate Change on Migratory Waterbirds within the African–Eurasian Flyway.* Bonn, Germany: British Trust for Ornithology.

Maclean, I. M. D., Boar, R. R. & Lugo, C. (2012). A review of the relative merits of conserving, using, or draining papyrus swamps. *Environmental Management*, **47**, 218–229.

Mafabi, P. (2000). The role of wetland policies in the conservation of waterbirds: The case of Uganda. *Ostrich*, **71**, 96–98.

McCarthy, M. A. (2007). *Bayesian Methods for Ecology.* Cambridge: Cambridge University Press.

Meltofte, H., Hoye, T. T. & Schmidt, N. M. (2008) Effects of food availability, snow and predation on breeding performance of waders at Zackenberg. *Advances in Ecological Research*, **40**, 325–343.

Mitchell, R. J., Morecroft, M. D., Acreman, M., *et al.* (2007). *England Biodiversity Strategy – Towards Adaptation to Climate Change.* Final Report to DEFRA for Contract CR0327. London: DEFRA.

Musters, C. J. M., ter Keurs, W. J. & de Snoo, G. R. (2010). Timing of the breeding season of black-tailed godwit *Limosa limosa* and northern lapwing *Vanellus vanellus* in The Netherlands. *Ardea*, **98**, 195–202.

Nash, J. C. & Walker-Smith, M. (1987). *Nonlinear Parameter Estimation.* New York, NY: Dekker.

Newton, I. (1988) *Population Limitation in Birds.* London: Academic Press.

Niehaus, A. C. & Ydenberg, R. C. (2006). Ecological factors associated with the breeding and migratory phenology of high-latitude breeding western sand-pipers. *Polar Biology*, **30**, 11–17.

Oksanen, L. & Oksanen, T. (1992). Long-term microtine dynamics in north Fennoscandian tundra – The vole cycle and the lemming chaos. *Ecography*, **15**, 226–236.

Orr, J. C., Fabry, V. J., Aumont, O., *et al.* (2005). Anthropogenic ocean acidification over the twenty-first century and its impact on calcifying organisms. *Nature*, **437**, 681–686.

Parmesan, C. (2006). Ecological and evolutionary responses to recent climate change. *Annual Review of Ecology, Evolution and Systematics*, **37**, 637–669.

Parmesan, C. & Yohe, G. (2003). A globally coherent fingerprint of climate change impacts across natural systems. *Nature*, **421**, 37–42.

Pearce-Higgins, J. W., Yalden, D. W. & Whittingham, M. J. (2005), Warmer springs advance the breeding phenology of golden plovers *Pluvialis apricaria* and their prey (Tipulidae). *Oecologia*, **143**, 470–476.

Pearson, R. G. & Dawson, T. P. (2003). Predicting the impacts of climate change on the distribution of species: Are bioclimate envelope models useful? *Global Ecology and Biogeography*, **12**, 361–371.

Perrins, C. M. (1991). Tits and their caterpillar food-supply. *Ibis*, **133**, 49–54.

Pienkowski, M. W. (1983). The effects of environmental-conditions on feeding rates and prey-selection of shore plovers. *Ornis Scandinavica*, **14**, 227–238.

Piersma, T. & Lindstrom, A. (2004). Migrating shorebirds as integrative sentinels of global environmental change. *Ibis*, **146**, 61–69.

Rehfisch, M. M. & Crick, H. Q. P. (2003). Predicting the impact of climatic change on Arctic-breeding waders. *Wader Study Group Bulletin*, **100**, 86–95.

Rehfisch, M. M., Austin, G. E., Freeman, S. N., Armitage, M. J. S. & Burton, N. H. K. (2004). The possible impact of climate change on the future distributions and numbers of waders on Britain's non-estuarine coast. *Ibis*, **146**, 70–81.

Robinson, R. A., Learmonth, J. A., Hutson, A. M., *et al.* (2005). *Climate Change and Migratory Species*. BTO Research Report 414: A Report for DEFRA Research Contract CR0302. Thetford, Norfolk: British Ornithological Trust.

Robinson, R. A., Baillie, S. R. & Crick, H. Q. P. (2007). Weather-dependent survival: Implications of climate change for passerine population processes. *Ibis*, **149**, 357–364.

Robinson, R. A., Crick, H. Q. P., Learmonth, J. A., *et al.* (2009). Travelling through a warming world: Climate change and migratory species. *Endangered Species Research*, **7**, 87–99.

Root, T. L., Price, J. T., Hall, K. R., *et al.* (2003). Fingerprints of global warming on wild animals and plants. *Nature*, **421**, 57–60.

Rubolini, D., Saino, N. & Moller, A. P. (2011). Migratory behaviour constrains the phenological response of birds to climate change. *Climate Research*, **42**, 45–55.

Schekkerman, H., Tulp, I., Piersma, T., *et al.* (1996). Growth and energetics of knot chicks in Taymyr, Siberia. *Wader Study Group Bulletin*, **79**, 28.

Schwartz, M. D., Ahas, R. & Aasa, A. (2006). Onset of spring starting earlier across the Northern Hemisphere. *Global Change Biology*, **12**, 343–351.

Seavey, J. R., Gilmer, B. & McGarigal, K. M. (2011). Effect of sea-level rise on piping plover (*Charadrius melodus*) breeding habitat. *Biological Conservation*, **144**, 393–401.

Stillman, R. A., West, A. D., Goss-Custard, J. D., *et al.* (2005). Predicting site quality for shorebird communities: A case study on the Humber estuary, UK. *Marine Ecology Progress Series*, **305**, 203–217.

Sunday, J. M., Bates, A. E. & Dulvy, N. K. (2012). Thermal tolerance and the global redistribution of animals. *Nature Climate Change*, **2**, 686–690.

Sutherland, W. J. (2006). Predicting the ecological consequences of environmental change: A review of the methods. *Journal of Applied Ecology*, **43**, 599–616.

Thaxter, C. B., Sansom, A., Thewlis, R. M., *et al.* (2010). *Wetland Bird Survey Alerts 2006/2007: Changes in Numbers of Wintering Waterbirds in the Constituent Countries of the United Kingdom, Special Protection Areas (SPAs) and Sites of Special Scientific Interest (SSSIs)*. Thetford, Norfolk: British Trust for Ornithology.

Tian, B., Zhang, L. Q., Wang, X. R., Zhou, Y. X. & Zhang, W. (2010). Forecasting the effects of sea-level rise at Chongming Dongtan Nature Reserve in the Yangtze Delta, Shanghai, China. *Ecological Engineering*, **36**, 1383–1388.

Underhill, L. G., Prysjones, R. P., Syroechkovski, E. E., *et al.* (1993). Breeding of waders (Charadrii) and Brent geese (*Branta bernicla bernicla*) at Pronchishcheva Lake, Northeastern Taimyr, Russia, in a peak and decreasing lemming year. *Ibis*, **135**, 277–292.

Van de Pol, M., Vindenes, Y., Saether, B. E., *et al.* (2010). Effects of climate change and variability on population dynamics in a long-lived shorebird. *Ecology*, **91**, 1192–1204.

Visser, M. E. & Both, C. (2005). Shifts in phenology due to global climate change: The need for a yardstick. *Proceedings of the Royal Society of London, Series B, Biological Sciences*, **272**, 2561–2569.

Walther, G. R., Post, E., Convey, P., *et al.* (2002). Ecological responses to recent climate change. *Nature*, **416**, 389–395.

Warnock, N., Page, G. W., Ruhlen, T. D., *et al.* (2002). Management and conservation of San Francisco Bay salt ponds: Effects of pond salinity, area, tide, and season on Pacific flyway waterbirds. *Waterbirds*, **25**, 79–92.

West, A. D. & Caldow, R. W. G. (2006). The development and use of individuals-based models to predict the effects of habitat loss and disturbance on waders and waterfowl. *Ibis*, **148**, 158–168.

Wiersma, P. & Piersma, T. (1994). Effects of microhabitat, flocking, climate and migratory goal on energy-expenditure in the annual cycle of red knots. *Condor*, **96**, 257–279.

10

The impacts of climate change on marine turtle reproductive success

LUCY A. HAWKES, ANNETTE C. BRODERICK, MATTHEW H. GODFREY, BRENDAN J. GODLEY, AND MATTHEW J. WITT

WHY MARINE TURTLES?

Ectothermic species are fundamentally affected by environmental temperatures, which largely dictate their metabolic rate. In marine turtles, foraging behavior, migratory patterns, and ultimately breeding success may be modulated by the environment and influenced by climate change. This has the potential to have both positive and negative effects. The seven species of marine turtles broadly occupy three foraging niches (planktivory, herbivory, and omnivory) and occur in almost every non-polar ocean basin in the world, from shallow coastal seas to open ocean habitats. The effects of climate change to marine turtles likely will be wide ranging and of direct relevance to other marine animals in these varied habitats. Marine turtles are a fascinating "canary in the coal mine" with which to study the effects of climate change in marine habitats, and there has been an exponential increase in interest in the effects of climate change on them in the last decade (Poloczanska *et al.*, 2009; Hamann *et al.*, 2010; Hawkes *et al.*, 2010). Marine turtles are also generally considered charismatic, making them ideal subjects with which to raise awareness of climate change effects to biodiversity and to increase support for effective management and conservation of marine environments.

In addition, marine turtles have survived dramatic climate change in the past. Marine turtles are among the most ancient of the marine vertebrates, with fossil evidence of leatherback turtles (*Dermochelys coriacea*) suggesting that they have existed in their extant form for at least 900 000 years (Dutton *et al.*, 1999). Over this period the climate has undergone dramatic fluctuations, and marine turtles have evidently adapted and persisted, surviving to the present day. However, many marine turtle populations are now

Coastal Conservation, eds B. Maslo and J. L. Lockwood. Published by Cambridge University Press. © Cambridge University Press 2014.

dramatically depleted, having been harvested for their meat, eggs, and attractive shells in huge numbers up until the end of the nineteenth century (reviewed in McClenachan *et al.*, 2006). Consequently, six of the seven species of marine turtles were added to the IUCN red list of threatened species in 1986 (www.iucnredlist.org; the seventh species, the flatback turtle (*Natator depressus*), was added in 1994), with many modern populations at relictual levels compared to historic past. For example, Caribbean green turtles (*Chelonia mydas*) are thought to be at only 0.3% of historic population numbers (McClenachan *et al.*, 2006; Bell *et al.*, 2007, 2009). Massive-scale population reduction of this sort can inhibit the ability of a population to recover through depensation, affecting fitness and reproduction, although evidence for this phenomenon is, as yet, lacking in marine turtles (Bell *et al.*, 2009). Although hunting pressure is now largely absent and some populations of marine turtles are thought to be increasing (Allen *et al.*, 2010), the modern threat of climate change will be set against a very different biological background than marine turtles would have experienced in the past.

Since its inception, the study of marine turtle biology has been biased toward studies on beaches, where marine turtles are more accessible for research than in the open ocean. Projects observe and record female turtles arriving on shore to lay nests of approximately 100 eggs at two-week intervals (although this varies by species) and often follow the clutches of eggs for up to two months until they hatch. The precocial hatchling turtles typically enter the water at night *en masse* and disperse to largely unknown developmental grounds. This window of opportunity for study has been used for some six decades, and much of the breeding biology of marine turtles, particularly a few key species and regions, is now well understood. The effects of climate change on it, however, are not.

In this chapter, we will describe the effects that climate change may have on the reproductive cycle of marine turtles (Figure 10.1), from adult turtles as they arrive in breeding areas to mate, to females ascending their natal beach to lay successive clutches of eggs, how the embryos themselves develop underground, effects of the incubation environment on hatchling morphology, sex, and survivorship, and finally as hatchlings emerge from the beach and depart to the ocean.

TIMING OF BREEDING

Marine turtles congregate to mate in the vicinity of their natal beaches, the region where they hatched some decades earlier (Limpus, 1993;

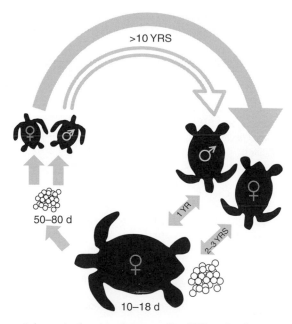

Figure 10.1 Schematic showing the generalized life cycle of marine turtles. Adult female turtles visit the nesting beach every 2–3 years, laying up to eight clutches of eggs at 10- to 18-day intervals. Adult male turtles are thought to visit the nesting beach annually. Nests (with 80–140 eggs) incubate for between 50 and 80 days, with incubation temperature determining hatchling sex. Hatchling and juvenile sea turtles develop in cryptic and poorly understood nursery areas before recruiting back to the adult foraging areas some decades later. (See color plate section.)

Fitzsimmons *et al.*, 1997; Lee *et al.*, 2012. Adult female turtles are known to breed every two to three years (Miller, 1997; Beggs *et al.*, 2007), while adult male turtles are thought to visit breeding areas annually (FitzSimmons *et al.*, 1997; James *et al.*, 2005a, 2005b; Hays *et al.*, 2010, but see Wright *et al.* 2012, which suggests that male green turtles in Cyprus may not breed annually). This tendency may reflect the differential overall investment of the sexes in reproduction, with females probably investing considerably more than males (Pearse & Avise, 2001). The resources for this investment will have been derived from foraging areas, the quality of which is linked to environmental conditions; therefore, a turtle's decision to breed or not in a given year may be affected by the changing climate (Kwan, 1994; Broderick *et al.*, 2001; Solow *et al.*, 2002; Wallace *et al.*, 2006; Saba *et al.*, 2007, 2008; Chaloupka *et al.*, 2008; Reina *et al.*, 2009). Given that seas are already warming and are expected to continue to do so in the future, we

Table 10.1 *Studies assessing changes in marine turtle nesting season onset and duration (nesting phenology) in response to increased sea surface temperatures recorded nearby the nesting beach.*

Species	Location	Nesting season onset	Nesting season length	Key reference(s)
Loggerhead	Archie Carr Wildlife Refuge, FL USA	Earlier	Shorter	Weishampel *et al.*, 2004, 2010
Loggerhead	Cape Canaveral, FL USA	Earlier	Shorter	Pike *et al.*, 2006
Loggerhead	Bald Head Island, NC USA	Earlier	Longer	Hawkes *et al.*, 2007
Loggerhead	Zakynthos, Greece	Earlier	No change	Mazaris *et al.*, 2009
Loggerhead	USA and Mediterranean	Earlier	Longer	Mazaris *et al.*, 2013
Loggerhead	FL, USA	Earlier	Longer	Lamont & Fujisaki, 2013
Green	Archie Carr Wildlife Refuge, FL USA	Earlier	Longer	Weishampel *et al.*, 2010
Green	Cape Canaveral, FL USA	No change	No change	Pike, 2009
Hawksbill	Long Island, Antigua	Earlier	No change	Ditmer & Stapleton, 2012

might expect phenological changes, that is, changes in the onset and the duration of the reproductive cycle, to be occurring (Witt *et al.*, 2010); indeed, there is evidence that this is happening (Table 10.1). Warmer spring sea-surface temperatures appear to elicit earlier onset of nesting, although the effect of temperature on the duration of the nesting season is uncertain (Mazaris *et al.*, 2013; Table 10.1). Additionally, there is no method at present to document the long-term arrival dates of male and female turtles to the breeding grounds (except to satellite track individuals at considerable expense per turtle). The effects of climate change to turtle mating phenology appear to vary in strength with latitude of nesting beaches (Mazaris *et al.*, 2013). Additionally, phenological changes in reproduction may be challenging to document for some nesting populations because the reproductive population may consist of cohorts of turtles that migrate from different foraging areas and are subject to varying environmental cues early in the reproductive cycle (Hamann *et al.*, 2007). Moreover, monitoring of nesting beaches may not occur early or late enough in the nesting season to document subtle changes in the timing of nesting. Nevertheless, phenological changes in reproductive seasonality may be one of the most tractable ways for marine turtles to adapt to climate change.

NESTING BEACH AVAILABILITY

Gravid female turtles are known to lay their clutches of eggs on or near their natal beaches. This mechanism promotes evolutionary selection for beaches that deliver successful incubation and hatching and selects against poor quality beaches from which fewer hatchlings successfully emerge (Freedberg & Wade, 2001).

Climate change may reduce the availability of nesting beaches by a combination of: (1) sea level rise; (2) coastal squeeze, where natural beaches cannot recede due to human coastal developments in the way (Fish *et al.*, 2005, 2008); and (3) coastal erosion due to increased frequency and severity of storms (Fuentes *et al.*, 2010, 2011). Marine turtles are poor locomotors on land, and consequently almost all marine turtle nesting beaches tend to be low-lying with short tidal ranges (Mortimer, 1990; Miller, 1997). In the simplest case scenario, sea level rise would mean a typical nesting beach would be inundated higher up the shoreline, reducing the net area available for egg-laying and successful incubation. In modeled case studies in Barbados, Bonaire, Greece, and Hawaii, up to half the beach was lost (Fish *et al.*, 2005, 2008; Baker *et al.*, 2006; Mazaris *et al.*, 2009). However, in most natural shoreline systems, beaches may not only be eroded but also accreted, and highly dynamic dune systems behind them simply retract and expand accordingly, with environmental forces governing their zonation (Thom & Hall, 1991). Such beach retreat has probably made suitable nesting beach available for marine turtles for millennia. Beach retreat, however, cannot occur where coastal development (e.g. buildings, sea walls, and coastal fortifications) exists close to the tide line (Nicholls, 1998; Fish *et al.*, 2005, 2008; Baker *et al.*, 2006; Jones *et al.*, 2007; Mazaris *et al.*, 2009; Witherington *et al.*, 2011a, 2011b). Coastal erosion takes place instead, often with loss of high value coastal property (as well as turtle nesting beach; Figure 10.2). As a consequence, shoreline protection (fortification of human coastal settlements using sea walls, jetties, and other hard-engineered structures) has been erected in many key turtle nesting areas, leading to partial or total loss of nesting beaches (Pilkey & Wright, 1988; Koike, 1996; Kraus & McDougal, 1996; Lutcavage *et al.*, 1997; Bouchard *et al.*, 1998; Burke & Maidens, 2004; Airoldi *et al.*, 2005; Zheng *et al.*, 2007; Dugan *et al.*, 2008; Schlacher *et al.*, 2008; Rizkalla & Savage, 2011).

Other projects seek to maintain the beach *in situ*, for example, using beach renourishment, but such approaches are yet far from ideal. This offshore-sourced material is not always suitable for nesting and incubation, having a high mud and silt content, which causes it to be compact and

Figure 10.2 (a) Nesting beach may be lost through coastal squeeze, where beach is eroded but coastal development prevents its retreat (here valuable coastal property in North Carolina, USA is defended by sand bags); (b) hatchling deformities, such as this two-headed green turtle (*Chelonia mydas*) from a nest in Cyprus, may result from altered nest incubation temperatures; (c) nests can be washed out by storms and unusually high tides. This nest has been exposed in the bank of an escarpment; (d) eggs that may fail to develop due to unusually high incubation temperatures or non-viable incubation conditions may be moved to hatcheries. (Photo credits: (a) Matthew Godfrey, (c) David Wright, (b, d) Lucy Hawkes.) (See color plate section.)

difficult for turtles to dig nests in. Dredged material may also be darker in color than the original sand it replaces, and may have a higher content of environmental contaminants, particularly if dredged from shipping channels where fuel and fouling chemicals may be concentrated (Crain *et al.*, 1995; Milton *et al.*, 1997; Rumbold *et al.*, 2001; Peterson & Bishop, 2005; Montague, 2008; Brock *et al.*, 2009). There has even been a suggestion to use ground glass cullet as a fill material (Makowski *et al.*, 2008), although to date, egg incubation has not been tested in this material. Ideally, beaches should be renourished with sand matched to the original grain size, material content, and albedo of the target beach, but ultimately renourishment projects provide only short-term (and high-cost) solutions to beach erosion and sea level rise, with subsequent nourishment usually required after only a few years (Montague, 2008). More long-term studies are needed to assess cumulative impacts of repeated beach nourishment projects on marine turtles.

The loss of nesting beaches may be compounded by an increase in the proportion of extreme weather events (Goldenberg et al., 2001; Webster et al., 2005, Cowell et al., 2006; Leslie et al., 2007), many of which may make landfall at turtle nesting beaches in temperate and tropical areas (Martins, 1996; Bengtsson, 2001; Ross, 2005; Pike & Stiner, 2007; Prusty et al., 2007; Van Houtan & Bass, 2007; Fuentes & Abbs, 2010). Extreme weather events may cause significant nesting beach loss, as well as washing out and terminating nests already incubating on beaches (Milton et al., 1994), which will not be replaced, unlike many other taxa such as birds that exhibit parental care and can re-lay after nest loss. How marine turtles respond to total beach loss remains to be seen, although some insight may be gleaned from Suriname and French Guiana. There, green, leatherback, and olive ridley (Lepidochelys olivacea) turtle nesting beaches are so dynamic that they may be completely eroded from one season to the next (Schulz, 1975; Girondot & Fretey, 1996; Rivalan et al., 2006; Kelle et al., 2007), yet high-magnitude, successful nesting persists in the region. This observation suggests a high degree of plasticity in nesting beach fidelity, at least in this region, and may belie more flexibility in nest site selection by marine turtles than is commonly accorded. Species with lower site fidelity (nests spread over a greater area) might be expected to be more resilient to the effects of beach loss than species with highly precise repeat nest placement (Pike & Stiner, 2007).

Evidence exists that marine turtles are able to colonize new beaches, with nesting having been recorded at both newly formed natural and artificial beaches (Hoggard, 1991; Bowen et al., 1993; Encalada et al., 1998; Bell et al., 2005; Mrosovsky, 2006; Hamann et al., 2007), and it therefore seems likely that beaches that were previously too cool for successful incubation may be opened to nesting by climate change. Leatherback and loggerhead (Caretta caretta) turtles are now nesting at their furthest north since records began (Rabon et al., 2004; Sénégas et al., 2008; Bentivegna et al., 2010), suggesting that this phenomenon might already be occurring. In addition, evidence exists that populations of turtles can be translocated – the critically endangered

Kemp's ridley turtle (*Lepidochelys kempii*) was subject to high levels of harvest at what was effectively its only nesting site in Mexico (Plotkin, 2007). In response, a conservation project moved entire clutches of eggs immediately after laying to beaches in Texas, USA, where they were afforded complete protection from harvest (Manzella *et al.*, 1988). Nesting by adult females from those clutches at these new natal beaches takes place today (Shaver & Caillouet, 1998).

NEST PLACEMENT

Marine turtles generally lay their eggs between the high-tide and vegetated line on temperate, subtropical, and tropical beaches, ensuring that eggs have a warm, dry incubation environment, safe from excessive tidal over-wash that can reduce hatching success (Caut *et al.*, 2010). Different species of marine turtles appear to have different selection criteria for nesting beaches (Mrosovsky, 1983; Whitmore & Dutton, 1985; Hays *et al.*, 1995; Kamel & Mrosovsky, 2004, 2005). For example, the huge leatherback sea turtle selects short, steep nesting beaches to minimize the distance over which it must crawl to reach dry sand, while hawksbill turtles (*Eretmochelys imbricate*), a smaller marine turtle species, nest on much less dynamic, flatter beaches, and may travel far into dunes to lay their clutches. Varying beach types will be differentially affected by sea level rise (e.g. flatter beaches might be more quickly inundated and lose a greater total area than steeper beaches) (Slott *et al.*, 2006), leading to greater impacts for some turtle species or populations. However, factors influencing nest site selection are not understood, making it difficult to predict how marine turtles might respond to changing shorelines. Comparative studies involving different species will facilitate better prediction of how turtles may respond to changing beach profiles (Mrosovsky, 2006; Wetterer *et al.*, 2009; Cuevas *et al.*, 2010; Garcon *et al.*, 2010).

SEX RATIOS

For marine turtles (as well as many reptilian species), sex is determined by the temperature of the incubation environment. Marine turtles have temperature-dependent sex determination (TSD; Ewert *et al.*, 2004), where females are produced at warmer temperatures and males at cooler temperatures, with 50% of each sex at the pivotal temperature (Mrosovsky, 1988; Figure 10.3). The shape of the relationship between temperature and sex is sigmoidal, such that there is a narrow range of

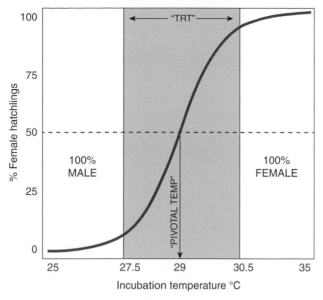

Figure 10.3 Schematic figure showing temperature-dependent sex determination (TSD) in a generic marine turtle species, where on a sigmoidal curve females are produced at warmer temperatures and males at lower temperatures. Production of equal numbers of males and females occurs at the pivotal temperature. A mixture of sexes can be produced in the Transitional Range of Temperatures (TRT), and eggs generally fail to successfully hatch outside of a ~10°C range of temperatures (26–36°C).

temperatures (the Transitional Range of Temperatures, TRT) over which both male and female offspring are produced (Yntema & Mrosovsky, 1980, 1982; Figure 10.3). Within each incubating clutch of eggs, temperature can vary; eggs at the periphery of the clutch are often cooler than eggs in the center, as are eggs at the bottom of the nest furthest from the penetrating warmth of the sun (Kaska *et al.*, 1998). A developing clutch of eggs produces enough metabolic heat to increase the overall incubation temperature by approximately 1°C; therefore, smaller clutches tend to be cooler than larger ones (Godfrey *et al.*, 1997; Broderick *et al.*, 2001; Zbinden *et al.*, 2006; Sandoval *et al.*, 2011). In addition, the extent to which the clutch is warmed by solar radiation will differ with sand albedo, as darker sands absorb and retain more heat (Standora & Spotila, 1985; Hays *et al.*, 1995; Reece *et al.*, 2002). Nests may also be subject to punctuated temperature changes. For example, rainfall events may reduce the clutch temperature by several degrees for a few hours (Godfrey *et al.*, 1996; Houghton *et al.*, 2007; Steckenreuter *et al.*, 2010). Daily thermal variance can have an impact on sex ratios of turtles with TSD (Neuwald & Valenzuela, 2011), although this effect is likely minimal for marine turtle clutches placed deep within beach sand. Finally, on some nesting beaches, conservationists sometimes translocate and rebury eggs in hatcheries (Figure 10.2d), where eggs are thought to be safer from predation (by humans and other animals) or poor weather conditions (i.e. storms and spring high tides). In general, hatcheries host a higher density of nests and are often further up the shore, making them warmer than natural incubation conditions (Morreale *et al.*, 1982; Chan & Liew, 1995; Baptistotte *et al.*, 1999; Naro-Maciel *et al.*, 1999).

Temperature-logging devices have been used in the field to record nest temperatures on many beaches, and published equations describing the relationship between temperature and sex are used to estimate with increasingly sophisticated modeling approaches the proportion of male and female hatchlings that are being produced (Fuentes & Porter, 2013). Many studies have demonstrated that nests are normally female-biased, and in some cases produce no male hatchlings at all (Hawkes *et al.*, 2010). Given that females are produced at higher temperatures and that the climate is expected to warm, these data suggest that an even higher proportion of female hatchlings may result (Hawkes *et al.*, 2007; Fuentes *et al.*, 2009; Mitchell & Janzen, 2010; Fuentes & Porter, 2013), potentially leading to a shortage or extirpation of males. If this were to happen, marine turtles would have to adapt or modify one or more of four traits to persist in this new climate: (1) pivotal temperature; (2) TRT; (3) nest site fidelity; and (4) nesting phenology (Mitchell & Janzen, 2010). Changing the pivotal temperature (for example, to be higher) could mean that more males would be produced for the same incubation temperature. Changing the TRT (for example, making it wider) would mean that mixed-sex clutches could be produced over a wider range of temperatures (and it would be less likely that one sex would be in short supply). This adaptation has been recorded in freshwater turtles (Hulin *et al.*, 2009), where a wider TRT is linked to more mixed-sex clutches, and, interestingly, appears to be correlated to latitude, with wider TRT at higher latitudes (Ewert *et al.*, 2005). Alternatively, reducing nest site fidelity could increase the chances of nests being laid in cooler parts of the same beaches (in more shaded areas, or in paler sands) or on different beaches, and therefore could produce more males overall. Finally, changing nest phenology would mean that nests might be laid earlier or later in the year when temperatures are cooler, which would also produce more males. For example, Tucker and colleagues (2008) showed that, for red-eared sliders, an overall male-biased sex ratio can occur even with increased climatic warming due to changes in the length of the nesting season.

Some recent studies have suggested that marine turtles might already be adapting to the changing climate; some populations are apparently nesting earlier in the season (Table 10.1) or at higher latitudes (Rabon *et al.*, 2004; Weishampel *et al.*, 2004; Doody *et al.*, 2006; Hawkes *et al.*, 2007). Even failing to adapt might not be detrimental; along with overall increasing temperatures, the future climate is expected to become more interannually variable (IPCC, 2007), so clutch incubation temperatures from one year to the next are expected to be very different. This will potentially maintain more variable sex ratios (Neuwald & Valenzuela, 2011), which may support population growth and new nesting site colonization (Kallimanis, 2010).

Despite some concern that few male hatchlings are produced (Hawkes *et al.*, 2007; Fuentes *et al.*, 2009; Mitchell & Janzen, 2010; Valverde *et al.*, 2010), it is important to assess if this is likely to be a problem in the future (e.g. Bell *et al.*, 2009; Schwanz *et al.*, 2010). Because adult male sea turtles rarely leave the ocean, it is more difficult to count them than it is adult female turtles that are tagged on nesting beaches and followed through many reproductive seasons. Because sea turtles are promiscuous and do not form long-term pair bonds, one way to try to gain an understanding of how many reproductively active male turtles are at large relative to reproductively active females (the operational sex ratio) is to measure the number of fathers siring each clutch of eggs (multiple paternity). This measure should reflect the relative numbers of males at the breeding area prior to the nesting season (Hays *et al.*, 2010; Stewart & Dutton, 2011). For example, if males were in short supply, one should expect to see few fathers per clutch, or even unfertilized eggs laid on nesting beaches. Multiple paternity has been shown to occur in all seven sea turtle species (Table 10.2), although it does not occur in all populations or in all clutches laid within a single population (Phillips *et al.*, 2013). Generally, at least some clutches will be fathered by multiple males (polyandry), but those same males may have mated with other females (polygyny). A recent study by Wright and colleagues (2012) has shown that in a population of green turtles with 30% of clutches exhibiting multiple paternity, the estimated adult breeding sex ratio was 1.4 males : 1 female. Further work by Wright and colleagues (2012) demonstrated similar sex ratios in subsequent years. Multiple paternity may be complex; its drivers may vary with population size and mating strategy (Jensen *et al.*, 2006), and its fitness consequences may be questionable (Lee & Hays, 2004). Nevertheless, its presence may at least suggest that the operational sex ratio may not yet be dramatically skewed. No data yet exist to describe if multiple paternity changes over time, but these data should be collected as a priority.

Table 10.2 *Studies recording multiple paternity in egg clutches of marine turtles (see also summary tables in Pearse & Avise, 2001; Jensen et al., 2006; Bowen & Karl, 2007; Uller & Olsson, 2008).*

Species	Proportion nests with MP (%)	Max. fathers	Country	Key reference(s)
Loggerhead	31.4	3	Florida, USA	Moore & Ball, 2002
Loggerhead	38.1	3	Mon Repos, Australia	Harry & Briscoe, 1988
Loggerhead	33.0	2	Florida, USA	Bollmer et al., 1999
Loggerhead	94.7	5	Greece	Zbinden et al., 2007
Loggerhead	50	2	Tunisia	Chaieb et al., 2010
Loggerhead	75	7	Georgia, USA	Lasala et al., in press
Loggerhead	43	3	Japan	Sakaoka et al., 2011[*3]
Loggerhead	46	3	Japan	Sakaoka et al., 2012[*3]
Green	30	4	Cyprus	Wright et al., 2012[**]
Green	55.6	5	Ascension Island	Lee & Hays, 2004
Green	9.01	2	GBR, Australia	Fitzsimmons, 1998
Green	100	>2	Ascension Island	Ireland et al., 2003
Green	100	3	Michoacán, Mexico	Lara-De La Cruz et al., 2013
Green	54	3	Sri Lanka	Ekanayake et al., 2013
Leatherback	39.5	2	US Virgin Islands	Stewart & Dutton, 2011
Leatherback	10.0	2	Pacific Costa Rica	Crim et al., 2002[*]
Kemp's ridley	57.7	2	Mexico	Kichler et al., 1999
Olive ridley	92.3	4	Costa Rica	Jensen et al., 2006[1]
Olive ridley	30.7	4	Costa Rica	Jensen et al., 2006[2]
Olive ridley	20.0	>2	Suriname	Hoekert et al., 2002
Hawksbill	10.0	2	Sabah, Malaysia	Joseph & Shaw, 2011
Hawksbill	9.3	2	Seychelles	Phillips et al., 2013
Flatback	69.0	3	Australia	Theissinger et al., 2009

[**] Wright and colleagues' study used parentage analysis and found no males sired offspring with more than one female.

[*] Denotes studies that documented polyandry – the same male mating with multiple females.

[1] Sampled for a population exhibiting "arribada" behavior (mass nesting).

[2] Sampled for a population that does not nest *en masse*.

[3] Turtles in captivity.

HATCHLING DEVELOPMENT

Hatchling success is tied to incubation temperatures, with low hatching success at temperatures that are too cool or too warm (below approximately 25°C and above 35°C, respectively) (Miller, 1997; Matsuzawa *et al.*, 2002). Increasing sand temperatures associated with climate change may therefore negatively impact hatching success, even making some areas completely unsuitable for hatchling production at least during parts of the year (Hawkes *et al.*, 2007). Changes in phenology of nesting seasons may mitigate some of the predicted negative impacts of higher incubation temperatures associated with climate change (Ditmer & Stapleton, 2012). Incubation temperature also has an impact on hatchling size and behavior (Reece *et al.*, 2002; Mickelson & Downie, 2010). For instance, recent work has suggested that turtle hatchlings emerging from warmer nests are smaller and are slower swimmers than hatchlings from cooler nests (Mickelson & Downie, 2010; Booth & Evans, 2011; Micheli-Campbell *et al.*, 2011), although the mechanisms for this are unknown. The implication is that hatchlings produced from warmer nests might be more susceptible to predation while swimming away from the nesting beach (Gyuris, 1994). However, there is little information on long-term impacts of incubation temperatures on the traits or fitness of marine turtles; studies of non-marine turtles suggest that at least some differential fitness impacts of the incubation environment are transient (e.g. O'Steen, 1998). More long-term studies of individual turtles are needed to fully understand the potential impacts of climate change on fitness associated with incubation temperatures. Finally, growth and maturation of hatchling turtles at sea, referred to as the lost years (Reich *et al.*, 2007), is the least understood of the marine turtle life stages, but may be affected by climate-driven alterations to ocean currents and wind patterns and represents a major knowledge gap for marine turtle ecology.

SUMMARY

While a complete understanding of the effects of climate change on marine turtle breeding ecology is still lacking, it is apparent that breeding ecology may be fundamentally affected (Van Houtan & Bass, 2007; Baez *et al.*, 2011). Climate-correlated changes in the timing of reproduction and colonization of new beaches have been recorded, and alterations to the availability of nesting sites, primary sex ratios, and hatching success may be expected. Current net habitat available for reproduction may be lost due to sea level rise, although increases in temperature could open up new areas of beach (either spatially at higher latitudes or temporally earlier/later in the year). The extent to which this is possible depends on the availability and accessibility of suitable beaches at higher latitudes and the adaptability of turtles to use new beaches. Further, a coherent understanding of fine-scale variability among females in nest site selection and subsequent consequences for their clutches/hatchlings is required, particularly as there is early evidence of thermal adaptation of eggs of some turtles on hotter nesting beaches (Weber *et al.*, 2011). The effects of altered thermal regimes may have the most dramatic and insidious effects if they undermine the fundamental ecology of marine turtle reproduction. In addition to changes to sex ratios, it is clear that the thermal conditions of the incubation environment affect the phenotype, survivorship, and growth rate of hatchling turtles and feed directly into demography. Such effects are likely to be difficult to monitor; therefore, pre-emptive management strategies could be investigated as a cautious approach going forward. Although there is much still to be understood about the potential effect of climate change on marine turtles, recent work has indicated that marine turtles and some other reptile species may be beginning to adapt (Iverson, 1991; Weishampel *et al.*, 2004; Doody *et al.*, 2006; Telemeco *et al.*, 2009; Weber *et al.*, 2011), which yields an exciting new field of study.

MANAGING FOR CLIMATE CHANGE

Managing for the effects of climate change should be an obligate part of any coastal biodiversity management plan and will be essential for successful conservation of habitats and species (Hansen *et al.*, 2010). Growing evidence of marine turtles already adapting to altered climate is noteworthy and suggests that interventionist management should proceed cautiously. For example, the current state of knowledge cannot dictate what the most appropriate primary or operational sex ratio or threshold of hatching success should be. Recommending management interventions is complex; for many aspects of marine turtle breeding ecology it is not yet possible to predict the direction, let alone the magnitude, of some of the expected changes. So far, protection of climate refugia, areas that might become important for marine turtle nesting as warmer climes move pole-ward, has been promoted (Baptistotte *et al.*, 1999; Hansen *et al.*, 2010; Hawkes *et al.*, 2010). This approach is essentially a no-risk strategy, as it does not try to manipulate the natural behavior of the population of concern. Higher risk, more invasive strategies have also been considered. Patino-Martinez and colleagues (2012) investigated the effect on hatching success and hatchling fitness of shading nests (cooling them and producing more males), while other studies have investigated the effect of moving clutches of hatchlings to safer incubation environments (Pintus *et al.*, 2009) or manipulating the thermal environment of incubating eggs (Naro-Maciel *et al.*, 1999). These novel approaches are worth investigation should they be needed in the future (Fuentes *et al.*, 2012), but it would seem prudent not to roll them out widely until greater certainty about the direction and magnitude of climate change effects have been established.

REFERENCES

Airoldi, L., Abbiati, M., Beck, M. W., *et al.* (2005). An ecological perspective on the deployment and design of low-crested and other hard coastal defence structures. *Coastal Engineering*, **52**, 1073–1087.

Allen, Z. C., Shah, N. J., Grant, A., Derand, G. D. & Bell, D. (2010). Hawksbill turtle monitoring in Cousin Island, Seychelles: An eight-fold increase in annual nesting numbers. *Endangered Species Research*, **11**, 195–200.

Baez, J. C., Bellido, J. J., Ferri-Yanez, F., *et al.* (2011). The North Atlantic Oscillation and sea surface temperature affect loggerhead abundance around the Strait of Gibraltar. *Scientia Marina*, **75**, 571–575.

Baker, J., Littnan, C. & Johnston, D. (2006). Potential effects of sea level rise on the terrestrial habitats of endangered and endemic megafauna in the Northwestern Hawaiian Islands. *Endangered Species Research*, **2**, 21–30.

Baptistotte, C., Scalfoni, J. T. & Mrosovsky, N. (1999). Male-producing thermal ecology of a southern loggerhead turtle nesting beach in Brazil: Implications for conservation. *Animal Conservation*, **2**, 9–13.

Beggs, J., Horrocks, J. & Krueger, B. (2007). Increase in hawksbill sea turtle *Eretmochelys imbricata* nesting in Barbados, West Indies. *Endangered Species Research*, **3**, 159–168.

Bell, C. D. L., Parsons, J., Austin, T. J., *et al.* (2005). Some of them came home: The Cayman Turtle Farm headstarting project for the green turtle *Chelonia mydas*. *Oryx*, **39**, 137–148.

Bell, C. D., Solomon, J. L., Blumenthal, J. M., *et al.* (2007). Monitoring and conservation of critically reduced marine turtle nesting populations: Lessons from the Cayman Islands. *Animal Conservation*, **10**, 39–47.

Bell, C. D., Blumenthal, J. M., Broderick, A. C. & Godley, B. J. (2009). Investigating potential for depensation in marine turtles: How low can you go? *Conservation Biology*, **24**, 226–235.

Bengtsson, L. (2001). Weather – Hurricane threats. *Science*, **293**, 440–441.

Bentivegna, F., Rasotto, M. B., de Lucia, G. A., *et al.* (2010). Loggerhead turtle (*Caretta caretta*) nests at high latitudes in Italy: A call for vigilance in the western Mediterranean. *Chelonian Conservation and Biology*, **9**, 283–289.

Bollmer, J. L., Irwin, M. E., Rieder, J. P. & Parker, P. G. (1999). Multiple paternity in loggerhead turtle clutches. *Copeia*, **1999**, 475–478.

Booth, D. T. & Evans, A. (2011). Warm water and cool nests are best: How global warming might influence hatchling green turtle swimming performance. *PLos ONE*, **6**, e23162.

Bouchard, S., Moran, K., Tiwari, M., *et al.* (1998). Effects of exposed pilings on sea turtle nesting activity at Melbourne Beach, Florida. *Journal of Coastal Research*, **14**, 1343–1347.

Bowen, B., Avise, J. C., Richardson, J. I., *et al.* (1993). Population structure of loggerhead turtles (*Caretta caretta*) in the northwestern Atlantic Ocean and Mediterranean Sea. *Conservation Biology*, **7**, 834–844.

Bowen, B. W. & Karl, S. A. (2007). Population genetics and phylogeography of sea turtles. *Molecular Ecology*, **16**, 4886–4907.

Brock, K. A., Reece, J. S. & Ehrhart, L. M. (2009). The effects of artificial beach nourishment on marine turtles: Differences between loggerhead and green turtles. *Restoration Ecology*, **17**, 297–307.

Broderick, A. C., Godley, B. J. & Hays, G. C. (2001). Metabolic heating and the prediction of sex ratios for green turtles (*Chelonia mydas*). *Physiological and Biochemical Zoology*, **74**, 161–170.

Burke, L. & Maidens, J. (2004). *Reefs at Risk in the Caribbean*. Washington, DC: World Resources Institute.

Caut, S., Guirlet, E. & Girondot, M. (2010). Effect of tidal overwash on the embryonic development of leatherback turtles in French Guiana. *Marine Environmental Research*, **69**, 254–261.

Chaieb, O., El Ouaer, A. Mafucci, F., *et al.* (2011). Genetic survey of loggerhead turtle *Caretta caretta* nesting population in Tunisia. *Marine Biodiversity Records*, **3**, e20.

Chaloupka, M., Kamezaki, N. & Limpus, C. (2008). Is climate change affecting the population dynamics of the endangered Pacific loggerhead sea turtle? *Journal of Experimental Marine Biology and Ecology*, **356**, 136–143.

Chan, E. H. & Liew, H. C. (1995). Incubation temperatures and sex-ratios in the Malaysian leatherback turtle (*Dermochelys coriacea*). *Biological Conservation*, **74**, 169–174.

Cowell, P. J., Thom, B. G., Jones, R. A., Everts, C. H. & Simanovic, D. (2006). Management of uncertainty in predicting climate-change impacts on beaches. *Journal of Coastal Research*, **22**, 232–245.

Crain, D. A., Bolten, A. B. & Bjorndal, K. A. (1995). Effects of beach nourishment on sea turtles: Review and research initiatives. *Restoration Ecology*, **3**, 95–104.

Crim, J. L., Spotila, L. D., Spotila, J. R., *et al.* (2002). The leatherback turtle, *Dermochelys coriacea*, exhibits both polyandry and polygyny. *Molecular Ecology*, **11**, 2097–2106.

Cuevas, E., de los Angeles, M., Liceaga, C. & Marino-Tapia, I. (2010). Influence of beach slope and width on hawksbill (*Eretmochelys imbricata*) and green turtle (*Chelonia mydas*) nesting activity in El Cuyo, Yucatan, Mexico. *Chelonian Conservation and Biology*, **9**, 262–267.

Ditmer, M. A. & Stapleton, S. P. (2012). Factors affecting hatch success of hawksbill sea turtles on Long Island, Antigua, West Indies. *PLoS ONE*, **7**, e38472.

Doody, J. S., Guarino, E., Georges, A. , *et al.* (2006). Nest site choice compensates for climate effects on sex ratios in a lizard with environmental sex determination. *Evolutionary Ecology*, **20**, 307–330.

Dugan, J. E., Hubbard, D. M., Rodil, I. F., Revell, D. L. & Schroeter, S. (2008). Ecological effects of coastal armoring on sandy beaches. *Marine Ecology – An Evolutionary Perspective*, **29**, 160–170.

Dutton, P. H., Bowen, B. W., Owens, D. W., Barragan, A. & Davis, S. K. (1999). Global phylogeography of the leatherback turtle (*Dermochelys coriacea*). *Journal of Zoology*, **248**, 397–409.

Ekanayake, E. M. L., Kapurusinghe, T., Sama, M. M., et al. (2013). Paternity of green turtles (*Chelonia mydas*) clutches laid at Kosgoda, Sri Lanka. *Herpetological Conservation and Biology*, **8**, 27–36.

Encalada, S. E., Bjorndal, K. A., Bolten, A. B., et al. (1998). Population structure of loggerhead turtle (*Caretta caretta*) nesting colonies in the Atlantic and Mediterranean as inferred from mitochondrial DNA control region sequences. *Marine Biology*, **130**, 567–575.

Ewert, M. A., Etchberger, C. R. & Nelson, C. E. (2004). Turtle sex determining modes and TSD patterns, and some TSD pattern correlates. In N. Valenzuela & V. Lance (eds.), *Temperature-dependent Sex Determination in Vertebrates*. Washington, DC: Smithsonian Institution Press, pp. 21–32.

Ewert, M. A., Lang, J. W. & Nelson, C. E. (2005). Geographic variation in the pattern of temperature-dependent sex determination in the American snapping turtle (*Chelydra serpentina*). *Journal of Zoology*, **265**, 81–95.

Fish, M. R., Cote, I. M., Gill, J. A., et al. (2005). Predicting the impact of sea-level rise on Caribbean sea turtle nesting habitat. *Conservation Biology*, **19**, 482–491.

Fish, M. R., Cote, I. M., Horrocks, J. A., et al. (2008). Construction setback regulations and sea-level rise: Mitigating sea turtle nesting beach loss. *Ocean and Coastal Management*, **51**, 330–341.

Fitzsimmons, N. N. (1998). Single paternity of clutches and sperm storage in the promiscuous green turtle (*Chelonia mydas*). *Molecular Ecology*, **7**, 575–584.

Fitzsimmons, N. N., Limpus, C. J., Norman, J. A., et al. (1997). Philopatry of male marine turtles inferred from mitochondrial DNA markers. *Proceedings of the National Academy of Sciences of the United States of America*, **94**, 8912–8917.

Freedberg, S. & Wade, M. J. (2001). Cultural inheritance as a mechanism for population sex-ratio bias in reptiles. *Evolution*, **55**, 1049–1055.

Fuentes, M. M. P. B. & Abbs, D. (2010). Effects of projected changes in tropical cyclone frequency on sea turtles. *Marine Ecology Progress Series*, **412**, 283–292.

Fuentes, M. M. P. B. & Porter, W. P. (2013). Using a microclimate model to evaluate impacts of climate change on sea turtles. *Ecological Modelling*, **251**, 150–157.

Fuentes, M. M. P. B., Maynard, J. A., Guinea, M., et al. (2009). Proxy indicators of sand temperature help project impacts of global warming on sea turtles in northen Australia. *Endangered Species Research*, **9**, 33–40.

Fuentes, M. M. P. B., Limpus, C. J., Hamann, M. & Dawson, J. (2010). Potential impacts of projected sea-level rise on sea turtle rookeries. *Aquatic Conservation-Marine and Freshwater Ecosystems*, **20**, 132–139.

Fuentes, M. M. P. B., Limpus, C. J. & Hamann, M. (2011). Vulnerability of sea turtle nesting grounds to climate change. *Global Change Biology*, **17**, 140–153.

Fuentes, M. M. P. B., Fish, M. R. & Maynard, J. (2012). Management strategies to mitigate the impacts of climate change on sea turtle's terrestrial reproductive phase. *Mitigation and Adaptation Strategies for Global Change*, **17**, 51–63.

Garcon, J. S., Grech, A., Moloney, J. & Hamann, M. (2010). Relative Exposure Index: An important factor in sea turtle nesting distribution. *Aquatic Conservation-Marine and Freshwater Ecosystems*, **20**, 140–149.

Girondot, M. & Fretey, J. (1996). Leatherback turtles, *Dermochelys coriacea*, nesting in French Guiana, 1978–1995. *Chelonian Conservation and Biology*, **2**, 204–208.

Godfrey, M. H., Barreto, R. & Mrosovsky, N. (1996). Estimating past and present sex ratios of sea turtles in Suriname. *Canadian Journal of Zoology – Revue Canadienne De Zoologie*, **74**, 267–277.

Godfrey, M. H., Barreto, R. & Mrosovsky, N. (1997). Metabolically-generated heat of developing eggs and its potential effect on sw ratio of sea turtle hatchlings. *Journal of Herpetology*, **31**, 616–619.

Goldenberg, S. B., Landsea, C. W., Mestas-Nunez, A. M. & Gray, W. M. (2001). The recent increase in Atlantic hurricane activity: Causes and implications. *Science*, **293**, 474–479.

Gyuris, E. (1994). The rate of predation by fishes on hatchlings of the green turtle (*Chelonia mydas*). *Coral Reefs*, **13**, 137–144.

Hamann, M., Limus, C. J. & Read, M. A. (2007). Vulnerability of marine reptiles in the Great Barrier Reef to climate change. In J. E. Johnson & P. A. Marshall (eds.), *Climate Change and the Great Barrier Reef: A Vulnerability Assessment*. Hobart: Great Barrier Reef Marine Park Authority and Australia Greenhouse Office.

Hamann, M., Godfrey, M., Seminoff, J., *et al.* (2010). Global research priorities for sea turtles: Informing management and conservation in the 21st century. *Endangered Species Research*, **11**, 245–269.

Hansen, L., Hoffman, J., Drews, C. & Mielbrecht, E. (2010). Designing climate-smart conservation: Guidance and case studies. *Conservation Biology*, **24**, 63–69.

Harry, J. L. & Briscoe, D. A. (1988). Multiple paternity in the loggerhead turtle (*Caretta caretta*). *Journal of Heredity*, **79**, 96–99.

Hawkes, L. A., Broderick, A. C., Godfrey, M. H. & Godley, B. J. (2007). Investigating the potential impacts of climate change on a marine turtle population. *Global Change Biology*, **13**, 923–932.

Hawkes, L. A., Broderick, A. C., Godfrey, M. H. & Godley, B. J. (2010). Climate change and marine turtles. *Endangered Species Research*, **7**, 137–154.

Hays, G. C., Mackay, A., Adams, C. R., *et al.* (1995). Nest-site selection by sea-turtles. *Journal of the Marine Biological Association of the United Kingdom*, **75**, 667–674.

Hays, G. C., Fossette, S., Katselidis, K. A., Schofield, G. & Gravenor, M. B. (2010). Breeding periodicity for male sea turtles, operational sex ratios, and implications in the face of climate change. *Conservation Biology*, **24**, 1636–1643.

Hoekert, W. E. J., Neufeglise, H., Schouten, A. D. & Menken, S. B. J. (2002). Multiple paternity and female-biased mutation at a microsatellite locus in the olive ridley sea turtle (*Lepidochelys olivacea*). *Heredity*, **89**, 107–113.

Hoggard, W. (1991). First recorded turtle nesting on Mississippi's man-made beach. *Marine Turtle Newsletter*, **52**, 11–12.

Houghton, J. D. R., Myers, A. E., Lloyd, C., *et al.* (2007). Protracted rainfall decreases temperature within leatherback turtle (*Dermochelys coriacea*) clutches in Grenada, West Indies: Ecological implications for a species displaying temperature dependent sex determination. *Journal of Experimental Marine Biology and Ecology*, **345**, 71–77.

Hulin, V., Delmas, V., Girondot, M., Godfrey, M. H. & Guillon, J. M. (2009). Temperature-dependent sex determination and global change: Are some species at greater risk? *Oecologia*, **160**, 493–506.

IPCC. (2007). *Climate Change 2007: Synthesis Report. Contribution of Working Groups I, II and III to the Fourth Assessment Report of the Intergovernmental Panel on Climate Change*. Geneva, Switzerland: IPCC.

Ireland, J. S., Broderick, A. C., Glen, F., *et al.* (2003). Multiple paternity assessed using microsatellite markers, in green turtles *Chelonia mydas* (Linnaeus, 1758) of

Ascension Island, South Atlantic. *Journal of Experimental Marine Biology and Ecology*, **291**, 149–160.

Iverson, J. B. (1991). Patterns of survivorship in turtles (Order Testudines). *Canadian Journal of Zoology – Revue Canadienne De Zoologie*, **69**, 385–391.

James, M. C., Eckert, S. A. & Myers, R. A. (2005a). Migratory and reproductive movements of male leatherback turtles (*Dermochelys coriacea*). *Marine Biology*, **147**, 845–853.

James, M. C., Myers, R. A. & Ottensmeyer, C. A. (2005b). Behaviour of leatherback sea turtles, *Dermochelys coriacea*, during the migratory cycle. *Proceedings of the Royal Society of London, Series B, Biological Sciences*, **272**, 1547–1555.

Jensen, M. P., Abreu-Grobois, F. A., Frydenburg, J. & Loeschcke, V. (2006). Microsatellites provide insight into contrasting mating patterns in arribada vs. non-arribada olive ridley sea turtle rookeries. *Molecular Ecology*, **15**, 2567–2575.

Jones, T. T., Reina, R. D., Darveau, C. A. & Lutz, P. L. (2007). Ontogeny of energetics in leatherback (*Dermochelys coriacea*) and olive ridley (*Lepidochelys olivacea*) sea turtle batchlings. *Comparative Biochemistry and Physiology Part A: Molecular and Integrative Physiology*, **147**, 313–322.

Joseph, J. & Shaw, P. W. (2011). Multiple paternity in egg clutches of hawksbill turtles (*Eretmochelys imbricata*). *Conservation Genetics*, **12**, 601–605.

Kallimanis, A. S. (2010). Temperature dependent sex determination and climate change. *Oikos*, **119**, 197–200.

Kamel, S. J. & Mrosovsky, N. (2004). Nest site selection in leatherbacks, *Dermochelys coriacea*: Individual patterns and their consequences. *Animal Behaviour*, **68**, 357–366.

Kamel, S. J. & Mrosovsky, N. (2005). Repeatability of nesting preferences in the hawksbill sea turtle, *Eretmochelys imbricata*, and their fitness consequences. *Animal Behaviour*, **70**, 819–828.

Kaska, Y., Downie, R., Tippett, R. & Furness, R. W. (1998). Natural temperature regimes for loggerhead and green turtle nests in the eastern Mediterranean. *Canadian Journal of Zoology – Revue Canadienne De Zoologie*, **76**, 723–729.

Kelle, L., Gratiot, N., Nolibos, I., *et al.* (2007). Monitoring of nesting leatherback turtles (*Dermochelys coriacea*): Contribution of remote sensing for real-time assessment of beach coverage in French Guiana. *Chelonian Conservation and Biology*, **6**, 142–147.

Kichler, K., Holder, M. T., Davis, S. K., Marquez, R. & Owens, D. W. (1999). Detection of multiple paternity in the Kemp's ridley sea turtle with limited sampling. *Molecular Ecology*, **8**, 819–830.

Koike, K. (1996). The countermeasures against coastal hazards in Japan. *GeoJournal*, **38**, 301–312.

Kraus, N. C. & McDougal, W. G. (1996). The effects of seawalls on the beach: Part I, An updated literature review. *Journal of Coastal Research*, **12**, 691–701.

Kwan, D. 1994. Fat reserves and reproduction in the green turtle (*Chelonia mydas*). *Wildlife Research*, **21**, 257–266.

Lamont, M. & Fujisaki, I. (2013). Effects of ocean temperature on nesting phenology and fecundity of loggerhead sea turtle (*Caretta caretta*). *Journal of Herpetology*, doi: 10.1670/12-217.

Lara-De La Cruz, L. I., Nakagawa, K. O., Cono-Camodio, H., *et al.* (2010). Detecting patterns of fertilization and frequency of multiple paternity in *Chelonia mydas* of Colola (Michoacán, Mexico). *Hidrobiologica*, **20**, 85–89.

Lasala, J. A., Harrison, J. S., Williams, K. L. & Rostal, D. C. (in press). Strong male-biased operational sex ratio in a breeding population of loggerhead turtles (*Caretta caretta*) inferred by paternal genotype reconstruction analysis. *Ecology and Evolution*, doi: 10.1002/ece3.76.

Lee, P. L. M. & Hays, G. C. (2004). Polyandry in a marine turtle: Females make the best of a bad job. *Proceedings of the National Academy of Sciences of the United States of America*, **101**, 6530–6535.

Lee, P. L. M., Luschi, P. & Hays, G. C. (2007). Detecting female precise natal philopatry in green turtles using assignment methods. *Molecular Ecology*, **16**, 61–74.

Leslie, L. M., Karoly, D. J., Leplastrier, M. & Buckley, B. W. (2007). Variability of tropical cyclones over the southwest Pacific Ocean using a high-resolution climate model. *Meteorology and Atmospheric Physics*, **97**, 171–180.

Limpus, C. J. (1993). The green turtle, *Chelonia mydas*, in Queensland: Breeding males in the Southern Great Barrier Reef. *Wildlife Research*, **20**, 513–523.

Lutcavage, M. E., Plotkin, P., Witherington, B. E. & Lutz, P. L. (1997). Human impacts on sea turtle survival. In P. L. Lutz & J. A. Musick (eds.), *The Biology of Sea Turtles*, vol. 1. Boca Raton, FL: CRC Press, pp. 387–410.

Makowski, C., Rusenko, K. & Kruempel, C. J. (2008). Abiotic suitability of recycled glass cullet as an alternative sea turtle nesting substrate. *Journal of Coastal Research*, **24**, 771–779.

Manzella, S. A., Caillouet, C. W. & Fontaine, C. T. (1988). Kemps ridley, *Lepidochelys kempi*, sea turtle head-start tag recoveries – Distribution, habitat and method of recovery. *Marine Fisheries Review*, **50**, 24–32.

Martins, R. E. (1996). Storm impacts on loggerhead turtle reproductive success. *Marine Turtle Newsletter*, **73**, 10–12.

Matsuzawa, Y., Sato, K., Sakamoto, W. & Bjorndal, K. A. (2002). Seasonal fluctuations in sand temperature: Effects on the incubation period and mortality of loggerhead sea turtle (*Caretta caretta*) pre-emergent hatchlings in Minabe, Japan. *Marine Biology*, **140**, 639–646.

Mazaris, A. D., Kramer-Schast, S., Tzanopoulos, J. *et al.* (2009). Assessing the relative importance of conservation measures applied on sea turtles: Comparison of measures focusing on nesting success and hatching recruitment success. *Amphibia–Reptilia*, **30**, 221–231.

Mazaris, A. D., Kallimanis, A. S., Pantis, J. D. & Hays, G. C. (2013). Phenological response of sea turtles to environmental variation across a species' northern range. *Proceedings of the Royal Society of London, Series B, Biological Sciences*, **280**, 2012–2397.

McClenachan, L., Jackson, J. B. C. & Newman, M. J. H. (2006). Conservation implications of historic sea turtle nesting beach loss. *Frontiers in Ecology and the Environment*, **4**, 290–296.

Micheli-Campbell, M. A., Campbell, H. A., Cramp, R. L., Booth, D. T. & Franklin, C. E. (2011). Staying cool, keeping strong: Incubation temperature affects performance in a freshwater turtle. *Journal of Zoology*, **285**, 266–273.

Mickelson, L. E. & Downie, J. R. (2010). Influence of incubation temperature on morphology and locomotion performance of leatherback (*Dermochelys coriacea*) hatchlings. *Canadian Journal of Zoology*, **88**, 359–368.

Miller, J. D. (1997). Reproduction in sea turtles. In P. L. Lutz & J. A. Musick (eds.), *The Biology of Sea Turtles*, vol. 1. Boca Raton, FL: CRC Press, pp. 51–82.

Milton, S. L., Leonekabler, S., Schulman, A. A. & Lutz, P. L. (1994). Effects of hurricane Andrew on the sea-turtle nesting beaches of South Florida. *Bulletin of Marine Science*, **54**, 974–981.

Milton, S. L., Schulman, A. A. & Lutz, P. L. (1997). The effect of beach nourishment with aragonite versus silicate sand on beach temperature and loggerhead sea turtle nesting success. *Journal of Coastal Research*, **13**, 904–915.

Mitchell, N. J. & Janzen, F. J. (2010). Temperature-dependent sex determination and contemporary climate change. *Sexual Development*, **4**, 129–140.

Montague, C. L. (2008). Recovering the sand deficit from a century of dredging and jetties along Florida's Atlantic coast: A reevaluation of beach nourishment as an essential tool for ecological conservation. *Journal of Coastal Research*, **24**, 899–916.

Moore, M. K. & Ball, R. M. (2002). Multiple paternity in loggerhead turtle (*Caretta caretta*) nests on Melbourne Beach, Florida: A microsatellite analysis. *Molecular Ecology*, **11**, 281–288.

Morreale, S. J., Ruiz, G. J., Spotila, J. R. & Standora, E. A. (1982). Temperature-dependent sex determination: Current practices threaten conservation of sea turtles. *Science*, **216**, 1245–1247.

Mortimer, J. A. (1990). The influence of beach and sand characteristics on the nesting-behaviour and clutch survival of green turtles (*Chelonia mydas*). *Copeia*, **1990**, 802–817.

Mrosovsky, N. (1983). *Conserving Sea Turtles*. London: British Herpetological Society.

Mrosovsky, N. (1988). Pivotal temperatures for loggerhead turtles (*Caretta caretta*) from northern and southern nesting beaches. *Canadian Journal of Zoology*, **66**, 661–669.

Mrosovsky, N. (2006). Distorting gene pools by conservation: Assessing the case of doomed turtle eggs. *Environmental Management*, **38**, 523–531.

Naro-Maciel, E., Mrosovsky, N. & Marcovaldi, M. A. (1999). Thermal profiles of sea turtle hatcheries and nesting areas at Praia do Forte, Brazil. *Chelonian Conservation and Biology*, **3**, 407–413.

Neuwald, J. L. & Valenzuela, N. (2011). The lesser known challenge of climate change: Thermal variance and sex-reversal in vertebrates with temperature-dependent sex determination. *PLos ONE*, **6**, e18117.

Nicholls, R. J. (1998). *Coastal Vulnerability Assessment for Sea-level Rise: Evaluation and Selection of Methodologies for Implementation*. Technical report R098002. Caribbean Planning for Adaptation to Global Climate Change (CPACC) project.

O'Steen, S. (1998). Embryonic temperature influences juvenile temperature choice and growth rate in snapping turtles *Chelydra serpentina*. *Journal of Experimental Biology*, **201**, 439–449.

Patino-Martinez, J., Marco, A., Quinones, L. & Hawkes, L. A. (2012). A potential tool to mitigate the impacts of climate change to the Caribbean leatherback sea turtle. *Global Change Biology*, **18**, 401–411.

Pearse, D. E. & Avise, J. C. (2001). Turtle mating systems: Behavior, sperm storage, and genetic paternity. *Journal of Heredity*, **92**, 206–211.

Peterson, C. H. & Bishop, M. J. (2005). Assessing the environmental impacts of beach nourishment. *Bioscience*, **55**, 887–896.

Phillips, K. P., Jorgensen, T. H., Jolliffe, K. G., et al. (2013). Reconstructing paternal genotypes to infer patterns of sperm storage and sexual selection in the hawksbill turtle. *Molecular Ecology*, **22**, 2301–2312.

Pike, D. A. & Stiner, J. C. (2007). Sea turtle species vary in their susceptibility to tropical cyclones. *Oecologia*, **153**, 471–478.

Pike, D. A., Antworth, R. L. & Stiner, J. C. (2006). Earlier nesting contributes to shorter nesting seasons for the loggerhead seaturtle, *Caretta caretta*. *Journal of Herpetology*, **40**, 91–94.

Pilkey, O. H. & Wright, H. L. (1988). Seawalls versus beaches. *Journal of Coastal Research*, **SI4**, 41–64.

Pintus, K., Godley, B. J., McGowan, A. & Broderick, A. C. (2009). Impact of clutch relocation on green turtle offspring. *Journal of Wildlife Management*, **73**, 1151–1157.

Plotkin, P. T. (2007). *Biology and Conservation of Ridley Sea Turtles*. Washington, DC: John Hopkins University Press.

Poloczanska, E. S., Limpus, C. J. & Hays, G. C. (2009). Vulnerability of marine turtles to climate change. *Advances in Marine Biology*, **56**, 151–211.

Prusty, G., Dash, S. & Singh, M. P. (2007). Spatio-temporal analysis of multi-date IRS imageries for turtle habitat dynamics characterization at Gahirmatha coast, India. *International Journal of Remote Sensing*, **28**, 871–883.

Rabon, D., Johnson, S. B., Dodd, M., *et al.* (2004). Confirmed leatherback turtle (*Dermochelys coriacea*) nests from North Carolina, with a summary of nesting activities north of Florida. *Marine Turtle Newsletter*, **101**, 4–8.

Reece, S. E., Broderick, A. C., Godley, B. J. & West, S. A. (2002). The effects of incubation environment, sex and pedigree on the hatchling phenotype in a natural population of loggerhead turtles. *Evolutionary Ecology Research*, **4**, 737–748.

Reich, K. J., Bjorndal, K. A. & Bolten, A. B. (2007). The 'lost years' of green turtles: Using stable isotopes to study cryptic lifestages. *Biology Letters*, **3**, 712–714.

Reina, R. D., Spotila, J. R., Paladino, F. V. & Dunham, A. E. (2009). Changed reproductive schedule of eastern Pacific leatherback turtles *Dermochelys coriacea* following the 1997–1998 El Nino to La Nina transition. *Endangered Species Research*, **7**, 155–161.

Rivalan, P., Dutton, P. H., Baudry, E., Roden, S. E. & Girondot, M. (2006). Demographic scenario inferred from genetic data in leatherback turtles nesting in French Guiana and Suriname. *Biological Conservation*, **130**, 1–9.

Rizkalla, C. E. & Savage, A. (2011). Impact of seawalls on loggerhead sea turtle (*Caretta caretta*) nesting and hatching success. *Journal of Coastal Research*, **27**, 166–173.

Ross, J. P. (2005). Hurricane effects on nesting *Caretta caretta*. *Marine Turtle Newsletter*, **108**, 13–14.

Rumbold, D. G., Davis, P. W. & Perretta, C. (2001). Estimating the effect of beach nourishment on *Caretta caretta* (loggerhead sea turtle) nesting. *Restoration Ecology*, **9**, 304–310.

Saba, V. S., Santidrian-Tomillo, P., Reina, R. D., *et al.* (2007). The effect of the El Nino Southern Oscillation on the reproductive frequency of eastern Pacific leatherback turtles. *Journal of Applied Ecology*, **44**, 395–404.

Saba, V. S., Spotila, J. R., Chavez, F. P. & Musick, J. A. (2008). Bottom-up and climatic forcing on the worldwide population of leatherback turtles. *Ecology*, **89**, 1414–1427.

Sakaoka, K., Yoshii, M., Okamoto, H., Sakai, F. & Nagasawa, K. (2011). Sperm utilization patterns and reproductive success in captive loggerhead turtles (*Caretta caretta*). *Chelonian Conservation and Biology*, **10**, 62–72.

Sakaoka, K., Yoshii, M., Okamoto, H., Sakai, F. & Nagasawa, K. (2012). Mate selection based on genetic relatedness of loggerhead turtles in captivity. *Chelonian Conservation and Biology*, **11**, 214–222.

Sandoval, S., Gomez-Munoz, V., Gutierrez, J. & Angel Porta-Gandara, M. (2011). Metabolic heat estimation of the sea turtle *Lepidochelys olivacea* embryos. *Journal of Thermal Biology*, **36**, 138–141.

Schlacher, T. A., Schoeman, D. S., Dugan, J., *et al.* (2008). Sandy beach ecosystems: Key features, sampling issues, management challenges and climate change impacts. *Marine Ecology – An Evolutionary Perspective*, **29**, 70–90.

Schulz, J. P. (1975). *Sea Turtles Nesting in Surinam*. Zoologische Verhandelingen (Leiden) No. 143. Leiden: Brill, pp. 3–143.

Schwanz, L. E., Spencer, R. J., Bowden, R. M. & Janzen, F. J. (2010). Climate and predation dominate juvenile and adult recruitment in a turtle with temperature-dependent sex determination. *Ecology*, **91**, 3016–3026.

Sénégas, J. B., Hochscheid, S., Groul, J. M., Lagarrigue, B. & Bentivegna, F. (2008). Discovery of the northernmost loggerhead sea turtle (*Caretta caretta*) nest. *Marine Biodiversity Records* (Online), 2.

Shaver, D. J. & Caillouet, C. W. (1998). More Kemp's ridley turtles return to South Texas to nest. *Marine Turtle Newsletter*, **82**, 1–5.

Slott, J. M., Murray, A. B., Ashton, A. D. & Crowley, T. J. (2006). Coastline responses to changing storm patterns. *Geophysical Research Letters*, **33**, L18404.

Solow, A. R., Bjorndal, K. A. & Bolten, A. B. (2002). Annual variation in nesting numbers of marine turtles: The effect of sea surface temperature on re-migration intervals. *Ecology Letters*, **5**, 742–746.

Standora, E. A. & Spotila, J. R. (1985). Temperature-dependent sex determination in sea turtles. *Copeia*, **1985**, 711–722.

Steckenreuter, A., Pilcher, N., Krueger, B. & Ben, J. (2010). Male-biased primary sex ratio of leatherback turtles (*Dermochelys coriacea*) at the Huon Coast, Papua New Guinea. *Chelonian Conservation and Biology*, **9**, 123–128.

Stewart, K. R. & Dutton, P. H. (2011). Paternal genotype reconstruction reveals multiple paternity and sex ratios in a breeding population of leatherback turtles (*Dermochelys coriacea*). *Conservation Genetics*, **12**, 1101–1113.

Telemeco, R. S., Elphick, M. J. & Shine, R. (2009). Nesting lizards (*Bassiana duperreyi*) compensate partly, but not completely, for climate change. *Ecology*, **90**, 17–22.

Theissinger, K., Fitzsimmons, N. N., Limpus, C. J. & Phillott, A. D. (2009). Mating system, multiple paternity and effective population size in the endemic flatback turtle (*Natador depressus*) in Australia. *Conservation Genetics*, **10**, 329–346.

Thom, B. G. & Hall, W. (1991). Behavior of beach profiles during accretion and erosion dominated periods. *Earth Surface Processes and Landforms*, **16**, 113–127.

Tucker, J. K., Dolan, C. R., Lamer, J. T. & Dustman, E. A. (2008). Climatic warming, sex ratios, and red-eared sliders (*Trachemys scripta elegans*) in Illinois. *Chelonian Conservation and Biology*, **7**, 60–69.

Uller, T. & Olsson, M. (2008). Multiple paternity in reptiles: Patterns and processes. *Molecular Ecology*, **17**, 2566–2580.

Valverde, R. A., Wingard, S., Gomez, F., Tordoir, M. T. & Orrego, C. M. (2010). Field lethal incubation temperature of olive ridley sea turtle *Lepidochelys olivacea* embryos at a mass nesting rookery. *Endangered Species Research*, **12**, 77–86.

Van Houtan, K. S. & Bass, O. L. (2007). Stormy oceans are associated with declines in sea turtle hatching. *Current Biology*, **17**, R590–R591.

Wallace, B. P., Seminoff, J. A., Kilham, S. S., Spotila, J. R. & Dutton, P. H. (2006). Leatherback turtles as oceanographic indicators: Stable isotope analyses reveal a trophic dichotomy between ocean basins. *Marine Biology*, **149**, 953–960.

Weber, S. B., Broderick, A. C., Groothuis, T. G. G., *et al.* (2011). Fine-scale thermal adaptation in a green turtle nesting population. *Proceedings of the Royal Society of London, Series B, Biological Sciences*, **279**, 1077–1084.

Webster, P. J., Holland, G. J., Curry, J. A. & Chang, H. R. (2005). Changes in tropical cyclone number, duration, and intensity in a warming environment. *Science*, **309**, 1844–1846.

Weishampel, J. F., Bagley, D. A. & Ehrhart, L. M. (2004). Earlier nesting by loggerhead sea turtles following sea surface warming. *Global Change Biology*, **10**, 1424–1427.

Weishampel, J. F., Bagley, D. A., Ehrhart, L. M. & Weishampel, A. C. (2010). Nesting phenologies of two sympatric sea turtle species related to sea surface temperatures. *Endangered Species Research*, **12**, 41–47.

Wetterer, J. K., Wood, L. D., Johnson, C., Krahe, H. & Fitchett, S. (2009). Predaceous ants, beach replenishment, and nest placement by sea turtles. *Environmental Entomology*, **36**, 1084–1091.

Whitmore, C. P. & Dutton, P. H. (1985). Infertility, embryonic mortality and nest-site selection in leatherback and green sea turtles in Suriname. *Biological Conservation*, **34**, 251–272.

Witherington, B., Hirama, S. & Mosier, A. (2011a). Barriers to sea turtle nesting on Florida (United States) beaches: Linear extent and changes following storms. *Journal of Coastal Research*, **27**, 450–458.

Witherington, B., Hirama, S. & Mosier, A. (2011b). Sea turtle responses to barriers on their nesting beach. *Journal of Experimental Marine Biology and Ecology*, **401**, 1–6.

Witt, M. J., Hawkes, L. A., Godfrey, M. H., Godley, B. J. & Broderick, A. C. (2010). Predicting the impacts of climate change on a globally distributed species: The case of the loggerhead turtle. *Journal of Experimental Biology*, **213**, 901–911.

Wright, L., Fuller, W., Godley, B., et al. (2012). Reconstruction of paternal genotypes over multiple breeding seasons reveals male green turtles do not breed annually. *Molecular Ecology*, **21**, 3625–3635.

Yntema, C. L. & Mrosovsky, N. (1980). Sexual differentiation in hatchling loggerheads (*Caretta caretta*) incubated at different controlled temperatures. *Herpetologica*, **36**, 33–36.

Yntema, C. L. & Mrosovsky, N. (1982). Critical periods and pivotal temperatures for sexual-differentiation in loggerhead sea turtles. *Canadian Journal of Zoology – Revue Canadienne De Zoologie*, **60**, 1012–1016.

Zbinden, J. A., Margaritoulis, D. & Arlettaz, R. (2006). Metabolic heating in Mediterranean loggerhead sea turtle clutches. *Journal of Experimental Marine Biology and Ecology*, **334**, 151–157.

Zbinden, J. A., Largiader, A. R., Leippert, F., Margaritoulis, D. & Arlettaz, R. (2007). High frequency of multiple paternity in the largest rookery of Mediterranean loggerhead sea turtles. *Molecular Ecology*, **16**, 3703–3711.

Zheng, J. H., Jeng, D. S. & Mase, H. (2007). Sandy beach profile response to sloping seawalls: An experimental study. *Journal of Coastal Research*, **SI50**, 334–337.

11

The effects of spilled oil on coastal ecosystems: lessons from the *Exxon Valdez* spill

JAMES L. BODKIN, DAN ESLER, STANLEY D. RICE,
CRAIG O. MATKIN, AND BRENDA E. BALLACHEY

INTRODUCTION

Oil spilled from ships or other sources into the marine environment often occurs in close proximity to coastlines, and oil frequently accumulates in coastal habitats. As a consequence, a rich, albeit occasionally controversial, body of literature describes a broad range of effects of spilled oil across several habitats, communities, and species in coastal environments. This statement is not to imply that spilled oil has less of an effect in pelagic marine ecosystems, but rather that marine spills occurring offshore may be less likely to be detected, and associated effects are more difficult to monitor, evaluate, and quantify (Peterson *et al.*, 2012). As a result, we have a much greater awareness of coastal pollution, which speaks to our need to improve our capacities in understanding the ecology of the open oceans. Conservation of coastal ecosystems and assessment of risks associated with oil spills can be facilitated through a better understanding of processes leading to direct and indirect responses of species and systems to oil exposure.

It is also important to recognize that oil spilled from ships represents only ~9% of the nearly 700 000 barrels of petroleum that enter waters of North America annually from anthropogenic sources (NRC, 2003). The immediate effects of large spills can be defined as acute, due to the obvious and dramatic effects that are observed. In contrast, the remaining 625 000 barrels that are released each year can be thought of as chronic non-point pollution, resulting from oil entering the coastal ocean as runoff in a more consistent but much less conspicuous rate. In this chapter, we primarily address the effects of large oil spills that occur near coastlines

Coastal Conservation, eds B. Maslo and J. L. Lockwood. Published by Cambridge University Press.

and consider their potential for both acute and chronic effects on coastal communities. As described below, in some instances, the effects from chronic exposure may meet or exceed the more evident acute effects from large spills. Consequently, although quantifying chronic effects from low exposure rates can be challenging and time-consuming, the results of such efforts provide insights into the understudied effects of chronic non-point oil pollution.

Spilled oil can accumulate and persist in coastal habitats, leading to ecosystem-level effects that range from acute to chronic, direct to indirect, and lethal to sublethal. We begin by briefly exploring a range of coastal habitats where large oil spills have occurred and the nature, magnitude, and duration of documented effects that occurred under an array of conditions. This evaluation is not intended to be inclusive or exhaustive, but rather illustrative of the range of habitats, species, and interactions that have been impacted by oil spills and the resulting chronic and indirect effects detected. We next describe some of the challenges inherent in trying to understand the effects of spilled oil in environments where there is often little under-standing of the status, trends, or variability of the system at the time of the spill.

We then turn our focus to work over the past 23 years on the biological effects of, and the process of recovery from, the 1989 tanker vessel (T/V) *Exxon Valdez* oil spill in Prince William Sound and the Gulf of Alaska. To that end we present an overview of the spill and the observed acute, chronic, and cascading or indirect effects, which in some cases have persisted for decades. Realized impacts were dependent on the magnitude and persis-tence of oil in the environment, and the phenology, behavior, trophic dynamics, and social structure of organisms. Acute and direct effects were most obvious and resulted in elevated and often high rates of mortality. Chronic and indirect spill effects were more difficult to detect. Generally, chronic exposure to persistent oil was reflected in reduced levels of individ-ual fitness, resulting in modest changes to survival and reproduction that ultimately modify population growth rates.

We follow this discussion with case histories from four species that demonstrated different vulnerabilities to oil as reflected through habitat, life histories, and behavior, each of which demonstrated protracted periods of recovery. These include the pink salmon (*Oncorhynchus gorbuscha*), killer whale (*Orcina orca*), harlequin duck (*Histrionicus histrionicus*), and sea otter (*Enhydra lutris*). We close by reviewing the lessons learned in responding to the *Exxon Valdez* spill with the intent to improve responses related to biological resources when the next such event occurs.

REVIEW OF PRIOR SPILLS

Although our knowledge of the effects of oil spills in marine environments continues to grow, because of high variability among spills, there are few generalities to be drawn from this body of literature outside of the classifications of shoreline types used to evaluate sensitivity to spilled oil (Gundlach & Hayes, 1978; Gundlach, 2006; Adler & Inmar, 2007). Rocky exposed coasts are generally considered least susceptible, with sensitivity increasing as exposure, sediment size, and slope decrease. In general, marshes, mangroves, and estuaries are considered most sensitive and capable of sequestering oil for decades (Gundlach, 2006), although *Exxon Valdez* oil has persisted in the Gulf of Alaska in both exposed and sheltered unconsolidated sediments for more than two decades (Li & Boufadel, 2010). Multiple factors, including variation in coastal geography and geology, ocean and atmospheric conditions, type, volume and rate of oil spilled, distance from the coast, and composition of biological communities all interact to influence the nature and degree of the disturbance caused by an oil spill (Kingston, 2002).

Low latitude

In 1986, more than 50 000 barrels of crude oil were spilled into nearshore habitats comprised of coral reefs, mangroves, and seagrass beds near Galeta Marine Laboratory in Panama (Jackson *et al.*, 1989). Studies following a previous spill in the same area in 1968, the *Witwater* (Rotzler & Sterrer, 1970), providing an unprecedented baseline of data to support rigorous examination of acute and chronic effects of the 1986 spill across these habitats. The 1986 spill contaminated approximately 82 km of shoreline and affected 16 km² of red mangrove (*Rhizophora mangle*) and 8 km² of intertidal and subtidal reefs. Acute effects of the spill included large-scale mortality of scleractinian corals, with total coral cover reduced by up to 76%, and intertidal sea grasses (*Thallasia testudinum*), but with little apparent effect on subtidal seagrass. Within a few months of the spill, a 27-km band of dead mangroves was evident where oiling had occurred (Jackson *et al.*, 1989). Additionally, a diverse suite of invertebrates, including mussels, barnacles, oysters, and stomatopods (mantis shrimps) exhibited reductions in abundance. Algal assemblages also were affected through acute mortality but recovered to pre-spill abundances within 18 months. Many of the acute effects of the spill and recovery processes were consistent with what was expected from previous spills in tropical shorelines, but other results were not. Duke and colleagues (1997) estimated that sublethal damage to mangroves was 5–6 times greater than direct mortality. The widespread mortality of subtidal corals and invertebrate assemblages associated with seagrasses was unexpected and illustrates the variability in responses to acute oiling of tropical coastlines. This event also illustrates that sublethal exposure to oil and indirect effects can have a marked effect on the structure and function of affected ecosystems. Of particular note was the shift in the size structure of stomatopods, an important prey for many consumers in the system, with smaller individuals dominating the community after the spill. In follow-up work, Guzman and others (1994) found that recovery of corals had not occurred five years after the spill and that lingering oil in the environment was a factor contributing to its reduced fecundity and growth. Long-term persistent oil in coastal mangrove and seagrass sediments was projected to delay recovery of this low-latitude tropical ecosystem by more than 20 years (Burns *et al.*, 1993).

In 2001, the T/V *Jessica* ran aground in the Galapagos Islands off Ecuador, releasing >5000 barrels of diesel and bunker oil (Edgar *et al.*, 2003). Although oiling was evident along shorelines, the effects on algae, invertebrates, fishes, and mammals generally were minor and did not persist (Born *et al.*, 2003; Edgar *et al.*, 2003; Salazar *et al.*, 2003). The moderate volume of spilled oil, a predominantly rocky shoreline, dilution of bunker oil with lighter diesel oil, offshore transport, moderate sea conditions, and warm temperatures were suggested as factors contributing to the minimal effects from this spill (Edgar *et al.*, 2003). One dramatic exception was a decline of 62% in marine iguanas from pre-spill abundance at an island affected by the spill (Wikelski *et al.*, 2002). The iguana decline was attributed to relatively low levels of residual oil in coastal waters that appear to have adversely affected digestive processes in the iguanas' hindgut. This example illustrates the complexity of mechanisms and cascading effects by which spilled oil can affect coastal marine communities.

Mid-latitude

In 2002/2003, the T/V *Prestige* spilled 460 000 barrels of bunker C, a heavy oil, off the northwest coast of Spain, eventually impacting 1000–2500 km of coastline and other marine habitats off the coasts of Portugal, Spain, and France (Juanes *et al.*, 2007; Penela-Aranez *et al.*, 2009). This event was unusual in that the leaking ship was towed 260 km offshore before it broke apart and sank in 3600 m of water, where it continued to release oil for > 8 months. Thirteen taxa, from plankton to seabirds, experienced acute population-level reductions, with most of the documented injuries among intertidal invertebrates, benthic invertebrates, and seabirds (Sanchez *et al.*, 2006; Alonso-Alvarez *et al.*, 2007; Penela-Aranez *et al.*, 2009; Munilla *et al.*,

2011). In one additional case, secondary exposure to oil through contaminated prey was responsible for both adult and egg mortality in the peregrine falcon (*Falco peregrinus*) (Zuberogoitia *et al.*, 2006). Investigations following this spill documented widespread chronic effects, primarily represented through continued exposure to polycyclic aromatic hydrocarbons (PAHs) from the *Prestige*. Chronic exposure in the animals was measured through either biomarkers of exposure or direct measures of tissue PAHs. Species that demonstrated chronic effects included benthic invertebrates, demersal fishes, and seabirds (Perez *et al.*, 2008, 2009; Martinez-Gomez *et al.*, 2009; Vinas *et al.*, 2009). Indirect effects resulting from the spill were noted in several cases. The European shag (*Phalacrocorax aristotolis*) suffered high female-biased direct mortality, which resulted in long-term reductions in reproduction at the population level (Martinez-Abrain *et al.*, 2006). In addition, chronic exposure to PAHs in yellow legged gulls (*Larus michahellis*) was correlated with reduced secondary sexual characteristics that likely resulted in reduced reproductive performance of individuals, potentially lowering population levels (Perez *et al.*, 2009). In a third example, Velando and colleagues (2005) observed a reduction in reproduction and declining chick condition in the European shag, attributed to a spill-induced reduction in its preferred prey, the sand eel (*Ammodytes* spp.). Lastly, Pineira and others (2008) found genetic-level effects on shell traits in the rough periwinkle (*Littorina saxitilis*) consistent with oil exposure. Despite the breadth of taxa that incurred acute or chronic spill effects, Penela-Aranez *et al.* (2009), in a review of the *Prestige* effects on biota, concluded that recovery was evident in less than two years. Alternatively, the work of others clearly indicates that chronic and indirect effects may have persisted and delayed recovery beyond 2004 (Velando *et al.*, 2005; Martinez-Abrain *et al.*, 2006; Martinez-Gomez *et al.*, 2009; Perez *et al.*, 2009).

High latitude

In January 1993, the grounding of the T/V *Braer* released ~600 000 barrels of light crude oil near the rocky shorelines of southern Scotland at approximately 60°N, during a period when high winds and currents and large oceanic swells rapidly dispersed and suspended spilled oil into the water column (Ritchie, 1993). Due to these conditions at the time of the spill, relatively little oil was washed ashore, and only minor or localized effects were detected on intertidal species and communities (Newey & Seed, 1995; Kingston *et al.*, 1996), with limited effects observed on seabirds and marine mammals (Goodlad, 1996; Hall *et al.*, 1996). Rather, it appeared that the oil was suspended in the water column and transported to distant sediment basins, raising PAH levels there up to 150 times greater than background levels (Davies *et al.*, 1996). These contaminated sediments were cause for concern related to the health of finfish and shell fisheries that were closed over an area of 400 km^2 for two years after the spill. Despite the comparatively minor damage documented in this spill, recovery times for affected species were up to a decade (Newey & Seed, 1995). A variety of factors appeared to have contributed to the comparatively low impact of this spill on coastal ecosystems, including a light crude oil, a turbulent sea, and a lack of oil-susceptible beaches, such as low-energy tidelands (Ritchie, 1993). The evidence gathered from this particular spill suggests that pathways of injury to marine ecosystems do not exclusively reside along shorelines and further highlights the fact that we currently have a relatively poor understanding of the mechanisms of damage from oil spilled at sea.

For a variety of reasons it is likely that the full extent of effects of any oil spill in the sea will remain unknown. Some of these reasons include design and statistical issues related to the lack of experimental controls and replication of the treatment (spill effect), and others relate to the repeatability of sampling methods (Weins & Parker, 1995). Perhaps the most common constraint to understanding spill effects, however, is an incomplete understanding and record of the ecosystem prior to the spill, in the form of baseline data. An appropriate baseline would include not only estimates of the numbers, ages, sex, and size of all organisms present, but also the suite of interactions and physical, biological, and ecological processes that resulted in the structure, function, and variability of that community prior to the spill; a tall order indeed. To some extent, proclamations of the lack of effects of spilled oil in marine ecosystems must stem from our limited knowledge of those systems and the various mechanisms of direct and indirect effects generated by spilled oil. However, accumulating evidence from more recent spills, when resources have been made available to explore effects more closely, clearly indicate the complexity of interactions and cascading effects that result from disturbances to ecosystems caused by large oil spills in the ocean (Peterson *et al.*, 2003, 2012). In other words, we suggest that determinations on the lack of effects following spills could result more from our limited ability to detect and measure, rather than from negligible impacts (Kingston, 2002). The biological significance of oil spill effects undoubtedly will continue to be a source of debate.

Administrative, procedural, and legal requirements at different organizational (governmental and corporate) scales present further challenges to improved understanding of oil spill effects. In the case of the *Exxon Valdez* (Paine *et al.*, 1996), state and federal trustees initially focused efforts on assessing the extent of injury caused by the spill, while Exxon Corporation focused on restoration of injured resources. The legal framework at the time of the *Exxon Valdez* spill required that Exxon Corporation pay for damages; therefore, an incentive existed to minimize damages, which pitted corporate-sponsored scientists against government-sponsored scientists, whose legal guidance focused primarily on documenting damage. Competing objectives and legal requirements occasionally produced conflicting conclusions in response to the same questions and at the least precluded scientists from working collaboratively to improve basic knowledge (Paine *et al.*, 1996). By nature, the timing and locations of oil spills are unexpected, and the window of opportunity to acquire pre-event data is limited. Responding entities generally have priorities other than ecological sampling, such as human health, spill containment, clean up, and rehabilitation. The limited capacity and priority of planning to acquire pre-event data remains a constraint to advancing our understanding of the effects of spilled oil on coastal and oceanic marine ecosystems.

THE T/V *EXXON VALDEZ* SPILL

Centered at approximately 60°N and 147°W, Prince William Sound (PWS) is a sub-arctic estuarine embayment of approximately 15 000 km², with more than 5000 km of shoreline. Glaciated fjords dominate the northern Sound with deep basins to > 870 m in depth dominating the central Sound. A complex shoreline results from hundreds of islands, bays and passages composed of rocky benches and unconsolidated sediments from boulder beaches to sheltered bays and estuaries of finer sediments. The marine ecosystem of PWS is influenced by cool temperatures, high precipitation, and glacial inputs. The Alaska coastal current is a dominant oceanographic feature that transports nutrients and productivity into the Sound where the presence of kelp and seagrass beds supplement microalgal production and provide additional habitat for a variety of invertebrates and fishes. The complex habitat and environment in PWS and the adjacent Gulf of Alaska results in diverse marine communities that can be broadly characterized by at least two distinctive food webs. In general, the marine phytoplankton/zooplankton community supports a diverse assemblage of forage fishes and higher trophic-level consumers, such as predatory fishes, seabirds, pinnipeds, and cetaceans. In contrast, a nearshore food web, where kelps and seagrasses supplement phytoplankton production, supports an assemblage of nearshore benthic invertebrates, such as crabs, clams, urchins, and mussels that feed consumers, such as sea ducks, shorebirds, and the sea

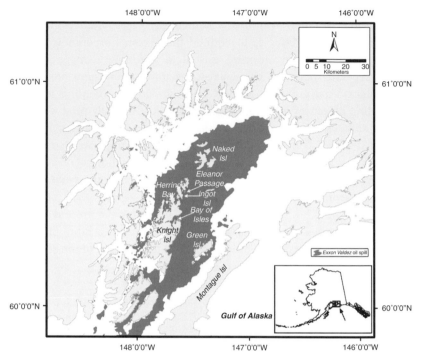

Figure 11.1 Prince William Sound and the area affected by the *Exxon Valdez* oil spill in 1989 (from Monson *et al.*, 2011).

otter. The functional distinction of these two food webs, as well as the life histories and behaviors of individual species, has important implications for the pathways and mechanisms of exposure and both direct and indirect effects of the oil spilled from the *Exxon Valdez* tanker.

On 24 March 1989 the T/V *Exxon Valdez* went aground on Bligh reef in northwest PWS, Alaska (Figure 11.1). The damaged ship eventually spilled an estimated 264 000 barrels of crude oil and ultimately contaminated > 2000 km of shore in PWS and the Gulf of Alaska (Bragg *et al.*, 1994). In the weeks following the spill, ~150 000 barrels of oil washed ashore on beaches in PWS (Wolfe *et al.*, 1994), contaminating 783 km of shoreline (Short *et al.*, 2004). Although oil also contaminated shorelines on the Kenai and Alaska Peninsulas and persisted for more than a decade (Irvine *et al.*, 2006), most of the work on acute, chronic, and indirect effects of the spill on species and communities was conducted in PWS, where we will focus the remainder of this chapter.

The initial acute effects of the spilled oil were dramatic and relatively well documented, at least among birds and mammals, through carcass collections and response activities, with acute mortality estimates of ~250 000 seabirds (Piatt & Ford, 1996), thousands of sea otters, and hundreds of harbor seals (*Phoca vitulina*) (DeGange *et al.*, 1994; Frost *et al.*, 1994a). However, less effort was directed toward quantifying acute mortality among the algae, seagrasses, invertebrates, and fishes, which suffered mortality from both direct oiling as well as clean-up efforts that included highly destructive high-pressure washing in intertidal habitats (Lees *et al.*, 1996).

Based on initial loss rates of oil in the years immediately following the spill, it was assumed that lingering oil would soon be negligible, spill effects would rapidly diminish, and recovery of affected populations would be evident within a few years (Neff *et al.*, 1995). However, long-term monitoring identified both unexpected persistence and magnitude of lingering oil in primarily unconsolidated intertidal sediments and evidence of continuing oil exposure in species of invertebrates, fishes, birds, and mammals occupying nearshore habitats (Peterson *et al.*, 2003; Short *et al.*, 2004). In the following sections, we will review published information on the persistence of lingering oil, the effects of acute and chronic oiling, and the range of mechanisms implicated in both acute and long-term exposure to spilled oil in coastal marine habitats.

LINGERING OIL

In the decade following the spill, several lines of evidence suggested that *Exxon Valdez* oil persisted in unexpected volumes in nearshore habitats and was related to the protracted period of recovery evident for some species. Evidence included both direct observations of oil in the intertidal zone (Hayes & Michel, 1999), the presence of hydrocarbons sequestered in the tissues of bivalves (Babcock *et al.*, 1996; Fukuyama *et al.*, 2000; Carls *et al.*, 2001), and biological responses in fishes, birds, and mammals (Duffy *et al.*, 1994; Trust *et al.*, 2000; Bodkin *et al.*, 2002; Esler *et al.*, 2002, 2011; Golet *et al.*, 2002; Jewett *et al.*, 2002).

In 2001, 12 years after the *Exxon Valdez* spill, Short and colleagues (2004) undertook a comprehensive field study to quantify the amount and distribution of lingering oil in PWS. Nearly 9000 pits were excavated in intertidal substrates that had been described as heavily or moderately oiled during 1989–1993. The team found that both surface residues and subsurface oil persisted on some beaches, including the majority of beaches that were classified as heavily or moderately oiled within four years after the spill. Oil deposits on beach surfaces were highly weathered and largely transformed into asphalt-like material, which was considered to have low toxicity and low bioavailability. However, subsurface oil was liquid and much less weathered than surface residues (Michel & Hayes, 1999; Short *et al.*, 2007), leading to concerns that the subsurface oil might be both bioavailable and toxic. Short *et al.* (2004) estimated that the areal extent of subsurface oil in 2001 was 7.8 ha (95% confidence intervals: 4.1–12.7 ha), and the mass of remaining oil was 55 600 kg (95% CI: 26 100–94 400 kg; one barrel of oil = 131 kg). These values were considered to be moderate underestimates, given several factors that would lead to a low bias (Short *et al.*, 2006). For example, subsurface oil was found lower in the intertidal zone than anticipated, at elevations not sampled during the 2001 effort, leading to an underestimate by ~30% (Short *et al.*, 2006). Despite uncertainty about the exact amount of lingering oil, all estimates were well under 1% of the amount thought to have stranded initially on PWS beaches. However, the mass and volume remaining and the toxic potential of subsurface oil elicited concerns about the effects of lingering oil on wildlife populations. For example, Short and colleagues (2006) reasoned that animals that forage in intertidal habitats, like sea otters and sea ducks, would be likely to encounter subsurface oil on multiple occasions during the course of a year in the most heavily oiled areas.

Subsurface oil on PWS beaches was distributed mainly in the middle to upper intertidal zone, although a significant proportion (~30%) persisted below 1.8 m above mean lower low water (MLLW) (Short *et al.*, 2006; Figure 11.2). Occurrence of subsurface oil in lower intertidal zones raises concerns, as these elevations tend to be biologically richer than upper zones and serve as foraging sites for many vertebrates, including harlequin ducks and sea otters.

Subsurface oil is expected to decline in occurrence and extent over time through disturbance of sediments associated with storm events, foraging by intertidal animals, including sea otters, and other weathering and degradation processes. However, the rate at which attenuation occurs is unknown and presumably becomes progressively lower over time, with oil persisting longest in areas that are least susceptible to depletion processes (Short *et al.*, 2004, 2007). It is well established that some oil currently remains within sediments underlying some beaches of PWS (Li & Boufadel, 2010; Xia & Boufadel, 2011), although the amount of lingering oil, and how much it has declined since estimates were made in 2001 (Short *et al.*, 2004, 2006), are not certain.

Lingering oil from other catastrophic spills has been observed in a number of other environments (Vandermeulen *et al.*, 1982; Corredor *et al.*, 1990; Burns *et al.*, 1993; Vandermeulen & Singh, 1994; Reddy *et al.*, 2002; Bernabeu *et al.*, 2009), suggesting that persistence of lingering oil is not an

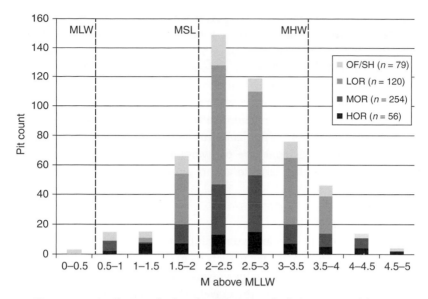

Figure 11.2 Distribution of subsurface lingering oil relative to intertidal zone elevation (*x*-axis, meters above mean lower low water) and oiling intensity (OF/SH, oil film or sheen; LOR, lightly oiled residue; MOR, moderately oiled residue; HOR, heavily oiled residue). The *y*-axis denotes the number of excavated pits meeting the indicated condition (from Short *et al.*, 2006).

issue that is specific to the *Exxon Valdez* spill. However, in the case of the *Exxon Valdez* spill, the extent of research directed at understanding persistence and distribution of lingering oil, as well as effects on wildlife, is unprecedented.

CASE STUDIES FROM THE *EXXON VALDEZ* SPILL

An extensive list of species was affected by the *Exxon Valdez* oil spill, but not all were affected equally. Some, such as the bald eagle (*Haliaeetus leucocephalus*), suffered acute oil-related mortality and reduced reproduction in 1989 but appeared to recover quickly (Bernatowicz *et al.*, 1996). However, a range of mechanisms and pathways of direct and indirect long-term effects from spilled oil on several species were revealed by the research completed in the decades following the spill. A comprehensive review of that research is beyond the scope of this chapter. Instead, we will focus on four species that perhaps reflect the breadth and complexity of mechanisms engaged when considering acute and chronic effects of a large-scale contamination event, such as an oil spill. We caution that the findings and conclusions of some of the research that we will report may not be universally accepted and that alternative conclusions may be found in the peer-reviewed literature (Boehm *et al.*, 2007; Brannon *et al.*, 2007; Harwell *et al.*, 2012). However, our intent here is not to review the various interpretations of data regarding spill effects, but rather to point to the various ways that spilled oil can affect individuals, populations, and ecosystems. While there will always be some level of uncertainty in understanding effects of events, such as oil spills, we believe that the breadth, depth, and duration of study following the *Exxon Valdez* spill clearly demonstrate pathways and mechanisms of potential spill-related effects that serve to aid in preparing for and responding to future events.

Pink salmon

For pink salmon, biology and vulnerability to spilled oil are linked. Pink salmon adults return in the fall to their natal streams, spawn in gravel beds, and embryos/larvae develop in the gravels until the following spring. Young of the year (fry) emerge from the gravel in the spring and are immediately swept downstream to estuarine marine waters where they convert from freshwater to seawater tolerance and from using yolk for energy to predation/feeding. Fry feed along shore for the first month as they migrate to the open ocean, returning as adults 1.3 years later. Spawning streams in PWS are relatively short (most < 1 mile long), but there are > 2000 of them. The most productive spawning habitat is in the intertidal portion of a stream where up to 75% of the spawning occurs. Unfortunately, this prime spawning area places developing embryos in the habitat where most oil was stranded and subsequently persisted. In addition to the potential for oil-exposed embryos, there was concern that out-migrating fry would receive exposure as they dispersed and foraged along contaminated shorelines.

At the time of the spill, fry were beginning to emerge from the spawning gravels, feeding along the shoreline and migrating through the estuaries of PWS. An estimated 31% of the pink salmon spawning streams in the southwest portion of the Sound were oiled to some extent. Acute mortalities of the out-migrating fry were never detected. However, immediate impacts on growth of fry, and on subsequent survival, were detected in 1989. Evidence of oil exposure included tissue PAH concentrations, induction of the biomarker enzyme P450IA (Carls *et al.*, 1996; Willette, 1996), and oil globules observed in stomachs and intestines (Sturdevant *et al.*, 1996). Wild pink salmon fry collected from nearshore waters in oiled areas grew at half the rate of fry from reference areas (Wertheimer & Celewycz, 1996), and Willette (1996) found lower growth in fry released from hatcheries collected in oiled areas than in unoiled sites. By 1990, fry grew comparably in oiled and unoiled reference portions of PWS with no evidence of increased P450IA enzyme induction or tissue hydrocarbons, demonstrating that reduced growth of pink salmon fry in the marine environment was restricted to the initial spill year when the shorelines were heavily contaminated during the migratory period.

In the fall of 1989, elevated pink salmon embryo mortalities were detected in spawning gravels of oiled beaches. This immediate impact was not unexpected as oil was still obvious on many beaches. However, further sampling continued to find elevated embryo mortalities up to four years past the spill (1993), although the differences in mortalities with reference streams declined over time (Bue *et al.*, 1994, 1996, 1998). The observation of mortality several years after the spill was unprecedented and raised questions about the exposure mechanism.

Oil exposure was initially assumed to be negligible as oil did not directly contaminate the spawning habitat (oil floats and the spawning gravels were always underwater). However, the continued elevated embryo mortalities stimulated re-examination of possible exposure mechanisms. Murphy and colleagues (1999) confirmed that lingering oil adjacent to streams was associated with elevated embryo mortalities. Further, embryo mortality was consistent with interstitial drainage of oil-contaminated water into spawning gravels from surrounding stream banks (Carls *et al.*, 2003). Concentrations of PAHs in gravels exposed to oil in this way must be very low, however, raising questions of whether a chronic PAH load would be of any significance.

In response, a series of controlled laboratory exposure tests were conducted to determine if chronic low-level exposure to PAHs could duplicate the field observation of elevated embryo mortalities. Acute toxicity studies prior to the spill required several parts per million to kill embryos (Moles & Rice, 1983), but the mechanism of exposure deduced from the field post-spill indicated that chronic exposure concentrations would be much lower, in the parts per billion (ppb). The embryonic development was long (90 days to hatch, more than 150 to emergence), and the high lipid content of the yolk suggested that long-term sequestering of low-level hydrocarbons was possible. Long-term exposure of embryos to PAH concentrations of 20–50 ppb resulted in increased deformities, slower development, histopathological damage, and lower survival (Marty *et al.*, 1997; Heintz *et al.*, 1999, 2000). Effects at these dose levels were unprecedented in the literature, but exposures were long-term, and the polycyclic composition was elevated (3–4 rings) compared to traditional acute bioassays where

1–2-ringed aromatic hydrocarbons dominated the exposure solutions. Chemical analyses for hydrocarbons in tissues and induction of cytochrome P4501A in embryonic tissues indicated the multi-ringed aromatics were easily permeating the outer egg membranes, resulting in lower growth and survival (Carls *et al.*, 2003).

The sensitivity of embryos to chronic exposure to PAH concentrations of 5–20 ppb was demonstrated through delayed impacts on growth and marine survival (Heintz *et al.*, 1999, 2000). In these experiments, pink salmon embryos were exposed to water contaminated with four different concentrations of PAH and then moved to saltwater pens for growth tests, or they were tagged and released to the environment to assess adult returns 1.3 years later. A delayed effect on growth was measured in juvenile salmon that survived embryonic exposure to a concentration of 18 ppb. Marine survival of salmon fry was tested using coded-wire tags to indicate the exposure dose during the embryonic life stage. Over a year later, the returning adults bearing the tags were decoded and counted to determine survival rates by dose (including controls treated and tagged similarly). Marine survival of pink salmon that had been exposed as embryos to 5 ppb in 1995 was reduced by 16%. Exposure to 19 ppb resulted in a 36% reduction in marine survival, indicating a dose–response relationship. The controlled laboratory exposure tests, followed by further environmental challenges (migration, growth, predation) are unprecedented and demonstrate that low-level exposures (ppb) at the embryonic life stage can affect fitness (growth) and have an impact at the population level (adult returns).

Collectively, the measure of elevated embryo mortality in the five years following the spill, identification of the exposure mechanism from contaminated beaches to spawning gravels, and measured effects on fitness following embryonic exposures provides compelling evidence of chronic impacts from lingering oil. Rice and colleagues (2001) calculated that a modestly sized run that produces 10 million eggs would produce 46 000 fewer adult fish if those eggs were exposed to 19 ppb total PAH. Such concentrations were still present in the interstitial waters of a number of salmon streams in 1995 (Murphy *et al.*, 1999).

Killer whale

Killer whales are considered a cosmopolitan species, found in all oceans. In the north Pacific, the species has been further classified into three distinct ecotypes based on genetics, diet, and behavior. These are referred to as residents, which consume fish exclusively and are organized into well-defined and stable social groups, or pods (Bigg *et al.*, 1990); transients, which consume exclusively mammals; and offshores, which consume numerous fish species, apparently specializing in sharks (Bigg *et al.*, 1990; Ford *et al.*, 1998, 2011; Herman *et al.*, 2005). These ecotypes are morphologically, genetically, acoustically, and dietarily distinct (Matkin *et al.*, 1999; Herman *et al.*, 2005). Killer whales are long-lived, some living over 60 years with females between the ages of about 15 and 40 typically producing a single calf every four to six years (Brault & Casewell, 1993). Although not well understood, it is thought that reproductively senescent females play an important role in maintaining the social structure and dynamics of the pod. Essential to assessing the effects of the *Exxon Valdez* oil spill, resident pods exist within a social organization of matrilines that exhibit no exchange of individuals among matrilines or pods. Some exchange of individuals may occur among transient groups, although this has not occurred within the oil-impacted AT1 transient population of PWS (Matkin *et al.*, 2008).

Understanding the effects of the *Exxon Valdez* spill on killer whales would not have been possible without the five years of data collected prior to 1989. During that period, photo-identification techniques allowed delineation of killer whale pods, including the number, age, and sex of individuals within each pod in PWS and the Gulf of Alaska (Matkin *et al.*, 1994, 2008; Scheel *et al.*, 2001). Additionally, comparable studies from southeast Alaska provided critical contrasts and allowed inferences regarding oil spill effects on killer whale populations and demographics in PWS. Because of the unwavering fidelity of individuals to their matrilines in resident pods and the lack of movement of individuals out of the AT1 transient population, resighting of individuals allowed for estimation of group size, recruitment, and mortality within the resident and transient populations of the region. Baseline data available on this species served to demonstrate the invaluable nature of pre-event data and provided an unprecedented opportunity to evaluate effects of the spill on one of the ocean's top predators.

The *Exxon Valdez* provided one of the first opportunities to evaluate the potential effects of spilled oil on killer whales. Between 1984 and the spill, 11 pods of resident whales and the AT1 population of transient whales were identified and annually censused in PWS and adjacent waters in the Gulf of Alaska (Figure 11.1). During the period prior to the spill there was general stability or a slight increase in the numbers of individuals in most resident pods (Matkin *et al.*, 2008). The AB pod, which was largely resident in PWS, had declined from 28 to 26 individuals during the 5 years prior to the spill, due to the loss of older females and fisheries interactions. The AT1 transient group remained stable at 22 individuals between 1984 and

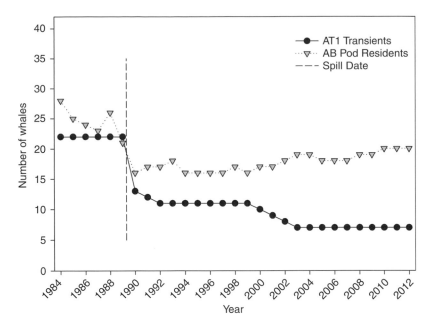

Figure 11.3 The number of killer whales (*Orcina orca*) in the AT1 transient group and AB resident pod, enumerated annually from 1984 to 2012. The vertical line in 1989 indicates the date of the T/V *Exxon Valdez* oil spill. This figure uses data that appeared in Matkin *et al.* (2008) but removes part of the AB pod (six whales) that split off in 1990 following the spill (AB25 pod). The remaining AB pod has not recovered in the 23 years following the spill, with fewer whales in 2012 than prior to the spill in fall 1988.

1989. In the days and weeks following the spill, both groups were documented swimming within the slicks of oil.

Matkin and colleagues (2008) reported a total of 13 mortalities from the AB pod following the spill. However, part of the AB pod (now known as the AB25 pod) split off permanently shortly after the spill. The matrilines, which still travel together and are now considered as the AB pod, lost 10 individuals (38%) following the spill (Figure 11.3). The individuals lost included three sexually mature females and seven juveniles. These are sex and age classes that generally demonstrate very low mortality rates (Olesiuk *et al.*, 2005). Since 1990, the AB pod has not recovered and numbered only 20 individuals in 2012. This annual growth rate of < 1% compares with a growth rate of 3.2% measured across all the unaffected pods in the Gulf of Alaska (Matkin, unpublished data, 2012). The delayed recovery of the AB pod is largely a result of increased mortality of mature and juvenile females shortly after the spill and the resultant decrease in production of calves

(Matkin *et al.*, 2008). However, social disruption resulting from acute oil exposure and mortality of key individuals cannot be ruled out as a factor contributing to delayed recovery and should be worthy of consideration when evaluating the recovery of highly social species.

At least four members of the AT1 population were observed and photographed in the oil within hours of the spill, and three of those four went missing and were eventually presumed dead when they were not resighted in 1990 and the years following (Matkin *et al.*, 2008). Nine of the 22 (41%) AT1 whales have not been observed in the 23 years since the spill and are considered fatalities (Figure 11.3). Additional mortalities reduced the AT1 population to 11 individuals by 1992, half of the pre-spill number, and by 2003 the group was reduced to 7 individuals. There has been no recruitment of calves into the AT1 population since the spill, and they are now listed as depleted under the Marine Mammal Protection Act of 1977.

The loss of 38% and 41% of the AB pod and AT1 group, respectively, following the *Exxon Valdez* spill is unprecedented in the decades of study of killer whales in the north Pacific (Ford *et al.*, 1998). Two avenues of exposure are likely to have caused or contributed to elevated mortality in killer whales, including inhalation of toxic fumes and oil and consumption of contaminated prey (Geraci, 1990; Lipscomb *et al.*, 1994). The latter may be particularly evident among transient whales that feed extensively on smaller marine mammals, such as harbor seals, which were known to have been exposed to and retained oil in fur and tissues (Frost *et al.*, 1994b; Lowry *et al.*, 1994). The lack of discovery of killer whale carcasses following exposure to spilled oil may not be surprising as individuals are known to sink after their death, but it does inject some level of uncertainty in assigning cause of death. However, the weight of evidence provided by Matkin *et al.* (2008) strongly implicates acute exposure to spilled oil as the dominant factor responsible for the declines in these two groups of killer whales.

It is likely that most acute killer whale exposure to oil occurred shortly after the spill, and that even without long-term effects, an extensive demographic lag in replacing lost individuals resulted in a recovery that has stretched over decades. However, the apparent disruption of the social structure of these highly organized groups of animals highlights the complexity of mechanisms and pathways that spilled oil or other sources of mortality can affect marine resources. Also to be considered are the trophic cascades and indirect effects on prey populations (e.g. seals, sea lions, and salmon) resulting from declines of these apex predators (Peterson *et al.*, 2003).

Harlequin duck

Harlequin ducks spend much of their annual life cycle in nearshore marine habitats and demonstrate a high degree of fidelity to relatively small areas of coast (Iverson *et al.*, 2004). As a result, they may not relocate in response to events that diminish the quality of their habitat (Iverson & Esler, 2006). They forage exclusively on marine invertebrates that occur in intertidal and shallow subtidal habitats, which put them in proximity to locations where lingering oil was known to persist (Short *et al.*, 2006). They are demographically characterized by long life spans (to 20 years) and low reproductive potential coupled with high adult survival. As a consequence, population dynamics are sensitive to even slight changes in adult survival. Overwintering in high-latitude marine environments, such as PWS, harlequin ducks exist close to their energetic threshold, which provides little margin for increasing caloric intake to meet elevated metabolic demands (Esler *et al.*, 2002), such as those resulting from exposure to PAHs.

For harlequin ducks, a number of factors indicated lack of recovery for the first decade after the *Exxon Valdez* oil spill, including reduced densities on oiled areas, numerical declines on oiled areas in concert with stable numbers on unoiled areas, and evidence of continued exposure to lingering oil (Trust *et al.*, 2000; Esler *et al.*, 2002). However, the most troubling finding was a significant depression of adult female winter survival on oiled relative to unoiled areas from 1995 to 1998 (Esler *et al.*, 2000; Figure 11.4). A similar study from 2000 to 2003 found that winter survival rates for both young and adult female harlequin ducks was similar between oiled and unoiled areas (Esler & Iverson, 2010; Figure 11.5), suggesting that the direct survival effects of lingering oil had subsided by this time.

Harlequin duck survival, as well as other demographic information including movements and fecundity, were compiled in a population model to estimate the timeline and process of population recovery (Iverson & Esler, 2006, 2010). Model results suggested that elevated female mortality, although likely highest during the first year after the spill, persisted for more than a decade and the mortality associated with the chronic phase of the spill (estimated at 772 females) was higher than the number estimated to have died during the first year after the spill (400 females). The harlequin duck population model also estimated that the most plausible timeline to full population recovery was 24 years (i.e. by the year 2013), with a range of 16–32 years (2005–2021) under best- and worst-case scenarios, respectively (Iverson & Esler, 2010; Figure 11.6).

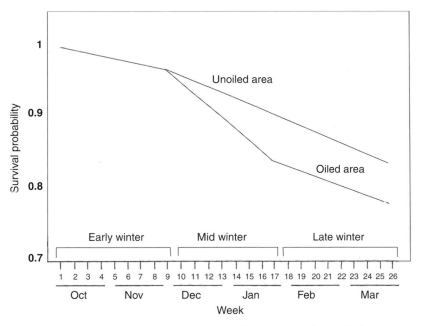

Figure 11.4 Cumulative winter survival probability of adult female harlequin ducks (*Histrionicus histrionicus*) in oiled and unoiled areas of Prince William Sound, Alaska, during 1995 to 1998 (from Esler *et al.*, 2000).

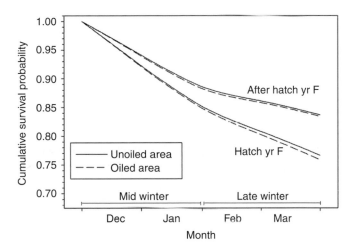

Figure 11.5 Cumulative winter survival probability of adult (after hatch year) and juvenile (hatch year) female harlequin ducks (*Histrionicus histrionicus*) in oiled and unoiled areas of Prince William Sound, Alaska, during 2000–2003 (from Esler & Iverson, 2010).

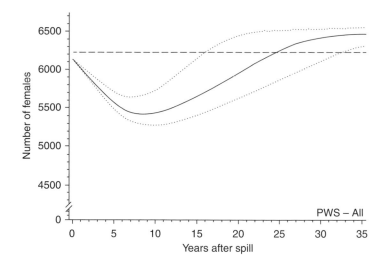

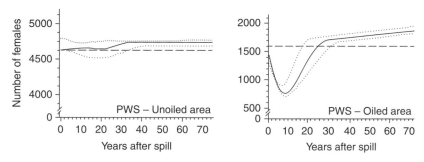

Figure 11.6 Results of a population model exercise projecting timeline to recovery of harlequin duck (*Histrionicus histrionicus*) numbers to pre-spill estimates (dashed line) following the 1989 *Exxon Valdez* oil spill. The solid line represents the most likely outcome, and dotted lines represent best- and worst-case scenarios, based on different permutations of model inputs (from Iverson & Esler, 2010).

Studies of harlequin ducks have generated the most complete data series evaluating cytochrome P4501A (CYP1A) induction since the *Exxon Valdez* oil spill. CYP1A is induced upon exposure to a limited number of compounds, including PAHs, and is widely used as a biomarker of oil exposure. In 1998, nine years after the spill, harlequin ducks from oiled areas of PWS had indicators of CYP1A that averaged nearly three times higher than those from unoiled areas (Trust *et al.*, 2000). Similar patterns were observed through 2009 (Esler *et al.*, 2010), suggesting that some harlequin ducks continued to be exposed to lingering *Exxon Valdez* oil for up to 20 years post-spill.

Unlike killer whales, for which acute oil exposure and mortality and subsequent demographic lags seems to be the most important factor constraining population recovery, harlequin duck population recovery was influenced by persistent, chronic exposure to oil that had demographic consequences for at least a decade after the spill. The importance of chronic exposure and the effects offers a novel perspective of the various mechanisms of population-level effects of oil spills, as well as insights to potential mechanisms of effects of chronic exposure to non-point source pollution.

Sea otter

Sea otters are non-migratory residents of shallow nearshore marine habitats of the north Pacific, mostly defined by the intertidal zone out to about the 40-m depth contour. Individuals display high fidelity to a relatively small annual home-range, which is usually from 10 to 100 km². Adult male sea otters defend small exclusive territories from other males, and female home-ranges can overlap several male territories. Because of small home-ranges with high site fidelity, the sea otter is susceptible to local disturbances or modifications to habitat at relatively small spatial scales (Bodkin & Ballachey, 2010). Adults have high survival. Females usually give birth to a single pup annually, and both sexes may live up to 20 years. These life-history attributes render populations sensitive to relatively small increases in adult mortality. Their habitat is defined by their need and ability to dive to the sea floor where they prey nearly exclusively on large benthic marine invertebrates, including bivalves, gastropods, echinoderms, and crustaceans. Most foraging takes place in shallow waters < 40 m in depth (Bodkin *et al.*, 2004). In soft sediment habitats, clams that require excavation can account for a high proportion of their diet. Lastly, reliance on dense fur and a high metabolic rate require that a sea otter consume ~25% of its own body mass daily, providing little latitude to increase energy intake in response to environmental stress, including that resulting from oil-contaminated habitat.

A number of lines of evidence indicate that sea otter populations suffered deleterious effects of the *Exxon Valdez* oil spill during both the acute and chronic stages of the spill (Bodkin *et al.*, 2002). Estimates of sea otter mortality due to acute effects of the oil spill in western PWS ranged from 750 to 2650 animals (Garrott *et al.*, 1993; Garshelis, 1997). The disparity among acute mortality estimates largely reflects the lack of accurate pre-spill estimates of sea otter population size. Using population models, Udevitz and colleagues (1996) predicted recovery of the western PWS sea otter population in 10–23 years, with maximum annual growth rates from

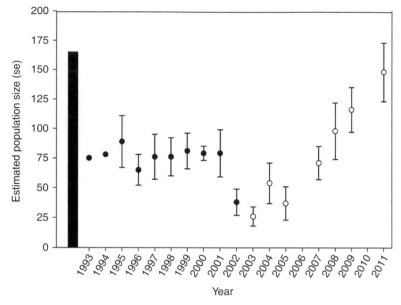

Figure 11.7 Results of aerial surveys to assess the recovery of sea otters (*Enhydra lutris*) following the 1989 *Exxon Valdez* oil spill. The survey area includes islands in the northern Knight Island Archipelago, from Herring Bay to Bay of Isles (Figure 11.1), where sea otter mortality approached 90% (Bodkin & Udevitz, 1994). The black bar reflects the estimated population size at the time of the spill based on the number of carcasses and live oiled animals removed for rehabilitation. White symbols represent the data used to estimate population growth (from Bodkin *et al.*, 2011).

10% to 14%. In the first decade post-spill, numbers of sea otters remained depressed at the heavily oiled northern Knight Island region (Figure 11.7), while recovery was evident to some extent through increases in abundance in areas less severely affected by oil (Figure 11.8). Also, population models based on age distributions of dead otters indicated that the survival of sea otters was depressed for at least a decade after the *Exxon Valdez* oil spill (Monson *et al.*, 2000).

Causes for the delayed recovery of sea otters residing in previously oiled habitats are likely related to elevated mortality rather than reduced reproduction (Bodkin *et al.*, 2002). Linkages between oil and increased mortality are documented in two studies. Ballachey and colleagues (2003) documented elevated juvenile sea otter mortality in oiled areas of PWS compared to unoiled areas. Monson and colleagues (2000, 2011) constructed mortality models based on ages at death acquired both prior to and after the spill. Elevated mortality was evident in animals that were alive at

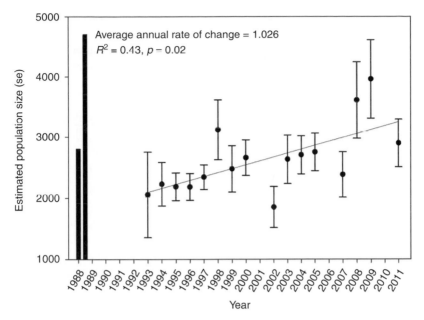

Figure 11.8 Results of aerial surveys to assess the recovery of sea otters (*Enhydra lutris*) following the 1989 *Exxon Valdez* oil spill in western Prince William Sound. The black bars reflect a range of possible pre-spill population sizes based on acute mortality estimates added to the 1993 estimate. The black bars reflect a range of possible pre-spill population sizes based on acute mortality estimates added to the 1993 estimate (from Bodkin *et al.*, 2011).

the time of the spill, as well as among those born after the spill, implicating lingering oil as a contributing factor (Monson *et al.*, 2000, 2011). Monson and colleagues (2011) estimated that the mortality associated with chronic exposure or long-term effects of acute exposure was 900 animals, suggesting that chronic exposure mortality was similar in magnitude to the known immediate, acute mortality represented by the number of carcasses recovered in 1989 following the spill.

While mechanisms of mortality related to acute oil exposure were evident through stranded live sea otters and carcass collections during the spill (Lipscomb *et al.*, 1994), pathways of exposure to relatively small amounts of lingering oil in the decades following the spill were not readily discerned. Sea otters excavate sediments when they forage for some prey, including clams, which constitute ~75% of their diet in PWS (Dean *et al.*, 2002). Sea otter foraging excavations routinely disturb sediments at depths below which lingering oil occurs (Short *et al.*, 2004). Therefore, if sea otters forage at sites with patches of lingering oil, they are likely to be exposed either through consumption of prey that have assimilated hydrocarbons or by disturbing oiled sediments and releasing lingering oil (Fukuyama *et al.*, 2000), which could then adhere to their fur and subsequently be ingested upon grooming. Bodkin and colleagues (2012) evaluated the degree of spatial and temporal overlap of foraging otters and lingering oil to determine whether these were plausible pathways of exposure.

Based on sea otters with abdominally-implanted time and depth recorders, Bodkin and colleagues (2012) found that, of more than a million foraging dives, most (82%) were subtidal and not a risk for encountering lingering oil. However, all individuals ($N = 19$) foraged in intertidal zones at least some of the time, averaging between 8 and 91 intertidal foraging dives per day. Within the intertidal zone, foraging dives occurred most frequently at lower elevations, where lingering oil was less common (Figure 11.2), but an average of 3–38 dives per day occurred at elevations > 1.8 m above MLLW, where most lingering oil persisted. Based on these foraging data and the distribution of lingering oil during 2001 and 2003 (Short *et al.*, 2004, 2006), Bodkin and colleagues (2012) estimated that sea otters would encounter subsurface lingering oil an average of 10 times each year, ranging from 2 to 24 times, depending on individual foraging routines (Figure 11.9). Perhaps more

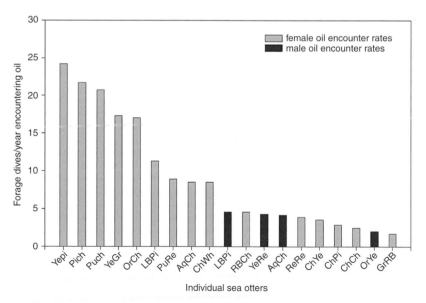

Figure 11.9 Estimated number of foraging dives per year in which individual sea otters (*Enhydra lutris*; $N = 19$) would encounter lingering, subsurface oil in intertidal zones of Prince William Sound, Alaska (from Bodkin *et al.*, 2012).

importantly, there was a strong seasonal component to intertidal foraging, with a pronounced peak from late spring to early summer. This is the period when most adult females will have small pups, making them most likely to encounter oil when they are least prepared physiologically to deal with the added metabolic costs associated with oil contamination.

Bodkin and colleagues (2012) also observed sea otter foraging excavations on soft sediment beaches within the heavily oiled northern Knight Island area, including beaches that were known to contain patches of lingering oil. Further, some sediment samples taken from or near sea otter foraging pits were determined to have elevated levels of PAHs. Collectively, the results of Bodkin and colleagues (2012) confirm that sea otter exposure to sequestered oil via their foraging activities was a likely pathway. These findings indicate that, as a function of their extensive foraging activity, the population of sea otters in the northern Knight Island area may have been an important agent in disruption and depletion of patches of lingering oil through their estimated excavation of more than a million intertidal pits annually (Bodkin *et al.*, 2012).

As another indicator of occurrence and effects of oil exposure, a technique for measuring differential gene expression in response to hydrocarbon exposure has been developed based on laboratory studies with mink (*Mustela vison*) (Bowen *et al.*, 2007). Gene transcript profiles indicated that sea otters from PWS in 2008 had differential transcription relative to those from captive and wild reference areas (Figure 11.10). Particularly for those otters captured near northern Knight Island, there were a number of genes with elevated transcription, including those related to tumor formation, cell death, inflammation, and heat shock (Miles *et al.*, 2012). These patterns were consistent with variation in gene expression of mink exposed to oil in lab studies (Bowen *et al.*, 2007), suggestive of exposure of sea otters to lingering *Exxon Valdez* oil and compromised health and physiological functioning (Miles *et al.*, 2012). Some of the factors indicated by differential gene expression (e.g. tumor formation) could be the result of historical, not necessarily contemporary, exposure in these long-lived animals.

In summary, sea otter populations residing in the path of spilled oil suffered high rates of mortality through acute exposure, resulting in large-scale declines in abundance that unexpectedly persisted for more than two decades. As a result of behavior that structures sea otter populations in relatively small geographical areas, those animals residing in habitats where lingering oil was sequestered in shallow sediments had potential access to that oil. Relying on a diet that is dominated by several species of clam that burrow in shallow sediments provided a direct pathway to

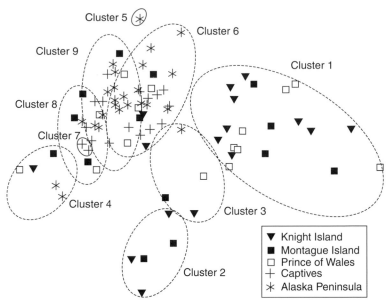

Figure 11.10 Multivariate, non-parametric, multidimensional scaling of gene transcription profiles of sea otters (*Enhydra lutris*) sampled at three locations in Prince William Sound, Alaska, at the Alaska Peninsula, and in captivity at aquaria. Statistics indicated significant separation among all clusters. Clusters 1 through 3 were dominated by sea otters from Prince William Sound, particularly heavily oiled Knight Island (from Miles *et al.*, 2012).

lingering oil. Chronic exposure to oil and possibly latent acute exposure effects apparently led to elevated mortality, contributing to a recovery period of more than two decades. Processes of population injury and recovery were very similar between sea otters and harlequin ducks, suggesting that ecological attributes may be stronger predictors of vulnerability to oil spill effects than taxonomic relationships.

LESSONS LEARNED

A diverse array of factors contribute to the magnitude, duration, and recovery from effects of marine oil spills, including the type of oil; magnitude, timing, rate, and duration of the spill; environmental conditions; and the physical, biological, and ecological conditions over which the spill occurs. Because of unique complexities and uncertainties associated with individual spills, predicting the full range of effects from future spills will remain problematic. However, the experience and knowledge gained from several decades of research into the effects of spills across a wide range of conditions provides lessons that may be used to better prepare for and document the effects of future spills. In the following three paragraphs we present our thoughts on generalities and lessons to be drawn from the literature on spills. In the final three paragraphs, we provide concluding remarks on our experiences specifically with the *Exxon Valdez*.

Initial short-term acute responses to oil spills and contamination of the shorelines are predictable and were most often reflected in direct mortality of birds and mammals. However, for most marine species (e.g. kelps and seagrasses, invertebrates, reptiles, and fishes), even acute effects remain poorly understood and require additional attention in preparation and response to future spills. Sublethal and chronic effects can lead to reduced fitness that may be translated into reduced survival rates, ultimately affecting recovery of injured populations. Long-term consequences of spills are significant, less predictable, and will remain difficult to document, and should be considered as potentially equal or greater in importance to acute effects.

If there is a single consistent message from those scientists that have studied the effects of past oil spills, it is that the lack of baseline data is the greatest single impediment to understanding the effects of spilled oil on marine ecosystems. Our ability to accurately and defensibly determine the effects of future oil spills on ecosystems, communities, and individuals, and subsequent recovery processes, will be determined largely on the quantity and quality of data available to describe the affected systems prior to the spill. Because ecosystems and populations are dynamic at various spatial and temporal scales, baseline data from one or more unaffected, or reference populations, immediately prior to the perturbation will be essential. Attempts to describe spill effects in the absence of baseline data for affected and unaffected populations will lead to uncertainty in conclusions and will be subjected to the valid criticism of an inadequate experimental design to assign cause to effect. Additionally, lack of accurate and defensible baseline data on populations hampers definition of meaningful restoration endpoints.

The work done to date associated with past spills highlights the diverse and often unpredicted pathways and mechanisms by which spilled oil affects marine ecosystems. It is not simply acute contamination of individual organisms that constitutes spill effects, but rather the complex interactions between the presence and persistence of oil in the environment and the ways in which it can affect organisms and communities. The examples from the *Exxon Valdez* we review above illustrate this complexity and highlight the need to consider and explore potential interactions between oil and individuals in the context of basic biology, behavior, and ecology.

Long-term oil persistence can lead to long-term consequences. The lack of recovery of sea otters and harlequin ducks in specific areas of PWS was alarming and after several years of study, was eventually linked to the presence of toxic subsurface oil. The apparent pathway of exposure was through diet and foraging behavior and mediated through the fitness of individuals causing relatively modest reductions in survival rates, rather than acute mortalities like those that were easily detected in the first months of the spill. Nevertheless, a localized population effect was detected, and full recovery was hampered for nearly two decades. In both sea otters and harlequin ducks, chronic mortality was nearly equal to or exceeded acute mortality. Response to future spills requires consideration of the potential for long-term consequences from persistent oil in the environment and from persistent effects from acute oil mortality, such as the disruption to the social structure and future reproduction in killer whale pods.

Recovery is dependent on many factors, including chemical recovery of the habitat and species' reproductive biology. Full recovery of pink salmon, sea otters, and harlequin ducks could not happen until the chronic contamination of lingering oil abated. Pink salmon, with high fecundity (2500 eggs per female) and a short life history (2 years), rebounded quickly when habitat oil exposure was removed. In contrast, long-lived/low reproductive potential species, such as the killer whale, may take decades to fully recover, if at all. Although the species affected by future spills will differ, biology, behavior, and ecology of affected species and communities should inform planning and response efforts in terms of the potential for both acute and long-term spill effects.

Lastly, we return to the finding that spills from transporting oil in marine waters represent only ~9% of the total amount of anthropogenic sources of oil entering the environment, and ultimately the oceans, where it is deposited in nearshore habitats. Evidence from laboratory experiments and acute marine oil spills clearly points to the adverse effects of elevated PAHs on both the fitness and health of individual organisms; yet accepting and understanding the potential for chronic oil exposure effects from the 91% of oil that enters the environment via human activities other than marine spills remains a challenge. The results of studies directed at monitoring the process of population recovery from chronic exposure effects of large oil spills provides a new perspective that demonstrates the potential for adverse effects from chronic oil pollution in coastal communities.

REFERENCES

Adler, E. & Inmar, M. (2007). Shoreline sensitivity to oil spills, the Mediterranean coast of Israel: Assessment and analysis. *Ocean and Coastal Management*, **50**, 24–34.

Alonso-Alvarez, C., Cristobol, P. & Velando, A. (2007). Effects of acute exposure to heavy fuel oil from the *Prestige* spill on a seabird. *Aquatic Toxicology*, **84**, 103–110.

Babcock, M. M., Irvine, G. V., Harris, P. M., Cusick, J. A. & Rice, S. D. (1996). Persistence of oiling in mussel beds three and four years after the *Exxon Valdez* oil spill. In S. D. Rice, R. B. Spies, D. A. Wolfe & B. A. Wright (eds.), *Proceedings of the Exxon Valdez Oil Spill Symposium*. Bethesda, MD: American Fisheries Society Symposium 18, pp. 286–297.

Ballachey, B. E., Bodkin, J. L., Howlin, S., Doroff, A. M. & Rebar, A. H. (2003). Correlates to survival of juvenile sea otters in Prince William Sound, Alaska. *Canadian Journal of Zoology*, **81**, 1494–1510.

Bernabeu, A., Rey, D., Rubio, B., *et al.* (2009). Assessment of cleanup needs of oiled sand beaches: Lessons from the *Prestige* oil spill. *Environmental Science and Technology*, **43**, 2470–2475.

Bernatowicz, J. A., Schemph, P. F. & Bowman, T. D. (1996). Bald eagle productivity in south-central Alaska in 1989 and 1990 after the *Exxon Valdez* oil spill. In S. D. Rice, R. B. Spies, D. A. Wolfe & B. A. Wright (eds.), *Proceedings of the Exxon Valdez Oil Spill Symposium*. Bethesda, MD: American Fisheries Society Symposium 18, pp. 785–797.

Bigg, M. A., Olesiuk, P. F., Ellis, G. M., Ford, J. K. B. & Balcomb, K. C. B. (1990). Social organization and genealogy of resident killer whales (*Orcinus orca*) in the coastal waters of British Columbia and Washington state. *Report to the International Whaling Commission, Special Issue*, **12**, 386–406.

Bodkin, J. L. & Ballachey, B. E. (2010). *Modeling the Effects of Mortality on Sea Otter Populations*. US Geological Survey Scientific Investigation Report 2010–5096. Reston, VA: US Geological Survey.

Bodkin, J. L. & Udevitz, M. S. (1994). Intersection model for estimating sea otter mortality along the Kenai Peninsula. In T. Loughlin (ed.), *Marine Mammals and the Exxon Valdez*. San Diego, CA: Academic Press, pp. 81–95.

Bodkin, J. L., Ballachey, B. E., Dean, T. A., *et al.* (2002). Sea otter population status and the process of recovery from the *Exxon Valdez* oil spill. *Marine Ecology Progress Series*, **241**, 237–253.

Bodkin, J. L., Esslinger, G. G. & Monson, D. H. (2004). Foraging depths of sea otters and implications to coastal marine communities. *Marine Mammal Science*, **20**, 305–321.

Bodkin, J. L., Ballachey, B. E. & Esslinger, G. G. (2011). *Trends in Sea Otter Population Abundance in Western Prince William Sound, Alaska: Progress Toward Recovery Following the 1989 Exxon Valdez Oil Spill*. US Geological Survey Scientific Investigations Report 2011–5213. Reston, VA: US Geological Survey.

Bodkin, J. L., Ballachey, B. E., Coletti, H. A., *et al.* (2012). Long-term effects of the *Exxon Valdez* oil spill: Sea otter foraging in the intertidal as a pathway of exposure to lingering oil. *Marine Ecology Progress Series*, **447**, 273–287.

Boehm, P. D., Page, D. S., Neff, J. M. & Johnson, C. B. (2007). Potential for sea otter exposure to remnants of buried oil from the *Exxon Valdez* oil spill. *Environmental Science and Technology*, **41**, 6860–6867.

Born, A. F., Espinoza, E., Murillo, J. C., Nicolaides, F. & Edgar, G. J. (2003). Effects of the *Jessica* oil spill on artisanal fisheries in the Galapagos. *Marine Pollution Bulletin*, **47**, 319–324.

Bowen, L., Schwartz, J., Aldridge, B., *et al.* (2007). Differential gene expression induced by exposure of captive mink to fuel oil: A model for the sea otter. *EcoHealth*, **4**, 298–309.

Bragg, J. R., Prince, R. C., Harner, E. J. & Atlas, R. M. (1994). Effectiveness of bioremediation for the *Exxon Valdez* oil spill. *Nature*, **368**, 413–418.

Brannon, E. L., Collins, K. C., Cronin, M. A., *et al.* (2007). Risk of weathered residual *Exxon Valdez* oil to pink salmon embryos in Prince William Sound. *Environmental Toxicology and Chemistry*, **26**, 780–786.

Brault, S. & Caswell, H. (1993). Pod-specific demography of killer whales (*Orcinus orca*). *Ecology*, **74**, 1444–1454.

Bue, B. G., Sharr, S., Moffitt, S. D. & Craig, A. (1994). Assessment of injury to pink salmon embryos and fry. *Proceedings of the 16th Northeast Pacific Pink and Chum Salmon Workshop*, AK-SG-94-02. Fairbanks, AK: Alaska Sea Grant College Program, pp. 173–176.

Bue, B. G., Sharr, S., Moffitt, S. D. & Craig, A. (1996). Effects of the *Exxon Valdez* oil spill on pink salmon embryos and pre-emergent fry. In S. D. Rice, R. B. Spies, D. A. Wolfe & B. A. Wright (eds.), *Proceedings of the* Exxon Valdez *Oil Spill Symposium*. Bethesda, MD: American Fisheries Society Symposium 18, pp. 619–627.

Bue, B. G., Sharr, S. & Seeb, J. E. (1998). Evidence of damage to pink salmon populations inhabiting Prince William Sound, Alaska, two generations after the *Exxon Valdez* oil spill. *Transactions of the American Fisheries Society*, **127**, 35–43.

Burns, K. A., Garrity, S. D. & Levings, S. C. (1993). How many years until mangrove ecosystems recover from catastrophic oil spills? *Marine Pollution Bulletin*, **26**, 239–248.

Carls, M. G., Wertheimer, A. C., Short, J. W., Smolowitz, R. M. & Stegeman, J. J. (1996). Contamination of juvenile pink and chum salmon by hydrocarbons in Prince William Sound after the *Exxon Valdez* oil spill. In S. D. Rice, R. B. Spies, D. A. Wolfe & B. A. Wright (eds.), *Proceedings of the* Exxon Valdez *Oil Spill Symposium*. Bethesda, MD: American Fisheries Society Symposium 18, pp. 608–618.

Carls, M. G., Babcock, M. M., Harris, P. M., *et al.* (2001). Persistence of oiling in mussel beds after the *Exxon Valdez* oil spill. *Marine Environmental Research*, **51**, 167–190.

Carls, M. G., Marty, G. D. & Rice, S. D. (2003). Is pink salmon spawning habitat recovering from the *Exxon Valdez* oil spill? In *Proceedings of the Twenty-sixth Arctic and Marine Oilspill Program (AMOP) Technical Seminar*, 10–12 June 2003. Victoria, British Columbia: Environment Canada, vol. 1, pp. 335–248.

Corredor, J. E., Morell, J. M. & Del Castillo, C. E. (1990). Persistence of spilled crude oil in a tropical environment. *Marine Pollution Bulletin*, **21**, 385–388.

Davies, J. M., McIntosh, A. M., Stagg, R. M. & Topping, G. (1996). The impact of an oil spill in turbulent waters. In J. M. Davies & G. Topping (eds.), *The Braer*. Edinburgh: HMSO, pp. 26–4.

Dean, T. A., Bodkin, J. L., Fukuyama, A. K., *et al.* (2002). Food limitation and the recovery of sea otters in Prince William Sound. *Marine Ecology Progress Series*, **241**, 255–270.

DeGange, A. R., Doroff, A. M. & Monson, D. H. (1994). Experimental recovery of sea otter carcasses at Kodiak Island, Alaska, following the *Exxon Valdez* oil spill. *Marine Mammal Science*, **10**, 492–496.

Duffy, L. K., Bowyer, R. T., Tests, J. W. & Faro, J. B. (1994). Chronic effects of the *Exxon Valdez* oil spill on blood and enzyme chemistry of river otters. *Environmental Toxicology and Chemistry*, **13**, 643–647.

Duke, C., Zuleika, S., Pinzon, M. & Prada T., M. C. (1997). Large scale damage to mangrove forests following two large oil spills in Panama. *Biometrica*, **29**, 2–14.

Edgar, G. J., Kerrison, L., Scoresby, S. A. & Toral-Granda, M. V. (2003). Impacts of the *Jessica* oil spill on intertidal and shallow subtidal plants and animals. *Marine Pollution Bulletin*, **47**, 276–283.

Esler, D. & Iverson, S. A. (2010). Female harlequin duck winter survival 11 to 14 years after the *Exxon Valdez* oil spill. *Journal of Wildlife Management*, **74**, 471–478.

Esler, D., Schmutz, J. A., Jarvis, R. L. & Mulcahy, D. M. (2000). Winter survival of adult female harlequin ducks in relation to history of contamination by the *Exxon Valdez* oil spill. *Journal of Wildlife Management*, **64**, 839–847.

Esler, D., Bowman, T. D., Trust, K. A., *et al.* (2002). Harlequin duck population recovery following the *Exxon Valdez* oil spill: Progress, process and constraints. *Marine Ecology Progress Series*, **241**, 271–286.

Esler, D., Ballachey, B. E., Trust, K. A., *et al.* (2011). Cytochrome P4501A biomarker indication of the timeline of chronic exposure of Barrow's goldeneyes to residual *Exxon Valdez* oil. *Marine Pollution Bulletin*, **62**, 609–614.

Ford, J. K. B., Ellis, G. M., Barrett-Lennard, L. G., Morton, A. B. & Balcomb III, K. B. C. (1998). Dietary specialization in two sympatric populations of killer whales (*Orcinus orca*) in coastal British Columbia and adjacent waters. *Canadian Journal of Zoology*, **76**, 1456–1471.

Ford, J. K. B., Ellis, G. M., Matkin, C. O., *et al.* (2011). Shark predation and tooth wear in a population of northeastern Pacific killer whales. *Aquatic Biology*, **11**, 213–224.

Frost, K. J., Lowry, L. F., Sinclair, E. H., Ver Hoef, J. & McAllister, D. C. (1994a). Impacts on distribution, abundance and productivity of harbor seals. In T. R. Loughlin (ed.), *Marine Mammals and the* Exxon Valdez. San Diego, CA: Academic Press, pp. 97–118.

Frost, K. J., Manen, C. & Wade, T. L. (1994b). Petroleum hydrocarbons in tissues of harbor seals from Prince William Sound and the Gulf of Alaska. In T. R. Loughlin (ed.), *Marine Mammals and the* Exxon Valdez. San Diego, CA: Academic Press, pp. 331–358.

Fukuyama, A. K., Shigenaka, G. & Hoff, R. Z. (2000). Effects of residual *Exxon Valdez* oil on intertidal *Protothaca staminea*: Mortality, growth, and bioaccumulation of hydrocarbons in transplanted clams. *Marine Pollution Bulletin*, **40**, 1042–1050.

Garrott, R. A., Eberhardt, L. L. & Burn, D. M. (1993). Mortality of sea otters in Prince William Sound following the *Exxon Valdez* oil spill. *Marine Mammal Science*, **9**, 343–359.

Garshelis, D. L. (1997). Sea otter mortality estimated from carcasses collected after the *Exxon Valdez* oil spill. *Conservation Biology*, **11**, 905–916.

Geraci, J. R. (1990). Physiologic and toxic effects on cetaceans. In J. R. Geraci & D. J. St, Daubin (eds.), *Sea Mammals and Oil: Confronting the Risks*. New York, NY: Academic Press, pp. 167–197.

Golet, G. H., Seiser, P. E., McGuire, A. D., *et al.* (2002). Long-term direct and indirect effects of the *Exxon Valdez* oil spill on pigeon guillemots in Prince William Sound, Alaska. *Marine Ecology Progress Series*, **241**, 287–304.

Goodlad, J. (1996). Effects of the *Braer* oil spill on the Shetland seafood industry. *Science of the Total Environment*, **186**, 127–133.

Gundlach, E. R. (2006). Oil spills: Impacts, recovery and remediation. *Journal of Coastal Resources*, Special Issue, **39**, 39–42.

Gundlach, E. R. & Hayes, M. O. (1978). Classification of coastal environments in terms of potential vulnerability to oil spill damage. *Marine Technology Society Journal*, **12**, 18–27.

Guzman, H. M., Burns, K. A. & Jackson, J. B. C. (1994). Injury, regeneration and growth of Caribbean reef corals after a major oil spill in Panama. *Marine Ecology Progress Series*, **105**, 231–241.

Hall, A. J., Watkins, J. & Hiby, L. (1996). The impact of the 1993 *Braer* oil spill on grey seals in Shetland. *Science of the Total Environment*, **186**, 119–125.

Harwell, M. A., Gentile, J. H. & Parker, K. R. (2012). Quantifying population-level risks using an individual-based model: Sea otters, harlequin ducks, and the *Exxon Valdez* oil spill. *Integrated Environmental Assessment and Management*, **8**, 503–522.

Hayes, M. O. & Michel, J. (1999). Factors determining the long-term persistence of *Exxon Valdez* oil in gravel beaches. *Marine Pollution Bulletin*, **38**, 92–101.

Heintz, R. A., Short, J. W. & Rice, S. D. (1999). Sensitivity of fish embryos to weathered crude oil: Part II. Incubating downstream from weathered *Exxon Valdez* crude oil caused increased mortality of pink salmon (*Oncorhynchus gorbuscha*) embryos. *Environmental Toxicology and Chemistry*, **18**, 494–503.

Heintz, R. A., Rice, S. D., Wertheimer, A. C., *et al.* (2000). Delayed effects on growth and marine survival of pink salmon *Oncorhynchus gorbuscha* after exposure to crude oil during embryonic development. *Marine Ecology Progress Series*, **208**, 205–216.

Herman, D. P., Burrows, D. G., Wade, P. R., *et al.* (2005). Feeding ecology of eastern North Pacific killer whales *Orcinus orca* from fatty acid, stable isotope, and organochlorine analyses of blubber biopsies. *Marine Ecology Progress Series*, **302**, 275–291.

Irvine, G. V., Mann, D. H. & Short, J. W. (2006). Persistence of ten-year old *Exxon Valdez* oil on Gulf of Alaska beaches: The importance of boulder armoring. *Marine Pollution Bulletin*, **52**, 1011–1022.

Iverson, S. A. & Esler, D. (2006). Site fidelity and the demographic implications of winter movements by a migratory bird, the harlequin duck *Histrionicus histrionicus*. *Journal of Avian Biology*, **37**, 219–228.

Iverson, S. A. & Esler, D. (2010). Harlequin duck population injury and recovery dynamics following the 1989 *Exxon Valdez* oil spill. *Ecological Applications*, **20**, 1993–2006.

Iverson, S. A., Esler, D. & Rizzolo, D. J. (2004). Winter philopatry of harlequin ducks in Prince William Sound, Alaska. *Condor*, **106**, 711–715.

Jackson, C. B. C., Cubit, J. D., Keller, B. D., *et al.* (1989). Ecological effects of a major oil spill on Panamanian coastal marine communities. *Science*, **243**, 37–44.

Jewett, S. C., Dean, T. A., Woodin, B. R., Hoberg, M. K. & Stegeman, J. J. (2002). Exposure to hydrocarbons ten years after the *Exxon Valdez* oil spill: Evidence from cytochrome P450lA expression and biliary FACs in nearshore demersal fishes. *Marine Environmental Research*, **54**, 21–48.

Juanes, J. A., Puente, A. & Revilla, J. A. (2007). The *Prestige* oil spill in Cantabria (Bay of Biscay), Part II. Environmental assessment and monitoring of coastal ecosystems. *Journal of Coastal Research*, **23**, 978–992.

Kingston, P. F. (2002). Long-term environmental impact of oil spills. *Spill Science and Technology Bulletin*, **1**, 53–61.

Kingston, P. F., Dixon, I. M. T., Hamilton, S. & Moore, D. C. (1996). The impact of the *Braer* oil spill on the macrobenthic infauna of the sediments off the Shetland Islands. *Marine Pollution Bulletin*, **30**, 445–459.

Lees, D. C., Houghton, J. P. & Drickell, W. B. (1996). Short-term effects of several types of shoreline treatment on rocky intertidal biota in Prince William Sound. In S. D. Rice, R. B. Spies, D. A. Wolfe & B. A. Wright (eds.), *Proceedings of the Exxon Valdez Oil Spill Symposium*. Bethesda, MD: American Fisheries Society Symposium 18, pp. 329–348.

Li, H. L. & Boufadel, M. C. (2010). Long-term persistence of oil from the *Exxon Valdez* spill in two-layer beaches. *Nature Geoscience*, **3**, 96–99.

Lipscomb, T. K., Harris, R. K., Rebar, A. H., Ballachey, B. E. & Haebler, R. J. (1994). Pathology of sea otters. In T. R. Loughlin (ed.), *Marine Mammals and the* Exxon Valdez. San Diego, CA: Academic Press, pp. 265–280.

Lowry, L. F., Frost, K. J. & Pitcher, K. W. (1994). Observations of oiling of harbor seals in Prince William Sound. In T. R. Loughlin (ed.), *Marine Mammals and the* Exxon Valdez. San Diego, CA: Academic Press, pp. 209–225.

Martinez-Abrain, A., Velando, A., Oro, D., *et al.* (2006). Sex specific mortality of European shags after the *Prestige* oil spill: Demographic implications for the recovery of colonies. *Marine Ecology Progress Series*, **318**, 271–276.

Martinez-Gomez, C., Fernandez, B., Valdeset, J., *et al.* (2009). Evaluation of three-year monitoring with biomarkers in fish following the *Prestige* oil spill (N Spain). *Chemosphere*, **74**, 613–620.

Marty, G. D., Short, J. W., Dambach, D. M., *et al.* (1997). Ascites, premature emergence, increased gonadal cell apoptosis, and cytochrome P450lA induction in pink salmon larvae continuously exposed to oil-contaminated gravel during development. *Canadian Journal of Zoology*, **75**, 989–1007.

Matkin, C. O., Ellis, G. M., Dahlheim, M. E. & Zeh, J. (1994). Status of killer whale pods in Prince William Sound 1984–1992. In T. R. Loughlin (ed.), *Marine Mammals and the* Exxon Valdez. San Diego, CA: Academic Press, pp. 141–161.

Matkin, C. O., Ellis, G. M., Saulitis, E. L., Barrett-Lennard, L. & Matkin, D. R. (1999). *Killer Whales of Southern Alaska*. Homer, AK: North Gulf Oceanic Society.

Matkin, C. O., Saulitis, E. L., Ellis, G. M., Olesiuk, P. & S. D. Rice (2008). Ongoing population-level impacts on killer whales *Orcinus orca* following the *Exxon Valdez* oil spill in Prince William Sound, Alaska. *Marine Ecology Progress Series*, **356**, 269–281.

Michel, J. & Hayes, M. O. (1999). Weathering patterns of oil residues eight years after the *Exxon Valdez* oil spill. *Marine Pollution Bulletin*, **38**, 855–863.

Miles, A. K., Bowen, L., Ballachey, B. E., *et al.* (2012). Variation in transcript profiles in sea otters (*Enhydra lutris*) from Prince William Sound, Alaska and clinically normal reference otters. *Marine Ecology Progress Series*, **451**, 201–212.

Moles, A. & Rice, S. D. (1983). Effects of crude oil and naphthalene on growth, caloric content and fat content of pink salmon juveniles in seawater. *Transactions of the American Fisheries Society*, **112**, 205–211.

Monson, D. H., Doak, D. F., Ballachey, B. E., Johnson, A. & Bodkin, J. L. (2000). Long-term impacts of the *Exxon Valdez* oil spill on sea otters, assessed through age-dependent mortality patterns. *Proceedings of the National Academy of Sciences of the United States of America*, **97**, 6562–6567.

Monson, D. H., Doak, D. F., Ballachey, B. E. & Bodkin, J. L. (2011). Effect of the *Exxon Valdez* oil spill on the sea otter population of Prince William Sound, Alaska: Do lingering oil and source–sink dynamics explain the long-term population trajectory? *Ecological Applications*, **21**, 2917–2932.

Munilla, I., Arcos, J. M., Oro, D., *et al.* (2011). Mass mortality of seabirds in the aftermath of the *Prestige* oil spill. *Ecosphere*, **2**(7), art. 83.

Murphy, M. L., Heintz, R. A., Short, J. W., Larsen, M. L. & Rice, S. D. (1999). Recovery of pink salmon spawning after the *Exxon Valdez* oil spill. *Transactions of the American Fisheries Society*, **128**, 909–918.

Neff, J. M., Owens, E. H., Stoker, S. W. & McCormick, D. M. (1995). Shoreline oiling conditions in Prince William Sound following the *Exxon Valdez* oil spill. In P. G. Wells, J. N. Butler & J. S. Hughes (eds.), Exxon Valdez *Oil Spill: Fate and Effects in Alaskan Waters*. Philadelphia, PA: American Society for Testing and Materials, pp. 312–346.

Newey, S. & Seed, R. (1995). The effects of the *Braer* oil spill on rocky intertidal communities in south Shetland, Scotland. *Marine Pollution Bulletin*, **30**, 274–280.

NRC, National Research Council. (2003). *Oil in the Sea III: Inputs, Fates, and Effects.* Washington, DC: National Academies Press.

Olesiuk, P. F., Ellis, G. M. & Ford, J. K. B. (2005). *Life History and Population Dynamics of Northern Resident Killer Whales* (Orcinus orca) *in British Columbia.* Ottawa: Canadian Science Advisory Secretariat.

Paine, R. T., Ruesink, J. L., Sun, A., *et al.* (1996). Trouble on oiled waters: Lessons from the *Exxon Valdez* oil spill. *Annual Review of Ecology, Evolution and Systematics*, **27**, 197–235.

Penela-Aranez, M., Bellas, J. & Vasquez, E. (2009). Effects of the *Prestige* oil spill on the biota of NW Spain: 5 years of learning. *Advances in Marine Biology*, **56**, 365–396.

Perez, C., Velando, A., Munilla, I., Lopez-Alonso, M. & Oro, D. (2008). Monitoring polycyclic aromatic hydrocarbon pollution in the marine environment after the *Prestige* oil spill by means of seabird blood analysis. *Environmental Science and Technology*, **42**, 707–713.

Perez, C., Munilla, I., Lopez-Alonso, M. & Velando, A. (2009). Sublethal effects on seabirds after the *Prestige* oil-spill are mirrored in sexual signals. *Biology Letters*, **6**, 33–35.

Peterson, C. H., Rice, S. D., Short, J. W., *et al.* (2003). Long-term ecosystem response to the *Exxon Valdez* oil spill. *Science*, **302**, 2082–2086.

Peterson, C. H., Anderson, S. S., Cherr, G. N., *et al.* (2012). A tale of two spills: Novel science and policy implications of an emerging new oil spill model. *Bioscience*, **62**, 461–469.

Piatt, J. F. & Ford, R. G. (1996). How many seabirds were killed by the *Exxon Valdez* oil spill? In S. D. Rice, R. B. Spies, D. A. Wolfe & B. A. Wright (eds.), *Proceedings of the* Exxon Valdez *Oil Spill Symposium.* Bethesda, MD: American Fisheries Society Symposium 18, pp. 712–719.

Pineira, J., Quesada, H., Rolan-Alvarez, E. & Caballero, A. (2008). Genetic impact of the *Prestige* oil spill in wild populations of a poor dispersal marine snail from intertidal rocky shores. *Marine Pollution Bulletin,* **56**, 270–281.

Reddy, C. M., Eglinton, T. I., Hounshell, A., *et al.* (2002). The West Falmouth oil spill after thirty years: The persistence of petroleum hydrocarbons in marsh sediments. *Environmental Science and Technology,* **36**, 4754–4760.

Rice, S. D., Thomas, R. E., Heintz, R. A., *et al.* (2001). Impacts to pink salmon following the *Exxon Valdez* oil spill: Persistence, toxicity, sensitivity, and controversy. *Reviews in Fishery Science,* **9**, 165–211.

Ritchie, W. (1993). Environmental impacts of the *Braer* oil spill and development of a strategy for the monitoring of change and recovery. *Marine Policy,* **17**, 434–440.

Rotzler, K. & Sterrer, W. (1970). Oil pollution: Damage observed in tropical communities along the Atlantic seaboard of Panama. *Bioscience,* **20**, 222–224.

Salazar, S. (2003). Impacts of the *Jessica* oil spill on sea lion (*Zalophus wollebaeki*) populations. *Marine Pollution Bulletin,* **47**, 313–318.

Sanchez, F., Velascoa, F., Cartesb, J. E., *et al.* (2006). Monitoring the *Prestige* oil spill impacts on some key species of the Northern Iberian shelf. *Marine Pollution Bulletin,* **53**, 332–349.

Scheel, D., Matkin, C. O. & Saulitis, E. L. (2001). Distribution of killer whales pods in Prince William Sound, Alaska over a thirteen year period, 1984–1996. *Marine Mammal Science,* **17**, 555–569.

Short, J. W., Lindeberg, M. R., Harris, P. A., *et al.* (2004). Estimate of oil persisting on beaches of Prince William Sound, 12 years after the *Exxon Valdez* oil spill. *Environmental Science and Technology,* **38**, 19–25.

Short, J. W., Maselko, J. M., Lindeberg, M. R., Harris, P. M. & Rice, S. D. (2006). Vertical distribution and probability of encountering intertidal *Exxon Valdez* oil on shorelines of three embayments within Prince William Sound, Alaska. *Environmental Science and Technology,* **40**, 3723–3729.

Short, J. W., Irvine, G. V., Mann, D. H., *et al.* (2007). Slightly weathered *Exxon Valdez* oil persists in Gulf of Alaska beach sediments after 16 years. *Environmental Science and Technology,* **41**, 1245–1250.

Sturdevant, M. V., Wertheimer, A. C. & Lum, J. L. (1996). Diets of juvenile pink and chum salmon in oiled and non-oiled nearshore habitats in Prince William Sound, 1989 and 1990. In S. D. Rice, R. B. Spies, D. A. Wolfe & B. A. Wright (eds.), *Proceedings of the* Exxon Valdez *Oil Spill Symposium.* Bethesda, MD: American Fisheries Society Symposium 18, pp. 578–592.

Trust, K. A., Esler, D, Woodin, B. R. & Stegeman, J. J. (2000). Cytochrome P4501A induction in sea ducks inhabiting nearshore areas of Prince William Sound, Alaska. *Marine Pollution Bulletin,* **40**, 397–403.

Udevitz, M. S., Ballachey, B. R. & Bruden, D. L. (1996). *A Population Model for Sea Otters in Western Prince William Sound. Exxon Valdez* Oil Spill State/Federal Restoration Final Report, Restoration Study 93043–3. Anchorage, AK: National Biological Service.

Vandermeulen, J. H. & Singh, J. G. (1994). Arrow oil spill, 1970–90: Persistence of 20-yr weathered bunker C fuel oil. *Canadian Journal of Fisheries and Aquatic Sciences,* **51**, 845–855.

Vandermeulen, J. H., Platt, H. M., Baker, J. M. & Southward, J. Y. (1982). Some conclusions regarding the long-term biological effects of some major spills. *Philosophical Transactions of the Royal Society of London*, **297**, 335–351.

Velando, A., Munilla, I. & Leyenda, P. M. (2005). Short-term indirect effects of the *Prestige* oil spill on European shags: Changes in availability of prey. *Marine Ecology Progress Series*, **302**, 263–274.

Vinas, L., Franco, M. A., Soriano, J. A., *et al.* (2009). Accumulation trends of petroleum hydrocarbons in commercial shellfish from the Galician coast (NW Spain) affected by the *Prestige* oil spill. *Chemosphere*, **75**, 534–541.

Weins, J. A. & Parker, K. R. (1995). Analyzing the effects of accidental environmental impacts: Approaches and assumptions. *Ecological Applications*, **5**, 1069–1083.

Wertheimer, A. C. & Celewycz, A. G. (1996). Abundance and growth of juvenile pink salmon in oiled and non-oiled locations of western Prince William Sound after the *Exxon Valdez* oil spill. In S. D. Rice, R. B. Spies, D. A. Wolfe & B. A. Wright (eds.), *Proceedings of the* Exxon Valdez *Oil Spill Symposium.* Bethesda, MD: American Fisheries Society Symposium 18, pp. 509–517.

Wikelski, M., Wong, V., Chevalier, B., Rattenborg, N. & Snell, H. L. (2002). Galapagos Islands: Marine iguanas die from trace oil pollution. *Nature*, **417**, 607–608.

Willette, M. (1996). Impacts of the *Exxon Valdez* oil spill on migration, growth, and survival of juvenile pink salmon in Prince William Sound. In S. D. Rice, R. B. Spies, D. A. Wolfe & B. A. Wright (eds.), *Proceedings of the* Exxon Valdez *Oil Spill Symposium.* Bethesda, MD: American Fisheries Society Symposium 18, pp. 533–550.

Wolfe, D. A, Hameedi, M. J., Galt, J. A., *et al.* (1994). The fate of the oil spilled from the *Exxon Valdez*. *Environmental Science and Technology*, **28**, 561A–568A.

Xia, Y. Q. & Boufadel, M. C. (2011). Beach geomorphic factors for the persistence of subsurface oil from the *Exxon Valdez* spill in Alaska. *Environmental Monitoring and Assessment*, **183**, 5–21.

Zuberogoitia, I., Martinez, J. A., Iraeta, A., *et al.* (2006). Short-term effects of the *Prestige* oil spill on the peregrine falcon (*Falco peregrinus*). *Marine Pollution Bulletin*, **52**, 1176–1181.

12

Overexploitation of marine species and its consequences for terrestrial biodiversity along coasts

LAWRENCE J. NILES, AMANDA D. DEY, AND
BROOKE MASLO

OVEREXPLOITATION, TROPHIC SKEW, AND THE CROSSOVER BETWEEN MARINE AND TERRESTRIAL SYSTEMS

The overexploitation of marine species for resource consumption is one of the most serious threats to coastal biodiversity. Examples of historic fisheries collapse are numerous (e.g. Boreman *et al.*, 1997; Myers *et al.*, 1997; Liu & De Mitcheson, 2008), and the unsustainable harvest of many species continues today (Coll *et al.*, 2008). Nearly 60% of global fishery stocks are collapsed or overexploited, with another ~33% fully exploited (Froese *et al.*, 2012), and the demand for fish for dietary protein is ever increasing (Pauly *et al.*, 2002). Species losses appear biased toward higher trophic levels, with total biomass of marine predatory fish reduced by at least 80% in many marine ecosystems (Pauly *et al.*, 1998, Worm & Duffy, 2003). This phenomenon is largely due to increased body mass and low reproductive rate (Byrnes *et al.*, 2007). However, recent analyses suggest that fisheries collapse is biased toward small, low trophic-level species (Pinsky *et al.*, 2011). In either case, overharvesting has severe direct impacts on targeted species.

The non-random loss of marine species also has several indirect impacts on marine ecosystems, including habitat loss and altered food webs (Botsford *et al.*, 1997; Jackson *et al.*, 2001). Prior research has focused on the top-down effects of the loss of marine predators. Reductions of top consumers can skew the distribution of biodiversity toward lower trophic-level species, affecting ecosystem function in several ways (Reynolds & Bruno, 2012). For example, in the Gulf of Maine, the loss of predator diversity in seagrass beds increased organic sediment loads (Duffy *et al.*, 2003). In addition, the

Coastal Conservation, eds B. Maslo and J. L. Lockwood. Published by Cambridge University Press.
© Cambridge University Press 2014.

overharvesting of top and intermediate consumers, combined with the introduction of lower trophic-level non-native species, has suppressed the recruitment of many native fish species (Levin *et al.*, 2002).

Impacts of marine species overexploitation can cross over to terrestrial ecosystems, affecting the functioning of a wide range of habitats. For example, the annual salmon (*Oncorhynchus* spp.) migration and spawning event in the Pacific Northwest is essential to the productivity of coastal freshwater systems. As the large-bodied salmon spawn and then die, massive amounts of ocean-derived energy and nutrients are deposited in these habitats, supporting organisms on all trophic levels (Gresh *et al.*, 2000). Pacific salmon have experienced long-term declines due to fishing, greatly reducing nutrient inputs to terrestrial ecosystems (Schindler *et al.*, 2003). The effects of these reductions are poorly understood, but evidence suggests that the impact to terrestrial biodiversity and productivity may be severe (Schindler *et al.*, 2003). Similarly, reductions of 40–80% of commercially harvested blue crabs (*Callinectes sapidus*) in southeast US and Gulf coast estuaries have resulted in massive die-offs of salt marsh cordgrass (*Spartina alterniflora*) by releasing the grazing marsh periwinkle (*Littoraria irrorata*) from predation pressure (Silliman & Bertness, 2002).

An understudied but potentially widespread impact of trophic skew is the removal of marine organisms that represent seasonal resource pulses for terrestrial species. Pulsed marine prey, such as the spawning runs of many marine and anadromous fishes, transcend biological realms and can affect both ecosystem function and predator population dynamics (Yang, 2004). Utilization of pulsed resources by predators has been shown to increase the breeding success of Stellar's sea lions (*Eumetopias jubatus*) and black (*Ursus americanus*) and brown bears (*U. arctos*), enhance survival of juvenile bald eagles (*Haliaeetus leucocephalus*), and fuel the migration of Thayer's gulls (*Larus thayeri*) and other migratory species (Willson *et al.*, 1998; Womble *et al.*, 2005). As suggested by Willson and Womble (2006), the overexploitation of these and other marine pulse species may have profound effects on those predators that rely on them.

Here we describe a now well-documented example of the catastrophic effect of the loss of a marine pulse species, the horseshoe crab (*Limulus polyphemus*), on a long-distance migratory shorebird, the red knot (*Calidris canutus rufa*). Incorporating the clash of socioeconomic factors, the influence of the fishing industry on the regulatory process, and the power of public perception, we present a case study on the overexploitation of horseshoe crabs and the consequential deterioration of the Delaware Bay migratory stopover.

THE DELAWARE BAY SHORE: A CRITICAL STOPOVER FOR MIGRATORY SHOREBIRDS

The Delaware Bay lies at the mouth of the Delaware River (Figure 12.1), between the US states of New Jersey and Delaware, and its shoreline consists of a mosaic of mudflats, salt marsh, and tidal creeks that are fringed with sandy beaches. Considered one of the most prominent migratory shorebird

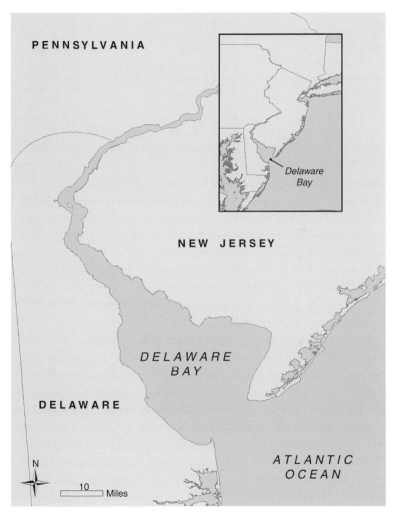

Figure 12.1 Delaware Bay lies at the mouth of the Delaware River between the US states of New Jersey and Delaware. Its shoreline is a mosaic of salt marsh, mudflats, and tidal creeks, fringed with sandy beaches.

Table 12.1 *Shorebird species using Delaware Bay as a migratory stopover. Species in bold type are largely dependent on horseshoe crab (*Limulus polyphemus*) eggs to achieve the weight gain necessary to fuel their flight to the Arctic breeding grounds.*

Species		Seasonal
American oystercatcher	*Haematopus palliatus*	YR
Black-bellied plover	*Pluvialis squatarola*	Sp, F, W
Curlew sandpiper	*Calidris ferruginea*	Sp (rare)
Dunlin	***Calidris alpina***	**Sp, F, W**
Least sandpiper	*Calidris minutilla*	Sp, F
Red knot	***Calidris canutus rufa***	**Sp**
Ruddy turnstone	***Arenaria interpres***	**Sp, F**
Sanderling	***Calidris alba***	**Sp, F, W**
Semipalmated plover	*Charadrius semipalmatus*	Sp, F
Semipalmated sandpiper	***Calidris pusilla***	**Sp, F**
Short-billed dowitcher	***Limnodromus griseus***	**Sp, F, W**
Whimbrel	*Numenius phaeopus*	Sp, F
Willet	*Tringa semipalmata*	Sp, Su, F

YR, year-round; Sp, spring; Su, summer; F, fall; W, winter.

stopovers in the US, the Delaware Bay historically supported some of the highest shorebird abundances recorded for the lower 48 states (Clark *et al.*, 1993). Delaware Bay is considered a stopover of *Hemispheric Importance* by the Western Hemisphere Shorebird Reserve Network (WHSRN), a *Wetland of International Importance* by the Ramsar Convention, and a globally significant *Important Bird Area* by BirdLife International (Mizrahi *et al.*, 2009; WHSRN, 2011). It joins the Wadden Sea (Netherlands) and Yellow Sea (China) as one of the top three ecologically valuable shorebird stopovers in the world (Senner & Howe, 1984).

Surveys conducted in 1991 estimated a total abundance of 1.5 million shorebirds using Delaware Bay (hereafter "the Bay") as a migratory stopover (Niles *et al.*, unpublished data), representing at least 13 species (Table 12.1). Five of these species rely heavily on the seasonal resource pulse provided by a single prey item, the eggs of the horseshoe crab, to fuel the last leg of their migration to their Arctic breeding grounds (Table 12.1; Myers, 1986; Castro & Myers, 1993; Tsipoura & Burger, 1999). The red knot relies almost solely on them (Tsipoura & Burger, 1999; Haramis *et al.*, 2007). The majority of the *rufa* subspecies of red knot uses Delaware Bay (Harrington, 2001), making the survival of the population critically dependent on the resource pulse provided by breeding horseshoe crabs.

Horseshoe crabs are marine arthropods that rely on low-energy beaches for successful breeding. Each spring, individuals leave overwintering areas along the Atlantic Continental Shelf and come into the Bay to spawn in May and early June before returning again to the ocean depths (Swan, 2005). Females come ashore at least twice (at the full and new moon high tides) and lay several clutches of eggs that sit approximately six inches deep in the sand. Males strongly compete to fertilize eggs, with a single male attached to a female and several satellite males surrounding her. These satellite males can fertilize 40–74% of the eggs in a clutch, providing greater genetic diversity in the offspring (Brockman, 2003). This significant evolutionary advantage is perhaps one reason why horseshoe crabs have persisted for > 445 million years (Rudkin *et al.*, 2008).

Although no baseline estimates of the Delaware Bay horseshoe crab population exist, local citizens described historic spawning events as "cobbling", where the vast numbers of crabs blanketing the beach made it look like an urban cobblestone street. With each female laying ~80 000 eggs, this plentiful pulse resource was enough to allow a shorebird to double its weight in less than two weeks (Tsipoura & Burger, 1999; Harrington, 2001; Haramis, 2003). In the early 1990s, mean egg densities were >50 000 eggs per square meter in the surface layer of sand (top 5 cm), with even greater numbers beneath the surface (Botton *et al.*, 1994). Continuous spawning activity caused bioturbation of the eggs, bringing them to the surface of the sand where they were readily available to foraging shorebirds (Jackson *et al.*, 2002; Smith, 2007).

Red knots, in particular, fly up to 10 000 miles from wintering areas as far south as Tierra del Fuego, South America. Their migration is timed to arrive in Delaware Bay precisely when horseshoe crabs are spawning (Harrington, 2001; Niles *et al.*, 2010), taking full advantage of this pulse event. In the past, the shores of the Bay were awash in high-fat content prey, allowing the red knots to attain the weight necessary for the final leg of the journey to the Arctic tundra. It was an elegant system resting on improbably unrelated ecological factors, and prior to the early 1990s it seemed immune to an immediate threat (Niles *et al.*, 2009). Rather, the more contemplated threats to this resource were oil spills, habitat destruction, and the lack of reliable scientific information (Delaware Bay Shorebird Working Group, 1992).

AN ELEGANT SYSTEM UNRAVELED: THE LOSS OF A MARINE PULSE RESOURCE AND ITS IMPACT ON SHOREBIRD SURVIVAL

The drastic decline of horseshoe crabs began with a seemingly unrelated phenomenon occurring well outside of Delaware Bay. Overfishing of Atlantic cod (*Gadus morhua*) in New England led to the collapse of that fishery in the early 1990s (Myers & Mertz, 1997), which put tremendous economic strain on cod fishermen. Looking for another fishery to sustain their livelihoods, fishermen began harvesting channeled (*Busycotypus canaliculatus*) and knobbed whelks (*Busycon carica*), commonly referred to as conch, and American eels (*Anguilla rostrata*) for overseas markets. The horseshoe crab provided an easy and inexpensive source of bait for commercial conch and eel pots. Female horseshoe crabs were, and continue to be, the preferred bait for American eel pots because allegedly horseshoe crab eggs make better bait. The > 400 million-year-old horseshoe crab suddenly had a profitable use and was free for the taking in the many bays along the US mid-Atlantic coast. Because horseshoe crabs were not previously harvested for commercial uses, they were unregulated and unprotected when the bait harvest exploded, and crab harvests prior to 1998 went largely unreported. Even though whelks are harvested marine species, their populations are not managed, and their harvest continues to be unregulated.

The nucleus of the horseshoe crab breeding population occurs in Delaware Bay. By 1995, fishermen from New England and the mid-Atlantic region were harvesting crabs on Delaware Bay beaches, also taking advantage of the crabs as a pulse resource. By 1997, coast-wide horseshoe crab harvests (Maine to Florida) reached three million, nearly two million from the Delaware Bay population alone (NJDEP, 2012; Figure 12.2). Models suggest that between the mid-1990s and 2003, the number of horseshoe crabs in the Bay declined by 7% each year (Davis *et al.*, 2006), with the population showing signs of collapse as early as 1997 (Michels *et al.*, 2011).

The collapse of the horseshoe crab population led to a virtual disappearance of their eggs on Bay beaches. By 2002, average crab egg densities on the surface of New Jersey beaches fell from the 50 000/m^2 observed in the mid-1980s and early 1990s to 2618/m^2 (Botton *et al.*, 1994; Hernandez, 2012). Compounding the problem, without large numbers of crabs digging up the beach, the relatively few eggs that were laid remained buried in the sand and thus inaccessible to knots and other shorebirds. Due to the reduced success rate of knots foraging for eggs buried in the sand, egg densities must exceed 19 000/m^2 to be energetically profitable for red knots (Gillings *et al.*, 2007). A portion of the red knot population, mainly individuals that winter in areas of southeastern US and the Caribbean and migrate a short distance, could feed on ephemeral mussel spat and ocean bivalves as an alternative on their stopover stay in the Bay. However, the majority of the red knot population winters in Tierra del Fuego, at the southern tip of South America. These long-distance migrants reduce their

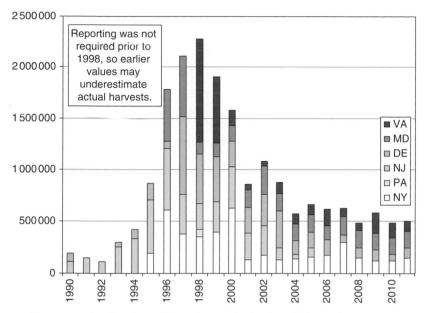

Figure 12.2 Landing data of horseshoe crab (*Limulus polyphemus*) harvests, 1990–2011. *Data source*: National Marine Fisheries Service.

digestive organs for long flights, and many do not arrive at the Bay until mid-May or later, leaving them less able to digest hard-shelled prey and only 10–12 days to double body weight before they must complete their migration (Piersma *et al.*, 2005). Suitable weight gain for these individuals, therefore, is achievable only on easily digested, fat-rich horseshoe crab eggs.

The sudden and dramatic reduction in horseshoe crab eggs resulted in significantly diminished weight gains for red knots and other shorebird species. At the start of the crab collapse in 1997, red knots were gaining 4 g per day while at the Bay for stopover, with individuals arriving later in May gaining at a rate of 2–3 times more (maximum 15 g per day). In 2003 and 2005, later-arriving knots could not achieve high rates of mass gain because of inadequate food supply (Niles *et al.*, 2008), and the consequences were catastrophic.

Without this pulse resource, shorebird numbers on Delaware Bay declined substantially between the mid-1990s and the mid-2000s. In 1982 and again in 1989, researchers counted > 90 000 red knots on Delaware Bay, but that number dropped to < 50 000 by the early 2000s and just above

Table 12.2 *Trends in the number of shorebirds recorded from aerial surveys of Delaware Bay beaches, 1998–2007.*

Variable	Ruddy turnstone	Semipalmated sandpiper	Sanderling	Short-billed dowitcher	Dunlin	All
Slope	−8145	−3017	−1039	−849	−1057	14.106
P value	0.001	0.545	0.102	0.097	0.424	0.071
Decline (%)	77	28	48	64	29	50

Niles *et al.*, 2009.

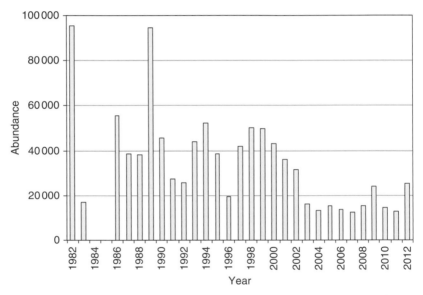

Figure 12.3 Peak counts of red knots (*Calidris canutus rufa*) in Delaware Bay during spring stopover, 1982–2012. Counts between 1982–2008 and 2010–2011 were conducted by air. Counts in 2009 and 2012 were conducted on the ground.

12 000 in 2011 (Dey *et al.*, 2012; Figure 12.3). Other species' numbers declined as well. Ruddy turnstones regularly peaked at > 100 000 birds during the 1980s and 1990s, but currently number < 15 000 individuals. The population of semipalmated sandpipers that passes through Delaware Bay has declined by 43%, and similar declines have been noted for least sandpiper (*Calidris minutilla*), dunlin, and short-billed dowitcher (Morrison *et al.*, 2006; Bart *et al.* 2007). Overall, migratory shorebird populations on Delaware Bay fell by an estimated > 50% (Niles *et al.*, 2009; Table 12.2).

HORSESHOE CRAB HARVESTS AND THEIR REGULATION

Shorebird researchers were warning of the imminent collapse of the Delaware Bay stopover as early as 1997, but a concrete understanding of the critical trophic link between red knots and horseshoe crabs did not yet exist. While it was obvious that the crab fishery needed to be managed, regulators were not yet convinced of the dire situation now present for red knots and other migratory shorebirds. At the time, no published studies on the importance of marine pulse resources to terrestrial species existed; therefore, conservationists could not point to other examples as precedents (Willson & Womble, 2006). Some regional and state regulations were enacted to conserve horseshoe crab stock levels in an effort to appease both sides (Mizrahi *et al.*, 2009). New Jersey imposed a temporary 2-year moratorium on the rapidly rising horseshoe crab harvest, and the US Atlantic States Marine Fisheries Commission (ASMFC), the agency responsible for marine fish management in state waters, adopted a horseshoe crab Fishery Management Plan (ASMFC, 1998). However, tensions between conservationists and fisheries managers were rising.

The modest protective measures within the horseshoe crab management plan failed to adequately protect the crabs from overharvest for three reasons. First, the main purpose of fisheries regulatory organizations is to manage the populations of commercially or recreationally valuable fish species; therefore, there was no immediate fisheries incentive for creating a horseshoe crab management plan until shorebird population declines became obvious. Second, the ASMFC used reported harvests from the early and mid-1990s as the reference period, or benchmark landings, to develop the fishery management plan. They proposed a 25% harvest reduction, which amounted to reducing take by < 500 000 crabs out of a total coastwide harvest of 3 million (ASMFC, 1998, 2002). Unfortunately, the population was so heavily exploited during these years that a 25% harvest reduction was not enough to reverse the downward trend.

Despite its limitations, there is some evidence that the horseshoe crab management plan helped to slow the decline of the crab populations on the Bay. Analysis of Delaware Bay spawning and benthic trawl surveys indicated that juvenile and male crabs were increasing and that the female population had stabilized (Michels *et al.*, 2011). However, without solid and comprehensive scientific information, the battle between wildlife conservation and economic gain pressed on, to the detriment of both the shorebirds and the crabs. More recent analyses have concluded that population increases have not been significant and continued harvest (although lessened) is preventing population rebound (Hata & Hallerman, 2012; Figure 12.3).

UNDERSTANDING RED KNOT DECLINES IN THE CONTEXT OF HORSESHOE CRAB OVERHARVEST

As management agencies worked to lessen the decline of horseshoe crabs (with limited success), the effort to establish a clear connection between the loss of crabs and the dramatic decline in shorebirds was itself causing controversy. The lack of scientific evidence identifying the cause of red knot declines triggered the introduction of several hypotheses by fishery scientists and administrators that could explain this decline. For example, the ASMFC Management Board posited that the decline in red knots was not caused by the rapidly declining horseshoe crab population in Delaware Bay, but rather by problems experienced elsewhere on the knots' migratory flyway. The now politically charged conflict between conservationists and fisheries constituents generated new research projects within Delaware Bay in an effort to provide irrefutable evidence of the imminent extinction risk of red knots (and other species) as a result of the overexploitation of horseshoe crabs.

Shorebird work on Delaware Bay was comprehensive, including aerial and ground counts, trapping, and banding of three shorebird species (red knots, ruddy turnstones, and sanderlings). Research was also conducted on food and foraging habits, competition and energetics, habitat use and horseshoe crab egg availability. At first, individual shorebirds were marked with color rings to identify yearly cohorts. In 2003, leg flags with unique three-character codes allowed identification of individual birds with binoculars and spotting scopes. This innovation, implemented first on Delaware Bay, allowed development of more accurate assessments of survival and turnover rates and provided a significant new tool for identifying migratory routes. Another scientific achievement was the deployment of light-sensitive geolocators (Niles *et al.*, 2010; Burger *et al.*, 2012a, 2012b, 2012c). These small devices track animal movements by recording time of sunrise and sunset, providing an estimate of global position in the same way as a sextant (Vsevolod, 2004). Geolocators are lightweight (~1 g), which allows their use on small birds, such as red knots. The use of geolocators is a labor-intensive research method because birds must be recaptured to retrieve the device and download data. However, the information gathered is priceless; data recorded from only a few recoveries provided the first glimpse into the intricate life of red knots, and potentially a whole suite of shorebirds that could not carry much heavier satellite transmitters. The devices allowed a new understanding of migration routes, flight duration, and the identification of many new stopover and wintering areas in North, Central, and South America that were previously unknown to shorebird researchers (Niles *et al.*, 2010; Burger *et al.*, 2012a).

Work was also initiated in both the Canadian Arctic breeding grounds and the wintering grounds in Tierra del Fuego, Chile. In the Arctic, red knot breeding areas were unknown except for estimated range maps outlining an area equal in size to the eastern US (Morrison & Harrington, 1992). Early identification of red knot breeding grounds, including Southampton Island and King William Island in Nunavut, occurred by attaching VHF transmitters to red knots on the Delaware Bay then relocating them from a single-engine aircraft flown deep into the Canadian Arctic (Niles *et al.*, 2008).

Concurrent ground studies of nesting densities on Southampton Island for red knot and American golden plover (*Pluvialis dominica*) (a non-Delaware Bay migrant) helped elucidate red knot declines. Because these two species nest in the same areas at similar densities, acute conditions (i.e. nest predators and severe weather) should impact both species in a similar way. Between 2000 and 2004, red knot nest density declined from 1.15 to 0.547 nests/km^2, while American golden plover nest density remained unchanged (0.765–0.984 nests/km^2), rejecting the hypothesis that the breeding ground conditions were contributing to red knot declines.

To address potential issues occurring in the wintering grounds, biologists began resurveying the main South American site, Bahia Lomas, at the southeast end of the Strait of Magellan in Tierra del Fuego, in 2000. The area had not been surveyed since the 1986 winter shorebird Atlas conducted by the Canadian Wildlife Service (CWS). The survey indicated that red knot numbers were similar to the 1986 Atlas survey at just over 45 000. Hudsonian godwit (*Limosa haemastica*), a non-Delaware Bay migrant that also winters in Bahia Lomas, was also counted and found present in numbers similar to the 1986 Atlas. As these two species forage and roost in Bahia Lomas, acute events such as oil spills or loss of invertebrate prey should impact both species in a similar way.

Subsequent surveys of Bahia Lomas from 2000 to the present have documented rapidly falling numbers of red knots. By 2002 red knot numbers fell by 53% to just over 21 000 individuals and ultimately to a low of just over 10 000 in 2011. Hudsonian godwit numbers in the same period increased slightly, but remained largely unchanged with ~31 000 and ~33 000 birds in 1986 and 2011, respectively. Therefore, no short-term or acute problems were occurring in the Tierra del Fuego wintering areas that could contribute to red knot declines.

Long-distance red knot migrants have a very short time on Delaware Bay in which to gain sufficient mass (10–12 days). These birds must realize extremely rapid weight gains (≥ 6 g per day) to reach the mass necessary to finish migration and survive on Arctic breeding grounds until food becomes available there. Baker and colleagues (2004) documented that red knots leaving the Delaware Bay without sufficient weight (≥ 180 g) had lower adult survival than birds leaving at > 180 g; adult survival was reduced from an average of 84.5% (1996–1998) for the larger body mass to an average of 56.4% (1999–2001) for the smaller body mass. The publication of a status assessment on red knots in 2007 and a monograph in 2008 provided comprehensive evidence that the overharvest of the horseshoe crab population left the red knot in danger of extinction (Niles *et al.*, 2007, 2008).

This research effort provided convincing data to support the major impacts of horseshoe crab overexploitation on red knot declines. The mounting evidence prompted the US Fish and Wildlife Service (USFWS) in 2009 to consider the red knot as a candidate for federal listing as an endangered species. At the same time, the ability to track individually marked red knots provided the necessary information to devise crab harvests that benefited shorebirds (McGowan *et al.*, 2011). Finally, complementary research on other shorebirds found significant declines in semipalmated sandpipers, sanderlings, least sandpipers, and dunlin, all of which rely on horseshoe crab eggs as a significant food source during migratory stopover stays on Delaware Bay (Morrison *et al.*, 2006; Jehl, 2007, Mizrahi *et al.*, 2009).

THE CONTINUED HARVEST OF HORSESHOE CRABS

Despite the considerable scientific evidence showing low horseshoe crab numbers and egg availability were causing the steep decline of red knots and other shorebirds (Andres, 2003), crab harvests continued. So why are commercial fishing interests allowed to continue harvesting a pulse resource known to be damaging to a globally significant migratory bird stopover site, particularly when there is no real recovery in numbers of adult horseshoe crabs or eggs since harvests were originally regulated? This is a crucial question, not only in its relevance to many other fisheries controversies, but also for the many conservation efforts facing opposition by high-level private interests. The answer is as complex as one would expect in a modern-day conservation conflict. Here we suggest the primary factors driving the continued harvest of horseshoe crabs.

Lack of baseline data

Shorebird science is intricate and unfolding. While research has been implemented for decades, much of it focused on fundamental questions, such as identification of wintering grounds and quantification of population sizes. Often this work focused on details of shorebird biology, such as the energy necessary to fuel a flight to the Arctic (Castro & Myers, 1993). Certainly such information was critical to our understanding of shorebird ecology and conservation; however, one of the main limitations to effective management of shorebirds was the lack of population estimates that pre-dated the massive increase horseshoe crab harvests. In addition, the critical trophic link between red knots and horseshoe crabs was not fully understood. The concept of the crossover impacts of marine species exploitation on terrestrial species was largely understudied.

Scientific uncertainty

While the early predictions of shorebird declines made in the late 1990s were accurate (e.g. Shuster, 1996; Swan et al., 1996), several hypotheses were put forth to explain these declines. For example, shorebird biologists debated whether red knots and other shorebirds were simply moving off the Bay and onto the Atlantic coast beaches to forage on alternative prey once horseshoe crab numbers declined. In addition, Robinson et al. (2003) suggested that an increasing trend in late-arriving individuals (those missing the peak of crab spawning) was responsible for the lower numbers of red knots observed in the early 2000s. Proving these hypotheses right or wrong took time and significant funding. Meanwhile, the lack of scientific certainty about the causes of declines in red knots on the Bay provided management agencies with no impetus for implementing strong action to reduce crab harvests.

Horseshoe crabs as a multi-use resource

In addition to its use for bait in the eel and conch fisheries, horseshoe crabs are also harvested for the extraction of *Limulus* amebocyte lysate (Berkson & Shuster, 1999). Lysate is an extract of horseshoe crab blood and is used to detect bacterial contaminants in all medical devices and injectable drugs. Most of the lysate used worldwide comes from Delaware Bay horseshoe crabs. Crabs are harvested, bled, and then returned alive to the water. Although industry reports suggest mortality estimates are ~8–15% (ASMFC, 2012), peer-reviewed scientific studies, which duplicated typical conditions under which crabs are collected, held, and bled, suggest mortality is more realistically 29% (Hurton et al., 2009; Leschen & Coreia, 2010). Lysate production is an extremely lucrative industry, and harvests for these purposes are largely unregulated (ASMFC, 2012). In addition, full disclosure of lysate extraction protocols and resulting mortality are protected by a confidentiality agreement (ASMFC, 2012). The degree to which the practice of bleeding horseshoe crabs is contributing to overall declines in crab numbers is not clear, and this uncertainly creates political and scientific obstacles to the implementation of harvest reductions.

Politics of science-based decision-making

Relying on best available science provides a strong platform for political decision-making. However, the use of scientific ambiguity to avoid or delay action is a well-used strategy in environmental conflict, especially when money is at stake, as is often the case in political battles involving marine fisheries exploitation (Sullivan *et al.*, 2006). Relying on science as a sole driver of policy was a problem on Delaware Bay because statistical certainty was difficult. Most estimates of population trends require years of surveying before any conclusions are reached. In this case, red knots were in rapid decline, leaving the species in jeopardy while management agencies awaited further data to be certain in their actions. Early action was paramount if agencies were to avoid costly restoration programs or species endangerment. The call for certainty and action were in conflict, requiring policy-makers to halt controversial uses by resource industries with strong political connections.

THE POWER OF PUBLIC OPINION IN THE BATTLE FOR SPECIES CONSERVATION

While scientists disagreed publically over relatively small issues, the harvests of horseshoe crabs continued. When the New Jersey Marine Fisheries Council chose to end New Jersey's moratorium on horseshoe crab harvest, a vocal segment of the public grew even more impatient with the mismanagement of the migratory shorebird stopover in Delaware Bay. Several environmental groups and self-identified wildlife-watchers in New Jersey actively opposed crab harvests. In addition, the 650 000-member New Jersey State Federation of Sportsmen's Clubs publically declared support for actions necessary to protect horseshoe crabs and the shorebird stopover.

In 2008, the Public Broadcasting System's (PBS) *Nature* series released *Crash: A Tale of Two Species*, which eloquently documented the overexploitation of the horseshoe crab and its disastrous effect on red knot and other shorebird populations. Featuring much of the work of scientists actively engaged in red knot conservation, the film presented information in a format that could be understood and appreciated by a lay audience. The result was a significant shift in public opinion and a momentum boost for the conservation initiative. Within weeks of the documentary's release, major conservation groups, including the New Jersey Audubon Society, American Littoral Society, and Delaware Riverkeeper Network, had secured sponsors for a legislated moratorium on horseshoe crab harvest in New Jersey. The proposed legislation not only banned the harvest of crabs, but required full recovery of horseshoe crab and shorebird populations before crab harvests could resume. The bill passed in March 2008 and was signed into law by the state governor.

The sudden upwelling of support for protection came after 15 years of similarly high-profile national and local media treatments, including *Life* magazine, *National Geographic* (TV and magazine), the Discovery Channel, the *Washington Post, New York Times,* and *Smithsonian Magazine.* Most of this reportage focused on the ecological wonder of the stopover or presented a superficial point–counterpoint between shorebird biologists and fishing interests, as if both sides were right. The PBS *Nature* documentary, however, explained why conserving the Delaware Bay stopover was worth the price of opposing industrial fishing concerns.

CURRENT CONSERVATION EFFORTS

To date, the Delaware Bay horseshoe crab population has shown no significant recovery (Dey *et al.*, 2012; Michels *et al.*, 2013; Hata & Hallerman, 2013). Despite these disappointing results, crab spawns between 2010 and 2012 did appear to improve, most likely as a result of better environmental conditions. The water temperature of the Bay was favorable for spawning, especially in 2012, which allowed spawning in early and mid-May coincident with the arrival of the majority of shorebirds (Niles *et al.*, unpublished data). Moreover, calm weather in the month of May in all three years allowed crabs to spawn on beaches usually exposed to wind-driven waves and thus unsuitable for crabs. This change allowed eggs to be more widely distributed, reducing competition between shorebird species and laughing gulls (*Larus atricilla*). These conditions were unusual, and settled weather cannot be relied upon to produce more widely distributed food resources every year. Nevertheless, the last three years may offer a new basis for recovery and allow conservationists to reassess the best way forward.

Many new regulatory programs offer more lasting hope. In 2012, the ASMFC adopted an Adaptive Resource Management (ARM) model, which initiated a new effort to set future harvests of crabs based, in part, on red knot population numbers (McGowan *et al.*, 2011). The ARM model will use yearly data from both horseshoe crab surveys and shorebird banding efforts to estimate the best harvest scenario for shorebird recovery. Early results suggest a daunting challenge; depending on the current estimate of crabs and birds, it may take 60+ years for the horseshoe crab population to fully recover and 20–40 years for red knots to recover (Smith *et al.*, 2013; D. Smith, personal communication, 2012). The model, however, provides a solid scientific basis for limiting harvests until there are clear signs of recovery. It can also help conservationists and biologists assess the best ways to speed recovery.

Finally, the frustration over recovering the Delaware Bay shorebird stopover has motivated public agencies and conservation groups to conduct one of the most important public land acquisition efforts on the Atlantic coast. In the last 20 years, thousands of acres of land along both sides of the Delaware Bay have been secured by either public land agencies or cooperating conservation groups, such as The Nature Conservancy and New Jersey Natural Lands Trust. These lands include substantial areas of beach and marsh fronting the bay, as well as entire small drainages flowing into the Bay. Although managers lack sufficient funds to properly manage these lands, this does not diminish the potential for superior conservation in the future or detract from the outstanding achievement it represents. Now much of the Delaware Bay shore is permanently protected.

MANAGEMENT OF MARINE PULSE SPECIES FOR WILDLIFE CONSERVATION

Only time will reveal the ending of the red knot story, but the conservation implication is clear. Marine pulse resources can and do play a critical role in the survival of terrestrial species. Managing these resources is incredibly challenging, due to at least two factors. First, when stressor and impact are spatially decoupled, such as is the case with marine prey and terrestrial predators occurring several miles apart, cause and effect is not obvious. The pulse species may fortify entire ecosystems through massive but short-lived nutrient inputs, increasing primary productivity and affecting terrestrial wildlife from the bottom up (Schindler *et al.*, 2003). Tying the decline of a terrestrial species through the indirect effects of marine overharvesting is mired in potential alternative hypotheses. Second, published studies on these interactions are scarce (Willson & Womble, 2006). While it is known that several species take advantage of seasonal marine resources, including whale sharks (*Rhincodon typus*), several fishes, and seabirds, it seems likely that an even greater number of examples of predator exploitation of marine pulse prey remain unidentified (Piatt, 1990; Heyman *et al.*, 2001; Taylor & Lum, 2005). The red knot/horseshoe crab conflict represents one of the only well-worked examples of the cross-trophic impacts of marine over-exploitation (Willson & Womble, 2006). The lack of advanced baseline knowledge and understanding of the strong food web linkage between both species prevented swift and decisive management action.

The need to investigate more closely the decline of terrestrial species that may have strong, albeit ephemeral, links to overexploited marine species is clear. As we have demonstrated here, the key to survival of the red knot population lies in the reliability of a brief, but bountiful pulse in prey. Identification of a similar link between other terrestrial and marine species may be paramount to effective adaptive fisheries management. With prior understanding of these trophic crossovers, we can model the effects of prey reductions on predator populations, incorporating realistic spatial and temporal interactions to ground model predictions in reality (Willson & Womble, 2006). The end result would be a healthy and evidence-based marriage of fisheries management and wildlife conservation.

REFERENCES

Andres, B. A. (2003). *Delaware Bay Shorebird–Horseshoe Crab Assessment Report: Biological Assessment*. Shorebird Technical Committee, US Fish and Wildlife Service.
ASMFC, Atlantic States Marine Fisheries Commission. (1998). *Interstate Fishery Management Plan for Horseshoe Crab*. Fishery Management Report no. 32. Arlington, VA: ASMFC.
ASMFC, Atlantic States Marine Fisheries Commission. (2002). *2001 Review of the Fishery Management Plan for Horseshoe Crab* (Limulus polyphemus). April 2002. 10 pages.
ASMFC, Atlantic States Marine Fisheries Commission. (2012). *2012 Review of the Fishery Management Plan in 2011 for Horseshoe Crab* (Limulus polyphemus). Report to the Horseshoe Crab Management Board. Arlington, VA: ASMFC.
Baker, A. J., Gonzalez, P. M., Piersma, T., *et al.* (2004). Rapid population decline in red knot: Fitness consequences of decreased refueling rates and late arrival in Delaware Bay. *Proceedings of the Royal Society of London, Series B, Biological Sciences*, **25**, 125–129.
Bart, J., Brown, S., Harrington, B. & Morrison, R. I. G. (2007). Survey trends of North American shorebirds: Population declines or shifting distributions? *Journal of Avian Biology*, **38**, 73–82.
Berkson, J. & Shuster, Jr., C. N. (1999). The horseshoe crab: The battle for a true multiple-use resource. *Fisheries*, **24**, 6–10.
Boreman, J., Nakashima, B. S., Wilson, J. A. & Kendall, R. L. (1997). *Northwest Atlantic Groundfish: Perspectives on a Fishery Collapse*. Baltimore, MD: American Fisheries Society.

Botsford, L. W., Castilla, J. C. & Peterson, C. H. (1997). The management of fisheries and marine ecosystems. *Science*, **277**, 509–515.

Botton, M. L., Loveland, R. E. & Jacobsen, T. R. (1994). Site selection by migratory shorebirds in Delaware Bay and its relationship to beach characteristics and abundance of horseshoe crabs (*Limulus polyphemus*) eggs. *Auk*, **111**, 605–616.

Brockman, H. J. (2003). Male competition and satellite behavior. In C. N. Schuster, Jr., R. B. Barlow & H. J. Brockman (eds.), *The American Horseshoe Crab*. Boston, MA: Harvard University Press, pp. 50–82.

Burger, J., Niles, L. J., Porter, R. R., *et al.* (2012a). Migration and over-wintering of red knots (*Calidris canutus rufa*) along the Atlantic coast of the United States. *Condor*, **114**, 1–12.

Burger, J., Niles, L. J., Porter, R. R., *et al.* (2012b). Using a shore bird (red knot) fitted with geolocators to evaluate a conceptual risk model focusing on offshore wind. *Renewable Energy*, **43**, 370–377.

Burger, J., Niles, L. J., Porter, R. R. & Dey, A. D. (2012c). Using geolocator data to reveal incubation periods and breeding biology in red knots *Calidris canutus rufa*. *Wader Study Group Bulletin*, **119**, 26–36.

Byrnes, J. E., Reynolds, P. L. & Stachowicz, J. J. (2007). Invasions and extinctions reshape coastal marine food webs. *PLoS ONE*, **2**, e295.

Castro, G. & Myers, J. P. (1993). Shorebird predation on eggs of horseshoe crabs during spring stopover on Delaware Bay. *Auk*, **110**, 927–930.

Clark, K., Niles, L. & Burger, J. (1993). Abundance and distribution of shorebirds migrating on Delaware Bay, 1986–1992. *Condor*, **95**, 694–705.

Coll, M., Libralato, S., Tudela, S., Palomera, I. & Pranovi, F. (2008). Ecosystem overfishing in the ocean. *PLoS ONE*, **3**, e3881.

Davis, M. L., Berkson, J. & Kelly, M. (2006). A production modeling approach to the assessment of the horseshoe crab (*Limulus polyphemus*) population in Delaware Bay. *Fishery Bulletin*, **104**, 215–225.

Delaware Bay Shorebird Working Group. (1992). *Report of the Delaware Bay Working Group*. Report to New Jersey Division of Fish and Wildlife.

Dey, A., Kalasz, K. & Hernandez, D. (2012). *Delaware Bay Egg Survey: 2005–2012*. Report to the Atlantic States Marine Fisheries Commission.

Duffy, J. E., Richardson, J. P. & Canuel, E. A. (2003). Grazer diversity effects on ecosystem functioning in seagrass beds. *Ecology Letters*, **6**, 637–645.

Froese, R., Zeller, D., Kleisner, K. & Pauly, D. (2012). What catch data can tell us about the status of global fisheries. *Marine Biology*, **159**, 1283–1292.

Gillings, S., Atkinson, P. W., Bardsley, S. L., *et al.* (2007). Shorebird predation of horseshoe crab eggs in Delaware Bay: Species contrasts and availability constraints. *Journal of Animal Ecology*, **76**, 503–514.

Gresh, T., Lichatowich, J. & Schoonmaker, P. (2000). An estimation of historic and current levels of salmon production in the Northeast Pacific ecosystem: Evidence of a nutrient deficit in the freshwater systems of the Pacific Northwest. *Fisheries*, **25**, 15–21.

Haramis, M. G. (2003). *Use of Stable Isotopes to Determine the Relative Importance of Horseshoe Crab Eggs in the Diet of Long-distance Migrant Shorebirds in Delaware Bay*. Science Brief PWRC 2003–33, Laurel, MD: United States Geological Survey, Patuxent Wildlife Research Center.

Haramis, M. G., Link, W. A., Osenton, P. C., et al. (2007). Stable isotope and pen feeding trial studies confirm the value of horseshoe crab *Limulus polyphemus* eggs to spring migrant shorebirds in Delaware Bay. *Journal of Avian Biology*, **38**, 367–375.

Harrington, B. A. (2001). Red knot (*Calidris canutus*). In A. Poole (ed.), *The Birds of North America Online*. Ithaca, NY: Cornell Laboratory of Ornithology. www.ban.birds.cornel.edu/BNA/account/Red_Knot/.

Hata, D. & Hallerman, E. (2013). *Results of the 2012 Horseshoe Crab Trawl Survey*. Report to the Atlantic States Marine Fisheries Commission Horseshoe Crab and Delaware Bay Ecosystem Technical Committees.

Hernandez, D. (2012). *Report on Horseshoe Crab Egg Surveys in New Jersey for 2012*. Stone Harbor, NJ: The Wetlands Institute.

Heyman, W. D., Graham, R. T., Kjerfve, B. & Johannes, R. E. (2001). Whale sharks *Rhincodon typus* aggregate to feed on fish spawn in Belize. *Marine Ecology Progress Series*, **215**, 275–282.

Hurton, L., Berkson, J. & Smith, S. (2009). The effect of hemolymph extraction volume and handling stress on horseshoe crab mortality. In J. T. Tancredi, M. L. Botton & D. R. Smith (eds.), *Biology and Conservation of Horseshoe Crabs*. New York, NY: Springer, pp. 331–346.

Jackson, J. B. C., Kirby, M. X., Berger, W. H., et al. (2001). Historical overfishing and the recent collapse of coastal ecosystems. *Science*, **293**, 629–637.

Jackson, N. L., Nordstrom, K. F. & Smith, D. R. (2002). Geomorphic–biotic inter-actions on beach foreshores in estuaries. *Journal of Coastal Research*, **36**, 414–424.

Jehl, Jr., J. R. (2007). Disappearance of breeding semipalmated sandpipers from Churchill, Manitoba: More than a local phenomenon. *Condor*, **109**, 351–360.

Leschen, A. & Correia, S. J. (2010). Mortality in female horseshoe crabs (*Limulus polyphemus*) from biomedical bleeding and handling: Implication for fishery management. *Marine and Freshwater Behaviour and Physiology*, **43**, 135–147.

Levin, P. S., Coyer, J. A., Petrik, R. & Good, T. P. (2002). Community-wide effects of nonindigenous species on temperate rocky reefs. *Ecology*, **83**, 3182–3193.

Liu, M. & De Mitcheson, Y. S. (2008). Profile of a fishery collapse: Why mariculture failed to save the large yellow croaker. *Fish and Fisheries*, **9**, 219–242.

McGowan, C. P., Hines, J. E., Nichols, J. D., et al. (2011). Demographic consequences of migratory stopover: Linking red knot survival to horseshoe crab spawning abundance. *Ecosphere*, **2**, art. 69.

Mizrahi, D. S. & Peters, K. A. (2009). Relationships between sandpipers and horseshoe crab in Delaware Bay: A synthesis. In J. T. Tanacredi, M. L. Botton & D. R. Smith (eds.), *Biology and Conservation of Horseshoe Crabs*. New York, NY: Springer, pp. 65–87.

Morrison, R. I. G. & Harrington, B. A. (1992). The migration system of the red knot *Calidris cannutus rufa* in the New World. *Wader Study Group Bulletin*, **64**(S), 71–84.

Morrison, R. I. G., McCaffery, B. J., Gill, R. E., et al. (2006). Population estimates of North American shorebirds. *Wader Study Group Bulletin*, **111**, 67–85.

Myers, J. P. (1986). Sex and gluttony on Delaware Bay. *Natural History*, **95**, 68–77.

Myers, R. A. & Mertz, G. (1997). Maximum population growth rates and recovery time for Atlantic cod (*Gadus morhua*). *Fishery Bulletin*, **95**, 762–772.

Myers, R. A., Hutchings, J. A. & Barrowman, N. J. (1997). Why do fish stocks collapse? The example of cod in Atlantic Canada. *Ecological Applications*, **7**, 91–106.

Niles, L. J., Sitters, H. P., Dey, A. D., *et al.* (2007). *Status of the Red Knot (*Calidris canutus rufa*) in the Western Hemisphere*. Prepared for the United States Fish and Wildlife Service, Ecological Services, Region 5, NJ Field Office, Pleasantville, NJ 08232, USA.

Niles, L. J., Sitters, H. P., Dey, A. D., *et al.* (2008). *Status of the Red Knot (*Calidris canutus rufa*) in the Western Hemisphere. Studies in Avian Biology*, 36.

Niles, L. J., Bart, J., Sitters, H. P., *et al.* (2009). Effects of horseshoe crab harvest in Delaware Bay on red knots: Are harvest restrictions working? *Bioscience*, **59**, 153–164.

Niles, L. J., Burger, J., Porter, R. R., *et al.* (2010). First results using light level geolocators to track red knots in the western hemisphere show rapid and long intercontinental flights and new details of migration pathways. *Wader Study Group Bulletin*, **117**, 123–130.

NJDEP, New Jersey Division of Fish and Wildlife. (2012). *Wildlife Populations: Horseshoe Crab*. Environmental Trends Report, New Jersey Department of Environmental Protection, Office of Science. www.nj.gov/dep/dsr/trends/pdfs/wildlife-horseshoe.pdf.

Pauly, D., Christensen, V., Dalsgaard, J., Froese, R. & Torres, J. F. (1998). Fishing down marine food webs. *Science*, **279**, 860–863.

Pauly, D., Christensen, V., Guenette, S., *et al.* (2002). Towards sustainability in world fisheries. *Nature*, **418**, 689–695.

Piatt, J. F. (1990). The aggregative response of common murres and Atlantic puffins to schools of capelin. *Studies in Avian Biology*, **14**, 36–51.

Piersma, T., Roger, D. I., Gonzalez, P. M., *et al.* (2005). Fuel storage rates before northward flights in red knots worldwide: Facing the severest ecological constraint in tropical intertidal environments. In R. Greenberg & P. P. Marra (eds.), *Birds of Two Worlds: The Ecology and Evolution of Migration*. Baltimore, MD: Johns Hopkins University Press, pp. 262–273.

Pinsky, M. L., Jensen, O. P., Ricard, D. & Palumbi, S. R. (2011). Unexpected patterns of fisheries collapse in the world's oceans. *Proceedings of the National Academy of Sciences of the United States of America*, **108**, 8317–8322.

Reynolds, P. L. & Bruno, J. F. (2012). Effects of trophic skewing of species richness on ecosystem functioning in a diverse marine community. *PLoS ONE*, **7**, e36196.

Robinson, R. A., Atkinson, P. & Clark, N. A. (2003). *Arrival and Weight Gain of Knot* Calidris canutus, *Turnstone* Arenaria interpres *and Sanderling* Calidris alba *Staging in Delaware Bay in Spring*. BTO Research Report, 307. Thetford, Norfolk: British Trust for Ornithology.

Rudkin, D. M., Young, G. M. & Nowlan, G. S. (2008). The oldest horseshoe crab: A new xiphosurid from Late Ordovician Konservat-Lagerstätten deposits, Manitoba, Canada. *Palaeontology*, **51**, 1–9.

Schindler, D. E., Scheuerell, M. D., Moore, J. W., *et al.* (2003). Pacific salmon and the ecology of coastal ecosystems. *Frontiers in Ecology and the Enviornment*, **1**, 31–37.

Senner, S. E. & Howe, M. A. (1984). Conservation of Nearctic shorebirds. In J. Burger & B. L. Olla (eds.), *Behavior of Marine Animals*, vol. **5**. New York, NY: Plenum Press, pp. 379–421.

Shuster, Jr., C. N. (1996). Abundance of adult horseshoe crabs, *Limulus polyphemus*, in Delaware Bay, 1850–1990. In J. Farrell & C. Martin (eds.), *Proceedings of the Horseshoe Harvest of* Limulus polyphemus *187 Crab Forum: Status of the Resource.* Lewes, DE: University of Delaware Sea Grant College Program, pp. 5–14.

Silliman, B. R. & Bertness, M. D. (2002). A trophic cascade regulates salt marsh primary production. *Proceedings of the National Academy of Sciences of the United States of America*, **99**, 10500–10505.

Smith, D. R. (2007). Effect of horseshoe crab spawning density on nest disturbance and exhumation of eggs: A simulation study. *Estuaries and Coasts*, **30**, 287–295.

Smith, D. R., McGowan, C. P., Daily, J. P. Nichols, J. D., Sweka, J. A. & Lyons, J. E. (2013). Evaluating a multispecies adaptive management framework: Must uncertainty impede effective decision-making? *Journal of Applied Ecology*, **50**, 1431–1440.

Swan, B. L. (2005). Migrations of adult horseshoe crabs, *Limulus polyphemus*, in the Middle Atlantic Bight: A 17-year tagging study. *Estuaries and Coasts*, **28**, 28–40.

Swan, B. L., Hall, W. R. & Shuster, Jr., C. N. (1996). *Annual Survey of Horseshoe Crab Spawning Activity Along the Shores of Delaware Bay: 1990–1995 Summary*. Lewes, DE: University of Delaware Sea Grant College Program.

Sullivan P. J., Acheson, J. M., Angermeier, P. L., *et al.* (2006). Defining and implementing best available science for fisheries and environmental science, policy, and management. *Fisheries*, **31**, 460–465.

Taylor, S. G. & Lum, J. L. (2005). *Auke Creek Weir 2004: Annual Report, Operations, Fish Counts, and Historical Summaries*. National Marine Fisheries Service, Auke Bay Laboratory, 22305 Glacier Hwy, Juneau AK.

Tsipoura, N. & Burger, J. (1999). Shorebird diet during spring migration stopover on Delaware Bay. *Condor*, **101**, 633–644.

Vsevolod, A. (2004). A miniature daylight level and activity data recorder for tracking animals over long periods. *Memoirs of the National Institute of Polar Research*, **SI58**, 227–233.

WHSRN, Western Hemisphere Shorebird Reserve Network. (2011). WHSRN List of Sites. www.whsrn.org/site-profile/delaware-bay.

Willson, M. F. & Womble, J. N. (2006). Vertebrate exploitation of pulsed marine prey: A review and the example of spawning herring. *Reviews in Fish Biology and Fisheries*, **16**, 183–200.

Willson, M. F., Gende, S. M. & Marston, B. H. (1998). Fishes and the forest. *Bioscience*, **48**, 455–462.

Womble, J. N., Willson, M. F., Sigler, M. F., Kelly, B. P. & Van Blaricom, G. R. (2005). Distribution of Steller sea lions (*Eumetopias jubatus*) in relation to spring-spawning prey species in Southeastern Alaska. *Marine Ecology Progress Series*, **294**, 271–282.

Worm, B. & Duffy, J. E. (2003). Biodiversity, productivity and stability in real food webs. *Trends in Ecology and Evolution*, **18**, 628–632.

Yang, L. H. (2004). Periodical cicadas as resource pulses in North American forests. *Science*, **306**, 1565–1567.

Zimmerman, J., Michels, S., Smith, D. & Bennett, S. (2013). *Horseshoe Crab Spawning Activity in Delaware Bay: 1999–2012*. Report to the Atlantic States Marine Fisheries Commission Horseshoe Crab Technical Committee.

Part III

Synthesis

13

A research agenda for coastal biodiversity conservation

JULIE L. LOCKWOOD AND BROOKE MASLO

OVERVIEW

Coastal ecosystems make up 4% of the Earth's land area and 11% of its oceans, but they house > 30% of the global human population (UNEP, 2006; Barbier, 2012). The settlement of coastal ecosystems is expected to increase exponentially over the next 100 years, with many people moving to "mega-cities" that are located near the coast (UNEP, 2006). Given these numbers, it should not be surprising that coastal habitats are disappearing at a very rapid rate (Barbier, 2012). This rate of loss will surely increase as the remaining coastal habitats are "squeezed" between rising sea levels on one side and development on the other (Jackson & McIlvenny, 2011; see also Chapters 3, 7, and 10). We can ill afford to lose these habitats given the substantial services they provide society (Barbier *et al.*, 2011), and the growing recognition of this dilemma has directed much-needed attention on finding ways to accommodate people on coastlines without losing key services (Chan *et al.*, 2006; Halpern *et al.*, 2012). However, the role of biodiversity in this conservation dilemma has thus far been murky. We assembled this volume to begin to fill this gap in knowledge. The chapters within have detailed the species associated with key coastal habitats, their links to ecosystem services, and the influence of various stressors on their persistence. There are several cognizant themes that emerge from reading these chapters, some of which we reviewed in Chapter 1 (e.g. the need to conserve the connections between habitats). Here we broaden the discussion and highlight three research agendas that can serve as mileposts going forward.

Coastal Conservation, eds B. Maslo and J. L. Lockwood. Published by Cambridge University Press.
© Cambridge University Press 2014.

TAKING STOCK

One of the defining characteristics of coastal ecosystems is their dynamic and interconnected nature (Sheaves, 2009). This characteristic makes it difficult to fully account for all the species that utilize coastal habitats, some of which vitally depend upon these habitats for their continued persistence. Such species may use coastal habitats in an ephemeral way, thereby making their detection within standard sampling protocols unlikely (Condan et al., 2012). Other species may be year-round residents, but they are cryptic (e.g. small body size, secretive behavior) or otherwise difficult to observe (e.g. exist in feasibly challenged areas, such as surf zones or salt marsh). Nevertheless, the full implementation of coastal management requires a detailed understanding of which species use these ecosystems and how, and how important these ecosystems are to a species' persistence (e.g. Barnes, 2013; Hale et al., 2013).

To answer these questions, we need both broad-scale and local inventories of coastal biodiversity. At the local scale, a detailed understanding of how species arrange themselves according to physical and biotic forces allows managers to formulate strategies that have a sound ecological basis – a result not often realized in most coastal management plans (Barnes, 2013; Dutertre et al., 2013). Efforts to better characterize local biodiversity enables the tailoring of ecosystem-based management actions to site-specific ecological flows and spatial structures (Barnes, 2013). Such research is often very "old school" in that it requires systematic observational sampling and the taxonomic expertise to identify the species observed, albeit sometimes it requires high-tech monitoring solutions (e.g. Condan et al., 2012). However, the benefit of such detailed local knowledge is immense, especially when considered from an ecosystem services point of view (see below). Perhaps in particular it is critical to know the identity and distribution of species that utilize coastal habitats, even the very rare ones, because it is the particulars of species' traits that seem to determine their role in delivering key ecosystem services and not necessarily the simple count of species in an area (Emmerson et al., 2001; Cardinale et al., 2006).

On a broad scale, there is the concomitant need to better track changes in biodiversity that do not rely on intensive, often expensive, short-duration observational surveys (Herkul et al., 2013). Given the scale at which coastal ecosystems are being modified, traditional biodiversity surveys are unlikely to give an adequate large-scale view of changes in species diversity that may result (Mcleod et al., 2010). Sea level rise is a clear example of such a large-scale change. Sea level rise is spatially diffuse but represents a fundamental alteration of the physical and biological forces that shape coastal biodiversity. The effect it has on the distribution and long-term persistence of particular species is just becoming clear (e.g. Haward *et al.*, 2013). The ability to broadly monitor a single species' response to sea level rise across its entire geographical range (e.g. sea turtles, Chapter 10), or to track changes to biodiversity in a single habitat across its worldwide distribution (e.g. mangrove forests), will provide key insights into how managers can mitigate such changes or adaptively manage coastal biodiversity in the face of continued sea level rise. We can imagine an equally compelling argument for tracking broad-scale changes to coastal biodiversity due to non-native species invasions, ocean acidification, oil spills, or urbanization.

WHAT ROLE DO SPECIES PLAY IN COASTAL ECOSYSTEM FUNCTION?

A consistent theme in this book, and broadly across recent literature on coastal conservation, is the high economic value of coastal ecosystems in terms of the services they provide to human society (UNEP, 2006). Estimates of service values range up to thousands of dollars (US) per hectare (Barbier *et al.*, 2011), making immediate efforts at preserving coastal ecosystems appear profoundly penny-wise and pound foolish. But what role does coastal biodiversity play in providing these valuable ecosystem services? The general answer is that some species are needed to continue the delivery of these services (Zedler *et al.*, 2001), and there is broad agreement that that these species should be native to any particular coastline under consideration (Burke *et al.*, 2001; Ruesink *et al.*, 2005).

It is the details behind this generalization that are difficult to discern. Because the traits of species determine in large measure the ecosystem services produced, which species must be present in order to continue delivery of a particular ecosystem service? At what abundance must these species be in for this service to be delivered at adequate rates? What role do non-native species play in the delivery of highly valued ecosystem services? The answers to these questions are not just relevant to coastal ecosystems; they permeate all of ecology (Cardinale *et al.*, 2006). However, the answers take on a more immediate and acute importance given the rate at which coastal ecosystems are being lost and degraded, and the social and economic importance of the services these ecosystems provide (Granek *et al.*, 2009).

The chapters in this book and the broader literature on ecosystem functions suggest three non-mutually exclusive gaps in our understanding of how coastal biodiversity influences the delivery of ecosystem services. First, given that coastal ecosystems are highly interconnected and dynamic, the role of species in delivering ecosystem services is likely complex, evincing non-linearities across time and space (Barbier *et al.*, 2008; Koch *et al.*, 2009; Barbier *et al.*, 2011). Most existing literature on the relationship between biodiversity and ecosystem function ignore such real-world complexities (Bulling *et al.*, 2008; Hillebrand & Matthieson, 2009). For example, how does small-scale heterogeneity in resources affect coastal species distributions and thereby the delivery of ecosystem services (Bulling *et al.*, 2008)? How does the often highly ephemeral occurrence of some species within coastal ecosystems influence the magnitude and stability of services produced (Godbold *et al.*, 2011)? If we were to remove ecological connections between coastal habitats, which services do we lose and to what extent (Barbier *et al.*, 2011)? These are all questions that are highly relevant to the production of coastal ecosystem services but that are currently understudied in the context of biodiversity and ecosystem function (Bulling *et al.*, 2011; Peh & Lewis, 2012).

Second, coastal ecosystems are uniquely vulnerable to aspects of global climate change (e.g. sea level rise) while also being subjected to several other more localized stressors. We do not yet grasp the mechanistic connections between these stressors on coastal biodiversity, much less how these changes in biodiversity influence the delivery of ecosystem services (Mcleod *et al.*, 2010; Bulling *et al.*, 2011). There is some evidence that suggests that coastal ecosystems may lose societal value relatively quickly as one or more environmental stressors begin to ramp up in their effects on constituent species (Lohrer *et al.*, 2012). Providing answers to questions of how multiple stressors devalue coastal ecosystems via their effects on biodiversity are, of course, difficult in the extreme. Here is where those "old school" surveys of coastal biodiversity can inform our understanding (e.g. Barnes, 2013). Knowing how these stressors structure biodiversity provides the appropriate starting point for the design of experiments or simulations on the role of species loss on ecosystem function (e.g. Dutertre *et al.*, 2013; Haward *et al.*, 2013).

Third, and related to the above, is the question of what role particular species play in the delivery of ecosystem services, and in the stability with which these services are delivered through time (Davies *et al.*, 2011). Species are not lost from ecosystems in a random manner; they are instead affected in accord with their life history and the stressor(s) affecting them (Cardinale *et al.*, 2006). In which case, we need to know which species are lost first from coastal habitats, according to what set of stressors, and then we can approach the question of how ecosystem services change as a result (Lohrer *et al.*, 2012). For example, overexploitation of fisheries can result in the non-random loss of higher trophic levels in associated coastal food webs. What impact does losing top predators or herbivores have on coastal ecosystem services (e.g. Carey & Wahl, 2011)? Our understanding of how different trophic levels influence ecosystem functions is underdeveloped in general (Cardinale *et al.*, 2006), but this question is of prime importance for many coastal ecosystem services. Even the role of species in the delivery of basic, but very highly valued, ecosystem services (e.g. wave attenuation) is not well understood (Koch *et al.*, 2009). All available evidence suggests that we should expect the effects of particular species on the type and magnitude of coastal ecosystem services provided will vary across space and time (Koch *et al.*, 2009; Barbier *et al.*, 2011).

WHAT TO MAKE OF URBAN COASTLINES?

There are several factors that make the conservation and management of coastal ecosystems difficult, despite their importance. We highlighted some of these in Chapter 1. Given that many major urban centers are embedded within coastal ecosystems, and that we can expect human populations to continue to grow within and nearby these centers, a remaining major conservation challenge is figuring out how to conserve species in the face of the urban onslaught (Perkol-Finkel *et al.*, 2012).

The growth in knowledge of urban systems is remarkable, but much of this research has centered on terrestrial ecosystems and ignored coastal areas (Bulleri, 2006; Chapman & Blockley, 2009). As a result, our understanding of how urbanization affects coastal biodiversity and what these species provide in terms of ecosystem services is relatively limited (Naylor *et al.*, 2012; Piwowarczyk *et al.*, 2013). What evidence exists clearly shows that urban coasts do not support the same number or types of native species, and that the presence of urban coastal structures can greatly deplete nearby undeveloped coastal habitats (Able *et al.*, 1998; Bulleri & Chapman, 2010). This result is almost certainly because coastal development for human use is not designed to conserve or promote ecological processes, but rather to prevent them (French, 2001; Bulleri & Chapman, 2010). Coastal defense systems disrupt aeolian and tidal dynamics, severing trophic links and reducing overall species diversity (e.g. Airoldi *et al.*, 2005; Martin *et al.*, 2005). The rate at which coastal areas are being urbanized and the need to increasingly armor our coastlines for protection against the impacts of sea level rise demands that ecologists engage in the challenge of designing coastal infrastructure that *does* provide basic ecological services (Chapman & Blockley, 2009; Naylor *et al.*, 2012).

From a biodiversity perspective, the relevant questions center around ways to enhance the range and types of species that occupy coastal ecosystems. By viewing urban coastal infrastructure as habitat, ecologists can document how the physical attributes of these structures determine the species that utilize them and the food webs that are created (Bulleri & Chapman, 2010). From this understanding, and the details of species distributions from more natural ecosystems (see above), comes insight into how to engineer structures to better mimic natural coastal structures and include these into urban planning practice (Chapman & Blockey, 2009; Naylor *et al.*, 2012). Like all of urban ecology, this effort will be inherently interdisciplinary and requires a shift in mindset away from the "forlorn hope that pristine [coastal] habitats can and will be restored" (Chapman & Blockley, 2009) to engaging in the "art of the practical" (Baird, 2005).

A critical aspect of designing urban ecosystems to better support coastal biodiversity is the explicit recognition of the extent to which habitats along shore, inland, and seaward are connected. This is a key theme within coastal conservation (Chapter 1), and surely urban coastal ecosystems are subject to the same connectivity principles. From this perspective, planning and engineering solutions that hope to enhance coastal biodiversity must explicitly recognize these connections, or lack thereof (Weinstein & Reed, 2005). The degree to which urban coasts are depauperate in native biodiversity due to massive changes in the physical dimensions of local habitats versus the severing of critical connections to nearby terrestrial and aquatic habitats is an open question. The degree to which these connections can be restored is also open for debate and certainly depends on the level to which a coastal habitat has been urbanized (Weinstein & Reed, 2005).

There is some possibility, of course, given the current rate of continued global carbon emissions and its impacts, that coastal species may be the winners in a future global climate scenario. With much of the global coastal population concentrated in and around major urban centers, it is plausible that the finite resources required to combat the rising seas and the increased frequency and severity of coastal storms will result in management decisions to leave much of the coastline to fend for itself. Shoreline retreat and saltwater intrusion may transform terrestrial and freshwater ecosystems to coastal ones, suddenly increasing resources and habitat instead of restricting them. However, given the other climate-induced impacts (i.e. ocean acidification) and anthropogenic stressors, we can expect these "new" coasts to be significantly different from their present-day counterparts. A solid foundation of coastal biodiversity and its role in ecosystem function will ultimately inform management of coastal habitats in a no-analog future.

FINAL THOUGHTS

There is something special about coasts. Maybe it is just the feeling of standing on the (terrestrial) edge of the world with the endless possibility of the ocean in front of you. Perhaps it is the natural bounty that the ocean and land bring together into one location that makes it appealing. Ecologically, coasts are a remarkable amalgamation of terrestrial, ocean, and freshwater realms. It is the place where aquatic and terrestrial species come to meet, and often eat, one another. The interest in conserving these special places has grown substantially over the past decade. We hope this book has high-lighted the unique character of coastal biodiversity and its all too often perilous existence. The challenges associated with researching and conserving coastal biodiversity are not trivial. In these pages, a reader can find several examples of what conservation actions to try, or research to explore. With any luck, a decade from now a follow-up volume on the conservation of coastal biodiversity will be able to report significant advances and some good news.

REFERENCES

Able, K. W., Manderson, J. P. & Studholme, A. L. (1998). The distribution of shallow water juvenile fishes in an urban estuary: The effects of manmade structures in the lower Hudson River. *Estuaries*, **21**, 731–744.

Airoldi, L., Abbiati, M. Beck, M. W., *et al.* (2005). An ecological perspective on the deployment and design of low-crested and other hard coastal defence structures. *Coastal Engineering*, **52**, 1073–1087.

Baird, R. C. (2005). On sustainability, estuaries, and ecosystem restoration: The art of the practical. *Restoration Ecology*, **13**, 154–158.

Barbier, E. B. (2012). Progress and challenges in valuing coastal and marine ecosystem services. *Review of Environmental Economics and Policy*, **6**, 1–19.

Barbier, E. B., Koch, E. W., Silliman, B. R., *et al.* (2008). Coastal ecosystem-based management with non-linear ecological functions and values. *Science*, **319**, 321–323.

Barbier, E. B., Hacker, S. D., Kennedy, C., *et al.* (2011). The value of estuarine and coastal ecosystem services. *Ecological Monographs*, **81**, 169–193.

Barnes, R. S. K. (2013). Distribution patterns of macrobenthic biodiversity in the intertidal seagrass beds of an estuarine system, and their conservation significance. *Biodiversity and Conservation*, **22**, 357–372.

Bulleri, F. (2006). Is it time for urban ecology to include the marine realm? *Trends in Ecology and Evolution*, **21**, 658–659.

Bulleri, F. & Chapman, M. G. (2010). The introduction of coastal infrastructure as a driver of change in marine environments. *Journal of Applied Ecology*, **47**, 26–35.

Bulling, M. T., Solan, M., Dyson, K. E., *et al.* (2008). Species effects on ecosystem processes are modified by fauna responses to habitat composition. *Oecologia*, **158**, 511–520.

Bulling, M. T., Hicks, N., Murray, L., et al. (2011). Marine biodiversity–ecosystem functions under uncertain environmental futures. *Philosophical Transactions of the Royal Society*, **365**, 2107–2116.

Burke, L., Kura, Y., Kasem, K. et al. (2001). *Coastal Ecosystems*. Washington, DC: World Resources Institute.

Cardinale, B. J., Srivastava, D. S., Duffy, J. E., et al. (2006). Effects of biodiversity on the functioning of trophic groups and ecosystems. *Nature*, **443**, 989–992.

Carey, M. P. & Wahl, D. H. (2011). Fish diversity as a determinant of ecosystem properties across multiple trophic levels. *Oikos*, **120**, 84–94.

Chan, K. M. A., Shaw, M. R., Cameron, D. R., et al. (2006). Conservation planning for ecosystem services. *PLoS Biology*, **4**, 2138–2152.

Chapman, M. G. & Blockley, D. J. (2009). Engineering novel habitats on urban infrastructure to increase intertidal biodiversity. *Oecologia*, **161**, 625–635.

Condan, F. J., Aguzzi, F., Sarda, M., et al. (2012). Seasonal rhythm in a Mediterranean coastal fish community as monitored by a cabled observatory. *Marine Biology*, **159**, 2809–2817.

Davies, T. W., Jenkins, S. R., Kingham, R., et al. (2011). Dominance, biomass and extinction resistance determines the consequences of biodiversity loss for multiple coastal ecosystem processes. *PLoS ONE*, **6**, 1–11.

Dutertre, M., Hamon, D., Chevalier, C. & Ehrhold, A. (2013). The use of the relationship between environmental factors and benthic macrofaunal distribution in the establishment of a baseline for coastal management. *ICES Journal of Marine Science*, **70**, 294–308.

Emmerson, M. C., Solan, M., Emes, C., Paterson, D. M. & Rafaelli, D. (2001). Consistent patterns and the idiosyncratic effects of biodiversity in marine ecosystems. *Nature*, **411**, 73–77.

French, P. W. (2001). *Coastal Defences: Processes, Problems, and Solutions*. London: Routledge.

Granek, E. F., Polasky, S., Kappel, C. V., et al. (2009). Ecosystem services as a common language for coastal ecosystem-based management. *Conservation Biology*, **24**, 207–216.

Godbold, J. A., Bulling, M. T. & Solan, M. (2011). Habitat structure mediates biodiversity effects on ecosystem properties. *Proceedings of the Royal Society of London, Series B, Biological Sciences*, **278**, 2510–2518.

Hale, S. S., Cote, Jr., M. P., Tedesco, M. A. & Searfoss, R. (2013). Management relevance of benthic biogeography at multiple scales in coastal waters of the northeast U.S. *Environmental Management*, **51**, 862–873.

Halpern, B. S., Diamond, J., Gaines, S., et al. (2012). Near-term priorities for the science, policy and practice of coastal and marine spatial planning (CMSP). *Marine Policy*, **36**, 198–205.

Haward, M. J., Davidson, M., Lockwood, M., et al. (2013). Climate change, scenarios and marine biodiversity conservation. *Marine Policy*, **38**, 438–446.

Herkul, K., Kotta, J., Kutser, T. & Vahtmae, E. (2013). Relating remotely sensed optical variability to marine benthic biodiversity. *PLoS ONE*, **8**, 1–8.

Hillebrand, H. & Mattheison, B. (2009). Biodiversity in a complex world: Consolidation and progress in functional biodiversity research. *Ecology Letters*, **12**, 1405–1419.

Jackson, A. C. & McIlvenny, J. (2011). Coastal squeeze on rocky shores in northern Scotland and some possible ecological impacts. *Journal of Experimental Marine Biology and Ecology*, **400**, 314–321.

Koch, E. W., Barbier, E. B., Silliman, B. R., *et al.* (2009). Non-linearity in ecosystem services: Temporal and spatial variability in coastal protection. *Frontiers in Ecology and Environment*, **7**, 29–37.

Lohrer, A. M., Townsend, M., Rodil, I. F., Hewitt, J. E. & Thrush, S. F. (2012). Detecting shifts in ecosystem functioning: The decoupling of fundamental relationships with increased pollutant stress on sandflats. *Marine Pollution Bulletin*, **64**, 2761–2769.

Martin, D., Bertasi, F., Colangelo, M. A., *et al.* (2005). Ecological impact of coastal defence structures on sediment and mobile fauna: Evaluating and forecasting consequences of unavoidable modifications of native habitats. *Coastal Engineering*, **52**, 1027–1051.

Mcleod, E., Poulter, B., Hinkel, J., Reyes, E. & Salm, R. (2010). Sea-level rise impact models and environmental conservation: A review of models and their applications. *Ocean and Coastal Management*, **53**, 507–517.

Naylor, L. A., Coombes, M. A., Venn, O., Roast, S. D. & Thompson, R. C. (2012). Facilitating ecological enhancement of coastal infrastructure: The role of policy, people and planning. *Environmental Science and Policy*, **22**, 36–46.

Peh, K. S. H. & Lewis, S. L. (2012). Conservation implications of recent advances in biodiversity-functioning research. *Biological Conservation*, **151**, 26–31.

Perkol-Finkel, S., Ferrario, F., Nicotera, V. & Airoldi, L. (2012). Conservation challenges in urban seascapes: Promoting the growth of threatened species on coastal infrastructures. *Journal of Applied Ecology*, **49**, 1457–1466.

Piwowarczyk, J., Kronenberg, J. & Dereniowska, M. A. (2013). Marine ecosystem services in urban areas: Do the strategic documents of Polish coastal munici-palities reflect their importance? *Landscape and Urban Planning*, **109**, 85–93.

Ruesink, J. L., Lenihan, H. S., Trimble, A. C., *et al.* (2005). Introduction of non-native oysters: Ecosystem effects and restoration implications. *Annual Review of Ecology, Evolution and Systematics*, **36**, 643–689.

Sheaves, M. (2009). Consequences of ecological connectivity: The coastal ecosystem mosaic. *Marine Ecology Progress Series*, **391**, 107–115.

UNEP, United Nations Environment Programme. (2006). *Marine and Coastal Ecosystems and Human Well Being*. A synthesis report based on the findings of the Millennium Ecosystem Assessment.

Weinstein, M. P. & Reed, D. J. (2005). Sustainable coastal development: The dual mandate and a recommendation for 'commerce managed areas'. *Restoration Ecology*, **13**, 174–182.

Zedler, J. B., Callaway, J. C. & Sullivan, G. (2001). Declining biodiversity: Why species matter and how their functions might be restored in Californian tidal marshes. *Bioscience*, **51**, 1005–1017.

Index